Medieval Christianity

Medieval Christianity

A NEW HISTORY

KEVIN MADIGAN

Yale

UNIVERSITY

PRESS

New Haven and London

Published with assistance from the foundation established in memory
of Calvin Chapin of the Class of 1788, Yale College.

Yale University Press books may be purchased in quantity for educational,
business, or promotional use. For information, please e-mail
sales.press@yale.edu (U.S. office) or sales@yaleup.co.uk (U.K. office).

Maps by Bill Nelson.

Set in Galliard type by Newgen North America, Austin, TX.

Printed in the United States of America.

The Library of Congress has cataloged the hardcover edition as follows:

Madigan, Kevin, 1960–
Medieval Christianity : a new history / Kevin Madigan.
pages cm
Includes bibliographical references and index.
ISBN 978-0-300-15872-4 (hardback)
1. Church history—Primitive and early church, ca. 30–600.
2. Church history—Middle Ages, 600–1500.   I. Title.
BR162.3.M33 2014
270.3—dc23
2014021498

ISBN 978-0-300-21677-6 (pbk.)

10 9 8 7 6 5 4 3 2

To my students

Discipulis meis eximiis

Contents

List of Illustrations, Maps, and Plans, xiv

Preface, xvii

Acknowledgments, xxiii

I. Early Christianity, ca. 150–600

Chapter 1. Pivotal Moments in Early Christianity, 3

    Nemesis: The Challenge of Gnosticism, 4

    Marcion and Marcionism, 7

    Montanus and Montanism, 9

    The Emergence of Normative Christianity: Creed, Council, Clergy, 11

    The Roman State and Persecution, 15

    Constantine, 20

    Augustine of Hippo, 22

    The End of Ancient Christianity, 29

II. Early-Medieval Christianity, ca. 600–1050

Chapter 2. Beginnings: The Conversion of the West and the Emergence of Celtic Christianity, 33

    Bishop Ulfilas and the Conversion of the Arian Kingdoms, 36

    The Conversion of the Franks, 40

Male and Female Ascetics in Gaul: The "Double Monastery," 42

Ireland and St. Patrick (ca. 390–ca. 461), 44

Early Irish Christianity and the Emergence of Celtic Christianity, 46

Chapter 3. Foundations: Monasticism, the Papacy, and Mission, 50

"The Finest Teacher of the Ascetical Life": Benedict of Nursia and
  Benedictine Monasticism, 51

The Monastery and the Mundane, 53

"Consul of God": Pope St. Gregory, "the Great," 55

The Anglo-Saxon Mission, 62

The Venerable Bede, 64

The Lindisfarne Gospels, 65

The Synod of Whitby (664), 66

British Missionaries on the Continent, 67

Chapter 4. Holy Empire? Christianity, Charlemagne, and
the Carolingians, 69

The Hammer: Charles Martel, 69

The Iconoclastic Controversy and Its Consequences, 71

Covenant of Kingdom and Papacy, 71

New Constantine: Charlemagne and the Church, 73

New Athens: Aachen and Its Culture, 76

Collapse of Empire, 78

Chapter 5. Parochial Life and the Proprietary Church, ca. 700–1050, 80

The Proprietary Church, 80

Physical Dimensions of Church Buildings and "Parishes," 82

Clerical Education and Lay Catechesis, 83

Liturgy and Sacraments, 85

Preaching, 87

Sacramentals, Parallel Liturgies, and the Question
  of "Superstition," 88

A "Folkloristic" Culture?, 91

Chapter 6. Christians and Jews, ca. 400–1100, 95

Roman Law, 96

Jews in the Visigothic Kingdoms, 97

The Ostrogoths, Imperial Rule, and the Lombards, 99

Early Frankish and Carolingian Era, 100

Chapter 7. Islam and Western Christianity, ca. 600–1450, 103

The Life of Christians under Muslim Rule, 104

"Reconquest," 106

The Idea of the Crusade, 107

The First Crusade, 109

Iter Sancti Sepulchri: On the Road to Jerusalem, 111

Western Christian Views of Islam, ca. 700–1450, 115

III. High-Medieval Christianity, ca. 1050–1300

Chapter 8. *Libertas Ecclesiae:* The Age of Reform, ca. 1050–1125, 119

Monastic Reform, 120

Cluny and Papal Reform, 123

The Role of the New Testament, 124

Moderate Papal Reform, 1050–1075, 126

Developments in Canon Law, 131

Kings and Episcopal Grace: Investiture, 132

The Norman Alliance, 134

Gregory VII and Empire, 134

The Conflict of Papacy and Empire, 1075–1100, 139

The Pamphlet War and Compromise, 143

Consequences of Reform, 145

Chapter 9. *Religiosi:* Monks and Nuns in the Monastic Centuries, 148

The Anchoritic Life, 149

Julian of Norwich, 150

The Desert Tradition Revived, 151

Carthusians, 152

Female Carthusians, 156

Wandering Hermits, Women, and Fontevrault, 157

Gilbert and the Order of Sempringham, 158

Regular Canons, 160

Premonstratensians, 162

Premonstratensian Women, 163

To the Letter of the *Rule*: The Cistercian Adventure, 164

Cistercian Women, 171

Chapter 10. Heresy and Its Repression, 174

Radical Gregorians, 175

Cathars, 178

Waldensians, 188

Repression: Crusade, 198

Repression: Inquisition, 201

Chapter 11. Dominicans and Their Sisters, 211

Dominic and the Dominicans, 211

Learning, 218

Beguines, Dominican Sisters, and the Friars Preachers, 219

Hounds of the Lord: Inquisitors, 223

Masters, 224

Chapter 12. *Fraticelli*: Franciscans and Their Sisters, 226

The Lives of Francis, 227

Lesser Brothers, 233

Clare, 236

Mission, Dismay, and Death, 238

The Pastoral Mission to the Cities, 241

Conflict and Controversy, 1226–1274, 245

Emergence of the Spirituals and Joachites, 249

Guglielma of Milan, 250

Secular-Mendicant Controversy, 251

Bonaventure, 253

Olivi and the Controversy over "Poor Use," 254

Shock: Papal Suppression, 255

Chapter 13. The Philosopher, the Fathers, and the Faith: Scholasticism and the University, 257

Monastic Schools, 258

Urban Schools, 260

A History of Calamity: Abelard and Heloise, 262

The University, 266

Teaching and Learning, 271

Aristotle and Scholasticism, 274

Universities and the Mendicants, 276

Thomas Aquinas, 277

The Aristotelian Crisis, 279

Scholasticism and Gothic Architecture, 283

Chapter 14. The Bid for Papal Monarchy, 287

Vicar of Christ: Innocent III, 287

Lord or Shepherd? Innocent's Petrine Doctrine, 289

Instruments of Papal Power, 292

Causes of Papal Resentment, 295

Chapter 15. To "Deepen Understanding": Means of Christianization, 1050–1250, 299

Learning through Texts, 300

Instruction through Worship, 300

Liturgical Drama, 301

The Pictorial and the Pedagogical, 302

Piety and Processions, 303

Religious Drama, 307

Preaching, 308

The "Revolution in Pastoral Care," 1200–1250, 309

Fraternities, Guilds, and Charities, 312

The Meaning of Marriage, 315

Money and Morality, 318

Chapter 16. Devotion: Saints, Relics, and Pilgrimage, 320

The Saint and Ideals of Sanctity, 320

Specialization, 322

The Shrine and the Supernatural, 323

Theological Issues and Problems of Authority, 325

Calendars and Feast Days, 326

Relics: Theft, Translation, Invention, 327

Pilgrimage, 329

Jerusalem, 331

Rome, 332

Santiago de Compostela, 333

Conques: Ste. Foy, 334

Canterbury: Thomas, 336

Tours: Martin, 338

"Virgin Most Powerful": The Special Place of Mary, 339

Critique, 342

Chapter 17. A Lachrymose Age: Christians and Jews, 1096–1492, 343

The Crusades, 343

Anti-Semitic Myths, 347

Caricature and Iconography, 354

The Medieval Passion Play, 356

Innocent III and the Fourth Lateran Council, 357

Money Lending and Usury, 358

Talmud Disputations and Talmud Burnings, 360

Disputation at Barcelona, 361

Expulsions and Massacre, 362

"Enough unto Our Sufferings": Spain, 363

IV. Later-Medieval Christianity, ca. 1300–1500

Chapter 18. Dark Ages? Popes and Councils, ca. 1300–1450, 369

The Clash between Boniface VIII and Philip IV, 370

The Avignon Papacy, 1309–1378, 374

Catherine of Siena, 377

The Great Schism, 1378–1417, 378

The Emergence of the Conciliar Solution, 378

Later Councils, 383

The Restoration Papacy, 385

Chapter 19. "Morning Stars" or Heretics? Wyclif, Hus, and Followers, 387

John Wyclif: Life and Thought, 387

The Lollards, 393

Hus, Bohemia, and the Hussite Revolution, 395

Radicalization in Prague, 400

Chapter 20. Late-Medieval Contours of Reform, 1380–1500, 403

Partial Reform, 403

Local and Provincial Reform, 406

Florentine Humanism and the Early Renaissance, 406

Savonarola and Florence, 407

The Sisters and Brothers of the Common Life, 410

Nicholas of Cusa's Papally Sponsored Reform, 412

Francisco Ximénez de Cisneros and the Reform of the
   Spanish Church, 415

Chapter 21. Late-Medieval Piety and Its Problems, 418

The Flowering of Mysticism in the Later Middle Ages, 418

Sybil of the Rhine: Hildegard of Bingen, 419

Books of Hours, 428

"Certain Mansions": Purgatory, 430

The Mass and the Eucharist, 431

The *Facere* Doctrine, 433

Chronology, 437

Notes, 441

Glossary, 459

Index, 465

Illustrations

1. Leaf of the Arian "Silver Bible," 36
2. Remains of beehive hut monastery, 47
3. Abbaye aux Hommes (Men's Abbey), St. Etienne, 55
4. Church of the Holy Savior, Spoleto, 63
5. Lindisfarne Gospel, 66
6. Throne of Charlemagne, Aachen Cathedral, 76
7. St. Martin in Zillis, Switzerland, 82
8. Crusaders' Chapel of the Virgin Mary, Church of the Holy Sepulchre, 108
9. Abbey of Cluny, 122
10. Scenes from the Life of Pope Gregory VII, 141
11. La Grande Chartreuse, 153
12. Hugh of St. Victor teaching, 161
13. Abbey of Fontenay, 167
14. Fountains Abbey, 168
15. Abbey of Santa María la Real de Las Huelgas, 172
16. Expulsion of the Albigensians from Carcassonne, 200
17. Detail of relief panel, tomb of Saint Dominic Guzman, 213
18. Habit of St. Clare of Assisi, 237
19. St. Francis of Assisi, 240
20. Church of the Jacobins, 243
21. Amiens Cathedral, 284
22. Reims Cathedral, 284
23. Pope Innocent III, 289
24. Virgin and Child in Majesty, 303
25. Processional cross, thirteenth century, 304

26. Crucifix, 1307, 305

27. Mont St. Michel, 323

28. Portico of Glory, Santiago de Compostela, 334

29. Reliquary of Ste. Foy, 335

30. Pilgrimage badge of St. Thomas Becket, 338

31. Chartres Cathedral, 341

32. Ritual murder of Simon of Trent, 350

33. Palace of the Popes, Avignon, 376

34. Anathema on and deposition of Pope Benedict XIII at Council of Constance, 381

35. Capture of Jan Hus at Constance, 382

36. Cathedral of Santa Maria del Fiore, Giotto's Bell Tower, and the Baptistery of San Giovanni, Florence, 407

37. Savonarola preaching to the Florentines, 409

38. Cardinal Ximénez's Complutensian Polyglot Bible, 416

39. Hildegard of Bingen, 420

40. Late-medieval book of hours, 428

41. Eucharistic cup and paten probably belonging to St. Francis and followers, 432

Maps and Plans

1. Germanic pattern of settlement, early sixth century, 35

2. Europe at the time of Gregory the Great, ca. 600, 60

3. Important monasteries of medieval Europe, 165

4. Plan of cruciform church (Chartres) with apsidal chapels, 285

5. Europe ca. 1250 with major bishoprics, 296

6. Major pilgrimage sites in western Europe, 330

Preface

By the early seventh century or so, the biblical culture today called medieval Christianity was *the* distinguishing and unitive religious and cultural mortar of European society. By the year 1000, six or seven monarchies, countless city-states, duchies, counties, and ecclesiastical fiefdoms organized the European land mass politically and geographically. By that time, the major ethnic groups of Europe (Celtic, Germanic, Roman, and Slavic) would all be settled and Christianized. Within the midst of this considerable political, ethnic, and linguistic mix, one tradition united the continent religiously and to some extent politically, socially, and economically: Christianity. Indeed, the church was the single institution that cut across the lives, political boundaries, and ethnic divisions that otherwise made local traditions and customs so strong a factor in early medieval Europe. One can go so far as to assert, as has the great British historian R. W. Southern, that the church was identical with medieval society and that it was this identity that distinguished it from societies that preceded and succeeded it. As Southern has also observed, the medieval church was a compulsory society in exactly the same way that the modern state is an unavoidably obligatory society. Our modern states require us to pay taxes for defense and public services, to obey their laws, and to subordinate our private desires to the good of the commonweal. Just so, baptism into medieval society required one to do all these things for the church. As Southern also observes, the medieval church was also very much like a modern state insofar as it collected taxes, administered justice in accordance with its laws, and had the power of life and death over its "citizens." It had a coercive power in the pope (coercion being expressed most usually through excommunication or the threat of it) and a purpose to its government: "to direct man into a single Christian path." Only the lack of a dependable army causes the analogy to break down.

The church not only formed the institutional framework within which one lived out one's life. Every important event for the individual from birth to death (including, from the ninth century, marriage) was marked by ecclesiastical ritual. The same set of sacraments (set at seven in the late twelfth century) punctuated the lives of Christians in northern England and Iceland, southern Italy, western Spain, and Poland. Monasteries, churches, chapels, parish churches, convents, cathedrals, and simple stone crosses covered the landscape—all professing or representing the same creed. Clergy—priests, bishops, deacons—were everywhere, as were monks, nuns, and other religious. More or less the same liturgy of the Mass was celebrated in the same language across the Continent. Certainly, there were "outsiders" in this culture—principally Jewish communities and sects of heretics—but they were "minorities" in every sense of that modern word. This culture was held together by religious belief expressed in ancient creeds whose authority very few challenged or from which they dissented. Very few would have doubted the existence of a triune God who had sent his "Son," both human and divine, to redeem humankind and to set the normative and salvific pattern for human life. Nor would many have doubted that life on this earth was a journey, or pilgrimage, to a domain more real, more permanent—indeed eternal—to be spent in everlasting beatitude with God or never-ending punishment.

A tremendous force for the unity of Christendom and for the possibility of a shared biblical culture was the possession of a common sacred language, Latin, which the church had inherited from Rome. This was a language used in all matters of religious culture, including "secular" diplomacy and politics. (The word "secular" is put in quotation marks, as medieval people did not distinguish, as we do in modern Western societies, between the sacred and the secular.) Western theological literature and art are saturated in imagery and idioms taken from the Latin Bible. The Christian liturgy was conducted in Latin, as were creeds, one of the major media for instruction in the rudiments of faith in all centuries of the Middle Ages (though only clerics would have known the Latin in some times and places, as most lay Christians were not Latinate). It was also the language in schools and, eventually, in universities.

In his pathbreaking analysis of the "making of Europe" in the central Middle Ages, historian Robert Bartlett has painstakingly charted the outward establishment of bishoprics, especially in the Baltic region, as Latin Europe expanded eastward and northward. He observes that in the process of expansion, new peripheries came to resemble the old center of Europe. It would not be going too far to say that something like a homogeneous culture emerged in the central Middle Ages. This culture had many shared elements, including shared military technology, agricultural practices and instruments, and the configuration of villages and towns. Yet it was a culture that also shared a common religious view of the cosmos, widespread religious beliefs, and shared religious practices. These, too, were essential to establishing a common European culture. It is on the establishment and evolution of this religious culture from ca. 500 to 1500 that I will focus in this book.

Many existing textbooks have laid out this very general picture of the Middle Ages. As is the case with most medievalists, textbooks on medieval ecclesiastical history are causing my bookshelves to groan. I have learned a vast amount from these volumes. Indeed, I owe their authors a profound debt of gratitude. The best of these textbooks are not merely works of synthesis (though synthesizing the scholarship on a millennium of history is no contemptible feat), but are also scholarly works in themselves, books that made us see the medieval church in new ways. I think, for example, of R. W. Southern's 1970 volume, *Western Society and the Church in the Middle Ages.* Southern's textbook brilliantly analyzed central figures, movements, and individuals, as well as relations with the Eastern church, in the high and late Middle Ages.

So why a new textbook? My hope in composing this volume was to synthesize the important new scholarly developments in the field of medieval Christianity in the four decades since the publication of Southern's book and to integrate them with some traditional themes and topics in medieval Christianity. I have attempted to write a narrative account of the Middle Ages without sacrificing analytical rigor or explanatory power, one that takes advantage of the many virtues of literature published in this field since the publication of Southern's textbook. For that reason, I have spent time in almost all chapters talking about the stories of real human beings and their lives, not merely because of the intrinsic interest of their stories, but also because of the illustrative power of their lives.

Readers thumbing through this text will have noticed, for example, that I have written at length on women in virtually every chapter of the book. Insofar as is possible, I have written about them in relationship not just to other women but also to men who venerated, wrote about, sneered at, or corresponded with them. Such a book could not have been written forty years ago. Now a book that sidelines women to a single chapter or single section would, or in my view should, be unimaginable. All historians of medieval Christianity are deeply indebted to leading historians of women in the Middle Ages, above all to Caroline Walker Bynum, who has revolutionized our field of study. So too have scores of other scholars. This book depends heavily on their enormously stimulating contributions.

Much ink has been spent since 1970 discussing "popular" religion and the problem of a "two-tiered model" of piety that attempts to explicate Christian practices in terms of the religion of the people and the religion of the prelates. While few Anglophone historians accept this historiographical model (people and prelates often participated in the same practices and murmured the same prayers), there can be little doubt that new ways of reading hagiographical sources, miracle stories, and *exempla* (illustrative stories used most often in sermons) have given us new appreciation for lived religious practice, practice that oftentimes originated "from below" and was disciplined, chastened, approved, and very often appropriated by sources of authority "from above." We now know much more about parish life and parochial Christianity, especially in the later Middle Ages, than we once did, thanks to the labors of historians like John Van Engen and Eamon Duffy.

Those once regarded on the margins of medieval Christianity have also attracted increasing attention, especially since the Second Vatican Council. This is the case not only with women, but also with mystics and mysticism. One need only think of the work of Bernard McGinn to appreciate how much more we now know about these spiritual virtuosi and the literature they left than we knew in 1960. The same can be said of visionaries. Some of these, like Joachim of Fiore (ca. 1135–1202), were also apocalyptic thinkers and writers, as well as biblical exegetes. Here again, McGinn and others produced many studies that have advanced our understanding of this captivating field enormously. Heretics and heresy are much better understood today and are of much more interest than they were before the Second Vatican Council, with major contributions from French, British, and American scholars. Much interest has been expressed in the way in which these and other out-groups, such as the Jewish communities of Europe, interacted with the Christian majority. In the early medieval period, these communities could, and did, live in something like comity in many parts of Europe. Scholars such as R. I. Moore have painted a different picture of relations among these communities at the start of the second millennium, as national states emerged and clerics, in his view, helped push such groups to the margin as Europe became, in Moore's view, a "persecuting society."

Contemporary history can shape scholarly agenda. Today there is great interest in interreligious relationships, hostility, and reconciliation. For that reason, and even more for reasons of deep scholarly interest, I have given significant attention to relations among Christians, Jews, and Muslims in the Middle Ages. Other scholars, such as Miri Rubin, under the influence of the "cultural turn" in history, have taken traditional materials, like sources on the Eucharist, and shown how they were expressed culturally and in practice. To all of this new literature, I am more indebted than I know and more grateful than I have the words to express.

I have also attempted to give readers some taste of the major debates concerning various aspects of medieval Christianity over the past forty years. I hope they come away with the conviction that history is an art of interpretation and with some sense of how sources are used in debates among scholars. Occasionally I will indicate briefly where I stand on these issues, but no student should take those verdicts as authoritative. Only deep immersion in the primary and second-ary sources allows one to take such a position. These debates are perhaps useful topics for papers written in courses in which this book will be read.

My intent in this book, then, has been to produce a volume that integrates the best of traditional scholarship with the rich and important developments that have occurred in the study of medieval Christianity over the past forty years or so. I have tried to synthesize the latest scholarship on the many cultures of conver-sion in the Middle Ages from Benedict in the early medieval period through the Cistercians and Mendicants in the high and the Beguines and Observants in the later Middle Ages. I have written on some traditional topics because they would be impossible and perhaps foolish to ignore: the emergence and then centraliza-tion of papal power in the high Middle Ages, medieval religious life, heresy and its repression, and conflicts between popes and royal figures—not to mention those great monuments to the Christian Middle Ages, the university, new ways of learning, and the many movements of reform that mark the high and late Middle Ages. As with most new textbooks, much is borrowed (if resynthesized by the author), and I again acknowledge my debts to my scholarly colleagues worldwide; some material, inevitably, is old, and some should certainly be new. This, then, is a history that is at once cultural, institutional, intellectual, spiritual, and histo-riographical. It is also a textbook in which I accept the traditional division of the Middle Ages into three periods: early (ca. 600–1050), high (ca. 1050–1300), and late (ca. 1300–1500).

Above all, I have written in a prose style and with, I hope, a narrative and in-tellectual depth that respects the kind of reader I have imagined to be interested in this subject matter. I have not attempted to write on every imaginable period, theme, practice, or subject of interest in this thousand-year period. Rather, I have attempted a narrative that, while selective, I aspired to make deeper and more complex than is traditional in a textbook. In addition, I have tried to respect the serious and mature reader without overwhelming the beginner, who is after all looking for an introduction to a period and to a civilization that may be, in every way, foreign. If there are ways I failed to achieve my aspirations and ways I can im-prove this book, I should be glad to hear from my readers care of Yale University Press, New Haven, Connecticut, 06520-9040.

Acknowledgments

As I suggested in my preface, I owe more than I can say to historians of medieval Christianity worldwide. I would like to thank them all, above all my teachers at the University of Chicago, Bernard McGinn and Robert Bartlett, now a member of the history faculty of St. Andrews, Scotland. Closer to home and to the present day, I must begin by thanking my colleagues at Harvard, particularly fellow medievalists on the Medieval Studies Committee, especially Beverly M. Kienzle, who generously helped me with issues on which she has written such important works, above all Catharism and the work of Hildegard of Bingen, and Amy M. Hollywood, for whose long friendship and acute perception, especially pertaining to the topic of medieval mysticism and women, on which she has written so illuminatingly, I am very grateful. Thanks, too, to other colleagues in religious studies and history: above all to Jon Levenson for his loyal friendship and brilliant wit; to the great Americanist David Hall for his intellectual companionship, wisdom, and fine suggestions on several chapters; and to my friend and dean, David Hempton, the distinguished historian of evangelical Christianity, for his constant support and interest in this book. To my editor, Jennifer Banks, I owe very much as usual, beginning with the idea of writing such a book. All authors should be so fortunate as to have so encouraging and supportive an editor. I also thank her colleagues at Yale University Press, Heather Gold and Dan Heaton, for their extraordinary dedication to and care for the developing manuscript. I thank my copyeditor, Bojana Ristich, for her sharp eye, sure instinct, and much-needed wit as we labored together to polish the manuscript. Thanks, too, go to two anonymous readers for the Press for many suggestions for improvements; I incorporated many of them in the final draft. To no other person do I owe so much than to my indefatigable research assistant, Carrie Bradley. She helped in myriad ways, above all in going through thousands of photographs and helping me to choose the forty-seven figures and maps included in this book. Her tireless research on dates and terms and figures discussed is reflected throughout the book and in the timeline and glossary in particular. To my wife, Stephanie Paulsell, and to my daughter Amanda, I give thanks for a happy home and much silly laughter. Finally, I wish to thank all of my students at Harvard. Many of them read drafts of these chapters and improved them by their characteristically brainy suggestions. All of them provided stimulation in the form of perceptive observations and questions in class that often stumped their instructor. It is to them, with much gratitude, that I dedicate this book.

I
Early Christianity, ca. 150–600

Pivotal Moments in Early Christianity

For more than sixteen centuries, historians of early Christianity, relying heavily on early Christian sources, took it as given that orthodox Christianity, as a rule—perhaps at all times—preceded erroneous or heretical forms of Christianity. They also usually presumed that heretical sects were smaller than orthodox groups. In his deeply learned and influential *Orthodoxy and Heresy in Earliest Christianity,* German historian Walter Bauer (d. 1960) demolished that long-held premise. Over the course of the decades following his book's publication in 1934, Bauer slowly proved to the satisfaction of a vast majority of historians that in many regions of the Mediterranean, so-called heretical groups were among the earliest expressions of Christianity. As a result of Bauer's work, heresy and orthodoxy are no longer viewed by most historians in terms of secondary and primary manifestations of Christianity. In addition, many historians are reluctant to label heresy as an obvious or inevitable deviation or to think of early or "proto-orthodoxy" (as I shall call the earliest forms of emerging Catholic Christianity) as self-evidently and necessarily correct. Proto-orthodox and then early Catholic Christianity were *forms* of Christianity practiced in the first and second centuries. Only eventually did primitive orthodoxy come, in part because of the dominant influence of the Roman church, to secure the majority of practitioners describing themselves as "Christians." It did so, however, largely by grappling with the doctrinal and practical challenges of the many Christian groups in the Mediterranean that came, ultimately, to be judged heretical. In so doing—and only in having to do so—did early Catholic Christianity come to define, in gradually more sophisticated and complex ways, its own understanding of the revelation handed down by the apostles. It also formed literary and institutional structures that would, it hoped, express and protect the "true" teaching and distinguish it for ordinary believers from the false.

Nemesis: The Challenge of Gnosticism

For over sixteen centuries, our knowledge of Gnosticism derived almost entirely from the writings of its opponents. That changed dramatically with the discovery in 1945 of the so-called Nag Hammadi library or collection. It is true that third- and fourth-century writers preserved some important texts written by Gnostics themselves, and it is also true that in the eighteenth century a number of Gnostic documents in Coptic were discovered in the Egyptian desert (including the *Pistis-Sophia,* a text purporting to be a dialogue between Christ and his apostles). Still, it remained the case for very long that our main sources for Gnosticism had been the hostile writings of Christian critics in the second and third centuries, writers such as Irenaeus (d. ca. 200), Clement of Alexandria (d. ca. 215), Tertullian (d. ca. 240), and Origen (d. ca. 254). Documents actually written by Gnostics were often destroyed by the orthodox or otherwise perished and disappeared from history.

Written originally in Greek, the Nag Hammadi collection contains more than fifty texts translated into Coptic (six of which were already known before the discovery). The collection also contains published writings, some of which are, because of the influence of popular fiction and film, fairly well known among the public. These include the *Gospel of Thomas,* a collection of sayings of the risen Jesus, including some parallels to sayings in the synoptic gospels (Matthew, Mark, and Luke); the *Gospel of Philip,* which gives us a window into Gnostic ritual; and the *Secret Book of John,* which is illustrative of many Gnostic texts insofar as it supplies a detailed cosmogony, or narrative, about the origins of the universe—in this case, a revelation of the risen Jesus to John. This text was certainly known to hostile church fathers like Irenaeus. Published in 1977 in English in its entirety, the Nag Hammadi collection provides strong evidence of Jewish sectarian influence on Gnostic speculation, and its contents have augmented enormously our knowledge of the teaching, ritual, and purpose of Gnosticism.

Among the greatest challengers to the triumph of orthodoxy were the numerous sects historians today classify, cautiously and often reluctantly, under the general rubric of "Gnosticism." The word "Gnosticism" is an umbrella term. It is meant to describe a wide variety of religious and philosophical movements and groups in the ancient Mediterranean world. One early church father in Rome wrote a refutation of no fewer than thirty-three groups he considered Gnostic. Here we will concentrate on those that originated or grew in strength and numbers in the second century. We must stress that these groups regarded themselves as authentic Christians. It is important to underscore that different mythologies and rituals characterized these groups, and some scholars have gone so far as to question whether "Gnosticism" can even be considered a coherent category. For the purposes of this book, I will assume that the category of Gnosticism does indeed have explanatory and heuristic power and will be stressing the commonalities among these groups.

The term "Gnosticism" derives from the Greek word for knowledge *(gnosis)*. Gnosticism in most of its forms was preoccupied with knowledge regarding the genesis of the world, the origin of evil, the destiny of the elect, and the knowledge or teaching needed to liberate one from the material domain, which it regarded as evil. The knowledge it imparted was to a small group of elect; the recipients of this revealed knowledge were a minority of humanity chosen to receive it and destined to return to their heavenly home once liberated from ignorance of their lofty destiny. As Theodotus, a second-century Gnostic teacher and follower of Valentinus, a leading Gnostic in Rome, expressed it, *gnosis* allowed the elect to ascertain "who we were, and what we have become; where we were . . . and the place to which we hurry; what truth is, and what rebirth is." Usually, the author of this knowledge was held to be Jesus, one of the apostles, or an enlightened teacher, who was believed to have received his knowledge via direct revelation. Gnostic salvation, therefore, was from *ignorance,* not from sin. That is, the fundamental problem in Gnosticism was not some inherited inclination to sin, nor the inability to do the good, nor our mortality as such; the problem was that a small group of elect were ignorant of the arcana critical to their destiny.

One crucial dimension of the secret knowledge imparted to the elect involved cosmogony, or the origin of the universe, and especially the way in which the evil material realm came into existence. Most Gnostic groups believed this world to be a domain of darkness and evil, fallen, by some cosmic disaster, from the heavenly world of goodness. Like the beginning of the book of Genesis, many Gnostic myths focus on the story of a fall from the heavenly realm. Some of these myths depict a figure like Eve, called Wisdom (Greek: Sophia), a young divine being who may have sought more than was ordained by the divine father—again rather like Eve in the opening chapters of Genesis. Other Gnostic myths tell of Sophia's giving birth to a dark creature with animal-like features. Like Eve after sin, this creature is ejected from the heavenly realm, called by the Gnostics the "fullness" (Greek: *plèroma*). Sophia's progeny creates the world in which we live. As an unskilled or malefic being, however, he creates a world of matter. Almost all Gnostics were united in their belief that this world of matter was evil—thus disdaining the belief, common to Jews and Christians, that God had created this world and that it was *good*. Thus, when contemplating the material order, Gnostics, unlike later Christian defenders of orthodoxy, refused to attribute its origin to the God of goodness. Rather, it was the result of some primeval disorder, some conflict or fall, some primal glitch.

As is apparent, many Gnostic myths are allegorical or symbolic readings of the Hebrew Bible, especially the book of Genesis. Indeed, some teachers of Gnosticism explained that Eve was a representation of Sophia and that the narrative of the first chapters of Genesis illustrated the way in which she alerted Adam to the truth. In fact, many of the second-century church fathers attempted to refute the Gnostics by rejecting their interpretation of Genesis. Several of the texts in the Nag Hammadi collection reflect Jewish thought about Adam and Eve. Other texts have literary parallels in Jewish apocryphal literature. In short, the evidence suggests that much of Gnostic mythology originated in heterodox Jewish circles, though scholars have not been able to identify who, precisely, belonged to these groups.

More clear is that many Gnostic Christian teachers were active in Alexandria, which had a large and educated Jewish community. Strong links existed between Judaism and Christianity in Alexandria. Some early Christian teachers like Valentinus (d. 165), perhaps traveling the grain road between Egypt and Rome, eventually made their way to the capital city of the Roman Empire. At first a member of the primitive orthodox community there, Valentinus eventually became an influential Gnostic teacher and prolific author. In any case, most Christian Gnostic teachers claimed to have understood the true revelation of Jesus Christ and to have preserved the secret tradition passed down by the apostles.

The knowledge so acquired and preserved was not gained by study but by revelation of secret knowledge. This was true even though the Gnostics knew and read the Gospels, as well as the letters of Paul, who deeply influenced their understanding of *gnosis*. Yet the Gnostics were convinced that they had achieved deeper insight into the scriptures than was available to simple, uneducated Christians (see 1 Corinthians 2:6–7). The Gnostics, to employ a biblical metaphor, consumed solid food, while ordinary, immature Christians drank the milk of simple teaching (see 1 Corinthians 3:2–4). For the Gnostics, the Scriptures expressed far more than what was given in the literal, plain sense of the text. Actually, the Gnostics were among the first Christians to read into the scriptures a second, higher or "allegorical" meaning. For the Gnostic the true meaning of the text was deeply hidden. It needed to be excavated in light of the *gnosis* that had been given the reader. It should be noted that here the Gnostics shared much, interpretively or hermeneutically, with their proto-orthodox and orthodox counterparts. This advanced doctrine was expressed, in much Gnostic writing, in intentionally mysterious language, so much so that it is extremely difficult, even for trained scholars today, to interpret these documents. In any case, the revelation supplied by the

Scriptures was, again, the knowledge that the Gnostic reader was a spirit trapped in flesh.

Many Gnostics also believed that in the primal fall, a spark of the spiritual or divine had entered into the bodies of *some* human beings. Consequently, the soteriological or salvific aim of Gnosticism was to receive the knowledge that enabled the practitioner to escape this evil material domain and to return to the heavenly realm—how they had found themselves in their present plight, to reveal to them that they were elected for a grand destiny, and to furnish them with the knowledge allowing them to be restored to their heavenly home.

Those Christian Gnostics who believed Christ to have been the revealer of saving *gnosis* were distinguished from their orthodox counterparts because they presumed that no divine emissary could have assumed human flesh; indeed, he only *appeared* in human form. Technically, this strain of Christology is called "docetic" (it derives from the Greek verb for "to seem," "to appear") and is characterized by its central conviction that the spirit Jesus only seemed to be human. Perhaps a spirit temporarily inhabited the human being Jesus, or he assumed a phantasmal human appearance. This was a critical point of disagreement between the proto-orthodox and the Gnostics because it centered on the issue of soteriology, or the doctrine of salvation. In the view of Gnosticism's critics, if the Incarnate Word had not assumed real human flesh, humanity was doomed. What was not assumed or taken on by Christ, in their eyes, could not be saved by him; had Christ not taken on human flesh, then humanity could not have been redeemed, elevated, transformed. For the Gnostics, it was self-evident that humanity and divinity could not be united and, therefore, that Christ did not experience any ordinary physical or psychological "passion" or infirmity. Instead, he only appeared to suffer on the cross, to die, and to rise from the dead. Rather, his heavenly soul left his quasi-human clothing at the time of the crucifixion. Teachings such as these genuinely alarmed proto-orthodox and orthodox teachers in the second and early third centuries. They soon would devise ways of sharply distinguishing themselves and their beliefs from those of their heretical arch-enemies.

Marcion and Marcionism

A teacher who shared much with Gnosticism (and indeed was counted among the Gnostics by Irenaeus), like belief in the inferiority and incompetence of the creator god, was Marcion of Pontus (d. ca. 160). He was among the very most influential "heretical" teachers of the second century. His teaching, and the many new churches he created, put new questions to the emerging orthodox church as challenging as those of the Gnostic teachers. Ultimately, most of the church fathers already mentioned, though most did not regard him as a Gnostic, felt compelled to respond to him vigorously.

Born in Sinope, a port city in the province of Pontus on the Black Sea, Marcion was the son of a bishop in that city. A wealthy shipowner and merchant, he traveled to Rome around 140 and joined the Christian community there, to which he donated a large sum of money. Having soon fallen under the influence of a Gnostic teacher named Cerdo (fl. ca. 140), he began to develop his own theological ideas, which he then proceeded to explain to the leaders of the Roman church. Horrified, the leaders returned his money and then, in July 144, excommunicated him. Undaunted and bent on spreading his teachings, Marcion founded his own church. It had a ritual and organization so similar to those of the Roman church that contemporary orthodox Christians felt compelled to warn their flocks not to enter a Marcionite church by accident. One contemporary Christian, Justin Martyr (d. ca. 165), asserts that Marcion's ideas were so rapidly and widely disseminated that they could be found everywhere in the Roman Empire by the middle of the second century.

Wholly characteristic of Marcion and his followers was the great ontological gulf they posited in the divine realm. Marcionites tended to view theological ideas in binary, dichotomous ways. Thus they separated an inferior creator god, or demiurge—the god of the Hebrew Bible—from the sovereign God of the New Testament. So far as sacred literature went, Marcion distinguished sharply between the Old and New Testaments, the former of which Marcion identified with law and the latter as gospel. According to Marcion, the creator god was thoroughly inferior. The creator of Adam, he had permitted evil into the world. Ignorant of Adam's whereabouts, he had to call out to find him. Every act of the creator god had its opposite or antinomy in a parallel act of goodness carried out by the Christian God. These antinomies Marcion laid out, in detail, in a book he entitled, appropriately enough, *Antitheses*. If the Jewish god taught an "eye for an eye" ethic, then, Marcion pointed out, Christ had urged his followers to love one's enemies. Only the God of Jesus Christ, as revealed in the New Testament, deserved the name of God.

Like the Gnostics, Marcionites were docetic in their Christology. Based on his assumption that matter was irredeemably evil, Marcion rejected the notion that Christ assumed a material body in the Incarnation. Nor could he accept the orthodox assertion that Christ had been born of a woman. These central and non-negotiable elements of the emerging Christian creed, challenged by Marcion so bluntly, would induce the orthodox to fashion fuller and more complex creeds by the end of the century.

Marcion's view on the sacred scriptures of Judaism and Christianity were, with respect to the evolving orthodox perspective, quite radical. Unlike most church fathers, who read the Hebrew Bible typologically or Christologically—that is, as consisting of many prophecies of a suffering Messiah—Marcion read the text quite literally, and he rejected the allegorical method of interpretation (here distinguishing himself, hermeneutically, from the Gnostics). He appreciated the Old Testament only as a historical document of the evolution of Jewish religion and because it bore an important ethical code. Even this he believed to have been abrogated at the beginning of the Christian era.

Marcion had an equally idiosyncratic view of the New Testament. Persuaded that Paul alone had correctly interpreted the revelation of Jesus's teachings, he rejected the apostles as Judaizers who simply taught another form of Judaism. On the basis of Galatians 1:8–9, Marcion concluded that there could be only one gospel, in his view Luke, whom he identified as a companion of Paul. Even still, both the letters of Paul and the Gospel of Luke had also been perverted by Jewish or Judaizing influence. Thus, any element of Paul that hearkened back appreciatively to the Hebrew Bible or elements of Luke, like the genealogy and infancy narratives, had to be purged.

Marcion's significance, then, is that he seems to have been the first to compile a list of authoritative Christian writings. His canon contained one gospel—namely, an expurgated version of Luke—and ten edited letters of Paul. Any part of the Pauline letters that hearkened back to the Old Testament Marcion rejected as Judaizing interpolations; he simply purged these. Marcion's canon encouraged Christians to begin to reexamine their own assumptions about the relationship between the two biblical testaments and stimulated them to begin to compile their own list of authoritative writings, or canon.

Montanus and Montanism

Another group that antagonized groups of emerging Catholic Christians was an ecstatic and prophetic movement known as "Montanism," after its first founder, Montanus (fl. second century). Emerging first in the late second and third centuries, it originated in Phrygia in Asia Minor and was thus sometimes known by contemporaries as the "Phrygian heresy." One interesting question having to do with geographical origins is: why Asia Minor? The most plausible explanation is that the Gospel of John, the one gospel in which Jesus proclaims the coming of a comforter or "Paraclete" (often identified as an inspiring Spirit), was very popular in Asia Minor. Asia Minor was also the setting for the composition of the Apocalypse, or the Book of Revelation, which is filled with visions and prophecies. Not surprisingly, adherents claimed to have received direct, ecstatic revelations from God, many of them eschatological, or more precisely, millennial, as most followers of Montanus believed, with local chauvinism, that the thousand-year kingdom promised in Apocalypse 12 would soon descend in Phrygia. Among the more interesting elements of this prophetic group is that without question, it had women prophetic leaders, and Montanus is mentioned in the sources (primarily the *Ecclesiastical History,* 5.16.13, 17, of the great early Christian historian Eusebius of Caesarea [ca. 260–337]) with the two most famous of them, Priscilla and Maximilla (fl. second century). All the prophets maintained strict practices of ascetical discipline, eating little, observing hours of fasting, and abstaining from marriage and sex.

It is quite clear that the Montanists were not doctrinally deviant in the way, say, that contemporary Gnostic groups were. What made them dangerous, in the eyes of many leaders in the Asian (and by 177 the Roman) churches was the very claim of experiencing new revelation outside the emerging channels of early normative Christianity. A series of synods was held in Asia Minor—the first in Christian history—and the result was that the Montanists (again according to Eusebius, *Ecclesiastical History,* 5.16.16) were excommunicated. Then, in 177, the Montanists were excommunicated by the bishop of Rome. Why? Again, they were not heterodox, and they practiced an admirably strict lifestyle. The issue was whether there could be prophecy or new revelation after the age of the apostles, and if so, could women be vehicles of it? Ultimately, bishops felt that prophets were too great a threat to their own precariously established authority; one group of bishops was so opposed to women prophets that it attempted to exorcise Maximilla. This was not before Montanism had captured its prize convert, Tertullian. In the end, it was concluded that the age of revelation had ended. We might say also that the age of the history of exegesis had begun. In addition, the controversy stimulated the development of a new, important structure in the history of normative Christianity: the synod or council. This was to become the preferred way to settle disputes regarding belief and discipline for two millennia in the history of Christianity.

Almost needless to say, orthodox Christians reacted strongly to Gnostic teaching. They criticized the multitude of Gnostic sects and warned that heterodox Gnostics could easily appear to be orthodox Christians. For their part, most Gnostics thought orthodox Christians were stupefied by their captivity to matter; this prevented them from perceiving the truth. For example, while orthodox Christians believed in the resurrection of the material body, Gnostics scoffed: resurrection actually referred to the union of the disembodied souls with their Savior. Again, orthodox Christians believe that the crucifixion of Jesus atoned for sin. Gnostics argued that to the contrary, such thinking was absurd; no heavenly being could possibly have died on the cross. In fact, the heavenly revealer had come in a material body that served simply as a vehicle during his earthly life, much as a spacesuit allows an astronaut to function in outer space. Gnostics found

hidden meanings in the Scriptures and derided Christians for reading Jesus's sayings and interpreting his actions in a plain literal sense. Simple Christians concentrated on the earthly life of Jesus and lived in ignorance of the revelations that
the resurrected Jesus gave to the disciples. While orthodox Christians believed
in a judgment at the end of time, Gnostics thought it occurred at death, when
the individual soul left the body. For them the end of the world referred only to
the disintegration of the dark material world, when all light would return to the
heavenly world.

Christian intellectuals retaliated essentially by affirming points denied by the
Gnostics and denying affirmations they proclaimed. Unlike the Gnostics, Christians identified and worshipped the God of Judaism and retained its Scriptures as
their own. It was that God who had created the world, who had made it good,
and who would resurrect his faithful at the end of ages. The father of Jesus Christ
and the God of the Hebrew Bible were, in their view, one and the same God.
Christian intellectuals emphatically rejected the docetic understanding of Christ,
according to which Christ came to the world in the angelic or phantasmagoric
body. They insisted, to the contrary, that Christ assumed true human flesh; that
he experienced the full spectrum of emotional and physical passions; and, above
all, that he suffered and died on the cross. This insistence has its roots in soteriology. Christian intellectuals asserted strongly that salvation depended on Jesus of
Nazareth, the Incarnate Word, having taken on a human body. Only that which
is assumed could be saved, they insisted. Redemption could not have occurred if
Jesus had not taken on human flesh.

The Emergence of Normative Christianity: Creed, Council, Clergy

It has been recognized that Christians formed three structures to express and
guard the truth of early Catholic Christianity: creeds or "rules of faith" (as they
were initially called), canons of scripture, and authoritative clergy, especially the
single bishop slowly recognized as the authoritative teacher in the community.

One of the most effective instruments devised by the proto-orthodox against
the hodgepodge of non-normative Christianities was the creation of laconic or
compact creeds. Few structures of early orthodox Christianity demonstrate as
clearly as these primitive "rules of faith" that early Catholic faith and thought
were shaped in the matrix of rivalry with ecclesiastical antagonists, above all the
many Gnostic groups in the empire. Some of the earliest rules of faith, and some
of the church's enduring creedal language, were first expressed in occasional letters written by proto-orthodox Christians. The example *par excellence* of this is
the letters of Ignatius of Antioch (d. ca. 107). While being transported from his
see in Syria to Rome for execution, Ignatius, once bishop of Antioch, wrote six

letters to communities in Asia Minor. In these letters, he warned the proto-ortho-dox to beware of those who spread false teaching; he meant Gnostic teachers or groups who doubted the actuality of Christ's human flesh, particularly those who denied the true physicality of the Incarnate Christ or the reality of his suffering, death, and physical resurrection. The language and categories he uses anticipate in content, and in some cases verbally, those used in the first Catholic creeds at the end of the second century. Consider, for example, his letter to the community of Smyrna, written in the first decade of the second century. In that Epistle, he proclaims Christ to have been descended from David "in the flesh." He asserts that he was "truly" born of a woman and that "truly" he perished on a cross; and he says very similar things in his other letters. Each of the clauses in his letter to Smyrna can be understood as having been aimed at a disputed tenet of Gnostic belief; each was intended to repudiate the Gnostic understanding of Christ's flesh and to promote that of the proto-orthodox. Asserting that Jesus had "truly suf-fered" so that we might gain salvation, Ignatius yokes the budding doctrine of the Incarnation (namely, that the Word had taken flesh) with the proto-orthodox primitive teaching regarding salvation, and he emphasizes the actuality of Jesus's physical being by repetition of the word "truly"—an adverb that would be ap-propriated regularly in later Christian creeds.

Derived from the Latin word for "I believe" *(credo),* creeds are more formal, often short, official, and authorized statements of the essential elements of Chris-tian belief. As already suggested, many early Christian creeds drew liberally on existing pre-creedal language, like the confessional letters of Ignatius. Such creeds were usually fixed in wording. Ritually speaking, they were by the mid-second cen-tury associated with baptism. Indeed, catechumens memorized and recited them publicly before baptism. From a theological and structural point of view, creeds eventually took on a Trinitarian form, though the heart of the earliest creeds was a series of Christological confessions. One of the earliest and best known of these is the so-called "Old Roman Creed," probably composed around 180:

> I believe in God the Father almighty;
> and in Christ Jesus His only Son, our Lord,
> Who was born from the Holy Spirit and the Virgin Mary,
> Who under Pontius Pilate was crucified and buried,
> on the third day rose again from the dead,
> ascended to heaven,
> sits at the right hand of the Father,
> whence He will come to judge the living and the dead;
> and in the Holy Spirit,
> the holy Church,

the remission of sins,
the resurrection of the flesh

The function of a creed (some of the clauses of which rhymed in Latin and were thus easily memorized) like this was to give simple believers a touchstone by which to distinguish the orthodox faith from the many varieties of heterodox Christianity to which they might otherwise have been vulnerable. It was intended to allow them to distinguish the slowly emerging proto-orthodox consensus from Gnostic and Marcionite views, especially regarding the nature of Christ. It was on this Old Roman Creed that many later western creeds verbally and theologically depended and that later Christians embellished, as they gave more metaphysical and linguistic precision to their understanding of God, the Son, and the relationship between them.

A second structure built to ground the faith of early Catholic Christianity was the formation of the New Testament canon. For the first century and a half of the Christian era, the term "New Testament" was not used. For the earliest Christians, the "scriptures" were the writings of the Septuagint, the version of the Hebrew Bible translated into Greek. Over the course of the 160 or so years from the death of Jesus of Nazareth, all sorts of written literature about him, his teachings, and his life and death had been produced: gospels, letters, apocalypses, sermons, and treatises. Almost all of these were written pseudonymously—that is, under the name of an apostle or group of apostles. Many of these were of Gnostic or Marcionite origin. Accordingly, early orthodox Christians began to draw up lists of writings believed to be inspired by the Holy Spirit and so to have the same authority as the Septuagint.

We do not know exactly how this canon was formed. It was surely important that the gospel be widely read in liturgy and attached to an apostolic name. But since so many claimed to be of apostolic origin, it seems that conformity with what was taught in rules of faith and creed turned out to be a decisive criterion. We assume that bishops of communities played an important role in distinguishing true from false writings. What is not in doubt is that by roughly the end of the second century, evidence suggests that early Catholics had adopted a canon very much like modern authoritative canons, even if some of the lists that exist contain or omit books not finally recognized as authoritative. For example, a fragment from about 200 CE, probably written in Rome (and known as the Muratorian Fragment after the scholar who, leafing through a volume in the Vatican Library, discovered it), knew the same four gospels as we: thirteen letters of Paul (and two he claims were pseudo-Pauline), the letter of Jude, two of John's letters, and the Apocalypse. In short, he knew twenty-two of the twenty-seven documents that were finally included in the authoritative versions of the New Testament. By 367, a canon produced by Athanasius (d. 373), bishop of Alexandria, that is identical to the New Testament canon as known today, existed. Still, the point to stress is that by roughly 200 CE, early orthodox Christian communities had established a list of authoritative writings and distinguished them from heterodox writings they had not accepted. Again, this was a crucial development in the emergence of normative Christianity, stimulated by the thought of heterodox thinkers, in this case Marcion above all. So, too, was the development of the monarchical episcopate.

Evidence from the second century suggests that a wide variety of models for local clergy existed throughout the Roman Empire. Yet the one to prevail was a three-tiered, hierarchical model. In this model, the bishop served as leader of the local community and was assisted by presbyters or priests (elders) and deacons. Again, this model was established in the Antioch of Ignatius, as he underscores emphatically the necessity of gathering for learning, ritual, and teaching around a single bishop. By the end of the century this three-tiered form of ministry had spread to most early Catholic communities throughout the empire, and it would soon become the sole authoritative manner of organizing local ecclesial communities.

Arguing against the Gnostic idea that revelation was secret knowledge passed down by charismatic teachers, the proto-orthodox argued that to the contrary, it had been transmitted by the apostles to their successors, duly-appointed bishops. Some local communities in the late second century drew "lines of succession" from contemporary bishops back to the community's founding teacher, often but not always an apostle, in order to demonstrate that the teaching of the local community was true and authoritative. Technically, this idea is called the "doctrine of apostolic succession." It was also stressed that the oldest apostolic churches— Rome and other churches mentioned in the New Testament especially—were sure havens of authoritative teaching. The consistency in the teaching of living bishops with one another was also stressed as proof of apostolic origin—this in contrast to the multifarious quality of Gnostic teaching. Irenaeus, for example, worked his way back from Eleutherus (r. ca. 174–189) all the way to the apostles Peter and Paul as commonly regarded founders of the Roman church, which he recognized as having special authority in doctrinal matters. He did the same for Smyrna, the town where he had grown up, claiming that Bishop Polycarp, who had been martyred in 155, had been appointed by the apostles. Again, the public succession of bishops from the apostles was, however tenuous historically speaking, used to fortify the conviction that a local bishop was a living witness to and bearer of the authority of the apostles in matters of revelation. Slowly, the many forms of Christian authority (such as "prophets," "apostles," and "teachers") gave way to the authority in each community of a single or monarchical bishop.

Through the establishment of creed, canon, and clergy, early Catholic Christianity was moving to take the shape it would assume for centuries to come. The challenge of Gnosticism had been met. At the same time, Christians were facing questions, trials, and occasionally tyranny from the Roman state.

The Roman State and Persecution

Enthusiasts of the films of Cecil B. de Mille and of historical fiction may be pardoned for imagining that early Christians were unremittingly persecuted by the Roman state—indeed, that the emperor himself issued imperial dictates that outlawed the young religion; that a vast multitude of Christians died at the hands of intolerant Romans, consumed by lions in the imperial Colossea; and that Christians had to be on guard against the ceaseless, ubiquitous threat of Roman persecution. In fact, until the mid-third century, Christians were only sporadically persecuted; there was no Roman law specifically outlawing the practice of Christianity (though laws against unauthorized societies could have been applied to Christian assemblies); persecution was local, usually mob-driven, or instigated by a magistrate under pressure from an inflamed local populace. Finally, it was often fleeting and, while often horrible, neither injurious nor mortal for most. Nor was it an impediment to the numerical or geographical growth of the Christian church. Indeed, until 250 or so, there are forty-year periods (e.g., ca. 211–249) for which there is simply no evidence anywhere in the empire of Christians suffering at Roman hands simply for being Christian. In the end, Christians would survive persecution, even when it turned ruthless. Then, the most serious problem bequeathed to the Christian church, one that would plague it for over a century, was essentially a theological one: how, if at all, to reconcile and reintegrate into the community those who had seriously sinned by apostatizing during the persecution.

Why were Christians persecuted at all? Far from intolerant toward other religions, the Romans were notably pluralistic and inclusive. Even when conquering other territories, the Romans brought back to the empire the gods of subjugated peoples. Indeed, the Romans worshipped the gods promiscuously, convinced that their military and political success depended on the support of as many gods as achievable. It is no accident that one of the most recognizable of all ancient temples in Rome is the Pantheon, dedicated, as its very name suggests, to all the gods. Only cults that seemed to encourage immorality or sedition fell under suspicion. Yet it was precisely on these grounds that Christian communities came to be oppressed, first by local mobs and magistrates.

Christians were suspected by their Roman neighbors of malfeasance, of which they were surely innocent. What did *not* cause hostility was Christian propensity to win converts or proclaim in public. In fact, there is very little evidence that in the second century Christians actively proselytized. On the other hand, clandestine religious practice and detachment from society—Christians by and large avoided the public baths that ubiquitously served as hubs of social life, intellectual activity, and even politics—were habits about which the Romans harbored reservations and suspicion. Christian cultic and theological language made neighbors believe Christians to be immoral and ghoulish. Thus, language about the consumption of flesh and blood sounded to Roman ears, understandably enough, rather like cannibalism. Just so, discourse about love of brother and sister appeared to suggest the practice of incest. Refusal to participate in the military (at least in the first three centuries of the new religion's existence because participation demanded official sacrifices and the kind of civil religion familiar to Americans and British today) irritated as well. Beyond that, Christians were mistrusted for supposedly meeting secretly and for being antisocial and taciturn. This caused the Romans to charge them with misanthropy or "hatred of the human race." Some Christian wives left their non-Christian husbands for a life of devotion—or martyrdom. Perhaps most galling was their rigorous exclusivity, devotion to the God of Jesus Christ, and stubborn refusal to participate in the cult of dead and living emperors. Also unbearable was the Christian conviction that all other cults were demonic in inspiration.

This notion that all other cults were demonic is the origin of the curious charge that the Christians were "atheists." Their contempt for pagan ritual (western Christians coined the term "pagan" to mean something like rubes who continued to practice traditional cults) and their religious exclusivity struck some as insufferable arrogance. Provincial governors who commanded Christians to worship the Roman gods were probably infuriated by nothing so much as their refusal to do so. For this obstinate refusal we know some, like Pliny (d. ca. 112), the Roman governor of Bithynia-Pontus, a province on the Black Sea, tortured and executed a number of Christians around 112. Here it is important to recall that the Romans connected public worship of the gods with prosperity or at least immunity from natural, economic, or political disasters. Finally, the Roman government and some of the populace were deeply suspicious of secret societies or political associations *(hetaeriae),* and some probably saw Christian assemblies in the categories of these outlawed groups. Others probably perceived them, more accurately, as a kind of burial society.

In light of this view of Christians, it cannot be surprising that suspicious and hostile Romans blamed and occasionally persecuted them, especially in times of adversity. Tertullian famously observed that the Romans "think the Christians [to be] the cause of every public disaster, of every affliction with which the people are visited. If the Tiber rises as high as the city walls, if the Nile does not send its waters up over the fields, if the heavens give no rains, if there is an earthquake, if there is famine or pestilence, immediately the cry is: 'Away with the Christians to the lions!'" The aforementioned Pliny persecuted local Christians in Bithynia-Pontus because of local economic factors. Similarly, regional factors, unknown to us, caused mob violence in Gaul in 177. Some Christians were brutally tortured, others tormented by animals in the amphitheater. Still others lapsed and, as the Romans ordered, worshipped the gods. In the end, the bodies of the martyrs were torn to pieces and deposited in the Rhone River, probably to discourage belief in their resurrection, as well as to prevent the recovery of the bodies for burial and the formation of martyrs' shrines.

In the case of the persecution in Gaul, the names of ten martyrs ("witnesses"—in these cases blood witnesses) survive, though perhaps four or five times that many died before, within a year or so, the persecution mysteriously stopped and the Christian communities in Lyons and Vienne survived. Martyrs were the first Christians recognized as saints by the early Christian community. They had died an agonizing death rather than deny their Savior. In so dying, they had imitated, as nearly as possible, the violent death of their Lord. Their deaths not only proved to be a powerful, and in some cases nearly irresistible, model to Christians themselves; they seem to have impressed at least some Romans as well. Theologically, it was understood that martyrdom was a sign of election by God. The martyr's sin was forgiven, and he was given the gift of a martyr's crown—assurance of eternal life. Practically, martyrdom was socially flattering, opening the real possibility of a saving death to slaves and free, as well as to women, none more illustrious than the North African aristocrat Perpetua (d. 203), who has left us with an account of her time awaiting persecution.

Perpetua's account consists of her prison diaries while awaiting martyrdom. Thematically, they focus upon her father's attempt to persuade his daughter to recant and thus to save herself. Some of the most poignant passages in the diaries have to do with Perpetua's struggles to overcome her maternal attachment to her newly born son. Eventually, she hands over her son to be brought up by her father. Her diaries are punctuated by four visions. One assures her that her prayers have delivered her brother from post-mortem suffering. The second and third are related to her own martyrdom, in one of which she says "she became a man" in the arena. In the fourth vision, Perpetua's slave, Felicitas, bears a daughter in prison; her baby girl is given over to a Christian woman to raise. The visions likely indicate at least that the editor of Perpetua's account was a Montanist, as he is persuaded that her visions are as authentic as any in the New Testament. Along with a handful of other catechumens (for the persecution was launched against catechumens, not those already baptized), Perpetua and Felicitas were torn apart in an agonizing battle against the wild animals in the Colosseum at Carthage. Their saintly fate was already sealed when the fifth-century North African bishop, Augustine of Hippo, preached four sermons on Perpetua's faith and heroic character.

This kind of example of supreme faith in the face of harassment and awful persecution shaped Christian practice and its primitive literature. Very early evidence suggests other Christians wished to be buried near the tombs of the saints so that they might be taken up in their power on the day of resurrection. These tombs also became pilgrimage sites. Some of our earliest datable Christian documents in the West are accounts of martyrdom. These helped fix the martyr as the supreme example of devotion and holiness in the early church. Even when the age of martyrdom ended, the church sought to keep continuity with the church of the martyrs by filling its calendar with feast days commemorating the saints who had given all for their faith. When monks succeeded martyrs as the highest exemplars of Christian life, they imagined themselves as latter-day martyrs, living out a sort of slow-motion martyrdom of bodily mortification and sacrifice on a daily basis. The martyr, given new contours and dimensions over the ages, would remain an ideal for Christians for centuries.

The chance to become a martyr increased dramatically in the second half of the third century. Until then, persecution had largely been sporadic, local, and unsystematic. No state-sponsored persecution occurred, nor were there attempts to exterminate the Christian population nor even, in any organized way, to curb the growth of catechumens. In the mid-third century, much of this changed. Why then? Beginning as early as the late second century and intensifying in the third, the Roman Empire was plagued by political instability, war, inflation, famine, infectious disease, and population decline.

As Rome's political and economic success had long been linked to the favor of the gods, many Romans could only conclude that their empire's dissolution was connected to the anger of the gods. Accordingly, near the millennial anniversary of Rome's founding, the emperor Decius (r. 249–251) issued an edict requiring a general sacrifice to the gods. This took the Christian church by surprise. Some Christians flocked to the temples to do worship to the Roman gods. Others held fast. Fabian, bishop of Rome (r. 236–250), was executed, as were the bishops of Antioch and Jerusalem. It was at this time that the great theologian Origen was tortured. Other bishops, like Cyprian of Carthage (d. 258), fled persecution and disappeared. Many Christians, including some bishops, like the Spanish bishops Martialis and Basilides, purchased certificates verifying that they had performed the sacrifice. In the end, perhaps hundreds of Christians died. But many more had lapsed, offering sacrifice to the gods. The question of their readmission or reconciliation to the church—even whether such reconciliation was possible—would dominate much theological debate about sin and penance for the next two centuries. It would also split the North African church for centuries.

After another brief persecution by the emperor Valerian (r. 253–260), the church enjoyed, for the second time in the third century, a forty-year period in which it was not terrorized by persecution, with the exception of a single Christian soldier who, when promoted, refused to sacrifice. The emperor Gallienus (r. 260–268) issued a decree that might be considered the first decree of toleration in Christian history. Returning confiscated property to the bishops, he allowed them, for the first time officially, to continue their episcopal duties. These forty years were decades in which Christians and their increasingly prominent buildings grew in numbers and visibility. By the dawn of the fourth century, some towns in the eastern part of the empire and some in North Africa likely had Christian majorities. Among these were at least some intellectuals and aristocrats.

These forty years of peace were to be dramatically interrupted during the reign of Diocletian (r. 284–305). Known for his administrative skill, Diocletian divided the empire bureaucratically into West and East, with an emperor (or Augustus) and vice-emperor (Caesar) for each vast region. It was he who launched the fiercest, longest, and most systematic purge of the Christians, traditionally called "the Great Persecution." Persuaded that the Christians were the cause of bad omens and also to blame for a deteriorating economy, the emperor issued a series of edicts that ordered, first, that all palace and military personnel sacrifice to the gods as a test of their loyalty; he then decided to "terminate" the Christian community for its refusal to participate. In November 303, Roman soldiers destroyed and looted a church in Nicomedia and burned its holy books. Soon an edict was published requiring the destruction of all churches and sacred scriptures. In response, Christians in the East revolted and burned some imperial buildings. Diocletian retaliated by burning almost three hundred Christians in Nicomedia. Another edict was issued: all higher clergy were to be imprisoned, but a third edict allowed them reprieve on the condition that they would sacrifice. A fourth edict raised the stakes by requiring all to sacrifice. The penalty was hard labor or death. This time, thousands, not hundreds, were tortured, mutilated, enslaved, incarcerated, or put to death.

In the end, the persecution failed. By the fourth century, many Christians had non-Christian friends or relatives who were disgusted by their torture or death. Western officials were notably reluctant to carry out the harsh decrees mandating death, willing only to comply with the edicts demanding the burning of scriptures. In the East, suffering was more severe. We have the names of about one hundred martyrs who died in Palestine alone; there must have been more. Still, the Roman state could not carry out a mass extermination of Christians, as there was far too much social resistance. In addition, the numbers of Christians had grown to the point where attempted liquidation would have been futile. Diocletian finally retired in 305. Soon the son of a Roman emperor, Constantine (r. 306–337), who was sympathetic to the Christians, emerged on the scene. According to several accounts, Constantine (and possibly his army) had dreams and visions in which he was ordered to impose the Chi-Rho sign (the first two Greek letters for the name "Christ") on the shield of his soldiers. He did, and in 312, he defeated his main rival for the imperial throne in the West, Maxentius (r. 306–312), who ruled Italy and North Africa while Constantine had taken Gaul, Britain, and Spain at the famous battle of the Milvian bridge in Rome. The first blush of a new morning for the Christians was visible, this time from the West.

Constantine

Not only was Christianity tolerated by Constantine, but the new emperor would also shower the church with gifts, buildings, and money. He built grand churches at the sacred loci of Christianity, including churches celebrating Christ's birth, baptism, and resurrection and Peter's death in Rome. Eusebius of Caesarea reports (in a document whose complete authenticity is doubtful) that Constantine even gave directions about how lavishly he wanted churches to be appointed.

Constantine's successors would continue this pattern. Many churches would become quite wealthy. Their clergy were exempt from taxation and other onerous obligations like labor. Although not baptized until near death (not uncommon at the time), Constantine was regarded so highly that contemporary Christian intellectuals considered him a virtual savior, designating him "a friend of the *logos*" and a Thirteenth Apostle. After establishing a new capital in Byzantium, which the new emperor renamed Constantinople (today known as Istanbul), Constantine died in 337. Roughly forty years later, one of his successors, Theodosius (r. 379–395), made Christianity the legal or "official" religion of the empire. Within a half-century, the Christian community had raced from a position of abomination and persecution to one of imperial privilege and munificence. The tables turned, "paganism," along with deviant forms of Christianity, would now be legally forbidden (though this hardly brought an end to pagan practice). At the beginning of the second century, the Christian community was perhaps .1 percent of an imperial population of maybe 60 million. By the time of Constantine, it constituted perhaps 10 percent of the population, with higher numbers in the East than the West. Now the number of converts began to soar. By the 380s, it may well have made up the majority of the imperial population.

The churches organized themselves along the lines laid down by the geography and political order of the empire. A city *(civitas),* along with its surrounding rural perimeter, the foundation of imperial organization, also formed the basic unit of ecclesiastical structure. Virtually every Roman city, many of them quite small, had its own bishop. He exercised his authority over a "diocese" that ordinarily coincided with the boundaries of the *civitas*. These dioceses were then grouped into provinces, over which a metropolitan, the bishop of a province's principal city, held sway. Eventually, provinces themselves were organized into large "patriarchates," each led by one of the five preeminent bishops of the church: those in Rome, Constantinople (called "New Rome," second in prestige to the Old), Antioch, Alexandria, and Jerusalem.

These bishops set an important precedent by meeting in local councils to discuss and rule on matters of doctrine and discipline. Some of their decisions, recorded often in letters, became the foundation of another key element in Christianity: canon law. The first large council of hundreds of bishops met in Nicaea in 325. It was called by none other than Constantine. This was another crucial precedent. The first seven "ecumenical" ("worldwide" in theory but not in fact) councils were gathered by the Roman (or, later, Byzantine) emperors. What they—and Constantine first of all—were to discover was that they could not contain the theological quarrels to which the church's priests and bishops were prone, this despite the fact that they were the acknowledged "heads" of the eastern churches.

These quarrels quite naturally centered on the nature of Christ, his relationship to God the Father, and the way in which humanity and divinity could coexist in a single human being who was also the incarnate deity. For example, the council at Nicaea was summoned because of a view of the relationship of the Father and the Son called "Arianism," after its founding teacher, the Alexandrian priest Arius (d. 336). The literary result of the council was the Nicene Creed, later emended at the second ecumenical council in Constantinople (381); it is still regarded as authoritative by Christians today. The bishops at the council concluded that the Father and Son were made of the same essence or substance *(ousia)*. Yet they could not prevent those who supported Arius's view, which imagined the Son to be a creature far inferior to the Father, from continuing to promulgate their views. Indeed, the Arians clung to their teaching ferociously, as would several emperors in the fourth century. For our purposes, Arius and his teachings are important, as varieties of neo-Arianism sprung up (or were thought by observers to have done so) throughout the history of Christianity, including the Middle Ages. They would attract the attention of orthodox clergy and face the same fate as Arius, whom the Nicene Council condemned and anathematized.

Just as Nicaea failed to establish the Christian doctrine of God to everyone's satisfaction, so another notable council, this one in Chalcedon (451), again called by the emperor, failed to solve the knotty problem of how a truly divine and truly human nature could come together and unite in the single "person" of Jesus

Christ, the Incarnate Word of God. Again, a creed was issued. It simply declared that Christ was "truly divine" and "truly human" and that these "natures" had come together to form a single, integrated "person." The creed succeeded in persuading some churches (like the Catholic in the West), while reinforcing theological divisions it had been called to heal in the East. The result, especially in the East, was a fracturing of the unity of the churches along dogmatic lines, divisions that defined the churches for centuries and to the present day.

As the Constantinian era wore on, some Christians began to feel their religion was losing the rigor required of the baptized during the times of persecution. They swarmed to the desert and established one of the institutions that would come to define medieval Christianity: monasticism. As medieval Christianity depended heavily—socially, intellectually, economically, in terms of religious influence, and in many other ways to be discussed—on the institution of monasticism and on monks, it is important to understand the emergence of this form of life in the deserts of Egypt, Syria, and Judea. As more serious Christians began to believe, not wrongly, that the skyrocketing numbers of converts were merely nominal or tepid believers, they began to move into the remote deserts, where they could dedicate themselves to a life of profound Christian commitment, asceticism and prayer, bodily self-mortification, and rumination on the scriptures. Some adopted an "eremitical," or hermit style, of life, of which St. Antony (d. 356) was the illustrious exemplar. Others followed a coenobitical, or communal form, of life, the form that would come to dominate in the West. Women as well as men (who far outnumbered the women) felt this call to the desert, and monastic establishments were built for them in the wild places. By the end of the fourth century, thousands of monks were living in the desert, making (in the words of Antony's biographer, Athanasius), "the desert a city."

The story of the transmission of this way of life to the West is a complex one. Part of the story is the enormous influence of the Latin translation of Athanasius's *Life* of St. Antony. A crucial development for the future unity of the church was that monks were often chosen to be bishops, a pattern exemplified by Martin of Tours (d. 397), who established the first monastery in Gaul, then, after his election as bishop in ca. 372, continued to lead a monastic life. Among those nudged to convert by the influence of Athanasius's *Life* and who would himself live an ascetical life once made bishop of Hippo was none other than St. Augustine (d. 430), perhaps the greatest theologian in the history of Christianity.

Augustine of Hippo

It would be impossible to do even minimal justice to the writings of Augustine in a short space. Here we will concentrate on a number of theological controversies in which he was deeply, aggressively, and (in the eyes of some) heartlessly involved. We will do so because his theological opponents, who usually ended up condemned as heretics, had ideas not dissimilar to a number of heretical (and even some orthodox) individuals and groups in the Middle Ages and, later, during the Reformation. When medieval clerics observed these groups, they imagined them, often, in the hostile terms conceived by Augustine. In other words, they thought they perceived the reemergence in their own day of the very enemies against whom Augustine had fought centuries earlier. In addition, Augustine established what we might call the authoritative Christian theology of the Jews.

Augustine was born in Numidia, a Roman province of North Africa. His mother, Monica, was baptized; his father was a non-Christian. In his *Confessions,* the major, semi-autobiographical source for much of his life, Augustine describes the classical education he received. A pivotal moment in his religious development occurred when he read Cicero's *Hortensius* (extant now only in fragments), then a regular part of the school curriculum, which had its intended effect of stimulating his desire for learning. Chronically unhappy, he was easy prey for the Manichaeans, who, like the Gnostics, preached a thoroughgoing dualism of good and evil and a complicated route to redemption. He resisted his mother's deeply heartfelt attempts to have him convert to Catholic Christianity. Reading the Hebrew Bible, he dismissed it as a collection of fables written in inelegant Latin.

While a Manichee, he was made professor of rhetoric in Milan, where he attended the sermons of the redoubtable bishop of Italy's second city, Ambrose (d. 397), which he found both philosophically substantive and theologically acute. By this time, he had become disillusioned with the teachings of the Manichees, which he had followed for almost a decade. Also protracted and deep was his desire for women and sex. In accordance with the custom of the era, he had taken a mistress, with whom he fathered a son, Adeodatus ("given by God"). He presents his final conversion to Christianity as a kind of divinely wrought liberation from sexual desire, but it was more complicated than that. In any case, after a long period of hesitation, he was finally baptized, by Ambrose, on Easter 387.

Not long thereafter, Augustine returned to Africa. While he was traveling through the town of Hippo to found a monastery (for his son had died), popular acclaim elevated him to the priesthood. The bishop of the city paved the way for Augustine to become his successor, and in 395, Augustine became bishop of Hippo. He would hold that position for the remaining thirty-five years of his life. It was a life spent pastoring the community and presiding for endless hours over the ecclesiastical court in Hippo. In addition, he wrote voluminously on the doctrinal and disciplinary squabbles that threatened the unity of the church in North Africa and, in his mind, the essence of the Christian gospel of grace.

The first of these threats originated during the Great Persecution by Diocletian. A group of African bishops was convinced that a bishop of Carthage, Caecilian, had been consecrated by three bishops, one of whom, Felix of Apthungi, was considered a traitor for surrendering sacred books over to the Romans. In the eyes of these bishops, called the Donatists (after Donatus, one of their number), this offense was so egregious that it made Caecilian's ordination invalid. He was a traitor (*traditor;* literally one who had handed over the scriptures), one whose ordination was ruined by collaboration with the diabolical state. By the time Augustine arrived in Hippo, the Donatist church there was larger than the Catholic, and a century-long schism between the two looked as if it might remain permanent.

The issue here was not exactly doctrinal; both, among other things, viewed the Nicene decision as orthodox. What divided the two churches were their views of ecclesiastical purity, the nature of the church (a society of sinners or of the perfect?), the character of the priesthood, and the validity of sacraments administered by lapsed priests and bishops. The schism was complicated by social and ethnic factors as well, as the Catholic church was associated with empire, power, the city, and the Latin language, while the Donatists were largely rural, of Berber stock and language, and settled farmers. The Donatist view of church was that it should be the pure bride of Christ, "without spot or wrinkle," the church of the perfect, the church of whom martyrs would have been proud to have been members. Like Noah's ark, it contained only a small minority of the pure. Sacraments dispensed by those disgraced and even contaminated by collaboration with empire, or associated with those who were, were ineffective and even polluting.

Augustine's view of church was that it was a "mixed body" of saints and sinners until it was perfected by God at the end of time. Wheat and tares (the parable [Matthew 13:24–30] to which Augustine habitually alluded in the controversy) would not be separated until the end of time. Noah's ark? It stank of animals, the stench a symbol of sin that all would have to tolerate. The baptized were made up of the morally mediocre for the most part, fallible sinners whose need for forgiveness was virtually constant and for whom the forgiving church was established.

The Donatists were not persuaded. Eventually, the North African bishops suggested that force be used by the empire and the Catholic church to eradicate the Donatists or bring them into conformity with Catholic orthodoxy. Augustine hesitated, but persecution of the Donatists, favored by his North African episcopal colleagues, proved effective in forcing them to embrace, at least nominally, the faith they had once despised. Augustine changed his mind. Now he urged that the Donatists be "compelled to enter" (as the master instructs his servants in the parable of the banquet in Luke 14:23) the Catholic church. For this stance, some have harshly, and not very convincingly, faulted him for fathering the Inquisition. Besides, the Donatists had their own terrorists, called Circumcellions, among the most aggrieved socially of the Donatist church, who intimidated many and (though Augustine may have exaggerated this) mutilated and killed priests. Be that as it may, force did not wipe out the Donatists. Ironically, both Donatists and Catholics, who accepted the Nicene view that the Father and Son were of the same nature, would be persecuted by Arian Vandals in the fifth century. The Donatists would disappear from the map of North Africa only in the seventh century, when Muslim Arabs swept through Roman North Africa and captured Carthage in 697.

Unlike Donatism, the debate over "Pelagianism" was doctrinal. Indeed, it touched on an issue that Augustine regarded (to use the modern term) as the very "essence" of Christianity—namely, the way in which sinful humanity is redeemed by the grace of God. What both movements, Donatism and Pelagianism, shared, however, was a belief in the possibility, even the necessity, of personal and ecclesial perfection. Though not perhaps a strict "Pelagian" himself (more on this question below), Pelagius (d. ca. 420), probably a British ascetic, did teach and write about the themes associated with this eponymous and large movement: the capacity for free choice of good or evil, the reality and nature of the help ("grace") given to humanity in moral choice, and the possibility of perfection. By the late fourth century, he found himself in Rome, the leader of many of the groups dedicated to a holy Christian life.

Appalled by Augustine's prayer in the *Confessions,* where Augustine pleads with God to grant him the grace to do what he commands—implying that humans were too damaged by sin to choose the good—Pelagius regarded Augustine's views as implying far too negative a view of human capacity. For Pelagius, the gifts of God given in creation were sufficient for humans to choose the good: the ability to discriminate between good and evil, the instruction of the scriptures, the examples of Christ and the saints, and the will to do the good. Almost needless to say, this view was based on a far more optimistic theological anthropology than Augustine's. Human beings sin, in Pelagius's view, not because of some inherited fatal flaw but because they imitate the bad habits of Adam and of their fellow human beings. Essentially, all have the freedom, because of the help of God given in creation, not to choose the bad. Pelagius in fact rejected the distinction between the life of religious perfection chosen by a few and the life of sinning and mediocrity preferred by the many. Indeed, he looked forward to the day when all would practice the virtues conventionally associated with the ascetical life.

Augustine regarded these views, especially as accentuated or distorted by Pelagius's followers, as a simple betrayal of the Christian message of God's deliverance of sinful humanity through his freely bestowed and unmerited grace. Those who had received grace had been mysteriously "predestined" by God without regard to merit; those not so predestined were doomed to perdition. Grace could not simply mean the gifts given in creation, for humanity was far too impaired in the Fall to choose the good without grace. By "grace," Augustine meant a power from God capable of transforming the soul so that it would so desire and love the good as to choose it spontaneously. Still, even if helped by God's grace, perfection was not a possibility in this life. The Christian life was a constant, daily struggle against sin, a pilgrimage *toward* the ideal of perfection. Augustine charged Pelagius with denying the Christian's need for grace. This is a charge that few historians today would credit; that is what they mean when they say that Pelagius was himself not a strict Pelagian. For he did not deny the need for God's grace; he simply imagined it in terms radically different than Augustine's, terms sometimes called "creationist," or given in creation (not to be confused with the modern definition of that view of divine creation).

Eventually, the cause of Pelagius was taken up by the talented bishop Julian of Eclanum (d. ca. 454), with whom Augustine waged a ferocious literary war in the 420s. Julian was not the only "Pelagian" sympathizer to argue that Augustine's Manichaean past had disastrously undermined his capacity to appreciate the Christian gospel; a tiger, he taunted Augustine, never changes his stripes. Augustine, despite his baptism, was captive to a view of human nature that was essentially non-Christian, a view of election ("predestination") that was deterministic, and of creation that was Gnostic. For roughly a century, the debate raged on, surviving the deaths of its originators.

Among those who repudiated the Augustinian view were monks from Gaul, who did not appreciate Augustine's views that their daily quest for perfection was futile, and indeed most of the Gallic church. An attempt to marry Pelagius's views on human freedom with Augustine's appreciation for the absolute need for God's grace—a sort of compromise between the opposed, extreme positions associated with Pelagius and Augustine—was finally achieved at a council in the Gallic town of Orange in 529. In the long run, for good or ill, Augustine's view of depraved human nature and the absolute dependence of humanity on God's healing grace would have a far more profound influence on western theology. His views of predestination were regarded as authoritative by many, but some who wished to be "Augustinian" found it awkward to embrace this harsh doctrine. It is, as many later theologians found, virtually impossible to preach the grace of God to a community of Christians whose God had for unknown reasons assigned a majority of them to damnation.

Long before Augustine's death, the Visigothic king Alaric (r. 395–410), another Arian, would in 410 capture and sack the city of Rome. Pagan critics charged, again, that disaster had befallen the Romans because of neglect of the gods and the spread of Christianity. Augustine countered with a massive book entitled *The City of God,* in which he demonstrated that wars, invasion, and adversity long antedated Christianity. He also distinguished two invisible communities, the City of God and the City of the World. Each had its own origin, destiny, and character. The City of God, which Augustine did not simply identify with the church, aimed for holiness and salvation; the City of the World, for mundane achievement, pleasure, power, and wealth. The City of God consisted of those predestined by God for salvation, and those of the City of the World, for damnation. However, some in the City of the World were also among the elect, dwelling temporarily in the spiritually foreign worldly city. Kingdoms and empires came and went. They were far less real, less permanent, and less important than the two cities. They could provide a minimal form of justice and, at their best, peace.

The City of God is one of the three or so works in which Augustine expresses his views about a very visible and ancient community in the Roman empire. Though two major rebellions in Palestine had been brutally put down by the Romans, Jewish communities were tolerated by law and had long been protected by the Romans. An ancient religion, Judaism had many admirers among the Romans. While Jews were not permitted to rebuild the Temple, destroyed by the Romans in the first rebellion in 70 CE (a disaster to which the Gospel of Mark alludes), nor to return to Jerusalem, they were permitted to exist, hold property, and perform religious services. On the other hand, it was not easy to secure permission to build new synagogues. Nor were Jews allowed to convert or attempt to convert others (contrary to widespread belief, Judaism in some of the Second Temple period was very much a proselytizing religion, a fact that accounts for why, especially in the eastern empire, the numbers of Jews soared), to hold political office, or to hold baptized slaves.

Augustine's views of Jews and Judaism—his doctrine of "Jewish witness"— might easily be regarded as the authoritative western view from the time of his death in the fifth century until the Second Vatican Council in the twentieth. Early in his writing career, Augustine, following a well-established Christian tradition, identified the biblical characters of Cain and Abel, from the book of Genesis, as symbols of the Jews and Jesus Christ respectively. For their guilt in the murder of Christ, the Jews (like Cain, who killed his brother Abel) were exiled from their land, and in exile they would continue to live, in sorrow, anxiety, and servitude, until the end of time. Bearing "the mark of Cain," they were to be permitted to live (though, again, only in subjugation) by gentile emperors and kings in whose lands they were dispersed.

In Augustine's view, it was thus God's will that Judaism should endure and Jews not be slain. Biblically, the survival of the Jews and their dispersion were, Augustine argued, mandated by Psalm 59:12. "Slay them not, lest at any time they forget your law; scatter them in your might." The survival of the Jews, as well as their continued practice of Judaism, was intended in several respects to witness to the truth of Christianity. First of all, their condition of dispersion and subjugation served to authenticate the triumph and truth of Christianity and the displacement of the synagogue by the church. Second, by preserving their scriptures, the

Jews unintentionally would preserve the prophecies concerning Christ contained within them. In this way, they proved to pagan critics of or recent converts to Christianity that the church had not forged those prophecies. Thus Jews served insensibly as custodians of the books that proved the messiahship of Christ and that contained prophecies of their own blindness and rejection. In short, if Jews had a continuing place in the drama of divine salvation, it was solely as a witness people, to vindicate the truth of the new religion.

This "doctrine of Jewish witness" was charged with mixed meanings for Jews, especially since it helped to shape the ways that Jews were treated by Christian leaders and peoples for millennia. On the one hand, no potentate could coerce Jews into ceasing the practice of Judaism, although this proviso was not always observed, even by Christian clerics. (As we have seen, Augustine did not extend the same tolerance to non-orthodox Christians, such as the Donatists, against whom he condoned imperial punishment.) On the other hand, they were to be permitted to practice Judaism only as a service of witness to the church. According to historian Jeremy Cohen, the invocation of Psalm 59, with its mandate not to slay "them," served as a "prophetic policy-statement" that not only prevented their liquidation, but also guaranteed them religious freedom. Yet the second half of the psalm—"scatter them in your might"—makes their dispersion a matter of divine will and human obligation. Less ambiguously, it was simply assumed, according to the eschatological scenario laid out by Augustine, that the Jews would convert to Christianity at the end of time. Moreover, the doctrine underscored the sole responsibility of the Jews for the death of Christ, emphasized their supposed stubbornness and blindness in refusing to acknowledge Christ as messiah, and viewed Jewish religion and the synagogue as essentially moribund.

The danger in this view of Jews and Judaism when put into practice, aside from the obvious psychological, social, political, and economic disabilities it could inflict, is that the religious and cultural presuppositions favoring and even demanding Jewish survival could change, wither away, or disappear altogether in different historical circumstances. A second, although less serious danger (yet not unknown in the Middle Ages or in the modern period) is that the principle could be ignored even among those for whom it remained theoretically authoritative. Thus the Augustinian doctrine was unable to prevent, in "Christian societies," instances of forced conversion, expulsion, and, in the Crusades and Black Death, mass murder. Ultimately, the tension between the two halves of Augustine's teaching proved, in the Middle Ages, difficult and then, in the modern period, tragically impossible to maintain.

In some ways, the end of Augustine's life symbolizes the end of the ancient Roman order and the dawn of a new biblical culture. That is not untrue, but much more needs to be said about this question, as we will see below.

The End of Ancient Christianity

Scholars debate the question of when the Christian Middle Ages began because so very much rides on historians' responses to it—namely, what distinguishes *this* period from the centuries that came before and the scores of decades that follow it? What are this religious tradition's unique characteristics, institutions, figures, thoughts, relationship to its past, events, practices, cultural realities, geographical reach, relations to "outsiders," forms of religious life, dissent, demographic challenges (or catastrophes)? And above all, how do these realities change over time within an established chronological framework? Historians can hardly avoid this latter, *diachronic* treatment of materials. Still, few approaches are so pure, and a treatment, like this one, that attempts to trace phenomena over time will also have its *synchronic* layers, dimensions, and moments. That is, it will step back at times to take a temporarily static view of a complex religio-cultural reality of particular importance.

Perhaps the most stimulating and persuasive examination of these questions is a book authored by Robert Markus, entitled *The End of Ancient Christianity*. Examining the period ca. 400–600 CE, when Christianization on a large scale began until the empire dissolved into a crazy-quilt of barbarian kingdoms, Markus argues that western Christendom was in these centuries undergoing a period of desecularization. Secular government, education, and culture were all collapsing. Western Europe, he argues, was being "drained of the secular," the secular being defined as that domain of life "not considered to be of direct religious significance." As the realm allowed to the secular shrank, the area occupied by the sacred grew. The process Markus describes is rather like the reverse of the modern process of secularization, where areas of life, thought, and activity are withdrawn from religious or ecclesiastical influence.

What were the signs of this process of desecularization in late ancient and early medieval Christianity? To start with, as the age of the martyrs receded into the distant past, Christians filled their calendar—sacralized it—with feast days of the martyrs. Relics, or pieces of the past, bridged the time between past and present. Time had been made holy, and something similar happened with space. In the fifth century, the western emperors left Rome for Ravenna, and the papacy expanded in an area removed from the political and civic center of "pagan" Rome. Bishops in Rome and other metropolises also began to take over municipal authority and assume civic responsibility for their episcopal cities. Christian churches multiplied in the towns; baths, theaters, and circuses disappeared. There was now such a thing as "Christian topography." Culturally speaking, secular and pagan traditions had disappeared by the 580s, replaced by a wholly biblical language and culture. Particularly significant was the way in which ascetic norms and attitudes entered the cultural bloodstream of the West, how monastic ideals came to be embraced by those outside the walls of the proliferating monasteries. The values of the desert came to be established in the city, as the distinction between those two geographical and cultural realms began to blur. Present in the city, monks influenced and inspired laymen and women. Bishops, many of them once monks, encouraged monastic reading practices in their dioceses, such as reading and meditating on the Bible. A way of life based on withdrawal moved to the city; the periphery and center collapsed into one. Ascetical ideals came increasingly to be appropriated not only by lay Christians, but also by priests and bishops. The walls that separated the lives of monks, the secular clergy, and the laity slowly crumbled. By the late sixth century, a new age had dawned.

II

Early-Medieval Christianity, ca. 600–1050

Beginnings: The Conversion of the West and the Emergence of Celtic Christianity

By the time of Augustine, the Roman Empire had famously been in "decline" for some three centuries. It would not be far wrong to say that the empire had achieved the height of its prosperity, socioeconomic well-being, and military power in the mid-second century. By the end of the fourth century, a new element would be introduced that would upset the empire's already delicate, precarious politico-economic ecology: the Germans. Sometimes called the "Germanic peoples," sometimes "the barbarian invaders," it is best to recognize that they were "German-speaking," not that they possessed a kind of ethnic purity or a set of shared social and political structures.

The great Roman historian Edward Gibbon (d. 1794) could speak glibly about "the ferocious temper of the conquerors." The truth is that the Germans had been pushed from their homelands near the Baltic Sea to the border of the Roman Empire by the truly menacing Huns, a nomadic tribe that had been routed by the Chinese and, in the wake of defeat, pressed westward. By ca. 375, the Huns had defeated the Ostrogoths, whom they would then dominate for nearly a century. The Germans, by contrast, were, by and large, not belligerent. Rather, they were attracted by qualities of Roman life, including the relative ease of agricultural production and trade. Very recent archaeological evidence suggests that the "border" between the Germans and Romans was somewhat porous, and some intermarriage occurred. In effect, the Germans were looking for a suitable homeland, free from the terror of domination by the Huns. In fact, one of the Germanic groups, the Visigoths, hoping to escape Hunnish control, applied to the Romans for permission to cross the Danube and enter imperial territory, a request that was granted.

Nonetheless, conflicts sometimes broke out. One, the battle of Adrianople (378) has been vested with special significance. It was there that the emperor Valens (r. 364–378) lost his life and his army to the very Visigoths his predecessors had allowed into western imperial territory. With the benefit of hindsight, we may say that this was the battle that began the "wandering of the German peoples"—or, if you like, the Germanic or barbarian invasions—into the western empire. Almost exactly a century later, in 476, the child emperor Romulus Augustulus (r. 475–476) would be deposed. The West would soon be invaded, occupied, and ruled by new confederacies of Germans: Visigoths, Ostrogoths, Vandals, Lombards, Franks, Angles, Saxons, Jutes, and others. Now political and religious forces would pull the old empire into three parts. In the West, the large Roman population would be ruled by more powerful German overlords. Roman emperors would continue to preside over the eastern or Byzantine Empire in Constantinople. Finally, in the seventh century, Muslim expansion would result in the taking of much of the old empire, including the Near East, North Africa, and Spain.

In the eyes of some scholars, like the great Belgian historian Henri Pirenne (d. 1935), the Muslim expansion marks the beginning of the history of the European West. Without Muhammad, Pirenne argued, there would never have been a European Christian emperor; without the effect of the Islamic expansion, which was to cut off western ties of trade to the East, the West would never have emerged with its own unique identity. The "Pirenne thesis," as it has been called, has been much debated. However one comes down on that thesis, it is clear that by 750 CE or so, a new political equilibrium had been reached. The old empire now lay divided into the Germanic and Roman West, the Byzantine East, and the Arab empire. The East had a common language, Greek, and was religiously Orthodox. The Arab empire also had a common language, Arabic, and a common religion, Islam.

The West had no common religion or language. Those Germanic invaders who were baptized were Arian; those not baptized worshipped their own gods. By the time of the deposition of the last Roman emperor in the West, not only did it seem as if linguistic unity would be impossible ever to achieve, but also religious unity seemed a very remote possibility indeed. In addition to hosting worshippers of the ancient Roman gods, Europe, no longer an empire but an aggregation of smaller kingdoms, now was home to practitioners of Germanic religions, to Catholic Christians, and to baptized Germans who practiced a form of Christianity that was regarded as dangerously heretical by Catholic Christians. How, if

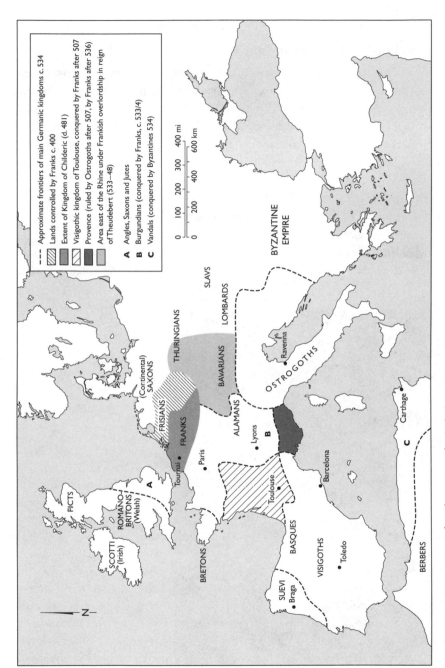

Map 1. Germanic pattern of settlement, early sixth century

Approximate frontiers of main Germanic kingdoms c. 534

Lands controlled by Franks c. 400

Extent of Kingdom of Childeric (d. 481)

Visigothic kingdom of Toulouse, conquered by Franks after 507

Provence (ruled by Ostrogoths after 507, by Franks after 536)

Area east of the Rhine under Frankish overlordship in reign of Theudebert (533–48)

A   Angles, Saxons and Jutes

B   Burgundians (conquered by Franks, c. 533/4)

C   Vandals (conquered by Byzantines 534)

0   100   200   300   400 mi

0   200   400   600 km

N

PICTS

SCOTTI
(Irish)

ROMANO-
BRITONS
(Welsh)

A

BRETONS

FRANKS

FRISIANS

(Continental)
SAXONS

THURINGIANS

SLAVS

LOMBARDS

BAVARIANS

ALAMANS

Paris

Tournai

Lyons

B

Toulouse

Barcelona

BASQUES

VISIGOTHS

Toledo

SUEVI

Braga

OSTROGOTHS

Ravenna

BYZANTINE
EMPIRE

Carthage

C

BERBERS

at all, would these various kingdoms reemerge into an empire united, religiously speaking, by Roman Catholicism?

Bishop Ulfilas and the Conversion of the Arian Kingdoms

Born of a Cappadocian Christian family that had been captured by the Goths, Ulfilas (d. ca. 381) was fluent not only in Greek and Latin but in Gothic as well. Consecrated bishop around 340 by Eusebius of Nicomedia (d. 341), an Arian who was then bishop of Constantinople, Ulfilas laid the foundation by which the Goths later became Arian Christians and Gothic became a written language based on Greek. Aside from preaching an Arian creed, he translated the New Testament into Gothic. In this way, his Arian style of Christianity passed from the Goths to other Germanic tribes and moved back into the western empire when the German tribes crossed the old frontiers, established kingdoms, and began to settle.

The western Goths, or Visigoths, terrified of the Huns (who were migrating westward from Central Asia), already occupied the banks of the Danube late in the third century, when Dacia was given to them by the Romans. As noted, in 378, in

1. A leaf of the Arian "Silver Bible," a page from one of the gospels, dating from Ravenna, ca. 520. More than half the Codex Argenteus, which was copied from the Gothic translation of Arian bishop Ulfilas, survives, including almost the entirety of all four gospels. The book may have been made for the Ostrogothic king Theodoric. Preserved now in Uppsala University Library. akg-images.

a conflict over land and food, they defeated the Romans at Adrianople. Emperor Theodosius I thereafter recognized them as Roman allies and confirmed them in their possessions along the Danube. By the end of the century, however, they were raiding again and ravaged the Balkans. As the Visigoths attempted to secure better land, agreements were made with the Romans and then breached. Hostilities over food provisions and other terms caused King Alaric to move into Italy, where he famously sacked Rome in 410.

From Rome, the Visigoths continued south, carrying with them as a hostage the emperor's sister, Galla Placidia (d. 450). They moved north again through Italy and southern Gaul, after an unsuccessful attempt to invade Africa. In 418, the Visigoths defeated the Vandals in Spain. In return they were allowed to settle in southwestern Gaul (Aquitania), where they had their capital in Toulouse. They were now recognized again as allies of the Roman Empire, in which capacity they crossed the Pyrenees in response to a call for military aid. Over the course of the fifth century, they expanded their hold in Gaul and in the fifth century joined with the Franks to defeat Attila (d. ca. 453) and the Huns. Between 453 and 466, the Visigoths occupied most of Roman Spain.

In the sixth century, some Visigothic leaders began to see advantages to closer cooperation with the Spanish ecclesiastical hierarchy. Meanwhile, a fusion of the Germanic and Roman populations gradually proceeded. A new Gallo-Roman culture emerged based on Roman law and education, Catholic Christianity, and Germanic politics and military prowess. Finally, the Visigothic king Reccared I (r. 586–601) formally converted to Catholicism in 587. In 589, the Third Council of Toledo declared Catholicism to be the religion of the Visigoths. Nearly all vestiges of Arianism rapidly disappeared in Spain. The same sort of pattern occurred with the enemies of the Visigoths, the Vandals.

The Vandals were Germanic peoples that originated in Scandinavia or the Baltic region. As a result of pressure from the Huns, they moved westward and crossed the Rhine frontier in 406, moved through Gaul, and in 409 across the Pyrenees into Spain. They may have converted to Arian Christianity before they crossed the frontier. As they continued to move westward, they for a time settled in Spain, but the Visigoths (now the allies of Rome) routed them from the Iberian Peninsula. They crossed the Straits of Gibraltar in 429 and occupied with little difficulty northern Africa, along with the islands of the western Mediterranean.

During the Vandals' long siege of Hippo, Augustine died in his episcopal city in 430. The Vandals, Arian Christians, permitted only the private observation of Catholicism. They occasionally persecuted Catholic Christianity, which consequently lost a number of churches. Some Catholic bishops were also sent into exile. In the early sixth century, the emperor Justinian's army, then attempting to reunite the eastern and western halves of the empire, attacked the Vandals; the emperor justified his attack, in part, as an attempt to eradicate the Arian heresy. By 533, the Vandal army was defeated. Justinian I (r. 527–565) restored Catholicism, returned its exiled bishops, and restored property taken by the Vandals. All remains of Vandal culture, including their religious culture, disappeared within a short period of time.

It was a Germanic king, Odoacer (r. 476–493), who deposed the western emperor, Romulus Augustulus, in 476. After deposing Romulus, Odoacer simply sent notice to the eastern emperor that he was now ruling Italy in his name. The Ostrogothic king Theodoric (r. 475–526) invaded Italy at the request of the eastern emperor in 483, murdered Odoacer, then established the Kingdom of Italy, which included not only the peninsula, but also Provence and the Dalmatian coast. He established his capital at Ravenna, where he erected a basilica to Christ the Savior. Theodoric proved to be among the more enlightened of the barbarian kings. Unlike some of the western Gothic kings, he was tolerant of Roman Catholicism and had close working relations with the senatorial aristocracy of old Rome. He also maintained good relations with the Byzantine Empire. He deeply respected much of the Roman administrative personnel and administrative system, including two of its leading lights, Boethius (d. ca. 524), whom he eventually turned against, and Cassiodorus (d. ca. 580).

Born into a prominent Roman family, Boethius was early taught two traditions, Greek philosophy and Catholic Christianity; both would inform his impressive literary legacy. Indeed, like the early Christian apologists, he used Greek philosophy to present orthodox Catholicism as rational and true. In addition to his intellectual accomplishments, he had an extraordinarily distinguished political career. In 510, he was made consul and then became a senator. Later, King Theodoric established Boethius's sons as consuls in Rome and then made Boethius one of the highest administrative officers in Italy, the "master of offices" *(magister officiorum)*.

Despite this auspicious beginning, Boethius was eventually implicated in a charge of treason against Theodoric. It is possible that his defense of orthodox Catholicism hurt him in the court of an Arian king. In any case, he was arrested in 523, incarcerated for an unusually long time in Pavia, and then executed ca. 524. While in prison, he wrote his final and most famous work, the *Consolation of Philosophy*, a meditation on innocent suffering and an attempt to reconcile human freedom with divine sovereignty. Boethius famously abstained in this short book from making any reference to the Christian scriptures or creeds. Instead, the *Consolation* is a work of a philosopher attempting rationally to comprehend the problem of evil and the difficulty of reconciling human free will and divine foreknowledge. Despite the absence of Christian vocabulary, the work was considered so important from the Carolingian era through the late Middle Ages that nearly every library of any significance, all of them Christian, had a copy made of it; consequently, the manuscript tradition is unusually rich. One of the first literary works to be translated into the emerging European vernaculars, its influence has led some historians to link Boethius together with Augustine, Ambrose, and Jerome as one of the founders of the Middle Ages.

Yet it was not just the *Consolation* that earned Boethius that honor. Sometimes called "the first scholastic" in Europe, Boethius established the essentials of the medieval educational program. He also commented on Aristotle and other ancient Greek authorities. In fact, Boethius in effect invented what he called the quadrivium, the four "mathematical disciplines" of arithmetic, geometry, music, and astronomy. The quadrivium would be standard in educational institutions for centuries. Boethius's credentials for being "the first scholastic" are that he wrote several important logical treatises and translated Aristotle's *Prior Analytics* and *Posterior Analytics*. These translations then went on to form the fundamental foundation of Aristotelian logic in the high-medieval scholastic period.

Like Boethius, Cassiodorus held a number of important positions at the Italian court in the sixth century. Born to an Italian senatorial family, he received an excellent education in the liberal arts and was brought to the Ostrogothic court as the official composer of letters and other documents for the king. Around 540, he took a turn away from politics and went to Constantinople to study theology. Fourteen years later, he returned to Vivarium, a monastery in Squillace, his birthplace, that he founded before his departure for Constantinople. It seems that he imagined it as a citadel for instruction in non-secular subjects, like theology, and as a scriptorium for reproducing important books. It was at Vivarium that he produced some of his most influential theological works.

Perhaps the most important of these is his *Institutions,* which he completed ca. 562. Designed as an introduction to the educational program for monks at Vivarium, the work is divided into two large books. In the first book, Cassiodorus documents the books at the library at Vivarium, instructs his readers on which heresies are to be shunned, and teaches the monks how to copy manuscripts. In the second book, Cassiodorus discusses the seven liberal arts, a treatment that was to be reproduced often and that influenced writers deeply in the Carolingian period. Cassiodorus's death also marked the demise of Vivarium. However, his works survived and were deeply influential. In addition, many of the books he had collected were copied by his monks and from there circulated widely through medieval cloisters. Cassiodorus's most important work would coincide with catastrophic war on the Italian peninsula.

In 527, Justinian became emperor. Under the command of Belisarios, Justinian launched his Italian campaign, part of his ambitious expedition to reunite the empire. The imperial forces conquered Rome in 536 and took the Gothic capital, Ravenna, four years later. Yet the Goths were remarkably resilient. One Ostrogothic king recovered almost all of Italy, and it took two more campaigns from Justinian's forces to subdue Gothic resistance, which ended only ca. 562.

The long years of warfare were disastrous for Italy, leaving a political vacuum to be filled by the bellicose Lombards, some of whom were probably converted to Arianism in the sixth century. Mentioned already by the Roman historian Tacitus (d. ca. 117), the Lombards initially occupied territory along the Elbe. During Justinian's reconquest of Italy, Lombards served as mercenaries in the eastern Roman army. In 568, they invaded Italy. By 572 they had subdued the entire Po Valley. Soon most of the peninsula, excepting Venice, Ravenna, Rome, and other coastal areas, fell under Lombard domination. For a time, it seemed as if all Italy might fall. But in 774, the Lombards faced and were destroyed by the most powerful of the Germanic kingdoms, that of the Franks.

The Conversion of the Franks

When they crossed the frontiers of the empire, the Franks had not yet been baptized as Christians. Early in the fifth century, they dwelt in the lower Rhine, partly in Gaul and partly in Germany. The emperor Julian the Apostate (r. 361–363) made them allies of the empire, in exchange for which they were expected to defend the region of the frontier in which they dwelt. That region, even in the third century, was called "Francia," land of the Franks. Once recognized by the emperor, many Franks had good relations with the Romans, and some even held high office.

During the fourth and fifth centuries, the Frankish people began to mingle and then emerge into two distinct groups, one western and one eastern. The integration of the western group occurred under the leadership of a family later known as the Merovingians. An exceptionally important Merovingian king for the future of western Christianity was named Clovis I (r. 481–511), the monarch who united all Franks, sometimes by annihilating close blood relatives. Clovis's military conquests, once extended by his sons, brought all of Gaul under Frankish overlordship.

At the time of their incursion to the west, the Frankish invaders were not Arians. In the end, it was Clovis's land lust and hunger for power that led him to Catholic Christianity. Most of central and southern Gaul was Catholic, while its rulers were Visigoths and therefore Arian. For political and military reasons, it was useful for Clovis to have experience of, and, if possible, the appreciation of, Catholic bishops. Even while conquering, he warned his warriors not to loot churches in territories just subjugated. In a story that seems to repeat itself in early-medieval history, it so happened that Clovis's wife, Clothilda (d. 545), was a

Catholic. The source of this story, the chronicler Gregory of Tours (d. ca. 594), reports that Clothilda had unsuccessfully attempted to convert her husband. Since early-medieval Christians were unabashedly instrumental in their view of religion, Clothilda and her fellow Catholics tried to convert Clovis by persuading him that he ought, for reasons of military success, worship the Christian God. Clovis pondered the argument. In a difficult battle with another Germanic tribe, his own gods derelict, he made a famous covenant with Clothilda's God:

> Jesus Christ, who Clothilda says is the son of the living God, you are said to give aid to those who are laboring and to bestow victory on those hoping in you. Full of devotion, I beg the glory of your help so that if you will grant me victory over these enemies, and if I may have experienced that power which the people dedicated to your name say that they have experienced from you, then I will believe in you and I will be baptized in your name. I have called upon my own gods, but, as I learn, they are far away from my aid. Hence I believe that they are endowed with no power, since they do not come to the assistance of those who obey them. I call on you. I want to believe in you, if only I am snatched from my enemies.

Because Clovis's warriors had not yet heard of Jesus Christ nor agreed to convert, Clovis was catechized secretly by Remigius (d. ca. 533), bishop of Reims. Finally, at a gathering of his warriors, Clovis persuaded them to convert; more than three thousand are said to have done so between 496 and 506.

This was a momentous development. The man who now controlled most of central and northern Gaul and who ruled the only stable kingdom in the center of western Europe had linked destinies with Catholic Christianity. A single, militarily powerful kingdom now had a Catholic ruler, soon recognized by the eastern emperors as consul. In their eyes, the kingdom of the Franks *(regnum Francorum)* continued the presence of Roman authority and tradition. This assessment was essentially a welcome development from the perspective of Frankish bishops, even though Frankish kings later interfered routinely in ecclesiastical affairs. They bestowed episcopal sees on friends and family and took ecclesiastical property as it suited them. Nonetheless, the Frankish leadership would be a champion and ally without whom the Catholic Church could not have survived the political and military calamities of the sixth and seventh centuries. The church was made even more content with them as the Franks absorbed elements of classical culture, not least of all Latin, which eventually evolved into contemporary French. They intermarried with the Romans whose territories they conquered; thus was created a Gallo-Roman culture, based religiously on Catholicism and linguistically on Latin. Frankish kings championed the growth of the monastic movement and of missionizing. Ironically, this once-pagan federation of tribes helped spread

Christianity by weakening or driving out extant pagan groups. The episcopal support that Clovis had sought gave the Franks some advantage in conflicts with the Visigothic and Burgundian kingdoms, which would be incorporated into the larger Frankish kingdom.

Male and Female Ascetics in Gaul: The "Double Monastery"

The wife of Clovis II (r. 639–657) was a woman from the lower orders of Saxon society in Britain; it was customary for men from the Merovingian line to ignore matters of "social class" when selecting wives. Named Balthild (d. 680), she was both politically astute and pious. A friend of powerful churchmen, she was also a sponsor and promoter of the monastic order. Around 660, she founded the important abbey of Corbie. Yet the monastic project dearest to her heart was Chelles, an abbey of nuns, established on a royal villa built by Clothilda, the wife of Clovis I. After expanding the villa, Balthild brought in a community of nuns from Jouarre and, after the death of her husband, lived out the rest of her life under an abbess whom she had appointed.

Both Chelles and Jouarre were "double monasteries." These were communities of male and female monks living in the same monastic precincts. This arrangement was made because women needed men to perform the liturgical ministry of priests, as well as some managerial and manual tasks thought to be beyond their powers. Essentially these double monasteries were first and foremost communities of women to which communities of men were attached. As we will recall, there was ancient, eastern precedent for this, the paradigm for men and women living in close proximity having been established in the deserts of Egypt in the fourth century by Pachomius (d. 346) and others.

Clothilda imposed a "double rule" of Columbanus and Benedict, which governed customs at the monastic communities of Luxeuil, St. Martin of Tours, and other important male houses. Followed by both men and women in the new Frankish monasteries of the seventh century, the first reference to the following of such a dual system of monastic government and custom comes from the foundation charter of Solignac. It surely derived its inspiration from the model of Luxeuil. We do not know how the Italian *Rule* of St. Benedict, which would ultimately govern western monasticism in all of Europe, reached the north. It is clear that the veneration of Benedict went hand-in-glove with the adoption of some aspects of his *Rule,* though which aspects were appropriated remains unclear. The adoption of the *Rule* and the cult of Benedict were buttressed after Benedict's relics were stolen and brought back secretly to Fleury (the abbey St. Benoît-sur-Loire); as we shall see in chapter 16, the theft of relics was common in the Middle Ages and even sometimes thought to be a holy act *(furta sacra),* performed on behalf of a saint. That Benedict had "chosen" to be buried in a

Frankish monastery (despite the later protests of the monks at Monte Cassino that no such request had been made and that his relics were still safely interred at the monastery he founded) heightened the reputation and accelerated the growth of Gallic monasticism. Eventually, as we shall see, it was through a Frankish king and in a Frankish empire that Benedict's *Rule* acquired its status as the standard everywhere in western Europe of monastic practice.

What strikes us most about these double monasteries, given later-medieval developments, was that these were governed by a woman, the abbess. The abbesses held and exercised impressive powers. During the seventh century a *Rule of a Father for Virgins* (possibly composed by Walbert of Luxeuil [d. 668]) assigns to the abbess many of the roles assumed by male abbots of the day. These included the power of hearing the confessions of her nuns and even of absolving them. In the custom of the day—a custom that was to have much staying power in medieval female nunneries—Walbert indicates that the abbess should be wise and holy and noble by birth, a criterion that would have barred Balthild herself. Be that as it may, the abbesses of these Merovingian monasteries were by and large well born, highly educated, and sovereign over their cloisters. The holiness of some of these women caused them to be sanctified by pious hagiographers. Accordingly, some high-standing families thus acquired a "dynastic" or house saint *(Hausheiliger)*. These female saints only augmented the already considerable status of the families who had endowed the monasteries in which they lived and whose abbesses appointed their own successors.

One of these double monasteries, Nivelles (founded ca. 640), was endowed, built, and governed by Itta (d. 652), the wife of Pippin the Elder (d. 640). She appointed her daughter, Gertrude (d. 659), its first abbess. That Gertrude intended this to be a foundation following Celtic and Columbanian customs is clear. She summoned monks from Ireland to instruct her sisters in chant. She was also determined to educate her nuns and sent agents to Rome to acquire books to build a library. Again, like other high-born abbesses, Gertrude appointed her successor, her niece.

The close religious links between Gaul and England caused the model of double monasteries to be introduced in England. As in Gaul, they were by and large aristocratic foundations and were governed by abbesses of noble and sometimes royal blood. Among the most famous of these abbeys is that at Whitby. Trained by the great Northumbrian monk and missionary Aidan (d. 651), Hilda, previously abbess at the house of Hartlepool, had the same position at Whitby from 657 until her death in 680. It was said that kings and princes sought her counsel, and of course it was her reputation and that of her house that caused King Oswiu (r. 642–670) to choose to summon the representatives of the Celtic and Catholic churches to Whitby to debate the question of the Easter controversy, which then divided the Celtic and Catholic churches of Northumbria. Like her Gallic colleagues, Hilda was a great sponsor of both her abbeys, and she encouraged education in both. No fewer than five monks from Whitby were to become bishops in the English church. Her foundation was to serve thus as a nursery of bishops, a center for education and pastoral activity, and a site that determined the very future of the English church. Her monastery would also serve as the famous locus of a debate between representatives of the Roman and Irish churches.

Ireland and St. Patrick (ca. 390–ca. 461)

What we know about Patrick's life is quite little and is dependent upon two sources, one a letter to a British warrior named Coroticus, about whom we know almost nothing. More important as a source for Patrick's life is his autobiographical account of his religious life, called the *Confession*. Aside from these two sources, a number of later *vitae* exist, as do a few short documents. However, this later evidence is, in general, mutually conflicting, frequently incredible, and in general of dubious historical veracity.

Born around 390, Patrick was raised in a partially Romanized region of western Britain. He was the son of a local *decurio* (member of a town council, the same position held by Augustine's father in North Africa at roughly the same time) named Calpurnius, a deacon and the grandson of a presbyter. (Needless to say, these data suggest priestly celibacy was not practiced in late fourth-century Britain.) Patrick's father owned some land. He was by no means poor; indeed, he may have come from aristocratic stock. Patrick tells us little else, except that he was not a terribly pious young man and, more important, that at the age of sixteen, he was captured by Irish pirates who were likely raiding his father's estate. For the next six years, Patrick shepherded in County Mayo in Ireland.

Eventually, in response to voices he thought divine, Patrick escaped two hundred miles on foot to a merchant ship, and, after three days (Patrick tells us— perhaps a buried allusion to symbolic resurrection), his pagan crew deposited him on the coast, probably of Britain. Eventually, he returned home. He began learning a simple catechism and familiarized himself with the Latin Bible, probably the Vulgate version of Jerome, which he quotes liberally in the *Confession*. While it is not impossible that some of his preparation occurred on the Continent, he probably trained with priests in Britain. In any case, this simple training sufficed to make him deacon and later to be ordained a priest. Once he was trained, the divine voices and visions resumed. Patrick's family, in view of the tribulations he had already endured, begged him not to leave them again. In one vision, he received a letter from "the Voice of the Irish." It implored him that he should "come again and walk among us." Despite the supplications of his desperate family, Patrick vowed to return to Ireland.

Ireland had never been occupied by the Romans. Consequently, early Irish society differed in significant ways from European culture. First, the basis of society was the tribe, each ruled over by a petty king. No central authority ruled over Irish society. As a result, small skirmishes and wars were endemic. This society was carefully layered into classes. For this reason, a Christian missionary would have been entirely exotic—an impediment that Patrick certainly had to confront. There were no towns or cities; the largest centers of dwelling were natural forts. Into these, women, children, and the oxen of a particular tribe could be gathered when a nearby tribe was raiding. The local tribal head might live in a house made of wood, but most of the tribe dwelt in tiny houses of turf and wattle. These tribes grew some crops but mainly raised cattle. The nature of early Irish society would shape Patrick's mission. For one thing, unlike continental bishops, who had fixed sees tied to cities, Patrick was an itinerant bishop.

No British or Gallic authority authorized Patrick's mission, and none consecrated him bishop. In fact, at the beginning of his *Letter to Coroticus,* Patrick informs us that he simply declared himself to be bishop. He had received his episcopal commission and orders, he tells us, directly from God. A later Irish tradition indicates that Patrick was sent to Ireland at the behest of Pope Celestine (r. 422–432), but that is plainly an attempt to vest him with the very authority he quite evidently lacked. Pope Celestine actually had in 431 sent Palladius of Auxerre (d. ca. 460) as first missionary to the Irish. Similarly, the medieval *Lives* of Patrick suggest he had a lengthy period of study in Gaul and Italy; again, these supply him with the educational background the actual lack of which, eventually, stimulated so much criticism of his mission.

Much closer to the truth is that ecclesiastical authorities regarded him as unsuitable for ministry. As Patrick confesses, thirty years before being made deacon, when a boy, he had committed a sin that contemporaries thought unfit him for orders. At the end of his life, Patrick says, he was a poor, ignorant orphan. Patrick's ecclesiastical superiors would have agreed emphatically. Nonetheless, Patrick's mission was, especially considered against this background, highly successful.

By the time of Patrick's arrival, Palladius had already Christianized many communities in the south of Ireland. For that reason, Patrick covered the northeast, western, and central regions of the island. His converts were people who had previously been untouched by Christianity. Patrick often approached the leaders of tribes or clans by bringing petty gifts of payment to tribal leaders or kings. In early-medieval fashion, again, once a clan leader accepted Christianity, many or all of his subjects would eventually be baptized.

It is quite clear from Patrick's writings that this method did not always work, and on occasion it resulted in severe opposition, even violence. This was the case with the king Coroticus, to whom Patrick complains in his letter. Coroticus enslaved and massacred a group of men and women who had, after the missionary efforts of Patrick, converted to Christianity. In this letter, Patrick shows himself to be especially concerned about Coroticus's female victims, many of whom had ignored the pleas of family members or husbands not to convert. Patrick himself faced other vicissitudes. He was imprisoned and tells us that he fully expected to be murdered. Having returned to Ireland as a bishop and missionary, however, he vowed never to leave the island again. His efforts were, in the long run, effective. By the time of his death, Ireland was, at least nominally, a largely "Christian" country. But Irish Christianity differed in important ways from that found on the Continent.

Early Irish Christianity and the Emergence of Celtic Christianity

"Celtic" is a category historians use to describe the practices, institutions, and peculiarities of a certain kind of Christianity and the areas of the world in which its adherents were active as missionaries: first, Ireland, Scotland, Wales, Cornwall, and Brittany; then the missionary regions of Anglo-Saxon England and the many monastic centers founded in Gaul, Italy, and Germany, of which Luxeuil, Péronne, St. Gall, and Bobbio hold pride of place. The Celtic-speaking peoples did not use the term "Celts" to distinguish themselves from other churches in the world of western Christianity. That said, early Irish Christianity, which developed as it spread into the broader phenomenon of Celtic Christianity, did differ in significant ways from its continental "Roman" counterpart. Still, there was no point in its history when Celtic churches threatened to break with Rome; nor did they ever refuse to recognize the juridical, theological, and disciplinary supremacy of the pope. Some of the particularities of Celtic Christianity were overemphasized by Bede and have misled historians for twelve centuries. That there were Celtic particularities in organization, liturgy, calendrical observance (these particularly problematic), piety, and intellectual life, originating in Ireland's physical isolation from the Continent, no historian denies.

First of all, early Irish Christianity differed in its pattern of ecclesiastical organization. As we have seen, the continental church was divided into administrative districts that corresponded to the old Roman cities, over each of which a bishop presided. As there were no cities then in Ireland, monasteries became the basic units of ecclesiastical organization. Ordinarily, each tribe had its own monastery. The abbot, usually a member of the clan leader's immediate family, ruled the monastery. Some priests, ordained as bishops, were consecrated to perform sacramental functions, such as ordinations and the dedication of churches. Yet abbots were the chief authorities of the church; bishops were subject to their authority. Usually ordained priests, they performed most duties of pastoral care for the local

2. Remains of a "beehive hut" monastery. Probably constructed between the sixth and eighth centuries CE. The monastery stands on a rock island dedicated to Michael in the Atlantic, off the coast of County Kerry in Ireland. One of many Christian sites dedicated to the holy archangel in early-medieval Christianity. Photo: akg-images/ ullstein bild.

community. So impressed was the Irish ecclesiastical system with the superiority of the abbot that when referring to the pope, they reputedly called him the Abbot of Rome. In any event, there is no question that the most impressive and distinctive feature of Celtic Christianity was its profoundly monastic character and its tendency to prize monks and monastic virtues.

The second way in which Irish Christianity came to differ from its European counterpart was in the severe austerity of its monasticism, which resembled ancient Near Eastern models more than western. The earliest monasteries were clusters of thatched huts, then stone beehive huts. Like their Egyptian or Syrian predecessors, early Irish monks were ferociously ascetical. Spending days in silence, fasting for great lengths of time, they sometimes prayed for hours while (a characteristic practice) they extended their arms in the shape of a cross, usually while standing. Some holy men genuflected or prostrated themselves hundreds of times through the night. Others practiced a form of ascetic immersion, plunging into icy water and remaining in the sea all night. The practice of *superpositio,* or fasting from food entirely, for two to as many as four days, was also widespread in Celtic-speaking churches. So, too, was the practice of individual self-flagellation, which would pass to the West as "the discipline" *(disciplina)*. Life in solitude was also characteristic of Celtic Christianity. Some dwelt in the wilderness as hermits absolutely alone; others attached themselves as anchorites to churches or monasteries. Such men were highly esteemed, and, like the "holy man" in ancient Near Eastern Christianity, they were consulted as advisers on issues of theology, discipline, and liturgy.

As already intimated, Irish monks were overcome with zeal to Christianize, and they often dedicated themselves to a life of voluntary, perpetual, missionary exile: *peregrinatio pro amore Christi* (pilgrimage for the love of Christ). Ironically, the practice may have originated in secular law, which required everlasting banishment for certain egregious crimes and was thus in its origins anything but voluntary. St. Columba (d. 597), for example, established on the island of Iona a monastery that served as a base from which he traveled to convert the Picts of Scotland. His efforts won him the title "Apostle to Scotland." From Iona, other Celtic missionary monks traveled to the north of England; the most famous and influential of them was St. Aidan. Columbanus (d. 615), named after Columba, eventually traveled to Gaul and established monasteries that again served as centers for evangelization. It was the work of these Irish monks that began the formidable job of converting the rural population of northern Europe to Christianity.

The particularly Irish manner of practicing penance influenced all the Celtic churches, the Roman British churches, and finally all of western Christendom. Until the seventh century, penance in the West was a public act. It resulted in the exclusion of the penitent from religious services, often for lengthy periods of time. For this system of public penance, the Irish substituted the practice of private penance. This practice originated in monastic sessions of spiritual guidance. Attempting to achieve perfection, many Celtic monks carefully scrutinized their consciences for any sin, even the smallest. These they confessed frequently to a superior in private. The superior would then impose for the traditional public penance a penitential practice to be performed privately and one that, in contrast to the traditional public form, could be repeated.

This form of penance also produced a distinct genre of literature: handbooks of penances that corresponded to different kinds and gravity of sins. Sexual sins got a treatment comprehensive in analysis and punishment, as well as risible or horrifying to the modern mind, as this seventh-century excerpt from a penitential written by Theodore of Canterbury (d. 690) indicates:

> Whoever fornicates with an effeminate male or with another man or with an animal must fast for 10 years. Elsewhere it says that whoever fornicates with an animal must fast 15 years and sodomites must fast for 7 years. If the effeminate male *(bædling)* fornicates with another effeminate male *(bædling)*,

(he is to) do penance for 10 years. Whoever does this unintentionally *(un-wærlice)* once must fast for 4 years; if it is habitual, as Basil says, for 15 years if he is not in orders and also one year (less?) so as a woman does. If it is a boy, for the first time, 2 years; if he does it again, 4 years. If he is a boy, for the first time, 2 years; if he does it again, 4 years. If he fornicates interfemorally [between the limbs], he must fast for 1 year or the 3 40-day periods. If he defiles himself [masturbates], he is to abstain from meat for four days. He who desires to fornicate [with] himself [i.e., to masturbate] and is not able to do so, he must fast for 40 days or 20 days. If he is a boy and does it often, either he is to fast 20 days or one is to whip him. If a woman fornicates [with another woman?] she must do penance for 3 years. If she touches herself in the same way, i.e., in emulation of fornication, she must repent for 1 year. One penance applies to a widow and a virgin; more [penance] is earned by her who has a husband if she fornicates. Whoever ejaculates seed into the mouth that is the worst evil. From someone it was judged that they repent this up to the end of their lives.

In interpreting this document, we must remember that not all that is written is enforced, and what is written can be primarily designed to discourage, rather than punish, particular behaviors. Be that as it may, the penances required by the penitential handbooks were, on the whole, severe in the extreme. The brother-in-law of Edward the Confessor (r. 1042–1066), after confessing that he had murdered a kinsman, walked barefoot from Bruges to Jerusalem in 1052 as penance. Though healthy and relatively young, he died in Constantinople on the journey home, depleted by the arduous journey. A very common penance for less serious sins was hardly lax: long fasting on bread and water. In any case, this form of private penances and the penitential handbook spread, ultimately, to the entire western church as a result of the influence of Irish missionaries, who carried to the Continent practices they had learned and perfected in Ireland. These private, personal, ascetical practices are among the most novel and distinctive characteristics of Celtic Christianity.

Foundations:
Monasticism, the Papacy, and Mission

In the fourth century, the mass of territory known to history as the Roman Empire broke up, as we have seen, into three distinct cultural and religious continents: the Byzantine East, where Orthodox Christianity was practiced and Greek spoken; the Muslim world, in which Islam was practiced and Arabic spoken; and the West, where Catholic Christianity and Latin and German were spoken. Of these three entities, western Europe was by far the least impressive culturally, politically, and economically. As Germanic marauders flooded over the Roman river borders, some brought Arian Christianity—heretical of course in Catholic eyes—while others, never Christianized, continued to practice different forms of Germanic religion. Yet seeds were sown for the formation of an early-medieval biblical culture and society. The key figures in the establishment of this ecclesiastical and biblical culture were the remarkable monk Benedict of Nursia (d. ca. 550); Pope St. Gregory I, "the Great" (r. 590–604); Bede, "the Venerable" (d. 735); and Roman missionaries, led by Augustine of Canterbury (d. 604), sent by Pope St. Gregory to convert the Anglo-Saxons in England. These missions would be sustained by papally commissioned monk-missionaries sent to Christianize the Germanic peoples in the northern fringes of Europe. The result was an early-medieval ecclesiastical culture based on the institutions of monasticism and the liturgical civilization it perfected; the papacy and its leadership in secular as well as in religious domains; and Christianization by a papally commissioned, disciplined corps of monks loyal to Rome and determined to spread a Rome-centered and Rome-loyal form of Christianity.

"The Finest Teacher of the Ascetical Life": Benedict of Nursia and Benedictine Monasticism

Though reverenced as the patriarch of western monasticism, Benedict went unmentioned by contemporaries. He left no writings, save the enormously influential *Rule*, which would set the pattern for western monasticism from the "Benedictine centuries" (roughly 600–1000), as John Henry Newman called them, down to the present day. Our knowledge of Benedict's life depends upon a single source, Pope Gregory's *Life of St. Benedict*, which takes up most of the second book of his *Dialogues*, a collection of the miracles performed by Italian saints. Written more than forty years after its subject's death, the work is therefore a piece of hagiography: a saint's life. No saint's life from the early Middle Ages is very trustworthy, historically speaking, because medieval hagiographers were not interested in producing biographies but in writing edifying literature for those aspiring to sanctity. Indeed, it would be wrong to call hagiographers "authors." They were compilers of inspiring and exemplary religious literature. In addition, Gregory was very likely relying on oral traditions, though two of the four abbots on whom he relies likely knew Benedict in his old age; they certainly knew the community's traditions about him. It is likely that Gregory also had read the *Rule*, as in one of his writings, a commentary on 1 Kings, he seems to refer to Benedict as "the finest teacher of the ascetical life" *(arctissimae vitae magister optimus)*.

With all this said, we are sure of certain facts. First, Benedict was born in the Italian province of Nursia, northeast of Rome, around 480, or about the time the last Roman emperor in the West was deposed. This is a coincidence of no little importance, as cloisters would from then on have to be robustly self-sufficient, in accordance with the increasingly localizing trends of the early-medieval period—developments caused by the disintegration of overarching social, economic, and educational systems and structures. We know, too, that Benedict was sent to Rome for education in the liberal arts. Appalled by the decadence of the city and by the debauchery of his fellow students, he left Rome and moved to the valley of Anio, where, under the guidance of a monk named Romanus, he spent three years in monastic solitude at Subiaco.

Eventually, Benedict attracted his own monastic disciples, whom he organized into groups under his guidance. With some of these monks, he then moved to a hill that rose high above the town of Cassino, roughly halfway between Rome and Naples. It was on Monte Cassino that he founded a coenobitical monastery and achieved fame regionally as a holy man. Before he died, he founded at least one more monastery and, more important for us, wrote a *Rule* intended to regulate life in the monastery over which he himself presided. He almost certainly did not expect or hope that his would emerge—though not for another two centuries—as the preeminent *Rule,* observed throughout Latin Christendom. Indeed, it was common in the sixth century for a *Rule* to regulate life only in the monastery in which it was written or in a small number of regional monasteries. Beyond that, monasteries often used several rules and borrowed from each what they wanted or needed. Indeed, it is worth emphasizing that it would be better to consider Benedict a compiler, as authorship was not understood by makers of rules to mean anything but the gathering, organization, and transmission of the ancient tradition of monastic observance and theology.

In fact, one of the discoveries made about the *Rule* in the twentieth century is that large portions of it, including some of its most influential and well-known sections (including the prologue and its first ten chapters), were almost certainly borrowed from a much longer, anonymous rule known as the *Rule of the Master* (or *RM*, just as the Benedictine *Rule* is abbreviated *RB*). There seem to be several reasons that the *RB*, completed ca. 540, late in Benedict's life, prevailed over the nearly contemporary *RM*. Aside from its brevity and freedom from irrelevant and extensive detail—it is around one-quarter the length of the fifty-thousand-word *RM*—and the later influence of Gregory's *Life of Benedict*, the *Rule* had intrinsic merits that recommended it. In his famous prologue, Benedict aspires "to ordain nothing harsh, nothing burdensome." Indeed, the asceticism he prescribes is, while rigorous, rather moderate in context. It allows for reasonable quantities of food and sleep, as well as generous provisions for reading and some fraternity. The abbot is far from an autocratic figure but is, rather, a spiritual father to each of the monks, with whom he is expected to have a genuinely paternal relationship. He represents Christ to his monastic sons. When an outgoing abbot nears death, the new abbot is not designated by his predecessor, as in *RM*, but elected by the community.

Still, the abbot, as was customary in monastic thinking, was to be obeyed without hesitation, and a monk vowed obedience to him, to the gospel, and to the *Rule* when he made his profession. The way of life to which he had vowed himself was a penitential one, based on the cardinal virtue of obedience. He also promised stability or lifelong residence in the community in which he had been professed and commitment to monastic virtue *(conversatio morum suorum)*. The purpose of the penitential community was the salvation of the monk's soul. No mention is made of apostolic, educational, or cultural obligations or purposes.

Benedict had imagined that the monk's day be essentially oriented to prayer in liturgy, the "work of God" *(opus Dei)*. Indeed, the monk's day was punctuated by the night office of vigils and seven daily offices (based on the psalmist's vow to praise God seven times each day in Psalm 118, a sign of the degree to which monastic culture was saturated in its very structure with biblical paradigms and language). Each office was devoted to the recitation of psalms, a hymn, readings from the Bible, and commentaries on both Testaments. In addition, Benedict imagined that his monks would, as a means of subsistence, labor agriculturally in fields for some seven hours a day or so (this varied slightly according to season).

Perhaps four hours daily were given over to "divine reading" *(lectio divina)*. By this term, Benedict meant to include the scriptures, saints' lives, the writings of the historian and admirer of Egyptian monasticism John Cassian (d. ca. 433), and writings and other monastic rules, such as those of Basil (d. 379), the patriarch of eastern monasticism. No educational or cultural purpose was intended; the cloister was, as Benedict said in his prologue, "a school for the Lord's service." Nonetheless, as young boys formed part of the community and because Benedictine life presupposed literacy, schools were established, letters taught, and Latin grammars and other classics owned by many cloisters. Finally, nearly the entire day was to be spent in silence, even meals, at which an elaborate sign language was developed to allow communication. Indeed, the only voice heard in the refectory was that of a monk reading edifying literature from the pulpit. This simple, balanced monastic day was to be radically refashioned by the time the *RB* had spread throughout Europe and, by the year 1000, became almost ubiquitously observed in its cloisters.

The Monastery and the Mundane

By the eleventh century, this uncomplicated division of the day was dramatically altered in order that monks might offer their lives to satisfying the social and religious needs of the political, social, economic—and of course spiritual—environment around which a cloister had been planted. No other service was so treasured as the monks' capacity to pray for society. Monks were imagined by those who founded and supported them as a sort of spiritual militia; they fought against the society's spiritual enemies, especially the archenemy Satan and his minions. Above all, donors of land and buildings expected that monks would satisfy for the sins they had committed against God by their prayers. Punishing penances could be satisfied not by the sinner but by his surrogate, the monk; he performed by his liturgical prayers the penances accumulated by lay sinners. Here the issue, religiously speaking, is that satisfaction was owed to God, who had been dishonored by sin. It did not matter who made that satisfaction; what mattered was that it was made and God's honor restored (just as a bank does not care who pays a debt owed to it so long as it is repaid with interest). By the eleventh century, this requirement for satisfaction resulted in the ordination to priesthood of the vast majority of the monastic community. No prayer, no devotional act, no ritual was believed to be so effective in making satisfaction as saying mass. Soon monks were reciting private masses and Offices for the Dead for much of the day, obligations that virtually eliminated the manual labor Benedict had envisaged.

Monasteries also increasingly served as safe havens for children, called "oblates," given by their parents to the cloisters. Allowing the family to avoid partitioning its estate, this practice was especially useful to noble families, as monasteries allowed sons born to the purple to live in relative security and comfort and with other children of the well-born. Aristocratic girls for whom no satisfactory marriage could be arranged also found homes in Benedictine nunneries. Eventually proscribed in 1215 by the Fourth Lateran Council, the recruitment of child oblates produced some of the most remarkable monks of the Middle Ages, including the Venerable Bede (discussed below), the Saxon-Norman monk Orderic Vitalis (d. ca. 1143), and others. In his book on ecclesiastical history, Orderic tells us what it was like to be "donated" by his British parents to a Norman monastery and the assurances given by his father:

> For he promised me for his part that if I became a monk I should taste of the joys of Heaven with the innocents after my death. . . . And so, a boy of ten, I crossed the English channel and came into Normandy as an exile, unknown to all, knowing no one. Like Joseph in Egypt I heard a language I could not understand. But thou did suffer me through thy grace to find nothing but kindness and friendship among strangers. I was received as an oblate in the abbey of St. Evroul by the venerable abbot Mainer in the eleventh year of my life. . . . The name of Vitalis was given me in place of my English name, which sounded harsh to the Normans.

For more than the fifty years that remained to him, Orderic spent his days, except for a few short trips ordered by his abbot, in the cloister of St. Evroul.

Other societal and political changes in the early-medieval period transformed Benedict's simple vision of lay monks pursuing their own supernatural perfection in isolation. Where Benedict had wished his abbots to be elected by the community, lay lords were, no later than the ninth century, either physically present at elections or involved in their direct appointment. In addition, familial relations with nobles led monks to perform still other duties for secular authorities, lay men and women, and ecclesiastical overseers. Some Benedictines served, anomalously to us, as leaders of military campaigns. Others advised kings or other civic luminaries; some acted as judges in secular courts. Still others taught or practiced medicine, architecture (monastic architecture is quintessentially Romanesque), or masonry. Some sat in parliaments and royal councils. Intellectuals produced not just religious literature, but also scientific and mathematical works. Others managed agricultural estates.

3. Abbaye aux Hommes (Men's Abbey), St. Etienne, west façade, Caen, France. Begun 1068. A fine example of a Romanesque Benedictine church. Compare with illustration 22. Photo credit: Foto Marburg/Art Resource, NY.

In the end, nonetheless, the essential work of the monks, from the point of view of the society that supported them, was intercessory prayer. A donor who endowed a monastery could be assured that no matter the enormity of his transgressions, regardless of the weight of sin he had accumulated, his penance would be "prayed down" by a community he founded, a community all then believed would exist in perpetuity. An institution that in Benedict's time was isolated and profoundly disinclined to offer service to surrounding communities, one that concentrated on the supernatural aspirations of its monks, came to offer both civic and spiritual benefits without which early-medieval society found it could not live.

"Consul of God": Pope St. Gregory, "the Great"

At the end of the sixth century, Benedict's monastery at Monte Cassino was sacked by the Lombards, one of the Germanic tribes that came, in the wake of imperial collapse in the West, to control the Italian peninsula. It is not impossible that the monks from Cassino fled to Rome and there acquainted Gregory with the *Rule,* to which and to whose author he would give such crucial and authoritative patronage and prestige. Gregory's enthusiasm for monasticism may well have been nurtured by Benedict and by the western tradition, well established in the late sixth century, of monk-bishops. By the beginning of Gregory's pontificate in 590, many monks had been made bishops in the West. However, Gregory was the first monk to be made bishop of Rome, or pope. A man of immense diplomatic and administrative skill, as well as holiness, his elevation to the throne of St. Peter at the dawn of the Middle Ages exemplified the crucial role monks would play in the life of the early-medieval church.

Gregory's elevation also symbolized the bishop's position in the West as defender of his episcopal city, in this case Rome. Like other bishops who found themselves faced with urban power vacuums, Gregory was, as principal citizen of the city, its informal "mayor" at a time of grave adversity for Rome and indeed for much of Italy. In addition, Gregory established geographical and ecclesiastical principles that, in time, would allow later-medieval popes to grow in authority, power, and prestige. A prolific writer who left many works, he is considered (along with Ambrose, Jerome, and Augustine) one of the four ancient "doctors" of the western church. His life and papacy are a fulcrum point between the old Roman society and the emerging sacred one. A loyal citizen of Rome, of whose benefits he partook and for which he exercised his administrative and practical skills brilliantly, he was also an energetic bishop who helped create a new society based on the papacy, monastic life, and biblical culture.

Gregory was fortunate to have been born into a patrician family that was also deeply dedicated to the church and its leadership. Already by his birth, his family had brought forth one and perhaps two popes (one of them, Felix III [r. 483–492], was Gregory's grandfather). Three other relatives were so devout that they would ultimately be proclaimed saints. Gregory inherited administrative skills as well. In this sense, we must understand that Gregory not only pointed the way forward, but he had also absorbed some of the assumptions of an imperial subject and many of the characteristics of a Roman civic leader or manager. Had he lived in an earlier century or even elected a secular path, he might have had a successful civic career. Gregory had no desire to break with the Roman Empire. Indeed, he assumed he was an imperial subject, knowing very well he lived on the western perimeter of that world, while real "Roman" power lay far to the East. He took it for granted that the emperor had not only the right but the duty to protect the western church. In fact, when he became bishop of Rome, he wished dearly that the emperor could have come to his city's aid in its distress. When he was elected bishop of Rome by the clergy and people of the city, he put off the traditional laying on of the hands of other bishops until he received permission from the emperor to proceed with the ceremony. As bishop, he was not only the principal citizen of Rome, but also its wealthiest inhabitant. His "Roman" qualities of organizational skill, fondness for order, and penchant for solving problems made him the natural choice to manage and defend his episcopal city and its surrounding territory, above all in a time of somber and quite grave tribulation. He was also forced into this position by simple political realities. No Roman emperor had lived in the city for more than a century. The Byzantine emperor's representative in Italy, the governor (or "exarch") of Ravenna, was far north and powerless to help.

Early in his thirties, Gregory assumed the prestigious and powerful position of prefect of the city of Rome *(praefectus urbi)*. If skilled, he was not enthusiastic about the position, and within a short period, he resigned to become a monk. As such, Gregory founded at least seven monasteries, six of them in Sicily. He joined St. Andrew's on the Caelian Hill in Rome, a monastery he himself had founded. Rigorously ascetic, he likely damaged his health, as many monks would in the Middle Ages, by the extent of his mortifications, and he was periodically ill until his death. Indeed, for the fourteen years of his pontificate, a stomach ailment laid him up for days and sometimes weeks.

To his familial reputation, ecclesiastical prestige would be added when Gregory was appointed one of the seven historic deacons of Rome. At the same time, ecclesio-political duties would soon mushroom. Educated men with practical administrative skill were very rare. Already the pope's closest adviser when made deacon, Gregory would be appointed papal ambassador in 579 to the court in Constantinople (where he began his enormously long biblical commentary, *Moralia in Job,* a meditation on the sufferings of Job and the necessity of defeating despair). There he lived the monastic life with the Latin monks who accompanied him. It was there, not when he was pope, that Gregory adopted the title "servant of the servants of God" *(servus servorum Dei),* one that he later applied to himself as pope, as all his successors on the throne of St. Peter have down to this day. He finished his diplomatic service after six years, having never mastered the Greek spoken ubiquitously around him. This of course was not because of want of skill but because of Roman snobbery, of the aristocratic conviction that Roman culture and language were superior to Greek. On his return, he became abbot of the monastery in Rome he had founded.

After the bishop of the city, Pope Pelagius II (r. 579–590), died in 590, Gregory was chosen to be elevated to the throne of St. Peter. He was about fifty years of age. Before him lay the tasks of ministering to the religious needs of Christians in his diocese, serving as a sort of unelected (if supremely well-prepared) city manager in an age of genuine crisis, and leading the universal church as chief bishop.

It was, to say the least, a trying time to be pope. There was very good reason for Gregory's conviction that the world was about to end. He was not the first Christian, nor hardly the last, to persuade himself that economic and political calamity, and the human suffering it caused, portended The End. Gregory's predecessor had died because of a plague—the same plague, the bubonic, that would take more than one-quarter of the population of Europe, and one-fifth of the world's, eight centuries later. Since the deposition in 476 of the last Roman emperor, Italy had been ruled by the Ostrogoths. In the years 535–555, Emperor Justinian attempted, as we have seen, a reconquest of Italy. The resulting war devastated Italy. For forty days in 549, Rome was empty, a ghost town. Milan destroyed, Rome itself came under siege three times in 546. Gregory came of age during this period of chaos. Eventually (554), as we saw in the previous chapter, the Ostrogoths were defeated, but the imperial rule of Italy lasted only fourteen years.

In 568, a Germanic tribe not nearly so amenable to Romanization as the Ostrogoths had crossed the Alps. A tribe as fearsome as it was land-hungry, the Lombards began to colonize large parts of Italy. Of the imperial conquests hardwon by Justinian, only coastal areas, such as Ravenna and Naples, could be saved. The Lombards came by Gregory's day to occupy the north, south, and east of the peninsula, and they eyed Rome covetously. In the eyes of Pope Pelagius II, the un-Romanized Lombards and the suffering they caused were far, far worse than that occasioned by Ostrogothic occupation: "So great," he observed, "are the calamities and tribulations we suffer from the treachery of the Lombards, in spite of their solemn promises, that no one could adequately describe them. . . . The Empire is in . . . [a] critical situation. . . . May God bid the emperor to come to our aid with all speed before the army of that impious nation, the Lombards, shall have seized the lands that still form part of the empire." As the Byzantine emperor, the traditional protector of Rome, had military problems of his own, he was not at all inclined to come to the aid of the Eternal City. Some 850 letters of Gregory survive, many of them describing his state of mind as military defender and lover of the old imperial ways. Pondering the lost grandeur that was once Rome, Gregory could only lament that the cities of Italy had been "destroyed, its fortifications ruined, its population depleted, and the earth a wasteland." Later in his life, Gregory commented on this scene of devastation: "We see what has happened to her [Rome]. She, once the mistress of the world, has suffered innumerable adversities in number and intensity. Her people are desolate, threatened by external enemies. Everywhere there is only ruin, nothing but ruin. . . . The remnant are menaced by the sword and tribulations without number. . . . We no longer have a Senate, no longer a people. For those still living only sorrows and tears. . . . Rome is deserted and in flames." As if to intensify the apocalyptic climate and amplify the scale of human suffering, the Tiber flooded the city, making the lowlands marsh.

In this dire situation, Gregory had been abandoned by his traditional protector. Consequently, Gregory assumed responsibility for those in flight from the barbarians, organized the defense of Rome, and treated with barbarian leaders. Refugees from the north flooded by the thousands into Rome. Gregory acted as "defender of the city" *(defensor civitatis)* as pope, organizing troops and dispensing advice to military commanders. When garrisons near Rome almost mutinied because of lack of pay, Gregory took five hundred pounds of gold from Rome's ecclesiastical funds. He attempted to negotiate with the Lombard king. Thousands now looked to him for sustenance.

But how to feed the hungry refugees and the people of Rome, as well as pay for the defense of the city? For these purposes, Gregory possessed a pearl of great price, the so-called "Patrimony of St. Peter," organized by Gregory into what historians would eventually call "the Papal States." These were parcels of lands that the apostolic see had received as legacies from grateful and generous Christians over the first Christian centuries. They were, fortunately, scattered far and wide in the West; not only could they be found in central and southern Italy, as well as its offshore islands, but also in North Africa, Gaul, and the Balkans. The military consequence of this scattering was that it was unlikely in the extreme that they could be conquered simultaneously. Economically speaking, they generated substantial income and produce, which Gregory used for refugee aid and defense.

All of this relief and defense activity very naturally brought Gregory into affairs of the commonweal in a time of desperate crisis. No one disputed that he had the right and the obligation, as the wealthiest and most capable man in the city, not to mention its bishop, to intervene in the civic affairs of the city. The effect, nonetheless, was to reverberate for centuries. The bishop of Rome had become, in a power vacuum, the secular leader of the city and the territory surrounding it. He had used the considerable resources of the Roman church to feed the refugees and defend the city of Rome. This secular rule was to be a mark of the medieval papacy. Like other bishops who presided over their sees, Gregory was in effect the civic ruler of the city of Rome. He was the first to be chosen pope. This, too, was an augury of the crucial, manifold roles to be played for centuries by the bishops of Rome, first in Italy and then, after the turn of the millennium, in much of western Europe.

One of Gregory's most influential books would be a volume written shortly after his accession to the papacy, entitled *Pastoral Care*. It was written in response to a request by his friend, John, bishop of Ravenna. Divided systematically into parts on the selection of clergy, the purity of life to which a pastor should aspire,

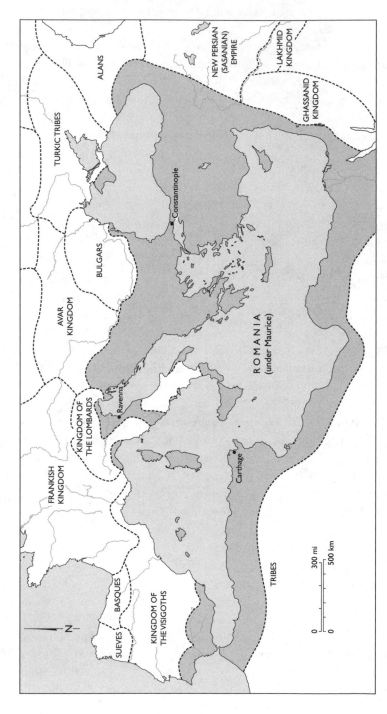

Map 2. Europe at the time of Gregory the Great, ca. 600

the different kinds of people whom one will encounter as pastor, and (with re-markable sensitivity) thoughts on the most appropriate approach to each, the fourth book urges the pastor to beware of personal ambition. This book had enormous influence not only in the western churches, including those in Britain, but also among the kings of the new European kingdoms and even with the east-ern emperor, Maurice (r. 582–602). The emperor, as well as many of the kings, demanded that copies be made and distributed to the bishops in their dioceses. As is clear here, not only the emperor but also kings saw themselves as lying, in ecclesiastical matters, very much within the church leadership and hierarchy, not outside the church but within it.

Needless to say, bishops in the kingdoms saw themselves to be the supreme authorities within their own dioceses. How did Gregory understand his role in relation to his fellow bishops? As successor to Peter, the prince of the apostles, Gregory certainly saw himself as having not only a primacy of honor, but he also assumed that he was vested with a general authority over other bishops (descen-dants of the apostles) that came down from Christ's commission to St. Peter, as represented in Matthew 16. This assumption comes through in Gregory's sev-enth book of *Pastoral Care,* as well as in his *Letter* 40: "To Peter the care and dominion *[Petro totius ecclesiae cura et principatus]* of the entire church" had been given. This authority rested in what in Gregory's day was called "St. Peter's See." Writing to the patriarch of Constantinople, he did not hesitate to assert his claim to the primacy of dignity among the five ancient patriarchates. That was not disputed, but the eastern bishops insisted on limiting the reality of the Roman bishop's primacy to one of dignity. None would have conceded that the pope could intervene in the internal affairs of another bishop's diocese. Even the bish-ops of the West were more prone to listen to their kings than to the distant pope. It will be obvious, then, that while Gregory was regarded with great affection, the practical power of the bishop of Rome in other bishoprics was quite limited.

After his death on March 12, 604, Gregory was canonized by popular acclaim. His tomb in Constantine's Church of St. Peter memorialized him as *consul Dei* (the consul of God). He was subsequently named a doctor of the church and is one of only two pontiffs (the other being Pope St. Leo I [r. 440–461]) to be vested with the title *Magnus* (the Great). He was a protector and promoter of monasticism and laid the foundation for the important alliance between monasti-cism and the papacy.

Above all, Gregory was the first medieval pope (though not the last) to take an active role in the conversion of the Germanic tribes, in his case the Anglo-Saxons. Gregory was not of course the first to have Christianized Roman Britain. Christianity had already arrived by the fourth century. Three bishoprics from that century are known. Germanic invasion in the fifth and sixth centuries, however, wiped Christianity from much of the map of lowland Britain. Left defenseless, the Romans had appointed Germanic Saxons, along with Angles and Jutes, to defend the island as mercenaries. It then occurred to the Germans that they could seize the land they were defending for themselves. They did and began to settle. Although Frankish bishops were only thirty miles from Kent, soon to be principal see of the English church, it was not they who undertook the conversion of the Anglo-Saxons. It was Pope Gregory in far-distant Rome. Six years into his papacy, Gregory wrote to two Frankish princes, expressing his will more than that of the Anglo-Saxons: "It has come to our ears that, by the mercy of God, the English race earnestly desire to be converted to Christianity."

The Anglo-Saxon Mission

According to an anonymous Anglo-Saxon biography of Gregory written ca. 710, Gregory's interest in the English originated before he became pope. He once encountered in Rome fair-skinned, light-haired, blue-eyed young men on the slave market. Gregory asked the young men to what tribe they belonged. Told that they were "Angles," Gregory is reported to have responded that they were "not Angles but angels" *(non Angli sed angeli)*. Gregory's biographer proceeds to report that Gregory received permission from the pope to go to Britain himself to begin the work of Christianization there but that the Roman people petitioned the pope not to allow him to quit the city. When he became pope, he wrote to the patriarch of Alexandria in 598. He told him of "the English race, who live in a corner of the world . . . [and] until now have remained unbelieving, wickedly worshipping wood and rocks." Gregory told the patriarch how he had sent one of his monks to begin converting the religiously depraved tribes. Letters had just reached him. His emissary, he learned, had baptized "more than 10,000 Englishmen."

While we can take that estimate with a grain of salt, two features of this account call for comment for their later significance. First of all, it was the pope who initiated and authorized the missionary effort, a precedent that would guide the Christianization of northern Europe in the centuries to follow. Second, monks, who were expected to do no missionary work—indeed, no pastoral work at all— were the ones Gregory selected to perform the work of Christianization. This too set a pattern: the paradigm of monks missionizing under the authority of popes, with whom they would correspond for counsel and encouragement, while planting a form of Christianity among the Germans that made Rome the center and its bishop the decisive arbiter of the faith.

By the standards of the day, Gregory showed remarkable pastoral sensitivity to the Saxons and their native religious traditions, which he was, in the end, deter-

4. The Church of the Holy Savior (Basilica San Salvatore), Spoleto, is one of the oldest in Italy. It dates from the late fourth and early fifth centuries. It is an excellent example of the early Christian practice (encouraged by Gregory the Great) of using Roman temples to build Christian churches. This was once a classical pagan temple, the inner sanctuary of which is now occupied by the choir. This transformation is a good example of one way in which the Roman Empire was physically Christianized. © Vanni Archive/ Art Resource, NY.

mined to eradicate. He urged his Italian monks not to destroy the Saxon temples but the idols in them. Had not God dealt similarly with the Israelites in Egypt? Their temples, if well built, should simply be consecrated with holy water and converted to the worship of the true God. With knowledge of the true God, they would more likely worship Him if they could "resort to the places to which they had been accustomed." There they would substitute solemnities like veneration of the holy martyrs in place of their diabolic practice of slaughtering oxen in pagan sacrifice. Gregory's advice represents some of the earliest Christian thinking on how the newly converted would assimilate to a novel religious culture, a topic to which entire libraries, especially in the early modern age, would eventually be dedicated.

It was not of course a single monk that performed all of the work in Kent. According to an account left by the great English monk-writer Bede, the Italian monk Augustine of Canterbury established a monastery dedicated to Sts. Peter and Paul; it was later to be named after St. Augustine himself. It was this monastery that served as the basis of the monks' missionary efforts. By 601, King

Ethelbert (r. ca. 560–616), whose wife was already baptized and in fact had in the king's house a Frankish bishop to minister to her spiritual needs, had converted. It is possible that much of the warrior aristocracy's conversion followed, in the customary early-medieval pattern.

Be that as it may, for some generations, both Anglo-Saxon bishops and kings began a correspondence with popes for direction on matters of faith, morals, liturgy, and organization. Occasionally, pilgrims sent by local bishops traveled to Rome to discuss such issues with the pope or to ask for his decision on a disputed matter. Such correspondence often took quite concrete forms. For example, when a new archbishop of Canterbury was chosen, he would write to Rome to receive his *pallium,* a woolen liturgical vestment conferred on newly consecrated archbishops by the pope. Again, these were developments of some significance. Fiercely loyal to St. Peter, this church, which lay on the perimeter of the world known in Rome, strengthened its connection to and affection for the successor to the Apostle, whom it saluted by confessing his religious authority. It was the first church outside of central Italy to do so.

The Venerable Bede

The account given us of Augustine's missionary efforts is from an early-seventh-century document called the *Ecclesiastical History of the English People.* It was written by a monk, Bede (ca. 672–735), later called "the Venerable." Usually regarded as the greatest and most influential writer in the West between Pope Gregory and Alcuin of York (d. 804), a monk in the court of Charlemagne in the early ninth century, some have described the period ca. 600–800 as "the age of Bede." To the *Ecclesiastical History,* Bede appended a brief summary of the facts of his life:

> I, Bede, servant of Christ and priest of the monastery of the blessed apostles St. Peter and St. Paul, which is at Wearmouth and Jarrow . . . was born in the territory of that monastery. At the age of seven, I was given to the most reverend abbot Benedict to be educated. . . . From that time, I have lived my whole life in the habit of that monastery, directing all my energy to the study of Scripture and, amid the observance of the regular discipline and daily duty of chanting in church, ever happily applying myself to learning or teaching or writing.

He was made deacon at age nineteen and ordained priest when thirty. "From the time I entered the priesthood to my fifty-ninth year of age," Bede says, "I have devoted myself to annotating briefly Holy Scripture from the tracts of the venerable Fathers, as I and my associates needed."

Bede was lucky to have so ambitious and adventurous an abbot as Benedict Biscop (d. 689), who founded the cloister at Wearmouth in 674 and that at Jarrow two years after Bede became oblate. Benedict traveled extensively on the Continent, from which he brought back books, not to mention the arch-chanter of St. Peter's in Rome, Abbot John, to Wearmouth-Jarrow. The education Bede would receive would be, thus, from some of the greatest teachers in Christendom and certainly the best-stocked library in Britain.

Bede wrote in a simple, intentionally "humble" style, the better to achieve the didactic purpose intended in all his writings. About half of Bede's literary output of roughly fifty works is scriptural commentary. For this purpose, Jerome's biblical commentaries and his translation of the Bible, the Vulgate, were critical; Bede relied on them heavily. He also had access to many of Augustine's writings, as well as those of Ambrose and Gregory the Great. Many of his other writings show us Bede the monastic schoolmaster. He composed textbooks on penmanship, spelling, elementary grammar, sacred geography, natural phenomena, versification, telling time (important, of course, for monastic liturgical life), and a Christian calendrical text. He created a martyrology in a book that supplies evidence of how rapidly the cult of the saints had grown. Yet the work that is his masterpiece is his *Ecclesiastical History,* "published" in 731. This is the work that earned him the sobriquet "Father of English History," even "Father of English Scholarship, History, and Literature." It was for the influence of that book and his scriptural commentaries that he was named a doctor of the church in 1899 and canonized in 1935. In the eleventh century, his relics were taken and translated to the spectacular cathedral of Durham, where they remain today.

The Lindisfarne Gospels

Just before Bede was ordained priest, monks in the scriptoria of Lindisfarne, sometimes called "the Holy Island," were about to finish one of the great achievements of medieval British culture. Richly illuminated, as well as glossed, the Lindisfarne Gospels are instantly recognizable by their spectacular ornamental vocabulary, including a broad range of colors, interlaced bands within frames, and uniquely decorated initials (sometimes filling an entire page), which are on virtually every page. Preceding each of the four gospels is a "carpet page," so called because, like a carpet, it is completely decorated, usually with interlaced ribbons. Based on Italian and wider Mediterranean models, the Lindisfarne Gospels may well reflect the sorts of manuscripts Benedict Biscop had brought from Rome. Only the Book of Kells rivals the Lindisfarne Gospels for artistic inspiration, as well as dedication to detail and splendor, as visitors to the British Library in London can today testify. It is perhaps no accident that these splendid cultural works

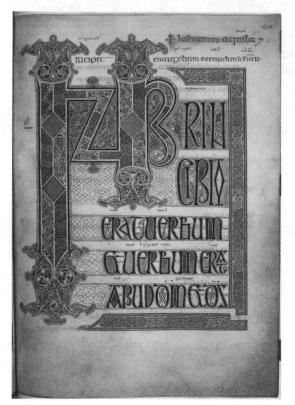

5. Lindisfarne Gospel. The first or incipit page of the Gospel of John (identified by the monastic scribe with his symbol, the *aquila*, or eagle: *In principio erat Verbum et Verbum erat apud Deum et Deus* (In the beginning was the Word and the Word was with God and God). A fine example of Hiberno-Saxon art, composed ca. 700–720. © British Library Board/ Robana/Art Resource, NY.

were produced on an island that, until the Synod of Whitby, was the spiritual powerhouse of Anglo-Saxon England.

The Synod of Whitby (664)

In ancient and early-medieval Christianity, religious pluralism was not especially appreciated. Tolerance for variety in matters liturgical, theological, and disciplinary was simply not part of the Christian worldview. Proper cult demanded that worship be performed everywhere the same. Calendrical matters, like observance of the date of Easter, were of great significance not only for this reason, but also because they functioned as symbols of the unity of the church. Through the mid-seventh century, Celtic and Roman missionaries worked in England without much evidence of mutual hostility. Each church followed its own liturgical traditions, including the dating of Easter observance. In the end, calendrical observances, especially the observance of Easter, were a disagreement that forced a confrontation, as it was causing division even within the royal court of Northumbria, where the king followed Celtic tradition and his wife, the Roman. If differences between Celtic and Roman disciplinary observances have sometimes been exaggerated, the hostility generated by this particular observance was felt cordially.

A debate summoned by the king ensued. Celtic and Irish bishops reported to the monastery of Whitby to decide the issue. When Bishop Colman (d. 676), the Irish prelate, conceded that St. Peter, the quintessential Roman saint, had been given the keys to the kingdom of heaven by Christ, the issue was decided. The king now chose the Roman ways. By the late seventh century, all of the Anglo-Saxon kingdoms had as well. The decision at Whitby, and its aftermath, only strengthened the English church's fidelity to St. Peter and his successor. With this in mind, it would be foolish to believe that Celtic Christianity and its particularisms simply disappeared from Britain. In fact, the process by which Celtic churches were placed under the jurisdiction of the See of St. Peter (that is, the bishop of Rome) would take centuries. Only by the end of the twelfth century, as a result of reforms of British monarchs (like Queen Margaret of Scotland [d. 1093]) and Welsh and other British bishops, had Celtic Christianity lost its independence and virtually all of its distinguishing characteristics.

British Missionaries on the Continent

The verdict at Whitby did nothing to take away from the severe asceticism and the desire to Christianize the pagans, qualities that were brought to Anglo-Saxon England by Celtic missionaries and later exported to the north of Britain. Indeed, it was from the north that many monks, loyal to Rome, would join the exodus across the Channel. They did not face the first obstacle—language—standing in the way of so many missionaries in ecclesiastical history. Speakers of a Germanic language, they probably had little difficulty learning local Germanic dialects. In any case, though Latinate, they likely taught in their converts' tongues.

The two outstanding monastic missionaries of the north were both notable for their organizational skills and their dedication to the papacy. A man who had spent a dozen years in an Irish cloister, where his zeal for missionizing grew, Willibrord (d. 739) would play a decisive role in establishing Roman-centered Christianity in parts of Europe that were rather hostile to him. At the end of the seventh century, his abbot sent him, along with perhaps a dozen companions, to continue the work of Christianizing the Frisians, a Germanic ethnic group concentrated in coastal enclaves in the Netherlands and Germany. He founded a monastery in Esternach (modern Luxembourg) ca. 700 as a base from which to conduct his missionary work. Realizing he needed authority to establish bishoprics where there had never been any, he requested permission from the pope. The pope not only gave him that permission but also made him archbishop of the Frisians. He also gave him the historic Roman name of Clement. The nexus of pope-monk-missionary, already strong, was fortified.

Renamed Boniface by Pope Gregory II (r. 715–731), Winfrith (d. 754) was a willing disciple of Clement. He ranged from the coast of the North Sea to Thuringia and Bavaria for four decades, both Christianizing pagans and reforming ecclesiastical life in realms where it had collapsed. Founder of another historic northern monastery, Fulda, Boniface was made "archbishop to the Germans" by the pope, who established his see at Mainz and by whom he was consecrated. He corresponded with four popes. With each, Boniface sought counsel or approval in a decision he made. Eventually, he crossed back to Frisia. There he was martyred in 754. His body was brought back to Fulda, where he was buried.

The mustard seed planted by Gregory a century and a half earlier had flowered beyond even that remarkable man's powers of imagination. Not only was all of Britain Christianized. So, too, now, were the northeastern regions of western Europe. Anglo-Saxon monks had planted a form of Christianity loyal to St. Peter and his successors. As a result, Rome-centered Christianity would spread to the Franks, with whom the political future of Europe lay.

Holy Empire? Christianity, Charlemagne, and the Carolingians

No empire in Europe from the early Middle Ages to the time of Napoleon was to be so grand in sheer territorial scope as the Carolingian. It extended to the southwest at the Pyrenees, to the southeast into central Italy, eastward into central Europe, and northward to the Danish march. It contained within its borders most of the western Christian lands. In the mid-eighth century, the Frankish dynasty formed an alliance with the papacy that was to change the future of both the Franks and the church. Frankish kings would see it as their solemn religious duty to protect the papacy and defend its lands. Consecrated by popes, these kings would issue laws governing religious affairs, including the conduct of bishops, priests, and monks, as well as laypeople. It was under the Franks that the *Rule* of St. Benedict was established as the standard of monastic observance in western Europe. Canon law was recognized as an expression of the highest ideals of the Christian community. The Carolingian court would produce most of the leading intellectuals, abbots, and bishops for generations. In the end, both internal and external forces caused the empire to disintegrate but not before its leaders defined and reformed Christianity. The relationship of imperial power and the papacy is certainly among the central themes in the history of Christianity, a storyline that, it could be argued, had its origins in the Carolingian era.

The Hammer: Charles Martel

Supporter of the missionary labors of Willibrord, Charles Martel (r. 723–741) by the early eighth century ruled the Frankish kingdom. His chief military and political aim was the unification and defense of his realm. In this connection, Charles fought in a battle that has been hallowed by legend and history; it was for his martial skills that he earned the sobriquet "Martel," or "the Hammer." By the early eighth century, Muslim invaders, having defeated the Visigothic kingdom in 711, crossed the Pyrenees and poured into southern France. For more than a generation they held land along the Mediterranean littoral. In 732, a Muslim raid near Tours was checked by Charles. It is sometimes said that this victory, by securing the southwest border of the Frankish kingdom, made the creation of Europe possible by impeding further Muslim incursion. That is a bit of an exaggeration, as in 735 the Muslims destroyed Arles and three years later sacked Avignon. For quite a time they controlled the region of Narbonne. Nonetheless, it can be said that Charles's victory ensured that the Muslims would never create a powerful stronghold north of the Pyrenees. From this point to the wars of conquest, Muslim strength would be confined to the Iberian Peninsula.

Charles viewed himself as a good Christian. For him, that meant endowing churches and monasteries and supporting the work of the missions to the north. It also meant that he could name or depose bishops and expropriate ecclesiastical revenues for his own purposes. He regarded himself as the practical or actual head of the Frankish church. This attitude caused tensions with the pope, but for the bishop of Rome to break with the most powerful king in the Occident would have been reckless, and Charles used that land to support warriors, soldiers who in turn protected the church.

When the titular Merovingian king died in 737, Charles chose not to replace him. This, perhaps more than the Battle of Tours, was to have great significance for the future of Europe and for the church. For this non-act was to allow his son to claim a vacant throne, announce that he was king, and begin to establish the Carolingian dynasty—named not for Charlemagne, as is often heard, but for Charles Martel—which would change the face of Europe and shape the history of early-medieval Christianity.

Already by the time of Charles Martel, the Merovingian dynasty's last strong king had been dead for a century. The power lay with the king's principal aid, the *maior domus,* or "mayor of the [royal] palace." He was a powerful civic official and leader of soldiers. In place of a ruler who was merely nominal, Pepin III (r. 751–768), sometimes "the Younger" or "the Short," wished to be recognized as king. At the same time, the papacy was threatened by the Lombards, who had already taken much of central Italy. This was territory that the bishops of Rome regarded as rightly belonging to them. Early in the eighth century, the Lombards had attempted to conquer all former Byzantine territories, including Rome. That crisis passed, but another time of danger began around the middle of the eighth century. In short, the Franks sought legitimacy; the popes were desperate for military protection. In the event, a theological controversy in the East prevented the papacy from appealing to its traditional protector, the Byzantine emperor.

The Iconoclastic Controversy and Its Consequences

In 726, Emperor Leo III (r. 717–741), for reasons that still remain a matter of debate, ordered the destruction of religious images, or icons. A reign of terror resulted in the mutilation and death of many eastern monks, who were the principal iconodules, or image venerators. It resulted as well in the confiscation of vast territories of monastic lands; perhaps expropriation was the emperor's actual motivation. Be that as it may, Leo's actions began a half-century of iconoclasm (image obliteration), an era of artistic destruction and human devastation that was sanctioned by the will of the emperor and implemented by policy devised by supporters. Western popes and intellectuals regarded iconoclasm not simply as a breach of tradition. It was rank heresy, as it seemed to compromise the central incarnational principle of Christian theology by maintaining that the material could not mediate the divine. In any event, the popes of the mid-eighth century took another momentous step toward making Europe an autonomous entity, the home of western Christianity, alienated permanently from its traditional imperial protector. Frantic at the threat posed by the Lombards, the popes turned to the only power willing and able to protect them—and in need of something from the papacy.

Covenant of Kingdom and Papacy

The marriage of the Kingdom of the Franks and the Catholic Church was arranged by necessity. Both sides needed something from the other. The Franks needed a rightful, indeed sacred, authority as respected and prominent as the bishop of Rome to recognize their legitimacy as kings of the Frankish realm. The Church needed a defender and a force capable of returning lands taken from it, unjustly by its lights, by the Lombards. A delegation therefore was sent from Pepin III to Pope Zachary (r. 741–752). At this meeting of Frankish and papal representatives, perhaps the most famous leading question of the Middle Ages was put to the pope: Should the king be the one who has the title but no power or the power but not the title? In response, Pope Zachary is supposed to have responded that "the one who had the power ought rightfully to be named king, so that good order not be upset." In other words, the *de facto* king should also be king *de jure*. In 751, therefore, Frankish bishops anointed Pepin.

A pope and his bishops had never before made a king, nor even claimed to do so, yet the pope here seems to have authorized, if not created, a new Frankish dynasty. At the same time, the papacy seemed to have conferred a sacramental quality and, so it seemed to Pepin and his successors, a place of prominence and responsibility within the church. In time, the papacy would come to regret this sacralization of secular office. Indeed, many later imperial-papal disputes had their origins in this moment of mutual need in the eighth century. Yet at the time, the pope had little choice but to turn for aid to the Franks.

In 754, Zachary having since died, his successor, Pope Stephen II (r. 752–757), crossed the Alps into Frankland. At a meeting between Stephen and the new king, Pepin agreed to the new pope's request to resist Lombard aggression in the papal lands. While there, the pope also anointed King Pepin, along with his wife and two sons, at the church of St. Denis (which would become in time the burial site of most French kings), to the north of Paris. He also bestowed on him the title "patrician of the Romans" *(patricius Romanorum)*. The exact meaning of this term is unclear, but it obviously was intended to augment Pepin's authority and prestige and to tie him to the dignity of the Roman imperial past—as well as to underscore his obligation to protect the Roman church.

In 756, Pepin kept a promise made sometime in the previous four years, invaded Italy, and routed the Lombards by the following year. In addition, he took the keys to twenty-two cities and had them sent to Rome. Sometimes called "the Donation of Pepin," this is a misleading term, as Pepin's action, in the eyes of the papacy, simply restored to its rightful owner—St. Peter—lands usurped wrongly by the Lombards; they were not therefore Pepin's to donate. A Byzantine representative protested the seizing of imperial lands, but Pepin simply responded, sincerely, that his actions had been motivated by affection for St. Peter. In any event, Pepin carried out his end of an agreement. Almost needless to say, there was some sort of *quid pro quo* prearranged and consummated here. In exchange for legitimate recognition as king of the Franks, Pepin returned the lands owed to St. Peter. Both sides satisfied, and were satisfied with, the terms of the agreement.

It is also important to emphasize that Pepin did *not* act in accordance with the most famous forgery in western history, the so-called "Donation of Constantine." The document, probably composed ca. 754–767, may have been drawn up by a cleric at the pope's Lateran Palace. It gives an account of the miraculous cure of the emperor Constantine by Pope Sylvester (r. 315–335), based on fifth-century legendary literature. In the document, Constantine, in gratitude for the papal cure, declares Peter's see to be exalted above all others. As a consequence, he grants Peter's successors the Lateran Church (the Church of the Savior) and allows to him authority not only over the city of Rome but all provinces, districts, and cities of Italy and regions of the West.

The document still astonishes by its audacity. But why was it written? Some have argued that this document was forged to underwrite Rome's claim to the

Papal States. Yet no such use was made of it in the eighth or ninth centuries. Since it seems to deny the eastern emperor's claims to overlordship in Italy, it may have been aimed less at western kings than at eastern emperors. As early as 1001, it was recognized to be a forgery. Still, it would later be trotted out to verify claims of papal supremacy in the West. The Waldensians and radical Franciscans would later mark this as a moment of declension in the church, when the material began to eclipse the spiritual, a tradition picked up and emphasized by many other militantly reformist groups in the modern era. Though Lorenzo Valla (d. 1457) is credited with having proven philologically that the Donation of Constantine was a forgery, its authenticity was often doubted by civil lawyers in the twelfth and thirteenth centuries, as it would be by no less a churchman than the fifteenth-century theologian and cardinal Nicholas of Cusa (d. 1464).

Having turned its back on the eastern emperor and turned to the Frankish ruler, Europe as a new conceptual and territorial entity was no longer centered geographically on the Mediterranean but in the north, in northern France and northern Iberia, the British Isles, western Germany, the Alpine regions, and northern and central Italy. In economic terms, a decisive transition had long occurred from a commercial, trading economy dependent on the sea to a rural and agricultural form of living sustained by arable plainlands. In the eighth century, events conspired to produce a synthesis of Germanic mores in military and government, Roman traditions of good order and language, and Catholic norms in piety and practice. Europe—and with it Christendom—had been born.

New Constantine: Charlemagne and the Church

When Pepin III died in 768, the Frankish kingdom was divided between his sons, Charles (r. 768–814) and Carloman (d. 771). With Carloman's death in 771, Charles, the greatest leader of the Franks (which is why he later became known as Charles the Great), became sole ruler and eventually presided over a prodigious empire. From that year until his death, Charlemagne ruled the Franks. Like his ancestors, Charlemagne was determined to extend the frontiers of his kingdom and to protect Christianity. He also sought to increase the number of Christians. Infamously, in 782, he slaughtered more than four thousand Saxons and forced survivors to convert to Christianity. His conquest of not only the Saxons, but also the Lombards, Bavarians, and peoples of northern Spain made him master of virtually the entirety of the Christian West. Only Britain, southern Spain, and southern Italy were not under his control. He launched an ambitious and successful program of educational reform (partly to supply competent administrators), and to his court he attracted some of the outstanding minds of his generation, including the Anglo-Saxon Alcuin of York.

According to his biographer and contemporary Einhard (d. 840), Charlemagne was quite pious. He tells us that Charlemagne dedicated a great portion of his days to liturgy and was concerned deeply with church and ritual furnishings:

> He was a constant worshipper at this church as long as his health permitted, going morning and evening, even after nightfall, besides attending mass; and he took care that all the services there conducted should be administered with the utmost possible propriety, very often warning the sextons not to let any improper or unclean thing be brought into the building or remain in it. He provided it with a great number of sacred vessels of gold and silver and with such a quantity of clerical robes that not even the door-keepers who fill the humblest office in the church were obliged to wear their everyday clothes when in the exercise of their duties. He was at great pains to improve the church reading and psalmody, for he was well skilled in both although he neither read in public nor sang, except in a low tone and with others.

As French medievalist André Vauchez has pointed out, the Carolingian era was, religiously speaking, a "liturgical civilization." A great premium was put on ritual carried out correctly, solemnly, and in good order, as this kind of ritualism was thought to be pleasing to God. This belief goes a long way toward explaining Charlemagne's determination to supply his churches with sufficient quantities of dazzling sacred objects and clothing. Indeed, it was a major aim of his to establish everywhere in his realm services properly performed and pleasing to God. He wished also to reform the clergy so that it might capably undertake missionary and pastoral work throughout the empire. To this end, much treasure was spent in educating clerics who were literate and thus capable of serving in the administration of empire. Like his father, Charlemagne had great affection for St. Peter. Charles, Einhard tells us, "cherished the Church of St. Peter the Apostle at Rome above all other holy and sacred places, and heaped its treasury with a vast wealth of gold, silver, and precious stones. He sent great and countless gifts to the popes; and throughout his whole reign the wish that he had nearest at heart was to re-establish the ancient authority of the city of Rome under his care and by his influence, and to defend and protect the Church of St. Peter, and to beautify and enrich it out of his own store above all other churches." Charlemagne wanted to drape Peter's church in such supernal glory that no other church could compare with it.

Certainly the most famous of Charles's visits to Rome occurred in the year 800, when Pope Leo III (r. 795–816) crowned Charlemagne emperor of the Romans. The meaning of this remarkable event, in which the leader of a Germanic people assumed the imperial title (though the empress Irene ruled in the Byzantine Empire) has confounded scholars, in part because of Einhard's report: "It was then [December 25, 800] that he received the titles of Emperor and Augustus, to which he at first had such an aversion that he declared that he would not have set foot in the Church the day that they were conferred, although it was a great feast-day, if he could have foreseen the design of the Pope."

First, Leo's motivations, which may have been complex, may at least have been to confirm Charlemagne's own view, stated four years earlier, about the appropriate relationship of church and kingdom:

> It is our task, with the aid of divine goodness, to defend the holy church of Christ everywhere from the attacks of pagans outside and to strengthen it within through the knowledge of the Catholic faith. And it is your duty, O Holy Father, with your hands raised high to God, after the manner of Moses, to aid our armies so that by your intercession with God, who is our leader and benefactor, the Christian people may always and everywhere be victorious over the enemies of His Holy Name, and the name of Our Lord Jesus Christ be proclaimed throughout the world.

Second, despite Einhard's protestations of Charlemagne's aversion and surprise, he almost surely was the author of the idea that the pope confer on him the imperial title. Third—as has tirelessly been pointed out by historians—the Holy Roman Empire created that day was neither holy, nor Roman, nor an empire. It was a northern empire with little imperial administration, a crazy-quilt of territorial holdings. Finally, for whatever the coronation was not, it certainly did seal the alliance between the papacy and the Franks, an alliance confirmed in 816 when Charles's son, Louis the Pious (r. 813–840), entered a "pact of confirmation" with Pope Stephen IV (r. 816–817). Both popes and imperial propagandists were anxious to depict Charlemagne as a counterpart to, and in some ways a competitor of, the Byzantine emperor.

Charlemagne was quite serious when he said to Leo III that he wished to strengthen the Christian faith, and he did much to do so. He encouraged reforms of law, clergy, monasticism, education, and mission. In 789, at a meeting of bishops, abbots, and aristocrats, he issued a set of orders called the *General Admonition* (dependent upon an earlier collection of canon law called the *Dionysio-Hadriana*). This collection of canons was directed to the reform of bishops and priests, including their education. In it, it is ordered that schools for educating to levels of basic literacy be established. It also mandated that texts essential for the liturgy be collected in monastic and diocesan libraries. Among the most successful religious innovations of the Carolingians was the Benedictinization of monasticism. Admired (wrongly of course) for being "Roman" rulers, Carolingian reformers, with the important aid of Benedict of Aniane (d. 821), persuaded monks across

6. Throne of Charlemagne, Aachen Cathedral, Germany; Carolingian. Cathedral (Palatine Chapel), ca. 800. The plan is likely modeled on San Vitale, Ravenna. Photo credit: Erich Lessing / Art Resource, NY.

the empire that as "sons of St. Benedict," they were to regard the Benedictine vision of the monastic life as normative. Among Charlemagne's most important achievements was the establishment at Aachen not only of his royal residence, but also of a church and school that attracted some of the finest intellects in Europe and stimulated a cultural renaissance.

New Athens: Aachen and Its Culture

Founded by the Romans, Aachen was an appealing locale because of the warm rising springs that made baths possible there. Charlemagne developed a major royal residence in Aachen, including the Palace (or Palatine) Chapel, a church possibly consecrated by Pope Leo III in 805 and certainly the one in which Charlemagne would be buried at his death. Of the construction of Aachen (or Aix-la-Chapelle as it is called in French), Einhard, himself an accomplished craftsman, tells us that the Chapel was adorned with gold and silver and doors of brass. Columns and marbles were apparently brought from Rome and Ravenna. All this made it a fitting architectural symbol of Charlemagne's reign. Charlemagne was an ardent collector of relics. Four are still kept in Aachen Cathedral, including the cloak of the Blessed Virgin, the infant Jesus's swaddling clothes, the loincloth worn by Christ on the cross, and the fabric that lay on the head of the Baptist after he was beheaded. There popes visited and imperial administration was centered. From Aachen, ecclesiastical synods and royal assemblies issued legislation. It was at Aachen, too, that Charlemagne gathered a distinguished circle of scholars whose collective efforts stimulated a great cultural revival, often called the Carolingian Renaissance, exemplified by the scholar Alcuin of York.

Born in Northumbria, Alcuin was educated at the cathedral school of York, where he began teaching in 768. He was a deacon who saw it as his vocation to teach. He never was ordained priest and may not even have been a monk. From 782 to 796, Alcuin headed the palace school in Aachen. Called by Alcuin a "new Athens," Aachen attracted the Italians Peter of Pisa (d. ca. 799) and Paul the Deacon (d. 799), the Visigoth Theodulph (d. 821), as well as Einhard, Charlemagne, his sons, daughter, sister, queen, courtiers, and others. Einhard tells us that Charlemagne learned Latin well and some Greek and spent much time learning from Alcuin. These individuals met to discuss theology and science and to compose and talk about poetry. They gave one another nicknames taken from the classical and biblical past. Thus Charles was "David"; his son Louis, "Solomon"; Alcuin, "Ovid"; and Einhard, "Bezaleel" (see Ex. 31:2).

Alcuin's educational program at Aachen encompassed learning all of the classical trivium and some of the quadrivium. Yet this learning was oriented to scriptural interpretation and the reform of the church. Both were based on classical ideals. The trivium focused on words: grammar, rhetoric, and dialectic. By focusing intently on the literature of the great writers of the past, the student was to learn to read, write, speak, think, and argue in correct and persuasive Latin. As noted, the quadrivium focused on numbers: geometry, astronomy, arithmetic, and music. Alcuin composed his own epitaph: "Alcuin was my name and wisdom always my love."

It is important to stress, if only because it is so often misunderstood, that the program of the Carolingian Renaissance was not the recovery of the ancient classical heritage. In fact, the great bulk of intellectual energy was dedicated to the reproduction of religious texts, especially the writings of the church fathers, sermons, saints' lives, and canon law. Nowhere do we hear of the importance of preserving the works of Virgil or Cicero. Nonetheless, because they were models of great literary Latin style, they were copied, if only to add splendor and glory to the service of God in language used in liturgy. Nevertheless, they were regarded as dangerous because of their paganism and what was perceived to be their immorality. That said, a small number of Carolingian scholars were in fact responsible for the survival of many ancient pagan authors whose works ceased to be copied as biblical culture took hold in the sixth century. In fact, most of the oldest surviving copies of manuscripts of Latin authors were in fact made by Carolingian scribes. Yet even these copies were dwarfed by the many copies made of the church fathers and hundreds of biblical and liturgical books. Many of these books were copied in a beautiful new form of handwriting called Carolingian miniscule, a clear and legible style of writing admired in the Renaissance for its "Roman" quality. For this reason, Carolingian miniscule was resurrected in the Renaissance. It became the basis of printed letters in books to the present day.

In the last years of Charlemagne, many of the ecclesiastical and political achievements on which he had prided himself had begun to disintegrate. No longer conquerors, the Carolingians were preoccupied with defensive actions. Counts and other lords gained power at the expense of the imperial court. In the church, corruption had spread again among the clergy. With his empire declining and the church to which he had dedicated so much treasure and time beginning to slip back to a state of disorder, Charlemagne died.

Collapse of Empire

It would not be long before Charlemagne's empire disintegrated. By the death in 840 of Charlemagne's son, Louis, who had inherited the crown at his father's death, civil war among three of his heirs weakened the monarchy still further. At the same time, Europe was being attacked from three sides. From the south, Muslim raiders, who had been making incursions along the Mediterranean coast since Charlemagne's death, actually looted St. Peter's in Rome, the holiest shrine in the western church. Far more dangerous than the Muslims, whose expansive energies were exhausted, were the Scandinavian invaders. Called by contemporaries "men from the North," we know them as "Vikings." Like those in the sixth century, they were Germanic invaders. Their main targets were Christian monasteries, which were virtually defenseless and had extremely valuable treasure. When Lindisfarne was looted and destroyed by the Northmen in 793, Alcuin wrote to its bishop: "The misfortune of your suffering saddens me every day, even though I am far away. The pagans defiled the sanctuaries of God and shed the blood of the saints in the vicinity of the altar. They ravaged the home of our hope and trampled the bodies of the saints in the temples of God as if they were dung on the street." One year later, Bede's monasteries in Northumbria and Wearmouth were looted and then burned. The next year, Iona was sacked. The conventional pattern of assault for the Northmen was to raid in the summer months and then to return to their northern homes before winter. In the 840s and 850s, however, they began to spend winters on the offshore islands of France and England. The new location allowed them to escalate the number of their attacks. Soon, much of Anglo-Saxon England was ruled by northern chieftains. Almost no Benedictine monastery was functioning.

While much of the eastern Carolingian realm had been spared from either Muslim or Viking incursion, the Magyars, from their base in Hungary, raided the west for booty and slaves. Still, this attack was modest and the damage minimal compared to that wrought by the Northmen. Many monasteries continued to function, and churches by and large escaped destruction. Slowly the Magyars settled into the pattern of agricultural life, and after defeat in 955 at the hands of the German king Otto I (r. 936–973), they stopped their raiding and even converted to Catholic Christianity.

In the wake of these internal and external threats, the old Carolingian Empire collapsed and split into three large territories: the East Frankish kingdom, the West Frankish kingdom, and the kingdom of Italy. The last Carolingian in the eastern line died without heirs in 911. There, the political future lay with three kings, each named Otto, and to the dynasty (Ottonian) to which they gave their name.

With the loss of an effective protector, the papacy became the object of jealous competition among the noble families of central Italy and the kings of Germany. From 850 to 1050, the average pontificate was roughly four years. Some candidates were flagrantly unsuitable. One pope, John XII (r. 955–964), was appointed at the tender age of sixteen. The appointments or elections of others were often attended by violence or unseemly subterfuge. When (as was the case with John XII) the pope was not appointed by a noble family, German kings either approved them or professed the right actually to appoint them. In this state of affairs, nonetheless, the pace of Christianization quickened. The Northmen of England and France were baptized. From 950 to ca. 1000, Denmark, Norway, and Sweden were all converted. On the eastern border, Christianity was accepted in Hungary and Poland in the late tenth century.

Still, everywhere canon law was either unknown or ignored. Church offices were bought and sold. Clergy were sexually immoral. Lay rulers appointed bishops and abbots. They also built private chapels without the supervision of bishops and appointed priests. It would have been impossible to see, in these conditions, that Christendom lay trembling just then on the brink of an epochal revival.

Parochial Life and the Proprietary Church, ca. 700–1050

What was parish life like at the end of the first millennium? Was it like modern parochial life? How did it differ? Interesting as these questions are, they are not easy to answer. The difficulty is one that often plagues historical inquiry: the number and nature of sources. In this case, the sources are too few, and say too little, about parish life as it was experienced (say) in the year 1000. Nonetheless, if the sources are not exactly voluble, they are not silent either. In fact, used with caution, they can provide us with an accurate general picture of rural parish life during the first feudal age. This was the age that came in the wake of the disintegration of the Carolingian political system, when a new order of feudal and vassalic institutions emerged and decisively transformed the character of the medieval parish and medieval religious experience. One of the most obvious and enduring ways in which this new system influenced religious sensibilities and gestures was that the sign used in paying homage to a feudal lord—hands folded—became the posture adopted in prayer not long before the year 1000. But there were other, even more significant, changes in European religious life, none more so than the emergence of the proprietary church.

The Proprietary Church

In 1000 CE almost all of the British Isles and the Continent were at least formally Christian. Still, western Europe had not yet been clearly divided into well-defined territorial parishes with resident priests chosen, ordained, and supervised by the local ordinary, who was in turn directed by the papacy. Indeed, the parish in the year 1000 was far from that ideal, ordered, hierarchical model. Instead, many different (often competing) churches, structures, and people overlapped in the organization of local religious life.

By the year 1000, Christianity in Europe had been developing for centuries. During all these years, many churches had been founded by a variety of patrons for a host of different reasons. Many of these were not parish churches in the modern sense. To be sure, there were many parish or "baptismal" churches in Europe, founded by some bishop in the distant past, endowed with a baptismal font, given rights to dispense ministerial services in their boundaries, and empowered legally to collect tithes and fees. But by the year 1000, this kind of church would have constituted only a minority of the churches in which Christians received religious ministration and an even tinier minority of the scores of thousands of religious sites (which would have included simple stone crosses; primitive, isolated wood or stone chapels; modest shrines; local churches; and more or less impressive monastic, collegiate, and cathedral churches) crowding the landscape of medieval Christian Europe. In fact, until the turn of the millennium, it was not at all uncommon for Christians at worship simply to gather, probably at irregular intervals, around a cross.

Actually, the most common type of church in the year 1000 was one founded— and governed—by a local lay lord rather than a bishop. At the time, few found this anomalous or objectionable, and almost no one, save a few Frankish bishops, perceived it to be outrageously uncanonical. It is impossible to calculate precisely how many of these churches there were, but they surely numbered in the tens of thousands. Indeed, they far outnumbered the baptismal churches controlled by bishops (many of which had passed into the hands of lay lords). Usually established far from the baptismal church in the territory, they were especially common in parts of Europe where the Germanic peoples had settled—that is, in Spain, Lombard Italy, England, Scandinavia, and Frankland. Because of the force exerted by the ancient, hierarchical, episcopal Roman tradition, this model, which was based on German property law, never took root in central and southern Italy.

These churches were built, endowed, and maintained by the owners of the property on which they were erected; these owners wished to establish on their estates places of worship for their family and their laborers. Because the churches were actually owned by their founders, they have come to be known as "private" or "proprietary" churches. While the local bishop had rights of visitation, it was the proprietor and his heirs who could (and usually did) appoint the cleric and who could, if desired, remove him. The owner also charged fees for religious services provided in his church. Consequently, such churches could be quite profitable for the owner, particularly if he compelled his subjects to attend services and pay fees there. The usurpation of tithes, fees, and (in some cases) baptismal rights by proprietary churches would become a major source of tension—and litigation—with the baptismal churches.

Physical Dimensions of Church Buildings and "Parishes"

Physically, what were these churches like? When we think about ecclesiastical architecture in the Middle Ages, it is hard not to imagine the splendid cathedral, rising spectacularly above a particular town, dominating the surrounding countryside, and being conspicuously visible for many miles. But cathedral buildings of any architectural style played a small part in the lives of the great majority of early eleventh-century Christians. In most parts of rural Europe in the year 1000 (about nine-tenths of the population lived in rural areas—and even large cities would have contained fewer than ten thousand people), the local church in which Christians received religious services would almost always have been an exceptionally modest structure.

Some churches and many chapels consisted of a single rectangular cell. More common, though, was the two-chamber structure with nave and chancel. Indeed,

7. St. Martin in Zillis, Romanesque church, Switzerland, 1130–1140. The simple design of this church would have been much more characteristic of this time than contemporary cathedrals. First church built as early as sixth century on a Roman cult site. It was named "the people's church" in 831. Renowned for its twelfth-century painted ceiling. Photo credit: Erich Lessing/Art Resource, NY.

this "cellular linear" plan was the most common church structure in England and northwestern Europe during this time period. Though some parish churches were very large, almost cathedral-like in their proportions, the local church would normally have been a rather humble structure, built often of wood and with dirt floors. In England, there would have been few if any architectural curiosities like apsidal chancels or side chapels or porches, though some churches may have had towers. No matter how humble the church, it would have possessed at least one crucifix. It was likeliest to be dedicated to the Blessed Virgin, though many churches, their founders hedging their bets, were also dedicated to All Saints. Many were consecrated to St. Peter.

Proprietary churches served very small territories, encompassing perhaps a village or two. It would be hazardous to generalize about the size of the congregations in such parishes. But we would probably not go far wrong to estimate that most parishes served 200–300 people spread out over several thousand acres. It was in front of these churches that people would gather and also trade at market, so the local church served as a social center as well as a religious one. However humble these churches, and however small the congregations, it was around these proprietary churches that the later parochial system of Europe largely developed. In fact, in some parts of Europe and the British Isles, later parochial boundaries virtually coincide with the boundaries of lay estates.

Clerical Education and Lay Catechesis

Obviously, the bishop was not an effective presence in local communities like these. Even if he wished to be more present, the medieval bishop could not have been: he was simply too busy with his own religious duties and with the crush of political and secular duties (like the management of estates). In fact, one of the reasons that the sacrament of Confirmation occurred fairly rarely is that bishops were too busy with other responsibilities to take on that one as well. We do have accounts of bishops confirming large crowds from horseback as they paused on their way to some destination or other. Consequently, by the year 1000 it was the priest who really emerged as the religious and even educational leader of the local church. What do we know about him?

The priest was selected by a local lay lord and was usually a free man. If not, he had to be freed before a bishop would agree to ordain him; in fact, it seems likely that the rural clergy was largely made up of freed serfs, some of whom continued to till land on the parish property after ordination. While fourth- and fifth-century canonical decrees required clerical celibacy, many (probably most) priests of rural churches at this time lived with women who were either their wives or "hearthmates." Many urban clerics (and even a few bishops) lived with wives or concubines as well. Although a few bishops and some synods in the early

Middle Ages insisted on clerical continence, their words were a dead letter. Simply put, virtually no rural parishioner or priest in the year 1000 regarded clerical concubinage or marriage as practically or canonically objectionable; it would be more than a century before this would change and we begin to have evidence of reforming lay groups demanding clerical celibacy. Given the difficulties of rural life, the economic motivations for having a wife, and the peasant origins of the clerical clergy, it was doubtless the case that celibacy was thought by many to be too lofty an ideal; some were probably even unaware that clerical concubinage or marriage was uncanonical. Additionally, the indifference or ignorance of parishioners and priests was reinforced by a regime of imperfect episcopal supervision, not to mention that the practices around clerical education and formation were barely adequate, and to describe them as such is being charitable.

In fact, there was no educational *system* for the training of parochial clergy. Such a system was not actually required by the church until the third session of the Council of Trent (1545–1563), and even that took a long time to develop into its present form, especially in poorer dioceses. In the year 1000, most candidates would have been trained for ministry by their local priest. Because clerical celibacy was not effectively enforced, that teaching priest could very well have been the ordinand's father. Thus a typical ordinand might well have learned the cure of souls just as other boys in the village learned their skills—namely, as apprentices to the master, in this case the village priest. Clearly, then, it would be anachronistic to think of a young man's entry into presbyteral life in the year 1000 in terms of the modern idea of "vocation." It is even less accurate to speak in these terms when we note that priests were often chosen by lords for reasons other than their pastoral suitability (many were selected for their willingness to take low pay or to pay high for a position). On the subject of "pay," these clergy were almost entirely unbeneficed. A benefice was a gift of property that generated revenue to support religious activities and offices, like those of bishops, abbots, or hospitals. But very, very few rural clergy were supported by endowment.

The major weakness in this system of apprenticeship was that moral and especially educational defects were passed on from one generation to the next. This was especially the case with Latinity, which was notoriously weak. The records of quite a few synods make it quite clear that many parish priests had only a formal knowledge of Latin. In an ecclesiastical culture where all of the priest's books—the sacramentary, lectionary, antiphonary, martyrology, and so forth—were in Latin, this was no trivial problem but rather a troubling defect. It is true that all priests received some practical instruction in reading and singing the Latin texts for public worship and administering the sacraments. But their linguistic and theological comprehension of these might have been quite superficial. It has been said that early-medieval Christianity was a religion more practiced than understood by the great majority of lay Christians, but this was true of the great majority of rural clergy as well. Indeed, so cursory and incomplete was their educational preparation for ministry that some have argued that the single greatest organizational deficiency of the early-medieval church was the lack of an adequate system of clerical education and formation.

Provision for the religious education of the laity was also quite unsystematic and spotty. In the year 1000, there was no written catechism for laypeople (though there were some for novices in monastic schools). Again, local synods produced legislation and clerics produced many treatises (eventually some in the vernacular) about how children were to be catechized and what they should be taught. Usually mentioned in the legislation and treatises were simple prayers, the major articles of the creed, the meaning of the sacraments and of the ecclesiastical year, and morals, with emphasis on the vices and virtues. It is important to emphasize, then, that while the overwhelming majority of the medieval laity in the early eleventh century could not have had access to, or comprehended, these written sources, it nonetheless remains true that those written norms very likely became their oral culture. Eventually, those norms would also shape not only ritual, but also art and cosmology. Instruction in the basic creeds and prayers may have been given by priests, perhaps on festival and saints' days, but very simple prayers would also likely have been transmitted by mothers to their young children.

Liturgy and Sacraments

One historian of medieval spirituality, André Vauchez, as we have seen, has dubbed this culture "a liturgical civilization." Generally speaking, that description holds true not just at the great cloisters of the period, but also all the way down to the simplest parish. Indeed, the major religious acts of the period were sacramental and liturgical so that almost the whole of the village priest's job was to make God present through sacraments and through a host of parallel liturgies (like blessings of families, crops, cattle, and hearths). It would not be going too far to say that the "cure of souls" was conceived almost wholly in liturgical, ritualistic terms. The notion that a parish priest should be trained and able as a counselor, a teacher, a preacher, a pastor of souls—as omnicompetent vicar of the learned bishop—that, too, is a later-medieval development. If this conception of the priest seems commonplace, even unremarkable, to us at the beginning of the twenty-first century, it is actually because of the enduring success of late medieval ideas. Few rural priests in the year 1000 thought of themselves in these terms. Far more central to presbyterial self-understanding, and to the expectations of simple village parishioners, was that the local priest should make God present in the Eucharist, sacraments, and other forms of blessings and prayers that would come to be called "sacramentals."

Though geographically, architecturally, and socially distant from the cathedral church and the grand monastic and collegiate churches, liturgically the village church remained a reasonable, if modest, simulacrum of them. In the cathedral church, mass was sung in the morning, and the canonical hours were observed in prayer. In imitation of the cathedral church, parishioners in a rural church could have heard daily mass in the year 1000, but not many would have done so because of the perpetual demands of labor. Many, though not all, would have heard mass on Sunday.

What was the experience of mass like for the lay faithful? It must be conceded that the general picture, insofar as we have access to it, is not terribly inspiring. First of all, the service was in Latin. (This is in contrast to common practice in the Slavic regions Christianized by the Byzantine church, where the vernacular was used in liturgy.) Even in the Romance-speaking regions of Europe, excepting much of Italy, almost no one could have understood the Latin of the liturgical services. By the year 1000, this linguistic alienation had been reinforced architecturally by the internal layout of the churches and by certain liturgical innovations. The altar was now situated near the back wall of the chancel, while the faithful stood in the nave. At the same time, the celebrant turned his back to the faithful and addressed God on their behalf in a low tone. The mass was altogether the priest's business; the laity were physically present but uninvolved. Though in the Carolingian era bishops insisted that the faithful respond to the priest and sing the *Gloria Patri,* the *Kyrie,* and the *Sanctus,* these chants soon came to be sung only by the clergy. At the same time, by the year 1000, the words in the canon relating to the laity, *qui tibi offerunt hoc sacrificium laudis* (who offer you this sacrifice of praise) were supplemented by the clause *vel pro quibus tibi offerimus* (or for whom we offer it to you).

This liturgical development underlines one of the basic changes in the understanding of the priest at prayer in the early Middle Ages: he was understood as one who offers prayers on behalf of the faithful rather than as a leader of prayers. It also reveals something absolutely central about early-medieval lay spirituality: religion was performed largely by specialists in rituals from which the laity hoped to benefit, or at least to protect itself from vicissitude, by contact with or proximity to the supernatural.

In the case of the Eucharist, proximity was often the only thing achieved. By the year 1000, the Irish-Scottish system of fixed-rate penances, with its heavy, long punishments, combined with the success of what can only be termed a theology of unworthy communication, caused laypeople to communicate very infrequently— perhaps only annually at Easter, if even then. Nonetheless, medieval parishioners knew well enough that the divine was made present in the Eucharist, and most would have made an effort to be present for the canon. At those rituals, they could behold their Savior and plead his sacrifice for their needs and for the destiny of their souls. (The certainty that their souls were destined for eternal beatitude or punishment is one of the few religious ideas that all medieval parishioners held with conviction, and it is this idea that perhaps best explains early-medieval parochial spirituality.) Here again, it is clear that external observance of the ritual and one's physical presence and proximity was thought (by the parishioner at least and probably by his priest) to be sufficient and efficacious to secure God's blessing, which was, perhaps, in the end, the supreme desideratum.

There is reason to believe that God's blessing may have been the only reason that many faithful attended mass at all. Again, the mass was the priest's business, not the parishioner's. There were probably no vernacular translations of the missal, and even if there were, the faithful could not have read them. In the later Middle Ages, we hear many bishops and higher clergy complain that men and women gossiped with neighbors inside churches (they could walk about freely since there were no pews or other seating) or lolled about outside them, and it seems probable that the same sorts of things had occurred earlier. Though canon law required that the mass be sung, the laity sung few if any hymns, and the services were generally performed without much reverence or dignity. Most masses lasted less than thirty minutes, and one ninth-century German theologian, as if intent on legitimating and reinforcing the general mediocrity of liturgical experience, required parishioners to attend only from the offertory to the final blessing.

Preaching

One reason the mass was so short was that sermons were exceedingly rare in the local parish church. It is true that in the cathedrals and monasteries, there was a good deal of preaching. But this preaching was subtle, learned, and allusive. And it was in Latin. Not only was a rural congregation incapable of understanding the conventional sermonic language—and even less of the complicated biblical and rhetorical allusions that comprised the standard homily—but also the priest was completely incapable of preparing such a discourse. After all, he had never been instructed in this art, despite the demands of the bishops and councils. In the ninth century, two German synods demanded that priests preach to their congregations in their own tongue, but, once again, this was a dead letter. Occasionally, Latin sermons had been paraphrased or written in the vernacular by those trained in the art (especially by a Benedictine named Aelfric [d. ca. 1010] in Anglo-Saxon England), but this was truly exceptional. The mendicant friars did much to make the sermon a part of the ordinary liturgical experience of late-medieval Europe. But in the year 1000, almost none of the priests could have prepared a homily, none of their parishioners expected it, and few would have valued it or even recognized it as an ordinary component of the liturgy. One of the few other ways that parishioners were asked to practice their religion was through the system of fasting and abstinence. Aside from the one long fast at Lent, the church also required the laity to keep fasts on the eve of the great feasts. In addition, Fridays and Saturdays were days of abstinence (meat and animal products were not to be eaten then, though fish was allowed).

Sacramentals, Parallel Liturgies, and the Question of "Superstition"

In addition to the weekly Eucharist and the days and seasons of fasting and abstinence, there was an entire network of parallel rituals, some of which were the result of lay initiative and some of which were holdovers from "pagan" religions. These practices the church did its utmost to discipline and chasten or to take over or forbid. Some—like the cult of the dead—the church took over with little difficulty, and it also easily met the demand for numerous blessings, exorcisms, and formulas recited over food, shelter, nautical equipment, ill and insane people, and wild animals. The prevailing piety of physicality, of tactility, and of proximity to the sacred, combined with canonical decrees requiring that all altars be dedicated with relics, ensured that relics were deeply treasured objects that, it was hoped, would bring safety to individuals and security to kingdoms. The veneration of relics and their use as vehicles for divine power were easily integrated into the church's own patterns of life and worship.

Nevertheless, it seems reasonably clear from the writings of a German bishop named Burchard of Worms that right around 1000, there were still many customs that some might call "superstitious" but that the faithful practiced. It is possible that many thought these to be more important and more efficacious, if categorically no different, than the Christian sacraments. Surely "practitioners" were impressed with the talismanic power of activities such as the recitation of secret sayings, charms, and incantations (often using Christian words); sacrifices at holy stones, at crossroads, and at wells; and the reliance on amulets, such as the use of holy girdles (to ease the pain of childbirth), and such powers included the consecrated host and relics, sometimes buried in fields for agricultural good fortune. Generally, these were highly practical and functional customs. They were used to harness the power of the deity, to master the elements, and to receive advantages, including protection from the evil forces that inhabited the cosmos of the parishioners and threatened to overwhelm them with adversity.

While we might be tempted to brand and dismiss these practices as contrary to Christianity, or "unchristian," that would be an anachronistic judgment. Those who resorted to these practices did not distinguish sharply between customs that were "Christian" and those that were "magical" or "superstitious." A good example is the invocation of saints and guardian angels, both of which were used to mobilize supernatural powers against natural and even diabolical powers. Is this a Christian or an unchristian practice?

We could not easily say, in part because medieval parishioners could not or did not. But another reason we could not say is that we little appreciate the sinister cosmos in which these vulnerable and often desperate parishioners lived their lives. Today, we might regard Satan as a symbol of the evil that perversely prevails in the world and that we, it seems, are powerless to eradicate. However, for the medieval parishioner, the Devil and his many henchmen were all too real. They were supernatural, invisible beings known to inhabit the world of the faithful— rather like events occurring on the atomic level that we are utterly certain occur in our world though they are not visible to the naked eye. One had to be on one's guard against these demonic beings constantly. In addition, the worlds of early-medieval people were populated—overpopulated—by other terrifying, if less obviously evil, forces. These included fairies and ghosts, who frightened and menaced the living. Beyond these, natural forces, both meteorological and astral, had power and touched the lives of rural parishioners, often detrimentally. Bad weather might ruin a food supply for a year or more. And the stars controlled individual and communal fate. Astrological influence was considered a natural pressure, like the weather. The difficulty of judging whether astrology was Christian or not is illustrated by the complex reality that some clerics reprehended it while others practiced and wrote on it or were at least interested in it. Moreover, to read the stars in order to predict the future was not something the church could easily deplore since prophets, which it recognized, did the same thing. Whether or not a practice was condemned could depend on who was practicing it, a cleric or a layman. In short, the layman and simple cleric were pawns of natural and supernatural powers they could not understand but against which they hoped to enlist supernatural friends and forces by engaging in practices by which they attempted to check the influence of malign powers—and, by so doing, to control their lives to some extent.

To multiply the analytical complexity, the church supplied a whole spectrum of rituals and practices, called "sacramentals," that often involved priestly participation and evolved alongside routine, conformist practice—and that remain part of approved Catholic observance today. Some of these practices the church itself classified as sacramental. These include articles that, in liturgical context, had been blessed at Candlemas (a winter feast celebrating the presentation of Christ in the Temple, among other things); in this case the objects were candles, or palms blessed on Palm Sunday. They also included water that had been blessed on ordinary Sundays. These practices certainly involved a belief in supernatural intervention and causation, and some were believed to protect against potentially catastrophic thunderstorms. The candles might also be lit around the bed of someone *in extremis* to prolong life and stave off death. These objects and practices can easily be included under the rubric of clerically approved practices since clerics participated in them.

Clerics were certainly also involved in—indeed presided over—votive masses. These were masses said with a special intention *(votum),* often the hope of sheltering local agriculture from misfortune like adverse weather, disease to animals, and so forth. They were also used to attempt to offer safety for someone traveling. These votive masses frequently involved the use of sacred objects to ensure the desired outcome, such as the burial of consecrated hosts in crop lands or the sprinkling of water or salt that had been blessed on certain crops. Overwhelmingly, these masses were seen in agricultural settings and were said for agricultural good fortune. Again, clerical involvement is noteworthy.

Other sacramentals did not involve clerics, like chants, incantations, and prayers used, again, for security against the forces of an often-malevolent cosmos. Some of these prayers we do not know, as they were said in oral form and never committed to writing. Others do appear in the sources, such as a prayer in the Carolingian era attributed to the emperor and thus known today as "the Prayer of Charlemagne." Addressed to the Holy Spirit, it asks for both pious and practical blessings. It could be said anywhere and anytime and therefore did not require clerical presence, oversight, or blessing.

To call these practices "superstitious" is deeply problematic. It would certainly be true to say that all of these sacramentals sought to control, somehow, the elements of the physical world. But it wasn't only that clerics were involved in many of these practices. It was believed that God and benign supernatural forces, like angels and saints, heard the pleas of practitioners and responded. For example, it was believed that the patronage of St. Christopher, gained by contact with his relics, would prevent one from dying on the day of association or touch. Where is the boundary line, in this example, between authorized Christian practice and belief and superstition? We could not say without being in danger of retrojecting modern, and therefore anachronistic, norms into medieval practice. The same objection could be raised if we denounced these practices as "magical." Yes, they were exploited in the hopes of controlling the physical world. But the participation of priests, not to mention the Deity, makes such a denunciation problematic. To call such practices superstitious or magical is to introduce a distinction not apparent in the sources but deriving instead from atemporal judgments of medieval Christianity. To emphasize: a boundary between superstition and magic, on the one hand, and Christian practice, on the other, simply was not obvious to those who used medieval rituals to control or resist the influence of the natural and supernatural worlds. But not all scholars agree.

A "Folkloristic" Culture?

Most scholars who have studied medieval culture in the twentieth century have assumed that it was at least minimally Christianized. However, beginning in the mid-1960s, several scholars (many of them French) came to challenge that central assumption. Their argument, reduced to its essentials, goes as follows. Those who were truly Christianized by even the early thirteenth century represented a tiny minority of clerical elite. Most medieval people, they argue, lived in a "folkloric culture" not unlike those studied in our own day by anthropologists in what is widely called the Third World. According to this view, most medieval parishioners were, at best, superficially Christianized. Indeed, Christian faith was not absorbed and practiced deeply until the dawn of the modern age, after the close of the medieval era—according to one French historian, not until the time of the Council of Trent. So far from being fully Christianized were these Christians in the Middle Ages that they actually wished for magical solutions to their mundane problems, and it was these that the church provided. One historian went so far as to proclaim, "The medieval church . . . appeared as a vast reservoir of magical power." Just as it is impossible to draw a line between religion and magic in primitive cultures, so was it equally difficult to draw such a line for the medieval West. Other historians went even further, arguing in essence for the existence of two distinct cultures: one was clerical and bookish, and the other was popular, magical, and oral. As their main sources of evidence, these historians used simple morality tales included in sermons (*exempla*) and inquisitorial records.

Definitional imprecision and its focus on the rare or unique have made this thesis difficult to sustain. It is often not clear what being "Christianized" means to these scholars, nor is it likely that scholars could ever agree on such a definition. For one thing (and this seems to have escaped the notice of many), what being Christian or Christianized consists of is historically conditioned—that is, it changes through the centuries. Moreover, the use of these sermonic and inquisitorial sources immediately led the "folklorists" down a dangerous road. It can hardly be surprising that inquisitorial records, for example, revealed the existence of outliers in medieval culture—millers, for example, who believed God evolved from a worm, that Christ was not divine, or that the moon was made of cheese. It is one thing to argue that such men existed. It is another to leap to the conclusion, from the inquisitorial record upon which this story relies, that such a person was representative of low medieval culture or to argue for the existence of two distinct cultures: the miller's "popular" culture and the high, clerical culture that examined him and produced the written document that allows us to know about him.

Why is this "two-tiered" model problematic? For one thing, the clerical class was hardly the monolith that this model suggests. The parish priests that were described above: where would they belong? Though they were clerical, it could easily be argued that in their understanding of the cosmos and the depth of their comprehension of the Christian faith, they shared more with the villagers among whom they lived and the parishioners to whom they ministered than they did with the bishops, deans, and canons in the cities. Beyond that, there is voluminous evidence to suggest that both peasant parishioners and powerful bishops struggled to gain access to the powers of a venerable saint and his bones—his relics. That is, there was a common Christian culture in which ordinary parishioners and prelates participated. In addition, the very existence of inquisitorial records suggests that the clerics who composed them were aware of "folkloristic" or deviant practices and beliefs and were attempting to channel or discipline them, rather than to simply allow them to perdure, on another socio-religious layer (so to speak), without any attempt to deepen the understanding of Christianity and its appropriate practice.

As American historian John Van Engen has forcefully pointed out, the parish ultimately came to be established as the seat of ritual and practice, a fundamental (if slow-developing) institution of medieval Europe, the center of medieval village life. The space parishioners inhabited, the time they lived through—all of these were imbued with Christian rituals, symbols, and practices that defined their lives. Major events in the life cycle were christened, beginning with the baptism of a child and ending with the last rites imposed by the priest at death. These sacraments established and reaffirmed membership in the Christian community. Confession would become routine in the early thirteenth century, an occasion on which to examine each of the christened in terms of what was a standard list of virtues and vices by then. In the early-medieval era, and for centuries, priestly manuals and synodical legislation demanded the knowledge of the Lord's Prayer and the Creed (both of which were among the earliest texts translated into European vernaculars). These would both have been recited at Sunday mass, and such recitation would have reinforced at least a fundamental understanding of Christian faith. Van Engen rightly points out that in medieval Christianity, "religious culture rested ultimately on 'faith' or 'belief,' meaning professed assent to certain propositions as well as inner convictions." This goes for simple parishioners as well as for learned theologians and bishops. Regarding behavior, conciliar decrees and priestly manuals demanded that Sunday be hallowed and that it, along with feast days, be observed as a day of rest. Van Engen does not want to argue that such parishioners were "deeply Christianized," nor does he wish to resurrect nostalgic nineteenth-century notions of the Middle Ages as "an Age of Faith" or as a perfectly Christian culture. He does, however, wish to underscore that the focus on sermonic and inquisitorial records inescapably, and not surprisingly, turns up outliers and exceptions.

One of the peculiar pieces of evidence studied, at book length, by French historian J.-C. Schmitt, in an attempt to distinguish and even sever clerical and "popular" religious cultures (and to prove the thesis of a lack of Christianization in the Middle Ages) is the case of St. Guinefort, or "the Holy Greyhound." Based on a timeworn tale, probably on a pre-Christian myth of a "faithful hound" found in most Indo-European cultures (and that can be found even today in Walt Disney popular films), Guinefort was, so the story goes, mistakenly killed by his owner, who believed his bloody teeth indicated he had killed the child with whom he had been entrusted. In fact, the dog, in his master's absence, had killed a serpent to protect the child. Eventually, the child is found, safe and sound. The dog, a sort of canine martyr, was then buried and venerated after his death, and a cult of *longue durée* was launched.

Sometime in the thirteenth century, the cult was discovered by the Dominican Stephen of Bourbon (d. ca. 1261), who reported that parishioners in the diocese of Lyons had been venerating the "holy hound." Pilgrims flocked to his grave in the hopes of securing miraculous cures for their ill children. Persuaded that the cult of "the sainted dog of France" was not an orthodox expression of Christianity, Stephen had the cult site destroyed after gathering the local parishioners to explain why the cult was heterodox. Schmitt uses this case in a village in France to argue for a widespread lack of Christianization and for the existence of a folkloristic culture untouched by the norms and expectations of the prevailing clerical culture. At the same time, he ignores the evidence that Stephen assembled the parishioners in order to make clear what lay *within* the boundaries of orthodox practice and what without. In other words, inquisitorial records point to *both* the existence of an unusual, perhaps heterodox, cult *and* the clerical attempt to eradicate it and to discipline and "Christianize" the simple parishioners. But Schmitt focuses on the former to argue for a popular Christianity largely unreconstructed by clerical norms.

It is worth asking if the case is made. Problems abound, but there are reasons to find the theory unconvincing. To begin with, we know of *human* saints named Guinefort venerated in other parts of France and Italy. It is not at all clear that pilgrims to these shrines were aware of the legend of the holy hound. Many were simply praying to a Christian saint with the name Guinefort. If this is true, then the allegation that medieval religiosity was folkloristic or even—as one French historian has said of such practices as this—"a species of paganism" becomes highly questionable. It is a judgment based on what a historian might imagine is the constant, undying definition of the "essence" of Christianity.

Other problems bedevil the presupposition of two strata of religious practice that are largely untouched by one another. While images of heresy trials and inquisitorial fires dominate the media-fed imagination today, the church was actually remarkably casual in suppressing popular expressions of faith; indeed, later in the Middle Ages it intervened only when there was evidence of outright deviance. Even more remarkably, it often followed the lead of popular thinking before issuing any authoritative or conclusive definition on a matter. Two examples will suffice.

Two of the most dynamic elements of medieval piety were, without question, purgatory and the cult of Mary. Many expressions of piety, as we shall see, were premised on purgatory. Nonetheless, popular belief in post-mortem purgatorial fire and a third alternative to heaven or hell predated the theological definition of purgatory as a noun and a place of purgative potential. Similarly, it was believed that Mary was generated without sin and bodily assumed into heaven by medieval Christians *well* before these beliefs came to be defined *de fide,* part of the deposit of Christian revelation. During the Middle Ages, the theory of the Immaculate Conception of Mary was vigorously debated by theologians. No less orthodox a figure than the Dominican Albert the Great (Albertus Magnus; d. 1280) could declare the doctrine "heretical, insane, and impious" even as parishioners in Europe could venerate Mary as immaculately conceived. The doctrine of the Immaculate Conception was not actually made an article of faith until 1854, and the doctrine of her assumption not until 1950.

These were unquestionably practices and beliefs that arose, so to speak, "from below," from the people. It is one thing to recognize this. It is another to say that these "popular" beliefs and practices were somehow sealed off from elite participation or approval, and it is even more absurd to believe that they are vestiges of a mythological or legendary culture. After all, priests and monks eventually fully embraced and developed the cult of Mary, in which she was venerated and called on for help. Part of medieval culture was a dynamic interaction between elements of the Christian faith sponsored by priests and those given life or popularity by the people. In attempting to understand medieval Christianity, we stray far from the truth if we imagine priests and people as inhabiting two different worlds of thought and practice or if we believe that the experience of ordinary medieval folk can be captured in the vocabulary of folklore and with the social scientific tools used to describe it today.

Christians and Jews, ca. 400–1100

In the middle of the twentieth century, the immensely erudite Jewish historian Salo Baron (d. 1989) railed vigorously against what he called the prevailing, "lachrymose" view of Jewish history. By that term, Professor Baron meant to indicate that many of his colleagues and predecessors had (understandably) viewed Jewish history in wholly desolate terms. In this view, which was sometimes linked with Heinrich Graetz (d. 1891), the nineteenth-century historian who identified the distinctive elements of Jewish experience as suffering and spiritual scholarship, and was magnified in the wake of the horror of the Holocaust, Jewish history is always the story of persecution, suffering, exile, and deprivation. This view is sometimes also represented as a "teleological" view of Jewish history because it sees in anti-Jewish legislation enacted in the Middle Ages the beginning of a road that would lead more or less directly to the Nuremberg Laws and the Holocaust. In an interview in 1975, Baron of course acknowledged that "suffering is part of destiny" but went on to add, "so is repeated joy as well as ultimate redemption." Jewish history ought not to be represented as "all darkness and no light," he insisted, and in his astonishingly prolific writing, he attempted to restore some balance to the Jewish experience and to bring Jewish history into the wider social, economic, political, and religious history of the times under consideration.

If we look back to the Christian patristic era, it could not be more clear that Baron was correct. The writings of the church fathers, which often seem (and superficially are) harshly anti-Semitic (I will use this controverted modern term for the sake of convenience and because its meaning is well understood), need to be put into context and interpreted carefully. The same is very much true of the canons pronounced by early ecclesiastical councils. Many scholars have read them, ham-handedly, within the theoretical framework of the lachrymose or teleological view of Jewish history just described. Yet these laws need to be read against the grain, with the understanding that the church was often *not* the dominant institution in society and that it often *lacked* real influence over kings and high officials and the political process in general. In fact, the truth is that much anti-Jewish legislation passed by ancient and early-medieval ecclesiastical councils was simply ignored; the church was, in this sense, politically impotent. It would be wrong to portray this legislation, as is still often done, as destructive in practice, vile as it was in intent. So, too, we ought not to imagine Jews as altogether lacking in power, small in number, and hatefully marginalized by early-medieval kings and emperors. So read, these writings often suggest that Judaism remained an attractive religious option to Christians well into the Constantinian age; that Christians, at various times, participated in Jewish religious festivals and liturgies; and that Christians and Jews sometimes intermarried, dined together, and enjoyed cordial relations. Such was true even, or especially, in the Gothic kingdoms, where, it has been reasonably estimated, perhaps 1–2 percent of the kings pursued policies that could genuinely be represented as in any way "anti-Jewish."

Roman Law

The eastern Roman emperor, Theodosius II (r. 408–450), compiled an official collection of the statutes issued by baptized emperors. It has come to be called the Theodosian Code *(Codex Theodosianus)*. In the thirtieth year of his reign, around 438, laws regarding the Jews were assembled and put into order in chapters 8 and 9 of the sixteenth book of the Code. Much of the Code seems to suggest that the position of Jews was in decline in the late Roman Empire. But, as always, we must distinguish between what a law code mandates and the degree to which it was enforced. The Code classified Jews as Roman citizens who lived under special limitations. These restrictions had to do with allowable religious practices and social relationships, especially with Christians. Jews were prohibited from circumcising Christian slaves (but the restrictions did not forbid Jews from owning them). On religious matters, Jews were allowed to appear before tribunals of their co-religionists. On civil ones, jurisdiction was reserved to the state. Jews were prohibited from taking part in transactions on the day of the Jewish Sabbath and other Jewish festivals, a prohibition that was not a serious hindrance. Jewish men were forbidden from marrying either Christian women or pagan women from the emperor's textile industry.

The eponymous Justinian Code *(Corpus Iuris Civilis)* was compiled during the reign of Justinian I. While Justinian's laws seem to attempt to curtail the legal independence in religious matters that Jews had traditionally enjoyed in Roman law, we must, as always, distinguish carefully between what was mandated in law and what could be or was prosecuted in practice. In the case of the Justinian Code, we can be quite sure that much of the anti-Jewish legislation was not enforced. For one thing, Byzantine officials of the emperor frustrated the anti-Jewish statutes and made little effort to enforce the law. A far-reaching effect, however, was felt in later Christian and Muslim law. Justinian formulated a view of Jews as second-class citizens, a view given a sacred imprimatur by later papal and ecclesiastical decrees in the Middle Ages.

In the Justinian Code, Judaism was no longer understood to be a permitted religion *(religio licita)*. The aim of this understanding, never realized, was to encourage Jews to convert to Christianity and to demonstrate the superiority of church to synagogue. Conversion from any religion to Judaism was theoretically punishable by death. Justinian's New Law *(Novella)* 146, "On the Jews" *(De Hebraeis)*, put Jewish religious services under the aegis of state regulation. In addition to recommending the Septuagint (though any version of the Jewish Bible could be read), the Code, for the first time, attempted to forbid the study of the Oral Law, or Talmud. In addition, whereas Judaism had previously been described in Roman law as "the national laws, customs, and beliefs of the Jewish people," it was now couched in the insulting rhetoric of triumphalist Christianity. Judaism was an evil sect, characterized by superstitious beliefs, law, and worship. Derogatory terms applied to Christianity in the pre-Constantinian era were now understood to pertain to Judaism, as were Christian understandings of Judaism in the economy of divine salvation, at least to the codifiers of the law. Still, we must stress that these laws were not enforced in the Mediterranean world. Other matters, like the Lombard invasion of the Italian peninsula, as well as attitudes of imperial officials, prevented the laws from actually being applied to the disadvantage of Jews—that is, until these laws were incorporated into Christian law books.

Jews in the Visigothic Kingdoms

As we have seen, until 589, the Visigoths, who ruled much of Aquitaine in southwestern Gaul and most of the Iberian Peninsula until the Muslim invasion in 711, were Arian Christians. By and large, they pursued a policy of tolerance, and Jewish communities under their rule flourished. Again, councils objected to close relations between Jews and Christians. As early as 506, for example, the Council of Agde issued decrees again denouncing the participation not only of Christian laymen but also of clergy in Jewish festivals. Dining at Jewish homes was also forbidden. As always, these canons issued by the council constitute strong evidence that the behavior deplored by the bishop was common. The behavior was especially unremarkable to Visigothic rulers and their officials. Among other things,

Jews were permitted to hold senatorial rank, and the Visigoths were happy to organize Jewish men for defense in their garrisons. One scholar has concluded: "It is clear that the Jewish communities in the major and minor cities of the Iberian Peninsula . . . were flourishing despite invasion, civil war and other similar troubles endemic to early-medieval Europe."

It is sometimes thought that with the conversion of King Reccared I in 589 to Catholic Christianity, the king also launched an anti-Jewish policy. Some scholars have argued that he established the first law requiring forcible conversion of Jews to Christianity in Visigothic Spain. But Bernard Bachrach, among others, has proven that "Reccared seems to have done no more in his legislation than accept the laws of his Arian predecessors," which, he notes correctly, were "tolerant." Nonetheless, nearly one-fifth of the monarchs who ruled Visigothic lands after Reccared did try to implement anti-Jewish policies. They aimed to take estates from Jewish landholders, markets from Jewish merchants, offices from civic officials, and even their religion and freedom. By around 711, Jews joined with some other disgruntled groups, such as the Goths, to support the Muslim force that overthrew the monarch Roderick (r. 710–711) and, with him, the Visigothic kingdom. For the next five centuries, Jewish communities would flourish in both Muslim and Christian Spain—and this despite the supersessionist terms in which some, like the archbishop of Seville, would view them.

Sometimes called "the last church father of the West," Isidore (d. 636) was archbishop of Seville from ca. 600 to the end of his life. He wrote a lengthy, though wholly unoriginal, treatise *On the Catholic Faith against the Jews.* Intended for the education of clerics, for whom the correct, negative image of the Jew was thought by the author to be of high importance, the work is highly dependent upon the works of Jerome and Augustine. In it, Isidore asserts that the Jews had been punished with the destruction of the Second Temple because of their criminal disbelief. For the same reason, they had lost their nation and their independence and were forced into exile. Not surprisingly, Isidore viewed the Jewish Law in supersessionist terms, arguing that it was null and void after the coming of Christ. Some scholars have argued that Isidore's anti-rabbinic polemics were more virulent than those of other fathers. Be that as it may, his was a fairly widespread and influential treatise. Some twenty manuscripts composed before the eleventh century exist. In the ninth century, the book was even translated into Old High German, an indication of the geographical scope of its influence. Isidore writes in his other works against the Jews, like biblical glosses, but these did not have the same influence.

As an aged man, Isidore presided over the Fourth Council of Toledo in 633. All of the bishops of the Iberian kingdoms were present. Many topics were taken up, including the establishment of seminaries in the cathedral cities. It has been argued that Isidore's theological anti-Semitism was translated into laws at the Council of Toledo, ten of which concerned the Jews, of which two would have lasting influence. Canon 60 called for the removal of Jewish children from their families and for their education by Christians. Of particular interest is Canon 65. This forbade Jews and even Christians of Jewish origin to hold public office. This law has led many scholars to question whether anti-Judaism began imperceptibly to change into anti-Semitism in the early Middle Ages. While intriguing, it is not at all clear that Isidore was thinking of Jews in ethnic or racial rather than religious terms. In any case, what is certain is that both these canons made it into the most influential medieval canon law collections, including those of Gratian (d. ca. 1160), Burchard of Worms (d. 1025), and Ivo of Chartres (d. 1115).

The Ostrogoths, Imperial Rule, and the Lombards

While not as numerous or politically significant as in Visigothic Spain, Jews in Italy under the Ostrogoths flourished in every way. Ostrogoth rule in Italy was remarkably favorable to its Jewish citizens, who were well represented at every stratum of society, from serf to senator. Jews were also among the most effective soldiers in Ostrogothic society, and they served in governmental positions as well. In his *Edict on the Jews,* King Theodoric (r. 493–526) reaffirmed the privileges granted Jews in the Theodosian Code, but he refused to restate the legislation that discriminated against them. Jews continued to flourish even in the chaos and political conquest that accompanied the Byzantine reconquest and Lombard invasions of the sixth century, despite the occasionally prejudicial writings of influential figures like Pope Gregory.

In his personal attitude toward Jews and Judaism, Gregory had absorbed the traditional anti-Semitism of the western patristic theological tradition, to which he was quite capable of giving sharp and apparently heartfelt expression, especially in those of his writings (like his biblical commentaries and letters, for example) that did not have the force of law or concrete empirical effect. Gregory could easily dismiss Judaism, as cultured Romans had dismissed early Christianity, as a ludicrous "superstition," and many of his attacks on Christian heretics began with the observation that they were blind or literal-minded like "the Jews." Beyond that, Gregory was also anxious to convert Jews to Christianity. On the one hand, he was emphatically opposed to the use of force and to any physical violence against Jews or the synagogue, even as coercion was being applied to Jews to convert in southern France at the very beginning of his pontificate. Yet while demanding that bishops neither use nor condone violence, he urged them to preach to the Jews in the short interval that was left before the end of the world, in order that they might convert to Christianity.

On the other hand, Gregory pursued a practical policy that can otherwise be described, in context, as benign. He guaranteed religious toleration, both theoretically and practically, and did much to protect Jewish rights as enshrined in Roman law. His famously influential encyclical, *Sicut Iudaeis* (598), is often seen (not entirely accurately) to have epitomized his policy: "Just as no freedom may be granted to the Jews in their communities to exceed the limits legally established for them, so too in no way should they suffer a violation of their rights." As has been observed by several scholars, if Gregory in his personal attitude was informed by the traditional animus of patristic anti-Semitism, in his actual dealings with Jews and Jewish communities, he was guided by the political and moral imperatives of Roman law. Even more significantly, it has been shown that he relied primarily on the older Theodosian Code rather than the more recently promulgated Justinian Code, which was notably less favorable to Jews. As one noted scholar has observed, "Thus, Gregory was not simply a legalist giving Jews their due, as might any unimaginative bureaucrat. Rather, he was an important political and ecclesiastical policy maker who chose a course of action that would seem to demonstrate a pro-Jewish stance regardless of the latest imperial legislation."

In practice, this pro-Jewish stance led Gregory on several occasions to prevent the confiscation of synagogues and sacred vessels and books and to forestall interference in Jewish ritual practice. Although Jews were not permitted to hold Christian slaves by either the Justinian or Theodosian laws, Gregory usually allowed the practice when it occurred (as he mock innocently put it) "in ignorance" or "accidentally." This, however, may have been intended less to inconvenience Jewish merchants than to placate imperial officials, who certainly knew about the slave trade and were loathe to impede it. There are other instances in which Gregory acted on behalf of Jewish economic interests even when Roman law forbade him to do so.

Ironically, then, Gregory, more than any other pope, happily violated his own injunction in *Sicut Iudaeis* not to go beyond legally established Jewish rights on behalf of the Jews. A pope who regarded Jews in his theological writings as "depraved" and "perfidious" and who attempted to convert them away from their "superstition," Gregory in the end demanded and achieved for individual Jews and Jewish communities—legally, economically, and politically—much more than either Roman law demanded or his pontifical successors would be willing to grant.

Early Frankish and Carolingian Era

It was in the nearly totally agrarian and feudal lands of northern France and western Germany that Ashkenazic Jewry would flourish. As is well known, this was a branch of Jewish culture that was to have far-reaching influence into the modern period. The Jews, like Bavarians or Saxons, were given recognition in Frankish law as a people with their own law. But the Jews were the only non-Christian group to be permitted to practice their own religion. Economically, Jewish merchants were treated well in the empire, in part because they had valuable trading connections with the Mediterranean and the East. Jews were encouraged in this merchant activity both within and on the boundaries of the empire, and they helped settle garrison towns on the Spanish frontier from which Christians had been expelled. One treasured Jewish merchant was sent to the Abbasid Caliph for a deputation, a trip from which he returned with an elephant, a gift from the caliph to Charlemagne.

Under Charlemagne's son, Louis the Pious, such policies as prevailed under the father were put into systematic form by the son. Louis protected the right of Jews to own and purchase slaves of all religions, including Christians. They were permitted to hire Christian laborers and own their estates, and they were encouraged to build new synagogues to meet the needs of a population quickly growing. In these circumstances, Jewish intellectual and religious life prospered. Great rabbinical schools were founded in Mainz and in other cities in the Rhineland, and academies thrived in southern Italy and Barcelona. Welcomed at the imperial court, Jewish scholars discussed religious matters there and even made converts—this despite the fact that making converts was contrary to various legal inhibitions.

Christian exegetes and scholars were helped in their labors by Jewish scholars. The first great intellectual produced by the Ashkenaz was Solomon ben Isaac of Troyes (d. 1105), known as Rashi (his acronym). His commentaries on the Bible and Talmud were to have an immense influence, including on medieval Christian biblical interpreters, who took Rashi's emphasis on the plain meaning of scripture. When Christian prelates, such as Archbishop Agobard of Lyons (d. 840), wrote anti-Jewish attacks and pressed for the implementation of anti-Jewish measures, the emperor simply ignored them. In fact, in the tenth and eleventh centuries, Jews, especially Jewish merchants, were treasured members of the empire and on good terms with kings and barons in the north of Europe. The same can be said of several archbishops and bishops. A famous charter issued in 1084 by the bishop of Speyer, announces that the bishop aimed to "bring honor" to his diocese by inviting Jews into his community.

The question of the constitutional status of Jewish communities in Europe is one on which scholars have invested much labor. It has sometimes been said, too generally, that Jews were understood to be "servants of the royal chamber" or "chamber serfs" *(servi camerae regis)*. Actually, there was, across time and space, no unvarying status except the recognition that all were Jews *(Iudaei)* and that all were dependent utterly on secular lords for all their rights. Such recognition did not, however, unambiguously define the legitimate scope of their activities. In fact, the vituperative writings of Archbishop Agobard can be traced to his frustration that legal parameters on Jewish activities did not exist. Such legal definitions emerge only in the eleventh century, most famously in a document written by Pope Calixtus II (r. 1119–1124), *Sicut Iudaeis* (ca. 1120)—not coincidentally, the same title as Gregory the Great's letter. This has been recognized as the first attempt to articulate papal policy toward the Jews in the central Middle Ages. It tried to attempt some balance between rights that were to be granted and restrictions to be observed. Thus, on the one hand, it promised full protection of the law, including due process. On the other hand, it demanded that Jews always obey the demands of the church. The balance to which Calixtus aspired was achieved and certainly defined and helped perpetuate Jewish existence. Yet the balance was so fine that in practice, it could be, and was, shattered again and again in succeeding centuries.

Islam and Western Christianity, ca. 600–1450

Muslim conquests of Christian lands in the Mediterranean, including the ancient heartland of Christianity, occurred immediately in the wake of the death of the Prophet in 632. The chronology of the earliest conquests is not certain. However, it seems likely that Damascus, as well as much of Syria and Palestine, had been conquered by the close of 636. Much of Persia, home to many Christians, also fell under Muslim rule. The fall of Jerusalem followed swiftly in 637, the same year that Antioch was struck down. Caesarea, the last significant Mediterranean city to fall to Muslim armies, was vanquished in 641.

The Muslim armies then moved west. Alexandria fell in 642 and with it all of Egypt in the same year. Muslim armies pressed further west into North Africa over the next generation; Carthage was taken by 694. By 703, Muslim armies had seized Tangier; some Islamic forces reached the Atlantic Ocean. In 711, the Muslim armies crossed the Straits of Gibraltar. From that date until 716, much of the Iberian Peninsula was conquered and the kingdom of the Catholic Visigoths destroyed. In 717–718, Constantinople, then the largest Christian city in the world was, for the second time, besieged (it had been attacked earlier, 672–678). It barely survived, and it would face repeated threats from Islamic armies for seven more centuries; raids into Byzantine territories occurred almost annually. Muslim armies in Europe pressed northward and were finally defeated in 732 by the Franks in a battle near Tours in Gaul. Further Mediterranean conquests were to come with the defeat of Crete and Sicily in 827 and Taormina in 902, the year that marks an end to Muslim expansion.

The military and political accomplishment was astonishing. Still, it is important to emphasize that these victories were not inevitable, as they seem in retrospect; in some cases the outcome of battles remained in doubt until their end.

In the century following Muhammad's death, Arab Muslims had secured control of the territory from Spain to Persia. Enormous numbers of Christians, perhaps the majority of Christians in the world, suddenly found themselves living under Muslim rule. Three of the five ancient patriarchates—Antioch, Jerusalem, and Alexandria—seemed to have vanished, though the patriarchs in those cities continued, with restrictions, to function. Only Rome (which would experience Muslim raids in the ninth century) and Constantinople (which would experience them much more often) remained. Conquered so rapidly, many of these lands would be fought over for much of the Middle Ages. The reconquest of Spain began not long after its defeat. In the eleventh century, the first of the Crusades to recapture the Holy Land for Christianity was launched by the papacy. From these encounters and the translation of Islamic sacred books, Christians would acquire a fairly accurate view of Islam. Yet for centuries the strictly monotheistic Muslims were misrepresented as heretics (not practitioners of another religion), idolaters, and polytheists. It was the beginning of a long, mutual misunderstanding.

The Life of Christians under Muslim Rule

Communities from Baghdad to Spain (or Al-Andalus) thus fell under Muslim rule. In some parts of the Muslim world, Christians formed the majority of the population. In others, Arabic was taken up for mundane purposes, while ancient languages were preserved for religious and liturgical purposes. The Qur'an was well aware of narratives from both Testaments and of elements of Jewish as well as Christian belief and practice. In fact, the Qur'an criticizes Christians (whom it calls "People of the Gospel" or "Nazarenes" and, along with the Jews, "People of the Book" or "Scripture People") for going astray and leading others astray (Qur'an 5.77) and expresses criticism of Christians' belief in the messiahship of Jesus as well as their belief in the Trinity (Qur'an 4.171). Nonetheless, friendships and cordial professional relations did in some times prevail.

There are no references outside the Qur'an to Christians until the close of the seventh century. These have to do with the conditions under which Christians and their officials would operate. These conditions would later be collected in the Covenant of 'Umar, a tricky legal document that underscored the Muslim duty to fight the "People of the Book" until they "pay the poll-tax submissively" (Qur'an 9.29). This would soon be followed by the construction of buildings and the minting of coins to declare the Muslim "testimony" to the truth of Islam and in an effort to eradicate public symbols of Christianity. Perhaps the best-known instance of this effort is the construction in Jerusalem of the Dome of the Rock. Ringed around the dome, as is well known, are Qur'anic verses freighted with contempt for Christian dogma.

The earliest Christian reactions to Islam appear in the eighth century. Composed in Greek, Syriac, and Arabic, they were written in Syria/Palestine. Most are imbued with apocalyptic fervor and see the rise of Islam in the apocalyptic idiom of the Book of Daniel. In typical early-medieval fashion, they interpret the Islamic conquest as punishment for Christian sin. One such text was the Apocalypse of Pseudo-Methodius of Patara. Written in Syriac in the late eighth century, it would be translated into Greek and Latin and then into several early-modern European vernaculars. In such form, it exercised a formidable influence on medieval western Christian attitudes toward Islam. Also highly influential would be John of Damascus's (d. ca. 750) Greek work *On the Heresies,* which views the "Ishmaelites" not as members of a discrete new religion but as heretics who had misunderstood shared biblical materials. While this work appeared from within the world of Islam, most Greek anti-Muslim texts would thereafter appear in Byzantium. Some of these were polemical and meant to disparage Islam and demean the Prophet, as well as ridicule the Qur'an and the religion founded upon it. Other works written in Syriac and Arabic were apologetical (that is, defensive) in character and attempted, like second- and third-century apologies to the Romans, to demonstrate the credibility and rationality of Christianity.

By the close of the first millennium, an "Islamic world" had been created. In this world, the day was everywhere punctuated by five daily prayers; the week, by the sermon in the mosque; and the year, by a new calendar, the pilgrimage to Mecca, and the month of Ramadan. From the beginning of the Muslim Conquest to the First Crusade, large numbers of Christians, including many illustrious intellectuals, inhabited this new world. In some parts of the Islamic world, like Baghdad, some degree of peaceful coexistence and intellectual interaction prevailed. This is sometimes thought to have been embodied in pre-Conquest Spain in the form of *convivencia,* a peaceful golden age of coexistence. Recently, some have gone far to expose as near-mythical a view that conceals the regular violence that characterized ordinary social life in these regions.

The truth is that places like Baghdad *were* highly exceptional and *convivencia* largely an imagined utopia ("nowhere") of unbroken peaceful coexistence that has little foundation in historical reality. In many Christian communities, Christians were treated quite badly and in some, as we shall see, were even persecuted. Many Muslims were exasperated by freedoms, like the freedom of speech, granted to non-Muslims. Jews and Christians were not, in fact, habitually classified as "People of the Book" but as infidels by the hostile (the same language, of course, would be used by the Crusaders to stigmatize their religious enemies). Some Muslims strongly objected to open religious exchanges among scholars.

Over the course of many centuries, Christian demography changed quite dramatically. Cities that had majority Christian populations in the conquered territories would, by the dawn of the Ottoman era, have, usually, only significant minority populations. One reason for this demographic diminishment was the social and economic attractions conversion to Islam held out to Christians who were ambitious. A second was an uncomfortable social condition, required by law, often identified by the neologism "dhimmitude."

In the Qur'an there is mention of a special poll-tax required for protection *(al-dhimma)* of the People of the Book. We hear there, too, of the fittingly docile and passive posture Jews and Christians should assume in paying it (Qur'an 9.29)—prescriptions later written into Islamic law. Submissive persons living under the condition of shelter or refuge of a superior people were known, pejoratively, as *dhimmi*. Still, Jews were safer in Baghdad than in Paris.

Until the eleventh century, the *dhimmi* were regarded ubiquitously as second-class citizens. They were subject to many legal disabilities, including prescriptions to wear distinctive clothing, to refrain from any public demonstration of their religious practice, and an absolute prohibition on attempting to convert Muslims away from Islam. Christian property and buildings (including churches, monasteries, and schools) were regularly seized, as, on occasion, were entire episcopal dioceses. In short, Christian populations had become subaltern communities. They were discriminated against, put at social and economic disadvantage, and, on occasion, persecuted. In these conditions, some resisted and were murdered, and an entirely new martyrological literature emerged that attempted to link their experience to memories of martyrdom under occasionally hostile Roman rule. Written in Arabic, Syriac, Coptic, Greek, and Latin, these martyrologies tell us of lethal encounters of defiant Christians and intolerant Muslims and, incidentally, much about the social conditions under which Christians lived.

Another genre of Christian subaltern literature to emerge in these conditions usually featured as protagonist a Christian monk in the court of an emir or caliph. Written in dialogue form by Christians, such stories were sometimes grounded in historically based realities. Inevitably, in the theological discussion at the center of these stories, the monk would triumph over his theological adversaries. Such works, designed not only to buoy up Christians in their faith but also to supply them with responses to Muslim critics, enjoyed great popularity in regions of Muslim rule. Eventually, attitudes toward interreligious relations would harden in the thirteenth century. By the Ottoman era, many early Christians found conditions so unendurable that they migrated to the West.

"Reconquest"

Long before the dawn of the Ottoman era—indeed shortly after the Islamic invasion of the Iberian Peninsula—a series of skirmishes and then more serious conflicts began. Yet the Reconquista proper dates to the eleventh century, when, inspired by ideas of a crusade against and depopulation of the infidel, Ferdinand of Castile (r. 1037–1065) took up the reconquest of Spain in a militarily earnest and systematic fashion. In either case, the reconquest would not end until 1492, when Granada finally fell to Catholic kings.

For some time, historians have debated whether the reconquest was essentially an ideologically or theologically motivated effort to take lands that had once belonged to the Visigoths or a conflict essentially political and economic in character. The response is not easy, as it depends on a precise specification of time and place. What seems clear is that from the late eighth century, the cult of St. James spread and grew in popularity and that this cult, which would eventually build up to the very popular pilgrimage to the Cathedral of St. James of Compostela, fed the imagination of those intent on reconquest. Soon, St. James was harnessed by ecclesiastical writers of the period. Popular legend held that an apostle mounted on a white horse—none other than St. James himself—rode on several occasions to rout the infidel and came to the aid of Christian knights. Once the idea of crusade to recover holy lands from the infidel took hold in the Christian imagination, the theological foundations for the Reconquest had been laid. This idea of course was to have an enormous and lasting, if ambiguous, legacy in the life of western Crusaders to the Levant and Bohemia and even to France (to suppress heresy) for the next two centuries and beyond.

The Idea of the Crusade

Though Christians had for centuries experienced the effects of the Muslim idea of *jihad,* the idea had no influence on Christian ideas of crusade. In fact, before the thirteenth century—by which time four Crusades had been launched—there was no Latin word to define "crusade." Nonetheless, popes, canon lawyers, and some Crusaders all recognized in it the familiar devotional and conceptual elements of pilgrimage (by the time of the First Crusade in 1096, the pilgrimage had been well established as an expedient for atoning for sin), as well as just war and holy war. During the eleventh century, prevailing ideas of holy war in defense of the church and the faith, or even of protecting the helpless or weak, were all common. Popes occasionally had called on armed militias to protect the church, as when Pope Leo IV (r. 847–855) in 853 adjured the Franks to defend Rome from Saracen pillagers. In 878, Pope John VIII (r. 872–882) proposed spiritual incentives to soldiers willing to defend the church against the hostile. The main incentive was remission of sin in the case of a soldier who died. No pope dared guarantee salvation. Yet it is not clear that a soldier distinguished remission of sin from a promise of salvation. In the eleventh century, the militantly self-righteous Pope

Gregory VII (r. 1073–1085) planned not only on encouraging but also on leading a campaign to defend Christians in the eastern empire. Building on the ideas of earlier popes, he aimed to create "an army of St. Peter" to undertake battle against Peter's foes, above all heretics and the infidel. During the eleventh century, popes awarded material and spiritual rewards to Christian warriors attempting to reconquer Spain and rout Muslims from "Christian" territory.

Eventually, canon lawyers would define the conditions under which Christian soldiers might punish heretics, excommunicates, infidels, and violators of the peace. They were considerably more reluctant than Pope Gregory to imagine clerics involving themselves in the shedding of blood. Yet in one proprietary sense, they were quite clear: the Holy Land "belonged" to Christians. Muslims held it illegitimately. They therefore could be routed by force. Canonists also defined the conditions under which one became a Crusader. Here, the key legal element was the vow to take up the cross in defense of the church against its enemies. The vow intentionally generated both obligations and rights for the Crusader; it may also have created powerful religious motivations for him to leave his family on a costly

8. Crusaders' Chapel of the Virgin Mary, twelfth century. Church of the Holy Sepulchre, Jerusalem, Israel. Gianni Dagli Orti / The Art Archive at Art Resource, NY.

expedition with little assurance of success or even survival. Taking the vow bound the soldier to take up the cross on behalf of the church. If he failed to do so, he could be punished by both clerical and civil authorities. His vow was symbolized by wearing a cross sewn to his clothing. He completed his vow by worshipping at the Holy Sepulchre in Jerusalem.

While this was an element of the Crusader's vow, it also functioned as an intoxicating religious motivation. In other words, it not only satisfied the requirements for the vow, but it was also a powerful religious motivator for soldiers yearning for sanctification and redemption, for being shrived of the sin that was necessarily committed in the practice of one's bellicose occupation. It undoubtedly aroused in the Crusader, praying at the site of Christ's triumph over death, powerful eschatological affections; at that site, he must have hoped that he, like Christ, would be raised from the dead by the power of God on the last day. Finally, canonists, working consciously in the tradition of just war theory, had to respond to the question of who was the legitimate authority required to declare a Crusade. They strongly emphasized the requirement of papal initiative. As only a pope could issue a Crusade indulgence, promising remission of sin, only he could declare a Crusade. It was the pope, too, who was responsible for securing certain rights for the Crusader, such as protection for his family and property. But the spiritual rights promised—the forgiveness of all previous sin and the restoration of the Crusader to a state of innocence in the giving of comprehensive remission of sin—were surely the gifts most treasured by the one who had taken up the cross. The pope had now sanctioned violence undertaken in an armed pilgrimage to liberate the Byzantine church and the Holy Land from the threat of the infidel; it is very important that he promised complete remission of sin to all who would go to Jerusalem to liberate the church.

The First Crusade

In a sermon in the field of Clermont (1095), it was with that promise that Pope Urban II (r. 1088–1099) appealed to Frankish knights to take up the cross. Anyone who went with pure motives on the pilgrimage to Jerusalem, he promised, could "substitute this journey for all penance." The magnitude of the response from northern and central Europe down through Italy to Sicily to this tempting petition—something on the order of sixty thousand people responded to the call and headed east for the Holy Land—is sufficient attestation to the strength of religious motivations (which, in many cases, must have been entirely mixed up with other, mercenary motivations). Some Crusader families already had a tradition of pilgrimage to the Holy Land; those who took up arms in addition to making pilgrimage were extending this ancestral tradition. Some extended family members went together on the journey. The desire for land or booty for younger sons has been perhaps overstated. In fact, few Crusaders actually settled in the Levant, and few returned rich, except perhaps in relics. In addition, very few young men would have been able to afford the enormous expense of the expedition. It has been estimated that one Crusader would have had to sacrifice four years' income to afford the horses, chain mail, and supplies required. Many mortgaged lands to finance the journey. When we take into account the severity of the journey; the financial and familial sacrifices demanded; the ordeal and privations of long, uncomfortable travel; the sheer misery of warfare (not to mention the genuine possibility of death en route or in battle); thirst; famine; and epidemic, not to mention long military odds, we can gain some appreciation of the power of the religious and devotional powers at play.

After preaching the Crusade to a largely clerical gathering at Clermont and exhorting the clerics there to undertake the cause of preaching themselves, the pope himself traveled through much of France to proclaim his message. To some degree, Urban's message and subsequent preaching were both responses to an appeal that had reached him while presiding in March 1095 at a council in Piacenza. There a legation from Constantinople appealed to him for military aid needed for the campaign against the Turks. As four surviving accounts of this sermon at Clermont exist and as all were composed after 1099, when the euphoria of victory in Jerusalem helped shape the final form of the speech given four years earlier, we cannot be sure exactly what Urban preached to his auditors.

Some things, however, are clear. First, in his capacity as pope, Urban certainly imagined himself as the legitimate authority required to call a just war. Like other popes, he imagined himself to be speaking in the person of and on behalf of Christ, and he regarded victories over Muslims in Spain and Sicily as clear expressions of God's will. Equally clear is that this war was not a response to injury suffered but a war of "liberation." Indeed, Urban used the word *liberatio* frequently in his campaign sermons. The liberation he imagined was twofold, one involving people, the other involving place, the latter infinitely eclipsing the former: it was the place of the Christians of the eastern churches (and especially the church of Jerusalem) and of the city of Jerusalem. All existing documents from the First Crusade mention the centrality of Jerusalem. Only there could the Crusader's vow be fulfilled. Many non-papal documents highlight the liberation of the Holy City as the purpose of the armed pilgrimage; one charter alludes only in passing to the liberation of eastern Christianity from the menace of the Turk. One chronicle relates that upon hearing the pope's appeal for a Crusade to free the Holy Land, the crowd cried out, "God wills it!"

At the same time, Urban's mind was preoccupied with freeing Spain—parts of which contemporaries were calling the "land of St. Peter"—from unjust occupation. Moreover, he imagined this campaign in terms indistinguishable from those in which he envisaged the Crusade. "Liberators" there were also promised a papal indulgence that would atone for all sin and all temporal punishment it incurred. Those who could not take up the cross were urged to contribute materially to the effort and promised that their penances, too, would as a consequence be commuted.

Both campaigns were reckoned as wider movements of liberation of the Christian church—a paramount concern of the Cluniac order, in one of whose cloisters Urban had once been a monk (see chapter 9). Though the goal of liberating Jerusalem, the Holy City of Zion (which the weekly monastic recitation of the psalter would have brought vividly to the mind of any monk of the period) was the central objective, Urban temporarily entertained the possibility of taking Egypt too. The centrality of Jerusalem is why the Crusade must be considered, in devotional terms, as a pilgrimage.

Urban attempted above all to recruit Franks, emphasizing the great deeds of Frankish warriors. He stressed to his audiences that the Crusade was an expedition to be undertaken primarily by laymen—that is, by knights and foot soldiers. He opposed the participation of monks and allowed clerics to join the expedition only under the condition that they secure the permission of their bishops. For the laity, the Crusade was a way to take up the cross and a means, thus, to remit for sin, a way of acting religiously that had previously been open only to monks and clerics.

The Crusaders had chosen, politically speaking, a propitious time to strike. Internecine struggles for power among different caliphates and princes left the Levant unprepared for a unified defense of the eastern Mediterranean. Meanwhile, four large armies of Crusaders formed. After converging on Constantinople in May 1097, they almost immediately achieved success. In July, the armies conquered the Seljuk capital city of Nicaea. Further victories followed, including an enormously important conquest near Dorlaeum, and this victory opened the route across Asia Minor. In March 1097 an army commanded by Baldwin of Boulogne (r. 1100–1118) established the first Crusader domain in the Near East, the county of Edessa; it was a sign of things to come. After a difficult siege, a relief army composed of an alliance of Muslim leaders was defeated in late June. The principality of Antioch, under Bohemond of Sicily (d. 1111), was established in January 1098. At that point, the Crusaders again took up their march to Jerusalem. In June 1099, they reached the Holy City, which they finally took in July.

Iter Sancti Sepulchri: On the Road to Jerusalem

Given the overwhelming odds against success, not to mention the Crusaders' awareness that they were weak, as well as poorly led, fed, and supplied, the Crusaders' improbable triumphs were quite naturally interpreted as signs of divine approval, benevolence, and intercession on their behalf. In letters written home, the Crusaders referred to their militia as the "army of God." They themselves were members in the "knighthood of Christ." Victory at Nicaea was not theirs but God's. Their expedition was far from a profane military odyssey; it was rather a "most holy" one, indeed one blessed by God. As the Crusaders moved from improbable victory to fortuitous outcome, they came to see themselves as charmed, favored with heaven-sent blessing. With this view in mind, they gradually came to see Muslim resistance as futile and pointless. What merely human army could defeat the will of God or His militia? He flummoxed and terrorized His enemies while miraculously protecting and fortifying the Crusaders. Indeed, they had been preselected, foreordained for the divine task they had taken on. If they suffered, their privations were like Job's. They were being purified by God. Their hardships were like those the Israelites had shouldered in their arduous journey from Egypt to the Promised Land, their leaders likened to Moses. Like the Maccabees, they fought a war for God's land, for Jerusalem above all. Some Crusaders began to imagine themselves as martyrs or monks. Of course, all the Crusaders wore crosses. Those who died in battle were understood to be martyrs who had justified themselves by their death. The spilling of blood in a sacred mission wiped away all sins.

The apparition of saints, coincidences, and the occurrence of natural portents only reinforced the conviction that the Crusaders had undertaken a sacred expedition. The Crusaders experienced at least three Marian apparitions. Mary was depicted on a banner as the Crusaders crossed Asia Minor. Oddly, Peter, the first pope, made relatively few appearances in this papally launched Crusade. Instead, saints associated with the East, like St. George and St. Andrew, appeared many times. Many major moments on the expedition occurred, not by accident it was believed, on sacred days. Jerusalem was captured, auspiciously, on the Feast of the Dispersion of the Apostles. The Crusaders breached the walls of Jerusalem at the very hour when Christ died on the cross. When the Crusaders had moved from Asia Minor into Syria, the sky was filled with supernatural portents. In 1097 a comet (documented not only in western but also in Chinese and Korean records), its tail shaped like a sword, flew through the night sky. Later that year, a light in the shape of a cross took shape in the sky, shortly after an earthquake. On the night of June 13, 1098, a meteor fell from the west onto Antioch. In June 1099, as the Crusaders came close to Jerusalem, an eclipse of the moon appeared. How could these signs be interpreted except as auguries of divine support and Christian victory?

The discovery of relics on the expedition only solidified even more the conviction of divine favor and inevitable victory. First of all, the Holy Land itself was a relic, imbued with the power drenched by contact with the prophets, with the apostles, and above all with Christ. Conquering and passing through famous land-marks must only have enhanced the burgeoning sense that the Crusaders were destined for a great triumph—cities like Tyre, visited by Christ; Caesarea, where Peter had preached; and Emmaus, where Christ had appeared after his resurrection. Jerusalem was the urban relic par excellence: the site of Christ's Passion and resurrection, as well, of course, as the patrimony of Christ and his followers. The very purpose of the Crusade was to liberate the city; that is why the Crusaders took the road to the Holy Sepulchre *(iter sancti sepulchri)*. Their purpose was to liberate it, purge it of pagan presence, and worship there. Actions were taken by the Crusaders explicitly "for God and the Holy Sepulchre." That, in fact, is what made a military expedition a holy pilgrimage.

Many Crusaders discovered amazing relics, like a ball of Mary's hair, torn out while her son suffered so grievously on the Cross. The discovery of the Holy Lance, the one that had pierced Christ's side during his crucifixion, was so exhilarating that it boosted Christian morale and was credited with the Christian victory in Antioch. It was said that anyone fighting near the Holy Lance was immune to injury. The most famous relic discovered was a fragment of the True Cross. It was brought into battle in subsequent Crusades until lost in a skirmish in 1187.

It will have been noticed that the Crusaders' experiences embodied different elements of Pope Urban's message. They succeeded because God Willed It. The celestial portents, discoveries of relics, and apparitions only reinforced this belief. It was God's will that Jerusalem be liberated. This was what made the Crusade righteous and meritorious. The Crusaders were like those undertaking a religious profession. Reaching the earthly Jerusalem was required; it was also a sign of the internal journey to the heavenly Jerusalem. They were knights, yes, but knights of Christ. They were warriors but spiritual ones.

In retrospect, the planned capture of Jerusalem seems an outrageous and al-most preposterously futile undertaking. That it succeeded continues to astonish, even as historians can provide convincing "explanations" for its success. Poorly coordinated armies had to overcome the lack of military choreography, unimaginable physical privation, and even want of crucial military equipment, like siege engines. That the Crusaders managed to capture Jerusalem requires us to under-score that they were obsessively fixated on their goal and single-minded in their determination to achieve it. Their religious motivations made them believe they were invincible, as did several improbable triumphs and sheer luck on the very hard journey. At the military level, naval support, especially in the sieges of Antioch and Jerusalem, was pivotal to their success. The disunity of Muslim political and military leaders was decisive. They had no way of knowing why such a fanatical military force was bearing down on them, nor could they imagine how calamitous a successful European expedition could be.

After victory, the territory in the Levant was soon carved up along feudal lines. The western warriors created a kingdom of Jerusalem, the principality of Antioch, and the counties of Edessa and Tripoli. Each of these was, in essence, a fiefdom. Though many of the warriors were Frankish, Italian merchants were quick to establish settlements in the conquered territories. Ecclesiastically speaking, Latin rites were established in churches in the domains of Jerusalem and Antioch. The conquered territories were organized into eight archbishoprics and sixteen bishoprics. Countless new monasteries blossomed in the sands of the eastern Mediterranean.

In terms of religious life, the most novel outcome of the First Crusade was that it spawned two new "military orders" charged with protecting and otherwise supporting those in the Latin kingdoms. The more well known of these were the Knights of the Temple, popularly known as the Templars. Founded in 1118 near the site of the Temple in Jerusalem, the Templars' *Rule* was prepared for them by no less a figure than Bernard of Clairvaux (d. 1153), who worked off the Cistercian founding documents to create it. The order would receive papal approval at the Council of Troyes in 1128 and become beloved in the West. It received many gifts, legacies, and endowments and quickly found itself rich—the cause of much suffering for members of the order at the hands of the French king Philip IV (r. 1285–1314) in the fourteenth century.

Almost needless to say, this was a hybrid order. Those who took vows were monks-in-arms. As such, they took the customary monastic vows and prayed the canonical hours. In addition, they promised to fight the infidel, protect pilgrims, and defend the Holy Land. No more perfect or concrete marriage of current Christian monastic and bellicose ideals could be imagined, except perhaps that of the great rivals of the Templars, the Knights of St. John (Hospitallers). Their foundation was made ca. 1080, when merchants from Amalfi founded a hospital in Jerusalem named for St. John the Baptist.

The Crusaders had succeeded, in part, because of Muslim political and military disunity. But that lack of unity was to prove ephemeral. The history of the improbable success of the Crusaders would soon take a different arc. Soon the Crusaders' nemesis, the Kurdish general and empire builder, Saladin (d. 1193), would unite Muslim power under his rule. He aimed to regain Jerusalem and to rout the westerners. By 1187 he would take Jerusalem and, very quickly, most of the Holy Land, thus rousing Europe to the Third Crusade. The westerners, who included Richard the Lionhearted (r. 1189–1199) and other European leaders, recaptured Acre, but despite great effort, Jerusalem remained under Muslim control.

The worst outcome of the Fourth Crusade (1202–1204), from the perspective of the Christian world, is the way in which it deepened hostility between the eastern and western halves of Christendom. The Crusaders from northern France were deterred from the Holy Land when Alexius Angelus IV (r. 1203–1204), son of the deposed eastern emperor, Isaac II (r. 1185–1195), appealed to them for help. He promised a large amount of payment money, as well as Greek submission to the Latin church. The Crusaders easily dethroned the usurper. But the son of Isaac could not keep his promises. The Crusaders plundered Constantinople over a course of three days, taking many precious relics. Constantinople and much of the eastern empire around it was divided among the knights and Venice. A Latin patriarch was consecrated in Constantinople and the Greek church declared to be subject to the pope. This was disastrous for the eastern emperor. It made his empire (which was regained in the mid-thirteenth century) weaker and much more vulnerable to attacks by the Ottoman Turks in the middle of the fourteenth century. It also deeply embittered the East's relations with the West, so much so that it has been suggested that the Crusaders' destruction of Constantinople hurt ecumenical relations more than any other single event or factor.

The subsequent Crusades were replete with folly and failure, even tragedy, as we shall see more clearly in chapter 17. In 1291, the last Latin holding in Palestine was lost. With its loss, the Crusades to the Holy Land were over. No permanent territorial gains were made. An expedition that started out in part to help the eastern church accelerated its destruction by Ottoman Muslims in 1453. Latin and Greek Christians now despised one another. Only the pope as a defender of Christendom and authorizer of Crusades benefited by acquiring a cheap form of prestige.

Western Christian Views of Islam, ca. 700–1450

Surely the most curious feature of western perceptions of Islam is how little they changed, once fixed, over eight centuries. Firsthand knowledge of Islam in the early Middle Ages and knowledge acquired about the Qur'an and sacred texts in the twelfth century did almost nothing to change the first Christian descriptions of Islam, which were inflected by hatred, ignorance, and religious rivalry, as well as fear of physical threat. From very early on in Islamic history, Christians portrayed Muslims, who were of course strict monotheists, as polytheists and idolaters. This was self-evidently false and shaped deeply by polemical aims, not descriptive ones. Another sign of the polemic distortion of Islam is that in the eyes of Christian writers, it was violent and carnal in nature. While some treated the Islamic conquests as God's just punishment for Christian sin, others came to the conclusion that the Muslim God must be the true God and so converted to Islam. But most Christian writers wondered if Muslims were really beasts riding in chariots and armed with swords, ever ready for violence in the name of God.

Christians also ridiculed Muhammad and his followers for their supposed carnality. Some polemical writers contended that Muhammad had false revelations so as to have many wives and satisfy his sexual affections. In addition, the afterlife he promised to faithful Muslims was portrayed as entirely devoted to carnal satisfaction. John of Damascus knew Islam intimately. He was an important financial administrator at the courts of two Umayyad caliphs. He nonetheless depicted Muhammad as a devious, false prophet who conceived of Islam after encountering an Arian monk. Thus, many Christian writers, John included, categorized Islam as a *heresy* rather than a non-Christian religious tradition. John too dwells on the Qur'an's discussion of polygamy and ridicules Muhammad for taking multiple wives.

Later-medieval Christian writers, even though they knew quite a lot about Islam, said much the same things about Muhammad, his revelations, the holy book, and the religion he had founded. They underscored the familiar themes of idol worship and carnality. It is curious that this came at a time when western Christians were gaining more and more direct knowledge of Islamic texts. For example, Peter the Venerable, abbot of Cluny (d. 1156) had the Qur'an and other sacred texts translated. But these efforts were all oriented toward ridicule and condemnation—or conversion.

One use famously made of the newly acquired knowledge of Islam in the West was a series of efforts in the thirteenth century to convert the Muslim world to Christianity. Both Dominican and Franciscan orders would be involved, but the most famous attempt by far was that of Francis of Assisi. In 1220, he explicated the essentials of Christianity to al-Kamil, the sultan of Egypt, with no success. Later missionaries probed the Islamic world for proselytes, their success negligible. In the end, Christianity seems to have had exceedingly little appeal for Muslims. An infinitesimal number of Muslims was baptized.

III
High-Medieval Christianity,
ca. 1050–1300

Libertas Ecclesiae:
The Age of Reform, ca. 1050–1125

The social and political origins of the reform movement of the eleventh- and twelfth-century church, a militant campaign that would transform Latin Christianity, lay in the near-anarchical conditions that prevailed in the wake of the collapse of Charlemagne's empire. To many in the church, it seemed not only advisable but imperative that churches everywhere put themselves under the protection of some lay lord or, preferably, a national monarch. This appeared, not unreasonably, to be the only alternative to potential disaster and even extinction. Ironically, the problems of lay proprietorship of ecclesiastical property, the selection and investiture of prelates, and their enjoyment of sacred status and prerogatives all came to be seen, by the eleventh century, as troubles badly in need of eradication, or at least as matters for reform. Yet these were quandaries created, in the first instance, by churchmen desperate for the health and survival of the institutions and people for which they felt responsible.

As noted, when ecclesiastical lands and buildings fell under the control of lay lords, they often came to be regarded by these lords as sources of revenue—profit-making enterprises from which they could benefit and over which they exercised all rights, including the right of clerical appointments. The men they designated often cared little for the high religious obligations and practices that were traditional to their spiritual vocation, not to mention regulated by canon law. In particular, the many parish priests who were either married or kept women would have scandalized canonical tradition. Also shocking was the high percentage of parish clergy who had purchased their offices, an act that canon law called simony, after Simon Magus, a sorcerer and apparent heresiarch whose confrontation with Peter is recounted in Acts 8. Both of these specific sins seemed to illustrate to the reform-minded a more pervasive, general transgression against the right order of things—namely, the subordination of the sacred to the profane and the ecclesiastical to the regal. Ultimately, the point of reform would be quite radical because it aimed to invert this perverse relationship.

An instance *par excellence* of the current disorder, and of the confusion of the sacred and secular, was the way in which kings imagined themselves as quasi-clerical sacred officeholders. This again was a case where the church, in desperation, had earlier imputed sacred qualities and obligations to monarchs, qualities kings were only too happy to accept. Because churchmen regarded kingship as the best stay against disorder and violence, in the ninth and tenth centuries they gladly gave it the justification of theology and imbued it with the aura of the holy. In particular, they themselves began to regard and to describe kingship as a sacred office. Kings were compared to the great monarchs of Israelite history—to Saul, David, and Solomon. They were ritually anointed in ceremonies that all too closely resembled those for the consecration of bishops. Hailed as ministers of God, they were set over the people in their realm and also their prelates, whose appointments they monopolized. Indeed, they invested the bishop with the pastoral staff and ring that were the insignia of his pastoral office and the visible signs of his capacity to dispense invisible grace. In short, royal theocracy, and all the privileges that went with it, had become customary throughout much of Europe. In the short run, this was a necessary stay against the fissiparous potentialities of early feudalism, but as canon law enjoyed something of a revival at the end of the millennium, it came to be seen as a gross violation of the legal tradition. As the need for sheer physical protection declined, canon lawyers and other prelates began to realize that reform would only be possible if the churches could extricate themselves from lay control.

Monastic Reform

At the same moment that lay lords and kings were assuming increasing control of ecclesiastical lands, institutions, and appointments, several movements of monastic reform sprang up independently of one another in Germany, France, and Anglo-Saxon England under St. Dunstan (d. 988). By far the most enduring and influential of these reforms came at the Burgundian house of Cluny, soon to be the mother house of a great monastic empire, in the early eleventh century. Founded in 910 by Duke William I of Aquitaine (d. 918), who felt guilty about a murder and wished to establish a house of prayer to pray down his supernatural debt, the house would soon become the mother of hundreds of daughter houses in much of western Europe. In the foundation charter, William stated his reasons for founding the monastery. His is a thoroughly conventional opening to an early-medieval monastic charter, in which a donor states his hope that the prayers of a community of monks established in perpetuity might save a soul deeply enmeshed in a world of war, bloodshed, and sin—and therefore punishment. But the following sentences were less traditional:

> Therefore, be it known to all who live in the unity of the faith and who await the mercy of Christ, and to those who shall succeed them and who shall continue to exist until the end of the world, that, for the love of God and of our Savior Jesus Christ, I hand over from my own rule to the holy apostles, Peter, namely, and Paul, the possessions over which I hold sway, the town of Cluny, namely, with the court and demesne manor, and the church in honor of St. Mary, the mother of God, and of St. Peter, the prince of the apostles, together with all the things pertaining to it, the villa, indeed, the chapels, the serfs of both sexes, the vines, the fields, the meadows, the woods, the waters and their outlets, the mills, the incomes and revenues, what is cultivated and what is not, all in their entirety. . . . I give these things, moreover, with this understanding, that in Cluny a regular monastery shall be constructed in honor of the holy apostles Peter and Paul, and that there the monks shall congregate and live according to the rule of St. Benedict, and that they shall possess, hold, have and order these same things unto all time. . . . And let the monks themselves, together with all the aforesaid possessions, be under the power and dominion of the abbot Berno, who, as long as he shall live, shall preside over them regularly according to his knowledge and ability. But after his death, those same monks shall have power and permission to elect any one of their order whom they please as abbot and rector, following the will of God and the rule promulgated by St. Benedict—in such wise that *neither by the intervention of our own or of any other power may they be impeded from making a purely canonical election.* Every five years, moreover, the aforesaid monks shall pay to the church of the apostles at Rome ten shillings to supply them with lights; and they shall have the protection of those same apostles and the defense of the Roman pontiff; and those monks may, with their whole heart and soul, according to their ability and knowledge, build up the aforesaid place. (Emphasis added.)

There are a number of points here that invite comment. First and foremost, in order to frustrate the practice of lay choice and investiture of an abbot, a practice that was not healthy for the religious condition of many houses, William explicitly grants to the monks of the new foundation the right to choose their own abbot. Beyond that, he makes them subject to no secular power. Indeed, they were accountable only to Sts. Peter and Paul—that is, to the papacy, which itself was warned against interfering too much in the internal life of the cloister. Given the distance between Rome and Burgundy, this dictum in effect made Cluny an independent house, free from all secular or ecclesiastical jurisdiction.

Under the leadership of a series of extraordinarily capable abbots, Cluny not only established an impressive and highly elaborate liturgical life and the preservation of Benedictine customs, but it also became the mother house of the many cloisters that adopted its usages in France, Italy, Spain, Germany, and, finally, England. Guesses as to the number of houses that subordinated themselves as priories to Cluny vary widely. But there were at least five hundred and as many as two thousand. Theoretically, the abbot of Cluny appointed the prior in all these many houses. Each novice monk was supposed to make his formal profession at Cluny. In addition, all Cluniac houses followed the same customs regarding observance of the canonical hours and the ecclesiastical calendar. While the influence of the Cluniac ideal on the eleventh-century papal reforms can be exaggerated, Cluniac monks were vociferous in their opposition to simony and clerical marriage. Above all, some reformers looked to Cluny as a model; this was a house that enjoyed Christian liberty *(libertas)*—that is, freedom from lay domination.

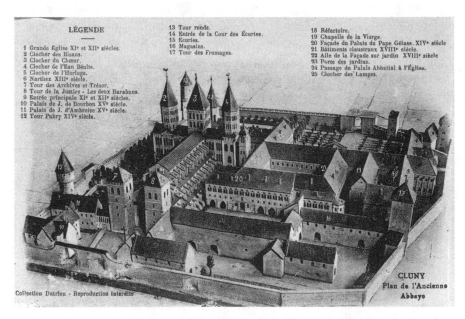

9. Cluny (Saône-et-Loire, France), Benedictine abbey (founded 910). Model of the medieval monastery. The largest church in Europe for five centuries, it exemplifies stone-vaulted Romanesque churches typical of Benedictine monasteries. Photo postcard, ca. 1900. akg-images.

Cluny and Papal Reform

There were many sources of dissatisfaction with the state of affairs in the eleventh-century church and, correspondingly, many visions of reform among the dissatisfied. Sometimes this bundle of reforms is called "the Gregorian Reform," but, for a variety of reasons to be discussed below, this is not a satisfactory way to describe the entire spectrum of improving practices that, within the short span of a quarter-century, dramatically transformed the western church. Nonetheless, the role of the papacy in these reforms was notable as it acted as the leader of an international movement of reform, revealed its willingness and indeed avidity to step into the affairs of other churches as a divinely appointed supreme authority, and succeeded in engaging non-Romans in the papal reform movement, either as popes or as influential cardinals and ideologues.

It was once widely believed that the impetus behind the thinking of the reformers was monastic, especially Cluniac. While it is true that monks did come to influence papal policy in ways that were essentially without precedent, this notion is only partly true. For one thing, some reformers, like Pope Gregory VII, were essentially men of action, not of contemplation. A far more complex understanding of the relation between the ideals and practices of Cluny and those cherished by the papal reformers is required.

Naturally, the aims and ideals of both groups often overlapped. It was very hard for Cluniac reformers to resist clerical abuses or ruination by secular rule. But in their attitude toward the more radical claims of the Gregorian era they had to be ambivalent. On the one hand, they were inclined to support the Gregorians in their desire to be free of lay or episcopal interference. On the other hand, the Cluniac empire was deeply indebted to the generosity of pious princes, and, especially in Germany, it collaborated with the royal family. Thus, they could not have endorsed the more radical claims of the Gregorians without flagrant self-contradiction. While free themselves from lay control, the Cluniac abbots and monks were curiously silent about the issue of lay control of ecclesiastical offices. Essentially, they approved of lay control of the church and simply urged lay rulers to exercise their ecclesiastical responsibilities with primary care for the good of the church.

Still, Cluniac monks provided moral support to the reforming popes. Cluniac abbots attempted to broker a truce when relations between the German empire and the papacy ruptured. Some of the Roman reformers, like Gregory VII, would see in Cluny a model for the reform of "Roman liberty," by which they meant ecclesiastical freedom from lay interference or control. Some Cluniac monks were chosen to serve in the papal curia. Finally, a former Cluniac monk was chosen pope. Taking the name Urban II, he is most famous for having launched the

First Crusade in 1096. Thus, the influence of new monastic currents of reform should not be exaggerated, nor underestimated, as a potent new source of religious energy and reform vigor that predated but inspired the thinking of reformers in Rome.

Still, it was from cloisters and dioceses in Lorraine, not Burgundy, that reform first touched the papacy in Leo IX (r. 1049–1054). This moderate reform was not only less monastically tinged, but also less papally inspired, less Italian, less clerical, less hostile to empire and emperors themselves, and less united than the term "Gregorian Reform" seems to suggest. Actually, the Gregorian Reform was part of a larger current of reforms, some of which gave it life but many of which antedated it. Moreover, some of the reformers from this larger current came to resent or defy Gregory's attempt to refashion the western church in the image of his ideas. We therefore need to distinguish the Gregorian Reform from the earlier papal reform that began in the 1040s and that would only become a part of the Gregorian efforts much later.

The Role of the New Testament

The papal reform that began around 1040 resulted from the coincidence of a number of currents of reform and political circumstances that allowed a new vision of the church to emerge—and then to seize the imagination as the only supposable one. Already in the early eleventh century, there was considerable hostility among the reformers to simony, or trafficking in sacred ecclesiastical offices. The same opposition existed to clerical marriage. There were canonical objections to both practices, but perhaps even more important were the exegetical objections to them. Neither practice corresponded to the vision of the apostolic life of the clergy as represented in the *Acts of the Apostles,* a book that, along with the gospels, gained ascendancy in these centuries for the supposedly faithful image of the life of Christ and the apostles depicted therein. Thus, the reform marks yet another important religio-cultural shift in the western church: the slow eclipse of the Hebrew Bible, with its models for action, codes of conduct, and patterns of worship, and the ascendancy of certain key books of the New Testament, especially those parts believed to represent the life led by Christ and the apostles. Many scholars have characterized this epochal shift as a "New Testament revival." While not untrue, it is a slightly uninflected interpretation. It was only certain key texts from the gospels and the *Acts of the Apostles* that were to have a massive, omnipresent impact on religious life from the eleventh through the thirteenth centuries at least, the ones that claimed to represent the life of Christ and the apostles. This form of life was known by the key term "the apostolic life" *(vita apostolica)*, which is ubiquitous in the documents of the period.

One distinguished historian of the Middle Ages has designated the early Middle Ages as a "Levitical period" for its emphasis on codes of behavior necessary in an age of anarchy and for the dominance of models of Old Testament kingship. How, then, do historians account for the massive shift in preference for the New Testament that included an effort on the part of many clerics and writers to suppress the appeal of models based on the Hebrew Bible? One explanation for this change is that sacred kingship was justified by reference to the Old Testament. Second, papal theocracy or overlordship was legitimated by texts in the New Testament, in which Christ makes certain promises to Peter regarding his authority over the church. Third, all of the texts in the New Testament pertaining to the quest to achieve the primitive or apostolic life were contained in the gospels and Acts. In Jesus's commission to the disciples (Mark 6:6–13 and parallels), there is an emphasis on preaching, renunciation of personal wealth, and the communal sharing of goods. The same sort of elements are present in the description of the apostolic community in Acts 4:32–5: "The whole group of believers was united, heart and soul; no one claimed for his own use anything that he had, as everything they owned was held in common. The apostles continued to testify to the resurrection of the Lord Jesus with great power, and they were all given great respect. None of the members was ever in want, as all those who owned land or houses would sell them and bring the money from them, to present to the apostles; it was then distributed to any members who might be in need." Such emphases and changes like these are difficult to explain. But the newly ascendant model of penniless, wandering, and begging preachers living chastely may have been a response to—and a symptom of revulsion toward—the values of an increasingly commercial society and the moral standards of urban culture. Be that as it may, religious reformers and papal reformers were united in their pilgrimage to the primitive as they sought to remold the church and themselves in the image of the earliest apostolic community.

Many papal reformers came to the conclusion that having embraced the communal life and renounced private property, the apostles must have been monks. Since clergy succeeded to the apostles, it followed that they, too, ought to live as monks. Convinced that these ancient monks were celibate, the reformers' drive to stamp out clerical marriage and concubinage and to restore celibacy received powerful, indeed sacred, justification from the pages of the gospels and Acts. The New Testament would now be harnessed to restore the discipline and order of the remote past, of the primitive church (or what the papal party conceived that order to be). New collections of ancient law would be used in precisely the same way. In the reformers' eyes, the buying and selling of church offices or clerical concubinage could of course find no legitimation in scripture, nor could they be justified by canon law. Around 1050, a reform movement centered on abolishing these offensive abuses took hold in Rome. The special political circumstances in Italy, which allowed appointments to be made by imperial authority, were ideal for the zealous passions of the moment.

Moderate Papal Reform, 1050–1075

The reform was launched when Emperor Henry III (r. 1039–1056) came to Rome. It is sometimes said that he came to heal a three-party schism, but that is not quite correct; he came to receive the imperial crown at the hands of the pope—this in accordance with the custom and practice of his predecessors, beginning with Otto I. Some have thought it ironic that Henry appointed the first serious reforming pope, as it was his son who would so dramatically clash with Leo's most intransigent successor, Gregory VII. But this overlooks the degree to which Henry III took his responsibilities to the church with the utmost seriousness—and the way in which he imagined himself, as many other contemporary kings did, as a high figure *within* the church. For example, he was conscious of his need to appoint bishops dutifully, and he did so without a whisper of simony. His was a pious and upright character, so much so that he earned the title *linea iusticie* (the measure of righteousness). From the citizens of Rome, he received the title of *patricius,* a high honorary title in republican and imperial Rome that was then thought to give him a decisive voice in the appointment of the pope.

In that capacity, Henry III selected in 1049 his cousin Bruno of Toul to succeed to the throne of Peter. Bruno was a bishop whose diocese led an important reform movement in Lotharingia, one inspired by two monasteries within his see, Cluny and Lorraine. He took the name Leo IX. His pontificate was short, but, as Colin Morris has put it, "in a few short years [it] changed the character of the Roman Church and its standing in western Christendom." It was from Lorraine that Leo gathered a remarkable group of like-minded advisers solemnly intent on reform, whom he brought to surround him at Rome. These included Humbert (d. 1061), a monk of Moyenmoutier (later cardinal-bishop of Silva Candida); the subdeacon Hildebrand (later Pope Gregory VII); and the hermit Peter Damian (d. 1072). By carefully choosing a group of leading churchmen from around Europe to help spearhead and support the reform program, the new pontiff had begun creating and internationalizing (or de-Romanizing) the cardinalate, a move that led one contemporary to call him that "marvelous pope" *(papa mirabilis).* The title of cardinal certainly existed before Leo ascended the throne of St. Peter. However, Leo transformed it. No longer was it an office conferred merely as a sinecure of status and benefit whose prelates would spend their time performing liturgical offices in the basilicas of the city. Rather, Leo had gathered about him men who had profound, even revolutionary, convictions about the church's place and prerogatives and the glorified place of the pope within that church.

These men would become leading ideologues and preachers. It is important to stress that by and large, they were non-Romans. Why does this matter? Because as foreigners to Rome (many, again, were from Lorraine), they could think of the pope in entirely more grandiose terms than was traditional in the city. Since the days of the Christianization of England and the north of Europe, Romans and the popes they produced generally had not imagined themselves as leaders of all Christendom—or even of the western Church—nor had they conceived of their office as an ecumenical power. They were far too caught up in Italian territorial questions and quarrels. Only occasionally did they intervene on a larger scale—for example, by adjudicating disputes between churchmen or by defining points of dogma.

It can hardly be surprising that all began to change only when a non-Roman pope was appointed by a German emperor and surrounded by non-Roman advisers. These were men who were not in thrall to long-standing custom and so could think in new ways about the regenerative uses to which the papacy might be put. For his part, the pope began to imagine that he had responsibility for the entire western church. This new responsibility was signified by a neologism that entered Latin at almost the moment Leo ascended the papal throne: *papatus*. This term, which means "papacy," was meant to indicate without ambiguity that there was a stratum of hierarchy higher than that of the episcopate *(episcopatus)* and that the bishop of Rome was higher and had more extensive powers than any other bishop. Surrounded by powerful cardinals, the reform papacy would attempt to eliminate traditional customs, now seen as iniquities, beginning with simony.

In the eleventh century, under the leadership of the new reformers at Rome, simony came to be seen as the worst sin imaginable for the clergy, despite the fact that at the start of the reform period, simony was virtually universal throughout Germany, Gaul, and Italy—to the dismay of the reformers, who complained bitterly of it in their writings. In canon law, simony had long been seen as a heresy. Defined primarily as the sin of giving money for the acquisition of holy orders or any ecclesiastical office, it also included the sin of even asking for an office.

The onslaught against simony was an attempt to purify the clergy for divine service by unyoking them from the world. It is instructive that this was the sin against which the reformers raged because it gives us a glimpse into the nature of medieval Christianity at the time. In the early eleventh century, what struck the reformers as offensive and intolerable indicates that Christianity was still imagined primarily as a cultic religion; what really counted was ritual and priestly purity, and what really revolted the reformers was imagined as an infection or contamination.

Other priestly characteristics, like the capacity to preach, would not become important until the thirteenth century, with the rise of the friars. It is only then that we can say something essential about Christianity changed.

A second aim of the reformers was to enforce clerical celibacy, and this was also motivated by the desire to achieve a pure clergy. By the time of the reformers, canon law had forbidden the marriage of clergy in major orders but not in the minor grades. Since the minimum age for the ordination of priests was thirty, many priests were already married and had families. In addition, concubinage was widely practiced among the clergy, and almost no one in society objected to it. So in 1050, a high percentage of clergy were living with wives or concubines. Again, the objection to this practice had its roots in the cultic nature of Christianity, as the reformers objected to the handling of Christ's body by those with impure hands. The reformers insisted that married men leave their wives when receiving holy orders. A primary aim of the synod of 1059 in Rome was to pass canons against anyone in holy orders—priests, deacons, and subdeacons—living with concubines. Peter Damian spoke ardently on the celibacy of priests and identified clerical marriage as a heresy of very ancient vintage—a suggestion that would have flummoxed most parish priests and their parishioners. It is of great significance that in 1059, the reformers gave instructions to the laity (with consequences they could not then have foreseen) to refuse to attend the masses of married priests. This was an instruction repeated by two subsequent popes, Alexander II (r. 1061–1073) and Gregory VII, and the repetition indicates both the refusal of priests to leave their wives immediately and the determination of these reforming popes to stamp out this "heresy" of impurity. Paradoxically, since the reformers made themselves something like neo-Donatists, they gave rise to a new sense of popular empowerment, which led to entire movements, also neo-Donatist, aggressively dedicated to priestly purity in the subsequent century. These occasionally developed, much to the reformers' dismay, into heretical movements.

Given the widespread incidence of clerical marriage, the reaction to these new canons was fierce. One bishop attempting to promulgate the new reform decrees in 1072 was driven from his diocese in Rouen. Two years later, there were chaotic and angry scenes in various parts of Europe, including Paris; there the clergy opposed the reforming decrees as unreasonable and therefore intolerable. Soon the reformers were insisting that children of clergy were bastards and were therefore not capable of inheritance. Eventually papal decrees referred to all consorts of priests, even if married, as concubines. These decrees were then enforced by the Second Lateran Council (1139), which proclaimed that any marriage entered into by a man in holy orders was not a legitimate marriage. The long sought-after aim was to establish a priesthood that was entirely celibate.

One of the tactics of the reformers in enforcing these measures was to harness the authority of St. Peter for the reform program. Like his namesake Leo I, who in some sense had founded the ancient Petrine doctrine, Leo IX had a strong sense of apostolic authority. Indeed, he believed that when he spoke, Peter was speaking through him to his Christian auditors (a sense felt all the more deeply by Hildebrand when he was made pope). Leo's own sense that Peter was speaking through him must have been profoundly felt by his terrified auditors. At Leo's first synod, held in Rome, the bishop of Sutri is said to have collapsed and died while attempting to defend himself against the charge of simony. Contemporaries recalled how Leo's denunciations of simoniacs sounded like the roar of the divine wrath. In addition to internationalizing the cardinalate, a second great achievements of Leo's was to hold a series of synods in Rome in which he promulgated new decrees against simony and clerical marriage.

In our current age, in which many of us have lived through the pontificate of John Paul II, the church is accustomed to a pope who is also a world traveler. But in the eleventh century, papal travel was not at all common. Leo's third great innovation was to travel north of the Alps through France and Germany. There he held a series of reform councils in which he announced and enforced his new decrees. Such councils were a novelty that brought papal power, and not just papal prestige, to the area. Bishops and other ecclesiastical dignitaries who had offended against one or more of Leo's decrees would be required to identify themselves. Sometimes they were deposed, often symbolically, and then reinstated. Sometimes they were simply deposed. Again the main issues were simony and clerical marriage. But the pope also demanded church appointments be made through elections by the clergy and people. Moreover, he denounced mistreatment of the poor, lay proprietorship of churches, and lay collection of fees for burial and administration of the sacraments. Leo transformed the consecration of some churches into ad hoc trials, like that at St. Remigius of Reims in 1049, during which he announced his reforming decrees and called for simoniacs to identify themselves.

The significance of Leo's travels in the northern lands can scarcely be exaggerated. He spent just over six months of his pontificate in Rome. In his first year in office alone, the pope would preside not only over synods in Rome, but also over councils in Pavia, Mainz, and Reims. Prior to his pontificate, the papal office, while venerable, had seemed remote, almost aloof. Now the Roman pontiff was acting as lawgiver and judge in the northern dioceses. The sheer novelty of the pope's being seen north of the Alps amplified the prestige of his office, and it gave hope to other reformers that their transformative vision might be achieved. Leo's own power seemed to have divine inspiration, and his compelling way of expressing divine dissatisfaction with simony and clerical concubinage convinced not only the clerical caste but also the laity to take it very seriously indeed. All of this made papal authority so real, so visible, and so effective that it won over the northern reformers, including the vast network of Cluniac congregations, whose enthusiasm and extensive network of priories would be used to good effect by the papacy.

As the feeling of reform overtook many in Lorraine and Burgundy, monks imagined reform primarily in terms of the moral improvement of the clergy. Geoffrey Barraclough has described well the fateful alterations that occurred when the forces of change made it to the Eternal City: "When the spirit of reform penetrated to Rome and came into contact with an Italian and Mediterranean environment, it was imperceptibly altered. For the Romans who joined the reformers, the first consideration was not moral rejuvenation." It was, rather, "the reinforcement of papal authority." This new emphasis would soon become clear in three ways: in relations with Constantinople and the Greek churches, in the development of canon law, and in Leo's impatience with Norman impunity in occupying part of the patrimony of St. Peter, one unacceptably close to the center of Peter's power.

The newly invigorated reformers, single-mindedly dedicated to their notions of papal authority and universality, soon caused a breach in relations with the East. The breach began when Pope Leo IX in 1052 tried to impose Latin liturgical usages on the Greek churches of southern Italy—at a time when the occupying Normans were taking churches from the Byzantine Empire. In retaliation, Michael Cerularius, the patriarch of Constantinople (r. 1043–1058), demanded that the Latin churches in his see adopt Greek practices. When they refused, he closed them down. In the following year, he wrote to Pope Leo IX and asked for negotiations. In response, Leo sent three legates in 1054, led by Humbert of Silva Candida, an aggressive and intransigent papalist. Humbert immediately made a bad impression by thrusting a letter at Cerularius from the pope (which he had drafted) outlining the place of Rome in the hierarchy of sees. After this inauspicious start, negotiations stalled. Eventually, Humbert lost patience and laid a bull of excommunication against Cerularius on the altar of Hagia Sophia just before Michael was about to begin the liturgy. In retaliation, Cerularius presided over a synod that anathematized Humbert. In short, this attempt at reconciliation left matters worse than they had been before, putting the two churches in open breach. The anathemas were lifted some nine hundred years later, at the close of the Second Vatican Council, but suspicion of Rome by the eastern churches did not magically lift with the anathemas. In any case, claims were made on behalf of the papacy that, when moved from the sacred to the earthly sphere, would become the basis of brash assertions later made by Gregory VII in his epochal conflict with Emperor Henry IV (r. 1056–1106).

Developments in Canon Law

The acute consciousness of the place of the popes as successors to St. Peter was reflected in contemporary developments in canon law. Until the middle of the eleventh century, the canon law was that collection compiled by Burchard of Worms in 1012, called the *Decretum*. Though hardly anti-papal, Burchard's collection reflects the view of the papacy before the reformers came to power. As a consequence, his collection made almost no reference to the pope and thus accurately reflected the modest role the pope played in contemporary ecclesiastical affairs. Burchard's concerns were not unlike those of the northern reformers, moral ones having to do with simony, clerical celibacy, and the indissolubility of marriage.

Around the accession of Leo IX, however, a new collection of canon law was assembled. Known as the *Collection in 74 Titles,* it was hardly concerned with moral reform. Rather, again reflecting the cares of the reforming party as it pertained to the pope, it was preoccupied with the position and privileges of the successor to St. Peter. For its sources, it drew not on the holy fathers or on synodical decrees but, rather, on papal letters, or decretals. Still, there was no attack on the rights of the emperor in the church, and there would not be until Henry IV's death in 1106. Until then, there was little sign of antagonism between the reforming party and the monarchy. These chronological markers are crucial in understanding when and how the reform movement took a new and revolutionary direction. Before that point, only one man at the papal court appears to have been opposed to Henry III's position with respect to the papacy: Hildebrand. But his time had not yet come.

One of Leo IX's irritations was the Norman conquest and occupation of southern Italy. Leo was convinced, partly on the basis of the "Donation of Constantine," that the papacy should hold dominion over the entirety of the region; the Normans, in his eyes, were occupying territory belonging to St. Peter and dispossessing him of goods that were his—that is, the saint's. Finally, Leo was driven to take military action against the invaders—leading the army south himself. This campaign ended unsuccessfully. His own cardinal, Peter Damian, condemned the whole military misadventure as undignified for a pope, and Leo's army was overwhelmed at Civitate in June 1053. The pope himself was taken into captivity for almost a year. In April 1054, shortly after his release, he died in Rome. But despite this inauspicious end, Leo's papacy was all-important. It had decisively reestablished the pope as the head of the western church, especially north of the Alps. Equally important, Leo IX had established and left behind a group of cardinal reformers who would sustain—and then radicalize—his legacy.

The next two moments of immense significance for the reformers—changes in lay investiture and alliance with the Normans—occurred during the brief pontificate of Nicholas II (r. 1059–1061). By the time of Nicholas, it seems clear that the more rigorist of the reformers at Rome had won the day. By 1059, Hildebrand had become archdeacon of the Roman church. This man, whom Peter Damian ambivalently but all-too-accurately dubbed his "holy Satan," was obstinate in his defense of the rights and prerogatives of Rome. He played a key role in negotiating the election of Nicholas II. Humbert, who has already been mentioned, also played an important part in this era of reform. Issues of authorship muddy the waters, but it is quite likely that Humbert wrote a pamphlet entitled *Three Books against the Simoniacs*. In this book, Humbert came finally to articulate his view that lay investiture was the most serious threat to the church—far more serious than either simony or clerical marriage.

Kings and Episcopal Grace: Investiture

To the minds of the reformers, lay investiture would come to symbolize much that was wrong with the church, if not the very source of its worst evils, in large part because its practice was built on custom and the accidents of history rather than canon law. The custom had originated in the ninth and tenth centuries. Once again, it was churchmen themselves who, in the anarchic conditions then prevailing and desperate for protection, had devised a theology and ritual of regal theocracy. No distinction between temporal and spiritual spheres was imagined or desired at the time. To the dismay of later reformers, when German emperors were crowned, they were acclaimed "vicars of Christ" on earth—a sacred honorific the papacy would soon jealously claim for itself. In any case, it was hardly surprising that the kingdom or empire over which such men presided was imagined as a unified church-state and that it was the king who appointed bishops. More precisely, a king or emperor "invested" the designated bishop with the insignia of his ecclesiastical office; in the case of a bishop, this meant his ring and staff. When the reformers came to challenge this custom, they were not merely challenging a ritual and what it seemed to symbolize (namely, that kings and princes had sacramental power and grace to consecrate a bishop). Nor were they simply trying to resist a ruler attempting to install an unsuitable candidate by force, though that was obviously highly objectionable. More profoundly, they were objecting to the prevailing ethos of royal theocracy with its notion that a king or emperor had primary authority within the church and, on a theological level, that the religious ought to stand in a subordinate relation to the profane and political. It may be the case that the reformers did not intend to subvert the existing order of society. Nonetheless, that was the inevitable outcome of their efforts to bring about change.

The first evidence of hostility toward the practice of investiture comes from 1058 and, predictably, from the pen of Cardinal Humbert. By this time, he and the reformers, wishing to return to the simplicity and practices of the apostolic church, had scoured the collection of ancient canons. What they discovered there was that bishops were supposed to be canonically elected and then consecrated— not by a lay ruler, of whatever rank, but by his fellow bishops. So far as Humbert and his fellow reformers were concerned, authority resided in the ancient canons, not in recent custom, and it was clear to all the reformers that the prevailing practice of lay investiture had no foundation in the canons. Humbert bitterly complained: "The sacred canons are being rejected and the whole Christian religion confounded because things pertaining to election are being done backward. . . . For the secular power comes first in electing and confirming, and then, whether they like it or not, there follows the consent of the clergy and people, and finally the judgment of the metropolitan bishop." For Humbert, this system was upside-down because it contradicted the sacred authority of the canons; therefore, it had to be toppled. "How," Humbert continued, "does it pertain to laypersons to distribute sacraments and episcopal grace, that is to say, the crozier staffs and rings with which episcopal consecration is principally effected?" In this jeremiad, he did not bring himself to acknowledge that such bishops would not only become chief priests of their provinces, but they would also achieve something like the status of counts or princes, with significant temporal holdings and responsibilities.

But Humbert went even further in his condemnation. In neo-Donatist fashion, he maintained that a cleric who had been raised to his position through lay investiture, rather than by clerical election, was no bishop at all. About the relations of priests and kings, he observed: "Just as the soul excels the body and commands it, so the priestly dignity excels the royal"—an argument of which later papal ideologues frequently availed themselves. Slowly, these theories won general acceptance at Rome among the reformers, and the theology of papal supremacy essentially became the foundation for papal reform for centuries.

For reform to be at all effective, the capacity of churchmen to appoint a reform-minded pope had to be secured. Consequently, in 1059 Nicholas held a synod at Rome and issued a decree on papal election whose importance is undoubted but whose interpretation is again debated. Clearly, the law meant to designate the cardinal-bishops first of all as those who would meet to debate the papal elections. Thus, the pivotal role in future papal elections was handed over to the cardinal-bishops. Other cardinals would then be invited to participate. Finally, the clergy and laity were invited to give their consent. All this is clear enough. But several interpretations of the decree need to be carefully examined.

Some see in this decree the application of the ideas of the rigorist reformers, schemes that would only fully be put into practice by Gregory VII after 1075. In this view, Nicholas not only reinforced Leo's reform legislation but also added a prohibition of lay investiture to it. In other words, this was a decree designed to free the papacy from all German and imperial influence, not to mention that of the feuding Italian nobility. The crafters of the decree knew that there was no tradition in canon law that legitimated imperial influence over elections; such influence was, rather, a customary imperial right given in the very concept of theocratic government. The reformers therefore tried to hedge on the issue by granting to the emperor the "due honor and dignity" given the position by the See of Peter. Actually, it is rather unlikely that this decree intended to remove the emperor from participating in papal elections altogether. Rather, it meant to signal to an emperor that any role he might play was conferred upon him by Rome and that the major role in papal elections would henceforth be taken by the cardinal-bishops.

The Norman Alliance

The second change that punctuated Nicholas's brief reign, which also marked a reversal in Leo IX's policy, was the settlement of an alliance with the Normans, whose occupation of the south of the peninsula had so annoyed that pope. Either Hildebrand or the abbot of Monte Cassino achieved a rapprochement with Robert Guiscard (d. 1085) and Richard of Capua (d. 1078), leaders of the Normans. The papal ambassador recognized the Norman right to most of southern Italy, some of which was then held by Greeks and Muslims. In return, the Norman princes promised financial and military assistance to the pope. Their promise of protection ensured that the papal election could be undertaken in accordance with the Decree of 1059; this was important in a world in which several forces might upset the determination of the reformers at Rome that the next papal election should be carried out according to the canonical demands of the decree. It was carried out, and Pope Alexander II was elected and held the pontificate for twelve long years. During this time the gains of the reformers were consolidated, and Hildebrand, the future Pope Gregory VII, emerged as the most powerful cardinal on the Roman scene.

Gregory VII and Empire

By the time he was elected to the throne of Peter in 1073, Archdeacon Hildebrand, now Gregory VII, had established himself as the most dynamic and certainly most pugnacious of the reformers gathered at the Lateran. Born in Tuscany to a family decidedly not high bred, Hildebrand became a monk (probably of the cloister of St. Mary's). We know almost nothing else about his early career except that he joined Pope Gregory VI, whose name he would choose when elevated to the papacy, in that pope's reforming activities and accompanied him into exile in northern Europe. Crucially, while in the north, Hildebrand became associated with the new party of reformers—whose spokesman and leader he would one day become. In 1049 he returned to Rome with one of those reformers, Bruno, sometime bishop of Toul, who became Pope Leo IX. He served all the succeeding reform popes in a variety of capacities. By 1061, he was the most powerful adviser at the papal court. Upon the death of Pope Alexander II in 1073, he was so evidently Alexander's successor that the papal election decree of Nicholas II was quite amazingly ignored, as a determined and unruly crowd of Romans sat him on Peter's throne without a canonical election. Amazingly, no cardinals conferred, and there was no discussion with the Roman court. This would prove to be fateful for Hildebrand. For a reformer, this lack of procedure was shockingly irregular, even uncanonical, and for this reformer's enemies, it would be a canonical abnormality with which they would torment Gregory for much of the rest of his life.

We have already noted the way in which even a fairly sympathetic figure and fellow reformer like Peter Damian could imagine Gregory as partaking of both the divine and diabolical because of his extreme commitment to the causes he fought for—even though Damian never harbored a doubt about the desirability and righteousness of those causes. In similar ways, Gregory polarized contemporary opinion. Some saw in him unambiguous good and righteousness, others a false monk (though he was never, as is sometimes heard, a monk from Cluny), an impostor—even a minion of Antichrist. How the next decade or so of ecclesiastical history unfolded—and how Gregory acted and thought of himself, his office, and others during that time—ended up amply justifying the way these qualitative polarities were applied to Hildebrand.

The testimony of Gregory's contemporaries is invaluable in understanding his personality. So, too, are the pontiff's own views of the world. Just as Damian imagined a man at once devout and diabolical, Gregory's own not infrequent blasts reveal, despite his occasional willingness to compromise, a mind that perceived the world in dualistic and belligerent terms—Manichaean even. Sons of Light (the Roman church and its friends and allies) struggled always against an overwhelming number of Sons of Darkness, who looked after their own self-serving interests rather than "those of Jesus Christ" (Philippians 2:21—an oft-used quotation). As one historian has put it,

He was a man who (as he said on his deathbed) loved and hated passionately, and he was not interested to convince his opponents by logical argument. That there might be truth on the side of his critics scarcely entered his mind; opposition was to him either stupidity or tantamount to criminal folly. He assumed throughout—and this is what alienated contemporary opinion— the identity of his own commands with those of God; hence his inflexibility, hence also in the guise of a return to the old order, the revolutionary nature of his claims he was . . . in spite of all precursors the great originator who stood absolutely by himself.

His enemies he did not hesitate to stigmatize in apocalyptic terms as minions of Antichrist, whose presence hinted of the imminent end of the world. He sincerely seems to have believed that those who disagreed with or obstructed him must have had not only low but diabolical motives for doing so.

As is the case often whenever scholars examine religious language so fraught with apocalyptic imagery, it is difficult to know for certain how literally Gregory took these terms. What is not in doubt is that they were terms used by someone with a mind that saw in others either good or evil and believed, messianically, that one was either with or against him. He seems to be one of those figures in history who could not imagine another state of things or judge others with moderation. Also not in doubt is that even when compared with popes like Leo IX, he had an overwhelmingly powerful sense of having been called, like a prophet from the Hebrew Bible, to serve and to take on the heavy yoke of papacy. He identified with Peter, experiencing an unparalleled intimacy with him, and it was to the Apostle's own will, he firmly believed, that he gave expression. Over the course of his life, willingness to obey his thunderous commands became the litmus test by which one's fidelity to him, to Peter, and to church could be ascertained.

What set apart Gregory from many of his fellow papal reformers was his determination to employ his powers not only to transform the church or to purify the clergy, but to create a righteous, if not pure, secular order as well. As holder of the keys to the kingdom, he had the power to demand of all men conformity to his vision of a purified temporal order. Part of the righteousness of this order involved an understanding that the secular ought to be subordinated to the superior spiritual order and that temporal lordship was inferior to the priestly and especially the papal. Indeed, so absolute and total were the pope's powers that he could mobilize all the resources of the secular for the purposes of St. Peter in whatever way he saw fit. (Here we see the seeds of the Crusades, which would flower under another Gregorian pope—Urban II.) The significance of this concept, in the history of Christianity, cannot be exaggerated. Gregory was attempting to shift decisively the essential ethos in Christianity away from the contemplative ideal of withdrawal to an active one of engagement with the world.

Broadly speaking, reformers and revolutionaries on the world stage have looked either forward or backward when imagining the world in new ways. Gregory, as we shall see, looked both ways in framing his papal policy. Far from having contempt for antiquity, as some have suggested, Gregory firmly believed that the Apostle Peter spoke through him. But for him, the entire apostolic age—its practices, beliefs, and norms—became the inviolable model and touchstone for righteous behavior and truth. Gregory was persuaded that such truth as could be grasped in this world reposed in the ancient canons of the church, and he gave active encouragement to compilations of ancient collections. This meant that customs that had built up could be trumped by the authority of law. Also precious to him was a small circle of trusted advisers, not just cardinals at court (whom he could imperiously ignore and thus aggrieve), but also countesses in Tuscany, including Matilda (d. 1115), who would play a role in one of the best-known episodes in medieval history. Gregory also established devoted resident legates of a new type who would take up dwellings in a particular see in Europe, often for a lengthy period. They loyally represented the pope and indeed acted on his behalf.

If Gregory could look back to the apostolic pattern as the benchmark for reform, he could also look forward. Put another way, he was capable of imagining new rules—new laws—if ancient ones did not suit or could not be located. This approach can be seen preeminently in a document called (by historians, not by Gregory) *The Dictates of the Pope (Dictatus Papae):*

1. That the Roman church was founded by God alone.
2. That the Roman pontiff alone can with right be called universal.
3. That he alone can depose or reinstate bishops.
4. That, in a council his legate, even if a lower grade, is above all bishops, and can pass sentence of deposition against them.
5. That the pope may depose the absent.
6. That, among other things, we ought not to remain in the same house with those excommunicated by him.
7. That for him alone is it lawful, according to the needs of the time, to make new laws, to assemble together new congregations, to make an abbey of a canonry; and, on the other hand, to divide a rich bishopric and unite the poor ones.
8. That he alone may use the imperial insignia.
9. That of the pope alone all princes shall kiss the feet.
10. That his name alone shall be spoken in the churches.
11. That this is the only name in the world.
12. That it may be permitted to him to depose emperors.
13. That he may be permitted to transfer bishops if need be.
14. That he has power to ordain a clerk of any church he may wish.
15. That he who is ordained by him may preside over another church, but may not hold a subordinate position; and that such a one may not receive a higher grade from any bishop.

16. That no synod shall be called a general one without his order.
17. That no chapter and no book shall be considered canonical without his authority.
18. That a sentence passed by him may be retracted by no one; and that he himself, alone of all, may retract it.
19. That he himself may be judged by no one.
20. That no one shall dare to condemn one who appeals to the apostolic chair.
21. That to the latter should be referred the more important cases of every church.
22. That the Roman church has never erred; nor will it err to all eternity, the Scripture bearing witness.
23. That the Roman pontiff, if he has been canonically ordained, is undoubtedly made a saint by the merits of St. Peter; St. Ennodius, bishop of Pavia, bearing witness, and many holy fathers agreeing with him. As is contained in the decrees of St. Symmachus the pope.
24. That, by his command and consent, it may be lawful for subordinates to bring accusations.
25. That he may depose and reinstate bishops without assembling a synod.
26. That he who is not at peace with the Roman church shall not be considered Catholic.
27. That he may absolve subjects from their fealty to wicked men.

In order to interpret these decrees properly, we should try to understand their origin, literary location, and purpose. Given how laconic they are, it is not surprising that scholars have differed on almost all of these issues. The issue of literary location is the most clear; the *Dictates* are found in the papal register. Gregory may have intended them as rubrics for future elaboration. When they were placed in the papal register is not certain, however, so it is difficult to say whether or not these were drawn up with the German empire in mind. Again, some scholars view them as Gregory's summary of the authority of the papacy. But an equally plausible view can be (and has been) suggested: that these were a novel collection of claims for which there was no precedent. One historian has suggested a third sensible possibility—namely, that when we look at the claims closely, we should understand that the purpose of the *Dictates* "was not to provide a blueprint for papal absolutism, but to define the emergency powers inherent in the Roman see to enable it to take action for the reform of the church. In this view, they were less an epitome of Gregory's reform program, as has often been suggested, and more an expression of the distinctive privileges of the church of Rome, especially in extraordinary circumstances." Some of these *Dictates* led to hostile relations with bishops, some of whom, we now know, were not guilty of simony or con-cubinage. But none so affected the church, the papacy, and the empire as the twelfth—the one that led to papal schism and civil war in Germany, alienated distinguished bishops (some of whom regarded Gregory as a truly dangerous and reckless pope), and, above all, locked Gregory into conflict with the German empire and its emperor, Henry IV.

Gregory may well have expected that his supporters would have found prec-edent in the biblical and canonical tradition for many of these rubrics. But such precedents would have been hard to find. Many of Gregory's claims are entirely new; they are without foundation in the ecclesial intellectual tradition and even revolutionary. Almost entirely novel and daring were the dictates relating to the pope's authority, the authority of legates, and the idiosyncratic interpretation of the ancient dictum that all churches must be in harmony with Rome; what was primarily intended was dogmatic harmony, but Gregory meant it to encompass matters of organization and rite as well.

Yet it was that twelfth dictate, the one that stated the pope could depose em-perors, that was potentially most revolutionary—and furthest from the central tradition of thought centering on the relation of the sacred and the secular, the papal and the imperial. For Gregory, such a notion was essential to secure the liberty of the church. If a king threatened that liberty, he ceased to behave righ-teously and became a tyrant who could be removed by the pope acting as succes-sor to St. Peter. This notion shattered the traditional belief, enunciated classically by Pope Gelasius I (r. 492–496), that the created order ought to be ruled in harmony by two powers, the royal and the priestly. Given Gregory's convictions, which made the once sacred king a removable official who could be judged and deposed by the successor to St. Peter, it was almost inevitable that he should come into conflict with the imperial power.

The Conflict of Papacy and Empire, 1075–1100

The occasion for the conflict was the determination of Henry IV to install his own candidate as archbishop of Milan. In December 1075, Gregory reacted with anger. He sent Henry a letter that began by asserting that he was king only insofar as he obeyed the Roman bishop. He had been disloyal to the church and had treated the apostolic decrees with contempt. Most important, he had ignored Peter, prince of the apostles. As if these accusations were not enough, Gregory almost certainly accompanied them with a verbal message stating that should Henry continue to act as an unfaithful son of the church, he would be excom-municated and deposed. For his part, Henry was not easily intimidated. He soon wrote a letter to Gregory that in its salutation brazenly addressed Gregory as a "false monk," announced that he was no longer pope, and declared that his king-ship came directly from God.

Now a crisis loomed. When Henry convoked a synod of German bishops at Worms that declared Gregory to be a usurper and unworthy of the papal office, the emperor was practically begging for a fight. By no means easily tyrannized, upon hearing this news in Rome in 1076, Gregory invoked his power of binding and loosing:

> Wherefore, relying upon this commission, and for the honor and defense of thy Church, in the name of Almighty God, Father, Son and Holy Spirit . . . I deprive King Henry, son of the emperor Henry, who has rebelled against thy Church with unheard-of audacity, of the government over the whole kingdom of Germany and Italy, and I release all Christian men from the allegiance which they have sworn or may swear to him, and I forbid anyone to serve him as king. For it is fitting that he who seeks to diminish the glory of thy Church should lose the glory which he seems to have . . . that the nations may know and be convinced that thou art Peter and that upon thy rock the son of the living God has built his church and the gates of hell shall not prevail against it.

In short, Gregory, applying the ancient Petrine doctrine with revolutionary implications, here deposes and excommunicates the emperor. The last lines of this text suggest that to Gregory, Henry was allied with the forces of darkness—an emergency circumstance for the church that abundantly justified the execution of the papal dictate, allowing him to depose the most powerful secular author-ity in the world. For his part, Henry responded quickly, writing a letter to the German bishops. In the letter (1076), he reprehended Gregory as the "so-called pope" who acted with the violence of a usurper, exercising his power with "Hilde-brandine madness."

Henry's enemies were not altogether united, though ordinary parishioners by and large regarded him as the instigating party. More ominously, the Saxons and others saw in this rupture an opportunity to remove Henry from power. In the end, the princes required Henry to swear obedience to Gregory, promising that they would not recognize him if he was not absolved within a year of his excom-munication. In addition, he was to meet at a council in Augsburg in 1077, with Gregory present. This assembly would decide whether to restore him as king.

The next chapter in the saga furnishes us with one of the most memorable episodes in all of medieval history. Gregory headed north in December 1076 for the proposed assembly. Meanwhile, Henry traveled south over the Alps. In Janu-ary 1077, he met the papal party at the castle of Countess Matilda in Canossa. At Canossa, Henry arrived barefoot, in a penitential frame of mind, wishing to

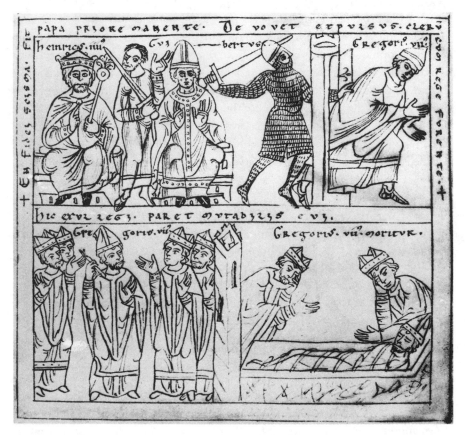

10. Scenes from the life of Pope Gregory VII. Top: Emperor Henry IV and Antipope Guibert expel Gregory VII from Rome by force of arms; bottom left: the expelled Gregory VII lays ban of excommunication on the clergy and king; bottom right: death of Gregory VII at Salerno in 1085. Chronicon of Otto von Freisig (d. 1158). Codex Jenesis Bose 9.6, fol. 79r. Ca. 1170. Universitaetsbibliothek, Jena, Germany. Photo credit: Foto Marburg/Art Resource, NY.

confess his sins and receive absolution. The king was supported by the powerful Countess Matilda and by Abbot Hugh of Cluny (d. 1109), his godfather. Gregory forced Henry to wait in the snow for three days to quench his anger. Gregory, by canon law, had no choice. He therefore conferred sacramental forgiveness on January 28, 1077, under the condition that Henry would meet at the princely diet with Gregory present.

Though he had no choice, from a canonical point of view, since any priest must absolve a sincerely penitent sinner (and sincerity is very difficult to perceive), Gregory's decision to absolve Henry hurt him tactically. Princes back in Germany felt that the pope had betrayed them. Henry, meanwhile, was able to return to Germany and win the support of the moderate bishops. Outraged, the opposition elected Rudolf of Swabia as emperor (r. 1077–1080), instigating a civil war. It was a disaster for Gregory. After three years of war, Gregory deposed Henry for the second time (March 1080). His letter is a tour de force of rhetoric that implores the apostles Peter and Paul to execute the papal sentence, refers to Henry as the one whom they *call* "king," and declares emphatically that while restoring him to communion, he had not reinstated him in the royal power from which he had deposed him. He again forbids all Christians to obey Henry as king.

It was not a propitious moment to take such actions. Many German bishops, not just imperialists but moderates, had grown impatient with the pope's intransigence. Gregory was not unaware of this. Still, it must have come as a shock to him when those bishops met in June 1080, declared that he had been irregularly elected, and elected Archbishop Wibert of Ravenna as Clement III (d. 1100). Now the church was in a state of formal schism. By 1084, thirteen cardinals, the staff at the Lateran Palace, and the papal chancellor had all changed their fidelity to Clement III. Gregory's position grew even more dire when Rudolf of Swabia died in battle in 1080.

Meanwhile, Henry built up his forces, and the imperial armies invaded and occupied Rome in 1084. Clement III crowned Henry emperor in St. Peter's. For his part, Gregory fled to the papal fortress of St. Angelo, from which he appealed to the Normans. They advanced from southern Italy and routed the imperial forces. Still, Gregory in a real sense had lost. The Normans looted the city and burned down about a third of it. Gregory left Rome. In 1084, he wrote an encyclical letter: "Ever since by God's providence mother church set me upon the apostolic throne . . . my greatest concern has been that holy church, the bride of Christ, our lady and mother, should return to her true glory and stand free, chaste and catholic." These were among the last words that he would write. The pope died in Salerno in May 1085 under the protection of the Normans. As his last words, he is supposed to have uttered an agonized rendering of Psalm 44: "I have loved justice and hated iniquity—and therefore do I die in exile."

They are poignant last words. Still, the verdict on his papacy cannot be a kind one. He had alienated many supporters—not just imperialist bishops and supporters, but also those who had supported his desire that the holy church return to its glory. He had been defeated by Henry and routed from Rome, his beloved city, which was then desecrated and damaged by his protectors, the Normans. He left the church in schism, and a number of formerly friendly bishops changed their allegiance to Clement III, the anti-pope. Though certainly he had had the help of fellow reformers, he had ruined the association of empire and papacy. Very few of his ideas made their way into the writings of canon law or those of later popes.

Some historians have suggested, perhaps too severely, that his pontificate was a "distraction if not a deviation." In any event, it was left to successors on both sides to pick up the pieces.

The Pamphlet War and Compromise

From the first excommunication and deposition of Henry until the dawn of the twelfth century, a pamphlet war between imperialist and papal controversialists flourished. Gregory and his supporters had claimed essentially a monarchical position within the church. In addition, they felt it was the pope's duty to bring sinning secular rulers back to the way of *iusticia,* to conformity with the demands of divine justice. To supporters of Henry IV and imperialist propagandists, this latter claim scandalized and incensed them; its novelty appalled them. To some, this exchange of competing ideas marks the beginning of western political thought. That may be going too far. The issues at stake were extremely narrowly defined, having to do with the justice of Gregory sitting on Peter's throne and of Henry's ruling over the empire. More broadly, there was the question of the propriety, or capacity, of a pope to depose a king and release his subjects from loyalty to him.

As the pamphleteers fought their literary war, the Gregorians finally regained the papacy with the election of Urban II. This pope was a dyed-in-the-wool supporter of Gregorian ideas for reform, and he vehemently decried the practice of lay investiture. With Urban's pontificate, the investiture controversy became *the* central issue with respect to ecclesiastical appointments. Extreme polemicists on each side wrote on the controversy, the imperialists arguing that a king was greater than the priests, the papalists countering that the king was essentially an administrator appointed by his people who could be removed, should he fail in his duties, "like a swineherd." Needless to say, these extreme views did little to move the two sides to resolution or reconciliation.

More sober and reasonable views soon began to emerge. Ecclesiastical canonists wanted to ensure that the emperor and all lay rulers understood clearly that they did not receive their spiritual office from secular powers. Only a duly ordained priest, usually a bishop, could confer spiritual grace and power. For their part, imperialists and royalists wished it to be clear that temporal power and jurisdictions were received from secular powers. The French canonist Ivo of Chartres pointed out that these two interests were not really in conflict. Ivo's suggestion was that, first, a canonical election should be held. Another canonist suggested that the ring and staff not be used in royal investiture since these were spiritual symbols of a bishop's office. The way was open for a compromise.

Before that compromise was formally reached, Paschal II (r. 1099–1118) proposed a radical solution that fell like a bombshell. Pascal suggested that the popes simply refuse their feudal lands and worldly jurisdictions. He proposed this because it was on the basis of their overlordship of lands that kings claimed the right to appoint bishops. If, Pascal suggested, popes simply renounced their secular powers, the king would lose his justification for interfering in ecclesiastical appointments. Beyond that, popes and bishops would again become simple pastors of souls, servants of the servants of God with no responsibilities for secular government. Intriguing as this suggestion was, prelatical reaction to it was swift and extremely unfavorable, and the plan never actually had any chance of success.

The understanding that finally concluded the contest was the Concordat of Worms (1122). The terms of the accord were not unlike those that had been agreed to by the archbishop of Canterbury and the king in England earlier in the century in the Concordat of London (a concordat is an agreement between the Roman see and a sovereign nation). Bishops would be canonically elected. For his part, the emperor would renounce the practice of investing the candidate with ring and staff. Still, he was permitted to be present at the election of the bishop. More important, he could refuse to accept feudal homage for the lands given to the church and thus retained some power over episcopal selection. In actual fact, secular rulers did have a large say in the appointment of bishops throughout the course of the Middle Ages. At the parochial level, the attack on lay control proved to be much less successful. The worst abuses, like simony, were broadly eliminated. But throughout the Middle Ages and beyond, nobles kept control of the appointments of local clergy. At the conceptual and practical level, though, a new vision of the clergy had prevailed. The clergy, now purified, were to be distinguished from the laity and were promoted in the social and celestial hierarchy.

Now the clergy were organized in a hierarchical line under the direction of the pope, who could trump the power of local custom, tradition, and even episcopal power. Below the pope stood the bishop. Responsible for maintaining clerical discipline and for overseeing the property of the church, he was answerable only to the pope. Only he could perform all the sacraments; he alone performed the sacrament of confirmation and by the sacrament of ordination passed on his power to others. Theoretically, canon law held that he would be elected by the clergy and people of his diocese. In practice, he was elected only by the canon priests attached to the cathedral. Considered high clergy, the canons aided the bishop in furthering his agenda, administering the diocese, and performing rituals at the cathedral church. At their head was the dean, the highest officer in the diocese. A diocesan chancellor supervised the cathedral school and issued licenses allowing clerics to teach and preach in the diocese. A treasurer oversaw finances, while a precentor managed the choir and organized the cathedral's musical program. Each diocese was divided into administrative districts, over which presided the archdeacons. Practically, these were powerful men; they were the bishop's legates, charged with enforcing discipline among the lower clergy, and therefore they were often quite unpopular. Nonetheless, it was a desirable office, as it often led to promotion within the hierarchy. The parish priests were answerable to them. Mostly drawn from the peasant class, these priests usually remained in their humble roles for a lifetime, though it was not impossible for them to rise.

Consequences of Reform

Exceptional practical issues were at stake in the conflict, and thus it was imbued with near-apocalyptic vigor. Both sides struggled over the issue of who would control the church and society. Neither side prevailed; both had to make concessions. In the end, the long struggle ended in a compromise. Some objectives were achieved; some were not.

On the positive side, from the reformers' point of view, was that the earliest and most constant causes of reform—namely, the creation of a church that was free from the contamination of simony and clerical concubinage—had received a cogent theological and canonical rationale. Moreover, this rationale came to be accepted by many who were at first not ready to receive it and in some cases were actively resistant to accepting it (though not all of these resisters were convinced). The success of this reform, which reached back to the pontificate of Leo IX, owed much to the sheer determination of a group of dedicated reformers, as well as their local legates and devoted canonists. Whatever practical successes the reform enjoyed, the reformers had won the war of ideas. The worst abuses came to be seen as abhorrent in common opinion. Indeed, the success of the reformers' appeal to the laity would not be underestimated; they heeded the reformers' prayer to boycott simoniacal clerics and those living with women.

As the years passed, reforming energies were concentrated on the issue of lay investiture. As we have noted, that issue had ended in compromise. However, at the ideological level, royal theocracy had been vanquished. The notion that the spiritual was superior to the secular gained increasing acceptance in all levels of society. Kings and lay lords came to be seen as simple laymen and not vicars of Christ, who, like all laymen, could be held to account to the clergy, at least in religious matters. Moreover, the prestige of the papacy grew steadily in the eleventh and twelfth centuries. Popes were now without doubt the heads of the churches and the entire body of Christians, called Christendom (*Christianitas*). More and more, Christians felt a primary allegiance to this supranational, supernatural corporate body, an allegiance that, many came to feel, superseded their fidelity and obligations to local or regional communities. The deeply felt emotions and commitments generated by the reform movement were harnessed by the papacy for centuries. The Crusades are only the most familiar expression of these deep religious affections.

As for the reformers' failures, despite the fact that they had created a new sensitivity to ecclesiastical purity, this was a vision that applied to the church as an international, somewhat abstract, body. When we ask if this new vision of ecclesiastical order affected the regional churches, we must conclude that it did so only marginally in many areas of the Continent. To be sure, the ideological war had been won, and on the ground, there were certainly fewer married canons in the cathedral and urban churches in the twelfth century than in the eleventh. But in the rural areas, old habits died hard. For a very long time, it remained conventional for priests in these areas to have families and for a son to inherit the church of his father. In other words, so much energy went into the ideological battle that the reformers lost their focus on the actual evils they were attempting to reform. Lost in this battle, too, was care for the pastoral experience of ordinary parishioners, a task that was badly in need of improvement.

At the same time that Christendom was consolidating itself around the office of the papacy and the term "Christianitas" entered the ecclesiastical thesaurus as a common expression, the reformers had created ruptures within the Latin community and without. Above all, the reform had distinguished clergy and laity. And though the importance of 1054 can be exaggerated, it does mark an important moment of breach in relations between the western and eastern churches. Launched by a Gregorian pope, the Crusades lastingly damaged relations between Christendom and the Muslim world. What is more, partly as a consequence of schism, Germany had been separated from the western kingdoms with which it had earlier enjoyed links and good relations. Perhaps most important, the once cooperative relations between empire and papacy had soured into open hostility. If the ideological battle against royal theocracy and lay investiture had been won, many practical advantages were conceded to the sons of Henry that scandalized Gregorian priorities: the holding of elections in the presence of the emperor, imperial intervention in disputed elections, and the humiliating act of homage performed before episcopal consecration.

Even the reformers' success with the laity was, in the long run, an ambiguous triumph. In the centuries to come, the laity's new affections could not easily be contained, much to the dismay of the papacy and the orthodox prelates. These affections sometimes ran outside approved ecclesiastical channels as a new lay activism was unleashed that touched even the lower classes. Public debate about married clergy led some laypeople, not without the encouragement of the papacy, to refuse the ministrations of unworthy priests. Most people by instinct became, in practice, neo-Donatist (though of course they could not have articulated it that way). Sinful priests, or those believed to be such, soon became targets of popular preachers whose language could border on the heretical or even spill over the line that, in the view of the papacy, separated orthodoxy and heresy. In fact, though it was thoroughly unexpected, one of the principal results of the reforms enacted in the centuries under consideration was the spread of popular heresy. This unforeseen consequence of the reformers' ideas would shake the church for the next two centuries.

Religiosi: Monks and Nuns in
the Monastic Centuries

In our discussion of the papal reform movement of the eleventh century, we focused attention upon the way in which the ancient and the time-honored became normative for cardinals, legists, and popes. The model of the ancient church and the "life of the apostles" *(vita apostolica)* were increasingly not just influential or suggestive. More and more, they were understood to be normative. As such, they superseded any practice that was regarded as merely customary or temporarily useful; evolution from ancient conventions slowly became seen as evidence of degeneration from treasured, pristine ideals, archetypes that the church ought, in the eyes of reformers, to embrace again. Reform was largely imagined, then, in terms of a restoration of usages that were imagined to have prevailed as disciplinary, ecclesiastical, moral, and legal norms in the apostolic age.

By and large, these same ideals prevailed in the domain of contemporary religious life. In the eleventh century, individuals and groups experimenting with different forms of religious life, often sharing the troubling sense that the Christian faith had fallen away from its primordial rigor, shaped their ascetical experiments around ancient ideals, models, and normative documents. In many cases, "innovators" tried to resurrect ancient ideals by reinvigorating communities or founding wholly new ones by attempting to return to the apostolic life, which meant a life of poverty, the communal sharing of goods, and, in some cases, itinerant preaching. Others imitated the eremitical model of the Egyptian and Syrian hermits of the desert. For still others, the canonical measure was another written document to be observed, now with the strictness and severity its author intended: the Benedictine *Rule* and the *Rule* of St. Augustine. A sign of the status of monks and nuns in this period is that they were called "religious people" *(religiosi);* ordinary lay people were described as "worldly" or "secular" *(seculari),* no matter how devout.

The Anchoritic Life

Many men and women after the turn of the millennium sought the strictly enclosed, wholly contemplative life. Among these, many lived in "anchorholds" or "anchorages" attached to the chancel of a parish church. In the ancient church, "anchorite" (from the Greek word for "withdrawal") and hermit were synonymous. However, by the twelfth century, distinctions between modes of life and, very often, gender, allow us to discriminate the two terms. Anchorites were usually women and thus more appropriately known as anchor*esses* and men as ancho*rites.* Unlike hermits, who wished to preserve their freedom to move about, an anchoress elected to be enclosed in a single room to devote herself to contemplation and to prayer. Some of these anchoresses had enjoyed long careers in convents as contemplatives and ascetics, but most had not. More often, they were older women who had occupations not in convents but in the family home as wives and mothers and who, late in life, wished to pursue the intensities of the enclosed contemplative life.

An aspiring anchoress could often have been "vetted"—that is, her background and character might be scrutinized by a cleric of some note. In theory, anchoresses were supervised by the local bishop; in practice, it was more often a neighboring priest who did the job. While some anchoresses were religious virtuosos, visionaries, or mystics, most were not. More commonly, they were involved in the religious community as spiritual advisers or religious educators. If contemporary criticism can be trusted, they were sometimes seen as being overinvolved in the community, receiving visitors, educating the young, and keeping funds safe—that is, functioning as bankers—for members of the local community.

The anchorhold was often sited in the center of a sizeable town or city. Yet contemporary evidence suggests that some anchoresses were sequestered from the distractions of urban life. Anchoresses were often enclosed by ritual act. As she was being sealed in her anchorhold, the anchoress was solemnly instructed by the presider (theoretically a bishop) about the solemnity of her ascetical commitment; he declared to the anchoress that she would henceforth be "dead to the world." Some rituals went so far as to bring the aspiring anchoress into her coffin while the Office for the Dead was said for her; in case this message did not get through, the anchorhold was simultaneously bricked up. There is evidence to suggest that some anchoresses may then have been given last rites. At this ritual entombment, a grave might be prepared and even kept open as a *memento mori*.

An anonymous rule or guide for anchoresses exists. Known as the *Ancrene Wisse* or *Ancrene Riwle* (names not given to the document by its author), the guide was apparently written at the request of three sisters early in the thirteenth century. The author was likely an Augustinian canon, though he may have been a Dominican; he may also have served as spiritual adviser to the three anchoresses. While the language in which the original rule was written is unclear (it was likely composed in English or French), it was clearly dependent, literarily and spiritually, on the Latin *On the Education of Clerics* by the Cistercian monk Ailred of Rievaulx (d. 1167). The guide lays out a strict regime of devotions, meetings with a spiritual adviser, and manual labor in a garden. It is interesting that it admonishes its readers not to teach, or to keep pets (unless a cat), or to gossip and entertain visitors (above all men). Yet we know that some anchoresses received visitors and dispensed advice on matters both religious and secular. The document may be responding to those realities, attempting to rein in women who were not accustomed to being managed.

Although the overwhelming majority of anchoresses remain anonymous and unknown to us to this day, it seems as if they were highly respected and even treasured members of their communities. Some were materially supported by local lords—and particularly illustrious ones by kings. As with communities of monks, benefactors felt that it was religiously advantageous to have an anchoress installed in one's town. Many of these anchoresses were fairly high born, but by no means all; the evidence suggests that a wide spectrum of classes and educational backgrounds was represented. At least one English anchoress, Eve of Wilton (d. ca. 1125), was highly Latinate and was reputed to have read voraciously.

Julian of Norwich

By far the most illustrious English anchoress was Julian of Norwich (d. ca. 1416). After a visionary experience, she would record a series of mystical revelations, usually known by the title *Showings* (or the longer title *The Revelations of Divine Love*), and she also gave spiritual advice to seekers, including to the autobiographer, inveterate pilgrim, and mystic Margery Kempe (d. ca. 1439). Some anchoresses in the north of continental Europe were equally if not more famous and influential at the time. The mother of Guibert of Nogent (d. ca. 1125), the illustrious Benedictine historian, dwelt for more than forty years in an anchorage she had commissioned after having been widowed. There she experienced dreams and visions and became renowned as a prophet.

Julian's visions occurred in May 1373, when, at the age of thirty, she became very ill and indeed nearly died. While she was surrounded by a coterie of family and friends, a priest held a crucifix before her. It was then that, over a period of roughly five hours, she experienced sixteen visions or "showings." It is interesting that as a small girl, she prayed to God for something like a vivid experience of Christ's Passion and crucifixion. Her visions in fact do center upon Christ crucified. Some-how—Julian and those present thought miraculously—these visions cured Julian. Shortly thereafter, she dictated her visions to an amanuensis. Twenty years later, she set down a much longer and profounder version. Julian addressed herself to fellow Christians who "wish to be Christ's lovers," but her simple language and her claims to be unlettered are to be taken with a grain of salt. She reflects profoundly on the major themes of Christian theology (creation, providence, redemption, sin, evil, the Trinity, and so forth). She dedicates three chapters of the longer version to a theme popular in medieval mystical writings and explored by Caroline Bynum and others: the motherhood of God. Proof of her learning can be detected in her many references and obvious grasp of ecclesiastical teaching and the Bible. She was also clearly familiar with the writings of other mystics, whose language she uses, to some extent, to communicate her own experience of the divine.

Despite these examples, we know quite little about the overwhelming major-ity of medieval anchoresses. Manuscript evidence proves that even Julian's *Show-ings* was not widely known or copied until the seventeenth century; only in the nineteenth century (and then until the present day) has it attracted widespread interest. Evidence suggests there were thousands of medieval anchoresses, but we can say something significant about only a few. This is perhaps because most wished to remain anonymous. In any case, when she died, an anchoress would be laid in the tomb that had been kept open for her meditation during the entirety of her time in her anchorhold. But we ought not to imagine the life of the ancho-ress as particularly dark or unattractive. Indeed, the sheer number of anchoresses in England and northern Europe suggests a widespread and growing avidity for the ascetical life and indicates that the construction of anchorages answered to a burgeoning religious need.

The Desert Tradition Revived

The lure of the desert, the yearning for a return to the simple life of the ancient Egyptian hermits, sequestration from the demands of lay society, and greater as-cetical severity all fueled a revival of the eremitical life in the early eleventh cen-tury, especially in secluded mountainous regions of southern Europe. This revival began in the cities of Italy, perhaps because of their proximity to Byzantine and other eastern cities and influences. The patriarch of the new movement in Italy was St. Romuald of Ravenna (d. 1027). Although he founded the new order of Camaldolese (the name is taken from the hills at Camaldoli in Tuscany), Romuald never intended anything more than to organize individuals and groups who, like he, aspired to a more ascetical and contemplative life than seemed available in the conventional Benedictine monastery. His aim, then, was to establish houses that were reformed Benedictine cloisters.

In 1012 Romuald founded a new community. The monastery followed Benedict's *Rule,* but the house of Camaldoli brought together the cenobitical and eremitical lives. Some of the monks led a communal life in a house at the foot of the slopes. This house was imagined as a nursery or training ground for the congregation of hermits, each inhabiting a hut higher up the slope. Romuald intended members of the thirty monasteries he established (mostly in Italy, though foundations were made in France and Spain) to fast, keep silence, and preserve strict solitude. Two houses of the order—Camaldoli and Fonte Avellana—were centers of religious and literary vitality; they attracted men of considerable talent. Popes appointed many Camaldolese monks to bishoprics in the Italian provinces of Umbria and Ancona. As we will recall, Peter Damian, who was a monk of the order, was one of the principal leaders of the Roman reform movement of the eleventh century, in which he vigorously opposed simony and clerical marriage. Made cardinal-bishop of Ostia in 1057, he still remained a committed ascetic. While a hermit, he promoted self-flagellation for the monk as a practice designed to master the temptations of the flesh. Even as a cardinal, he recommended these austerities; they were an effective means of resisting the seductions of the simoniacal, corrupt church.

Perhaps it is not surprising that this was a way of life that only a few would ever embrace. During Damian's lifetime, Fonte Avellana probably numbered some twenty monks. Meanwhile, north of the Alps a new form of eremitical life emerged that wedded a life of rigorous ascetical observance with a form of "preaching." It became so popular that it attracted groups of men and women from all social classes.

Carthusians

By far the most stable, lasting new eremitical group was the Carthusian order. It preserved such a high level of rigorous observance, and so consistently, that no fewer than three popes (the last being Pius II, in 1460) said, not unjustly, that the order had "never been reformed" because it had "never been deformed." This lofty level of observance animated not only the Camaldolese, but also the Cistercians, the spectacularly successful order that sprang from it, at Cîteaux.

11. La Grande Chartreuse, France; sited high up in the Alps, near Grenoble. Note the individual cells for hermit-monks. Given to St. Bruno in 1084. © Franck Guiziou/ Hemis/Corbis Rights Managed (RM).

The Carthusian order began when Bruno of Cologne (d. 1101), chancellor and master of the diocesan school of Reims, resolved to remove himself, along with six of his companions, to the cold desert some three thousand feet up in the Alps, roughly thirty miles from Grenoble. Bruno's hagiographer tells us that, compulsively attracted by the example of the desert hermits, Bruno decided to quit his posts in Reims around 1080 in order to join hermits already living in the forest of Colan. Soon Bruno received from Bishop Hugh of Grenoble (d. 1132) a lofty, sequestered site in an alpine valley. It was there that Bruno established his "charterhouse," forever known as the "Grande Chartreuse" (an old French word for "charterhouse"). Like Bernard of Clairvaux later, Bruno could not be considered the founder of the order, though both are revered for being the patriarchs of their respective congregations. Bruno never got the chance to live out his desert idyll; he was called in 1090, by Pope Urban II, once his pupil at Reims, to service in Rome. He obediently left and never returned to the charterhouse.

Like so many foundations established during this time of experimentation in the eleventh century, this one seemed doomed for gradual decline and then disappearance until it was saved by the infusion of new blood. This arrived in the form of Guigo I, the dean of Grenoble. It is Guigo (d. 1136) who must be considered the administrative genius and founder of the order. By 1130, it was he who had

committed the customs and practices of the growing order to writing. In so doing, he largely followed the vision of Bruno.

Like Romuald, Bruno never intended to found a new religious order. Rather,
he wished to fuse in one house both the eremitical and cenobitical forms of life
and to be governed by the *Rule* of St. Benedict. The *Customs* or *Consuetudines*
that Guigo drew up imagined a life in which each monk would courageously confront the solitude of his own cell within the context of communal life. Approved
by Pope Innocent II (r. 1130–1143) in 1133, the *Customs* received the papal imprimatur, and a general chapter held eight years later marked the Carthusians' official
beginning as an order. It was understood that the prior of the Grande Chartreuse
presided over the order as prior general and was responsible for the government
and discipline of the order.

Over the course of the next three centuries, three emendations to the *Customs*
reduced the number of fasts. Still, the life remained quite austere. The emphasis
on self-purification through the practice of utter silence and almost total solitude
was never changed. As Guigo wrote: "As water is needful for fish and folds for
the sheep, [let the monk] regard his cell as necessary for his life and salvation."
Within the context of this strict solitude, the monks would meet daily for Vespers
and the night office. All other services were recited by the monk in the solitude of
his own cell. The very spartan diet the monks consumed, in which meat was not
permitted, was prepared by each monk alone. He ate one meal in the winter and
two in the summer. The severity of this solitude was relieved only on Sundays and
major feast days. Then mass would be heard, a chapter held, and dinner eaten in
common in the refectory. Only on the afternoons of these days was the strict rule
of silence relaxed for a short period of conversation. Among the various lifelong
mortifications the monk accepted was a hairshirt. Within his cell, the monk could
work on artistic or intellectual endeavors, and he could cultivate the small garden
in front of his cell. Any external preaching or teaching was forbidden. Each charterhouse could house only twelve monks, plus the prior; all houses were subject
to an annual visitation, and all priors that had maintained discipline and good
observance met annually in general chapter at the Grande Chartreuse.

Although the Carthusians built their houses in various locations—in the
mountains, valleys, and villages; outside large towns; and even within town walls
—everywhere a uniform architecture functioned to screen the monks from the
world and to serve the specific needs of the monastery. A fortified wall usually
surrounded the entire monastic compound. The thirteen individual cells (each a
miniature house with several rooms and a small garden) encircled three sides of an
open cloister; community buildings—church, chapter house, lay brothers' lodgings, kitchens, refectory, barns, stables, and guest houses—occupied the fourth

side. Buildings were simple in order to reflect and reinforce the form of life the brothers had chosen.

The work for which each charterhouse was constructed was the making of books. In fact, each cell of a charterhouse was a small scriptorium, equipped with all the implements of contemporary bookmaking: parchment, quills, ink, and rulers. For Guigo, the production of books had more than an intellectual purpose. For the solitaries who produced them, they were a way of spreading the word of God and also a way for them to serve the ecclesial communities from their forested and secluded fastnesses.

The Carthusians were creative spiritual writers as well as hagiographers, and some produced hagiographical works and spiritual treatises that had a relatively wide impact. Guigo I not only produced the Carthusian *Customs,* but he also wrote a *Life* of St. Hugh of Grenoble. Guigo II (d. 1188), prior of the Grande Chartreuse between 1174 and 1180, produced the influential spiritual treatise entitled *The Ladder of Monks.* Later in the Middle Ages, Denis the Carthusian (d. 1471) was perhaps the most prolific late-medieval commentator on scripture, the *Sentences* of Peter Lombard (d. 1160), and other philosophers. Denis also composed a treatise entitled *On Contemplation.* These men and the works they produced were admired by the current and next generation of religious leaders, men the caliber of Peter the Venerable (d. 1156), Bernard of Clairvaux, and others.

The dedication of the monks to contemplation, their reluctance to have any truck with secular society, and the time they spent in bookmaking led them to adopt lay brothers or *conversi,* men who had come to the monastic life as adults. These were usually illiterate men, and they were expected to remain so for the entirety of their lives. The visible sign of this unique social distinction was that the lay brothers did not wear the cowl, which distinguished the choir monks, and they did not take part in choral office. These men performed most of the agricultural labor and managed most of the business transactions for the community. The *Customs* of the communities restricted their number to twenty. They lived in the so-called "lower house," separate from the full-fledged monks; this arrangement was modeled after the Grande Chartreuse, where the lower house was located further downhill than the charterhouse. Guigo assumed that they would remain illiterate, but that does not mean they did not participate in the life of the community. Indeed, when the bell was rung for the chanting of the night office, the lay brethren would rise, proceed to an oratory constructed for them, and listen in silence while their leader, called a procurator, would chant their office for them. They knew when to bow and how to recite *Paternosters.*

Given the austerity of the life of the Carthusians, this was a vocation that drew relatively few aspirants. In each charterhouse dwelt the apostolic number of twelve monks, along with a prior. Late in his life, Bruno could observe: "The sons of contemplation are fewer than the sons of action." Still, by the late eleventh century, there were nearly forty charterhouses of men and two of women. As the Middle Ages unfolded, the number of charterhouses grew further, and many more mystics were drawn to the contemplative austerities of such a life.

Female Carthusians

Neither Bruno nor Guigo seems to have anticipated the attraction their order would have for groups of female fellow travelers. In fact, Guigo mentions them in the *Customs* only to warn his monks against them and to bar them from Carthusian enclosures: "We by no means allow women to penetrate our boundaries, knowing that neither the wise man, nor the prophet, nor the judge, nor the guest of God, nor the sons, nor the first man himself formed by the hands of God were able to escape the charms and deceptions of women." Roughly a decade after these words were written, a group of nuns at the convent of Prebayon in Provence became the first to ask to be admitted to the order. Three popes approved their affiliation.

Carthusian women never lived exactly the same kind of life as their male counterparts. Never did they achieve the strict austerities of the charterhouses, nor did they pursue the solitary life with the same degree of fervor. These differences can partly be traced to something so concrete and simple as architecture. Houses that converted to Carthusian observance were often originally Benedictine or otherwise communal in their observance. They lacked the detached, self-sufficient cells that were the necessary architectural hallmark of the disciplined male Carthusian religious life. We know from some female Carthusian sources that women gathered daily in church for mass and to sing the divine office. While men took their meals in their cells, alone, women gathered in a refectory to eat a communal meal.

In some ways, these women seem to have more in common with Benedictine nuns than Carthusian monks. What distinguished them was the double consecration bestowed on them. From the bishop they received a virginal consecration, at which they received the veil and ring, and a diaconal consecration, at which they received the stole and maniple. This allowed the Carthusian women to read the Epistle at mass and to read the gospel at the night office. This seems to suggest that the women who entered the order were literate when they arrived or were taught to read and write (and in this respect they were like their male counterparts). The privilege of consecration thus gave women a role in liturgy that few women would enjoy. And despite the differences, male and female Carthusians shared some practices. Rigorous fasting throughout the year is an important example.

The movement was never large, but other female Carthusian houses were founded in the next few centuries, though a tiny number next to the hundreds founded for and by men. As with the male houses, they also provided a context within which some writers could flourish and influence. Their literary productions remain interesting today for their profound reflections on the relationship between the act of writing and the cultivation of the religious life and the dilemmas of inexpressibility when writing about the divine.

Wandering Hermits, Women, and Fontevrault

If the Carthusians imagined themselves "preaching" through their production of sacred literature (as indeed they did), other groups attempted to marry the life of the destitute hermit with the life of the wandering preacher. Scores of such preachers, many of whom attracted sizeable companies of followers in the forests of the north, existed in the eleventh century. Anxiety, scandal, or the death of the charismatic leader would often lead a bishop to encourage their now leaderless members to adopt a more conventional religious life, which included elements foreign to the apostolic life as they comprehended it: stable residences, separation from the secular world, observance of an approved rule, regular patterns of worship, fixed incomes, and traditionally hierarchical organizations.

No individual epitomizes this pattern so well as the reforming preacher Robert of Abrissel (d. 1117), nor any community as perfectly as Fontevrault, the monastery Robert founded around 1100. After studying as a scholastic in Paris, Robert took flight to the forest of Craon in 1095, where he realized his dream of living as a hermit dedicated to prayer, meditation, and self-mortification. Soon, however, he came to understand the apostolic life as a way of Christian life that included public preaching. He was so powerful a preacher, and his calls to repentance and renunciation of the world so compelling, that he was soon joined by a large number of enthusiastic followers. These included people from all social classes, from lepers to nobles, clerics to laypeople, and, perhaps most interesting, women as well as men. Some of his preaching was anti-clerical in tone, and there is no question that Robert was a burr in the saddle of many local prelates. But what caused real difficulty was his association with women, prostitutes whom he had brought into the woods, with whom he experimented in a way of life that was (in the eyes of those hostile to him) flagrantly uncanonical and dangerously intimate. Later, Robert would be criticized for his continuing practice of sleeping with women so as to arouse carnal desire for the express purpose of mastering it. One colleague admonished him: "Divine and human laws are both clearly against this association. Sin began with a woman, and it is through her that death comes to us all. Without doubt, you cannot long be chaste if you dwell among women."

As a result, Robert decided in 1101 to establish a permanent site where his followers would live in a regulated communal life. The site he chose was Fontevrault, in the diocese of Poitiers, whose bishop was a fervent supporter of Robert. In time, Fontevrault would become the mother house of a small order of a novel congregation. Fontevrault was a mixed monastery of men and women. Robert was an unusual man for his day. He sympathized with the religious aspirations of his female followers and was favorable to, even enthusiastic about, their participation in his penitential group.

Accordingly, he settled a group of women who would become nuns dedicated to the contemplative life; they followed the Benedictine *Rule*. Alongside them, he established a community of monks, one that contained both clerics and lay brethren. The men provided for the sacramental and material needs of the women as well as the men. The women far outnumbered the men, and the community expanded quickly. Wishing to continue his itinerant preaching, Robert appointed two women to govern both monasteries. He then left on a series of trips in western France to preach and to found priories dependent upon Fontevrault. He followed this pattern of preaching and founding of dependent priories for the rest of his life.

As Robert grew ill beginning around 1115, he focused his efforts on the organization of Fontevrault, which had already been given special status by Pope Paschal II in 1113. In 1115, the first abbess of Fontevrault, Petronille de Chemillé, a widow (not a virgin) was elected, and again Paschal II confirmed the choice. In February 1117, Robert died at one of the Fontevrist priories he spent his last year visiting and administering. His body was taken to Fontevrault. After a public ceremony that was attended by a vast crowd, including many prelates and secular worthies, he was buried at the abbey he had founded. Much later in the century, Eleanor, duchess of Aquitaine, chose this as the burial place for King Henry II (r. 1154–1189), so it became the recognized burial place of all monarchs in the Angevin line. Again, the swift growth of this order and the rapid inrush of ascetical and contemplative enthusiasts indicate that the mixed monastery was responding to a widespread and deeply felt religious need.

Gilbert and the Order of Sempringham

It is possible that the arrangement of double monasteries at Fontevrault helped shape the configuration of a modest but enduring female order in England, often known, after the name of its male founder, the "Gilbertines." Gilbert of Sempringham (d. 1189) was neither a hermit nor a wandering preacher. He was a secular clerk who served two churches in Lincolnshire. The order he founded, therefore, originated not in his own ascetical or contemplative aspirations but in the kindness and alacrity with which he responded to the religious yearnings of young women in his parish.

Upon learning of these aspirations, Gilbert first responded by building the women a house and cloister against the north wall of his home church. Gilbert must have imagined his job was done and must have been surprised when this thoughtful act brought attention, funding, and grants of land from a number of baronial families with daughters who harbored ascetical aspirations. Gilbert had had no intention of founding a monastic order, but now the problem of organization and discipline had to be confronted. His hope of affiliating his houses with the new and burgeoning Cistercian order was rudely rebuffed in 1147. At this point, he may have taken inspiration from Fontevrault and resolved upon an order of double monasteries.

Gilbert began to settle small groups of canons regular with each convent. They heard confessions, celebrated the Eucharist, and administered last rites to dying nuns. The canons also managed the nuns' property. From the local peasantry, Gilbert drew lay brethren to chop wood and carry out other essential jobs. Lay sisters cooked and performed menial tasks. The layout and discipline of the typical Gilbertine monastery was as follows. The female community occupied living quarters on one side of the conventual church; the male community occupied the other side. The nuns recited the hours in the choir, the priests in their oratory. The priests also celebrated mass for the nuns in the conventual church.

An appalling story—usually simply called the "story of the nun of Watton" after its anonymous protagonist—may have led to a more strict separation of the two communities than had prevailed in the early years of the order. One of the nuns at the community of Watton (probably the largest house in the order), who was reputedly put in the convent against her will, and a lay brother fell in love; the nun was then discovered to be pregnant. She was eventually put in something like solitary confinement. If the original testimony is to be credited—and it may be doubted—her hapless companion was supposed to have been castrated at the hands of the nuns themselves. Though several brothers successfully secured the command of the pope to separate the nuns and canons, Gilbert's powerful episcopal friends wrote Pope Alexander III (r. 1159–1181) in 1167 to assure him that the houses were appropriately segregated. Still, later constitutions indicate that the "nun of Watton" incident may have resulted in even stricter segregation. In the common church, the two communities were hidden from one another by a screen, and communion was passed from one side to another by a turntable. When nuns traveled, they were required to do so in a cart concealed by a cloth; that way they could not see out, nor could anyone peer in.

Still, not all consequences were negative for the nuns. The preoccupation with mutual segregation left nuns with a measure of independence they had not previously enjoyed. They controlled the material resources of their convents, and prioresses were answerable only to Gilbert and to his successor masters. Perhaps the most striking lesson from the whole sad incident was the readiness of the pope and others to believe that men and women simply could not live in proximity to one another without endangering one another's commitment to celibacy. Be that as it may, thirteen double monasteries and sixteen for canons survived until they were dissolved in the Reformation.

Regular Canons

The regular canons adopted a form of apostolic life that might best be understood as a hybrid order of priest-monks. Without question, they came into being as a consequence of the Roman reformers' belief that the apostles were monks and that the secular clergy ought to fashion their lives after them. Given their conviction that the apostles owned nothing individually and were celibate, the reformers sought to enforce celibacy and communal wealth by settling priests together in community (making clerical marriage impossible) and encouraging them to pray on a monastic schedule. Around the middle of the eleventh century, groups of priests began to organize themselves into corporate bodies called canonries. In some cases, the decision to order themselves this way was not made voluntarily but imposed upon them by the bishop of a cathedral. These secular canons could closely resemble houses of monks, especially since most Benedictine monks were being ordained by the eleventh century. Probably the single disciplinary characteristic that distinguished secular canons from monks was the emphasis put on the virtue of moderation. Unlike monks, canons could eat meat and wear linen clothes. They said the choral offices, but the office used was that of the secular clergy, which was briefer than that followed by monks. Almost no emphasis was placed on manual labor.

Many regular canons also had lives of active pastoral care, so much so that it has been said by a distinguished historian that the monks played the contemplative role of Mary in the church and the canons played the active role of Martha. But it would be a gross generalization to say that all did. Some assisted the bishop in the government of his diocese. Others carried out various kinds of pastoral care. Still, many viewed the care of souls as incompatible with the practice of the apostolic life and refused to be involved in pastoral care at all. Some orders and many houses of canons chose the contemplative and intellectual life. Probably no abbey of medieval canons was as distinguished intellectually or spiritually as the Abbey of St. Victor in Paris. Founded by the retired scholastic William of Champeaux (d. 1121) in 1108, the Victorines produced Hugh (d. 1142), who was so accomplished a theologian, exegete, and spiritual writer that he became known as

12. Hugh, an Augustinian canon, teaching to his students at St. Victor in the twelfth century. akg-images.

a "second Augustine." Hardly any house in Europe produced so fine a cluster of ascetical theologians and interpreters of scripture as did St. Victor.

The regular canons (*regula* is Latin for "rule") are also often known as the "Augustinian canons" because they were vowed to live a common life under the so-called "*Rule* of St. Augustine." The textual and manuscript history of Augustine's *Rule* is enormously complicated. Reduced to its essentials, the story goes as follows. After Augustine's sister entered a religious community, her famous brother wrote her a letter that included a lengthy treatment of the virtues of charity, chastity, and communal unity. Sometime in the fifth century, changes to the letter were made so that it seemed as if it was addressed to a male rather than a female community, and very broad instructions on the monastic life were added. Much later, around 1120, some of the detailed parts of the *Rule* were cut. What remained is what we know as "the *Rule* of St. Augustine," an extremely general document that nonetheless proved enormously popular. Indeed, its very generality and thus flexibility is what has made it so attractive and so widely used from the twelfth century to the modern day. Because it gave so little practical guidance (as contrasted, say, with the Benedictine *Rule*), it was almost ubiquitously augmented by local customs that gave more specific instructions to a community as to how to organize its day. In any case, it quickly became recognized as a source from an unimpeachable and ancient authority for the organized apostolic life. So many thousands of communities used it in the Middle Ages that R. W. Southern has concluded, "it must be judged the most prolific of all medieval religious Rules."

Premonstratensians

Southern has argued that the followers of the *Rule* of St. Augustine fell into two schools. The first he calls the "broad" school (exemplified by the Abbey of St. Ruf near Avignon) and its daughter houses, which played the role of Martha—that is, they "sought in some humble way to repair the ruins of the world" by rebuilding decrepit churches, providing poor relief, caring for the sick and infirm, and working for the restoration of religious life. The second, exemplified by the priory at Prémontré, he calls the "severe" school, which insisted on traditional monastic virtues of silence, manual labor, psalmody, and abstinence.

The Premonstratensians took their name from their mother house. The founder of the order was Norbert of Xanten (d. 1134), who had been a canon of the cathedral in his hometown since he was an adolescent. In 1115, he became an itinerant preacher. Although his brothers protested, he had a sympathetic bishop, who gave him the chapel of Prémontré in the forests nearby. As with Robert of Abrissel, around Norbert there soon gathered a group of hermits and preachers. This group also included not only clergy but also laity of both sexes. In 1120, the group formally adopted the *Rule* of St. Augustine. They took a habit of bleached wool; thus they became known as the white canons. Norbert soon had to leave the community when he was elected archbishop of Magdeburg (whose cathedral chapter he turned into a community of regular canons).

In 1134, Norbert drew up the first statutes of the order. These emphasized both an ascetical life lived in community and evangelization through preaching. However, Norbert's successor drew up new statutes. These decisively moved the order in a new direction, and in practice, it soon became almost indistinguishable from a form of monasticism dedicated to contemplation and free of apostolic obligation. In some ways, the order split over this dual interpretation of the Augustinian *Rule*, with some following Norbert's vision of a communal life of poverty and preaching, while others followed Norbert's successor and increasingly withdrew from commitments that would distract them from contemplating the divine. In this way, the Premonstratensians reflect the distinction within the regular canons as a whole between those who emphasized the active and those who pursued the contemplative forms of the apostolic life.

Premonstratensian Women

As with nearly all monastic innovators in the eleventh and twelfth centuries, the presence of a sizeable and enthusiastic body of female followers caused problems for Norbert. Again, it was assumed that the association of women with men would as a matter of course lead to sexual sin, and ecclesiastical custom and law left no room for women to engage in itinerant preaching. As one monastic historian has put the prevailing sentiment, "There was a deep conviction that the only safe place for a woman who had no husband was behind the high walls of a nunnery or perpetually immured in a hermitage."

Like Gilbert, Norbert responded to the ascetical aspirations of female disciples by establishing double monasteries. He began at Prémontré, where he installed a house for women next to the one for the canons. Yet the men there allowed the women only the role of maidservants. Though they did attend church when the canons sang the office, they spent the rest of their time taking care of the male community, washing and sewing its clothes, or serving as caregivers for the terminally ill. Nonetheless, many women continued to profess, and the number of double monasteries multiplied rapidly, particularly in the Low Countries. A canon of Laon tells us, with pardonable exaggeration, that around 1150, more than a thousand women were associated with Prémontré alone, with some ten thousand in the order as a whole. They were serving God, he concluded, in rare severity and silence.

As this chronicler was uttering his praise, misogynists in the order were agitating to expel and dislodge the women permanently. Near the end of the twelfth century, the general chapter announced that it would receive no more women in the order. A prior of the order stated the reason for this decision as follows: "We and our whole community of canons, recognizing that the wickedness of women is greater than all the other wickedness of the world, and that there is no anger like that of women, and that the poison of asps and dragons is more curable and less dangerous to men than the familiarity of women, have unanimously decreed for the safety of our souls, no less than for that of our bodies and goods, that we will on no account receive any more nuns to the increase of our perdition, but will avoid them like poisonous animals." This sort of outpouring of venom led to the decision to abolish all double houses. However, it did not demand that women disaffiliate themselves from the Premonstratensians. Instead, it required them to establish and dwell in communities far from the mother abbey. While it was not always easy to find or fund new houses, the abolition of double houses in some ways improved the lot of the female community. For one thing, they ceased to be the handmaidens for the male communities. For another, they became full-fledged canonesses, singing the canonical hours and essentially pursuing the same regime as the male Premonstratensians. Still, their independence was not without limits. The women were supervised by a prior. Beyond that, mother abbeys became increasingly reluctant to support their daughter priories materially. Finally, the order decided in 1198 on a policy of complete detachment: no more women would be admitted to the order. Once approved by Pope Innocent III (r. 1198–1216), this decision destined the female branch of the Norbertines to a slow disappearance.

The plight of the female Norbertines is sadly illustrative of the predicament in which many religious women found themselves in the twelfth century. To start with, women needed priests and, ideally, spiritual advisers to lead the sort of religious life to which many of them aspired. However, many of the new orders of the twelfth century were unwilling to undertake the religious direction, supervision, or provision of sacramental services for women that only men could provide. Occasionally, they resisted providing these services even in the teeth of papal directives that they do so. Many monks felt that they had to forsake their own spiritual quest and life in community—the very reasons they chose the cenobitic life—in order to relocate near a female house to satisfy the needs of the nuns therein. We have already had occasion to mention the fear, almost ubiquitous, that proximity to women could occasion for the monk the possibility of sexual transgression. Beyond the desires of individual monks, orders as a whole were reluctant to assume economic responsibility for women's religious houses in addition to their own.

This latter problem was made even more complicated by the canon law forbidding women from becoming priests. Donors were anxious to endow a monastery because the ordained monks could offer something very valuable to them—an unceasing fund of masses for the souls of the family's dead; but this was something, of course, that nuns could not do. As a consequence, in the competition for endowments, women suffered in relation to men. We know, for example, that there were roughly three times as many Benedictine monasteries as nunneries in eleventh-century England. Not until the thirteenth and fourteenth centuries, when women began living in small groups in private apartments and living off their own handicrafts, family resources, or donations, was the supply of houses sufficient to meet the booming demand. Even then, nuns would soon be haunted by charges of heresy and promiscuity.

To the Letter of the *Rule*: The Cistercian Adventure

By any measure, the most successful new experiment in religious life in the twelfth century was the Cistercian Order. Be it the number of houses founded; the rapidity of the order's expansion and extent of its geographical scope; the number of Cistercian bishops and cardinals chosen (even one pope was elected);

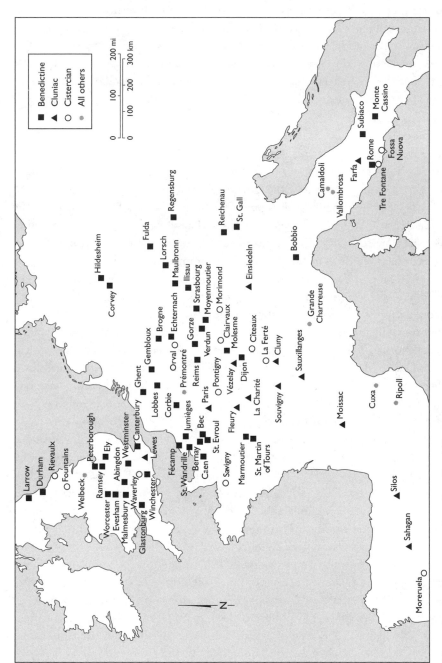

Map 3. Important monasteries of medieval Europe

the opening of the religious life to very large numbers of peasants through the institution of the lay brotherhood; the development of unsettled land in Europe; constitutional innovations that made the order the first actual and operative international organization in Europe; the simplicity and beauty of the Cistercian Order's architecture; the contribution of the order to monastic theology and piety; and, above all, the sheer power of its reforming ideal—by any of these criteria, the Cistercians dominate the monastic history of the days before the coming of the friars.

The order had its origin in the desire of Robert of Molesme, the abbot (d. 1111), and Alberic, the prior (d. 1109), to lead a group of monks (traditionally twenty-one in all) from the monastery of Molesme to the "new monastery" (*novum monasterium*—for that is how the new foundation was known to its first settlers) in a valley among the hills of Burgundy known as Cîteaux. This occurred in the spring of 1098. At the time, their hope was not at all uncommon: they wanted to live a life along eremitical lines in utter solitude and poverty and provide for their needs by the exercise of manual labor. Almost immediately there was trouble. The monks at Molesme protested their abbot's departure, and the papal legate ordered him back to his monastery; he took with him those monks "who did not," according to a contemporary document, "love the wilderness."

Fortunately for the fledgling order, the two next in line to Robert were among those who had followed him to the wilderness. Robert's first successor was Alberic. Under Alberic, the monks adopted their characteristic white habit; this is why, in contrast to the Benedictines, known as "the black monks," they were recognized as "the white monks" (for contemporaries, this was also a symbol of their arrogance and ostentatious purity, for which they were vigorously criticized). Stephen Harding (d. 1134) succeeded Alberic on his death in 1109 and presided over the community for the next twenty-four years. Under Stephen, the order experienced its first expansion with four important foundations being founded at La Ferté (1112), Pontigny (1114), Morimond (1115), and finally Clairvaux (1115). It was under Stephen (who, unlike the leaders of other orders, was an administrative genius) that some of the constitutions of the order that would eventually be so innovative and influential were contemplated.

The author of Bernard's *vita* suggested that under Stephen the monastic experiment was in danger of extinction until the arrival of the young Bernard of Fontaine (later Bernard of Clairvaux; d. 1153), along with some thirty brothers and relatives, an influx that preserved the community and was the pivot-point in its early history. This turn of events is unlikely. By the time Bernard and his relatives arrived, sufficient recruits had signed on, and enough property had been acquired, that the order would have survived. Whether it would have achieved its subsequent prominence, growth, and influence without Bernard is of course an

13. Abbey of Fontenay, France; nave toward west. It is typically Cistercian in its ornamental austerity, single-story nave, square eastern end, and lack of ambulatory or chapels. Photo credit: Anthony Scibilia/Art Resource, NY.

entirely different question; it is likely that it would have remained a small order like the Camaldolese. In any case, it was in 1115 that Bernard was sent to establish one of the original four daughter houses of Clairvaux. This is the monastery over which he would remain abbot for almost forty years, until his death.

The signature of the Cistercian reform program was the commitment to observe the Benedictine *Rule* to the letter. But, again, the early sources are problematic; thus, the issue of *when* it became the center of Cistercian observance remains a matter of dispute. We must be cautious in saying that literal observance of the *Rule* is the most "original" or "novel" component of Cistercian reform. After all, the monks at the "new monastery" made no claims whatsoever to novelty. Quite the contrary: they aimed to rehabilitate what they took to be original or primitive observance. Among other things, this meant that all of the elements that were regarded as accretions to the purity of the *Rule* were eliminated in a single stroke.

Many of these accretions were the very things we would associate with Cluny and its dependencies: comfortable clothes and bedding, superfluous meals,

14. Fountains, a Cistercian abbey founded in North Yorkshire in 1132, is the largest monastic ruin in Britain. Note the River Skell (right side of image) and the long nave of the abbey church, now carpeted in grass. © Adam Woolfitt/Robert Harding World Imagery/Corbis Rights Managed (RM).

elaborate ritual, involvement in feudal society (above all, any form of income not mentioned in the Benedictine *Rule*), and lukewarm observance of the *Rule*. The decision of the Cistercians to reject the customary sources of monastic revenue (altar offerings, rents, or tithes) was not just a matter of a wish to withdraw from feudal society. It was also a symptom of the new enthusiasm for voluntary poverty. As an early Cistercian document put it, the white monks were "the new soldiers of Christ, poor men with the pauper Christ." This sentence perhaps best captures the militant and poor ideals to which the young order aspired. No better concrete expression of these ideals can be found than in the austerely simple churches they built across Europe. All of their altar accessories were simple, and they explicitly rejected the gold and silver that had ornamented contemporary monastic churches.

As a consequence, wishing to retreat to the desert and not involve themselves in the affairs of the outside world, the white monks chose sites far from towns, locales that were generally uncultivated and not near any population center. This decision was to have three important consequences. First, because it was so inexpensive for a donor to endow uncultivated land, the Cistercians could expand very rapidly by receiving lands of little value to nobles and lords. Second, the monks were able to cultivate much of Europe that had previously been unproductive wasteland. Third, because the choir monks could by no means have managed the immense job of clearing wastelands and making them productive without help, they hired *conversi*. Their services were so desired and the new vocation was so popular that they usually far outnumbered the choir monks, sometimes by a ratio of roughly 5:2.

The acceptance of lay brethren was of course an anomaly for an order vowed to observe the *Rule* of Benedict to its letter: they are nowhere mentioned in the *Rule*. In addition, there was another very important way in which the order deviated from the *Rule*. No Cistercian cloister accepted child oblates, who were mentioned in the *Rule* and who made up a large percentage of the pool of recruits to Benedictine monasteries in the Carolingian era. Nor was there any school to educate boys from inside or outside the monastery. Only men who were of the age of discretion and capable of deciding for themselves were permitted to join. The monastic life was being then reimagined as a vocation chosen in freedom by an individual in response to a call from God. This was an important moment in cultural history. The twelfth century may not have "invented" the individual, but the Cistercian choice reflected an age in which increasing emphasis was placed on the choice of the individual for vocation. Accordingly, the long moribund novitiate, the one-year probationary period, was reintroduced.

The government and organization of the Cistercian monastery was also different from that of the completely independent Benedictine abbey or the semi-autonomous Cluniac priory. When a new or "daughter" monastery was founded, it was by a group of monks from the "mother" house. In each case, the mother house had obligations to its daughters. To start with, the abbot of the mother house was normally received by the daughter houses yearly in order to ensure discipline and strict observance of the *Rule*. Once a year, all the Cistercian abbots would gather at Cîteaux. This annual chapter would consider the problems of the order as a whole. Second, the abbots of the four senior daughter houses were endowed with the authority to visit Cîteaux and to ensure discipline there—even being given the authority to remove the abbot of the mother house if necessary.

The amazing growth of the Cistercian Order must be attributed in part to a man who would become not only the abbot of Clairvaux, but one of the most influential, charismatic churchmen of his time. During the 38 years he presided as abbot of Clairvaux, Bernard's abbey established 68 daughter houses alone; Clairvaux was soon the mother house of nearly half the Cistercian order. By his death there were nearly 350 Cistercian abbeys—a monastic empire so immense, influential, and rapidly expanding that its race to supremacy can only be attributed to a preternaturally powerful personality. By 1200 there were 525 Cistercian houses. Not only was the growth of the order remarkable, but the size of its individual houses was often stupendous. For example, Rievaulx in Yorkshire, founded in 1132 as a daughter of Clairvaux, had in its heyday some 140 choir monks and 500 *conversi*.

The Cistercian triumph was traceable not only to Bernard's successful recruiting and propaganda efforts for the order. It also had to do with his own fabled austerities, which in the end left him quite ill and about which his biographer spares us no sickening detail. Bernard eventually developed a severe gastric problem that prevented him from keeping food down. This required that a ditch be dug next to his stall in choir. Some of his brothers found Bernard's physical presence so repulsive that, for a time, Bernard had to live separately from them.

Bernard's severe illness did not prevent him from working tirelessly as the foremost recruiter of the order and apologist for the monastic life. In letters and sermons, he called for a complete renunciation of the false promises of the secular world. He also repeated with sincerity the stock monastic theme that the only sure way to salvation was by a life spent in the cloister. A serious religious person had only one option: the monastic life, of which the Cistercian was the most perfect. "We are the restorers of lost religion," Bernard once observed when contemplating the role of his order, a statement that was written in reaction to charges of Cistercian novelty and smugness. Soon Bernard wrote at length on grace and free will. Around 1130, he wrote an encomium in praise of the Knights Templar, a new military order he helped to found. Some five hundred letters from Bernard to kings, popes, prelates, and other secular powers exist. He wrote in every literary genre in use by churchmen of his time. He even wrote a disputed question, a quintessentially scholastic literary exercise, when he vigorously disputed with the brilliant scholastic Peter Abelard (d. 1142) and the entire scholastic enterprise. He advised the French king, Louis VII (r. 1137–1180). In a disputed papal election, he spoke so eloquently that his speech brought Innocent II to the throne of St. Peter. He traveled widely, and wherever he traveled, monasteries sprang up in his wake. In 1146, after the fall of Edessa and the call for Crusade, Bernard helped raise troops and passion for the expedition. The Crusade failed so completely and brought so much suffering upon innocents (like several Jewish communities) that it brought Bernard humiliation, though he had written heroically against anti-Semitism at its start.

Bernard, though a monk, was a colossus on the historical stage. He made and unmade popes and kings. He had Peter Abelard and others condemned. He defended his order fiercely and attacked the empire of Cluny for not following the Benedictine *Rule*. He deposed unworthy bishops. He converted many to the monastic life by his preaching and letters and by the fame of his own sanctity. He sent the knights of France and Germany on a Crusade. His monks became abbots, bishops, and cardinals; one even became pope. He gave a rule to the Templars.

As an intellectual, he is regarded as the last of the church fathers. His writings on devotion to the human love and suffering of Jesus and Mary were immensely influential on contemporary piety. Indeed, he gave decisive impetus to the cult of Mary. His contemporary, John of Salisbury (d. 1180), a brilliant rhetorician, designated Bernard the greatest preacher since Gregory the Great. He is, without doubt, one of the greatest religious and intellectual figures of the Middle Ages.

Cistercian Women

As we have seen when discussing the Gilbertines, the early Cistercians were not at all disposed to admit women to their society, nor to take on oversight of their pastoral care or management of their affairs. This attitude toward women was expressed in the statutes of the Cistercian Order. For example, abbots were forbidden to bless novices, and female visitors were not even permitted to visit Cistercian cloisters. However, there is evidence that these statutes could be ignored. Some abbots blessed new foundations for women and aided women with counsel. Meanwhile, across Europe, nunneries were increasingly fashioning their observances on the Cistercian paradigm. Until the very end of the twelfth century, the official acts of the order steadfastly ignored the existence of this group of Cistercian companions. By then, Cistercian abbesses in Castile and Burgundy were already holding annual chapters. In effect, these women were happily incorporating themselves without the consent of male fellow travelers. In her study of the first century of Cistercian women, Janet Summers has called this a period of "silent incorporation."

Once the Premonstratensians declined to allow any more women in their order or any more female foundations to be made, this quiet consent soon became explicit. Conversions to Cistercian nunneries multiplied. The Augustinian canon Jacques de Vitry (d. 1240), who had witnessed the construction of seven Cistercian nunneries in his diocese of Liège in a very short time, observed: "After the Premonstratensian decision to bar women, the nuns who professed the religion of the Cistercian Order multiplied like the stars of heaven and vastly increased— convents were founded and built, virgins, widows and married women who had gained their husbands' consent, rushed to fill the cloisters." Still the Cistercians ignored them.

Eventually, the pressure of numbers, and especially of powerful secular sponsors (like King Alfonso VIII of Castile), became impossible to disregard. Alfonso (r. 1158–1214) demanded that a female foundation he started be recognized as a daughter house of Cîteaux; such powerful royal voices could not easily be ignored. Early in the thirteenth century, the general chapter finally admitted that some nunneries could be incorporated into the order. In 1215, it produced the first set

15. Abbey of Santa María la Real de Las Huelgas, Cistercian; the royal nunnery of King Alfonso VIII, near Burgos. It enjoyed many regal favors and became the burial place of the royal family. It was also the site of many royal weddings. akg/Bildarchiv Monheim.

of statutes intended to govern their observance. Not surprisingly, the ordinance emphasized the importance of strict inclaustration. It also emphasized the responsibility of abbots to visit and oversee discipline at women's houses that had affiliated themselves to theirs.

In a pattern that in some senses reflects Premonstratensian female experience, the general chapter in 1222, seven years after the production of the first statutes, ordained that no more female abbeys be incorporated into the order. In 1228, this prohibition was reiterated in more emphatic form: "If any convent of nuns not yet associated with the order or not yet built wishes to imitate our institutes, we do not forbid it; but we will not accept the care of their souls or perform for them the office of visitation."

Why the about-face? Numbers count. The sheer number of nunneries founded in Germany and the Low Countries, where they came to greatly surpass the number of male foundations, made it impossible effectively to supervise those nunneries that had explicitly affiliated themselves. Beyond these nunneries, there were the female foundations that were independently following Cistercian observances without having secured, or sought, Cistercian permission from the male general chapter. There is also ample evidence to suggest that it was difficult to enforce discipline or to supervise nunneries. Abbots who tried to carry out their duties and visit nunneries sometimes found that the doors were firmly barred against them. The aristocratic women within were not used to being supervised by men. For instance, in 1250, the prioress at Colonges died. Two abbots went to supervise the election of her successor, only to find that the convent simply refused to cooperate. The abbots walked away, and the convent simply proceeded to elect and install a new abbess.

In the end, the decree of 1228 failed to have an effect. In the Low Countries, foundations of women continued to be encouraged and spiritual direction given. Again, it became difficult to ignore the requests of the highly placed. In 1248, the Cistercian Order complacently received the request of Queen Margaret of France (d. 1318) to affiliate three of the foundations she had made. Similar requests from the powerful in England were submissively received. The Cistercian women had broken down the doors debarring them and thus had found a permanent place within the order.

Heresy and Its Repression

Truth is the daughter of time.
—Bernard of Chartres (d. 1124)

One of the paradoxical and wholly unforeseen outcomes of the reforms enacted during the Gregorian era was the emergence of new movements of reform. As Colin Morris has rightly observed, "The Gregorian movement itself was the cradle which nursed the emergent heretical ideas of the twelfth century." In many cases, these became viewed, treated, and punished as depraved heretical factions. For roughly half a millennium, there had been no evidence of popular heresy in the West. In the eleventh and twelfth centuries, that changed. New groups of heretics proliferated, at times, it seemed, uncontrollably and, to the established church, ominously. One north Italian cleric in the 1170s could observe, to his horror, that "cities, suburbs, villages and castles are full of false prophets"—by which he meant heretics. The Cistercian Caesarius of Heisterbach (d. 1240) would record, with appreciable exaggeration, that a thousand cities had been infected by heresy. He thanked God that the faithful had cut them down; otherwise they would have poisoned all Christendom with their spiritual infection.

By the time of Caesarius, popular heresy *had* become a serious and fairly widespread phenomenon. But even during the half-century from ca. 1000 to 1050, evidence suggests the appearance of individual heretics and their followers. Unfortunately, this evidence is extremely fragmentary. Often, it is not confirmed by other sources, and on occasion, there are internal contradictions. Be that as it may, some common heretical themes would come to light in these fifty years: emphasis on detachment from the world (a motif that would later become radicalized), commitment to poverty, sexual abstention, and asceticism. Some urged doing without meat, while others recommended that goods be held in common—a thoroughly orthodox idea, sanctioned in the book of Acts (e.g., Acts 2:45) and practiced, in addition, by newly emerging, and wholly inoffensive, monastic and eremitical groups.

The social and economic background to the rise of these few and scattered individuals and groups is less in doubt. They emerged from the reurbanization of the West and the increase in literacy associated with economic development in the growing cities. Still, this half-century does not constitute a coherent story. For nearly six decades after the 1051 heretical groups mentioned in sources, no further groups were observed until ca. 1120. It is then that the history of popular heresy can be said to begin.

As mentioned, the ecclesiological source for these new heresies is wholly paradoxical. Without question, it was the papacy. Specifically, it was the teaching and preaching inspired by the Gregorian reform movement. As we will recall, popes from 1050 to 1125 led a vigorous campaign against what they perceived to be a corrupt priestly caste. Many priests had wives or concubines; others had bought (or sold) their offices; still others were in different ways covetous, greedy, and unscrupulous. Pontiffs acted and fulminated against these abuses, many of them violations of canon law. Pope Gregory VII skirted the Donatist view when exhorting French laity to abstain from services conducted by fornicating priests. His chief ideologue, Cardinal Humbert, went further and openly embraced the Donatist heresy by proclaiming the sacraments of simoniacal priests invalid. Augustine would have wept. In short, the preaching and teaching of the reformers alerted the laity to the sorry state of the clergy and appeared to legitimate neo-Donatist activity or even open schism. It can hardly be surprising that in the wake of these papal reformist fiats, radical Gregorians would emerge to rail against the pitiable clergy, to attract followers, and to demand that the clergy return to the apostolic model and the canonical observances promoted by the papacy.

Radical Gregorians

Soon they did. As they began their reforming message, and as they and their followers perceived that the clergy were not, on the whole, improving, their denunciations became ever more severe, then radical and, in the eyes of even honorable clergy, heretical. Two wandering preachers from the first half of the twelfth century exemplify how itinerant critics of the clergy could drift from permissible denunciation to radical anti-clericalism and, finally, to openly heretical preaching.

One, Henry of Lausanne (d. after 1145), left his monastery to begin his career of preaching against the flagrant sins of the clergy. Historians have differed over whether he ought to be characterized as a proponent of apostolic simplicity or as a radical anti-clerical fomenter of lay rebellion. Either way, he loudly rejected central aspects of established belief and practice. Rebuffing traditional notions of original sin, he could not, in consequence, accept the theology of baptism, believed to wipe away the stain of Adam's primordial transgression. Prayers for the dead he rejected as utterly futile. Since so many orthodox sacerdotal and monastic acts were organized around delivering dead souls from purgatory to heaven by prayer and mass, this was, to orthodox clerics, a truly dangerous idea. The ordained priesthood, corrupt as it was, should, Henry concluded, simply vanish. Sinful Christians should merely refuse priestly, auricular confession and feel free to confess sins to one another; priests, after all, had no power to bind and loosen. Rejecting the notion of the Eucharist as a sacrifice, he proposed eliminating it altogether. As for marriage, reciprocal consent sufficed; no need for clerical participation there. As church buildings violated the New Testament simplicity to which he was dedicated, they were not necessary. In short, anything not explicitly authorized by the New Testament, and practices and beliefs accumulated over the centuries since the days of the apostles, could—and should—be cast aside. As these included the notion that the clergy should have no special prestige, status, or particular functions, his radical Gregorianism was bound to land him in hot water. It did. Around 1120, he was implicitly condemned by papal decree. Still, we hear of him preaching, in Toulouse, a quarter-century later.

Another contemporary itinerant preacher, Peter of Bruys (d. ca. 1131) expressed similar ideas. His followers were not only radical but could also lapse into violence and were encouraged by him to do so. Ecclesiologically, he viewed the church not as a hierarchical structure but as a congregation of faithful Christians. Unlike Henry, he went so far as to deny the authority of the Hebrew Bible (yet again a hint of things to come). In addition, he held and advocated beliefs not unlike those of Henry, including the rejection of infant baptism, the theology of the Eucharist, prayers for the dead, the veneration of the cross, and singing in church. To his mind, none had scriptural justification. All were impediments to the practice of true religiosity and to the individual's responsibility for working out his own salvation. Again, underlying these negative views lay a positive commitment to observe the apostolic structures literally portrayed in the gospels.

By mid-century, Peter the Venerable, abbot of Cluny, was anxious enough about Bruys's followers that he wrote a treatise against them entitled *Against the Petrobrusians*. The Petrobrusians also troubled Bernard, abbot of Clairvaux, who led a preaching campaign against Peter. Thus, two of the greatest abbots of the age would anxiously brood over these radical Gregorian reformers. Nonetheless, it is still impossible to gauge how serious a threat they were and how widespread an impact they had. To be sure, they generated anti-clerical turmoil wherever they traveled. But they never converted entire regions or recruited to their ranks the plenitude of heretics that so vexed Caesarius of Heisterbach. Beginning in the 1140s, however, heretical groups emerged that *did*, it seems, threaten to convert large regions of southern Europe to what clerics believed to be "heretical depravity."

Seen as types, these heretics fall into two large categories or genuses, with many species within each. The first category of new movements was, from the beginning, so dramatically different from orthodox Christianity, dogmatically speaking, that it was obvious that it included heretics in a broad, imprecise sense. The groups in this category held religious, and in particular theological or cosmological, opinions radically at odds with those defined by the established church. One can even wonder whether such groups were in fact Christian, although members of these groups seemed like simple "good men" or perfect practitioners of apostolic Christianity, much closer to the apostolic exemplars than clerics in the established church.

Our second category of dissidents, inspired by fervor for the faith of the newly ascendant New Testament and the life of Christ and the apostles depicted therein, began as neo-Donatist agitators. Spawned in the new urban communities, increasingly literate and critical, touched by Gregorian ideas, these groups were rarely dogmatically deviant at their start. Typically, they *evolved* into anti-clerical, and often anti-institutional, movements intent on returning the church to New Testament austerity. It was, or became, their conviction that all Christians ought to imitate the life of the apostles, which included a commitment to an austere, itinerant life of preaching. Normally, they became more radical and *then* theologically dissident, following ecclesiastical repression.

It would be important to observe here that despite these neat definitions and distinctions, the line between this category of heretics and other eleventh- and twelfth-century apostolic and ascetic movements, like the Carthusians and Cistercians, is not always easy to draw. Indeed, the distinction between orthodoxy and heresy was not always obvious or even perceptible to contemporaries. Beyond that, the language in which they were described by clerics, who left most of the sources through which we know them, has misled historians.

Some of these groups breached the subtle, sometimes shifting boundary separating orthodoxy and heresy. This is true even when the transgressing groups were, doctrinally speaking, initially hardly distinguishable from groups that would gain papal approval, ecclesiastical endorsement, popular affection, and, occasionally, even patronage. Yet they persisted despite ecclesiastical and royal resistance—and, in cases, in part because of powerful secular protection. As a result, the two groups regarded by the institutional church as the most menacing, most profoundly unregenerate and unreformable, threatened to take and keep a vast swath of territory north of the Alps, to the Pyrenees, and beyond.

Not coincidentally, this was a region of Europe that was, at the moment, politically fragmented. By comparison, when one of the two groups sent two missionaries to England, which was united under a monarch who would not suffer the presence or proselytizing of heretics, the king himself had them turned out naked in winter and forbade his subjects from aiding them under pain of death. The penultimate clause of the Assize of Clarendon, an act of King Henry II (1166), states: "Moreover the lord king forbids that any one in all England should receive into his land or jurisdiction or any house of his, any of the sect of those apostates who have been excommunicated and branded at Oxford. And if any one receives them he shall be at the mercy of the lord king; and the house in which they were shall be carried outside the village and burned. And every sheriff shall take oath to maintain this, and he shall cause to take the same oath all his ministers and the baron's stewards, and all the knights and freeholders of the counties."

With a king willing to marshal his formidable resources in the service of repression, heresy could not get a toehold in England in the twelfth century. On the Continent, the task of rooting out heresy fell to a series of papally appointed men, including diocesan bishops and members of the Cistercian Order. When these men failed, Pope Innocent III, frustrated, launched an "internal" crusade of knights from the north to wipe out nobles from the south of present-day France who were protecting heretics in their land. This ruthless but effective military action left the southern heretics vulnerable to detection, interrogation, and varying degrees of penances once the Inquisition was established by Pope Gregory IX (r. 1227–1241), one of Innocent's successors. In the minds of popes and prelates, these heretics were wolves in sheep's clothing, predicted in scripture (Matthew 7:15), carriers and transmitters of a religious contagion; they endangered the eternal souls of men and women. As such, neither they nor the heresy they embraced and spread could be tolerated.

Cathars

A caveat is, or several cautions are, in order as we begin to describe what the western church considered the most grievous "dogmatic" error of the central Middle Ages. We must remind ourselves that our distinction between the two "types" of heresy just described is a tool for historical understanding. As such, they can falsify historical reality as well as illuminate it. The way in which, in this case, they falsify it is that the Albigensians (after one of their Occitanian strongholds, Albi), the Patarines (as they were called in thirteenth-century Italy), or the

Cathars (as their opponents came, beginning in the 1160s, to call them more generally—although they called themselves by that name rarely) shared much, in the practice of the Christian life, with countless other groups dedicated to the perfect practice of the apostolic life, both orthodox and heterodox. Like so many other such groups, the Cathars wandered, preached, renounced possessions, and tried, in the eyes of many contemporaries, with profound sincerity, to achieve the high spiritual and ethical standards set by the example of the apostles and their lord.

As such, and again in the eyes of contemporaries, the Cathars seemed, by contrast to some opulent clerics, to be simply good men or women or admirable Christians. Their simplicity surely aroused some clerical antagonism and aggression. Indeed, it was clerical perception and hostility that made them seem, to some contemporaries and modern historians, uniquely evil and dangerous. Like other such groups, by their practice and sometimes by their preaching, they revealed their anti-clerical convictions and their rejection of, and sometimes revulsion with, the established ritual, sacramental, and liturgical life of the orthodox church.

Indeed, it is at the intersection of apostolic poverty and preaching, ritual, and morality that our two categories overlap. For many, especially the non-elite, simple followers of the Cathars, *practice,* and not thought, was very likely primary, and it is even advisable to believe that the sometimes complex conceptual framework of elite Cathar belief was either unknown or unimportant to them. What counted was austere application of conviction. Intriguingly, here they overlap, in practice, not only with other heretical groups, but also with new and unimpeachably orthodox monastic and eremitical groups who strove, just as heroically, to achieve the lofty demands of the apostolic life. The clean lines historians draw today would have been hard to produce then. All were united in their enthusiasm for a new religious ideal. Having expressed that caution, we can now go on to observe that many among those known as Cathars *did,* in fact, cling to beliefs (which of course informed their practice, as well as their view of the orthodox system of belief), contrary to those proclaimed by the established church, often in the face of pursuit, aggression, and persecution.

So what do we know about this group, the so-called Cathars or Albigensians? What *did* they believe? Why *did* their beliefs so vex the church of Rome that the latter felt it necessary to preach against and then persecute them? Once persecuted, what was their fate? First of all, as already suggested, the name "Cathar" (likely derived from the Greek word for "pure," though it is not impossible that they were believed to be cat-worshippers, as they were certainly accused of conducting diabolical rituals) was imposed on them by clerical observers. This began in 1163, when Eckbert, a Benedictine monk and then abbot of Schönau (d. 1184)—not to mention brother of the more famous visionary Elisabeth of

Schönau (St. Elisabeth; d. ca. 1165)—claimed that the Cathars were, geographically speaking, well represented not only near him, in the Rhineland, but also in France. Elisabeth, along with Hildegard of Bingen (d. 1179), also wrote and spoke polemically against the so-called Cathars. While not unrepresented in the north, they were particularly strong and tenacious in southern France, or Occitania, often called the Languedoc, and in Flanders. Strongly represented as well in Italy, they were identified also by a number of other terms of opprobrium and derision, such as Manichaeans, Patarini, Publicani, Bulgars, and even "sodomites."

Informed clerics, who knew about ancient dualistic groups, like the Manichees, thought that the Cathars were, in fact, modern Manichees; indeed, a twentieth-century book written by an eminent historian of the Cathars, relying perhaps too heavily on the accounts of medieval clerical observers, is entitled *The Medieval Manichee*. Others called them "weavers," leading to debates among historians regarding their social origins (as we shall see, socially if not theologically they were catholic and confined to no one social group and, indeed, were well represented in the upper classes). Later, especially in inquisitorial documents, which are both rich *and* misleading, they are identified by the Dominicans' notaries, simply, as "heretics" and their beliefs as "heretical." Terminology is not unimportant here. The Cathars and those who admired, followed, or merely sympathized with them called them, equally simply, "Good People" or "Good Christians." What you call a group profoundly shapes how you understand its members and the attitudes you take toward them.

The mention of inquisitorial sources should remind us that, as is the case with almost all groups deemed heretical, in ancient as well as medieval Christianity, almost all we know about the Cathars derives from authors and sources who were openly hostile to them and who feared their capacity to convert others to their (in their eyes) genuinely damnable ways and beliefs. For this reason, almost everything about Cathar religious belief, practice, and fate has been fruitfully disputed among historians. Of the many writings composed by the Cathars, only a tiny number has survived. Among these are three Cathar rituals (two in Occitan, one in Latin), an Occitan Bible, an anonymous treatise for Cathar preachers, and quasi-scholastic apologies (written, as such literary refutations usually are, to defend the suspect sect, in this case using the categories employed by the hostile). Written both in the vernacular and in Latin, these were produced, by and large, in the twelfth and thirteenth centuries.

As for hostile sources, we have the rich but not unproblematic inquisitorial sources of the thirteenth and fourteenth centuries, which are supposed to contain depositions given by the Cathars before inquisitorial tribunals; these must be treated with caution. Several Cathars were, improbably, converted back to Catholicism, and one, Raynier Sacconi (d. 1263), was not only converted in the mid-thirteenth century, but after training, he also became a Dominican and then the Grand Inquisitor for Lombardy in northern Italy. His testimony is that of an insider, but it is written at a time at which he was no longer sympathetic with his sometime co-religionists. His *summa* (or summary), *On the Cathars and the Poor of Lyons,* was, nonetheless, extremely well known in the Middle Ages and survives in a large number of manuscripts, likely an indication of its wide influence.

Precursors of the Cathars began to appear in western Europe even before people knew how to identify or categorize them. It has now been fairly well established that they had connections with the so-called Bogomils of Bulgaria and other parts of the eastern church (from which they may have borrowed perfectly orthodox practices as well). Who were the Bogomils? Again, they were a group that was ascetic, though radically so. In this case, there can be no doubt but that they held to theological and especially cosmological ideas that the western church found incompatible with what it taught.

The theological beliefs of the Bogomils (which were probably disseminated along trade routes from east to west) on the origins of the cosmos, and especially of evil, link them conceptually with the ancient Manichees; however, few historians today credit the idea that there was a continuous Manichaean tradition that survived through the tenth century, when the Bogomils from the Balkans probably began to missionize those who would appear in the chronicles of westerners and extend their influence to the West. Like Catharism in its mature form, Bogomilism developed cosmological accounts, relying partly on the scriptures, in an attempt to address the mystery that has so flummoxed Christians (and co-religionists) throughout the centuries: why does evil exist? That it did exist, and the conviction that the world was evil, they did not doubt. Accordingly, they tried to distance themselves, insofar as possible, from involvement in or dependence upon the material world and certainly could not accept the orthodox Christian belief, based on the words of the Creator himself in Genesis, that the creation was "good." This belief, incidentally, explains why both the Cathars and Bogomils rejected the veneration of icons—a practice that, of course, connects them, theologically, with eastern iconoclasts; none could accept the idea that the material could represent or mediate the divine.

We should be cautious about imagining that belief in the irredeemably evil nature of creation in itself separated the Bogomils spectacularly from orthodox practice. Instead, we must remind ourselves of the long tradition of Christian asceticism and monasticism, whose practitioners similarly attempted to deny their fleshly desires and needs; separated themselves from ordinary society and established, "institutionalized" Christianity; and were profoundly suspicious of the temptations of "the world." Accordingly, not only did the Bogomils refuse sexuality and frown on procreation, but also they would eat nothing they believed to be the product of procreation, such as meat, eggs, milk, or cheese; it has been suggested, not utterly implausibly, that refusal to consume these products may have reflected respect for animal life. As practitioners, so they hoped, of the apostolic life, they repudiated what they did not find in the evangelical sources; this encompassed nothing less than the entire complex of structures, beliefs, rituals, thought, and organization of the western church. Like other contemporary movements, they thus had no church buildings, rejected the sacraments, did not venerate those recognized by the church as saints, disdained the established interpretation of scripture, and repudiated the priesthood. One orthodox prayer they did accept, and prayed often, was the *Paternoster*. Rejecting baptism (likely because it required the use of created matter, in this case water), Bogomil aspirants were inducted into the sect by the laying on of hands, by which they understood themselves to be imparting a baptism of the spirit.

Early in the eleventh century, three reports document the appearance of individuals and groups who clung to beliefs and practices remarkably similar to those of the Bogomils just described. One source, a chronicle, reports that a group in Orléans also did not partake of sacraments involving the material. In addition, its members abstained from eating meat. Theologically, they doubted either that Christ was born of a virgin or that he had in fact died. Socially speaking, they consisted of nobles and canons. Claiming access to what might be termed neo-Gnostic illumination, they utterly rejected "the fabrications of men written on animals' skins"—that is, the canonical scriptures, written on parchment. In this last sense, they of course differed from apostolic groups aspiring literally to imitate the life depicted therein. They would pay a high price for their convictions. Punishment came in the form of burning—the first time, so far as we know, that the church would burn heretics (five in this case).

Another group appears, at roughly the same time, in Liège. Its system of beliefs appears to be quite like that of the group from Orléans, though it more conventionally attempted to imitate the apostolic pattern as shown in the gospels. Finally a group in the Piedmont, again like many contemporary apostolic movements, appears to have held the sacerdotal hierarchy in contempt. Aside from rejecting the ministrations of unworthy priests (again like the ancient Donatists), its members refused to be baptized, persuaded that obedience to the "precepts of the gospels and the apostles" would suffice. They, too, agreed to abstain from sex, believing that, lacking carnal knowledge, they would procreate without coition, "like bees." The source on which we depend for our knowledge of this group reports that its members were determined to conclude their lives "in torment" as a way to avert the graver consequences of undergoing eternal agony. Theologically, they too refused to accept prevailing understandings of the mode of the divine-human union in Christ. The doctrine of the Trinity they took to be a mysterious allegory and rejected the notion of a triune God. All of this evidence, much of which has been extensively disputed, strongly suggests the infiltration of Bogomil missionaries and the acceptance in the West of Bogomil beliefs imported from the Balkans or other parts of the East. Intriguingly, the one belief that we cannot be sure they absorbed is the central tenet of the Bogomils and the mature Cathars—theological dualism—and this despite observers sometimes confidently pronouncing them "Manichees." Despite some of the characteristics just described, their commitment to sexual abstention, severe asceticism, and separation from the mundane all link them with new forms of orthodox monasticism. Mysteriously, we hear nothing more about such groups for roughly a century.

At that point—in the 1140s—references, if fragmentary and historically indigent, begin to multiply. Again, there was little in early Cathar practice to distinguish the Cathars from itinerant preachers never declared heterodox. Aside from dressing simply and living severely, all denounced the affluent, all-too-worldly clergy, whom they excoriated for purchasing, or selling, ecclesiastical offices. This is further proof that these groups were, ironically, brought forth by the potent reform currents originating in the Gregorian period of priestly critique and attempted regeneration—not to mention clerical inducement to neo-Donatist refusal to accept the ministrations of unworthy clerics.

Again in the 1140s, another group rejecting baptism appeared in Cologne. In place of baptism, its members preferred the laying on of hands. Refusing to consume milk or meat, they too never married. Their food they blessed with the *Paternoster*. A group cryptically named "Arians" emerges on the scene in Toulouse at roughly the same time; it is impossible to know exactly what its members believed theologically. However, if the source is at all to be trusted, it would seem that they, too, rejected the orthodox doctrine of the Trinity. Finally, a group explicitly called "Cathars" is, as mentioned, identified in Cologne by Eckbert in 1163. Two years later, the "Good Men" held a debate near Albi before an audience of luminaries, including several bishops, the countess of Toulouse, and the viscount of Béziers. It is important that though excommunicated by Catholic bishops, the Good Men were not pursued, nor even bothered by, the secular powers of southern France. The Cathar interlocutors simply drifted off and responded to the episcopal action by excommunicating the Catholic bishops.

As mentioned, these sources are frustratingly taciturn. We can conclude, nonetheless, that the groups appearing in the 1140s were likely converts of Bogomil missionaries, as they share so many of that group's characteristics. Good evidence suggests contacts between eastern Bogomils and especially Italian Cathars continued for some time. From the early to mid-thirteenth century, sources from Italy, not to mention writings produced by the Good Men themselves, allow us to reconstruct Cathar beliefs, practices, and organization in far more satisfying detail.

Some specialists argue that a practice, the *consolamentum* [the laying on of hands], should be regarded as central. Peter Biller seems closer to the truth when observing, "At the heart of Catharism was knowledge." Perhaps *the* central belief of mature Cathar dogma is cosmological dualism. Profoundly troubled with the conundra of how evil could exist in a good world or how God might have been tied up with the creation of an obviously evil one, they came to the conclusion that there could not simply be one good Creator God. Instead, relying (as we shall see below, ironically) on Genesis and some books or fragments of apocrypha, as well as the New Testament, they despised the world and scorned much of the Hebrew Bible. Like Marcion and his followers, the Cathars understood most of the Old Testament to be the revelation of the evil God; that did not prevent them from accepting some of its books as authoritative. Satan, for them, was the God to whom Genesis referred. Enthusiasm for the New Testament and the apostolic life led them to view with disdain the venerable patriarchs, like Moses, whom the Cathars regarded as the mouthpiece of Satan. The prophets? They were figures whom the Devil used to deceive, mixing their truthful oracles with his evil ones.

It was the angelic Christ who, of course, revealed true Cathar doctrine and the place, plight, and destiny of humanity. Human beings, in this view, were spirits caught in matter, like jewels secreted away in a mound of dung or virtuous and innocent souls incarcerated in the fetid prison of the flesh. As the extant Occitan ritual summed up the matter, the "spirit is imprisoned" and "the flesh born of corruption." Salvation or liberation began, then (again, as with ancient Gnosticism), with awareness and acknowledgment of the unfortunate human condition, contempt of matter (again something like but distinct from the orthodox tradition of *contemptus mundi,* or contempt for the world), and slow disengagement, by Cathar practice, from detention in the jailhouse of creation. Should a Cathar be so unfortunate as not to achieve perfection, or status as a perfect (see below), before his death, he would be punished, again, by immediate incarceration in another created body, either human or animal. Some scholars have observed, correctly, that the intermediate movement of souls from life to life mirrored the then fairly novel notion of purgatory in orthodox belief. These deeply held views about the incompatibility of matter and spirit very naturally shaped what we should call Cathar "Christology."

Again, and not surprisingly, conceptual (though not historical) links on this issue connect them with ancient heretics, like many Gnostic groups and the Manichees. None could believe that Christ had assumed real flesh. Had he not been incarnate, he could not have suffered, nor been crucified—and if not crucified, not, of course, resurrected. Many, certainly before the thirteenth century, did not consider Christ divine but, instead, an angel who had never sinned. Whatever his metaphysical reality (divine, angelic, human), he was regarded primarily as an exemplar and pedagogue whose mission it was to conduct the fallen angels back to their home in heaven. Likewise, the Cathars' opinion on the Trinity, which was quite underdeveloped, was unorthodox. The Trinity they regarded, perhaps, as three names for a single God or a mystery with fine symbolic meanings.

Some debate about the status and relation of the two eternal principles occurred among the Cathars. Using categories that would have been unrecognizable to Cathars themselves, modern historians distinguish between "absolute" or "radical" and "moderate" or "mitigated" dualism. The former held that the two principles or powers, good and evil, were both eternal and equal in power; the latter, that the evil power was a rebellious son or perhaps fallen angel or Satan himself. It is interesting that sources give us some insight about how debate among the Cathars on this issue could unfold. Almost amusingly, the issue of "orthodox" dualism came up in debate among the various theological camps. Some historians consider it likely that the prevalent form of Cathar dualism, to this point in the group's history, was moderate or mitigated.

That narrative centers on a figure named Niketas (or Nicetas). A convinced radical or absolute dualist from the Balkans, he appeared around 1170 in western Europe. There, in Italy, he found adherents of moderate or mitigated dualism. After some discussion in council at St.-Félix-de-Caraman (a town situated in the Lauragais region between Toulouse and Carcassonne where adherence to Catharism was strong), Niketas persuaded the moderates to accept the more extreme version of dualism to which he clung. Our sources for this episode reveal that the bishops of Albi and the north of France, as well as leaders from communities in Carcassonne, Toulouse, and, likely, other towns were present at this meeting. (If, as is suggested by the sources, representatives from Constantinople, where the Latin Cathar ritual was likely written, were also present, we cannot but call this an international church.) At that point, Niketas and a man named Mark, whom Niketas had, in the style of the ancient Donatists, reconsecrated bishop (along with two other moderate dualist bishops) by the conventional method of the laying on of hands, then went to Occitania, or southern France. The council also elected bishops for Carcassonne and Toulouse, as well as other cities, and "diocesan" boundaries were drawn.

Cathar society was divided into two groups, the "perfect" *(perfecti)* and "believers" *(credentes)*. (The Cathars, it should be noted, rarely used the term "perfect"—another clerical imposition.) Be they absolute or mitigated dualists, theologically both groups participated in a fairly standard set of rituals and practices. The central ritual, without doubt, was the *consolamentum*. This enabled the fully fledged adept to say the *Paternoster* (though evidence suggests believers said it as well) and to begin the return journey to his or her supernal home. In the early history of Catharism, a long period of preparation was required, a time of probation during which the initiate would undergo numerous fasts and thus establish his capacity to be liberated. Having been inducted into the sect, liberated, absolved, and "ordained" all at once, the initiate experienced the equivalent of three Catholic sacraments in a single ritual. Once consoled, the perfect would generally relinquish his worldly goods (if any) and begin the itinerant apostolic life of preaching and poverty, as well as sexual and nutritional purity, and a rigorous regime of fasting. He or she would commit whatever life remaining to supporting and exhorting sympathizers and to assisting others to transfer from the realm of darkness to that of light, whence they had come and to which, after death, they would return.

Matters of marriage, childbearing, and relations between the sexes were all at issue for the perfects. Committed to chastity, all gave up conjugal relations, even if married. If with child, no woman could be consoled, and her progeny were viewed as evidence of diabolical activity. When women were consoled, they took on a veil; it hid them and precluded the possibility, theoretically, of sexual activity. Over the course of time, an adherent would be consoled only on his deathbed, rather like catechumens in the early church receiving baptism at the end of their lives; it would be impossible, or difficult, to sin then. It has been suggested that some would then simply fast to their deaths, a practice that came to be called the *endura,* but this has been disputed.

It has been well established that women perfects also preached, gave pastoral care, and consoled. Again, practice was probably primary for women, as was familial belief—family connections were another channel by which Catharism was spread and received. Female believers, by contrast, did not engage in these activities. Indeed, they may have been indistinguishable from their Catholic neighbors. Like them, they married, bore children, and raised families. For these women, too, doctrine likely had little impact on their lives or their view of the world. Interestingly, it has been established that at least the French Cathars became increasingly misogynistic in the fourteenth century. Then it was taught that a woman could achieve salvation only if she was fortunate enough to be reborn a man. In addition, women could only be consoled if very close to death. Such beliefs are all by contrast to those of Italian Cathars. It seems as if the misogyny that affected French Cathars was something to which their Italian fellow travelers remained steadily immune. Yet this is not certain, as there is evidence of some interaction between the French and Italian Cathars.

Male or female, there was a neo-Donatist element to the administration of the ritual. The efficacy of the rite depended on the capacity and perseverance of the perfect who administered it. Should he ever lose his purity, he would lose his powers. As a consequence, all those whom he had consoled, even those who had achieved their heavenly destination, would lose their status as perfects. Much, therefore, rested on the capacity of the perfect to remain so. For less serious sin, the perfects gathered monthly to confess in a ritual they called the *apparellamentum*. Naturally, many could not maintain perfection, leading to schism, as sexual impropriety occurred, or was alleged, and the search for an authentic perfect, and reconsolation, ensued. Ultimately, at least six distinct Italian Cathar churches existed. By contrast, the Cathar churches of Languedoc remained united, even though there the churches were separated by belief in the nature of dualism.

Always much smaller in number than the perfects, the believers were not so consoled and therefore did not take on the regime of severe asceticism assumed by the perfects. Still sinful, they could not address God as father. They were, nevertheless, expected to commit themselves to a life of sinlessness, simplicity, and spare use of goods. Their nutritional purity consisted of abstention from consuming meat, milk, and cheese, and they attempted sinlessness in refusing to take oaths or participate in any form of extreme violence. (It is intriguing that the abstention from dairy products may have been influenced by contemporary Greek Christian practice.) As it was believed that fish were generated spontaneously by water, without coition, they were consumed. The fairly significant number of believers in the twelfth century from august families and courts did not always observe these rules for food consumption. Always, however, they venerated (and genuflected before) the perfect as a paradigm of purity, who would then bless and pray for them. Many believers of all classes—and the Cathars penetrated all classes, with stronger penetration than the Waldensians into the noble and urban patrician classes—did anticipate a time when they, too, should become consoled and follow the path of perfection. In addition, they supported the perfects materially, housed them, and, once the Inquisition began hunting them, gave them sanctuary. Not surprisingly, the Cathars became more clandestine over the years, sometimes desperately seeking safe haven in woodland houses or tents.

In terms of organization, the Cathar church constructed a structure that mirrored the ambient Catholic ecclesiological forms and hierarchies. We have already mentioned bishops in Occitania and Italy. Eventually, they were elected, but by the perfects alone. Only they could consecrate fellow bishops and those of lesser office. By the end of the twelfth century, a sort of hierarchy had begun to develop, and we begin to hear of "greater" and "lesser" sons; they likely succeeded bishops who had died. By 1170 or so, we hear of deacons. Like bishops, they could console—or at least male bishops and deacons could. Deacons also often organized and ran the domiciles harboring perfects, and they frequently led rituals and consoled the dying.

Reliable statistics on the number of Cathars, whether perfects or believers, are impossible to establish, though contemporaries did occasionally guess or pronounce on numbers. One frustrated priest near Toulouse complained that his entire parish was Cathar. This is likely a great exaggeration, as hyperbolic as those estimates of contemporary historians who have suggested that thousands of perfects existed in Occitania alone. Some have suggested that sympathizers numbered in the hundreds of thousands. By contrast, Raynier Sacconi figured there were four thousand Italian perfects in his time, and, even closer to historical reality, an early-thirteenth-century bishop of Béziers, which had around ten thousand citizens, found himself able to identify only around two hundred believers. As a consequence of effective persecution (as well as other factors to be discussed), only fifteen or so perfects remained in the early fourteenth century. By then, the sun of the Cathars had set.

Waldensians

If any group in the high Middle Ages was quintessentially unexceptionable, in a dogmatic sense, and drawn into dissent by ecclesiastical disapproval, it must be the Waldensians. Initially, they were a reform-minded movement. Indeed, there is evidence to suggest that their origins are tied up, ironically, in the struggle against the great heresy of the age, Catharism. Their leader, Waldes (d. ca. 1218), was a wealthy merchant of Lyons who wished to embrace fully the apostolic model of poverty and preaching. In this, he bears an uncanny resemblance to Francis of Assisi, who would gain the sanction of the papacy for his proposed way of life just three decades later. Yet the followers of Waldes would eventually be declared heretics, while those of Francis, at least initially, would be regarded as obedient sons of the church. Why?

To begin to respond to this question, we have to turn to the roots of the movement in the personal turning point of its founder's life. Until 1173, Waldes was an unremarkable if successful merchant. However, it was in that year that he heard the story of St. Alexius sung by a minstrel. It was to be a fateful moment in his life. Alexius was an early Christian saint (fl. fifth century). The conscience-stricken scion of a wealthy Roman father, he absconded from his wife (purportedly on their wedding night) and journeyed all the way to Syrian Edessa. There he embraced a life of severe austerity. He returned many years later to his father's house, destitute, to beg beneath his father's home, in which he then died, unrecognized and apparently unappreciated (the echoes of this narrative with the Parable of the Prodigal Son [Luke 15:11–32] are several—a clue that the account may reflect hagiographical embellishment).

The impact of this story on Waldes was immediate and profound. He soon took counsel from a master of theology. A thorough and cautious businessman, he inquired directly about the surest avenue to salvation. The theologian replied in the words of Christ given in response to the query of the Rich Young Man: "If you wish to be perfect, go, sell your possessions, and give the money to the poor, and you will have treasure in heaven; then come, follow me" (Matthew 19:21)—the text that launched many on their ascetical careers from the third century through the thirteenth and beyond.

If some of the details of this account are not altogether reliable, these and similar criticisms of wealth in the scriptures seem to have had a heartfelt and radical effect on Waldes. After providing sufficient wealth to his wife and dowries to his daughters (who soon entered the convent of Fontevrault), he flung the remainder of his own family wealth into the streets of Lyons. The distinguished historian of heresy, Malcolm Lambert, has acutely noted "a Franciscan touch in [Waldes's] religious passion, throwing money in the street, rejecting the usurious business methods that had brought him wealth." Part of this dramatic, if utterly sincere, performance may reflect the availability of Waldes's mind to the power of the enveloping cult and culture of voluntary poverty. But there is more. After experiencing the power of the Matthean story of the Rich Young Man, Waldes commissioned from two clerics extracts of parts of the scriptures in the vernacular tongue. He did so because the Bible then was available in a language, Latin, that a common layperson could not understand, and sermons explaining the scriptures to laypersons were not to become ordinary until the following century. He also requested some extracts of the church fathers. It is this interest in self-instruction by means of vernacular translation of the gospels and fathers, several historians suggest, that truly distinguishes Waldes from the mass of wandering preachers in previous decades.

Waldes's instant perception of a gulf between the life the gospels seemed to prescribe and the one he was leading may help to account for the force and feeling of his radical conversion to poverty from wealth. In other words, it may have been the explicit, forthright, and directly felt words of the gospels, as much as the ubiquitous cultural zeal for voluntary poverty, that best explains the intensity of his conversion experience. Waldes seems to have been especially captivated by another enormously influential text from the gospels, Jesus's commissioning of the apostles: "As you go, proclaim the good news. . . . You received without payment; give without payment. Take no gold, or silver, or copper in your belts, no bag for your journey, or two tunics, or sandals, or a staff; for laborers deserve their food" (Matthew 10:7–13).

Again, the effect of this text on Waldes is arresting for the similarity of its impact on Francis thirty years later. Like Francis, Waldes dedicated himself to what he took to be evangelical perfection—not excellence but *perfection*. This devotion to apostolic flawlessness, incidentally, implies a view of human nature and possibility rather at odds with orthodox "Augustinian" views on the matter and more consistent with heretical "Pelagian" opinion. In any event, like Francis, he would, precisely as Jesus ordained, take no money with him to purchase consumables or temporary housing but rely on the providence of God; this was not simply a lofty ideal to which he aspired but a divine command that he resolved to observe to the letter.

This resolution implied not only poverty but also the obligation of public exhortation—preaching—to be poor. That is, he not only adopted a life of poverty, but he also admonished others to do the same. The precise sources and contents of his preaching are otherwise unknown, but it has been plausibly suggested that he simply preached in public what he had learned by heart from the extracts made for him by the two clerics. If the translation for laymen of sacred books into the vernacular seems to have caused relatively little, if any, anxiety, the transition from untutored lay merchant to public preacher may have inspired more fear.

One historian has correctly perceived that in the emphasis on preaching, there lay a "fundamental divide" between Waldensians and Cathars. If the Waldensians wished to exhort, to encourage, to make people sin less and be more good, the same could not be said of the Cathars. There was, Peter Biller observes, "no rationale in [Cathar] theology for the moral improvement of their flock." Those who had not been consoled were still participating fully in the evil world—by which the Cathar meant marrying, procreating, and consuming forbidden food. For the Cathar perfect, there was no point in trying morally to improve simple believers. When interrogated, deposed Christians reported over and over, Biller concludes, that "Cathars talked about doctrine and Waldensians talked morals." It seems as if Waldensian exhortation consisted of simple admonitions (to contemporaries, some of them would have sounded more dangerous): to refuse oaths, never to kill, nor to lie, nor to do evil unto others. Some of this exhortation was of course also utterly innocuous.

It is difficult from the sources to tell just how unusual public preaching was at the time or how nervous ecclesiastical authorities, and which ones, grew anxious about it. Be that as it may, some clerics, perhaps alarmed that Waldensian preaching might grow more anti-clerical in tone and jealous of a privilege traditionally theirs (guaranteed as a monopoly to clerics by canon law), may have grown concerned about or contemptuous of—most assumed, not incorrectly, that laypeople were theologically deficient—untrained and potentially fault-finding preachers drifting around their dioceses and generating interest, recruits, and, possibly, anti-clerical animus, as well as revulsion with conformity. Just then, the Cathars were becoming a serious threat in the Languedoc, and it is possible their success played into attitudes toward the followers of Waldes. Still, it remains unclear whether such a fear reflects feeling at the time or was later retrojected into the early history of the movement by those hostile to it, when it had become reckoned a loathsome heresy.

Less doubtful is that Waldes began to attract sympathizers, both male and female, to his way of life. (Women may have played a special role in preserving Waldensian memory and tradition.) Like Waldes, all brothers and sisters were enthusiasts for voluntary poverty and, like their leader, felt it not only their right but also their duty to preach poverty and to do so publicly. This they began to do in 1177. In fact, it was the issue of the right to preach (and this in an age when the distinction between lay and cleric was being ever more emphatically reinforced) that pushed the Waldensians from a harmless poverty-practicing gospel movement to a disobedient and thus heretical one.

The beginnings of this decisive transformation began, it seems, with Waldes's dawning recognition that the archbishop of Lyons and his clergy would never give the poor of Lyons permission to preach. Indeed, the archbishop seems to have formally forbidden them from doing so—though, again, this proscription may have been retrojected from later sources to an earlier time period by a Waldensian sympathizer. Still, it seems likely that Waldes and his followers felt pressure not to preach. This was a particularly inauspicious moment to begin a preaching movement, as it was the very hour when the heretical Cathars were growing extremely powerful in the Languedoc; the possibility of a home-grown, heretical, and anti-clerical group must have seemed especially undesirable to the clergy of Lyons at that moment.

As it happened, the archiepiscopal prohibition, if it indeed occurred, would have been issued at almost the same time the Third Lateran Council (or Lateran III) was gathering (1179) in an effort to resist the growing Albigensian heresy. In a pattern already traditional and one that would intensify over the next century, the aggrieved party—in this case, the poor of Lyons—elected to go over the head of the local ordinary and appeal directly to the pope, Alexander III, who would preside over the council.

This they did. At the council a line of theological questioning (though not from the pope) designed to deride the competence of the Waldensians to preach did succeed in ridiculing them. According to one account, the pope actually embraced Waldes and lauded as well as blessed his dedication to voluntary poverty. There the enthusiasm ended. Pope Alexander decreed that unless requested by local clergy to do so (a more far-fetched possibility is difficult to imagine, even though Innocent III later allowed some lay groups to "exhort" against heresy), the Waldensians were not to continue preaching. From the point of view of the pope, this must have seemed a reasonable, Solomonic compromise. Both he and the Lyonnais clergy were all too aware of charismatic preachers, often defiant of ecclesiastical authority, originators sometimes of frightening heresies that could spread and result in increasing venom for clergy and a violent end for the heresiarch in question. Of such men and women, the English cleric Walter Map

(d. ca. 1209), who may well have attended Lateran III, inquired disdainfully: "Shall, therefore, any wise pearls be cast before swine, and the word given to lay-men, who, as we know, receive it foolishly, to say nothing of their giving what they have received? No more of this, and let it be rooted out!" Again, similar decisions were made in connection with analogous movements, such as the Humiliati of Lombardy. Given recent experience with men like Henry of Lausanne and Peter de Bruys, and the now alarming growth of the Cathars, prudence and caution must have seemed the rational course of action. Yet the prelates at the council probably did not help their cause by the derisive way in which they treated Waldes and his followers.

Ironically, Lateran III had been called specifically to quell and, if possible, van-quish the Cathars, and the poor of Lyons began it by professing their desire to serve the pope by preaching against that very heresy. At the end of the council, they were now confronted with a fateful choice: to comply in obedience with the decrees of the council and the pope or to resist them and thus to leave the ecclesiastical domain of orthodoxy and cross over into the territory of the hetero-dox—alongside the hated Cathars. The decision of the pope, the outcome of the council, and the future of the Waldensians would all shape the way in which a later pope, Innocent III, would treat the leaders of a poverty-and-preaching movement originating in Assisi.

Ironies multiply, as it was at this time that Waldes subscribed to, within a year or so of the council, a Profession of Faith (not written by but drawn from him by a papal legate) designed to demonstrate his dogmatic distance from the Cathars and, in general, to prove his theological orthodoxy. In fact, one way of reading the Profession is, in effect, to perceive that it denies everything the Cathars affirm; in that sense it *had* to reflect ecclesiastical orthodoxy, as well as anxiety about Albi-gensian error. Thus where the Cathars were convinced that John the Baptist was damned, the Profession declares he was inspired. Again, if the Cathars vigorously denied the reality, or even what we should call the metaphysical possibility, of the Incarnation, Waldes assented to the orthodox view of the Trinity, which includes, at least implicitly, the understanding that the Second Person of the Trinity as-sumed flesh and partook in the human condition. While the Cathars preached the transmigration of souls after death, Waldes accepted the traditional belief that the resurrected would be raised in their own bodies. He denied, again against Cathar affirmation, that the consumption of meat was reprehensible. Accepting the now traditional view that Catholic liturgical and devotional practices, such as the mass, the giving of alms, and "works," benefit the dead, he also (and crucially) rejected the neo-Donatist notion that sacraments (all seven of which he recognized) ad-ministered by an unworthy priest were thus invalid. Indeed, at one point, Waldes explicitly repudiated the neo-Donatist, anti-clerical tone that would later characterize branches of the movement: sacraments are valid, "even though they may be administered by a sinful priest," he declared. In short, the whole Profession was absolutely free of even a hint of heterodoxy; it was, instead, from a dogmatic point of view, unimpeachably orthodox.

The Profession concludes by advocating a way of life that is hardly distinguishable from that which Francis would propose decades later. The Waldensians would live poorly and accept no money but only necessities from the alms of others. The evangelical counsels they promised to follow to the letter. In short, they would attempt to live the perfect apostolic life. This last proposition is the trickiest to interpret, as there can be no doubt that for Waldes and his followers, it meant the privilege—or rather, the dominical charge and therefore obligation—of preaching.

Auspicious as this Profession might seem for relations between the poor of Lyons and the institutional church, it was not long before the relationship ruptured irretrievably. It would not be quite true to say, in the immediate aftermath of the Third Lateran Council, that the Waldensians became heretical. Nonetheless, from the point of view of the clerical class, they soon slipped into schism. Confronted now with the choice between obeying Christ's evangelical mandate to preach or the conciliar and archdiocesan decisions that they could not, they chose to respect the former. As they might very well have seen it, they chose to side with the apostles rather than their putative, even false, successors. As they are themselves reputed to have put it around 1182–1184, quoting Peter, the prince of the apostles, "We must obey God rather than men" (Acts 5:29).

With this act of defiance, the Waldensians found themselves excommunicated and expelled from Lyons, though they soon established themselves in other towns of southern France and Italy and Alpine areas, such as eastern France and Switzerland. What seemed like fidelity to the scriptures and to Christ to Waldes and his followers would be interpreted by the pope as acts of provocation and temerity. Accordingly, Pope Lucius III (r. 1181–1185) issued in 1184 the decretal *Ad Abolendam*. The document names as heretical several groups (the Cathars first of all), including the Waldensians. Here still, the issue is not dogmatic deviance; it is defiance of authority, specifically for preaching without ecclesiastical permission. The Waldensians, despite Lucius's decretal, would, by the time of their leader's death (sometime between 1205 and 1218), begin to spread widely over Europe. By the end of the century, they could be found not only in France but also in northern Italy and Germany (where they dwelt to the Reformation and beyond), as well as its Slavic frontiers and Catalonia. By the fourteenth century, they were well represented in central Europe, including Bohemia (we know because at least several hundred died at the stake, according to recently discovered inquisitorial records), Poland, Transylvania, Hungary, and Austria. Inquisitorial records survive in greatest numbers in southern France, leading historians to conclude that the numbers of Cathars there were much larger than of Waldensians. However, the recently discovered records (as well as the number of executions of Waldensians) have suggested to some recent historians that even there, in what has traditionally been regarded as the stronghold of Catharism, Waldensians outnumbered Albigensians.

Because of repression, felt with increasing severity over the course of the century, Waldensians would find refuge in the Alpine fastnesses—where, indeed, some communities of them dwell even to this day. If we were to draw a large contrast, it would be fairly safe to say that the Cathars were better represented, generally, in Romance-vernacular southern Europe and the Waldensians in Germanophone north and northeastern Europe. Neither group was well represented in England, northern France, or Flanders. In each of these areas, there was strong central authority and a desire not to see heresy or, if present, to repress it.

Eventually, the poor brothers and sisters evolved from a schismatic group to a clearly heretical one. In relatively short order, the followers of Waldes generated a heretical point of view extraordinary for its detail, radicality, and comprehensiveness—not to mention the rancor of its anti-clerical and anti-canonical vitriol. To be sure, we must not disregard significant doctrinal variations based on territory. Still, we can speak, despite these regional disparities, of a common, even conventional, set of convictions that together added up to a view of church and world that, for coherence and exhaustiveness, was matched only by the Roman church it increasingly came to loathe, disparage, and abandon. More, we can begin to speak of a different and nonconformist church, so at odds were these doctrines with those of orthodox Christianity.

Mention of the Cathars leads us to underline a point often underemphasized in the past. Like the Cathars, the Waldensians existed at two "levels" or degrees of commitment. As some historians have observed, the first bore close resemblances to the mendicant orders considered in the next chapter (except for having to live in clandestine fashion). Not only did they take the three traditional vows of chastity, poverty, and obedience, but they also were "regular"—at least in the sense that their days were punctuated by disciplined prayer, by listening to sermons, and by receiving instruction in special houses.

Houses were constructed for Waldensian sisters as well as brothers, and women, according to inquisitorial records, not only preached domestically but also in public, and they may have assumed priestly functions as well—but the evidence for this is not as strong as that for their preaching. In clothing, too, they resembled the friars, as they adopted a distinctive habit. Like the friars, these Waldensians held general annual meetings. To these, brothers and sisters would travel, usually to northern Italy and southern France (but occasionally to Germany) for what the Cistercians and friars would call yearly chapter meetings. The second level at which the brothers and sisters existed was that of "friends," structurally similar to the "believers" of the Cathars. Like the believers, they married; unlike them, they continued to participate in parish churches, where they would hear mass, confess, and have their weddings and funeral services. In addition, they would (here clandestinely) also go to the special houses of brothers, where they would receive further, often different, instruction and confess for a second time, this time not to priests but to non-clerical brothers. This too would be mirrored in the history of the friars, whose devout followers would confess to parish priests and then to members of the mendicant orders. In effect, they led double lives, participating fully in Waldensian instruction *and* the ordinary sacramental life of local churches, even while criticizing or rejecting it.

The ecclesiology of this church can, therefore, with some caution, be called neo-Donatist. Like the fourth-century Donatists of North Africa, the Waldensians grew to be quite hostile to the established clerical class, ecclesiastical authority, and sacerdotal rights and privileges. Corrupted by its association with wealth, ruined by its sin, the priestly class had lost all rights and power to administer valid sacraments or to preach. It followed, remorselessly, that a ruined priest ought not to be obeyed. But the Waldensians went further. It was the entire church—not simply individual priests—that had been wrecked.

Again, it followed that such a church could be held only in contempt. This contempt is something that orthodox churchmen, including inquisitors—came to realize in horror as they learned about Waldensian belief. Perhaps more alarming was the invitation to any Christian with merit, including any meritorious woman, to preach and, some have argued, on rather weak evidence, to administer sacraments in the Waldensian church.

Because they could find no express justification in the Bible for the doctrine of purgatory, the Waldensians soon came to turn their backs on that critical doctrine as well. Why critical? Because purgatory was associated with a host of ritual and sacramental practices—monastic prayers, indulgences, saintly intercession for the deceased, and, above all, the mass—conceived, or appropriated, to deliver the dead from their intermediate, temporal post-mortem state to the eternal state of beatitude in heaven. Renouncing purgatory, therefore, was a very loud way of announcing a more sweeping revulsion with and repudiation of practices and beliefs (non-Christian ones in the Waldensian view) that lay very close to the center of life in the church in the central Middle Ages. That it was a sweeping revulsion is especially true if we regard the medieval church, as some reductionistically do, as an institution designed primarily to deliver the believer from death and permanent damnation.

Wholly unconventionally, the schismatic and scorned Waldensians began to see the Roman church in the colorful categories and *dramatis personae* of the

Apocalypse. It was the "synagogue of Satan," the whore of Babylon, poisoned by acceptance of Constantine's catastrophic gift of temporal rule and jurisdiction over not just Italy but the entire West. Since Constantine's unintentionally disastrous act of generosity, the true apostolic line of priests remained hidden— invisible for nearly a millennium, until Waldes came forth to restore the church to purity. In the construction of this useful legend, Waldes now emerges with a new Christian name—Peter—to signify the apostolic authority, the purity (was it not Peter the Apostle who proclaimed that the true band of Christ's followers ought to obey the commands of God rather than of men?) and the true foundation on which the Waldensian counterchurch had been constructed.

It would be fruitless (and possibly tedious) to attempt a statistical analysis of "membership numbers" in the Waldensian churches over the last three centuries of the Middle Ages. Some sources, with as much exaggeration as imprecision, simply describe them as "countless." Suffice to say, they were numerous enough and were seen by the Roman church, not inaccurately, to be sufficiently institutionalized to represent a serious threat to its religious monopoly. A more interesting question would be: why and how had they become so popular, and why were they so revered? Here, as is usual in the Middle Ages, the response has much to do with *how* they lived their lives and the way in which their lives mirrored their preaching. It has almost nothing to do with *what* they thought.

Indeed, such influence as the Waldensians had on other medieval Christians should be measured in terms of their effects on the practice and intensity of devotion. Much of this was not original to them. Like a multitude of groups in these centuries, they came under the mesmerizing influence of the notion of the "apostolic life." Accordingly, they led lives of great and appealing simplicity. Historians habitually add that these lives were striking for the way in which they egregiously contrasted to the opulence of "the clergy." But this is far too uninflected. It needs to be remembered, constantly, that "the clergy" were, in the centuries under consideration here, themselves socially and economically (as well as educationally and theologically) heterogeneous. Therefore, it would be truer to say that Waldensian simplicity struck much of the laity as being very different and closer to the gospel ideal than the lives led by simoniacal or married priests or the minority of clerics who held bishoprics or abbeys or lived on great landed monastic estates. Nonetheless, the contrast is real and was perceived and felt at the time—and expressed emphatically by the followers of Waldes himself.

The story of the followers of Waldes is then, in part, the story of seemingly incessant friction in the high and late Middle Ages between privileges asserted by a zealous band of preachers, practitioners of poverty and simplicity, on the one hand, and, on the other, a hierarchy who felt stung by their claims and the simplicity of their lifestyle, as well as what must have seemed a usurpation of their canonically guaranteed clerical rights.

Still, it needs to be stressed, too, that *clerics* cautioned against overly harsh treatment of the Waldensians, perhaps perceiving that they had been nudged into schism and then heresy by an unimaginative papacy and institution that could not find useful space for the evangelical work they longed to pursue, the way Innocent III could for the brothers of Assisi just decades later. At the same time, one must concede that composure and understanding on the part of the Waldensians (such as was demonstrated, for example, by their founder), rather than tenacity and utter self-assurance about what the gospel required and grim persistence, might have earned them a more generous hearing from the clergy and archbishop of Lyons, not to mention the papacy.

In the end, then, the story of the Waldensians is an account of how a thoroughly orthodox and devoutly intentioned evangelical group could be forced, against its will and that of its leader, into the ranks (from the perspective of the western church, of course) of loathed and dangerous heretics. It is also the story of the effect of the lives of Waldensian believers on the practice of other Christians. Perhaps most interesting and most original, the followers of Waldes always, it seems, held a special appeal for women, who could be found preaching—in violation of canonical prohibitions on female preaching—in places like Pomerania and Strassburg as late as the end of the fifteenth century.

Otherwise, much that could be said of them could be said of other heretical groups. Yes, they were critical of ecclesiastical wealth and power. Of how many central- and high-medieval heretical groups could that *not* be said? Yes, they were persecuted and even hunted down, and some burned, by the Inquisition. Yet, it was the Cathars, not the followers of Waldes, against whom the Inquisition was principally aimed. They had virtually no strictly intellectual influence on contemporaries or successors and certainly no illustrious thinkers. That was not their collective *métier*. Rather, they demonstrate the power and grip of an extremely powerful ideal, in this case, desire—determination—to imitate perfectly the life of Christ and the lives of the apostles, the tenacity of a group, in the face of occasionally fierce opposition, to cling with heartfelt power to its ideals; to be received with reverence by those who chose to remain orthodox but not to persecute; and simply to survive until they could be absorbed by the reforming movements of the early modern period.

Heresy is a word that comes down to us via Middle English and Old French from the Greek word "to choose." Thus what united these two categories of groups was that both *chose* from competing alternatives: normative, orthodox Christianity and, rejecting that alternative, a better (to their collective appreciation of the gospel and what it required), more appropriate, more faithful form of the religious tradition as expressed or pictured in some or all of the scriptures (of which laymen increasingly had vernacular translations). Thus, what made one a heretic, properly speaking, was teaching and holding beliefs, like reincarnation or the existence of dual deities or competing eternal principles (one good and one evil); or pursuing and encouraging practices, like preaching; or rejecting some or all the sacraments, from which the church had forbidden them. It was, in the end, disobedience or stubborn defiance of ecclesiastical authority that made one a heretic in the Middle Ages. Heterodoxy, or different belief, the institutional church could tolerate—if one recanted it; heresy, or contumacious defiance of its authority, it could and did not. This it felt it had to detect—and to repress.

Repression: Crusade

As discussed, heresy was regarded as a serious sin by the institutional church, indeed something like a fatal spiritual infection. Not only was it regarded, from the viewpoint of civic law, as treason against the state, but clerics also regarded it as rebellion against the divine. From the point of view of many clerics and the most powerful pope of the age, there was no question but that its continued existence could not be tolerated. The only question was how it could be eliminated. Various methods were tried. When preaching, described as the "way of charity" *(via caritatis),* failed, more serious measures began to be considered. Bishops were urged to seek out heretics in their dioceses. This "charitable" tactic too failed. Repression then turned violent, and in this case, brutality was, if repulsive to the modern mind, effective in its aims.

As has always been clear, Pope Innocent III, whose career we will discuss in chapter 14, was no shrinking violet. This is, perhaps, nowhere more evident than in his attitude toward and, finally, his treatment of heretics and their protectors. Indeed, he could state to the bishops of Occitania, early in his time on the throne of St. Peter, that he in no realm of his pontificate was stricter than in his attempt to eliminate heresy. He promised those who joined him in the battle against error the same indulgence received by pilgrims to international shrines. In the second year of his pontificate, he began searching (canon lawyer as he was) for crimes analogous to heresy in the civil law, and, not surprisingly, he found not only the crimes, but the penalties for them as well.

Heresy he likened (not altogether originally) to treacherous behavior in the secular sphere and concluded that heresy should, like treason, be met with confiscation of the guilty party's goods and punishment of his inheritors (a punishment picked up in several decades by the Inquisition). To princes who confiscated that property, he offered a papally secured deed. The Cistercians and then St. Dominic's young order he charged with preaching against heresy, a milder form of the use of ecclesiastical power, in the Languedoc.

It would nevertheless be incorrect to suppose that Innocent favored only the *via potestatis,* or way of power, in dealing with heresy. A thoughtful (if forceful and decisive) man, he was willing to try several approaches, a symptom of how serious prelates thought the problem was, and he resorted to the velvet glove as well as to the fist. He recognized, again very early in his papal career, that intolerance could embolden heretics, confound the simple, and perhaps convert the orthodox to heterodoxy. With several heretical groups of the day, he was able to formulate ingenious solutions to win back those in error to orthodoxy. Even the Waldensians, who had been radicalized by previous and less imaginative popes, were won over, as several of their members returned to the Roman church after Innocent in 1208 approved a society for the "Catholic poor." Less than two years later, he was able to bring the potentially anarchical band of brothers from Assisi within the bounds of orthodoxy and made them among the most effective and loyal orders the church has ever known.

Innocent's campaign for preaching was, on the whole, quite unsuccessful. Having promised an indulgence to actors against heresy, his mind must have been ruminating upon more aggressive measures, including the use of force, a measure that had similarly promised remission of the temporal punishment for violence when it was harnessed on behalf of the rights and safety of Christendom. In two successive years (1204 and 1205), therefore, he begged the king of France, Philip II (r. 1180–1223), to "eradicate heretics from the French kingdom." Innocent felt that he had to turn to the secular power. In the south of France, not only did Cathars live and preach unmolested, but they also enjoyed the protection of local powers. Innocent's legate on the scene, Peter of Castelnau (d. 1208) pressured Count Raymond VI of Toulouse (d. 1222), whom some northerners thought, wrongly, to be a potentially effective hammer of heretics, to move against the southern Cathars. He refused. Peter then excommunicated him. In 1208, Peter was murdered. Though Peter was resented and likely loathed by many Cathars, suspicion fell on the count. His legate's murder infuriated Innocent and, without doubt, deepened his determination to eliminate the Cathars. He resolved to launch a crusade; in this case, that all-purpose instrument of papal foreign policy was employed, so to speak domestically, against internal or domestic enemies. While King Philip refused, despite pressure, to participate, a sizeable northern French army gathered in 1209. The result was a brutal campaign of violence against the southern Cathars and their secular (and ecclesiastical) protectors; it was known as "the Albigensian Crusade."

With the launch of a crusade, Count Raymond reversed his position, so much so that he actually himself enlisted in the crusade against the southerners. In

16. Expulsion of the Albigensians from Carcassonne in 1209 (ca. 1300–1400). Culmination of the crusade against the Albigensians (or Cathars), wearing "nothing but their sins." From Les Chroniques de France. British Library, London. Photo credit: HIP/Art Resource, NY.

July 1209, the crusaders marched on Béziers, a town totally unprepared for violent attack. A later story of dubious veracity reports that the papal legate, Arnald Amaury (d. 1225), informed that good Catholic orthodox lived in the town alongside wicked Cathar adepts, cruelly replied, "Kill them all! God will know his own!" Still, the man of God did nothing to arrest the indiscriminate slaughter, and a shameful massacre ensued. The next month, the stronghold of Carcassonne fell, also to force, and the Cathars left the town, according to an unsympathetic northern chronicler, destitute, bearing nothing, he concludes smugly, but their sins. Soon Simon de Montfort (d. ca. 1218) was elected lord of the vanquished territories. By the end of Innocent's pontificate, Simon possessed a large territory, including almost the entirety of the county of Toulouse. Southern bishops were replaced with prelates and abbots who were more determined than their predecessors to eliminate heresy. In the same year these Languedocian towns fell, canonical decrees were passed in Avignon demanding that in each parish, a priest and several laymen should take an oath to report suspected heretics. In the succeeding three years, large numbers of heretics were detected, then burned, in Lavaur, Minerve, and Cassés. This reign of terror had its desired effect. Not only did it eliminate simple Cathars and result in the pursuit, then murder, of their leaders, but it also panicked sympathizers.

The crusade also had important political results (and perhaps motivations). Once Louis VIII (r. 1223–1226) became monarch, he consolidated the conquered lands and expanded his kingdom and, of course, his control of much of what had been previously independent of royal oversight or power. He also strengthened Catholic control over the region. Once the Cathar protectors had vanished from the scene, all that was required for the utter elimination of heresy was a way of detecting, interrogating, reconverting, imprisoning, or, in extreme cases, killing heretics in more or less systematic fashion. The stage was set for the establishment of the Inquisition.

Repression: Inquisition

Those who have acquired their information about "the" Inquisition from popular film or literature and believe that they understand its motivations and functioning are sadly misled. The film based on Umberto Eco's brilliant novel, *The Name of the Rose,* not only represented monks and monasticism, the papacy and its envoys, and the local peasantry in the most grotesque possible clichés. It also grossly misrepresented the Inquisition and the famous (or infamous) Dominican inquisitor, Bernard Gui (d. 1331). Gui in fact did serve as inquisitor of Toulouse for roughly fifteen years, during which he interrogated more than nine hundred suspects in the early fourteenth century, and he wrote the most influential of many manuals on how to conduct heretical inquiries. Understandably, the film based on Eco's novel depicted the Inquisition, and Gui in particular, in the received, fallacious formulae of Hollywood: above all, hectoring, fanatical, sadistic, eager to torture and mutilate, satisfied with false confessions, and motivated by a lust for blood and the spectacle of a heretic going up in flames. While it is true that there were a tiny number of fiendish torturers (many of whom were relieved of their duties for overreliance on physical abuse), the straw man of Hollywood and of popular fiction, with the rarest exception, simply does not correspond with what we know historically—and it is a great deal, owing to the richness of the records—about inquisitorial incentive and procedure.

The stereotype originated with anti-Catholic animus, especially in Elizabethan England, and with unfamiliarity with inquisitorial procedure; ironically, it is Protestant historians who have helped to correct the most common misunderstandings, in part because of the recognition that Protestant intolerance prevailed throughout the early modern period, and suppression of heresy, and even the execution of heretics, was thought necessary by many Protestants and almost all Protestant theologians, ecclesiastics, and leaders. They, too, inhabited a world dedicated to religious orthodoxy, to the notion that truth is one, and to the persistence, or establishment, of a religiously pure society.

Neither they nor their Catholic or secular brethren would today (one hopes) ever wish to resurrect the Inquisition, much less justify or defend it; they simply wish to understand how it worked and why it was felt necessary to establish it in the context of the fight against heresy. Historians are more or less unanimous in their conviction that the age of persecution for religious ideas and ideals, as well as the Inquisitions that persecuted dissidents, remains one of the most gloomy chapters in medieval history—or rather of western history, as persecution for religious unconformity continued in the West long after the close of the Middle Ages (and began in Greece before the Common Era). Nonetheless, they are more interested in dispelling stereotypes than in issuing often anachronistic, moralistic verdicts or in inventing crude power narratives.

One of the first of the aforementioned false stereotypes is that there was *an* Inquisition. In fact, there were several, separated by chronology, intent, and architect. Here we are talking about the medieval or Papal Inquisition, *not* the Spanish or Portuguese Inquisitions, nor the Roman Inquisition of the early modern period. We go awry, too, when we imagine the Papal Inquisition as an "institution" or faceless bureaucracy with a clearly defined hierarchy and with physical plant and permanent presence. It was not. Rather, it should be understood as a legal *process*, an inquest *(inquisitio)*, developed in ad hoc fashion to deal with a current, and in the eyes of its creators, chronic and grievous problem. It involved detecting, then interrogating, those suspected of being heretics or heresiarchs. It was not without precedent. The sort of decisive action taken by the English king discussed above was rare (though laws against heretics were written into the codes of Germany, Spain, and France in the twelfth century, and the penalty, carried out by secular authorities, was death by burning). In the mid-twelfth century, the papacy asked again that rulers take action against heretics and recommended certain penalties, such as incarceration and confiscation of property. In southern Europe, this recommendation met with total failure. (By this time, secular and ecclesiastical authorities working in concert in northern Europe had begun to have, from their perspective, more success in repression.) When this call to action failed, Pope Lucius III asked bishops in 1184, in the bull *Ad Abolendam*, to conduct episcopal inquisitions of those who had been denounced as heretics. None of these inquisitorial proposals was effective (bishops were far too busy with other matters, for one thing), nor was the sort of preaching against heresy undertaken by members of the Cistercian and then the Dominican orders. Moreover, it was not easy for bishops to detect heretics in far-flung dioceses. Nor was there an established mechanism to interrogate them.

As numbers of Cathars (in particular) and other heretics grew, so did fear of heresy. Again, it is crucial to recall in a pluralistic age like ours that the church believed heretics to be in grave spiritual error and capable of jeopardizing the

salvation of others by conversion of those with whom they came into contact—
rather like the Center for Disease Control might regard a deadly worldwide flu
spread rapidly by airline travel today. It was the good—the eternal good—of
the souls of these people that motivated the church to act, and the church felt
profoundly responsible for the eternal good of the souls God had, in its view,
vouchsafed to its care. (Lest we believe this sort of attitude or harsh behavior toward dissidents was a strictly western practice of the Catholic Church, we should
note that many heretical Paulicians and Bogomils were put to death by Empress
Theodora [r. 1042–1056] and Emperor Alexius I [r. 1081–1118] respectively.) It
is not surprising to find Pope Lucius III in *Ad Abolendam*, a sort of foundation
charter for the hunting of heresy, declare that indentifying and punishing heretics
is licit, "since it is well and truly a matter of driving out sins." Accordingly, Pope
Gregory IX, who saw heresy in the same terms as Pope Lucius, in 1231–1232 issued
a series of letters that established the Inquisition (in part, it seems, to stem the
power of an imperially established secular inquisition by the Hohenstaufen)—or,
more precisely, he definitively, and this time effectively, reinvigorated legislation
already issued by prior popes. Because the skills needed were pastoral and priestly,
the inquisitors were, by and large, friars (especially Dominicans) who had been
trained as priests and not as lawyers, as virtually all popes of the age were.

Almost as soon as Gregory issued his letters, inquisitors began to extend over a
large and increasing area: first in Germany, soon in France, then in the Rhineland,
Spain, and Lombardy. In other words, they were most active in southern and
central Europe, especially the Languedoc, Lombardy, Germany, Aragon, Toulouse, Provence, Montpellier, and Carcassonne. The Franciscan friars were active
as well in Sicily, Savoy, Provence, parts of Italy, and the Dauphiné. By the close
of the fourteenth century they were represented in most parts of Europe, with
the notable exception of England, the Iberian Peninsula (there the government,
under Ferdinand and Isabella, would of course establish the Spanish Inquisition
late in the fifteenth century, though for different purposes), Aragon, Scandinavia,
and most of northern France (near the center of French royal power). Again, it
is important to remember that the Inquisition was founded primarily to detect,
combat, and in some cases punish the Cathars. In fact, in surviving documents,
like from the period under consideration here, the Cathars are sometimes simply
synonymous with "heretics."

We have emphasized that the Inquisition was staffed by and large by friars,
especially Dominicans. This is so because the primary motive of the inquisitor
was to convert or reconvert the heretic to orthodoxy, not to convict, incarcerate,
or murder. How did the Inquisition work in practice? If we could be present,
how would it have looked to us? First of all, it was normal for inquisitors to travel
in pairs, though occasionally they traveled alone. They were accompanied by a

phalanx of aides, including notaries to take reliable testimony. As traveling in this fashion became unsafe by the midpoint of the thirteenth century, inquisitors became less and less itinerant. In these conditions, witnesses had to be summoned from their villages or towns to the nerve center of the local inquisition.

Before 1250 or so, inquisitors arrived at a town or village believed to be inhabited by, or harboring, heretics. One of the inquisitors would call the people into the town square or church and typically preach a sermon on the wickedness of heresy (a sermon that parish priests often would deliver again, in essence, from their own pulpits); he would also pronounce a call for confession and (after 1235) a period of grace, conventionally lasting one or two weeks and sometimes as long as four, as well as a promise of canonical penance (again, not punishment). He would also deliver a summons, typically to those suspected of dissent, that would be delivered by parish priests. Refusal to respond to the summons within a year was tantamount to an admission of guilt and was so treated. Failure to respond could result in arrest.

Because the Inquisition possessed no powers of coercion of its own, villagers could conspire not to cooperate in supplying evidence while the inquisitors dwelt impatiently in their rooms. In some villages and towns, retaliation was a threat for anyone who did deliver information to the inquisitors. In these cases, there was little the inquisitors could do, lacking coercive power as they did, and, in most cases, they simply moved on to some other village or town.

Nonetheless, the arrival of the Inquisition could and often did result in confessions. On rare occasions a Cathar perfect would, as mentioned above, confess and, as in the case of Raynier Sacconi, become an inquisitor after being educated by the Dominicans. This *was* exceptional. Much more common was the examination of a witness who had been given a summary of charges against him, as well as some time to respond. He would not be represented by legal counsel; few lawyers would want to risk being themselves charged with defending or harboring an accused heretic, and defending one could end a legal career. Witnesses were brought in; they could include other heretics, other excommunicates, spouses, and even children (again, from several categories of witnesses not allowable in other forms of legal inquiry). The suspect was never told who had accused him, and the identities of witnesses were never revealed. This was, after all, an age of family vendetta. However, inquisitors were well aware that, as with later witch hunts, accusations could be made by those who had social or economic grievances. Accordingly, the accused was asked at the beginning of inquiry to name anyone who might bear him malice. Should he name the accuser and prove him guilty of malevolence, his case would be dismissed; the accuser would then be charged for perjuring himself before the Inquisition—an unlawful act that could itself lead to serious punishment.

The interrogation was held *in camera*—that is, in a chamber with the judge and very few others present. Conspicuous by his or her absence was any member of the public, any lawyer, and any bailiff. Aside from the inquisitor or inquisitors, a notary took record of the testimony of the witness (it was recorded in Latin, though given in the vernacular), and two witnesses from the inquisitorial staff were charged with verifying the accuracy of the deposition. The witness was asked if he had any contact with a heretic, had participated in a heretical religious ritual, had accepted heretical beliefs, or had harbored a heretic. One main purpose of the interrogation was not simply to identify guilt but to encourage the witness to name other heretics he knew, as well as those who sympathized with or harbored them.

These procedures all sound quite terrifying, and in some villages, many must have been panicked. In fact, most witnesses probably answered confidently, assured of their innocence (sadly, some of the innocent were still found guilty). In Toulouse, for example, almost six thousand witnesses were interrogated in 1245–1246; of these, less than one-tenth confessed to having had contact with heretics. Having given his or her testimony, the witness then promised to abjure heresy, avoid dissidents, and aid in their detection. Those guilty who were regarded as small fry—minor offenders and simple believers—were usually then simply dismissed and told to remain in town to wait for their penance to be established. Occasionally, the guilty had to provide money or the assurances of friends that they would not try to escape. Such a step was probably unnecessary because, with few exceptions (like mercenaries), simple villagers had extremely limited horizons; were profoundly tied to their families, communities, and hamlets; and truly could not imagine, in an age and environment that was not in the least cosmopolitan, how to escape or what to do once one had done so. Nonetheless, some did attempt to escape, and we do hear of fugitives. Leaders of heresies, Cathar perfects, relapsed heretics—in short, those found guilty of more serious offenses—were detained to wait for their sentences to be issued.

Much as one might wish, the historian cannot avoid the grisly issue of torture when discussing the Inquisition. Again, those who rely for their information on the cinema or popular fiction are likely to supply the least reliable information. To start with, the Inquisition did not, and could not, use torture for the first two decades of its existence. Nonetheless, frustrated inquisitors must have felt it was necessary, and they were granted power in 1252, after the inquisitor of Lombardy was killed by a group of Cathars, to use torture, under putatively restrictive conditions (sadly, not always observed), by the bull of Innocent IV (r. 1243–1254), *Ad Extirpanda (In Order to Root Out)*. Inquisitors resorted to the use of torture most often not on those who refused to abjure their heresy but on those who would not divulge wanted intelligence on local heretical networks. Theoretically, torture could not go so far as to cause bodily disfigurement or crippling, the spilling of blood, and of course the death of the suspect, and it was supposed to be used no more than once.

To their everlasting shame, some inquisitors routinely violated many of these procedures. Some put witnesses, not suspects, on the rack. Inquisitors themselves were rarely involved in the act of torture itself (though Pope Alexander IV [r. 1254–1261] seemed to permit it in the mid-thirteenth century by allowing inquisitors to absolve one another for participation in the infliction of pain), as it was usually administered outside the courtroom, and canon law demanded that clerics not be implicated in the shedding of blood. Some accounts reveal that a confession was made truly and freely only to disclose later in the same deposition that the suspect confessed freely after having been tortured.

It is impossible to say how often torture was used. Again, we must be careful not to caricature or exaggerate. No inquisitor was ever relieved of his duties for being too benign; only those known to be pitiless were relieved of their duties. Some of the most experienced inquisitors of the Middle Ages recognized what seems obvious to us: that a confession can be legitimate only if made freely, but torture *coerced* the suspect to confess. The frightful history of torture became only more monstrous over time, and in our day, we have come to realize that very, very few can tolerate outrageous physical persecution without blurting out something, true or not.

What happened to those who confessed or who were found guilty? Again, one has to remember that inquisitors were priests. Consequently, they handed out canonical penances to those who admitted guilt but repudiated their error. Before the penance was given by the inquisitor, the local bishop had to concur in its justice—a way to ensure that authority was not abused or ecclesiastical supremacy allowed to lapse into capricious ill treatment. It was also possible, but impossibly costly, for those on the brink of destitution to appeal a sentence to the pope, who had, awkwardly, both to head the struggle against heresy and to hear appeals of sentences from those whom he had appointed as shock troops against dissidence. Nonetheless, a high percentage of such appeals was successful.

Unlike modern Catholic practice, which ordinarily requires the penitent to utter a small number of traditional prayers in a seemingly perfunctory private ritual following absolution, medieval penances could be relatively stiff. After inquisitorial trials, judgments and penances were declared in public. The verdict was announced in a religious service called the *Sermo Generalis,* a short sermon followed by the announcement of acquittal of the innocent and conviction of the guilty. Penances for those found guilty were then pronounced. The penances ranged from fasting, to more regular or heavier church attendance, to pilgrimage to local or regional shrines (or international ones, like Rome, Compostela, Cologne, or

Canterbury—a hardship, not a lark, for the penurious and physically distressed) for more serious offenses; proof of having made the pilgrimage had to be presented upon return from these punishing and costly religious journeys. To reiterate: these penances were identical to those with which priests saddled penitents in routine acts of confession.

One exception, and a greatly feared one, was the requirement that the guilty wear a yellow cross, and in time this became the most common penance inquisitors came to levy. On the face of it, such a penance seems clement, even lenient, as it did not involve the financial and physical strain or absence from home or costs associated with the aforementioned penances. However, over time, it caused the suspect to become a community pariah with grave economic and social consequences, such as difficulty or impossibility in finding employment.

Naturally, many, especially Cathar perfects, did not recant. There is almost no evidence that they attempted to draw a veil over their beliefs and practices. To the contrary, they seem to have faced death and even exquisite physical agony phlegmatically. They responded to questioning directly. They seemed sure that they were in the right; they were thus unflappable, satisfied that God would save their souls after the boredom and physical hardship of incarceration or the anguish of fire.

Amazingly, even the dead could be convicted of heresy. In these cases, two witnesses would have to be deposed, and both would have had solemnly to swear that the deceased had been a heretic. If evidence suggested an eleventh-hour conversion to orthodoxy and the reception of extreme unction (last rites), the accused was naturally not sentenced. But in some cases a Cathar, for economic and social reasons (for example, to secure his children's inheritance), would receive ecclesiastical last rites and then call in a perfect to console him. In any case, if found guilty by the Inquisition, his bones would be disinterred and incinerated in public; the community had to be purified of the corpse that contaminated the burial ground. Even if absolutely orthodox, his descendants could suffer. None, for example, would be allowed to hold public office for two generations. In addition, costs associated with prosecution and incarceration were always contested and even perfectly orthodox Catholics, whose grandparents had been convicted two generations earlier, sometimes watched helplessly, and doubtlessly with resentment, as their property was confiscated to help defray expenses.

Occasionally, the state would confiscate the property of the guilty. Though such confiscation was not part of any inquisitorial sentence, no inquisitor ever objected. It would be wrong, however, to suspect an economic motive lurking behind the establishment and operation of the Inquisition. We must remember that these heretics pursued lives of strict poverty; they had little property and less revenue. If her husband were found guilty, a wife's dowry was never confiscated, as this would have left the woman utterly destitute. When an obdurate heretic received his sentence, he was handed over to the secular authorities for punishment. The sentence included an insincere plea for mercy, intended to shield the sentencing priest from violating the canon law forbidding involvement in the shedding of blood. At the risk of tedious repetition, it is crucial to note that inquisitors burned far fewer of the guilty than is widely believed. Again, records are imperfect and statistics unreliable. For some times and regions, however, we have good evidence. For example, in Carcassonne and Toulouse, two regions of intense inquisitorial activity in the mid-thirteenth century, roughly one of one hundred penalized were burned at the stake—in accordance with laws established by the state or political entity in question.

More common was incarceration in inquisitorial prisons. Perhaps 10–15 percent of the guilty received this penance, which was by no means an attractive one. Two types of prisons were established, the "broad wall" *(murus largus)* for those guilty of less weighty transgressions and the "narrow wall" *(murus strictus)* for heresiarchs, Cathar perfects, and the like. The lot of the latter group is truly awful to contemplate. Unlike prisoners in the broad wall, who inhabited cells with windows allowing in light and air and were allowed exercise, those in the strict wall were chained in cells with no windows and no occasion for exercise. Even beyond the physical hardships, the boredom must have been excruciating. The most such prisoners could hope for were visits by spouses, which occurred because the lay workforce could be, to the frustration of the papacy, easily bribed. A Cathar auditor could also hope for a perfect to dare to attempt to console him before death, an outcome the perfect himself would suffer if detected.

How effective was the Inquisition in eradicating heresy—that is, in achieving the goals set out for it by the papacy? No definitive response to this question is possible. To begin with, the Inquisition probably affected Cathars in different ways. Those with no previous connection to the Cathars, sympathizers, auditors, and the perfect all reacted differently; the auditors, or "listeners," the Inquisition likely frightened back to orthodoxy, the perfect it sentenced to more or less severe penances. Some argue that it is likely, in the end, that the Inquisition was just one factor in the disappearance in western Europe, within a century of its establishment, of Catharism. The Inquisition certainly made it more difficult to establish and operate conventicles (houses of the perfect). Popular preaching certainly improved. It has also been argued that the popular doctrine of the goodness of creation was more attractive to most than the grim view of the cosmos favored by the Cathars. Some argue that the heresy was already in decline and that the Inquisition merely hurried the process along. Almost all agree that the appearance on the scene of the orthodox perfect—the Dominican and Franciscan friars dedicated to poverty, preaching, and the apostolic life—accelerated the decline.

All this said, it is still likely that persecution and violence were the single most significant factors in the elimination of the Cathars. Good evidence suggests that repression of the Cathars in both the north and south of France produced defectors and refugees. The disappearance of Catharism in Germany corresponds very closely to the thirteenth-century career of Conrad of Marburg (d. 1233), who was the most devoted (and loathed) inquisitor there. In short, the role of preaching and orthodox witness were not unimportant, but persecution probably deserves the dubious prize for most effective agency in the crippling of the Cathars and the weakening of the Waldensians.

Having played a significant role in the eradication of the Cathars, the Inquisition then ironically turned its attention in the thirteenth and fourteenth centuries against dissident or "Spiritual" Franciscans, four of whom were burned in the marketplace of Marseilles in May 1318. In addition, nearly a hundred or perhaps more lay sympathizers (the "Beguines" or "tertiaries") were burned during the 1320s. In the following century, the Inquisition pursued sorcerers or those so accused. Of these, by far the most famous is Joan of Arc (d. 1431)—though it was an *episcopal* inquisitorial team that convicted her. Equally well known is the posthumous "nullification trial," resulting in a papal reversal of this decision in the mid-fifteenth century and the anomalous canonization of a convicted heretic who had been burned at the stake, now made, along with luminaries like St. Denis and Martin of Tours, a patron saint of France. In the fifteenth century, one of the most famous literary works of the Inquisition was produced. Written by two Dominicans with experience as inquisitors, it was entitled *The Hammer of Witches (Malleus Maleficarum)*. It would be used by Protestant as well as Catholic hunters of witches.

The Inquisition took new form (the "Spanish Inquisition") under Isabella (r. 1474–1504) and Ferdinand II of Aragon (r. 1474–1516) in Castile and Aragon, where, because it was an office of the government, it was efficiently and horribly brutal. The two monarchs were anxious about Jews and Muslims who had claimed, falsely it was alleged, to have converted to Christianity and wanted to ensure that they were practicing Catholicism rather than reverting to their old cults. The justly infamous Torquemada (d. 1498), a Dominican and very possibly of Jewish ancestry, supported the expulsion and burning not only of accused crypto-Jews and Muslims, but also of their books, including the Talmud. Thousands of victims were burned during his decade and a half as inquisitor. Like Gui, Torquemada was immortalized, though to shame rather than glory, in a literary work—in his case by no less a figure than Victor Hugo, who used him to protest against the anti-Semitism in France. He has also appeared in other literary works (like Dostoevsky's *Crime and Punishment,* in the guise of the Grand Inquisitor), operas, and films. All associate him with triumphalist and even fanatical Catholicism. In 1832 his enemies disinterred and burned his bones in a well-justified orgy of revenge and rancor.

The Reformation in the north of Europe profoundly and permanently changed the shape and practices of the old western church. What did not change was the conviction that religious coercion was required to intimidate, try, and penalize heretics. Nor did the reformers challenge the ancient Catholic idea that religious orthodoxy was unitary and given by God. Religious belief was simply not, as today, a matter of private judgment but of deep communal and ecclesiastical concern. Very few reformers doubted that orthodoxy had to be safeguarded, and most agreed that severe punishment and even death was not only licit but obligatory. Jerome Zanchi, a reformed theologian at the University of Heidelberg, crisply summed up the current view: "We do not now ask if the authorities *may* pronounce sentence of death upon heretics. Of that there can be no doubt, and all learned and right-minded men acknowledge it. The only question is whether the authorities *are bound* to perform that duty." With his Catholic adversaries, as well as his reformed colleagues, he concluded that, in fact, they *were* so obliged. Intolerance of religious dissent did not begin, nor did it end, with the Middle Ages.

Dominicans and Their Sisters

Part of the crisis the friars faced was, of course, heresy, and there can be little doubt that simply by their way of life, they did much to check its spread. But they also ministered to a new, urban, commercial population that had been largely despaired of, ignored, and given to believe that it was, at best, demi-Christian. The story of the Dominican and Franciscan response to these crises is largely a narrative of towering pastoral and intellectual achievement. These orders became masters of the art of preaching, of confessing, of teaching, and of serving royalty and the papacy. They Christianized the life of merchants and townfolk and created a new piety for those seeking holiness outside the precincts of the monastery. Virtually every master of note in the new universities was a friar. Eventually, they would bear the Christian message to the Far East.

Dominic and the Dominicans

The beginnings of the Dominican Order are intimately linked to the growth of the Cathar heresy in the south of France. The Dominicans are associated, too, with the failure of previous attempts, on the part of papal legates and members of the Cistercian Order, to restore orthodox order in the region. To reestablish conventional belief in the Midi (the south of France), orthodox preachers would have to match the austerity of the Cathar perfects and earn the reverence of Cathar supporters and sympathizers. In Dominic's view they would also have to be trained in theology and preaching in order to win converts back to orthodoxy. It was Dominic's genius to perceive that no preachers could compete against the Cathars unless they could effectively preach, so to speak, as orthodox perfects. The conviction that learning, poverty, and fairly traditional monastic observance could prepare preachers for this task, combined with the profound confidence that heresy was intolerable for the church—and mortally dangerous to souls—gave Dominic's new order its initial shape and mission, as well as many of its enduring features.

Dominic of Caleruega (d. 1221) was born in Castile—that is, in a region of Spain known for militant opposition to Muslim invasion and occupation, as well as for the avid practice of, and attachment to, orthodox Christianity. Dominic would later translate that regional combative zeal into international fervor against groups he would perceive to be a menace to orthodox Christianity. Probably born into an aristocratic family, Dominic was educated in liberal and scriptural studies as a cleric in the schools of Valencia. That, too, is an important fact from his early life. For the order that would bear his name would, from the start (and in stark contrast to the order founded by Francis), be a learned and clerical one.

Once his education was complete, Dominic took a canonry in 1196 at the Cathedral of Osma, the diocese into which he had been born. The cathedral chapter, at the time Dominic joined it, had recently established itself as a community of regular canons. They therefore observed the *Rule* of St. Augustine, and Dominic became an Augustinian canon. Not long after vowing to observe this rule, Dominic was ordained a priest. In 1201, he was elected subprior of his chapter. Contemporary sources do not give us for Dominic the relative abundance of personal and biographical information that they supply for Francis, and his personality remains thus somewhat enigmatic. But we are told, by both contemporary sources and those connected with his canonization process, that he was committed to profound scriptural study and that he treasured the monastic writings of John Cassian. He seems to have been both charismatic and genuinely humble. As a sign of simplicity, he walked unshod; he would put shoes on only as he entered a town, lest he seem to be advertising his humility.

His zeal for orthodoxy and his personal growth and development in a region of Europe vigorously committed to the Reconquista are personal traits that emerge in the subsequent narrative of his life. In 1203, Dominic was chosen to accompany his bishop, Diego d'Azevedo (d. 1207), on a diplomatic mission to Denmark. It was on this occasion that Dominic first encountered the Albigensian heresy. While staying overnight in Toulouse, he was horrified to learn that his host was a Cathar. Characteristically, he stayed up with him all night, attempting to argue him out of his heresy; our source tells us, perhaps not entirely convincingly, that Dominic brought him back within the bounds of orthodoxy. He also had a legendarily famous dispute with Cathars at Fanjeaux, west of the Cathar stronghold of Carcassonne. Three years later, this time returning from a mission to the Danish court, Dominic and his bishop ran into the Cistercian monks who had been selected to preach against the Cathars. From them, they heard a report of failure and dis-

17. Detail of relief panel, tomb of Saint Dominic Guzman, San Domenico, Bologna. From *Cathar Heretics before Saint Dominic, 1170–1221; the Dispute of Fanjeaux,* by Nicolo Pisano (ca. 1220–1284). At Fanjeaux, near Carcassonne, forbidden books were burned. Photo credit: Gianni Dagli Orti / The Art Archive at Art Resource, NY.

appointment. They had reconverted no one; moreover, they had been ridiculed and treated as frauds by the Cathars.

Diego at once perceived the problem. Their efforts were bound to be futile, he observed, traveling as they were with horses, large retinues, and in the style of ecclesiastical dignitaries. If they were to succeed with the perfects or, more likely, with those who sympathized with and supported them, they too had to live a life of evangelical austerity. As it was, their evangelical message stood in stark, hopeless contrast with their prelatical style. Living as they did, they could only expect to fail with the Cathars. With this observation, Diego and Dominic persuaded the Cistercians to join them in a new preaching mission. All sent home servants and horses and adopted the now culturally familiar appearance and behavior of the itinerant preacher, setting out shoeless and propertyless, utterly dependent upon alms-giving for food and other necessities.

It is not impossible that this mission had been discussed in Rome with Pope Innocent III on the Spaniards' return from Denmark. But there is no doubt that the mission corresponded with the pope's own anti-heretical agenda. Not surprisingly, the pope lent the anti-heretical mission his unqualified support. With papal enthusiasm for this mission, the abbot of Cîteaux, Arnald Amaury, accompanied by numbers of his brothers, joined Diego and Dominic. The company of monks and canons traveled at a rapid pace from town to town. We hear of many disputes with the Cathars in the sources and even of some converts to orthodox Christianity. It is sometimes said that the convent of Prouille was at this point established for women converts from Catharism. This, however, is now uncertain; more certain is that it would become a center of orthodoxy and a preaching center for the Dominicans and, in the end, an orthodox convent for Dominican nuns. In any event, not long thereafter, Diego, having helped Dominic launch his preaching mission, would die in Osma.

Staffed as it was, in part, by Cistercian monks, the preaching mission led by the Spaniards had, of necessity, to be ephemeral; the white monks would soon return to their cloisters. As this preaching mission broke up, a brutal but effective crusade was, as we saw in the last chapter, launched against princes protecting the Cathars in the south of France. By 1215, once the war had been won by the northerners, Dominic received property in Toulouse from some of the victors. More than that, the bishop of the city, Fulk (d. 1231), invited Dominic in 1215 to launch and manage a new preaching mission. With Fulk's support and approval, Dominic organized a group of preachers designed to stamp out heresy and also to instruct people in faith and morals. At this point, the preachers had authority to work only in the diocese of Toulouse. But the Dominicans—the Order of Preachers—had been established.

In 1215 Dominic sought from Innocent III papal confirmation of his order. This was at the very moment when the Fourth Lateran Council, just then meeting, was attempting to put the brakes on what it perceived to be the uncontrolled proliferation of orders and unbridled experimentation in forms of religious life. In this context, Dominic was encouraged rather to choose an existing, traditional rule. It is not surprising that as a canon, he chose the *Rule* of St. Augustine, which he supplemented with statutes that would govern the details of his new order's religious observance. Canonically speaking, the Dominicans were thus a singular group of canons regular. Part of their singularity consisted in their renunciation of property (save churches, which they would need, as canons regular, to say the offices) and their resolve to travel and preach in apostolic poverty. As their order evolved, they would eventually need and acquire more property, and they never exhibited (and could even find fault with) Francis's fanatical zeal for absolute corporate destitution.

In January 1217, Pope Honorius III (r. 1216–1227) approved the name of the new order, the "Order of Friars Preachers" (Ordo Praedicatorum, usually abbreviated O.P.) and empowered the entire community with the right to preach—a novelty in the history of the church, as the privilege of preaching had traditionally depended on episcopal approval and authorization (as the example of the Waldensians vividly recalls for us). Several months later, at the Pentecost chapter, Dominic announced a mission whose scope would far exceed the one imagined by Bishop Fulk of Toulouse, who was not pleased with the Spaniard's vastly more ambitious plans. Much had changed since Dominic had become a canon regular. Given episcopal permission to preach to heretics in Toulouse, the small order with a tightly focused charge quickly transformed itself into an order with an international mission.

Now Dominic was intent, with papal approval, on a universal preaching operation—that is, not simply in the province of Narbonne, but also to the nations of Europe—to Christendom. While retaining houses in Prouille and Toulouse, he sent friars to establish communities in Spain and other parts of France and Italy. Fatefully (and intentionally) for the future of the order and its impact, the cities to which Dominic chose to send his friars included Paris (a group of seven friars, the largest, was sent here) and Bologna, the sites of the two greatest universities in Europe, the former distinguished for the study of theology, the latter for law.

The new order would grow in these university cities and around the universities. By 1218, it had taken possession of the hospice of St. Jacques, on the left bank of the Seine in Paris, which would eventually house St. Thomas Aquinas and a succession of distinguished scholars for centuries. In Bologna, the preaching friars accepted the gift of the church of St. Nicholas (later named after Dominic), which stood in the center of the university quarter; soon a convent was established to house scholars. Three years later, the friars crossed the Channel and arrived in England. The archbishop of Canterbury offered them a residence in that great episcopal town. Yet the friars pressed on, settling in Oxford, the academic center for which they had, apparently, been aiming all along.

The desire to target centers of university learning naturally had implications for the demographics of recruiting. Most of the friars preachers were drawn from the sons of lesser nobility, the burgher class, and other sorts of professionals, like notaries. By the 1240s, the Dominicans were even drawing recruits away from several monastic orders, including the Cistercians. Above all, the Dominicans would target students and masters at the newly established universities of Europe. Dominic's successor as minister general, Jordan of Saxony (d. 1237), would similarly concentrate his visitation and preaching itineraries in the university cities, with outstanding success. In 1226, for example, more than twenty friars were recruited in Paris from the ranks of masters of arts and bachelors. Three years later, in

Oxford, another large number of recruits donned the black habit in Oxford. It would not be long before Paris and Bologna had definitively replaced Toulouse as the center cities of the order.

As we have seen, the Cistercians had begun the custom of admitting *conversi,* or lay brethren, to their cloisters—and in large numbers. The lay brethren were badly needed in order to help develop the sizeable estates of a rapidly growing order located in the uncultivated rural regions of Europe. The Dominicans, as town dwellers, possessed no lands and thus needed no labor for agriculture. Nonetheless, the friars preachers did throw open their doors to lay brethren, though on a much smaller scale than the Cistercians. Brought in with the explicit aim of freeing the clerical brethren for study, the lay brethren performed essential manual labor in the Dominican houses.

Yet it would be a mistake to assume that the same sort of social discrimination and separation that existed in the Cistercian cloisters prevailed in the Dominican convents. Not only did the lay brethren join the clerical brothers in choir for offices (something, we recall, the Cistercian lay brethren did not do, in part because they were laboring in distant fields at the canonical hours). The Dominican *conversi* also served as sextons, in charge of liturgical vestments and vessels. Moreover, they joined in the diurnal search for alms and occasionally joined the clerical brothers on their preaching and recruiting journeys. In other words, socially speaking, the Dominicans were, in the world of religious orders, revolutionaries, as the Franciscans would be. Both orders eliminated social distinctions within the cloister, distinctions that outside the convents seemed hard and fast—even ordained by God.

Not long before he would die, Dominic convened the first general chapters of the order. Meeting in Bologna in 1220 and 1221, the Dominicans memorably stated in the prologue to the constitutions enacted at the first chapter that the purpose of the order was "the health of souls," especially by preaching, and that their "zeal should be chiefly and ardently directed to the end that we can be useful to the souls of our neighbors." Seen against the backdrop of the Benedictine *Rule,* this is an important moment in the history of Christian religious orders. The goal of one following the Benedictine *Rule* was his own supernatural perfection; the aim of the aspiring Dominican was the spiritual direction and guidance of his neighbor.

Beyond this significant shift in the direction and purposes of the religious life, the constitutions passed in Bologna also enacted statutes intended to augment those adopted in 1216. Among other things, the order dedicated itself to mendicancy, or begging. The statutes enacted at Bologna prohibited the ownership of property or fixed revenues. They allowed the friars to keep only the properties and priories already standing; in the long run, it would become obvious that the friars preachers, who were destined to be an order of students and masters, would need convents in which to study, as well as churches in which to say their offices (and then attract large audiences of sermon-hearers). Initially, though, like the Franciscans, the Dominicans had chosen corporate poverty and begging; Jordan of Saxony, who was also Dominic's biographer, suggests that he initiated these statutes in order to liberate the brethren from the duty of managing property, so that "preaching [would not be] impeded." Some, relying perhaps too heavily on contemporary Franciscan testimony, have suggested that the friars preachers' decision was influenced by the pattern established by the Friars Minor (that is, the Franciscans; see chapter 12).

The organizational structure of the Dominicans was completed by the general chapter of 1221. It divided the order into provinces, ratified statutes for their government, and launched friars to establish houses in Denmark, England, Germany, Hungary, and Poland. The English group was the largest, consisting of thirteen friars, who were soon enrolled as students at Oxford. The statutes enacted by the order for the governance and organization of the provinces are in many ways, if not wholly unprecedented, an important moment in the movement from monarchical or autocratic to representative and constitutional forms of government. Indeed, it has been credibly suggested that the construction of such forms of government in the religious sphere encouraged their development in the secular realm. Be that as it may, the minister general of the order was elected by a general chapter; he could be corrected and even removed by the chapter. Each province had a provincial; he also was elected, as was the prior of each convent. With these epochal constitutional successes, which several orders imitated, Dominic died in August 1221. His death occurred in Bologna, which thenceforth would serve as the capital city of the order. At his death, he had established one of the great orders in the history of Christianity.

Yet Dominic, visionary though he was, could not have anticipated the rapid growth of the order under his successors, beginning with the supremely competent Jordan of Saxony. In 1221, at Dominic's death, there were some twenty houses scattered across Europe. Not fifteen years later, there were one hundred. By 1280, that number had quadrupled to four hundred. By the mid-fourteenth century, there were something on the order of thirteen thousand friars scattered across twelve thriving provinces.

Everywhere, the friars preachers formed themselves in the new or newly revitalized cities of Europe. The fifth minister general of the Dominicans, Humbert of Romans (d. 1277), explained in part why the friars preachers had chosen cities: "There preaching is more efficacious because there are more people, and the need is greater, for in the city there are more sins." Naturally, it followed for Humbert that contrition and confession must occur regularly in urban areas. In addition, heresies generally thrived in cities, and it was, by and large, on urban battle-grounds that the struggle for orthodoxy would be fought. In addition to these demographic and religious factors, there is the simple economic fact (which the friars' enemies would soon use to pour scorn on them) that only cities could, with surplus housing and wealth, support groups of mendicant monks, who would arrive in town and begin begging.

Learning

Another, decisive aspect of Dominican settlement strategy was the founder's intent from the outset that his be a learned order and that the brothers be set up in centers of education. Jordan of Saxony made this aim a major part of his life's work and of his indefatigable travels to recruit at universities. One brother reports that Jordan devoted all his energy to attracting to his order concentrations of scholars, above all in Paris. His efforts were reflected in the constitutional, educational, and even architectural structure of the order's houses.

Each Dominican convent was equipped with a classroom. There all the clerical friars heard lectures and participated in disputation. The educational leader of the convent was a trained master or a professor, called a *lector*. His main job was to lecture the brothers on the Bible. He would also lecture on the enormously influential *Historia Scholastica (Scholastic History)* of Peter Comestor (d. ca. 1180)—the name means "Peter the Eater," bestowed upon him for all the learning he, the chancellor of the cathedral school of Notre-Dame-de-Paris, devoured. The *Scholastic History* presented itself as a universal history book and was based largely on the Bible, other ancient but secular sources, and some of the writings of the church fathers. It would be widely read in the universities, translated into scores of vernaculars, and printed frequently. The friars, who would become popular confessors across Europe, were also given training in moral theology, penance, and the sacrament of confession by studying the treatise, composed in 1242 on those subjects, by Spanish brother Raymond of Penaforte (d. 1275).

Outside the convents, but still within a system of Dominican schools, brothers who had demonstrated an aptitude for study began to study the logical works of Aristotle (or, as the Dominican statutes repugnantly referred to them, "the books of the heathen"). Aristotle's logical works were an indispensable preparation for study of all forms of scholastic theology and biblical exegesis. Yet anxious that the brethren not learn their Aristotle in the uncontrolled environment of the universities, the Dominicans supplied this essential philosophical background in their own schools.

The most able friars were destined for one of the order's "general schools" *(studia generalia)*. These were all located in university centers, of which by far the most distinguished was Paris. But eventually very fine *studia generalia* were established at Bologna, Oxford, Cologne (which Albert the Great's massive learning would make famous), Montpellier, Barcelona, and Florence. The lives and even living arrangements of these friars were constructed around study. Yet none of this study was intended for the educational or cultural enrichment of the friar. Rather, education had, especially at this elite level, a religious or, better, an ecclesiastical, purpose: readying those who were preparing to preach.

Certain modifications to the normal Dominican monastic regime were introduced to enable certain brothers to pursue their studies or pastoral work. One of Dominic's intentions was to maintain a monastic framework to the friars' day. While his intentions were only decisively organized by Raymond of Penaforte during the latter's time as minister general (1238–1240), no one disputes that Raymond's plan represents the vision of Dominic himself. As with regular canons, the days of the friars preachers were punctuated by regular choral recitation of offices in choir. Other monastic practices, like daily chapter, perpetual silence (except in certain places in the convents), and periods of fasting were also observed.

Yet Raymond's program very intentionally included modifications and concessions for study and for the pastoral mission of the order. For example, he suggested that offices be sung "briefly" in order that the student brethren be allowed time for study. Again, no brother, except for lay brethren, was to be involved in manual labor. Priors of any convent were allowed to release any brother from office for either study or preaching. Friars studying at Paris in order to become conventual theologians, or lectors, were given even broader permission to absent themselves from liturgical offices for the purpose of academic work.

While many continue to imagine the Dominicans in the caricatured images of sinister friars staffing the Inquisition, there are other sides of their mission that have come to be better known and, in our age, appreciated and admired. For example, the friars transformed the concluding office of the monk's day, compline, from a private to a public service. Eventually, this attracted a large number of city-folk, who had by then finished their day's work; it became a very popular service among townspeople in the churches of the friars preachers across Europe.

Beguines, Dominican Sisters, and the Friars Preachers

The Dominicans also were deeply and interestingly involved in the religious lives of women who wished to follow them in their way of life. We have already mentioned the foundation at Prouille. Dominic himself established convents of women in Madrid in 1218 and in San Sisto in 1221; in fact the sole extant text from his pen is a letter of unknown date addressed to the Dominican sisters in Madrid. In accordance with socio-ecclesial norms of the day, Dominic could not picture his female fellow travelers as active partners collaborating with his friars in their itinerant preaching mission. Instead, he provided for them a more traditional regime, based upon the conventional monastic system, above all strict inclaustration. Yet he was very far from opposed, as later brethren could be, to affiliation with his order. As the thirteenth century wore on, increasing numbers of convents sought affiliation with the Dominicans.

These nunneries were, by and large, socially exclusive. However, that was not true of a new form of religious life in the cities of the Low Countries, Germany, and northern France: that undertaken by the so-called Beguines. Unlike their Dominican sisters, Beguines by and large were daughters (or widows) of the commercial classes; some were quite poor and earned their living as nurses or maids in hospitals and leprosaries. Others wove. Again, unlike the Dominican sisters, the Beguines took no irrevocable vows but did renounce personal wealth. Some scandalized social convention by begging for their food; other Beguinages, as their houses were called, were generously endowed by patrons or recruits. Some worked in the cities where their houses were located. As the Beguinages were situated in the towns of Europe (beginning in the Low Countries but spreading widely in Germany and then to most parts of Europe), the Beguines found themselves in the same cities as the Dominican friars. The assistance of these, as spiritual directors and confessors, they sought and often received.

These relationships were so successful that many Beguinages eventually sought incorporation into the Dominican Order. Though their way of life initially drew strong support from illustrious admirers like Robert Grosseteste (d. 1253), a British theologian and ultimately bishop of Lincoln, and though the papacy took the Beguines under its protection beginning with Gregory IX, they were often suspected of heresy (leading some to ponder a verbal connection between "Beguine" and "Albigensian," suggestive of the taint of heresy). Nonetheless, they flourished in the fourteenth century. In Cologne, for example, there were more than 160 houses at the turn of the fourteenth century. Two hostile decrees enacted against them began their decline, but visitors to towns in Belgium and elsewhere can still see many fine Beguinages, in part because they were revived in the early modern period and today serve as handsome apartments.

Perhaps it is even more remarkable that strong relationships developed between some friars preachers and Dominican nuns, Beguines and others, whom they guided. Recent study has shown that some friars so admired the women with whom they were associated that they vigorously encouraged them to record their spiritual experiences. On occasion, the friars drew up their own records of their female associates' religious experiences. In some cases, both nun and friar did, and in these cases there is often evidence of bowdlerizing on the part of the friars, an attempt to reconcile their female associates' extraordinary religious experiences with traditional, canonical, and accepted norms of female religious conduct. In other cases, where personal relations were maintained by epistolary correspondence, it is quite clear that these men and women had profound affection for one another and, in cases, maintained friendships through letter writing. Intriguingly, it also seems as if roles were occasionally reversed, and the friars received spiritual inspiration from those they were supposedly guiding.

These trends may have begun as early as the minister generalship of Jordan of Saxony. In this case, Jordan helped to establish the Dominican convent of St. Agnes in Bologna, of which the patrician Diana d'Andalo (d. 1236) became patron and first prioress. Jordan served Diana as spiritual director. But a remarkable series of letters written over fourteen years (1222–1236) indicates that the two established a warm friendship. Those of Diana have not survived, but Jordan's indicate that Diana sometimes imperiously stood in judgment of the pastoral performance of the local friars. She urged Jordan to intervene with the secular clergy, some of whom questioned the relationship of her community with the Dominican Order.

In some cases, as noted, it seems as if the men in the relationship came to depend upon the inspiration and guidance of charismatic women, and conventional relationships of authority were reversed. For example, Peter of Dacia (d. ca. 1289), a Swedish Dominican, carried on a correspondence with a Beguine, Christine of Stommeln (d. 1312). In addition, he made numerous visits to her. Here, the charismatic figure is Christine. A visionary from age five, she was said to have received the stigmata at the age of fifteen and repeatedly had sensational encounters with the Devil. Again, a lifelong friendship with Peter was established. In this case, it is she who seems to have authority in her relationship with Peter, who openly acknowledges the religious blessings and gifts he receives from his charismatic, if not institutional, superior. Indeed, he practically admits to having been a religious mediocrity until he met Christine, whose experiences set his soul afire and with whom he maintained a passionate, if chaste, friendship.

Perhaps no better illustration of these themes is embodied than in the relationship between the Dominican nun Margaret Ebner (d. 1351) and her secular confessor, Henry of Nördlingen (d. ca. 1351). Around 1330, Henry persuaded Margaret to make a record of her religious experiences. She did. Entitled *Revelations,* the text is written in the vernacular (Middle High German) and belongs to a specific genre of medieval women's mystical writings, which it both reflected and helped to shape: the autohagiography, or record of religious experiences composed by the one having them rather than by a pious admirer. In female autohagiographies of the period—in female religious writing in general from this era—physical illness often induces, accompanies, or follows upon extraordinary religious experiences. This was the case with Margaret. For three years (1312–1315), she was quite ill. Having recovered, Margaret embarked upon an extraordinary regime of asceticism. She mortified, flagellated, and starved her body; in this sense she reflects a pervasive devotional theme of the moment, when women's religious experiences were inscribed on their bodies. To select just one illustration from Margaret's remarkable array of experiences, one of her visions, sparked by intense reflection on a small wooden figure of the Christ child, led to an experience of miraculous lactation after the figure in her devotion asks Margaret to nurse him. There is no doubt but that Margaret had an intense devotional relationship with this carved figure, for which she cared, sometimes swaddling it, then cradling it, then rocking it to sleep. We know for certain that Margaret's *Revelations,* and texts like it, were found and used in Dominican monasteries, chock full as they were with narratives of devotional regimes and sanctified lives thought worthy of imitation by those who acquired them for their cloisters.

While there are profoundly somatic and visual components of Margaret's religious experience, textual influences and exchanges were important as well. The letters between Margaret and Henry reveal, among other things, that Dominican sisters were quite familiar with the writings of their Dominican brothers, figures like Meister Eckhart (d. ca. 1328), John Tauler (d. 1361), and Henry of Suso (d. 1366)—some of the greatest male mystics and mystical writers of the later Middle Ages. The letters also establish, again, that the two Dominicans, one a nun and one a friar preacher, had established a friendship both mirrored by and strengthened in the exchange of their letters.

Similarly, later in the Middle Ages, the Dominican friar Raymond of Capua (d. 1399) would befriend the forceful Dominican tertiary Catherine of Siena (d. 1380). Indeed, he would write her *vita,* presenting her in conventional categories (like bridal mystic) even as she wrote about herself and acted in all-but-traditional ways. In this case, it is probably fair to say that we would not know of Raymond if it were not for the accomplishments of his more famous Dominican sister, Catherine. In almost all these cases, there is tension, more or less explicit, between the traditional male prerogatives of authority, on the one hand, and, on the other, the friars' candid fascination with and admiration for those they admitted to be their spiritual, pious, or mystical superiors. In most cases, the friars preachers saw (and in cases envied) their confessees' relationship with God as unlike theirs—indeed privileged, unique, direct, and very different than their own, dryer, indirect experience.

This brief picture should not be taken to represent the views of the male Dominican Order as a whole in its understanding of its relationship to female confessees, spiritual advisees, or those to whom they dispensed sacramental services. Indeed, even one with so happy a relationship with women, and so powerful a position as minister general, as Jordan of Saxony could find himself powerless, during his generalate, to stop the annual chapter from strictly limiting the extent of fraternal ministry to Dominican nunneries. In the chapter of 1240, statutes were enacted that went so far as to forbid friars to administer sacraments to nuns, save the hearing of confessions. Papal intervention preserved Dominic's own foundations at Prouille and Rome in securing exemptions from these harsh measures. Even so, for a time, it seemed as if the Dominican nuns (like so many twelfth-century religious orders) stood in grave danger of being abandoned by their male brethren. Only with the support of the Dominican cardinal Master Hugh of St. Cher (d. 1264) and Humbert of Romans was it understood that the friars preachers had an obligation to care for the religious and spiritual needs of their Dominican sisters. Yet the whole story illustrates how precarious was the very existence of female religious orders in the twelfth and thirteenth centuries, how dependent upon the whims of brothers who could be variously motivated by sincere desire to concentrate on the order's primary mission or, at the other end of the spectrum, by frank misogyny.

Hounds of the Lord: Inquisitors

Having touched on these decidedly happier elements of the Dominican mission, we turn now to their role as papal inquisitors. Once Pope Gregory IX established a permanent inquisition, he delegated the task of inquisitors to the friars preachers. Almost simultaneously, two domains of France were put under the control of the Dominicans. In fact, the north of France was given over to the infamous Robert le Bougre (d. 1263). He was one of the very few Cathars who not only reconverted but, like Raynier Sacconi, also functioned as an inquisitor. Like many converts to any religious group, he was among the most dedicated—and the most ruthless. In 1239, he presided over one inquest at La Charité-sur-Loire that eventuated in a terrible burning of large numbers of the convicted there. Once the Inquisition was established in France, it was then set up in Italy. Again, the Dominicans were, at first, entrusted with what, to the papacy and to the order, was an essential task. Like France, Italy was divided into two areas of inquisitorial activity, the north and the central, with Dominican provincials heading both and appointing friars to their jobs. Their dedication to the reconversion of the heretical eventually earned the Dominican inquisitors the nickname *Domini canes* (hounds of the Lord).

Why were the Franciscans initially not more involved? We can only speculate, but the significantly lay portion of the friars minor in the first decades of the operation of the Inquisition may have discouraged Pope Gregory. Perhaps he trusted a clerical order that was, from the start, learned, as well as pledged to the eradication of error and the establishment of orthodoxy. It was the Dominicans, in the end, who provided many of the literary monuments to the Inquisition. As early as 1242, the Dominican Raymond of Penaforte composed a manual designed to guide friars in their inquisitorial activity. Raynier Sacconi, the sometime Cathar, wrote a more elaborate manual, only to be outdone by his Dominican brother Bernard Gui, whose *Conduct of Inquiry Concerning Heretical Depravity* (ca. 1307–1323) runs to roughly four hundred folio-sized pages and still serves as a major source of our knowledge of heresy and inquisitorial procedure in the fourteenth century. The Dominican hegemony over the literature of inquisition was almost complete. However, in the fourth and fifth decades of the thirteenth century, Pope Innocent IV began to recruit Franciscans for the task. It was he, too, who, in the wake of the murder of Peter of Verona (d. 1252), the Dominican inquisitor of Lombardy, authorized the use of torture in his chillingly entitled 1252 bull *Ad Extirpanda*. Eventually, Italy would be divided into eight inquisitorial districts, of which fully six were given over to the Franciscans. By this time, the friars minor resembled the Dominicans in that they were a clerical, learned order.

As the murder of Peter of Verona suggests, the friars who staffed the Inquisition were not just feared but loathed. One historian, somewhat implausibly, has suggested that Pope Innocent IV mobilized the Franciscans out of fear that the fervor of the Dominicans in carrying out their task had aroused popular hostility to a murderous intensity. Yet there is no evidence to suggest that the Franciscans pursued their task any less eagerly, nor that they were received popularly with any more affection. Indeed, *any* friar inquisitor very naturally would have been regarded, at best, with suspicion and fear and, at worse, with mortal hostility—this regardless of the inquisitors' intentions. At the end of the thirteenth century, a riot occurred in Bologna after the Dominican friars conducted an inquest there. They were popularly denounced as bloodthirsty and avaricious. Some identified the inquisitor himself as the Antichrist and, ipso facto, a heretic who himself ought to be burned—along with the other friars in his retinue. Only where the friars enjoyed the cooperation of secular powers and where political authority was strong were they safe and effective. Kings and emperors, as well as lesser political figures, viewed these heretics as what we might call political dissenters (the distinction between the religious and secular does not truly apply to this world) and agreed with the pope and friars that they needed to be repressed, violently if necessary.

Masters

Nonetheless, it is not for their predominant role in the Inquisition that the Dominicans have earned the affection and admiration of recent generations of popes and theologians. Rather, it is because the order produced an astonishing series of prominent theologians, professors (or "masters"), and intellectuals. These friars would bequeath to the academy and church an astonishing corpus, both in size and intellectual caliber, of biblical commentary and theological work. No order so successfully cast Christian theology in the categories of Aristotelian logic and metaphysics. It may be that no other medieval order produced so many intellectual giants—friars like Thomas Aquinas, whose influence runs down to our own day. To this narrative we will turn below.

Fraticelli: Franciscans and Their Sisters

By those who admired and followed him, Francis was regarded as a new, second, or "another" Christ *(alter Christus)*. Historians in search of the historical Francis are, like those in quest of the historical Jesus, challenged in their attempts at reconstruction by a remarkably similar array of critical issues. Just as there has been a scholarly quest (several quests, actually) for the historical Jesus, so there has been a "Franciscan Question." The followers of both men, and especially those who wrote about them, regarded them as figures of pivotal significance in the history of salvation. Consequently, they generated many literary and oral sources about the men whom they venerated. In both cases, these sources require cautious handling and critical scrutiny.

The major sources for both men are not, strictly speaking, biographies, though both include some reliable historical and biographical information. But biographical facts were not the essential interest. Rather, those who wrote about them were more interested in the cosmic and messianic significance of both men; they thought their subjects carried a message from God (as, indeed, their subjects surely did), and this matter decisively shaped the picture they presented of their divine heroes. In the *Paradiso,* Dante imagines Francis as a rising sun (*Canto* 11:52–54). Later, his rigorist followers would identify him with the sixth Angel of the Apocalypse (Apoc. 9:13–15) and "another Christ," sent providentially to convert the world. For that reason, it has proven difficult to distinguish historical fact from later devout fabrication or hagiographical embellishment. Beyond that, later sources depend on earlier ones, and those later sources were written, in part, because of different, in some cases incompatible, views regarding their subject's character and soteriological significance.

All sources were written primarily with a theological or religious point to make; none is transparent to the figure whose life it claims to mirror. Finally, all are separated in time from their subjects, to a greater or lesser degree (one life of Francis is separated from its author's death by only two years, yet it is still not historically unproblematic), and the fragility of memory, as well as the ferocity and ubiquity of ecclesial "politics," distorts, and many, it is very clear, depend on tradition, not the testimony of eyewitnesses.

In the case of Francis, we have a few short writings; Jesus wrote nothing at all. Neither was, in his way of life or teaching, wholly novel; both can be fit comfortably into their religio-cultural environments. Yet both taught and lived *something* new. Both were uncompromising in the demands they placed on themselves and their immediate disciples. Yet the sources mediating them to us are written to audiences that could not possibly imitate the radicalism of their lifestyle or conform to the severities of their teaching. To borrow a concept from the German social scientist Max Weber (d. 1920), their charisma had, if it were to perdure in some sense, to be institutionalized—and thus, inevitably, flattened. This process of institutionalization would ultimately split the order and cause unwelcome papal intervention.

In the case of Jesus of Nazareth, many authors, dependent on a complex array of common and particular sources, wrote "gospels," which contain *and* conceal biographical information regarding this ancient Mediterranean Jewish prophet. Of the many gospels written in the century or so following Jesus's death, four, the so-called "canonical" gospels, entered lists of the authoritative New Testament texts. Three of these, the "synoptic" gospels (Matthew, Mark, and Luke), overlap considerably, though close analysis reveals that each of the synoptic evangelists viewed Jesus somewhat differently than the other two; each, as we would say today, had his own "Christology." None can be reconciled, scholars agree, without offense to the literary-theological aim of the evangelist or the fabric of his text. This is in part because there was, we now recognize, an amazing variety of "early Christianities." Put another way, each distinct party of Jesus-Jews and, then, Jesus-Gentiles had its own interpretation and its own traditions regarding its Lord. Even more difficult to reconcile are the synoptic gospels, as a group, with the Fourth Gospel, the one traditionally credited to John. His Christology is so different, so much "higher" than that of the synoptics, that theological reconciliation is impossible, and his narrative so unlike that of the synoptics that historical reconciliation is unimaginable.

The Lives of Francis

Uncannily similar difficulties plague the historian in search of the historical Francis. Again, scores of sources issued from the quills of pious champions of

Francis and the way of life he embodied. From this array of sources, three major "lives" (or hagiographical *vitae*) came, within roughly four decades of Francis's death, to achieve authoritative status, though the first two eventually, so to speak, lost their imprimatur, owing to changing circumstances in the young order's self-understanding. Yet another major source was produced in the fourteenth century. This last, the so-called *Little Flowers* (or *Fioretti*) is, if not as incompatible as John with the synoptics, highly inflected by the bitter disappointment and feelings of betrayal on the part of its multiple compilers. Each of these texts had its own (if the term may be excused) "Franciscology." All are conditioned by debate about who Francis "was," in the religious and theological sense of this term, and what his order was or should be and became. These Franciscologies are likewise incompatible and attempts at clear historical harmonization futile.

Almost certainly the most trustworthy of the three major thirteenth-century *vitae* of St. Francis is the *First Life (Vita Prima)*, written by Brother Thomas of Celano (d. 1260). Still, as already suggested, this life is not entirely reliable. Among other things, like many saints' "lives," it is shaped profoundly by the hagiographical tradition. In this case, it is quite clear that Thomas makes Francis in the image of both St. Martin of Tours and St. Benedict. Nonetheless, Thomas had met Francis. Commissioned by Pope Gregory IX, Thomas's *Life* was begun within two years of Francis's death. It contains a meticulously written account of the canonization ceremony that took place, in Assisi, in July 1228, at which the author, clearly moved, was present. Moreover, it was composed before disputes over the future of the order began to whittle away the radicalism of Francis's and Thomas's harsh critique of wealth and the merchant class, as well as to expurgate embarrassing episodes in the early life in the order (like, for example, the deposition of Francis's hand-picked successor, Brother Elias).

Less than two decades later, the minister general of the order, Crescentius of Iesu (d. 1263), asked Thomas to gather any memories of Francis from now-aging brothers who had known or at least had encountered him. Three brothers responded with a rich collection of anecdotes and reminiscences, now lost. In 1247, Crescentius commissioned a second *vita* from Thomas, which almost certainly incorporates the "little flowers," or *florilegium* (that is, not an unbroken narrative), of recollections supplied by the three brethren.

Yet what Thomas put in with one hand, he took out with the other. This *Second Life (Vita Secunda)* clearly mirrors reactions to the *First Life,* as well as the disputes that had begun already before Francis's death in 1226 and mushroomed thereafter. Accordingly, Thomas excises some uncomfortable scenes and texts (including his own loud blast aimed at the depravity and decadence of the sons of Assisi) and skates lightly over other episodes judged, now, to be awkward or unedifying. A number of stories reflect apprehension that the order had begun already to betray the high and uncompromising ideals of its founder.

Yet a third—and, the order hoped, authoritative—*Life* was ordered in 1260 by the general chapter of the order, which met in Narbonne that year. Commissioned to do the writing was no less a figure than Bonaventure (d. 1274). Then the premier Franciscan theologian in Paris, he was also minister general of the order. Like the *Second Life* of Thomas, Bonaventure's *vita* is a work that shapes Francis in the image of his hopes for the order over which he presided—especially the hope that the order would not be ruptured by now opposed wings mutually alienated by disagreement over the authority of Francis's writings and observance of ideals and rules connected with austere living. Again, we see a hagiographer at work, discreetly bowdlerizing here, reshaping there. With the publication of the Seraphic Doctor's *Life* (the so called *Legenda Maior*), the chapter of Paris in 1266 ordered the destruction of Thomas of Celano's first two *Lives*. It was only their retention in Benedictine and Cistercian monasteries, where, of course, Franciscan decrees could not touch them, that preserved them for posterity.

Yet it is not, in the end, Thomas's *Lives* that are most precious for reconstructing Francis's own thoughts and ideals, invaluable as they are for helping us to assemble the framework and details for a short life history. Intellectual life was unimportant, even spiritually dangerous for him. Yet despite not understanding himself at all to be an author, Francis has left a small number of writings, most of them connected to the religious life or, as he would put it in his final writing, the power to do penance.

These writings include two *Rules* written for the order, including the one approved by Pope Honorius III in 1223; one composed in 1209, the first Francis compiled, is not extant. Francis also composed a rule for hermits. Just before he died, he drew up, or dictated, a brief statement of will for his order, the sternly toned document that has come down to us known as *The Testament of St. Francis*. This contains some valuable memories of the early history of the order, all delivered in a tone of regret—a sure sign that at the moment of his death, Francis had grown dejected with the direction his order had taken or was threatening to go. Several letters of his also survive. Finally, several lyrics, of which the most famous by far is the *Canticle of Brother Sun,* have come down to us in Francis's vernacular, Italian. Treated carefully, these, along with Celano's *Lives,* allow us to reconstruct Francis's life in brief but accurate form.

The man who would become probably the most widely venerated and revered saint in the Middle Ages, if not in the history of the church, was born and baptized Giovanni Bernardone around 1182. The place of his birth was Assisi, in the central Italian province of Umbria. His father, Pietro, was, like Waldes, a prosperous cloth merchant; he almost certainly wanted his son to follow, professionally speaking, in his footsteps and to lead his life as a member of the new bourgeois class. Accordingly, Francophile Pietro nicknamed his son Francesco (Frenchman). French was the language of European commerce and France the destination of his many business trips; it was also possibly rather, or in addition, a reference to his mother's ancestry. It was thus that Francis lost his baptismal name, John, and acquired the one by which he would be known by posterity and from which his enormously influential religious order would take its informal name. Though none could perceive it at the time, it was the first of many changing identities, each less superficial than the last.

One indication that Francis was meant to become a merchant was that no provision was made for higher education, which was nearly useless for taking over a family business. In school, Francis acquired the essentials of literacy and numeracy. He had an interest in poetry, and evidence suggests he grew fond of Provençal songs and legends. Given the way he concluded his life, and his nearly irresistible desire to retire as a hermit, one wonders at the reports that he delighted in friendship, that he was exuberant and vital—even that he was a sort of ringleader among young mischievous friends. It is amazing to contemplate that, in dress, he was reputed to be flamboyant.

Less in doubt is that Francis dreamed of military glory. While fighting against nearby Perugià, he was incarcerated and held for a year. A year of freedom followed, punctuated by bouts of curious illnesses. The following year (1205) he set off under Walter of Brienne on a military expedition on behalf of the papacy against the imperial army. This, however, was aborted in nearby Spoleto when, again, he became ill. While dreaming there, he heard the call of Christ, who summoned him to renounce his commitment to vanities and to undertake a life fighting for a different, divine cause. His conversion—long, complicated, and often distressing—had begun.

For the next four years or so, Francis slowly peeled away the trappings of his old character and, at a profounder level, began laboriously to construct a wholly new identity, with little continuity with his inherited one. Here Francis was groping for his life's work as well. It is not unimportant to recall that he would have encountered, in the course of his military and business travels the Camaldolese, other Italian hermits, the Waldensians, and many practitioners of the apostolic life; these passing images now began to impress. A quest had begun, but he could hardly have been expected to perceive or imagine its improbable end.

Naturally, so radical a turnabout was not psychologically or spiritually easy. Francis experienced trying, even agonizing, periods of revulsion with his old life, as well as deep, persistent frustration at not knowing what his future would hold. He reacted step by step, slowly alienating himself from the familiar and familial structures of his existence, abandoning not just silly frivolities, but also old friendships and even family. All, he inchoately perceived, he had to surrender, though he knew not what he was about to embrace. Rejecting the familiar, he drew close to the unfamiliar and even that which he had once found repulsive. As he himself recalls in his last writing: "When I was in sin, the sight of lepers was too bitter for me. And the Lord himself led me among them, and I pitied and helped them. And when I left them, I discovered that what had seemed bitter to me was changed into sweetness in my soul and body." It was this experience, he tells us, that gave him his superlative power: "the power to do penance." This change in perception and character led insensibly to the next, momentous step, one that would nearly complete his rupture with the past: "Shortly afterward," he tells us in his *Testament*, "I rose and left the world."

Knowing only that the Lord had given him "faith in churches," he began working on Santa Maria degli Angeli (better known as the Portiuncula) and the church of San Damiano, just outside the town walls of Assisi, then in a dilapidated state. While there one day, he had a vision in which he thought the crucifix depending above the altar spoke to him: "Francis, go, and repair my house, which you see is falling down." Altogether characteristically, Francis ("stupefied" and "nearly deranged," Celano tells us) took the words literally; after all, he accepted words like these, inevitably and significantly, as a personal revelation *for him*. Under divine instruction, or so he thought, he determined to rebuild the church. He was beginning to enact his dispossession spontaneously, symbolically, and histrionically, even before comprehending it consciously. Or, to use the contemporary language of Thomas of Celano, the exterior stigmata that would reveal publicly his absolute identity with Christ had, in this incident, been imprinted on his heart.

Almost before he knew it, Francis had supplanted his earthly father for his heavenly Father. The use and sale of cloth became an important, sometimes almost comic, theme in his conversion. In order to purchase the stones to rebuild San Damiano, for example, he sold cloth taken from his father's warehouse. Perhaps understandably, his earthly father was not pleased. Appalled at the ragged condition of his son, the cloth merchant was enraged and even house-imprisoned him for a time.

His mother liberated him. Finally coming to the conclusion that he could not persuade him from his divinely ordained mission (still hazily sketched in his mind), Pietro had Francis formally renounce his patrimony. Happily, Francis complied. Again, he enacted his response symbolically and histrionically (uncannily, the symbolic communication of message and intent is yet another trait that links him with Jesus of Nazareth). He simply stripped, returned his clothes to his father, and stood naked in the company of all present, including the bishop of Assisi, who, both stunned and impressed, covered Francis with his own robe. When attempting to understand Francis's character, the depth of his determination to chase his divinely revealed call to the letter, his refusal to obey his equally stubborn father Pietro, his new refusal to touch money—when contemplating all these things, it is healthy to wonder whether traditional images of Francis—as the soulful, poetic lyricist; the gentle *poverello;* and the intimate of rabbits and fish and enthusiast for attentive birds, to whom he would preach (what moral exhortation a bird might require to live a good avian life still teases at the mind)—are categories that open him up to us or, rather, wrap him in a veil of sentimentalities.

For roughly the next two years, Francis roamed in and around Assisi, restoring churches and ministering to the poor. Then, in February 1208, while attending mass in the Portiuncula, he heard the gospel as if it were a concrete divine message intended, again, *for him.* The gospel for that day (the feast of St. Matthias) was Matthew 10:7–14: "Preach as you go, saying, 'The kingdom of heaven is at hand. . . . Take no gold, or silver, nor copper in your belts, no bag for the journey, nor two tunics, nor sandals, nor a staff, for the laborer is worthy of his food.'" This, we recall, was the text crucial for Waldes's conversion. Francis asked the presiding priest to explicate the text to him. Having received his explanation, Francis is reported to have cried out with joy, sure now that he had received his divine vocation in the most specific form imaginable: "This is what I want; this is what I am seeking." Taking Christ's instructions quite literally, he proceeded to remove his sandals and made himself a tunic of very rough material. One of the reasons he was later so reluctant to see modifications of his original vision is that these were not simply alterations in the fabric of *his* vision. Much more seriously, they were amendments to what Francis quite seriously believed, again, to be a divine *revelation:* "No one showed me what I should do," he reminds us in the *Testament,* "but the Most High *revealed to me* that I should live according to the form of the holy gospel." If we take a wider cultural view of Francis's revelations, and his determination to live them out without improvement, equivocation, or mitigation, it seems clear that this is a moment of double significance. Not only does it represent the definitive ascendancy of the New Testament in western ecclesiastical history, but in the history of its reception, Francis's own dedication to literal imitation in practice also marks the growing ascendancy of the literal over the allegorical reading of the Bible (a trend, it must be stressed, that continued to and through the medieval period), especially of the gospels.

Living according to the form of the holy gospel meant, for Francis, preaching penance. This is sometimes misunderstood. For Francis, it of course meant contrition and amendment of ways. But we must remember, always, that Francis was an obedient son of the church and had been given by God, he reports in his *Testament,* "faith in priests" (here note the contrast with the Waldensians) and in the established media of salvation. Therefore, we must remember that these movements of conscience were intended by Francis to precede *sacramental confession*—that is, the channel provided by God through which sins could not only be regretted but also forgiven. Contrition meant little without confession or being shriven (as Francis was not a priest, he would have had to bring or direct the penitent to one—but the Franciscans would soon become a traditional sacerdotal order).

Lesser Brothers

Living according to the pattern provided in the gospels also meant practicing poverty at its most radical, both for Francis and for the brothers—"lesser brothers" (*fratres minores*), as they called themselves (thus the Order of Friars Minor), or (to use Francis's word) *fraticelli*—who began to gather around him. As we have noted, Waldes and his followers embraced what they took to be apostolic poverty. So did countless other movements of lay inspiration, not to mention contemporary eremitical and cenobitical orders. Francis went much further. For him and for his young brotherhood, Francis intended corporate destitution. Again, he states this emphatically, not gently, in the beginning of his first *Rule:* "The brothers shall appropriate nothing to themselves, neither a place nor anything; but as pilgrims and strangers in this world, serving God in poverty and humility, they shall with confidence go seeking alms." For a Benedictine, or even a Cistercian, living in stable residences and worshipping, often, in grand churches, "poverty" had a different meaning.

Francis did not intend a spiritual, asomatous poverty for himself or for his brethren. Rather, they were to wander into towns by day, where they would preach in the *piazze*, or marketplaces; acquire their food by begging (or mendicancy—the reason they, along with other orders, like the Dominicans, are sometimes known as the "mendicant" orders); and find shelter at night in abandoned tents, barns, or caves outside of town. Not satisfied with relinquishing individual property, Francis and his earliest companions held no property in common. (For those supposedly dedicated to the literal imitation of the apostolic life, this principle could be understood as an over-literal, or ultra-ardent form of observance.) All of this made them a rather ragged bunch. Shoeless, sheathed in tattered habits made of coarse material fastened by a rough cord tied around the waist, they would arrive in a town square to beg or, sometimes, to perform menial labor.

This was not a prospect that could have pleased the bourgeois parents from whom the burgeoning order recruited many of its members (it filled the aristocratic parents of Thomas Aquinas [d. 1274], who was determined to become a Dominican, with a combination of anger and dread). For it was not the poor classes that formed the pool from which the Friars Minor drew their recruits. Those classes usually aspired to *escape* the poverty by which fate had trapped them and left them physically and mentally oppressed. By contrast, the Friars Minor by and large were born into classes that rarely if ever experienced scarcity and even often enjoyed abundance: the merchant and knightly classes and the gentry, along with a smattering of artisans and peasants. Soon, with repercussions—and, in Francis's mind, costs—for the shape and future of the order, it would recruit with enormous success among scholars at the universities north of the Alps.

There is yet another respect in which the disheveled appearance, untidy arrival in town, and social composition of the young order could have displeased wealthy families. At no time in the central Middle Ages could it be said that any part of Europe was organized, socially and economically, along egalitarian lines. Indeed, the distinction of classes was ordinarily assumed simply to be given, even divinely ordained, and little, if any, thought was given to its abolition; it was the natural order of things. This was true even, or especially, in Benedictine cloisters. Hildegard of Bingen could write that only girls of the noble classes be admitted to cloisters, lest ones of the lower orders be humiliated by their class status. Men, including bishops, were admonished in foundation charters of Benedictine nunneries to ensure that only the well-born be admitted. More broadly, medieval society as such, for almost all times and places in the millennium we are considering, was deeply stratified.

In this connection, then, Francis's young brotherhood was quite exotic, even radical. No distinction was made, in the order's origins, between layman and cleric, peasant and nobleman (this would change over time). All embraced, and all shared, the same spartan diet, the same frugal disciplinary culture, and the same cramped sleeping quarters. This was a true *fraternitas*—a word of which Francis and his early brethren were fond—a real and not just notional brotherhood. C. H. Lawrence suggests that this "fraternalism [was] based on a pragmatic but deep-seated conviction . . . that in the sight of God all human beings are equally worthy of respect." Lawrence further speculates that this conviction may have been "peculiarly Italian."

That may be right, even though that profound conviction, held by the baptized at large, played no role in transforming Italian society as such; it would be anachronistic to believe that this conviction implied an equally profound certitude that all should enjoy the same political, economic, and social rights. That is a post-medieval idea, as foreign (if not horrifying) to a wealthy and powerful Italian medieval layman as it is familiar to those who legally possess those rights in western democracies today. In any case, Lawrence is certainly correct to assert that it constituted a real challenge to "the conventions of a sharply stratified society." In this connection, it is well to remember the observation of Robert Fossier: "The medieval world had little pity for the unlucky and the *disgraciés.* . . .

The blind man's mistakes were laughed at, the sick were excluded and the weak scorned. . . . At best, they were feared and people fled from them; at the worst, they were exterminated. . . . It was better to give a vineyard to the Church than a kiss to a leper." The friars challenged convention by deliberately associating themselves with and ministering to social outcasts in medieval society, especially lepers (those categorized as such making up perhaps 2–3 percent of the population in Francis's lifetime), socially segregated and innocently incarcerated for life in their ghastly dwellings.

According to Thomas of Celano, the first to join Francis in his *forma vitae,* or "way of life," was a devout layman of Assisi. Thomas does not name him, however, and he remains anonymous to us. We do know the names and a few facts about those who subsequently joined—for example, Bernard of Quintavalle (d. 1241), Peter of Cattani (d. 1221), and Giles of Assisi (d. 1262). When the companions numbered eight, they dispersed in the four directions of the compass to preach, in apostolic style, two by two. Once the apostolic number of twelve had been reached—perhaps hagiographical invention designed to link the order with Jesus's innermost circle of followers—Francis resolved to secure approval for his way of life from Pope Innocent III. He summarized his form of life in what is sometimes called a "rule" but is more accurately characterized as an assemblage of passages from the gospels having to do with Christ's commission to the apostles (e.g., Matthew 10:7–14; Matthew 19:21; Luke 9:3; Matthew 16:14).

All of this, which occurred in 1210, recalls Waldes's near-identical action in 1179. In this case, not only popular media but even great art have misled us. Giotto's famous fresco of the dream of a pope (traditionally identified as Innocent) of Francis shouldering the basilica of St. John Lateran (part of the cycle now decorating the upper basilica of San Francesco in Assisi) has led many to believe that Innocent promptly approved Francis's way of life. In fact, the ragged band from Assisi was not at once admitted to the papal curia, and Innocent apparently hesitated to give the *nihil obstat* (no objection) to their way of life. Nonetheless, he was not reactively hostile to lay poverty-and-preaching movements. In fact, he approved in 1199 a rule for the Humiliati, a group that had been anathematized at the Council of Verona in 1184, though he limited the scope of their preaching to "exhortation"—that is, to moral improvement and penance, not dogma. Eventually, Innocent likely gave his verbal approval (no written approval from 1209 exists), and tradition has held that he authorized the Friars Minor to preach ubiquitously and had them tonsured, a sign that they were approved preachers of penance and had status as minor clerics—Francis would be ordained a deacon, though, like most of his followers, never a priest—before they left Rome. As a new fraternity, they were to meet twice annually in chapter. By 1215, Pope Innocent certainly had approved them. In that year, he announced, the Fourth Lateran Council's ban on new religious orders did not apply to the Order of Friars Minor; they were then *already* an order.

Clare

One indication of the influence of contemporary itinerant preaching movements on Francis is that he, too, seems to have imagined that women would take their place, in some way and with certain fixed restrictions, in his ministerial enterprise. Traditionally, Clare (d. 1253), yet another of the noble children of Assisi attracted to apostolic poverty and ministry, is presented as having approached Francis. Again conventionally, Francis is then depicted as responding to Clare by organizing a community of religious women and then housing them at the familiar church of San Damiano, the very church in which Francis had received the command to repair "my house,"—that is, the church—which was then "falling into ruin." Francis soon tonsured Clare, thus making her unfit for marriage. Like many aristocratic families appalled that their children had chosen the mendicant path, Clare's soon sent knights in search of her. She meanwhile had taken refuge in a nearby Benedictine church. Only when Clare revealed her tonsured head to the knights did they quit; they realized she would never be a bride. Soon, Agnes and Clare, after giving up their substantial dowries to the poor, attracted others; they formed the first community of Franciscan women.

At Francis's death, Cardinal Hugolino assumed responsibility for the organization of the many female groups of penitents and those attracted to the mendicant ideal. Many, like Clare, had been attracted by the vision of apostolic poverty embodied by Francis. The later Gregory IX could not imagine women embracing this vision and imposed acceptance of the Benedictine *Rule*. Clare, not pleased, succeeded in securing from Pope Gregory in 1228 a guarantee that would preserve her devotion to living in poverty, as well as that of the sisters in San Damiano. In practice, this meant that the sisters could accept alms rather than be required to depend on a regular system of material support. Almost needless to say, despite her wishes, she could not follow Francis or the brothers in itinerancy, mendicancy, or preaching; even Francis could not breach those societal conventions. Nevertheless, Clare became something of a local saint quickly, profoundly respected and loved within her convent and without, as she took on the most odious jobs within the monastery and cared for ill brothers sent her by Francis. She also received with great tenderness laypeople in Assisi who came to her either for corporal works of mercy, like aiding with their sick children, or spiritual ones, like petitions for prayer.

18. Habit of St. Clare of Assisi. Now in the church dedicated to her, Santa Chiara, Assisi. akg-images/Gerhard Ruf.

The privilege of poverty was one granted only to Clare's house at San Damiano. Other houses of the second order, eventually to be known as the "Poor Clares" (but then simply known as "Damianite houses") were, despite that name, generally refused that privilege. This refusal came at a time when houses were established on the model of San Damiano in Umbrian towns like Foligno, Perugià, Arezzo, and Spello. (Claims that these communities were founded either by Clare or Francis have been disproven, though it is obvious they were inspired by those two.) Ordinarily, this privilege would require residence at the female monasteries of Franciscan brothers, there to supply the spiritual and secular needs of the sisters. By mid-century, Pope Innocent IV demanded that these houses accept ownership. Again, Clare had to stare down the papacy. She did, rejecting the papal legislation and instead composing her own "form of life," which the pope approved as Clare lay on her deathbed in 1253. While Clare intended her form of life to govern all Damianite communities, it seems as if her vision was not widely realized.

Two years after her death, Clare was canonized. Ironically, she was immortalized in the conventional hagiographical categories for women, remembered as a cloistered contemplative nun. The life of the great female follower of Francis's mendicant vision was completely redrawn, and Clare, in hagiographical literature, became a conventional example to be followed by all inclaustrated contemplatives.

Mission, Dismay, and Death

The same year Francis brought Clare within the scope of his ministry, he sailed, not for the first time, out of Italy in order to attempt to convert Muslims in the Levant. In this case, the trip was aborted by rough seas. In 1214, he tried again. His journey to Morocco was cut short in Spain, where Francis was struck by a grave illness; he would have to return home again, yet not before establishing the first communities of Spanish brothers. Yet he was undeterred and would try again. In 1219, Francis set out by sea for Syria and then to Egypt. Amazingly, he reached the court of the Ayyubid sultan al-Kamil (r. 1218–1238) and conversed with him at length. Francis begged the sultan to convert and accept baptism, but in vain. A good indication of Francis's deep conviction and sheer tenacity is that all this occurred as the Fifth Crusade (1218–1221)—which was an attempt to retake Jerusalem by beginning to conquer Egypt first of all (Francis encountered the Crusaders in Damietta)—was in progress.

By the time Francis had met with the sultan, his order had burgeoned and developed—in some ways of which Francis could not approve. With the convocation of the Fourth Lateran Council, at which Innocent announced that the Friars Minor had already been founded, the order had already grown to a size of perhaps several hundred members. By 1217 they were far more numerous and had spread to every corner of the Italian peninsula. By the Whitsun (Pentecost) Chapter, held at the Portiuncula in May–June 1217, it is likely that the brothers numbered in the thousands.

Significant decisions were taken here, some, in hindsight, ominous for the future unity of the order. Here six provinces in Italy were formed. An additional eleven were established, as the brothers decided to extend their mission beyond Italy and into France, Germany, Spain, Hungary, Morocco (where five friars would be martyred while Francis was in Syria), and even the Levant. Superiors were appointed for each of these new provinces; all, theoretically, were answerable to Francis, still regarded as the founding head of the order.

In fact, it was during these very years that Francis was endeavoring to convert the Muslims that others stepped forward to make decisions in his absence. No less a figure than Cardinal Hugolino, a nephew of Innocent III, as well as the later

pope Gregory IX—whom we have already met as author of the Inquisition—
became "protector" of the order. In effect, this position made him the chief pow-
erbroker for the order at the Roman curia and the pope's agent in restructuring
it so as to accept work the papacy increasingly relied on it to undertake. At the
moment Francis was meeting with the sultan, his brothers received a house as a
gift in Bologna—again, fatefully, not only because acceptance of it breached a
fundamental principle for Francis, but also because Bologna was a center of university life.

When he learned of this (in Acre, where a brother found him to reveal what
had been occurring in his absence), Francis was so infuriated that he immediately
set out for Bologna to supervise the physical ejection of the brothers from the
house—no placid *poverello* here. At this point, Hugolino stepped in to declare that
he owned the house. The Franciscans did not; they merely *used* it. This distinction
between ownership *(dominium)* and use *(usus),* a legal fiction, is language that
would soon enter papal decrees and would generate acrimonious debate, as well
as help propel the order toward a rancorous and finally disastrous intramural split
over the next century or so.

In 1220, Francis resigned as head of the order. In his stead, he appointed Peter
of Cattani, one of his earliest companions, as his successor; Peter died in about
a year. The following year, Elias (d. 1253), the first provincial minister in the Levant, was appointed vicar. At the same time, Francis, with the help of some of his
companions, composed a new version of the *Rule* (the so-called *First Rule,* or
Regula Prima). This one, too, consisted mostly of biblical passages, rather like
the primitive rule *(Regula Primitiva)* of 1209. Despite the claim that Innocent III
had given it his blessing, it was actually not approved; thus it has become known
to history as the *Regula non bullata* (the rule not approved by the papacy). From
1221 to 1223, Francis devoted much of his energy to producing a rule that would
capture—and shield from drastic modification downward—the strict requirements of his original vision for the fraternity. In this, he was to be frustrated.

At the chapter of 1223, he presented the rule that would be approved by papal bull *(Regula bullata)* by Honorius III. Much of Francis's rigorism had been
moderated. The "approved rule" does not demand that the brothers carry nothing with them when traveling, nor does it oblige the friars to complete renunciation of possessions. The original requirement that the friars travel by foot has
dropped out.

What are we to make of these modifications? To start with, it seems clear that
Francis felt betrayed by those whom he had long trusted. Additionally, it seems
obvious that some brethren and Hugolino collaborated in pressuring Francis to
draft, or dictate, a rule that would reflect the realities of the enormous expansion
and evolving character of the order. Celano's *Second Life* has Francis expressing

feelings of profound anger in very strong language at these acts of temerity: "Who are these who snatched my Order and my brethren out of my hands?" Hugolino would later take credit for the final form of the draft. He and the ministers at the 1223 chapter had overwhelmed the founder of the order. It seems as if, on virtually every important matter, Francis had fought them—and lost. Something of his disappointment, tempered by time and illness, can be gathered in his observation in his *Testament* that the early fraternity was "content with one habit . . . and we refused to have anything more." The newer brethren and their curial supporters had taken the order in a new direction and had done so by watering down the primitive, powerful ideals of strict poverty and simplicity. Disenchanted, Francis moved soon to Grecchio, a hill town in Lazio. There, with friends, he reenacted the scene of the birth of Jesus of Nazareth, to which, it might be said, the annual Christmastime veneration of the crèche might be traced.

Francis grew increasingly remote from the affairs of his own order; in fact, he did not even bother to attend the Pentecost Chapter of 1224. With only the companionship of his closest friends, he climbed Mount Alvernia, above Arezzo.

19. St. Francis of Assisi as an old man. Detail from *Madonna and Child with Angels,* by Cimabue (1240–1302). Photo credit: Scala/Art Resource, NY.

There he is said to have received the stigmata on his hands, feet, and side in what is often imagined as a mystical vision of a crucified seraph (an incident portrayed in anecdote and art so as to call up echoes in the imagination of the Transfiguration). His intense identification with the suffering Christ had now been made visible on his body.

To the distress occasioned by unwanted developments in his order were soon to be added a series of physical infirmities and painful, useless medical interventions. During his last two years of grievous illness and physical suffering, Francis dictated his *Testament*—his last act as founder of the order of lesser brothers. Perhaps hoping against hope, he demanded that the *Testament* be read with, and as a guide to, the *Rule* and that no gloss—that is, no moderating language—be allowed to blunt the sharpness of its requirements; the simple *poverello* had, prophetically, seen the future and tried to prevent it (fruitlessly, it turns out). In September 1226, Francis, well aware that "sister death" was near, asked to be taken to the Portiuncula. He died on October 3, 1226, as the story of Christ's Passion, at his request, was being read to him.

The Pastoral Mission to the Cities

To a degree that can hardly be exaggerated, the narrative of the friars is a story of colossal and reverberating importance, achievement, and triumph. Today we often remember the friars for their intellectual accomplishments—and not without reason. But to the ordinary layperson living in the towns in the thirteenth and fourteenth centuries, they were welcomed as bringers of the good news of Christianity, a message that some of them had not heard before or had heard in profoundly qualified—and insulting—form. No friar ever told a layperson in the towns that he or she had little hope of salvation, or that his religious yearnings were silly, or that she had to rely on the merits accrued by cadres of monks or secular priests praying for her otherwise imperiled soul. No friar ever shut his door to a spiritually serious lay Christian. To laypersons in ordinary occupations not content with the conventions of impersonal or vicarious piety, the friars brought the possibility of living a fully Christian life in the towns. The friars' genius was to have recognized these aspirations as authentically Christian and heretofore unsatisfied and to have directed them in orthodox Christian channels. As these religious desires were akin to those that gave rise to heretical groups, this was a delicate task; the friars were able to carry it off successfully, possibly because of the excellent education they had received—the first clerics in Europe really to have received a systematic education in pastoral care.

There were four main ways the friars appealed to their lay urban audience and revitalized the church: by reviving lay preaching, by transforming the practice of preaching, by emphasizing the importance of contrition and penance and of hearing confessions, and (this not so well known) by educating parochial clergy so that they might do their jobs better—do them, that is, more like the friars. Each of these dramatically improved the quality of the parochial experience and, one can only assume, the secular life lived in the towns. At the time the friars appeared on the scene, the church was in a parlous, fragile state, confronted by an unevangelized urban population, afflicted by heretical groups that threatened its unity, and having an educational system unsuited to new social and economic realities. Moreover, it had no pastoral theology or clerical personnel prepared to satisfy the longings of city parishioners; largely through their work, the friars left the institution they found in so dilapidated a state—indeed, "falling into ruin"— substantially rebuilt and, in many respects, quite robust.

As has been noted, the early Middle Ages were not indifferent to preaching; even so august a figure as Charlemagne mandated that each priest possess a copy of Gregory the Great's *Forty Gospel Homilies*. Later Frankish councils issued canons decreeing that sermons be given in the vernacular. Yet, as always, there is a gap between a decree and its realization in practice. In practice, public preaching was, before the twelfth century, given by bishops and canons. In the twelfth century, we see a noticeable uptick in itinerant reform preaching, some of it fiercely anti-clerical in tone and message. Learned preaching continued in Latin and in the cloisters of both men and women—women of the education and caliber of Hildegard of Bingen. Yet the messages of these sermons, however brilliantly constructed, were not designed for the new city dwellers, and parish priests were almost never trained to give sermons. Nor were churches designed, architecturally, for large urban crowds to hear sermons until the coming of the friars.

The friars made the sermon a part of ordinary liturgical experience in the thirteenth century. In turn, the friars excelled at sermon making and sermon delivery. This ability was directly linked to the seriousness with which Dominicans and Franciscans took the writing of instructional literature in the art of homily making. For example, the friars produced model sermons in the thirteenth century. These were essentially sermons in sketch or diagram form. A few large points would be supported by sundry biblical texts. The preacher would begin with the model sermon, then flesh it out by ornamenting it with reference to his own experience. He would also elaborate sermons by the addition of *exempla*, a literary genre of anecdotes, often garnered from hagiographical literature and designed to make a moral point and to stimulate his audience. These *exempla* would travel in collections made specifically for the purpose of sermonizing.

The friars also produced other literature that assisted in the construction of sermons. No less a figure than the Dominican minister general Humbert of Romans produced a manual, *On the Instruction of Preachers*. Other Dominicans composed treatises on the art of preaching. Above all, there survives a large number of col-

20. Church of the
Jacobins, Toulouse,
France; built thirteenth/
fourteenth centuries. The
cloister of the church is
Thomas Aquinas's burial
spot. Note the massive
interior space for urban
crowds to hear Dominican
preaching. akg-images/
Doris Poklekowski.

lections of model sermons. In addition, biblical concordances produced by Dominicans in Paris were assembled mainly to furnish the preacher with a reservoir of suitable allusions to passages of scripture.

What is the content of these sermons? How did the friars address their lay urban auditors? It has been argued that the friars attempted to captivate their urban audiences, many of whom were involved in commerce, by availing themselves of commercial terminology and tropes. The friars, so the argument can go, successfully cultivated the parishioners involved in trade by presenting a new gospel or theological message. Rejecting the notion that it was difficult for a merchant to be saved, which had grown out of a largely agricultural economy, this new theology of commerce focused, in part, upon the advantages to society that the merchants generated.

While not entirely untrue, this new theology can easily be overstated and even, in its extreme form, be slightly insulting both to the friars and to the merchants. In fact, when we inspect collections of sermons compiled by the friars, the burden of the typical sermon is usually quite conventional: the necessity of contrition and repentance, followed by sacramental confession, reconciliation with those whom one's actions have injured, and the responsibility to be charitable to the poor. Where the friars concentrated on merchants, they habitually warned that merchants often lied, stole, and perjured themselves or were avaricious, fraudulent, and, in their commercial transactions, guilty of lending money at unconscionable rates of interest, or usury.

Furthermore, the friars focused on other classes and stations of life, not simply the merchant, and their message was not limited to economic benefits and commercial sin. In fact, the friars popularized the sermon *ad status* (to a particular station in life), not only to merchants, but also to servants, scholars, rulers, and the married. To the last group, the married, the friars offered a much more sympathetic, approving, and even enthusiastic message than had been heard in the sometimes misogynistic writings of the monks. For all laypeople, the friars brought a new interpretation of the meaning of the gospel. It was a hopeful, not a pessimistic, message, one that recognized them as fully Christian and fully capable of salvation. No longer was the monk regarded as the only real Christian or confinement in a cloister the only way to salvation. Instead, the married, the lay, the merchant—all could lead a fully Christian life in the world, and none had to rely upon vicarious merits accumulated by professional religious in the cloisters.

To those in the city yearning to live actively as Christians and not depend passively on the prayers of the monks, a new, highly successful and enduring institution surfaced to meet their needs: the confraternity. Often called "third orders," these were regarded as penitential brotherhoods and sisterhoods that allowed their members to practice piety and corporal works of mercy. Here was an institution that provided the framework within which members could dedicate themselves to personal sanctification without reliance on another. Here those who had secular and lay commitments but devout yearnings were given exercises, fasts, and devotions in the organized framework of the confraternity. The friars often directed them, offered their services as spiritual advisers, and maintained the orthodoxy of their devotional practices. Had such an institution not been available, it is imaginable that these laypeople would have been attracted to the Waldensians or Cathars. Lay men and women no longer had to understand themselves as half-Christians and the professional elite as the only true Christians. Rather, they could live a fully Christian life by sanctifying their everyday duties and ordinary responsibilities. The religious reforms of earlier centuries had generated devout desires among the laity; now those desires were being satisfied in orthodox ways.

Another crucial dimension of the friars' mission was their expertise and humanity in hearing confession, which was always imagined as the aim of the sermon. Part of the reason the friars were in such demand as confessors was that unlike most parochial priests, they were trained carefully for their role. All were instructed in the theology and practice of penance and confession. Again, the Dominicans led the way in the production of literature, and each Dominican convent owned a copy of the manual written by Raymond of Penaforte. All of this instruction and the content of Raymond's manual produced a different kind of confessor. At one time a confessor simply resorted to the conventional penitential manual, which matched sins with appropriate penance. The friars, however, were taught, in ways that anticipate later developments in moral theology, to evaluate the sinner's confession in light of his or her intentions and condition. This approach sometimes led to the charge that the friars were easy confessors, rather like the way some professors acquire the reputation of being easy graders. Even Chaucer satirized the light penances the friars were reputed to assign. In any case, yet another reason for the popularity of the friars as confessors was their obviously sincere way of life. In contrast to the secular clergy, who were sometimes seen as overly concerned with professional advancement, or the monasteries, which were socially exclusive and, in corporate terms, quite wealthy, the friars' commitment to corporate destitution and to the perfection of the apostolic life earned them the respect and admiration of their grateful parishioners.

Finally, at the end of the thirteenth century, under the direction of the papacy, local bishops sent parish priests to the schools of the friars. Needless to say, they represented a great improvement over the ad hoc, apprentice-style and unstructured style of formation conventional in agricultural settings. Indeed, nothing so improved priestly formation and education until the Council of Trent required the establishment of seminaries. It has been argued that the lack of systematic education of the parish clergy was one of the gravest defects of the medieval church. If so, the friars, by throwing open the doors of their schools to the secular clergy, did as much as any other religious institute to remedy this defect.

In the end, it would be hard to exaggerate the impact the friars had on ecclesiastical life in the thirteenth century, a time of challenge and even crisis. In a time when heretical movements seemed to overwhelm the capacity of the authorities to deal with them, the friars offered a way of being perfect *and* orthodox by word and deed. The widespread desire for a personal, devout life they were able to manage and control and finally nudge into orthodox channels of practice. To those yearning to be pure, they brought the message—a new message—that the Christian life was one open to all classes and vocations. It was also a life, they demonstrated, that could be lived within the orthodox church. Soon the western church would be faced with another crisis, an intellectual one: how to treat the newly available works of Greek philosophy and science. It was the friars who would take on this challenge, too, and produce a remarkable synthesis that has outlasted the Middle Ages.

Conflict and Controversy, 1226–1274

It is possible to interpret the changes Francis opposed as the triumph of "institutional," "clerical," or "priestly" religion over the religion of spirit and charisma. On the other hand, it is possible to view these as inevitable or at least necessary and even wise changes for an order developing, numerically and vocationally, as the young Franciscans were. However, what is today an issue of interpretive possibility was, in the wake of Francis's death and the order he founded, a matter of the true meaning of *francescanesimo*, of Francis's meaning for history; his vision for the order; the authentic way of observing Franciscan poverty and humility; religious integrity and compromise; obedience (to Francis first? to conscience? or to the pope?); and internal relations within the order and external relations with the papacy. Debate about these issues would quickly involve the order in bitter intramural dispute, then rupture, and finally decisive papal intervention. Men of good will and strong principle might disagree on these issues; they had done so during Francis's life. What one man regarded as fidelity to principle, another regarded as obstinacy, if not betrayal; what one friar regarded as necessary compromise, another might view as evidence of corrupt laxity. All the ingredients were present for a prolonged verbal civil war, and, indeed, one would unfold over the next fifty years.

It would be difficult to organize the half-century of Franciscan history between the death of Francis and the accession of Bonaventure to minister general of the order without recourse to categories of disagreement, incompatibility and extremity of opinion, adversity, and even perhaps inflexibility. It could hardly have been otherwise, as the order began to acquire buildings and books, to recruit among intellectuals, and to clericalize itself. Sheer numbers also played a role. In 1210 there were around twelve Franciscans. Forty years later, there were perhaps thirty thousand. This kind of expansion alone was a significant factor in compromising the original rigor of the order. Perhaps even more significant was that popes, kings, and governments all recruited the friars to serve in a variety of positions that either encouraged or forced them to use worldly power and enjoy higher living standards.

Indeed, controversy started even before these developments began. Almost at the moment Francis died, Brother Elias acquired the land in Assisi above which would be raised, rapidly, an enormous two-storied basilica dedicated to the saint and housing his relics; he would also raise the funds for construction. Some of the friars felt that Francis should have been buried (and would wanted to have been buried) in the Portiuncula. But Elias won out and, in the end, turned Assisi into a pilgrimage site like Compostela and even Rome. In 1228, Hugolino, now Pope Gregory IX, arrived in Assisi. Simultaneously, he laid and consecrated the foundation stone of the church, announced that Francis was to be canonized, and ordered Thomas of Celano to draw up a life of the saint. In 1230, Francis's corpse was transferred to its resting place (today it is in the lower basilica, where it is surrounded by the bodies of four of his earliest companions).

In that very year, the charged issue of Franciscan poverty exploded. Superficially, the issue was whether the friars could own any properties at all and whether they could ever have fixed dwellings. This issue was connected to the ever-deepening involvement of Franciscans in study at university and the evident need for books and lodgings. Francis was not enthusiastic about his brothers' learning. "We were unlettered," he looks back wistfully late in his life, "in the service of all." Conversions should occur by example, not learned lucubration. A second issue was clericalization. As the friars evolved into a more traditional order, they had to be able to administer the sacraments, and this meant ordination to the priesthood. These needs were felt to be especially acute, as the Friars Minor arrived in towns in northern Europe at roughly the same time as the Dominicans—that is, an order that was educated, clerical, and committed to preaching but with the modest amenities of a movement dedicated to living in simplicity and poverty. Competition with the Dominicans unquestionably influenced the future shape of the Friars Minor.

At a deeper level, the issue was whether the Franciscans would, as they moved into the future, interpret Francis's wishes strictly or loosely—and who would decide or intervene authoritatively when matters of controversy arose. In the event, it was the papacy, in the person, again, of Gregory IX, who resolved both the superficial and profounder issues at once. By his very intervention, Pope Gregory ensured that it would be the papacy that would function as the authoritative arbiter in matters of difficulty and dispute—of which there would soon be a multitude. In his bull *Quo Elongati* (1230), he expressed his authority in the interpretation of Franciscan issues by first declaring that Francis's *Testament* was not legally binding. This was the pope's most significant legal and interpretive move, as Francis had concluded the document by forbidding glosses to it. Pope Gregory argued that it could not be binding on Francis's successors, as he had written it without taking their advice and without securing their consent. Now the way was open for a glossing of Francis's *Rule*. The friars, Gregory declared, had the capacity to appoint a "spiritual friend" or trustee *(nuntius)* to whom they could apply for necessities. There is no question but that Gregory had been put in a delicate place, between the strict and loose constructionists of Francis's writings.

Equally true is that *Quo Elongati* marks a pivot point in the history of the Franciscan Order. It represents a moment when the order turned away from corporate destitution and dependence upon Providence and toward the model of a traditional monastic order, with secure dwellings, books, and necessities acquired by money—in short, withdrawal from the inflexible and categorical form of life to which Francis and his earliest companions had dedicated themselves. Some in the order saw this as inevitable; others could wonder *what* the sometime cardinal protector of the order was preserving of the founder's vision. Fifteen years later, Pope Innocent IV would issue *Ordinem Vestrum* (1245). This vested ownership of all properties and goods with the papacy; it granted to the friars their use. Innocent thus allowed the friars, by the letter of the law, to preserve their theoretical commitment to absolute poverty, but its spirit had clearly been breached. Francis's original revelation of propertyless, homeless, wandering, unlearned preachers imitating the life of Christ in dependence on Providence now lay, for better or worse, in tatters.

Many of the brothers who had not forgotten Francis's original vision, or who were still alive at the time Gregory's 1230 bull was issued, lay the blame for these developments at the feet of Elias, who was a strong supporter of the pope and had been made minister general in 1232. Elias encouraged study in every province (and he increased the number of provinces to thirty-two from seventeen); he supported stable housing, commissioned the decoration in the lower basilica of San Francesco by fresco, and began construction of the new convent (the "Holy Convent" or Sacro Convento) adjacent to the new basilica (now spread out panoramically against the Assisi hillside).

None of these efforts would likely have put Elias into difficulty. However, this original companion of Francis, an intimate and trusted friend of the founder—so it was frequently alleged—lived elegantly, ate lavishly, dwelt in opulent surroundings, and had a large retinue and stable of horses. On top of all this, Elias became increasingly autocratic; among other things, he attempted to exercise authority over the order without bothering to summon general chapters. He sent out visitors to provinces who often were regarded as spies or who ended up taking powers away from those they were supposedly visiting. In these ways, Elias was quite clearly acting and living in ways inappropriate to the minister general of the order of Friars Minor.

Yet the issue that distressed Elias's most implacable opponents would presumably have pleased Francis. Elias conservatively resisted the clericalization of the order and preferred laymen for key positions over clerics. Soon, the leading scholars of the order and their powerful secular supporters (such as Robert Grosseteste) warned the pope by letter that Elias was in danger of damaging the order. In 1239, at a general chapter in Rome, Gregory spoke movingly of his dear friend Elias. Yet, bringing forth evidence of widespread lack of support, he proceeded to depose him. In the wake of his deposition, Elias then began associating himself with the excommunicated emperor Frederick II (1194–1250; r. 1220–1250), an act that caused Gregory to excommunicate Elias himself. Elias had disgraced himself and scandalized the order. For the rest of his life, he tried to defend himself. Only at his death in 1253 did reconciliation occur. But damage had been done again. Elias managed to offend both the early disciples of Francis by building a grand basilica and the order's new intellectuals and clerks, who regarded him as a rude layman. All were offended by his love of luxury and worldliness. In later literature, he is sometimes portrayed as a Judas figure who betrayed his master, Christ. That is perhaps too harsh, but he ended his life with few allies in the order and none at the Roman curia.

Emergence of the Spirituals and Joachites

By 1245, strict constructionists of Francis's writings, frustrated at the mitigation of Francis's original vision, began to emerge under the minister generalship of Crescentius of Iesu. Crescentius reported to the chapter that had elected him that groups of friars, some of them Francis's companions, were refusing to inhabit convents in the Marches of Ancona—always a hotbed of Franciscan rebellion in the thirteenth century. Instead, they were intent on preserving the primitive tradition of living without fixed residences and lacking property of any kind. These rebels are among the first Franciscans to seem to be familiar with the writings of the immensely influential apocalyptic commentator and monk Joachim of Fiore (1135–1202), who was understood by many Franciscans to have prophesied the rise and role of the order in the dawning age of both anti-Christian persecution and perfection. In the thirteenth canto of the *Paradiso*, Dante was to immortalize Joachim as one "endowed with the prophetic spirit." Yet he would be criticized by the Fourth Lateran Council for his Trinitarian views, and his followers took his thought in directions of which he would not have approved and indeed that were recognized to be heretical. Some of Joachim's followers in the Franciscan Order inspired Joachites to rebel against the papacy in the thirteenth and fourteenth centuries.

Joachim's most famous apocalyptic scheme of history is Trinitarian in nature. According to this scheme, salvation history unfolds in terms of three successive, overlapping "states" or "ages" *(status)*, each primarily under the aegis of one of the persons of the Trinity. Each *status* is also characterized by a particular way of life, or *ordo*. The *status* of the Father, which is coterminous with the seven ages of Old Testament history, began with Adam and ended with the coming of Christ. Its characteristic way of life was that of the married *(ordo coniugatorum)*. Since the three *status* are overlapping, those of the Son and the Holy Spirit have their beginnings *(germinationes)* in the previous *status*. The *status* of the Son began with King Josiah, achieved fruition in Christ, and would end shortly. Its characteristic way of life was that of clerics *(ordo clericorum)*. The *status* of the Holy Spirit had its beginning in St. Benedict, would reach fruition in the relatively near future, and would last until the end of the world. Its characteristic way of life was that of monks *(ordo monachorum)*. Joachim usually places himself explicitly at the beginning of the third *status*. The beginning of this *status* was to be marked both by an extraordinary advance in the understanding of the Bible and a frightening increase in the persecution of the spiritual church by the forces of evil. Uncannily,

Joachim also prophesied the coming of two new orders of "spiritual men" *(viri spirituales)*, one of contemplatives and one of preachers, both of whom would resist the Antichrist in the dawning third age of the Holy Spirit.

Though hardly the only order that found itself bound by a magnetic attraction to Joachim's thought or seized by the conviction that they would play a pivotal role in the coming age of the Holy Spirit, many Franciscans—especially those designated rigorists or "Spirituals" and destined to be considered heretics by some—were captivated by Joachim's writings, in part because they were persuaded that the Calabrian abbot had prophesied their genesis and emergence as "spiritual men." On them, a profounder, "spiritual" understanding of the gospel would be bestowed. Some Dominicans also saw themselves as one of the new orders of spiritual men *(viri spirituales)* prophesied by Joachim. But there can be little doubt that the intellectual and religious impact of Joachim on the Franciscans was far more profound. Naturally, the Franciscan Joachites, in the manner of all apocalyptic groups, modified Joachim's own writings to correspond more closely with their own convictions. For example, while Joachim did not say much about poverty in his authentic writings, for Franciscan Joachites it became a characteristic feature of the dawning third age; those who downplayed its significance might be understood as agents of Antichrist.

By the 1240s, several Franciscans, some in very high places, began to read Joachim with profound fascination—and conviction that he had foreseen that something crucial in salvation history would happen in the life and work of their founder. One of these Franciscans was John of Parma (d. 1289), who, to the satisfaction of the zealous wing of the order, had been elected minister general in 1247. All were persuaded history was drawing to its close, and as the church prepared itself to face the onslaught of Antichrist, not to mention the final judgment, God had sent Francis and his order to renew the church and to imitate the life of Christ and the apostles—and Joachim, under the influence of the prophetic spirit, had prophesied these things. Those zealous for the practice of absolute poverty, as described in Francis's *Rule* and *Testament,* were extremely enthusiastic to hear about the messianic, eschatological role their order would play. They had been chosen by God to help bring the end times to conclusion and to lead the church into the final Age of the Holy Spirit. It is no wonder that they were among the most active in spreading Joachim's message and works.

Guglielma of Milan

It was not only to Franciscan friars that Joachim's ideas appealed. They appealed also to women in the north of Italy, and some of their ideas resembled ideas for which Franciscan men, like Gerard of Borgo San Donnino (d. ca. 1277), had already been solemnly condemned. But even that observation hardly suffices to capture the radicalism of their thought and the limits to which they stretched Joachite ideas. Possibly by means of oral transmission, both authentic and spurious Joachite texts seem to have reached northern Italy. In any case, in the late thirteenth century a Bohemian princess, named Guglielma (d. 1281), who was by then established in Milan as a local holy woman, was identified by a follower, Andreas Samarita (obviously a man), as the incarnation of the Holy Spirit. She thus was the one earmarked to usher in the third age of the Holy Spirit. Among her followers, one woman, Maifreda da Pirovano (d. ca. 1300), would, her followers believed, ascend to the throne of Peter, to which only men had been raised for thirteen centuries. This was, to put it mildly, to be a new age. If Maifreda became pope, not only would all women be cardinals, but also all higher offices in the church would be occupied by women. In her capacity as *papessa*, Maifreda would convert Jews and Muslims (Joachim predicted Jews would be converted in the end times). The canonical gospels would be superseded by four new ones, written under the inspiration of the Holy Spirit. Needless to say, these were exceedingly dangerous ideas, the last the one for which Gerard, whose conviction on the matter never wavered, had been incarcerated for life.

Guglielma never accepted her followers' belief in her divinity, a rejection of deity reflected in the title of the latest book about her: *I Am Not God (Io non sono Dio)*, yet that disbelief had no effect on her followers. One follower claimed to have seen and to have washed her fleshly stigmata, a remark that connected her not only with Francis but, by extension, and even more daringly, with Christ. Guglielma was buried at the Cistercian convent at Chiaravalle. Some of the north Italian public expectantly waited for her to be canonized. That was certainly implausible but not impossible. But, in addition, some of her followers would gather at Chiaravalle, apparently waiting for her, like Christ, to be resurrected. In the end, a Dominican tribunal charged Guglielma's followers with heresy. Maifreda and Samarita died at the stake. Guglielma herself was posthumously condemned. Inquisitors even exhumed her bones and burned them so as emphatically to discourage expectation that she would soon be resurrected—as the Romans in the second century did to Christians in Gaul. Still, her cult thrived. Eventually, it spread to the peripheries of Lombardy. Even in tiny, secluded villages like Brunate, on the northwestern tip of the Italian peninsula, one can still find a fresco of Guglielma. Amazingly, she is depicted in the act of ordaining Maifreda by imposing her hands on the latter's head. Despite her condemnation, her cult improbably endured.

Secular-Mendicant Controversy

The rebels in the Marches of Ancona, under the bewitching influence of Joachim, likely saw themselves living on the cusp of the Age of the Holy Spirit, under whom they claimed to be guided—never a happy proclamation for those in authority. Direct guidance from the Holy Spirit also made instructions from priestly authorities irrelevant. Crescentius responded by denouncing them before the entire chapter of 1244. But it was too late. The "zealous" wing of the order or, as they would better become known, the Spirituals, had been born. By 1280 or so, they had hardened into a recognizable, distinct wing of the order, in contrast to the less rigorist (and sometimes lax) "Conventuals." The Spirituals would torment a whole series of ministers general and finally—and disastrously—the papacy. Some of the more radical Spirituals were also enthusiastic Joachites. The most radical believed that Joachim's message was "the everlasting gospel," his writings in effect a second Bible. They would scandalize the church and deeply damage the order in the coming conflict with the secular clergy in Paris, the so-called "secular-mendicant controversy."

The dispute began at the University of Paris as a conflict of interest over theological chairs, pupils, legacies, and ecclesiastical jurisdiction. By 1253 the mendicants had taken three of the twelve chairs of theology at the university, and they were preparing to take a fourth. Particularly galling to the seculars was that former colleagues (such as Alexander of Hales [d. 1245] and John of St. Giles [d. ca. 1260]) took the mendicant habit and then continued to teach at their orders' respective friaries. In so doing, they cut into secular control of the professoriate. The secular monopoly of student clientele was also broken by the friars' success in attracting sizeable numbers of young recruits to their own schools. Other members of the parochial clergy resented the presence of the friars because their popularity as preachers and confessors drew parishioners away from local parish churches. Dying penitents often chose to be buried in the friars' churches, depriving parish churches of mortuaries and legacies. Finally, many bishops were opposed to the presence of unknown persons working in their dioceses since they had no authority over them.

The prominent theologian William of St. Amour (d. 1272) was among the first and most vociferous spokesmen for the secular cause. The timing of his first attack was no coincidence. In 1254 the Joachite Franciscan Gerard of Borgo San Donnino published his *Introduction to the Eternal Gospel*. Among other things, Gerard, convinced that the Age of the Holy Spirit was about to dawn, announced that Joachim's writings would supersede the canonical testaments. In addition, the "carnal" church (always contrasted by Gerard with the true, "spiritual church") would fall into decay, as would institutions like the priesthood and the papacy. The spiritual clergy of the new age were not the parochial clergy but the friars.

William quickly exploited Gerard's colossal blunder. Armed with a list of thirty-one errors extracted from the *Introduction,* William and three colleagues set out for the papal curia. Once there, they convinced the pope that the friars were a serious threat to ecclesial order. Innocent IV soon published the bull *Etsi animarum* (November 1254), rescinding all privileges enjoyed by the friars at secular expense. The secular clergy had struck a decisive first blow. Its success was, however, somewhat short-lived. Innocent soon died, only to be succeeded by the former cardinal protector of the Franciscans. Upon ascending the throne of Peter, Alexander IV immediately began to act on behalf of the friars, first annulling *Etsi* with his own *Nec insolitum* and then restoring fraternal privileges at the University of Paris with his *Quasi lignum vitae* (April 1255). Still, the damage had been done. Not only had Gerard connected the Franciscans with what could only be regarded as insane heresy (indeed, his book was condemned as heretical in 1255), but his enormous gaffe led the pope to ask, reluctantly, for the resignation of John of Parma, who, a moderate Joachite untouched by Gerard's radical views, was regarded by all as pious and scholarly. This caused considerable dismay at the chapter of 1257. Once the brethren learned that the papacy had pressured him to resign, however, they asked him at least to nominate his own successor. Without wavering, he nominated Bonaventure of Bagnoregio, who would, not without reason, become known as the "second founder" of the Franciscan Order.

Bonaventure

When nominated minister general, Bonaventure, one of the great pupils of Alexander of Hales, had been a master in the theological faculty at Paris and without doubt among the greatest scholars in the order. By no means was Bonaventure untouched by Joachite speculation. He identified St. Francis as the angel of the sixth seal in the Apocalypse. That, along with his personal sanctity, dedication to poverty, and modesty all commended him to the zealots. (He had no enthusiasm for the idea of an age unfolding under the aegis of the Holy Spirit, a stance that probably commended him to moderates.) The Conventuals appreciated that he accepted the reorientation of the order to learning, to clericalization, and even to some deviation from primitive Franciscan observance. In any case, in interpreting Francis's own writings and wishes, he cut a path between the strict and loose constructionists, the Conventuals and the burgeoning Spiritual wing of the order. He was not a Franciscan fundamentalist. Rather, he looked to the founder as a source of inspiration, not of imitation, and to the founder's writings broadly, not as a code of law or commandments. He did not hesitate to interpret Francis's writings in light of papal decrees and dispensations. His writings included a commentary on Francis's *Rule* and an inoffensive, somewhat anodyne *Life of St. Francis,* certainly one the Spirituals could not exploit for inspiration or direction. In addition, in the constitutions passed at the chapter of Narbonne (1260), over which he presided, he managed to establish, by regularizing the ideal of "sparing" or "poor use," a *via media* between laxity and radical rigor. He standardized the ideal of "sparing" or "poor use" *(usus pauper)*. He could hardly have known that this idea would rock the order, agitate the church, and invite the papacy, disastrously, into the half-century dispute over what "poor use" meant and how it was or was not embedded in a friar's vow to observe the *Rule*.

Olivi and the Controversy over "Poor Use"

The roots of the restricted use of goods, or *usus pauper,* controversy lie not only in Bonaventure's inspired if imprecise idea, but also in the profound transformation of the Franciscan Order from a small band of itinerant preachers to a large, powerful, and even wealthy order exercising important functions on behalf of the pope and secular administrations. Over the course of the fifty or so years after Francis's death, the order grew phenomenally in numbers, as noted. Once Franciscans started assuming positions in ecclesiastical, royal, or city governments, the order came to be viewed as a road to worldly advancement rather than renunciation. Further, the gifts of generous benefactors brought the order into even more intimate contact with the wealthy and powerful, and for a variety of reasons, these gifts were not always easy to refuse. The result of all these developments was a somewhat understandable decline in standards. Since many of the order's new functions were either approved or ordered by the pope, it was clear that some adjustment in the observance of *usus pauper* would have to be made.

All these developments helped to give rise to the *usus pauper* controversy. Properly speaking, however, the controversy, which began about 1279, did not start over the issue of how restricted Franciscan observance should be or even over the issue of whether Franciscans were obligated to observe restricted use of goods. All Franciscans in 1279 were in agreement that they were obligated to observe restricted use, and the debate over the appropriate level of observance was not new. As David Burr has proven, the distinguishing characteristic of the *usus pauper* controversy was whether the observance of restricted use was imposed upon members of the order by their vow. In Burr's words, the "most characteristic element [of the controversy] was not a debate over whether Franciscans were obligated to live modestly, or even over how modestly they were obligated to live, but a debate over the source of their obligation in this regard." The debate began because Peter Olivi (d. 1298) argued that *usus pauper* was included in a friar's vow to observe the *Rule,* while his opponents insisted that their vows obligated them only to renunciation of dominion or ownership. By 1283, Olivi's views on *usus pauper* had been examined by the Parisian commission of seven theologians. They denied that *usus pauper* was in any way included in the vow and said that to affirm the opposite was erroneous. The commission was quite ambiguous or even silent about what precisely it found objectionable in Olivi's view. Perhaps the commissioners themselves did not know. The problem was a very new one. Olivi was among those Franciscan lectors most enthusiastic about Joachim. Not surprisingly, he suggested (though never explicitly stated) that opponents of his view of Franciscan poverty, and especially of "poor use," were agents of Antichrist.

For Olivi, these opponents included laxists within his own order, some Dominicans (including Thomas Aquinas, with whom he had a bitter literary exchange), and even the pope himself. Not long after the 1283 condemnation, Olivi was rehabilitated and lived out his career as a lector in Florence and the south of France. After his death, controversy continued over his views on poverty. The year after his death his writings were condemned by the minister general, antagonizing the now distinct and well-formed Spiritual wing of the order, who could only interpret the condemnation as evidence of imminent apocalyptic tribulation. It is clear that after Olivi's death, some of his works were translated into the vernacular, and pious laymen gathered to read them, the writings of one whom they regarded as a saint. The cult of Olivi was quite active in southern France, especially at Narbonne, where he was buried. These followers (or *sectatores*, as they were called) did Olivi few favors. Some argued that Olivi's views had been revealed to him by the Holy Spirit. Others viewed him as an apocalyptic figure, usually an angel, predicted in the Apocalypse. These beliefs made Olivi appear only more dangerous, even heretical, in the eyes of authorities.

Meanwhile, Michael of Cesena (d. 1342) was chosen as minister general of the Franciscans and John XXII (r. 1316–1334) as pope. Both were opposed to the Spirituals and particularly to their distinctive squalid clothing, dress intentionally designed to distinguish them from their Conventual brethren. In 1318, twenty-four Spirituals were brought before the inquisitor of Provence. Of these, nineteen recanted their heresies, which included the belief that authority in the church had passed from the carnal church, led by the pope, to the spiritual church, whose members truly observed the gospel of Christ. Four were burned in the marketplace of Marseilles on May 7, 1318. In October 1319, several lay supporters were burned. To Olivi's followers, this could only mean that in persecuting the true observers of evangelical poverty, the pope and the carnal church were functioning as agents of the Antichrist.

Shock: Papal Suppression

To this point, the Conventuals were not unhappy with the hostile attention paid by the pope to the Spirituals. But from 1321 on, John XXII began to focus on Franciscan poverty as such, believing it to be the source of so much trouble and conflict within the order and for the church, not to mention a fountainhead of heretical thinking that identified the pontiff with the Antichrist. Accordingly, he first issued the bull *Ad Conditorem Canonum*. Very much against the will of the Conventuals as well as the Spirituals, it revoked papal dominion of the friars' goods and returned to them the property they claimed they did not own. Then, in November 1323, the pope issued the bull *Cum inter nonnullos*. To the shock, again, of the Conventuals as well as the Spirituals, it condemned as heretical the notion that Christ and the apostles owned nothing individually or in common. John was not deterred by the fact that forty-three years earlier his predecessor had affirmed the very doctrine he now denied. Here both the Franciscans and the pope found themselves in curious positions. Franciscans argued that as *Exiit qui seminat* (1279), the bull that affirmed this decree, had been issued by the pope infallibly, it could not be reversed by anyone—even another pope. For the pope, infallibility was not the issue. Rather, it was the fact that this was the error that had split the church and caused such divisive controversy.

The Conventuals ultimately panicked. The minister general, Michael of Cesena, once the pope's ally, fled to the imperial court after having been deposed by John XXII. Other Franciscans fled to the court of John's sworn enemy, the emperor Louis the Bavarian (r. 1314 –1347), who just then was making claims to the imperial throne that the papacy had refused to recognize. Louis declared Pope John a heretic and placed a new man, who took the name Nicholas V (d. 1455), on the throne of Peter. For their part, the Franciscans then reelected Michael of Cesena. A century of triumph had concluded in flight and tragedy, and all the sound and fury had originated in the attempt by a simple man to live the perfect life of Christ and the apostles. That doctrine—that Christ and the apostles had lived a life of perfect poverty—now stood condemned. All of the practical and disciplinary customs that flowed from that fundamental understanding lay in ruins. The distinction made in *Quo Elongati* between ownership and use had been rescinded by the papacy. With a stroke of the pen, John made the Franciscans what it had seemed to critics—an order holding property. Having been sheltered and showered with privileges by the papacy, the order was now utterly alienated from it.

The Philosopher, the Fathers, and the Faith:
Scholasticism and the University

We have already discussed the rapid demographic and economic changes that transformed medieval society in the three centuries from 1000 to 1300. Many of these changes, especially changes in the economy, in the growth of governments, and in the rise and renewal of cities, are important factors in the correspondingly dramatic rise in literacy in these centuries—and in precisely those areas where economic, social, and political growth was most pronounced—namely, the cities. The utility of literacy in turn was tied to the need on the part of merchants, notaries, those in the legal profession, clerks, and what we might call civil service employees or bureaucrats—that is, government officials—to be able to interpret contracts, financial account books, and written decrees. Men were eager to acquire the skills of literacy and perhaps command of a body of knowledge that would guarantee them employment in the financial and legal sectors of the proliferating bureaucracies of this era. In other words, economic factors and the prospects for employment, in the first instance, gave rise to the development of new modes of medieval education.

Among the governments that pioneered commitments to writing and the establishment of binding written agreements was the papal curia. Indeed, the papal court had the most sophisticated legal and bureaucratic apparatus of any government in Europe in these three centuries. But there were many other bureaucracies needing men competent in the reading, interpretation, finance, and execution of contracts. These were needs for which the traditional monastic schools were neither designed nor developed. If the new economic and bureaucratic needs were to be met, new systems of education had to be established. Eventually, these would develop into the first universities, shortly after the works of Aristotle, referred to in medieval writings as "the Philosopher," would transform learning in the West for centuries.

Monastic Schools

The primary cultural loss of imperial collapse and subsequent chaos was the disintegration, with the crumbling of the Roman Empire, of an extensive public and municipal system of education. While it is true that some schools survived in northern Europe, schools that communicated classical literature and culture largely vanished in the early Middle Ages. As monasteries were sovereign, self-governing, and economically self-sustaining institutions, they were, to a large degree, immune to the vicissitudes of empire. Sited outside the foundering cities, and sequestered from the ubiquitous decaying of the political order, the monastery stood alone as a viable site for the educational enterprise in Europe. Indeed, from the definitive collapse of the empire at the end of the fifth century until the emergence of schools in the cities in the eleventh, monasteries monopolized education and learning. This is in part because the liturgical offices that punctuated the monk's day required liturgical books. The generous time allocated by Benedict for divine reading *(lectio divina)* also required that monasteries have a library. Moreover, the *Rule* required that monks be capable of reading and interpreting the two testaments of the Christian scriptures; the writings of the authoritative church fathers; and writings, like Cassian's works on ancient monasticism, as well as hagiographical literature. Aside from the fact that ancient schools were not designed with such curricula in mind, such schools had by and large vanished from the scene. If a monk were to become literate and to participate in the literate pious culture of the cloister, the monastery would have to provide for its own schooling and its own schools. This was especially true when it became common, by the Carolingian era, for parents to donate their children as oblates to monasteries. It was these children who made up the majority of students in the monastic schools under the guardianship of teachers who would shepherd them for the decade and a half that normally preceded, by that era, ordination to the priesthood.

Subjects taught and learned in these schools were not oriented toward cultural enrichment but to induction into literate monastic culture, particularly rumination on the works of scripture, which was the beginning of the monk's worship of the divine. Piety and contemplation of (and commentary on) the scriptures were thus intimately tied in the cloister. For a young monk to participate in this form of literate piety, he had first to learn Latin. Latin was for him, as for students today, a foreign language, and it was the language in which the literature on which he meditated, beginning with the Bible and commentary on it by the church fathers, was composed. Not only competence but eloquence in Latin was treasured in the cloister so that sermons, letters, and other literature be attractively written. Accordingly, part of the young monk's education necessarily included mastery of the classics of pagan antiquity, though these were usually preselected very carefully and arrived on a novice's desk, on occasion, in excerpted form, or *florilegia;* but even the works of Ovid were read and digested. Instruction in these classics was designed to form the young monk into a writer whose literary eloquence reflected and augmented the felt glory of God in the sacred precincts of the cloister; his writing, as well as his reading, had a pious, even prayerful, devotional element to it. Even the slow, patient making of beautiful books, constructed in monastic leisure without the pressure of deadlines or worldly headache, was felt to be an act of devotion to God. Learning and the love of God, as the great monastic author Jean Leclercq has memorably taught us, were intimately united in the thought, prayer, and literary productions of the cloister throughout the monastic centuries.

Though constructed primarily for aspiring monks, monastic schools had other constituencies. Young men, for example, who were learning to become secular clergy rather than monks could be found in the monastic schools. As the monastery school stood alone, educationally, in most regions of Europe, it eventually admitted young men aspiring neither to the monastic nor the priestly life. For the few monasteries that could afford it and that had a sufficient number of students, it was possible to segregate boys with a religious vocation from young men with no such expectations. It was also thought desirable to shield religious novices from the secular norms, aspirations, and temptations brought to the cloister by this class of young men. These monasteries, which were often the wealthiest in Europe, typically addressed this issue in the most concrete way possible: they created two schools, an "internal" school designed for the education of oblates and an "external" school, often constructed on the outer boundary of the monastery, for the instruction of other students. In actuality, it was usually the case that there were *not* enough students, or sufficient resources, to justify the construction of two schools. In these cases, both groups of young men were taught together.

With the revitalization of towns and the reestablishment of the schools in the cities, the ambivalence traditionally felt by monks toward the enterprise of learning not explicitly oriented to the cultivation of the soul turned to hostility. In the twelfth century, the great monastery of Cluny shut its doors to external students entirely. But it is in the reaction of the Cistercians to the new schools, new forms of learning, and even the corresponding temptations of city life that we really catch the depth of antagonism to the new educational enterprise. No less a figure than Bernard of Clairvaux led the crusade against the novelties of the age. In fact, he traveled to Paris expressly to turn students away from the urban schools, filled as they were with doubt and disputation, as well as staffed by masters, in his severe opinion, of dubious competence. "Flee this Babylon," he exhorted them, "and save your souls." Hoping to convert these young men to his own order, he urged them to "fly to the monasteries of the wilderness, where solitary rocks and forests teach more piety than mortal masters." There, in the tranquility of the monastic school, far from the imperfections, conflicts, and temptations of the city, they would learn from the one true master, Christ.

Contemplating these words, we feel, correctly, as if witnessing a cultural transformation, originating in the social and economic changes of the century. Education, teaching, and learning were passing from the forests and cloisters to the schools and cities (compared, now, by wary monks to Sodom, Gomorrah, Nineveh, and other cities notorious for wickedness and other sites detested by God). In this transition, it was not only the locus of education that would change, though that is hardly unimportant, as social setting shapes all economic and cultural enterprise. More significantly, the very forms, purposes, and aspirations of the custodians of learned culture would dramatically change, and its sacred character would suffer drastic reduction.

Urban Schools

The differences between monastic and scholastic education can be, and have been, exaggerated. We need to remember that even those schools in cities were for clerics training for ordination. Almost needless to say, all "believed in" and serviced the Deity. No scholastic ever claimed to have invented a portion of revelation. Rather, he worked within the very framework of the deposit of faith and attempted, by the strict application of reason, to understand it more profoundly. In other words, in ways that may seem backward to some today, he sought to understand what he already knew to be so. Belief preceded understanding; the latter clarified and reinforced the former. Some monks, notably the astonishing Anselm of Bec (d. 1109), a Benedictine monk and later archbishop of Canterbury, could devise a rigorous, logical, revelation-free proof for the existence of God, one with which philosophers and theologians are wrestling a millennium after his death. Anselm's intellectual program can be summed up in the subtitle of one of his books: "faith seeking understanding" (*fides quaerens intellectum*).

Still, differences there were. Those who would seek education in the cities rather than the forests were not monks. Rather, they were frequently men who aspired to high positions in the church—bishoprics, archdeaconries, and canonries—or at the very least posts in the presbyterate. Their education was not undertaken by a monk but a *scholasticus*—a scholastic—whose very name signals that he would be transmitting a wholly different kind of education. He taught not in a cloister but in the complex of buildings round the cathedral precincts. He was not part of a cadre of instructors but worked solo. Sometimes a bishop, he was more usually a member of the cathedral chapter. His school conferred no primary degrees. His students would either progress to ordination to the priesthood or, in a pattern sadly familiar to students today, his education would suddenly cease when resources were depleted. Scholastics *theoretically* taught the trivium and quadrivium in order to prepare the student for the study of the Bible (or the *sacra pagina*—the sacred page) in order that he might, ultimately, ruminate upon a verse of scripture to fix it in memory and aid in the worship of God.

In a sense that would intensify over the subsequent decades, the scholastic *was* the school. Over the course of the twelfth century, certain city schools slowly established reputations (again because of the presence of a particular master there) for excellence in advanced disciplines. Thus Laon and Reims, in northern France, developed a reputation for theology, as well as the liberal arts, that Paris soon would surpass; Orléans, for Latin and the liberal arts in general; and Chartres, for science and also for the liberal arts. A student avid for knowledge in all these fields easily could, and would, move from school to school to school in the relatively small geographical domain encompassed by these towns. On the Iberian Peninsula, Toledo would shape the future of learning by its translations of scientific works from the ancient Greek and Arab cultural worlds. In the south of Europe, medicine was taught with distinction in Montpellier and Salerno. While of course Bologna would achieve preeminence in law, it was also taught with excellence in the three French towns of Paris, Orléans, and Montpellier. A contemporary preacher could observe this scene and lament (all this before the outrages of web-surfing in class) that the only thing not taught in these schools was good manners.

Romantic views of the high Middle Ages and exaggerated, if not erroneous, views of "Augustine as Father of the Middle Ages" have led some to believe that what Augustine recommended must actually have occurred (in this as in all realms). Again untrue, perhaps to the dismay of those who would like to lay all the blames of western culture at the feet of that provincial North African bishop. While it is true that in his book on biblical exegesis and preaching, *On Christian Teaching,* Augustine recommended the trivium (grammar, rhetoric, logic) and the quadrivium (geometry, astronomy, music, arithmetic)—pagan gold, rightly stolen—for the goal of interpreting scripture, this ideal curriculum was honored far more in the breach. In ways inevitably governed by limitations of the lone-ranger teacher, the school essentially taught what the scholastic knew. Nonetheless, nearly every school had to have taught reading and writing. Each probably also taught one challenging foreign language: Latin.

In this, they would be supported by the papacy. Pope Alexander III decreed, from the Third Lateran Council, that each cathedral chapter support financially one scholastic to teach the rudiments of grammar without charge to poor students. When this was unheeded, Pope Innocent III not only renewed the decree in 1215, but he also demanded that metropolitan chapters supply a master in theology. Each of these decrees expresses papal aspirations; they ought not to be taken to reflect social realities but the importance, at the papal curia, of the cathedral school. Each would also predict the strong papal support of the newly emergent universities.

Those scholastics not tied by a benefice or position to a cathedral chapter were wanderers, or peripatetics *(vagantes)*. Again, their habits and conventions of labor mirrored those of their ambient culture. Like merchants, they traveled from city to city to trade in their product: learning. We see such a type already by ca. 1050. For Anselm's efforts, he earned a stern rebuke from the redoubtable Bernard of Clairvaux. Yet that was nothing compared to the blast the Cistercian abbot would deliver to the exemplary peripatetic teacher Peter Abelard, who would suffer other indignities over the course of his distinguished and disastrous career.

A History of Calamity: Abelard and Heloise

With the possible exception of his own outstanding pupil, John of Salisbury, no single master exemplifies the changes in instruction and learning nor the shift from monastic to scholastic styles of learning better than Peter Abelard. We know quite a lot about Peter, in large part because he left an account of his life, which he entitled, all too accurately, *A History of My Calamities.* Seven additional letters, to and from the woman with whom posterity will forever link him, Heloise (d. 1164), fill out the picture. A fully rounded character emerges: one avid for learning and teaching, charming, eloquent, arrogant, vain, paranoid, lecherous, contemptuous, impetuous, proud, prolific, and brilliant.

The scion of a knightly family at the southern edge of Brittany, Abelard first studied philosophy, or logic (then called "dialectic") at Loches and Tours, then, in 1100, at Paris. Moving next to Laon, the home of the celebrated biblical scholar Anselm of Laon (d. 1117), he began to display his withering wit, along with his arrogance. He would pick apart the greatest biblical scholar of his generation, dismissing his lectures as "smoke without a flame," and entrepreneurially dare to set up a rival school in the same city. A restless gun, he moved his school to Paris, Melun, Corbeil, and other towns in Champagne. He was, or perceived himself to be, constantly under attack by academic adversaries—not surprising for one who *was* frequently *on* the attack. Somewhere around 1105, he likely suffered what we should call today some sort of mental breakdown. He was, however, loved and admired by crowds of students who heard or followed him.

Abelard eventually became a canon at Notre Dame with an ample student following. As if scripted by a brilliantly ironic writer, it was here, at the height of his fame, that his calamities began to multiply. Engaged by his fellow canon Fulbert to tutor his niece, he soon fell helplessly in love with Heloise, and she with Abelard. Happy with the progress of his niece's studies, Fulbert startlingly encouraged the two to spend more time together so that she might learn more from Peter. She did. As Abelard remembers: "With our studies as an excuse, we gave ourselves to love. We withdrew to a private room, ostensibly for study, but our books lay unread before us. We spoke more of love than of books, and there was more kissing than learning. My hands were more often on her breasts than on our books." Before long, Fulbert, to Abelard's everlasting misfortune and to his niece's everlasting grief, caught them *in flagrante delicto*. Soon enough, Heloise found herself pregnant and gave birth to a son, called Astrolabe. Abelard overrode the objections of Heloise, who feared that marriage would ruin his teaching career, as one had to be a cleric and unmarried to teach. Thus Abelard wed her in a secret ceremony. He then sent his new wife to a nunnery outside Paris. That, not fornication, was the act that sealed his fate, for Fulbert (who did not know they had wed) interpreted this as an attempt by Abelard to free himself of his niece by dispatching her to a nunnery, where she could be conveniently forgotten. Once Heloise's uncle thought Abelard was trying to rid himself of Heloise, the enraged and dishonored Fulbert had his niece's former tutor emasculated by kinsmen. As the media might say today, news of the castration went viral, to the periphery of Christendom. His students gathered in tears outside his apartment. Yet not all were sympathetic. One of his teachers unkindly observed that he could no longer call himself Peter; that, after all, was a masculine name. Soon Abelard entered the royal abbey of St. Denis, just north of Paris, as a monk.

Abelard soon alienated the monastic community there. Long before he was expelled for denying that Dionysius the Areopagite, the follower of Paul (Acts 17:34) and supposed author of highly influential mystical writings, was founder of St. Denis, he grew quickly estranged from his community. (That Abelard was right—Dionysius was a sixth-century Syrian monk who wrote pseudepigraphally—made no difference, for that insight would not be verified and accepted for roughly three centuries.) This new brother quickly denounced the monks as worldly and their abbot as decadent. He was sent to a priory near Champagne. In this episode, we catch something remarkable about Abelard's character. Just humiliated, Abelard confidently and, without harboring doubts, criticized those he barely knew. He suffered no fools, intellectual or religious, yet he was hotheaded and reckless, indelicate and slightly inhumane in his harsh verdicts, even if correct.

Soon Abelard turned from dialectic to divinity; again no doubt about his capacity to make such an abrupt intellectual shift entered his mind. And for good reason: between 1118 and 1121, he wrote a treatise, on which he would work for much the rest of his life, entitled *Theologia*. It is to him, more than to any other contemporary, that credit (or, depending on one's perspective, fault) must be assigned for popularizing the term "theology."

Naturally, the book got him into trouble. His contemptuous conduct at Laon much earlier came back to haunt him. Enemies conspired to charge that he had resurrected the ancient heresy of Sabellianism; wrongly, if often, called "tritheism," this was a way of understanding the triplicity of God that suggested that God had acted in history in three ways: as creator, savior, and sustainer. Abelard was called up on heresy charges at the Council of Soissons in 1121. There his views on God were condemned. So deeply did Abelard feel the mortification of this sentence that he pronounced it worse than the sting of castration. He returned to St. Denis, only to be expelled again, for it was on this occasion that he questioned the identity of the abbey's patron saint.

Taking flight, Abelard lived as a hermit near Troyes. There an oratory was built. Abelard named it, after the Holy Spirit, "the Paraclete." Students soon found and flocked to him, and Abelard established a school there. There, too, he wrote one of his most famous and influential books, *Sic et Non (For and Against)*, a classic, a monument to learning and deep scholarship. It detected thousands of apparent contradictions in the works of ancient or early-medieval Christian thinkers. In the end, Abelard compiled 168 questions on which he found contradictory patristic opinion—for example, "Should one believe in God?" While Abelard himself did not offer opinions on the questions he raised—that task would be left to subsequent theologians of great distinction—he did offer principles for harmonizing existing conflicts. In addition to recommending that the authenticity of each text be determined, that context be established, and that various types of opinions distinguished, he strongly recommended that the rich semantic meanings of a single word be differentiated; in this way, dialectical reasoning, based on the mastery of grammar and logic, would enable the theologian to reconcile venerable authorities and show them to be in harmony. His aim was therefore emphatically *not* to call into doubt the authority of the patristic fathers who appeared to disagree on critical theological questions.

Anselm of Laon and Abelard, both "prescholastic" thinkers, herald a new era in the history of Christian thought, one that would be brought to brilliant consummation in the marriage of Aristotelian logic and the data of revelation in the thirteenth century. It was scholars like Abelard and Anselm that, for good or ill, helped along the process by which, in the thirteenth century, theology became a "science"—a science that aspired to understand more deeply, by the exercise of rational thought, what had been given, and believed, in the vehicles of revelation.

Amazingly, the monks of the monastery of St. Gildas in western Brittany, which overlooked the sea, elected Abelard as their abbot around 1125. Their astonishingly bad choice was compounded by Abelard's in accepting the position. When he attempted to reform these Celtic monks, with whom, culturally and intellectually, he had little in common, they retaliated. We are told by Abelard that they attempted to poison the Eucharistic wine and thus remove him by killing him. Interpretations of this incident vary. Yet it does not quite ring true; it may have been that Abelard's occasional paranoia colored his view of the monks, who, murderous or not, did not want him there. One way or another, he received the message, and he found reasons to be absent from St. Gildas. It has been suggested, and not implausibly, that Abelard was not at all paranoid but intentionally exaggerated the danger he was in at St. Gildas in order to make his way back to Paris and to teaching.

It was at this time that Heloise, now abbess at a community, found her community expelled from Argenteuil. Abelard gave the exiled community of nuns the Paraclete. Around 1131, Abelard wrote his autobiography. Somehow, Heloise found herself with a copy, and reading it gave her the heart to respond; this inaugurated their famous exchange of letters. She poured out her heart to him: "I have ever loved you," she said with obvious sincerity, "with a boundless love." With brutal honesty, she blurted out the details of her inner life: "It would," she professed, "be more precious and more honorable to me to be called your whore than the wife of the emperor." At the highest moments of the mass, she confessed, "lewd images of our pleasures seize my hapless soul." Coolly, Abelard admonished her to pray.

As if in punishment, he now had to face an enemy whose power was then unparalleled, even by the pope. With a character perhaps even less attractive than Abelard's, Bernard of Clairvaux, who loathed Abelard as much for his theological presumption as for his character, pursued him with aggression not usually associated with monks. In one of his letters, Bernard sums up his grievances: "Outwardly he appears a monk, but within he is a heretic, having nothing of the monk about him save the habit and the name. . . . He is a monk without a rule, a prelate without responsibility, an abbot without discipline." Bernard concludes this list of complaints: "He argues with boys and consorts with women." Infuriated, the abbot of Clairvaux decided to bring Abelard down by theological litigation, and he staged the trial of the century at Sens in 1141. Excited by the prospect, the king of France, many nobles, bishops, abbots, and other luminaries attended the legal festivities. The abbot of Cîteaux himself took on the role of prosecutor.

The verdict was predetermined. Knowing this, Abelard simply appealed to the pope and left, leaving behind a disappointed audience. On his way to the papal curia, Abelard stopped at the famous abbey of Cluny, then presided over by Peter, rightly called "the Venerable." Wisely and patiently, the abbot of Cluny counseled him not to proceed to Rome. Why not stay at Cluny? That was good advice, as the sitting pope, Innocent II, a tool of Bernard, condemned Abelard and may even have watched with satisfaction as, on his orders, Abelard's books were burned in the church in Rome that bore the author's name. As Abelard took up residence at a priory of Cluny, his health began to fail. Happily, he and Bernard were reconciled before his death. He was even absolved of the papal condemnation.

With these events, Abelard died in April 1142 at the age of sixty-three. Characteristically, Peter the Venerable responded to Heloise's request and personally accompanied Abelard's body to the Paraclete. There, in the sanctuary of the chapel, Abelard's body was put to rest. Twenty-two years later, his wife's corpse was placed next to his. Sometime during the French Revolution, their tombs were molested. Still, today, they are said to rest together at the cemetery of Père Lachaise in Paris.

The University

The universities, which evolved from the cathedral schools (particularly those concentrated on the left bank and on the Île-de-France of the Seine in Paris, like that at Notre Dame cathedral), originated in the late eleventh century. By the dawn of the early modern period, three hundred years later, perhaps seventy or eighty universities existed. This remarkable institution had multiplied and spread across Europe. A combination of adventitious factors, such as geographical locus and the specialization of a master or group of masters, resulted in certain cities achieving distinction in certain of the professions. Thus (as noted), for theology, Paris and Oxford were preeminent, as was Bologna for law and Montpellier and Salerno for medicine. These institutions were originally called "totalities of scholars" or "universities of masters." Why?

In order to comprehend the academic and economic structure of the medieval university and of the professoriate, we must appreciate some of the features of medieval guilds, to the characteristics of which the new universities and their academic leadership would closely correspond. Medieval guilds were first and foremost organized, much like unions today, for the common profit of their members. Our term "university" actually derives from the Latin term for guild (*universitas*). In the Middle Ages, a "university" simply meant the totality of something—in this case, of men organized to protect common economic interests and to treat with political authorities. Thus there were "universities" of, say, smiths or shoemakers and other makers of goods and those possessing particular skills. Such universities or guilds were also preoccupied with the admission of members, requirements for demonstrating competence, and the upward movement in skill from novice to master.

We might imagine this structure as what we today would term a career ladder. At the bottom of the ladder, so to speak, stood apprentices. These were young men just beginning to learn their trade under the supervision and instruction of a man at the other end of the career ladder and trade skill, the master. Next up the ladder were journeymen (men who worked for the day—think of the French *journée*, "the whole day"). These journeymen could also be called bachelors, so-called as they could not support a family because unable, possessing only intermediate competence, to set up their own businesses. Naturally, the journeyman aspired to move up the ladder to the next and final rung. At the top of the ladder were masters, who alone had achieved, partly by producing some sort of final project demonstrating expert command of their trade (in time this would evolve, in academic circles, into a final thesis or dissertation), full membership in the guild. Masters also had, and indeed were required to have, some sort of economic independence to achieve and maintain full membership in the guild.

The resemblance of this structure to that of the academic *universitas* is striking. An apprentice represented a novice in his trade. Beginning students were like apprentices. Unlike modern American first-year college students, students at the medieval universities in the north were quite young—"early teens," as we should say today. Most, indeed, were no older than students enrolled in modern secondary schools. The rough equivalent of a journeyman in the academic guild was called a "bachelor." A student with considerable experience, he would lecture and otherwise aid apprentice students and serve masters, somewhat in the fashion of teaching assistants in modern research universities. In what we today call theology, a bachelor would then have to pass through two stages on his way to becoming a master: that of "bachelor of the Bible" and that of bachelor of the standard scholastic textbook, the *Sentences* of Peter Lombard (whose production, structure, and profound influence we will discuss below). On each of these authoritative texts, he would lecture, minimally, for a year. The terminal degree was that of master (or *doctor*—someone learned). The student had attained the position of master in a trade guild. As such he could teach, by license, in his own university and, finally, ubiquitously.

In any case, the coupling of students and masters into collective groups organized for mutual protection, for freedom from external harassment or interference, and, above all, for administrative frameworks for admission—or academic guilds—gave rise, around 1200, to the university, one of the leading and enduring cultural contributions of the Middle Ages to the modern world. Note that this institution was in its origins not a place; it was a movable feast of scholarship and master scholars.

The loci for excellence in learning in the late twelfth and early thirteenth centuries and for the emergence of a new educational institution, the university, were Paris, Bologna, and Oxford. At many of the universities, both the student body and the professoriate were foreigners. The cathedral schools that had monopolized advanced education in northern France, southern England, and western Germany were international. Many drew students from Ireland and Scotland in the West and other parts of Germany and Slavic lands in the East. For example, if Paris were the chief center of theological learning in these centuries, it is true that its greatest professors were Italian and English. How were these students and professors, drawn from the center and peripheries of the Continent, to teach and learn, to speak and to comprehend? By employing a dead language that had been revived: Latin. Just as Hebrew has been reanimated in the modern state of Israel after a long period of desuetude, just so Latin was brought back to life as a language of instruction and learning—and, in certain theological schools of Europe, like those in Rome, it remained so until relatively recently. Not only would Latin remain the language of learning and instruction in universities, but it would also be used for administrative and legal proceedings and decisions as well.

The mention of foreign students and masters reminds us again of the guild origins of the medieval university. Citizens of Paris must, by and large, have regarded both students and masters as foreigners; even students we might today call "French" would have been so reckoned. This is so because citizens of medieval towns and universities had, and anxiously guarded, rights, both economic and legal, that "foreigners" did not possess. "Town-and-gown" friction only intensified when students carried out petty pranks, committed serious crimes, or even rioted. These students had received the tonsure and were thus technically considered clerics—even those who did not aspire to a career in the church. In cases where tonsured students had committed crimes, they were liable only to the somewhat soft justice of ecclesiastical courts.

For their part, masters and students nursed their own grievances against local merchants, booksellers, and vendors of food, all of whom were believed to charge foreigners exorbitant fees for their products. Even the local police forces were believed to treat students more harshly than they would locals. The most serious complaints among the clergy were not against the secular but the ecclesiastical authorities of Paris. Masters were located in the vicinity of both the bishop and chancellor of Paris, and the latter had the right (conferred by canon law) to license teachers, determine many aspects of the curriculum, and even confer degrees. Masters chafed under his control.

Because the medieval university had so few unmovable possessions, it had a powerful weapon at its disposal against both secular and ecclesiastical authorities: the strike. Universities also had the support of the French kings and the papacy. Each of these powerful allies was brought to bear in the wake of a violent incident that occurred in 1229 in the student quarter in Paris. On the day before Lent that year (called Shrove Tuesday, which survives today as Mardi Gras), a dispute between drinking (and probably drunk) students and a tavern owner over a bill led to a physical altercation, one that left many students injured and one dead. For two years, the horrified and angry masters struck and quit the city. Hostile though they often were to students, merchants were worried: students might have been unruly, but they were also a good and, until then, reliable source of income.

Much more important was the concern felt at the highest levels of state and church. The king of France was troubled that a source of prestige, not to mention intellectual and administrative skill, had been lost. At the same time, the papacy was deeply distressed that the premier center for training in theology in Christendom had been shut down. Paris, after all, had, by the time of the strike, become the indispensable center of training not only for officials at the royal court but also for future bishops and other high-ranking churchmen, as well as preachers. Two years after the strike, in 1231, Pope Gregory IX (himself an alumnus of the University of Paris) issued a bull, *The Mother of Sciences (Parens Scientiarum),* with the approval of the French king, Louis IX (r. 1226–1270). The bull deferred wholly to the masters, conferring upon them, and taking from the Parisian chancellor, the right to govern the university, a step that in effect secured its independence. From this time on, both popes and kings showered students and masters with a host of privileges and exemptions. No longer could the chancellor impose his rules, determine the curriculum, or confer degrees. Now these privileges had, by the highest authorities in Christendom, been authoritatively turned over to the masters. Incidentally, the strike at Paris allowed Toulouse to attract some Parisian scholars to that French town to establish a university, and a strike at Oxford in 1209 caused professors there to depart permanently to Cambridge, where of course they founded one of the greatest universities in Europe.

It is common and essentially correct, if slightly simplistic, to say that two archetypes of universities emerged in the late eleventh and twelfth centuries, one northern and the other southern (slightly simplistic, as there were some hybrid forms). The northern one, based on the Paris model, was magisterial, insofar as this type of *universitas* was controlled by the masters, or professors. The southern one, based on the Bologna exemplar, was controlled by the slightly older students in that Italian city.

Organizationally, the University of Paris was divided into four faculties: arts, medicine, law (civil law would be proscribed after 1219, so canon law is meant), and theology. The arts faculty dominated in several ways, especially in its foundational relation to the professional schools (much the way a liberal arts college at a major research university is the foundation for professional study today) and in the sheer number of masters. Indeed, this structure reflects the self-understanding of the masters of the arts faculty, which considered itself the "mother" of the professional faculties. Again as pertains to organization, the faculty of arts was divided, by 1250, into "nations": the French (those from the Île-de-France and the Latin countries), the Picard (which included the Low Countries), the Norman, and the English, later called the English-German. Further divided into provinces, each nation required members to have achieved the rank of masters of arts; each was headed by a proctor. All had patron saints, whose feast days were celebrated annually with academic and religious gravity. The arts faculty, alone among the faculties, had a rector, who would eventually become head of the university; the others had a dean. With few exceptions, the Paris archetype would be imitated, with some adjustment for local circumstance and composition of the masters, by almost all universities established in the north of Europe.

In the south, Bologna would function as the university archetype. Already by 1150, Bologna had established itself as a center for legal studies, as many illustrious legal scholars had installed themselves there. In addition to its well-deserved reputation as a center for legal learning, Bologna was known for training notaries and civil servants. Because foreign students enjoyed no legal privileges in the eyes of the commune of Bologna, they, too, organized themselves for protection, and thus it was they who, formed first, came to control the university. Because so many of the students, cismontane (that is, students from Italy) and ultramontane (from outside the peninsula, "beyond the Alps"), arrived in Bologna with some work experience, typically administrative, they tended to be older and more mature than their counterparts in Paris. Eventually, the cismontane and ultramontane students (each group of which was also divided into nations) united to form a single "university of scholars" and elected their own rector to run the university.

To the older and more mature students at Bologna fell the responsibility of negotiating not only with authorities from the commune but also with the masters, and it was on students that the masters depended for much (except admission to the guild, which was a privilege, almost the only one, reserved to the masters). In a manner that would make today's professoriate aghast, students controlled not only masters' appointments, chairs, and fees. If this were not humiliating enough, masters, should they wish to miss a day of lecture, had to request student permission. When leaving town, the professor was required to post bond. Failing, when lecturing, to attract an audience of more than five pupils, the master was simply treated as absent—and his pay correspondingly docked. Students also monitored his punctuality, and if tardy, he was treated like a schoolboy receiving a pink slip; the students also imposed punctuality in other ways, requiring the master to maintain pace with the established syllabus. So habitually—I almost wrote daily—do professors today breach one or more of these norms that they would, if such a regime were resurrected, be pauperized (if imaginable) even more severely or, like their hapless doctoral students, made jobless. Be that as it may, again, the pattern established at Bologna prevailed in most universities founded in the south of Europe.

As the thirteenth century wore on, new universities were founded less and less by striking professors and more by the conscious act of foundation. In the early thirteenth century, there were four universities in Europe. Around 1500, there were roughly seventy educational institutions that called themselves "universities." Before the Black Death, which ruthlessly shrunk student populations, the oldest universities, like Paris, might enroll five thousand students or even more. Their smallish size, however, was wholly disproportionate not only to their intellectual but also to their economic and cultural impact. Students—especially those not well born—matriculated at universities because a degree opened paths to profitable and rewarding careers in the service of the church, state, or municipality. Undoubtedly, the surest way to such a career was by acquiring a degree in law. Nonetheless, many careers required no more than a master of arts degree. At the same time, such a degree was essential, almost mandatory, to acquire a desirable position in state or church, in much the same way a bachelor's degree is required today in order to secure a white-collar position or to move to advanced studies or a professional degree.

If their impact on economic opportunity and life was deep, the universities' influence on intellectual life, art, music, literature, and, of course, ecclesiastical culture was even more profound. In theology, law, and medicine, almost all surviving works, many of which are extremely highly evolved and intricate, were composed by those who had studied, many for quite a few years, at university. Whether the emphasis on logic and legal thinking on the character of the church in those centuries was advantageous or detrimental is an open question. What is not in doubt is that it was the thinking and writing of men trained in the sciences of logic, law, and theology that deeply shaped the character of the church—especially ecclesiastical government—in the high and late Middle Ages.

Teaching and Learning

We must begin our discussion of teaching and learning by emphasizing that while scholasticism emerged as the dominant mode of teaching and learning in the Middle Ages, it did not technically originate in medieval Europe. Already in the ninth century, something very like what would become the Latin scholastic method had emerged in Islamic thought in Abbasid Mesopotamia, and it was far from undeveloped in Byzantine milieux.

That said, in the schools and in the new universities, a common pattern of learning emerged that prevailed across all the undergraduate and professional disciplines, including theology, canon and civil law, and medicine. Learning and teaching began with the reading *(lectio)* of one or more of the hundreds or thousands of available authoritative written texts *(auctoritates)* composed by acknowledged, usually ancient, masters in a particular field. Thus, in civil law (where it was taught), the authority on which discussion could begin might be a text from Roman law; in canon law, it could be an ancient conciliar canon or decree; and in theology it could be a statement regarding the Trinity, the mode of union of divine and human in the Incarnate Christ, or any number of theological or exegetical comments from the ancient and medieval authorities. In theology, a scriptural verse was also, and often, treated as such an "authority."

Reflection on these authorities would begin, as mentioned, with the *lectio* (the Latin word, of course, from which the English word for "lecture" derives), in which a professor would simply read texts out loud to the students. Early in the history of scholasticism, it was discovered that these authoritative texts, distressingly, could be in conflict with one another, or self-contradictory, or even inconsistent with what, by the scholastic period, had been accepted by the church as orthodoxy. Scholastics understood their job to be, by the exercise of Aristotelian logic, to harmonize these apparently conflicting authorities or to make the ostensibly self-contradictory ones make analytical sense. Obviously, the profound assumption of the scholastics, very foreign to the modern critical sense, was that most ancient authorities were, in fact, in agreement with one another.

Another assumption was that Aristotelian logic was the master tool for harmonizing authorities apparently in conflict. If there was a reason for the emphatic curricular concentration on logic in the schools and new universities at the undergraduate level, it was the assumption that logic was indispensable for succeeding in the professional curricula of the university. While presenting authorities through reading, the master would habitually pose a question *(quaestio)* to the students that often had to do with perceived contradictions among authorities that arose during the reading from the textbook. Then followed an oral argument or disputation *(disputatio)* in which, as part of their training, students would use grammar, logic, and other "dialectical" methods in which they had been so thoroughly trained in order to respond to the question posed by the master. Just as Abelard had recommended in the beginning of *Sic et Non,* his collection of apparently conflicting authorities, students would argue about the authenticity of a particular text and, above all, use their finely honed grammatical and logical skills to distinguish distinct meanings of a single word. Using these methods, they would attempt to demonstrate that the conflicts among authorities were resolvable, by and large, by careful semantic and logical differentiation. In any case, the sequence of reading-question-disputation was ubiquitous in medieval universities and still influences the conduct of instruction, especially in seminars, in western universities.

If Abelard carefully laid out the methods by which theological authorities could be brought into harmony, he left it to his successors at Paris to attempt to provide responses to the questions he had raised. This was a task undertaken by Peter Lombard, who, a year before his death, became bishop of Paris. Around fifteen years before that, Peter had begun teaching at Notre Dame in Paris. As his name suggests, Peter was born in northern Italy, at Novara. Eventually, he studied at Bologna, Reims, and Paris. He was that rare man who could have been both friendly with Bernard and, likely, a student of Abelard. By the early 1140s, he was, partly as a result of the recommendation of Bernard, teaching at Notre Dame in Paris. He was quickly recognized as a theologian of supreme competence, if not of rare brio or originality. His great contribution to theological literature and education was the production between 1155 and 1158 of his *Four Books of Sentences,* "sentences" *(sententiae)* meaning essentially the same thing as "authorities"— namely, statements, opinions, and judgments of the ancient fathers of the church, as well as biblical texts, organized around current theological questions. These sentences and questions were then structured into four books, the first of which dealt with the properties of God, the second with creation, the third with the Incarnation and redemption, and the fourth with the sacraments and the "last things" (death, judgment, heaven, and hell). Lombard's textbook aspired thus to encompass the entirety of theological issues and to arrange them in systematic order. Like Abelard, Lombard also recognized apparent inconsistencies in patristic opinion. Unlike Abelard, he would, by the conventional methods of dialectical analysis attempt to reconcile conflicts. He would offer his own opinion (*sententia,* or "resolution" or "determination") on the question at issue, sometimes at surprising length. Because of the logic of its arrangement and the comprehensiveness of its content, the work became immensely popular. Indeed, it became the new authoritative textbook for instruction in theology (its status would be boosted when its Trinitarian doctrine was explicitly approved by the Fourth Lateran Council in 1215) and remain so for roughly four centuries.

Before long, masters in theology began to lecture on the *Sentences* themselves and then to produce commentaries on the book, hundreds of which still exist. By 1250 or so, largely as a result of its popularity among the mendicant orders, a bachelor (then an advanced student in theology) would be required to lecture on the *Sentences* for an academic year. With the book's having by then become a part of the theological curriculum, lecturing on the "Master of the Sentences" became a step along the long road to the doctoral degree (or license) to teach theology *(licentia docendi)*. In this way, it prepared the path for the production, in the following century, for the great summaries *(summae)* of theology, like the most famous and influential one, the *Summa Theologiae (Handbook of Theology)* of the Dominican Thomas Aquinas. It would be a long time before Thomas's *Summa* overtook the *Book of Sentences* as the authoritative textbook in the universities. Not only did Thomas himself write an influential commentary on the Lombard, but late-medieval theologians would do the same, and even the great early Protestant reformers, like Luther and Calvin, would comment on or quote from Lombard's *Sentences*.

Like theologians, canon lawyers soon began to detect a whole host of apparently conflicting authorities from the decrees of councils and popes. Several compilations of such authorities were attempted. Of these, the most successful and influential was the work of Gratian, a canon lawyer who taught at Bologna. Author of a book entitled *Concord of Discordant Canons* (more usually known by its shorthand Latin title, the *Decretum*), Gratian too employed scholastic dialectic in order to reconcile the massive number of legal contradictions he had perceived and compiled. Like Peter Lombard's *Sentences,* Gratian's *Decretum* became a standard textbook, in this case for students of canon law in the universities of Europe. So useful and influential an introduction was it that only the publication, in the early twentieth century, of the *Code of Canon Law* rendered it of interest only to scholars. Throughout the Middle Ages, it served as the fundamental source of canon law. Celebrated as "the father of the science of canon law," Gratian was placed by Dante with the doctors of the church in the *Paradiso.*

Aristotle and Scholasticism

The works of Aristotle, so profoundly influential on medieval Christian thought, actually reached the West, by and large, through the heroic efforts of Muslim translators and Jewish and Islamic commentators on "the Philosopher." Until 1150, only Aristotle's logical works, known collectively as the *Organon,* had been translated into Latin. His writing on metaphysics, ethics, and science had not been. Islamic translation was concentrated, geographically speaking, in Syria, Constantinople, and Sicily and, above all, in Spain (where intellectual exchange was made possible by the Reconquista, as well as by trade)—that is, in major cities of the once massive Muslim empire.

By the late eleventh century, Christian scholars and translators had begun gathering in Toledo, following its reconquest, in search of manuscripts to translate from Arabic (or occasionally Spanish) into Latin. Later, translations into Latin were made directly from the Greek. In short, the passage of Aristotelian learning into Christendom, so critical for the future of theology in the north, occurred, in large part, on the backs of Islamic work on Aristotle in Spain or work that had been transmitted to Spain. By the dawn of the thirteenth century, northern scholars had acquired virtually the complete corpus of Aristotle's writings in Latin translations, some rough. These included his *Metaphysics,* Aristotle's work on psychology *(De Anima),* the *Physics,* and a set of authentic and spurious works on science, the *libri naturales.*

Both Islamic and Jewish commentators also produced a set of profoundly influential commentaries on Aristotle that also made their way to the West by way of Spain. One does not have to read very much of Thomas Aquinas to realize how deeply influenced he was by Moses ben Maimon, better known as the Jewish thinker Maimonides (d. 1204). Like Thomas himself, Maimonides would write a work, *Guide for the Perplexed,* that would attempt to cast revelation in the new categories of Aristotelian learning. Certainly the two most important Muslim commentators in the West were Avicenna (d. 1037) and Averroës (d. 1198), court philosopher to the caliphs in Cordova. Averroës's main intellectual project, not entirely realized, was to purge Aristotle's thought of any trace of Platonic influence. Nonetheless, his commentaries were received in the West, translated into Latin of course, and regarded as the authoritative interpretation of Aristotle's works. Enthusiasm for and adoption of much of the teaching of Averroës would eventually lead to a radical form of Aristotelianism on the faculty of Paris in the late thirteenth century.

It has been suggested, and not implausibly, that the rise of scholasticism and the new institution of learning did not together have a positive effect on women. Aristotelian biology famously held that women were incomplete or deformed men. It also asserted that the woman was the passive partner in reproduction; thus the male had the entire role to play in embryonic development. While some famous women, like Christine de Pizan (d. ca. 1430), resisted Aristotelian concepts of gender, it nonetheless remains true that Aristotelian physiology, with its many binary oppositions (like active and passive, shaper and shaped, strong and weak) were authoritative throughout much of the later Middle Ages and helped to reinforce religious views on the inferiority of women. As these very views excluded women from ordination, and as ordination to minor orders slowly became a prerequisite for study at university, women were institutionally excluded from the European university until the twentieth century. This is one reason we do not hear of women the intellectual caliber of Heloise or Hildegard in the later Middle Ages.

Universities and the Mendicants

One of the exceptionally creative periods in intellectual history and the history of theology in particular resulted from the fortuitous coincidence and mix of three ingredients: the retrieval of the whole of the Aristotelian corpus, the rise of the medieval university, and the determination of the mendicant orders to form preachers and scholars of the first order. By the time the friars emerged on the scene at Paris, theologians there, like masters in the other professional schools in Europe, already had their own set book, the Bible, just as the law faculty at Bologna had the Justinian *Code*, Gratian's *Decretum,* and papal decretals—decrees from the popes on points of canon law. As with Justinian's *Code,* the Bible soon received its own authoritative, standard annotation or commentary, called, not surprisingly, *The Standard Gloss (Glossa Ordinaria).* Long thought to be the work of a Frankish monk from the Carolingian period, Walafrid Strabo (d. 849), we now know that it was twelfth-century masters at the school of Laon (including Anselm, whom Abelard had dismissed with disdain) who took on the monumental task of assembling writings from the church fathers on each verse of the Bible. In the end, the result was a colossal pastiche of patristic opinions on the entirety of the scriptures. By the thirteenth century, the *lectio* consisted of reading not only from the *sacra pagina* of the Bible, but also from the patristic comments written between the lines and in the margins of the manuscript of the Bible. For this reason, distinction is sometimes made between the interlinear and marginal glosses. Incidentally, it was the school of Laon that began to compile this patristic opinion separately into books of "sentences." In this way, it prepared the way, ironically, for Abelard's *Sic et Non;* Abelard, in other words, relied for one of his greatest contributions to theology on the school on which he had heaped contempt.

As part of their ordinary teaching, the friars would lecture on the Bible. Many friars lectured on many books of the Bible. One Dominican, Hugh of St. Cher, led a team that produced a prodigious, comprehensive work relying heavily on magistral commentaries of the twelfth and thirteenth centuries that commented on every book of the Bible. This work remained in use in classrooms through the entire course of the Middle Ages and would eventually be among the first books printed. Members of Hugh's team also acquired knowledge of Greek and Hebrew—adumbrating developments in the later Middle Ages—and thus were able to compare Jerome's Vulgate translation with the original biblical texts. Hugh's team also produced one of the earliest biblical concordances in existence and other aids to textual study of the Bible. Hugh's Dominican confrere, Thomas Aquinas, known to posterity primarily as a theologian, would comment extensively on many books of the Bible, as would his Franciscan contemporary, Bonaventure.

Thomas Aquinas

Thomas is celebrated for many reasons. But one reason to acquaint oneself with the outlines of his career is that it exemplifies the sort of peripatetic calling an academic mendicant had undertaken (not inappropriate for a disciple of Aristotle). In addition, his literary output illustrates the whole spectrum of scholastic theological literature produced in the new university environment in Paris. Perhaps, along with Francis, the most widely recognized mendicant in the Middle Ages, Thomas was actually born to the purple. Born near Naples to the counts of Aquino (thus "Aquinas" refers to the place of his birth and is not, in modern fashion, a surname) and related to the German emperor through his mother, Thomas received his elementary education in the nearby monastery of Monte Cassino, the cloister of which Benedict had once been abbot; Thomas's family likely cherished hopes that he, too, would ultimately become abbot of the historic mountain-top monastery nearby. From Monte Cassino Thomas moved on eventually to the University of Naples. It was there that he first encountered the blackfriars (as the members of the Order of Preachers came to be called) and began to aspire to become a Dominican. Much to his parents' and family's distress and perhaps embarrassment, he did indeed choose the mendicant vocation. Hagiographical sources indicate that the family's humiliation was so acute that his brothers abducted him, detained him in family homes, and even arranged to have prostitutes attempt, unsuccessfully of course, to seduce him. Unable to nudge Thomas from his chosen path, his family finally released him.

In 1245 or so, his Dominican confreres, having recognized Thomas as a budding genius, sent him to Paris to study with the order's most distinguished scholar, Albert the Great, whom, in 1248, he followed to Cologne. There he lectured as a bachelor on the Bible. In 1252, he returned to Paris, serving first as a biblical bachelor, in which capacity he lectured and produced commentaries on Isaiah, Jeremiah, and Lamentations, and then as a bachelor of the *Sentences,* in which he lectured on and finished his first major theological work, his *Commentary on the Sentences*. In 1256, he received his license to teach. It was an inauspicious time to graduate as he, like Bonaventure, both ready to incept in theology, were caught up in the controversy with the secular clergy. Soon, however, Thomas was made professor of theology at Paris.

From this time until his death in 1274, Thomas was absorbed in teaching and writing in Paris and in many Dominican convents across Europe. In this way, too, his life is illustrative of a mendicant academic's career in the age of high scholasticism. After training with the Dominicans in Naples, Cologne, and Paris, he began his career in Paris. Yet he spent no more than three years there and, in 1259, was sent to Rome. There he spent only two years before he was sent to his home priory of San Domenico in Naples, again for two years, after which he was made lector at the Dominican priory at Orvieto. Again, roughly two years later, he was assigned to Rome in order to establish the school at Santa Sabina for the friars in the province at Rome and where he taught—yet again for a period of two years. From Rome, he went to Viterbo and served as lector in the priory there. In 1269, his superiors sent him back to Paris for a second time; he left in 1272. He then returned to Naples, where he set up another school for the order in that city. From there, he left for the Council of Lyons (1245) but fell ill and died at the Cistercian monastery of Fossanova.

Given all this to-ing and fro-ing, it is amazing and humbling to gaze at the collected works of Thomas; the sheer volume, not to mention diversity of genres, is staggering. Many editions of his *Opera Omnia (Collected Works)* have been printed, of which one runs to thirty-four volumes. They encompass the entire range of theological literary activity undertaken in the thirteenth century—and more. As mentioned, Thomas commented extensively on the scriptures and on the Lombard's *Sentences*. In addition, he commented voluminously on Aristotle. A series of commentaries that was intended not only to enable Thomas to master the writings of the Philosopher, but also to provide an orthodox guide to students in the arts faculties, it took him roughly two decades to complete. He left at least five hundred writings (many of which were recorded by auditors outside the lecture halls) on disputed theological questions, and he wrote many "quodlibeta"—from the Latin words meaning "what you please," arguments on issues of interest to the author, often given at the Christmas and Easter holidays. Though not widely known, he left liturgical writings and a number of lovely and famous hymns, including "Pange Lingua" (Sing, My Tongue).

Thomas's two most famous and influential works nonetheless are *summae,* or summary handbooks. The first, the *Summa contra Gentiles,* was composed in the early 1260s for use by Dominican friars preaching against Jews, Muslims, and heretics in Spain. The second, the book that immortalized him, is, of course, his *Summa Theologiae,* left unfinished at the time of his death. Students encountering the foreign terminology and difficult, if clear, thought of this masterpiece are usually astonished to discover that it was written as a handbook for beginners in the study of theology. Since the early church father Tertullian famously asked about the relationship of Athens and Jerusalem (that is, Greek philosophy and Christian revelation), many Christian theologians have attempted to synthesize the two.

It would be difficult to imagine an equal to the *Summa* for boldness of synthesis or the clarity, comprehensiveness, and brevity to which the author aspired. The entire work is structured into three parts. The first treats God, the Trinity, and creation; the second is divided into two parts, ethics and the virtues; and the third treats the Incarnation, redemption, and the sacraments. The whole addresses over six hundred *quaestiones,* themselves subdivided into more than three thousand articles, and in it Thomas responds to more than ten thousand objections. Without question, the *Summa* stands as one of the classics of western theology and indeed of western civilization. It has been printed countless times. Once it was recognized as a piece of orthodox genius, it replaced the Lombard's *Sentences* as the touchstone of Catholic theology, and it remained such for centuries.

The Aristotelian Crisis

Discussion of Thomas Aquinas leads us naturally into discussion of perhaps the mendicants' greatest theological achievement, the fusion of most of the main characteristics of Aristotle's philosophical system with the content of biblical revelation so as to establish a new and enduringly influential scholastic theology. Yet that makes the mendicant theological accomplishment sound too straightforward and facile. By the time the friars began to construct their impressive systematic theologies, it was already well known that Aristotle's system contained doctrines that were not easily reconcilable with the data of revelation. For example, Aristotle's belief in the eternity of matter seemed obviously in conflict with the Christian doctrine of creation from nothing *(ex nihilo),* and that is hardly the only crucial case where the two systems clashed. Through the early decades of the thirteenth century, prelates, councils, and even popes attempted to prohibit the study of Aristotle and his commentators. But the very fact that these condemnations had to be repeated indicated that there was a craving and determination for the study of Aristotle that could not be inhibited by prelatical or even papal bans. Ironically, books prohibited by Pope Gregory IX in 1231 appeared on lists of required set books in the faculty of arts at Paris in the mid-thirteenth century.

The friars who became the great scholastic theologians of the thirteenth century, like Albert the Great and Thomas Aquinas, not only embraced the language and syllogistic style of Aristotle's logic, but they also adopted many of his metaphysical categories, his view of the structure of the universe, his physics, and his views of physiology. In addition, they also accepted his view of the cognitive process, which holds that the mind derives ideas from data given to it by the senses. In constructing this Christian theology, these great Dominicans not only used the writings of a pagan Greek philosopher, but they also employed, and argued with, the commentaries on Aristotle of Averroës and Avicenna. Unlike some contemporary masters, they were comfortable with a quite clear distinction between what is knowable by faith and by reason, though, not unimportant, they did not believe what was given in the order of revelation to be in conflict with what is received by the order of reason. Thus, they were comfortable with the notion that God is knowable, albeit in different ways, both by faith and by reason; thus, for Thomas Aquinas at least, the existence of God is known via reason, but the Triune nature of God is known only by revelation. In any case, Thomas and his Dominican colleagues had taken up, with astonishing verve and inspiration, a task that had occupied theologians from the start of the Christian era: the relationship between Christian revelation and the culture of classical civilization.

Another complicating caveat is very much in order. While mendicants, especially Dominicans, embraced Aristotelian logic, "Platonic" and Neoplatonic elements continued to shape both the comprehensive structure and discrete doctrines of their works. It has been argued, convincingly, for example, that the overarching form of Thomas's *Summa,* which is positively replete with Aristotelian terminology and explanation, is essentially "Platonic." Beyond that, it would be quite erroneous to suggest that all mendicants accepted the use of Aristotle in theology. Not only conservatives within the Dominican order but, above all, many Franciscans were profoundly and sincerely opposed to the appropriation in Christian "sacred teaching" *(sacra doctrina),* or theology, of a pagan philosopher, many of whose metaphysical positions stood in flat contradiction to the central beliefs of the Christian faith; others used Aristotle much more cautiously and even warily. An Englishman who was formerly a canon and thus a member of the secular clergy, Alexander of Hales, at age fifty or so, donned the Franciscan habit (and was the first Parisian scholar to give decisive importance to reflection and commentary on the Lombard's *Sentences)*—and in this way, he became the first Franciscan master at Paris (he had been a secular master there since 1220). He is a good example of a Parisian master in whose works Aristotelian terminology can be found. But the use of Greek philosophy and science to explore the data of revelation is something he could never swallow whole. Neither could Bonaventure, who simply did not partake in the enthusiasm for Aristotle with the passion of his confrere Thomas. Some of their Franciscan contemporaries and successors were even less keen and indeed anxious that the Aristotelian transfiguration of sacred teaching was so grave a danger as to be capable of compromising certain presumably settled issues in Christian theology.

The issue for both Alexander and Bonaventure and indeed for all mendicants was the relationship of reason and faith, theology and faith, the teaching of Christ and that of Aristotle. The acceptance of Aristotle at Paris had seemed to broaden a historic distinction into a yawning and treacherous gap. The works of the two Franciscans, Alexander and Bonaventure, reflect the pressure of this new issue. Yet they equally clearly demonstrate that the arrival of Aristotle was, in some senses, irresistible. One does not have to read very far into the works of either to recognize that both Franciscans employ some of his logical distinctions. Yet both were quite anxious not to cause a rupture between philosophy and theology, to which the use of Aristotle might lead. Accordingly, both attempted to preserve fidelity to the Anselmian notion that belief leads to understanding, to the notion that Christ is the one universal master and that faith is the principal and fundamental condition of rational analysis. Both also attempted to preserve allegiance to what we might, somewhat weakly and a bit inaccurately, call "Augustinianism." Indeed, some have argued, just slightly too simplistically, that Franciscan theology was, in the last analysis, Augustinianism preserved, renewed, and expressed in the new and sometimes exotic nomenclature of Aristotle.

The reason this label of "Augustinianism" is imprecise is that Augustine's works were the common possession of all religious orders and all approaches to theology. In addition, Augustine was the most frequently cited authority among all authors in the field of theology. The reason that it is not entirely inaccurate is, of course, that there is something to the traditional stereotype. We can contrast the epistemological positions of Thomas and Bonaventure to illustrate the more conservative, Augustinian cast of the traditionalist Franciscan school. Against Thomas's essentially Aristotelian account of the process of knowing, Bonaventure embraced Augustine's view (itself heavily inflected by Neoplatonic thought and thus itself a product of reflection on Greek philosophy) that the mind received universal ideas through the action of divine illumination. Implicitly, this is a rejection of the Aristotelian and Thomistic notion that abstraction occurs by knowledge acquired through sensory perception. In general, the Franciscans and conservative Dominicans were more chary of the naturalistic and rationalistic assumptions of Greek thinking, especially as they seemed to clash with the supernatural elements of Christian revelation and those not clearly available to rational inquiry, like the doctrine of the Trinity.

Far more radical than either the Dominicans, who may be said to have occupied an intermediate and transitional position, and the Franciscans, who could, again loosely, be argued to have occupied a rather more conservative, "Augustinian" position, were the secular masters in the faculty of arts, who have often been called radical Aristotelians. It was this group of masters, sometimes also designated "Latin Averroists" (a term fixed on them by none other than Thomas Aquinas), who attempted to establish reason as an independent faculty and philosophy as a sovereign discipline. They were led, intellectually, by Siger de Brabant (d. ca. 1279), a figure from the Low Countries who would suffer condemnation and death under suspicious circumstances (he was probably murdered by his demented secretary), who distinguished himself from even enthusiastic Dominicans like Aquinas by his unbridled enthusiasm for Aristotle and his commentators, especially Averroës. In other words, for thoroughgoing Aristotelians like Siger, philosophy was a discipline that could, and should, proceed untouched and unaltered by creedal beliefs—even fundamental ones, like faith in creation and the activity of divine providence—and, as an independent science, it should proceed unimpeded by the conclusions and implications of revealed teaching. Not all prelates viewed Aristotle, as did Siger and his colleagues in arts, as an exciting and even revolutionary new way of understanding the created order. Largely because of Aristotle's belief in the eternity of the world and the lack of any sort of doctrine of divine providence, the bishop of Paris, Stephen Tempier (d. 1279), condemned many of the tenets of Aristotle's expositors in 1277.

Again, a caveat is in order. Neither Siger nor his colleagues ought to be understood, in anachronistic terms, as skeptics or freethinkers who had rejected Christianity. It is better to appreciate them as having different intellectual aspirations than even the less conservative Dominicans, who had attempted to bring into harmony the order of philosophy with that of biblical revelation. The intellectual project of Siger and sympathetic colleagues was to push Greek philosophy and science, especially Aristotle, as far as it could go without attempting to force it into conformity with Christian dogma. As intellectuals, they took Aristotle, especially as interpreted by Averroës's commentaries on him, as the supreme authority for knowing. As philosophers, they relied first on the faculty of reason, whose qualities they wanted to develop or push to their limit without resorting to the findings of theology or rules of faith. In this sense, they could and did detect genuine and serious contradictions between Aristotle and revelation. These were not, to their way of thinking, to be ignored, nor explained out of existence. Eventually, this approach caused Siger and his colleagues to be charged, not entirely without reason, with teaching a doctrine of "double truth." Hardly a compliment in the thirteenth century, this allegation essentially charged that the radical Aristotelians maintained that it was possible that something could be true by the exercise of reason and that something different, even its contrary, could be maintained through faith or by revelation. Still, as a Christian believer, Siger did defer to the superior truth of revelation where contradictions existed; this is why, perhaps, he had to embrace something like a concept of double truth. He simply took no interest in the traditional scholastic project of attempting to reconcile authorities. Accordingly, he was not deeply distressed, as a scholar, by contradictions between Greek and Christian authorities, nor the divorce of philosophy and theology. Given Siger's profound intellectual differences with Thomas, it remains mysterious that Dante, arriving with Beatrice in the abode of the wise in Paradise, not only places Siger in the presence of eleven other brilliant intellects, including Peter

Lombard, Albert the Great, and Thomas himself, but he also has Thomas, who had vigorously rejected his teaching, praise Siger as one who established new and unpopular truths (*Paradiso,* 10:136).

With the notion that Siger's propositions were unloved, Thomas could certainly have agreed, and he certainly would not have appreciated their novelty. Indeed, it may have been the felt need to preserve a modified Aristotelianism for the use of Christian theology that prompted Thomas to publish, in 1270, a scathing philippic against Siger and his colleagues entitled *On the Unity of the Intellect against the Averroists,* which argued that Siger had written erroneously because of overreliance on Averroës, not Aristotle. In the end, Thomas could not accept the notion that the truths of reason and faith could conflict, only that the former could be augmented and made more intricate by the latter.

Both Siger's own views and Thomas's disapproval of them eventually brought down condemnations on the heads of both. Today, we think of Thomas as one of only thirty-five doctors of the church. We know him as the theologian whom Pope Leo XIII (r. 1878–1903) designated as the standard of Catholic theology and whose works were required reading in Catholic seminaries and universities. In 1880, he was named, and remains, patron of all Catholic educational institutions.

Yet none of this could have been predicted at Thomas's death in 1274. In 1277, Stephen Tempier, probably under hostile Franciscan influence, condemned 219 propositions. These were aimed mainly at the Averroists at Paris, but some targeted theses had been put forward by Thomas. That is, a future doctor of the church was censured for positions that a future pope would declare normative and orthodox. In any case, the Dominicans soon responded, and in 1309, the order adopted Thomas's theology as its official doctrine. Though unimaginable in 1277, the influence of Thomas's writings perdured long after the close of the Middle Ages, in an age that produced an institution, the university, which has continued to have a profound influence on intellectual and cultural life to the present moment.

Scholasticism and Gothic Architecture

One of the most famous attempts to link an intellectual and artistic project from the high Middle Ages was expressed in a book whose title says it all: *Gothic Architecture and Scholasticism.* The author of the book was the great Erwin Panofsky (1892–1968). An emigré from Nazi Germany, he spent much of his career at Princeton's Institute for Advanced Study. In 1942, he was invited to give the Page-Barbour Lectures. For the lectures, Panofsky chose "The Gothic Style" as his theme. The result is a brief but brilliant book that has become both a classic

21. Soaring central nave of Amiens Cathedral, Amiens, France; Gothic, begun 1220. Compare skeletal architecture with mural architecture of Romanesque churches. Nave vaults are 144 feet high (cf. Chartres at 118 feet). Compare with illustration 28. © DeA Picture Library/ Art Resource, NY.

22. Reims Cathedral, western façade. Early thirteenth century. High, highly sculptured Gothic façade; many large openings in towers; rose window; pointed arches; tall pinnacles over portal. Compare with illustration 3. Hervé Champollion/akg-images.

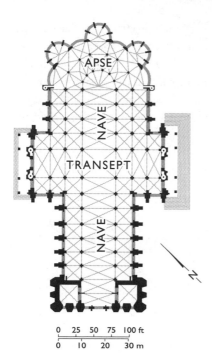

0 25 50 75 100 ft
0 10 20 30 m

Map 4. Plan of cruciform church (Chartres) with apsidal chapels

and an ambitious, if highly controversial, attempt to connect different phenomena from the same era, in this case the twelfth and thirteenth centuries.

It can be no accident, Panofsky argued, that the intellectual style of early scholasticism grew up at the same time, and in the same place (Paris), as the style of ecclesiastical architecture now known as "early Gothic." He observes that "early scholasticism" emerged at roughly the same time as early Gothic architecture was first given expression by Abbot Suger at St. Denis. Between scholasticism and Gothic architecture, he claimed, there was a "concurrence."

By "concurrence" Panofsky meant that certain patterns of thinking current in the twelfth century led to two cultural products, one written on the page, the other in stone, that bore a parallel or corresponding relationship to one another. Between high scholasticism and high Gothic architecture he perceived a nearly "analogous" or perfect relationship. Thus, in high scholasticism, the large structure of a theological treatise will be broken down into smaller and smaller logical units. In an inspection of Thomas's *Summa,* for example, it is obvious that Thomas divides treatises into books, then into questions, which are in turn divided into articles. Articles themselves are logically divided into objections and then answers to the objections. Just as in the thrust-and-parry of scholastic disputation (reflected in the argument and objection of the article), so in the Gothic cathedral, we see the thrust and counterthrust of force; just as in the highly systematic organization of the scholastic treatise, so the iconographic sculptural programs of Chartres and church portals everywhere are constructed. In short, the *Summa* and the cathedral are both structures, arising at roughly the same time, built up out of smaller and smaller parts that make for a unified and all-inclusive whole and mirror the architectonic structure of each other. Each monumental work attempted a comprehensive treatment of the vast entirety of Christian story and faith; taken together, they attempted to give the pilgrim Christian an experience of the majestic totality of the Christian faith under two species. While no documentary evidence has survived that proves Panofsky's thesis and his book has opened itself to other criticisms, the hypothesis remains dazzling.

The Bid for Papal Monarchy

The dreams of the Gregorian reformers had by no means died. Popes in the thirteenth century kept them alive and even briefly made them real and concrete. Yet the domination of both spiritual and temporal realms was to prove costly, in every way, to the papacy. Secular authorities never accepted the papacy's claims to temporal oversight. In the ecclesiastical realm, as popes increased their power, they also caused suspicion and frustration among the faithful. As popes claimed more and more authority and acquired more power over Christendom and as the curia became a sort of Supreme Court of Christendom, the successors of St. Peter, ever in need of more money, resorted to a tactic hated in the Middle Ages more than today: taxation. In many other ways, the papacy was believed to have departed from apostolic practice. These deviations from normative practice and the fathomless need for revenue slowly robbed the papacy of affection and respect, with profound consequences in the centuries to come.

Vicar of Christ: Innocent III

Born around 1160, Lotario da Segni, the future Innocent III, was the scion of wealthy landowners in the Roman countryside and of city patricians. Brought up and educated in Rome, he went to study theology in Paris, as did many talented young men at the time. The theological side of this man is too often underestimated. As pope, he remembered his theological studies with affection, and he appointed many men with whom he had studied in Paris, including prelates the caliber of Stephen Langton (d. 1228), later archbishop of Canterbury, to high offices. By the time Lotario arrived in Paris, Peter the Chancellor (d. 1205) was dominating the theological scene. Peter deemphasized the abstract prejudice of high scholasticism in favor of the pragmatic preparation of preachers and confessors; for him, moral and sacramental theology were more important than the dogmatic or systematic.

Thus, Innocent was much more than a canonist. Indeed, it might be argued that he was more influential as a theological writer than as a legal one. He wrote two works of theology that must be counted among the most influential books of the Middle Ages. One, *On the Mysteries of the Mass,* reflected his own care with saying mass and the attention and feeling with which he urged that altar furnishings be maintained. The book was so influential that it was taken almost verbatim into the standard textbook of the later Middle Ages. As cardinal, he wrote a book entitled *On the Misery of the Human Condition* (1196), just two years before being elevated to the papacy. This was an unusual work for an active cardinal and soon-to-be pope because unlike many books in the tradition of "contempt of the world" theology, it does not advocate withdrawal from active participation in the world. Something of its popularity can be gathered when we appreciate that it survives in almost seven hundred manuscripts.

In the past, it has often been written that Innocent spent considerable time studying law under great canonists like Huguccio (d. 1210). Actually, Innocent spent at most two years in Bologna. Moreover, there is no evidence that he had formal training as a canonist. True, he was to earn a reputation for his wise judgment (he was reverently named Solomon III by admirers), but he may have picked up such judgment by his experience in the court. In short, his Bologna training was much less influential on his character and subsequent career than has been previously believed, while the influence of Paris has been understated.

In any case, Lothario da Segni was elected pope in January 1198 and took the name of Innocent III. His young age at the time of his election—he was just thirty-seven—has long been a cause for wonder. He was one of the youngest men ever elected pope, and it is reasonable to ask why. By that age, he had already exhibited administrative ability and piety and had achieved two influential publications, all of which probably made him attractive. More important, a Roman noble who had a Paris education must have seemed like a man who could stand strong against German power and the hated Hohenstaufen dynasty.

The cardinals who elected him rightly sensed that Innocent would act decisively for the papacy against German interests. Taking advantage of the death of Henry VI (r. 1190–1197), whose son was in his minority, Innocent established authority over what we have since called the Papal States. Henry died in possession of a large part of the Patrimony of Peter and the Kingdom of Sicily. Throughout his eighteen-year pontificate, Innocent strove to prevent the reunification of the empire and Sicily. At the same time, he intervened in a disputed imperial election in Germany. In 1200, he explained to a consistory of cardinals that while the princes of

23. Pope Innocent III. Mosaic, thirteenth century CE. Museo di Roma, Rome. Photo credit: Scala/Art Resource, NY.

Germany had the right to nominate a king, the pope had the responsibility of examining a candidate's suitability for the imperium before crowning him emperor. By this move, Innocent gave himself the capacity to decide a disputed election.

Lord or Shepherd? Innocent's Petrine Doctrine

As it happened, there was indeed a dispute after a split German election between Otto IV of Brunswick (r. 1209–1215) and Philip of Swabia (d. 1208). (Innocent had taken Henry's infant son, Frederick II [r. 1220–1250], under his protection and upheld his hereditary right to the crown of Sicily.) The dispute suddenly ended in 1208 when Philip was murdered by an enemy. In 1209, Innocent unenthusiastically crowned Otto emperor after the latter promised to give the papacy the lands it claimed as its patrimony. Innocent grew even less happy when Otto made no move to return the lands of the Papal States and, to add insult to injury, gathered an army to invade Italy. Without hesitating, Innocent excommunicated Otto and also announced that he had been stripped of his imperial title. He then made the young Prince Frederick emperor, but not before securing a promise from him that before receiving the imperial title, he would renounce his claims to Sicily. When Otto was defeated in battle at Bouvines in 1214, Innocent's victory was complete. The significance of this episode can hardly be stressed enough. In the eleventh century, emperors had appointed popes without consulting any Roman prelate. Now the pope had chosen an emperor.

This was not the last "political" conflict, or victory, during Innocent's pontificate. Innocent was involved in disputes with King Philip II of France for attempting to divorce Ingeborg of Denmark and with King John of England (r. 1199–1216), who refused to accept Innocent's choice of Stephen Langton as archbishop of Canterbury. Innocent threatened both kings with excommunication and placed both kingdoms under interdict, a step that prevented certain ecclesiastical rituals from being performed without excommunication. He won resounding victories in both cases. In order to receive absolution, King John gave England as a fief to the papacy, and Philip was forced to choose Ingeborg as queen. In a short time, Innocent had twice chosen an emperor and won battles with the other two major states in western Europe, as well as victories over smaller states, like Portugal and Castile. To a greater degree than any pontiff before or since, Innocent achieved the dream of Gregory VII and became, in fact as well as in theory, the undisputed leader of Christendom.

Historians have debated whether these essentially political actions were taken on the basis of accepted papal doctrine or whether they reflected a novel understanding of papal supremacy. In truth, there is a certain incoherence in Innocent's doctrine, which may have evolved during his pontificate. Some of his statements seem quite modest and indicate no desire to usurp the rights of the monarchy. Others, however, seem to recognize no limit to his temporal power. For example, on the anniversary of his consecration as pope, he delivered a sermon in which he asserted: "To me is said in the person of the prophet, 'I have set thee over nations and over kingdoms, to root up and to pull down, and to waste and to destroy and to build and to plant' (Jeremiah 1:10). To me is also said in the person of the apostle, 'I will give to thee the keys of the kingdom of heaven.' . . . Thus the others were called to a part of the care but Peter alone assumed the plenitude of power. You see then who is this servant set over the household, truly the vicar of Jesus Christ, successor of Peter, anointed of the lord, a God of Pharaoh, set between God and man, lower than God but higher than man, who judges all and is judged by none." It was humble of Innocent not to claim divine status here, but the phrase "plenitude of power" *(plenitudo potestatis)* suggests that he thought his power extended to the temporal realm. Indeed, it is impossible to read this text in any other way than as an assertion of supreme authority in the temporal as well as the religious realm. He made such a claim explicitly in an 1198 letter to the archbishop of Ravenna, opining that ecclesiastical liberty is best preserved "where the Roman church has full power in both temporal and spiritual affairs." He expressed similar sentiments the following year in a letter to the patriarch of Constantinople, John Kamateros (r. 1198–1206), a figure of great stature, in which he blithely declared that James, the brother of the Lord, "left to Peter not only the universal church but the whole world to govern." If Gregory saw himself as the agent of Peter, with whom he had a sense of a powerfully intimate kinship, Innocent viewed himself explicitly as the vicar of Christ, priest and king, who possessed unrivaled temporal and religious authority. Still, as suggested, his imagery and rhetoric were not always hieratic. Sometimes, he would argue that he could intervene in secular affairs occasionally and only for particular cause *(casualiter)*, especially when a high secular official had sinned. It would therefore be incorrect to conclude that the ideological aim of his pontificate was to claim that all temporal power inhered in the papal office or in the successor to Christ. But neither was he consistent in his emphasis on the traditional theory of two independent powers acting in harmony. His legacy, rather, is a mix of varied images, language, and theories, as well as actions based on some of these theories.

One must hasten to add that no secular prince accepted Innocent's exalted theoretical claims or consented to the full-blown doctrine of the papal "plenitude of power." What is more, Innocent's claims were often unsuccessful in practice. For example, in order to make even his titular claims to lordship over the Papal States effective, he had to hand them over to a fief—the Marquis Azzo VI (d. 1212)—for only such a man had the military power to make effective the pope's claims for overlordship. Even within the curia, the administrative machinery was simply not sufficient to realize all of Innocent's grand dreams. It would be the job of Roman canonists, legates, and popes in the wake of Innocent's pontificate to develop just that machinery, to seize traditional local and episcopal power, and even to create business for the pope, thereby making Innocent's dreams real in practice. (Some of these activities were under way by the time of Innocent's pontificate, but they grew after his death, sometimes by orders of magnitude.) Future canons and popes achieved these dreams primarily by developing the canon law, by convoking western councils, by hearing thousands of cases in Rome from litigants streaming in from all over Europe, by seizing oversight in the canonization of saints, and by taking over appointments to ecclesiastical offices, and by providing other papal benefits. All of this would have been impossible without the general acceptance that the pope was the vicar of Christ and the growing sense of Christians, nourished by the reforms of the eleventh century, that they were part of a supranational entity, Christendom (*Christianitas*), and that their primary loyalty was to that body and to the pope as head of Christendom, rather than to any local, regional, or even national entity.

Instruments of Papal Power

In the thirteenth century, it was accepted that the canon law, which regulated affairs now the responsibility of the state (marriage, wills, and so forth), was the law of Christendom. Where popes had been consulted on disciplinary, liturgical, or theological matters, they responded with letters rendering their judgments. These letters, as noted in chapter 8, were called decretals and those who studied them, "decretalists." In effect, the decretals were the routine name for the main legislative form prevailing in Christendom. In the thirteenth and fourteenth centuries, no fewer than three collections of decretals were officially approved by the pope. Along with Gratian's *Decretum,* these laws together became known as *The Body of Canon Law (Corpus Iuris Canonici).*

In relation to the gradually growing power of the papacy over Christendom, the essential issue in this immense and sophisticated apparatus of law was dispensation from its often quite exacting punishments. Increasingly, dispensations were sought from the pope. As nearly every law regarding ecclesiastical discipline was capable of some sort of dispensation, thousands of supplicants flocked hopefully to the papal courts to seek them. Naturally, this enhanced the authority of the pope prodigiously since he could grant or deny a petitioner's request for dispensation from the letter of the law. But this power also implied that it was the papacy that was the source as well as the arbiter of the law.

Between the seventh and early twelfth centuries, virtually no councils were held. From a western perspective, those that were convoked were almost irrelevant, meeting as they did in Byzantine territory under the aegis of the eastern empire. Only legates of the pope attended, and they always played an insignificant role. As R. W. Southern has observed of this five-century period, "The whole picture is one of western inertia and papal impotence."

Over the course of the next two centuries, this picture would change dramatically. In 1123 Pope Calixtus II convoked the first "ecumenical" council in more than two centuries. It met not in Byzantine territory but in the Lateran Basilica in Rome. By the early fourteenth century, no fewer than six more general councils were summoned. Each was called by the pope, not the Byzantine emperor, and the pope set the agenda for each. He presided over all, and he was understood to be the source and guarantor of all the decrees issued. By force of will and energetic exercise of power, the general council had been made an instrument and symbol of papal authority.

This period of frequent church councils coincided with an exercise of papal power, often accomplished by decisive intervention by the pontiff in the form of letters in response to significant cases brought to the Roman curia from all over Europe. In some ways, this development was the fulfillment of the theoretical claim made by the papacy in the early Middle Ages that it should preside over very important court cases. Although there was an extensive network of "appellate" courts in existence, over which presided bishops, archbishops, and lower prelates, many litigants refused to accept their verdicts as final. Now aggrieved parties in cases involving everything from church offices and elections to wills and probate and marriages and divorces were heard at Rome. Thus, through a process encouraged by litigants themselves, the pope ipso facto became Christendom's chief justice as well as its chief legislator. In this respect, the curia became not unlike the U.S. Supreme Court in terms of the kind of business it conducted. By 1300, popes and cardinals, to whom the pope in his role as chief justice delegated work, spent much of their day hearing cases.

As with American Supreme Court cases on issues of major import (for example, free speech, equal protection, and privacy), the rulings on very significant cases became precedents for future jurisprudence. Canonists incorporated these decisions in collections of papal decretals, as law professors today collect them in textbooks of constitutional law. These collections would then themselves become law books for lawyers and judges and textbooks for aspiring students.

The sheer volume of letters produced and the remarkable increase of papal output furnish us with powerful evidence of how rapidly papal power grew from the early twelfth century to the early fourteenth. Historian R. W. Southern has calculated that in the early eleventh century, the curia produced about one letter a year. By the middle of the century, when the papal reform was under way, that number had risen to 35. By the time of Innocent III, that number had risen roughly tenfold; Innocent wrote 280 letters in his eighteen-year pontificate. His second successor, Innocent IV, wrote nearly 750. By the pontificate of John XXII, that number had soared to more than 3,500 letters per year.

Papal power was also augmented by the appointment of legates (who had usually attained the status of cardinal). These were men understood to possess the power of the papacy and to act on the pope's behalf. They spread all over Christendom, bringing Rome's authority and prestige to all the major cities and towns of Europe and some small ones too. They presided over small local councils, heard legal cases, received monies for the pope, and mediated conflicts—sometimes national and international conflicts. When they felt unable to decide a case, or when a conflict seemed impossible to resolve, the legate would send the case back to Rome—yet again enhancing papal authority and prestige. Through decretals and legates, the pope very much ceased to be a distant, venerable figure not active locally in each diocese. In fact, the tentacles of papal power now seemed to reach into every diocese of Christendom, even the most remote. To be sure, not everyone in the dioceses, least of all their heads, was entirely euphoric about this development. The losers in this development were of course the bishops and archbishops, who slowly and grimly observed their customary prerogatives and powers eaten away by the encroaching, all-powerful center. At the ecclesio-cultural level, this is a momentous development. The traditional localism of the Middle Ages was giving way—and rapidly—to an inexorable tide of centralization.

How exactly did this happen? It had been the prerogative of bishops officially to recognize local or diocesan saints before the twelfth century (even if the desire for canonization bubbled up from below, from the masses). The bishop's approval was expressed through the removal or translation of the saint's body into a church. Sometimes these translations actually occurred during the meetings of bishops. The first record of a pope having made a man a saint comes from 973, but that was not an augury of the immediate or distant future. By the time of Pope Alexander III, again during a time of papal assertion of authority, Rome began to demand that popes be involved in the official recognition of a saint. The traditional episcopal role came to be completely eliminated when Gregory IX reserved the right of canonization to the pope alone. In the eyes of diocesan bishops, the pope's omnicompetence was purchased at the considerable cost of their increasing irrelevance and loss of dignity.

Perhaps an even more grave loss was a change in the traditional definition of "church." Traditionally, it had been understood as the communion of the faithful, the community of Christians. Centralization, however, put the curia in the middle or the top of that communal image. If the curia was at the center, then the church was understood as clerical and hierarchical. This meant of course that the communion of all Christians was pushed out, theoretically, to the periphery. On the ground, this theoretical distance would be expressed by an ever-increasing resentment at papal encroachment, particularly around the fiscal invasions to generate papal revenue. This invasion came with a sense that the curia was increasingly bankrupt, spiritually as well as financially, having made the traditional unit of ecclesiastical administration, the diocese, a hollow casing and its ordinary, the bishop, an emasculated figurehead. Worst of all, centralization, which often if not inevitably involved papal provisions of benefices to cronies (many of whom held plural benefices and were thus absentees in some of their parishes), resulted in the gross deterioration of pious and spiritual life in the parishes and dioceses. The desperate hunt for livings, the accumulation of benefices, the obvious materialism of the candidates—all disgusted observers. The fact that respected bishops, intellectuals, and chroniclers all complained, more or less simultaneously, indicates that there was a widespread revulsion. It also suggests that papal control over benefices was one way in which the augmentation of papal power truly hurt the church—and hurt it in perhaps the most grievous way imaginable. At the political level, it succeeded in alienating not only bishops but also other local dignitaries and prelates, as well as abbots, town councils, and lay patrons. This all augured badly for the papacy. Writing of the deleterious consequences of centralization, papal historian Geoffrey Barraclough comments as follows:

> The result . . . was a growing scepticism about the validity of the ecclesiastical order, which seemed to have departed far from apostolic poverty. The elaborate legal and institutional system appeared to have little direct relation with the teachings of the Gospels, which more and more were set up as the only valid standard of Christian life. The upshot was a reaction against the hierarchy, which quickly took shape in the twelfth century on the heels of the new centralization, and was perhaps its inevitable sequel. The papal curia had the atmosphere of a law-court or business-office; inevitably the best elements turned elsewhere for spiritual leadership.

Among the most serious consequences following on the perception that the ecclesiastical order had departed from the practice of apostolic poverty was the emergence of groups, some heretical, that practiced it with a vengeance and criticized those, especially among the clerical cast, who failed to match their austere standards.

Causes of Papal Resentment

As if to reinforce the view of the papacy as an essentially secular court of business or law, the papacy in the thirteenth and fourteenth centuries began increasing taxes and fees for existing services and charging more and new taxes. Traditional papal revenues included income gained from papal landed estates and a number of other, relatively minor, sources, including Peter's Pence, a small annual tax; tributes from monasteries under the protection of St. Peter; and so forth. The point of no return came when the papacy began to tax the income of the clergy. Initially, it did so to pay for the Crusades. Later, these funds were used indiscriminately, and the rates at which the clergy could be taxed were equally promiscuous. Finally, the tax went from being an occasional impost to becoming a general tax, from which the papacy derived a dependable stream of revenue by the mid-thirteenth century. There is some grim irony in contemplating that when it came to taxing its main constituency, the papal government was far ahead of its secular counterparts.

Also deeply alienating was the slow monopolization of ecclesiastical benefices by papal provision, from the highest (archbishoprics) to the lowest (cures for village churches). This development was tied to the fiscalism just described; those who received a papally provided benefice began to pay a tax calibrated to the assessed value of the office. Because the appointment to bishoprics could be quite lucrative, beginning under Innocent IV, the appointment became "reserved,"

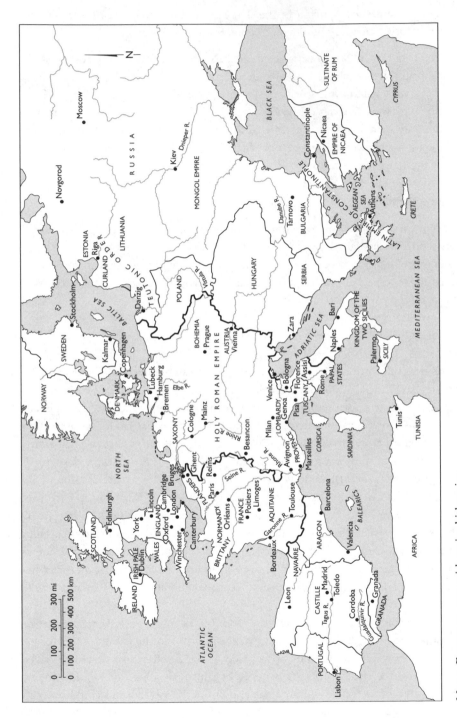

Map 5. Europe ca. 1250 with major bishoprics

forming part of the unstoppable train of centralization and fiscalism. Following the rule that one occasion, when repeated, soon becomes a habit and norm, Innocent's first general reservation became a principle, one that was frequently renewed by avaricious successors. These provisions and reservations were closely, and increasingly, tied in with the fiscal system. Soon minor benefices would be reserved to the papacy and then, all of those that had been vacated by death. Eventually, a wholesale system of reservation would be rationalized, to the obvious financial benefit of the papacy.

The papal court, eager to eke out every pence from the pockets of appellants, began demanding payment for the ink and parchment used during proceedings. Symbolically, this action may be regarded as the proverbial straw that broke the camel's back. The response to these developments was a bitter chorus from many sectors of European society that the papacy had become too greedy, had charged too often and too much, and had reached into the pockets of parishioners when it had no right to do so. The papacy had been doing "new and unheard of" things (to use the phrase of King Louis IX of France, later St. Louis), and these very practices, some hinted, were the source of evil in the church. Popes began to be viewed as the primary subverters of the ancient ecclesiastical order. Unsurprisingly, the foundation of good will on which all papal activity depended, and which had been laboriously and painfully constructed for centuries, began to crack under the perception that like any other secular court, the curia was above all interested in money.

Soon critics were openly complaining of papal "extortion." Papal power and control had reached its height, but it had lost much affection and good will. Some began to wonder whether the "plenitude of power" was not a doctrine that had ruined the papacy. Perhaps constitutional checks of some kind should be applied? The centralization of the church had also resulted in its bureaucratization. The church at its center seemed less like a religious body and more like a governmental institution; the pope was not the spiritual leader of Christendom but a man of business, a lawyer. His aims seemed less governed by a religious agenda than a political one. And, always, he was asking for more and more money. Bernard of Clairvaux had complained of this in the twelfth century. By the end of the thirteenth century, his voice had been completely ignored. Yet it was needed more than ever.

Disillusionment began to set in during the pontificate of Innocent IV. Political considerations prevailed during Innocent's years as pope. Almost immediately after taking office, he became obsessed with a desire to break the power of the Hohenstaufen dynasty. The issue at stake was the overlordship of Sicily. Innocent deployed every imaginable means to break the power of Germany, including calling the Council of Lyons specifically to deal with the emperor, whom he had deposed; Frederick II sensibly chose not to appear. In frustration and anger, Innocent soon shifted preaching and plenary indulgences for the original Crusade to a war against the emperor, and in an attempt to weaken him, Innocent created and financed several anti-emperors. After a brief moment of triumph, Innocent died with imperial troops in possession of Sicily; much sound and fury had occurred, but nothing but contempt for the papacy was gained.

Relations within the church also suffered grievously during Innocent IV's pontificate. Ominously, the French clergy complained bitterly that agents of the papacy treated bishops like servants. In order to obtain money and control appointments, they used the dark tools of excommunication and loss of benefices, which then often went to foreigners, especially to Italians. In addition, Innocent was charged with favoring the religious orders, with whom he had better relations, in providing benefices, to the detriment of the secular clergy. Pluralism, or the holding of several benefices simultaneously, became a neuralgic problem during Innocent's pontificate.

Innocent did not escape unscathed. It was not only the French who complained about papal "extortion"—for that is now what they called it; the English did as well. A realization was dawning that reform of the "members" by the "head" was no longer needed; it was the head itself—the pope—that stood most in need of reform. The papacy's "new and unheard of" actions were subverting the ancient ecclesiastical order and had shattered the apostolic model on which the church had ostensibly been built. The entire system of episcopal government had been ruined by centralization. The only remedy, it seemed, was for a reforming council. Cries for such a solution indeed began to be heard, a clear sign that some, at least, believed an ecumenical council to be above the pope. These cries would become louder, and much more urgent, in the decades to come.

To "Deepen Understanding":
Means of Christianization, 1050–1250

The principal burden of ecclesiastical authorities, such as diocesan bishops, was to confirm that the Catholic faith was taught to all baptized Christians and, in some regions and at some times, to disseminate it to potential converts. They also had to defend against thought coming from individuals or groups deemed patently deviant. In this chapter, we will discuss efforts by popes, councils, bishops, and priests to Christianize more deeply the already baptized in their dioceses and parishes. Special attention will be paid to the forms, settings, and institutions established, or perfected, in the period ca. 1050–1250, whose purpose was to communicate, render more explicit, and foster a more profound appreciation of the Christian faith—to "deepen understanding" (see Philemon 1:6). Thus, we will consider the following as modes of instruction: worship; musical liturgy; expressive gestures; visual expressions (images, icons, painting, and sculpture); nonliturgical drama; preaching (still occasional and rare); canonical regulation (with special attention given to the epochal Fourth Lateran Council and its decrees regarding penance and communion); and the confessional.

We will also examine not just Christian *faith*—that is, what was believed, taught, and thought—but also Christian *practice*. Thus, we will discuss institutions (often founded by the laity) designed to express charity, which all Christians were taught to regard as the highest of virtues and to make manifest—as a state of soul and an attitude toward neighbor. Believers were encouraged to express charity in concrete ways, above all in poor relief. We will conclude with an analysis of new social teachings from the church on the institution of marriage and on the practice of money making.

Learning through Texts

In the period under consideration, book learning and reading and, especially, the skill of writing were uncommon talents. Ordinary parishioners were nonetheless aware of the mysterious significance, however inaccessible, of texts and language, and they knew that the faith they embraced reposed in documents and was expressed in words. Even the simplest parishioner was likely to be impressed with the power of words by virtue of the fact that at almost any imaginable religious occasion, priests either recited or read texts. Some of these were undoubtedly internalized through the exercise of memory. The capacity to hear public religious reading and to commit it to memory was a skill of great significance in the Middle Ages. We rightly associate memory with the life of monks and those vowed to a regular life. After all, they knew the Psalter by heart, and evidence suggests some must have known other parts of the Bible (not to mention key commentarial texts) equally well. But some lay Christians who did not read also knew a phenomenal volume of religious literature as a consequence of highly developed skill in aural acquisition and memorial prowess.

In a splendid book on memory in the Middle Ages, historian Mary Carruthers rightly argues that "medieval culture was fundamentally memorial to the same profound degree that modern culture in the West is documentary." Though they could not read *books,* medieval parishioners could still memorize *texts.* In addition, common parishioners were very likely to be able to respond, by either intuition or imitation, to common public written texts, such as prayers on tombs to pray for the souls of the deceased. Historian R. N. Swanson nicely calls this "passive literacy," a skill probably more widespread than we have imagined. Thus, though books were inaccessible to the parochial laity, nonetheless they were instructed, or instructed themselves through these skills, and we should not underestimate the extent of learning acquired by the very best of them. But the best then, as now, would still have constituted only a small minority of the parochial community.

Instruction through Worship

Worship seems an obvious means for instructing a laity that, for the most part, could not read books. However, as mentioned above, the language of worship, Latin, was not understood, at least not outside the Italian peninsula. This made weekly worship relatively ineffective as a medium of teaching and learning the faith. More insight into the faith they professed may well have been achieved by parishioners in extraordinary times, such as the feast of Good Friday, when the cross was adored, or on Easter, when a new fire was started—and in some parts of Europe, this fire would have been taken into homes. A very powerful impact indeed could have been achieved by these acts of nonverbal ritual and ceremony. Yet it remains true that clergy did not succeed in using worship as a mode of instruction, primarily because they did not even attempt to use it in that way.

Why? Part of the response has to do with the lay reform movements discussed above and part with the expectations and desires of the clergy. Both clerical and lay reform movements focused on the clergy and particularly on the purity of the clergy. (Of course, this is in addition to the focus on eliminating simony and the lay control of churches.) The clergy were not interested in making the liturgy a more useful mode of instruction, and even less in engaging the laity more in the liturgy or sacraments. What mattered were the administration of water in baptism and the consecration of the elements in the Eucharist, all expressed using correct, traditional formulae. This emphasis had the effect of reinforcing the community's role as *witnesses* of the sacraments rather than as *participants* in it. The priest and the cultic acts he performed on behalf of the community assumed center stage. Here theatrical metaphors are altogether appropriate: priestly ritual acts were solo performances, and the congregation, so to speak, was merely the prop against which the priest's operations were staged. The ancient rite of worship, in which a priest (sometimes a bishop or "president") led services, with the help of deacons, readers, and choir, had long since vanished. Again, the purposes of the mass, and the hopes of the parishioners attending, had not changed much in the century or so since the turn of the millennium. In the words of one French bishop's gloss on the meaning of the mass in 1113, the mass was offered "against the peril of fire, for our homes; against drought or tempest, for our crops; against sickness, for our animals; against other losses, for everything else." In offering the sacrifice on behalf of the community, it was the priest who secured these blessings. Evidence from the first half of the twelfth century suggests that priests were encouraged to say readings and antiphons in a low voice. The uninvolved laity present could only hope that his sacrifice would be accepted and, for them, be efficacious. That the purpose of the mass was to secure mundane blessings can be seen in the proliferation of private masses. These were paid for by sponsors hoping to secure temporal or eternal benefits or by penitents paying down their supernatural debt.

Liturgical Drama

As these shifts occurred, other ceremonies developed that communicated the Christian message in musical and dramatic form. Needless to say, drama existed in the Greek and Roman cultural worlds. But it had been forbidden in the age of Constantine. From the fifth through the ninth centuries, there is no evidence of drama in Europe, except for an extremely short-lived revival at the court of

Charlemagne. It was only liturgical drama that maintained the tradition of western drama until the appearance of mystery plays and secular drama in the thirteenth century.

These ceremonies had explicitly didactic aims. For example, musical or liturgical plays, some of them very simple and thus effective as teaching tools, developed during this period. One of the very earliest (it may have originated in the tenth century) was the *Whom Do You Seek? (Quem quaeritis?)*. Perhaps performed as a ceremony called the "Collecta" prior to mass on Easter morning, this was a simple telling of the visit to the Easter tomb on Sunday morning. It is important to emphasize that these plays primarily took place within the church as a quasi-liturgical ceremony, though one French play composed in 1150, an augury of the future, was designed to be performed outside, perhaps in a public square. More intricate Easter plays emerged, as well as dramas about the shepherds in the fields and the coming of the Magi.

Rubrics—the red instructions written in a liturgical manuscript—occasionally underlined the importance of indicating the meaning or importance of a particular scene through expressive gestures. These helped a congregation to understand the meaning of the Virgin and Child being adored or the exhibition of the grave clothes of Christ. No parishioner, even the simplest, could have failed to apprehend the broad meaning of these performances, especially since the priest, in some parts of Europe, doffed his liturgical garments and wore angel wings or strung a star to his garments to indicate he was playing one of the Magi. Visible clues would have been important in a religious culture in which the parishioners were ignorant of the ecclesiastical language and unable to read books. Such meaningful and pregnant gestures are a recurring characteristic in the religious culture of the period. One would have witnessed them often; they were a favored way to teach.

The Pictorial and the Pedagogical

These simple musical dramas were inevitably bound up with another pedagogical device, the striking and impactful image. For example, the drama on the Magi concluded with an image of Virgin and Child being placed on the altar, which could then be venerated. Over the course of the 1100s, simple wooden statues became more common. Painted in natural colors, these saintly statues seemed so lifelike to parishioners that they nodded in response to a prayer or question—or so it could seem to medieval parishioners (and they continue to come alive for modern believers too). By far the most common image (and a window into the piety of the period) was that of the Virgin and Child. Conventionally, the Virgin was seated on a throne; the Christ child, who appeared like a miniature adult, sat on her lap. Some two hundred of these survive, and it suggests that many larger

24. Virgin and Child
in Majesty, 1150–1200.
Made in Auvergne,
France. Oak, polychrome,
gesso, and linen. Overall
measurements: 31 5/16 x
12 1/2 x 11 1/2 inches.
Image copyright © The
Metropolitan Museum
of Art. Image source: Art
Resource, NY.

churches would have owned one. And drama was not the only practice in which these were used. In the church, the image was placed on the altar, or on a stone behind it, and venerated; outside the church, it was also carried in processions on festival days.

Piety and Processions

Closely linked with drama and having similar dramatic and didactic effects were processions. These occurred often in the high Middle Ages and well beyond. Prominent as they became in Christian practice, the medieval church did not invent processions. Their roots lay in classical antiquity. In late April, the Romans annually observed the Robigalia, a procession to honor the gods, to whom they prayed for the protection of crops. The early Christian church took over processions (many to the burial sites of martyrs); even emperors would participate (or be the ones ordering the processions) in times of civic peril, such as war. For instance, bishops in Jerusalem traveled to sanctified places in the Holy City in the fourth

25. Processional cross, thirteenth century. Silver and gilt. Notice serenity of figure in triumph; contrast with illustrations 26 and 40. akg/De Agostini Pic. Lib.

century. So numerous and varied were these processions that Emperor Justinian eventually felt compelled, in 527, to establish requirements for them. By then, scores of processions were held in Rome for papal "stations"—that is, processional dates in the Roman calendar for Marian feasts, Christmas, Epiphany, the Sundays of Lent, Easter, Pentecost, Advent, and many other feast days.

By the twelfth century at the latest, entire towns participated in events that were indistinguishably civic and religious. These functioned to unite all parishes of a diocese, bind laity to clergy, and yoke high prelates with lower clergy. Some processions were designed to solidify parish identity and generate affection by circumambulating parochial boundaries, sometimes very ancient ones. In such processions—and in many other kinds—cathedral relics would be solemnly displayed en route to the short journey's end, usually a church. As in antiquity, processions were sometimes connected to a communal hazard or the fear of it. More common were processions held on major feast days, with children sometimes taking a role and even animals, if the narrative connected with the procession suggested it. Palm Sunday processions, for example, typically featured a "palm ass" and concluded at a church with the adoration of the cross.

Over the course of the period ca. 1050–1200, a large cross, or "great rood," became increasingly and unmistakably eye-catching in northern European churches.
The increasing prominence of the crosses almost certainly suggests a surge in
passion-piety in this period, which coincides not only with the first Crusades to
the Holy Land, but also with the return of pilgrims, for whom the Crusaders had
opened a route and whose relative safety warrior-monks tried to guarantee. A
number of small liturgies focused on the cross, such as carrying the cross in processions on Palm Sunday and the feast of the Holy Cross in September. In some
parts of France, artisans produced small enamel crosses, now used for private
devotion.

As is well known, this is also the era during which the representation of Christ
on the Cross underwent a dramatic refashioning. Once depicted in regal finery,
or as a fearsome if impassive judge, or represented as the Second Person of the

26. Crucifix Dévôt-Christ in Perpignan,
1307. The suffering of human Jesus is
emphasized. akg-images/Jean Dieuzaide.

Trinity, Christ was now portrayed as an intensely suffering man. Not surprisingly, this change coincided with the increasing devotional emphasis on identification with the suffering Christ and imitation of the life of Christ and the apostles. The change marks a crucial pivot point in the history of Christian piety.

Not only large "Romanesque" churches, but also small parish churches were painted from top to bottom—sometimes, to modern taste, quite garishly—in ways not easily imagined by the European traveler of today. In addition, sculptural decoration proliferated on the capital of arcades and on the west façade of churches. The façade, too, was luxuriantly painted. At northern cathedrals, laser light shows can now demonstrate how exuberantly a façade could be decorated and painted (as summer visitors to northern French cathedrals can attest). Even at more modest churches, such decorations could not have failed to make a memorable impact. What is less clear is the motivation behind this production of art and the precise nature of the impact it made on those viewing or venerating it. Was it made to instruct or warn? To serve as a devotional aid? Or to glorify God?

It is impossible to give a blanket response to these questions. Motivations differed with buildings. But obstacles arise when imagining that some church decoration, like splendid stained glass, was effective as a medium of instruction. Aside from being cast in complicated symbolic and typological forms, much stained glass was simply too high off the ground for parishioners to see, much less to interpret. Yet even if these forms failed to communicate a precise message, they could not but have conveyed a powerful image of divine glory and majesty. A number of art historians have argued, though unconvincingly, that some Romanesque sculpture conveyed an explicitly anti-heretical message. This presumes understanding on the part of the parishioners entering a church that contained such sculpture. Some lavishly decorated capitals would have been hidden in Romanesque choirs and thus invisible to the laity. Others, in churches just miles away, presented biblical stories that the laity must have comprehended at some fundamental level.

Pope St. Gregory the Great once famously remarked that images had the sort of effect on the non-Latinate as texts did on the literate. They were "books for the unlearned." Colin Morris has observed, "Romanesque art was essentially poster art" designed "to present bold subjects in an eye-catching way." Colorful glass, paintings on walls, and sculpture abounded. We simply cannot surmise how much ordinary layfolk understood all this.

Glass, icons, paintings, and statues may not have had a primarily didactic purpose; we just do not know in many cases. Images and statues of saints could remind a parishioner of the story of a saint, just as a crucifix would presumably remind him of the Passion of Christ, or his obvious carnality and susceptibility to suffering, or even the entirety of his earthly mission. Even here we must take care. Images of St. Christopher were almost everywhere in the churches of medieval Europe, *not* to remind the viewer of his story but to ward off untimely death. The darkness of buildings and the unlearnedness of parishioners undoubtedly prevented full appreciation of what was intended, which itself is unknown. What seems less in doubt is that this profusion of glass, painting, and sculpture was designed to have some enlightening effect on parishioners. Perhaps it was intended as a form of mute, aesthetic (and frequently exquisite) preaching intended for their edification, appreciation, or instruction. That, minimally, is what Pope Gregory would have wished.

It seems likely that these goals, and perhaps more, were achieved. Cyclical depictions in glass and sculpture must have communicated much of what the laity knew about the Bible. Simply by setting two related images (usually one from each testament), artistic genius could suggest a figurative or tropological interpretation. We see such creative genius operating in major French cathedrals and in Canterbury Cathedral. From cathedrals such as these, perhaps, more sophisticated minds could infer multiple senses of scripture. Other glass art and paintings were more explicitly didactic. Some depicted the sacraments or the corporal works of mercy, which must have conveyed to alert believers the moral duties to which their baptism had obliged them.

Religious Drama

We can say frustratingly little with confidence about the broad impact of Romanesque art; the evidence pales in comparison to the considerable volume of data we have on the tradition of medieval drama. Drama was, without question, intended to aid in the transmission of the basic message of the churches. This is not to deny that the staging of religious-didactic plays included a "secular" element of entertainment. Even still, these plays were intended to contain, communicate, and culminate in a message that was connected with a preexisting understanding of an element of Christian faith. Not surprisingly, then, the earliest liturgical dramas were intended to illuminate the meaning of the major ceremonies of the church's calendar. In the thirteenth century, plays developed that effectively recapitulated key moments of salvation history as recorded in the Bible; they must have functioned, therefore, as a major source of biblical knowledge for the illiterate playgoer. Soon dramatic "cycles" were drawn up, with each play in a cycle revolving around key moments in the Christian story from Creation to the Last Judgment. Intriguingly, some of these plays incorporated apocryphal literature or elements that had creedal but no biblical foundation (such as the harrowing of hell). Many so-called "morality" plays treated specific virtues or vices (like the deadly sins) or focused on prayers (like the *Paternoster* prayer, centering on the meaning of the "Our Father") or the Creed (around which a very lengthy play was constructed), as well as on other themes and figures (especially Mary) in the Christian story. Others communicated an unmistakably anti-heretical message.

We can say with a high degree of confidence that even given the inevitable civic element involved (plays could be staged to bring in tourists and funds and so had to have a component of "entertainment"), these plays functioned primarily to communicate or underline the historical and religious message of the churches. For example, dramatic "asides" were included to teach and explain intricacies of the faith and to point unambiguously to the relationship between stories in the two testaments. Regarding these connections, it has been convincingly argued that plays, more than any other medium of church instruction, were intended (as were certain forms of "cyclical" art) to introduce laity to the notion that the Bible had multiple layers of meaning. Did the laity comprehend? Again, it is impossible to say. But we can reasonably assert that when considering the didactic aim and impact of this tradition of plays, it is probably most useful to imagine them as dramatized sermons. This is so even though they occasionally contained comic and bawdy elements.

Preaching

As the twelfth century wore on, there are hints in our sources that preaching to the laity, while remaining infrequent, did occasionally occur. Some of this preaching transpired outside the routine frameworks of mass attendance and other parochial devotions. For example, we have evidence of many wandering preachers of the apostolic life and several preaching tours, like that of Bernard of Clairvaux, launched in 1145. Much larger preaching expeditions were initiated by the Crusades, including, again, one of Bernard's (1146–1147). When a new church or altar was consecrated, a sermon was usually prepared for the occasion. However, these sermons were narrowly framed and could not have served as a medium of instruction for most of the laity.

Yet there are whispers in some sources that sermons were given to the laity. In the mid-century sermons of urban clerics, we detect lessons that could only have been intended for the laity, as the sermons instruct the auditor in correct behavior in what we should call the secular life. Some sermons seem to address particular social classes, foreshadowing a mode of discourse called *ad status* sermons (sermons intended for laity who have a particular station or occupation in life, like the married or tradesmen). In the skillful hands of the friars, these would become very popular in the thirteenth and fourteenth centuries. On those occasions when sermons were preached to the laity, it was almost certainly in the vernacular. Most of this preaching must have occurred at large urban churches; it remained the case that country priests rarely gave sermons or were expected to preach.

By the twelfth century, however, there was an occasion in the mass, called the "prone," in which the priest could teach in the vernacular. What did he teach? Contemporary writers stress the congregation's obligation to know the Creed and the Lord's Prayer. During the prone, the priest had an opportunity not only to teach these basic texts, but he might also summarize the gospel—in the vernacular. Again, we have no way of knowing how often or how well priests exploited this opportunity, but it is imaginable that the basic texts for understanding the faith were taught on these occasions. Colin Morris rightly cautions us, however, to remember that such teaching "does not modify the general conclusion that the people of the time were witnesses of a ritual rather than holders of a faith." But that was about to change.

The "Revolution in Pastoral Care," 1200–1250

Some have argued, to make a point forcibly, that the church at the end of the twelfth century discovered the laity. Clerics from the popes on down to the bottom of the ecclesiastical hierarchy began to focus attention on what Robert Markus (in a discussion of Augustine) calls "Christian mediocrity"—that is, those Christians who were neither heroically good (the saintly) nor abominably bad. One symptom of this focus, theologically, was a clearer idea of the doctrine of purgatory. All knew that paradise received the souls of the saintly and perfect and hell those of the ungodly. But what was the destination of everyone else, the vast majority of whom were neither spotless nor wicked? For longer than is usually imagined and probably before clerics embellished the idea, medieval Christians thought that the ordinary or mediocre would undergo some sort of purgative fire after death, perhaps by a brief experience of the superior regions of hell. Much earlier, Augustine—not, to be sure, a mediocre Christian—relying on 1 Cor. 3:11–15, spoke of intense purgatorial flames but not of a locus for them in which to burn. Around 1170, however, theologians in Paris (and Cistercian monks before them) ceased to speak merely of purgatorial fire and began to speak, locatively and nominally, of "purgatory" *(purgatorium)* as a place and as a noun. This was the destination of those who were neither very good nor very bad—the *mediocriter boni*, or tolerably good, not perfect. It was universally taught (except by the Waldensians and Cathars and other heretics, who repudiated the doctrine) that even the least disagreeable purgatorial pains were more agonizing than the most intense mundane suffering. These were imagined to be bearable only because the sinner was confident of heavenly beatitude once he had made satisfaction for his sins. In any case, the doctrine and its theological refinement in the twelfth and thirteenth centuries is simply one illustration of the growing interest in the laity and their instruction in the Christian faith.

As always, we must ask, why at this time? The response very likely has to do with the emergence of popular heresy. No less a figure than Innocent III spearheaded the effort to prepare the laity to be able to identify heretics, who begin to emerge at the end of the twelfth century and who were claiming to live according to the prescriptions of the New Testament. Innocent implemented his vision at the Fourth Lateran Council, and to be sure, it was this vision of the pontiff that was put into place. Although the council was attended by some four hundred bishops and cardinals and more than eight hundred abbots and religious superiors, Innocent aimed mainly to reinvigorate the health of the local churches, which he found failing. No single decree presented by Innocent was more influential than Canon 21, the famous decree *Omnis utriusque sexus* (1215): "Let every member of the faithful of either sex, once he has reached the age of discretion, confess faithfully all of his sins once a year at least to his own parish priest; and let him strive . . . to fulfill the penance imposed, receiving reverently the Sacrament of Eucharist at least during the time of Easter." In a book on the history of auricular confession, the great medievalist Henry Charles Lea (d. 1935) once called this canon "perhaps the most important legislative act in the history of the church." Another great medievalist and sometime prefect of the Vatican Library, Leonard Boyle, has argued more recently that the council and this decree generated a "revolution" in pastoral care. This may be true, but the punishment theoretically proposed for disregarding the decree—excommunication and refusal of Christian burial—was severe. Quite evidently, it was meant to communicate the solemnity of the pope and his cardinals in crafting the decree.

Now the priest could use the confessional in order to assess the religious knowledge of the laity and, if possible, to improve upon it. Moreover, in the decades after 1215 bishops and other diocesan officials who managed pastoral care could more securely hope that a priest was competent, in part because manuals of instruction were regularly composed and distributed to the clergy. Boyle believes 1215 marks a revolution in the history of pastoral care because it generated this new type of literature, manuals of popular theology (as he calls them) that lay out the pastoral obligations of priests and instruct them on how to care for their penitent parishioners. Among other things, these manuals make explicit what the laity is expected to know. Before 1215, as we have seen, clergy had received some elementary education and could probably construe some Latin but did not profoundly comprehend, theologically, the texts they recited at service.

After 1215, and according to the requirements made binding by the Lateran Council, cathedral chancellors were required to furnish their diocesan clergy with some instruction in theology. As always, we are not sure about how and the degree to which such requirements were observed. It is likely that sermons and other conversations at diocesan synods provided the occasion for further instruction.

Here, too, diocesan clergy were taught what was required by way of conduct and learning. Much synodical legislation revolved around the requirement that clergy possess copies of codes produced by synods themselves—and the requirement that they produce these copies at later synods (bishops returned home with copies of the decrees). However, as there is no evidence that suggests that country priests were ever required to attend diocesan synods, it is difficult to say how many of the rural, unbeneficed clergy received any instruction at all. For these men, some form of the traditional instruction, apprenticeship, probably still had to suffice in many cases. A significant proportion of the canons deplored priestly misconduct—a signal that clerics likely continued to find frivolities like hunting and fowling to be irresistible. The council also forbade clerical participation in judicial ordeals by water and fire, and other canons suggest that the eleventh-century reforms demanding celibacy had not fully taken hold.

Three consequences of the new canon on annual confession invite further reflection. First, as a consequence of a more fully developed doctrine of purgatory, priests could feel free to relax the often grueling penances demanded by the old Scottish-Irish "tariff" system of penance. After all, if penance could only be consummated in post-mortem suffering that was unfathomably more onerous, it made little sense to impose excessively harsh penances. For one thing, penances might be ignored. Worse, if too severe, well-meaning priests might discourage further confession and make the new canonical requirement a dead letter. This would achieve the opposite of what the canon desired—namely, a parishioner who was no longer a mere observer or passive participant in parish ritual but a self-consciously committed Christian.

Another consequence of the new canonical requirements was the gradually formed consensus that absolution for sin came from the hearing priest. Like the power to confect the elements of bread and wine into divinity and thus to become a "God maker," this view of priestly power and sacramental operation served to augment appreciation of clerical status. Yet it could and did boomerang, as lay reformers and critics contrasted the lofty sacerdotal ideal promoted by theologians with the less exalted reality on the ground, and priests became more vulnerable to harsh (if all-too-often accurate) criticism.

A third result was that certain ways of life, and entire social classes of people, could no longer simply be dismissed as incorrigible or irredeemable. The whole spectrum of social ranks, especially as found in the cities, had to be taken into account pastorally and in the confessional. Priests understood that moneylenders and merchants—the "not-so-good," to use Innocent III's term for those destined after death for purgatory—were vulnerable to daily temptation and may have found sin, as then defined, virtually unavoidable. Such men were conventionally presumed unfit for salvation. Now, priests used the confessional in order to counsel such men and to establish new benchmarks of what was morally acceptable. No wonder some have argued that the enterprising spirit was sanctified and Christianized from the confessional stall. To say that confession was a mode of "social control" (as is often asserted) is to state an obvious fact. But it falls well short of expressing the whole truth, for the confessional, in a way no one anticipated, made certain classes of people admissible to the ranks of the reunited and reconciled and rendered certain previously illicit and sinful activities permissible and licit. Over the course of the twelfth and thirteenth centuries, these parishioners were brought into the church truly and not just notionally and were considered among those capable of salvation. Moreover, these parishioners increasingly took charge of their own religious life, in part by founding institutions to promote piety and prayer, none more important than the fraternity.

Fraternities, Guilds, and Charities

The heading of this section suggests we are talking about three different sorts of lay medieval institutions. Actually, we are describing one institution that went by these names and others in different parts of Europe—and was an institution in which the relationship and weight of social, devotional, and charitable activities varied by time and space. Its founding lay deep in Germanic history and had long predated the thirteenth century; we know that similar institutions existed already by the Carolingian period. But they exploded in numbers, impact, and popularity in the high Middle Ages. This may be so not only because of the profound social and religious aspirations to which they ministered, but also because so very little, by way of material resources, was required to found one. A group would decide to pray together. Perhaps it would also decide to hire a priest to join in and preside over mass. That was sufficient. By the late Middle Ages, countless of these mini-institutions existed everywhere, so much so that the fraternity became what many have regarded as, institutionally speaking, the most typical expression of late-medieval Christianity.

What functions did such groups satisfy? Again, it is difficult to generalize about all of Europe since, as is often the case in the Middle Ages, local, regional, and chronological variation must be taken into account. It has been argued that some Italian fraternities in the cities essentially replaced the parish as the center of ecclesiastical life. But these would have been exceptional and probably depended on the vitality (or lack thereof) of local parish life; even these were originally intended to *supplement* what was available at the parish, not to replace it. Some were little more than societies for regular meals. From this flowed what might be the uniting characteristic of nearly all fraternities: mutual support and the reception of benefits for members.

The benefits most treasured by members, and lavished upon them by their brothers, were post-mortem ones. Fraternities usually promised a Christian funeral for their members (building up subscription funds or membership fees for such purposes) and offered prayers for the departed. Before death, a member could receive benefits from the common fund when ill or especially needy. A few wealthy fraternities had their own burial grounds or vaults; some could afford to hire a priest to say daily mass for all members, the quick and the dead. Later, when indulgences came to be offered with membership, the post-mortem benefit eclipsed all other functions. Some international prayer unions existed for which no cash fee was required; one had simply to recite a certain number of prescribed prayers, usually *Paternosters* (Our Fathers) and *Aves* (Hail Marys). A good example is the monastic confraternity, in which a cleric or lay noble was permitted to receive spiritual benefits from powerful cloisters, like Cluny. Some fraternities were dedicated to particular saints or devotional practices (like dedication to the Passion) or feast days (such as Corpus Christi). Others were penitential societies. In these, the social and post-mortem functions were clearly subsidiary to the religious ones.

Needless to say, if fraternities could also be known as guilds, economic practices and interests might be the ties that chiefly bound members together. Still, even here there arises a chicken-and-egg question: did the desire for religious association or economic protection come first? It is difficult, if not impossible, to say. There can be little doubt, though, that some members joined because they first had a desire to make commercial connections. In any case, practitioners of one trade would assemble to memorialize a saint—the patron saint of that trade—and to worship at a particular building, not always the parish church. Accordingly, these guilds would often have transgressed parochial, geographical, and sacerdotal boundaries. Still, there is little if any persuasive evidence to suggest these groups were anti-clerical in origin or evolution or that parish life was generally unsatisfying.

At the same time as members were seeking benefits of the most mundane kind, some fraternities imposed strict moral rules on their members. Brothers were warned not to fornicate or commit adultery, not to swear, and not to sin in any other social way. To what degree violations were policed or punished is difficult to say. But guild membership brought prestige to individuals, and loss of this cachet (not to mention a fear of eternal punishment) may have functioned to discourage deviant religious and social behavior. And prestige ran two ways. Some guilds recruited and were proud to reel in local worthies, such as bishops, earls, or—in very rare cases—monarchs.

Newcomers or foreigners to a particular region might establish their own guilds for mutual protection and support. In Toledo Conversos (converts to Catholicism in Spain and Portugal in the later Middle Ages) set up their own guild in the Middle Ages. So did the sick. Lepers formed associations that were regarded, by their contemporaries, as fraternities, or "leprosaries." These sometimes had houses, or *ladreries,* perhaps founded when a wealthy leper formed or joined one; these existed outside the walls of a town (contemporaries knew the disease spread by contagion, so lepers were segregated); these houses were, by contemporary standards, not uncomfortable. Some were founded by nearby cloisters or their benefactors.

Through all of this variety in form and function ran the common thread of charity. Even those guilds not expressly founded as charitable associations (many were) felt the strong weight of that quintessentially medieval religious obligation, charity to those in need. Again, nomenclature is important. It is important to remember that at the time, the term "charity" was used interchangeably with "guild" or "fraternity." The sheer range of needs met and services provided overwhelms any attempt at comprehensive summary. "Charities" ran hospitals, ministered to the poor in numberless ways, gave alms, sheltered travelers, ran leper houses, and cared comprehensively for the destitute and deprived. It may be that these charitable activities also functioned as a way for the newly rich merchants and urban patriciate to manage the guilt that came while contemplating their piles of riches. What is certain is that despite the seriousness with which members took their obligation to be charitable to the needy, for several reasons the network of fraternities and guilds ought not to be imagined as a precursor to the modern European or American welfare state. First, only members received the fullness of charity from their guilds. Moreover, surviving account sheets suggest that monies spent on devotional candles almost always were greater than the amounts spent on external charity and almsgiving to non-members. Finally, it bears repeating that the commercial opportunities and contacts supplied by the guild could often have eclipsed the devotional and charitable purposes for which it had ostensibly been founded.

Motives can be, and usually are, mixed. Being glimpsed by neighbors in certain processions would have enhanced the social prestige of members of some guilds. For these reasons, suspicious prelates and legates who visited them could conclude that some guilds were achieving neither Christian charity nor unity. That skepticism, however, should not blind us to the immense good these widespread associations achieved, nor to the prodigious volume of spiritual and secular charity received by the poor and anguished in the high and late Middle Ages. It was never heard, as it often is in the West today, that the needy bore responsibility for their own misfortune and therefore deserved no help from wealthy individuals or social institutions. Even still, the rich probably gave more willingly to the voluntary and holy poor than to those who had been born or lapsed into destitution.

Many charities were founded by women for reasons that overlapped with the motivations for founding a male fraternity: charity and devotion. Women also joined fraternities that were mixed-sex. Scholars have debated recently how much power and agency women exercised in these associations. On the one hand, one Italian fraternity dedicated to the Virgin stated in its 1262 statutes that as no distinction existed between the souls of women and men in the sight of God, women were surely free to receive the religious blessings of such associations. Their sheer numbers in some confraternities suggest that women played a significant role. The confraternity of Misericordia Maggiore in Bergamo, for example, had almost two thousand women members. Other scholars have argued that the mere fact that women had matriculated in these associations does not necessarily imply their exercise of leadership or an escape from the norms that prevailed outside the charity's walls. It seems almost certain that any influence they might have exercised waned as time passed.

The Meaning of Marriage

It has sometimes been argued that the medieval church harbored a "virulent hostility" to marriage. This is inaccurate, in part because it does not explain regional and chronological variation and change and in part because it does not account for the way in which marriage customs were tied to social station. It is especially misleading when applied to the high- and late-medieval centuries. In the twelfth century, several theoretical and practical changes occurred that transformed the institution of marriage. A first had to do with prohibitions concerning degrees of consanguinity; a second had to do with the indissolubility or permanence of marriage; a third had to do with the notion that marriage was made not by contract, nor by coition, but consent. These changes, especially the third, opened the way for a new appreciation of marriage; this appreciation may also have been fed by contemporary cultural trends like courtly love literature, which understood marriage to be founded on romantic love and personal desire. All of these theological, canonical, and cultural developments set the context for the creation of a marriage service that, in modified forms, still exists today in the Christian churches.

Existing canon law in the twelfth century had defined the limit of relations of blood within marriage to the seventh degree of consanguinity. However, Roman and Germanic practices differed in their calculation methods. Eleventh-century legists, including Pope Alexander II, whose opinion was discussed and elaborated by Gratian, clarified the mode of calculation and trimmed the traditional prohibitions to four degrees. This decision was also ratified by Lateran IV.

In the early Middle Ages, marriage had usually been regarded in a secular and social sense as an alliance between two (often noble or regal) families. Parents in these cases almost always chose spouses for their children, some of whom were betrothed in infancy and married in their adolescent years. That is, marriage was an institution designed to augment or protect material wealth, especially property, as well as social and political rights or privileges. The revolution in twelfth-century thinking resulted in a new understanding that consent—and only consent—made a marriage. Theologians and canonists increasingly began to take seriously the Pauline doctrine (in Ephesians 3) that marriage was a covenant like the one Christ had entered into with humanity. The greatest theologian of the twelfth century, Peter Lombard, declared emphatically, and authoritatively, "The effective cause of marriage is consent," a view given even greater authority by the approval of Pope Innocent III. To be sure, there were certain requirements for consent to be valid. One had to have reached what might be called "the age of consent," which seems shockingly early to our modern view: a girl was expected to be at least twelve and a boy fourteen. No girl or boy could be married against her or his will. Thus, the new teaching of consent moved desire for a marital union from families to the members of the couple who would spend their lives actually living with one another.

Initially, the only formalities required were a public declaration of intent before witnesses, where the bridegroom would state, "I [name] take thee [name] to be my wife." These new developments corresponded with more sweeping religio-cultural trends in the period, in which individual preference was honored. The Cistercians famously rejected the notion of child oblation, and most orders concentrated on adult recruitment. The old argument that the "individual" was created in the twelfth century can be debated ad nauseam. But evidence like this, in marriage and in the religious orders, certainly poses a question of profound historical and cultural interest.

In ways that prefigured the shape of the modern theology of the institution, marriage ceased to be regarded along the lines of a contract that could be revised or repealed capriciously. In the twelfth century, comprehensive consideration of the nuisances and complications that might end a marriage occurred. In the end, all were rejected. Notions of exclusivity and permanence were promoted by the recognition that marriage was a sacred institution. Once permitted under certain conditions, divorce was now emphatically banned. Separations were allowed in cases of cruelty, infidelity, apostasy, and heresy. But illness or hardship did not meet the test. Spouses were supposed to live even with partners who had contracted leprosy. As an institution with sacred character, marriage was "for better or worse" and understood to be a lifetime commitment. By no later than the thirteenth century, it was understood that marriage was a sacrament whose sacred character created a relationship that could not be destroyed. Ecclesiastical courts were now in a position to enforce the marriage laws, and they did so.

One further theological and social evolution that might seem surprising to us—and destructive to the old chestnut that medieval people (especially clerics) harbored a comprehensive prejudice against marriage—was an emphatically expressed appreciation for the romantic and affective delights and dimensions of marriage. Again, Peter Lombard, a celibate cleric and consummate theologian, could celebrate marriage as a "union of minds" and a "conjugal society." Arguably, Gratian and Pope Alexander II went even further when they wrote movingly of "marital affection." It has been noted that vernacular literature then circulating through ecclesiastical courts was produced roughly contemporaneously with this ecclesiastical, Latin literature. But did courtly love literature help form ecclesiastical teaching on marriage? It seems unlikely because this type of literature originally glorified passionate love *outside* marriage.

Early in the twelfth century, we see evidence in northern churches of marriage ceremonies that express the new theology of consent. The wedding took place on the porch of the church. There, questions about any known impediments (especially regarding relationships between prohibited degrees of consanguinity) were solemnly posed. A contract followed, with the exchange of rings and a blessing. If this appears familiar to the modern reader, it is because our marriage ceremonies descend directly from ones like these. Also familiar to us are ideas that may not have had their origin in the high Middle Ages but were reinforced by clerical writers—that is, celibate priests and canon lawyers—that God had ordained marriage in paradise and intended for men and women to form a conjugal society; that marriage had been honored (some would soon say instituted) by Christ's presence at Cana, an event that made the once secular transaction a sacrament; and even the marvelous proposal that marriage was the first of the religious orders.

All of this is not to suggest that the church's novel teachings about marriage revolutionized the position of women therein. Though it must be observed that women did not always and everywhere experience marriage as oppressive, nonetheless, we ought not to imagine that the new ecclesiastical teaching, especially that on consent, made women the equal of men. Ironically, contemporary theology—or, if you like, ideology—could not allow that. For we must remember that this was also the age in which Aristotle's natural philosophy became available and taught in the universities. Aristotle's well-known views include the notion that women were, like children, incomplete, or even deformed men. They were the passive partners in reproduction. Woman's naturally imperfect state needed perfection through union with a male. Unless controlled by a male, she could be dangerous, incapable as she was of controlling her desires. It would take a woman's voice, that of the powerful fifteenth-century writer Christine de Pizan, to resist the Aristotelian traditions that had been inherited, taught, and ubiquitously believed until she wrote the *Book of the City of Ladies* in the early fifteenth century and, later, a poem celebrating Joan of Arc that exclaimed of the young maid, "What an honor for her sex!" But even Christine's spirited and amazingly learned riposte could not put an end to the influence of Aristotle's views in the later Middle Ages and far beyond.

Money and Morality

With few exceptions, the church was quite suspicious toward the new economy and commercial activity. Popes as early as the fifth century had concluded that commercial transaction perforce brought the two parties to sin. Leo I could conclude that merchants were incapable of pleasing God; their souls were sullied by involvement in business. Some of the church's earliest councils included canons that forbade clerical involvement in usury, usually citing Psalm 15:5: "He who does not put out money at interest" is blessed.

With the revival of the cities and the creation of a money economy, the church initially intensified its vilification of tradesmen, commercial activity, and the sins thought inescapably implicated in it. Cupidity was promoted to a new status as the cardinal sin. Nothing could be worse than avarice. Citing 1 Tim. 6:10, the papal reformer Peter Damian denounced it as the "root of all evil"; he both reflected and shaped the then prevailing clerical view that merchants had little chance of salvation. They lied, swindled, and served themselves only; little did they practice charity, if at all. Other churchmen, including canon lawyers and popes, condemned usury and simply identified it as theft. This was so profoundly believed that the ancient prohibition against clerical participation in usury was extended to all laity by the Third Lateran Council. Convened in 1179 and attended by Peter Waldes, this council occurred at a historical moment when the engine of commercial economy was everywhere thrumming. We live in an age in which the church is ignored or discredited by some for being "out of touch" for its magisterial teaching on everything from abortion to contraception, divorce, and other social issues. It was these economic teachings at the Third Lateran Council, a sign that the Gregorian impulse to extend the church's teaching to every sector of "secular" society was very much alive, that could then have been received by merchants, tradesmen, artisans, the nouveau-riche, and urban worthies as colossally off point and irrelevant.

It seems there is evidence here to justify the old chestnut that the medieval church's magisterial teaching was reflexively adverse to commerce and to the seemingly ineluctable progress of capitalism. Yet the canon law soon changed to reflect changing economic realities and to permit in practice what it had once and even then condemned as unlawful, making it possible for parishioners to participate licitly in commerce. By 1300, the church's lawyers had designated very precisely the conditions—thirteen in all—in which one could charge interest for loans. The new theology of confession and purgatory also helped ease the way for the church grudgingly to tolerate the practice of trade. Treatment of the sin of usury was relocated from the court to the confessional and thus to the conscience of the tradesman. This helped ease the way for the recognition that there was nothing intrinsically sinful in routine commercial transactions. The taking of gain, though never Christianized, was religiously curable not only by the confessional and the giving of charity, but also in the reality of post-mortem purgative suffering. Only those who outrageously capitalized on the helplessness of the poor earned the opprobrious term "usurer." Despite the reservations of the church, the ordinary merchant could, after all, be saved.

16

Devotion: Saints, Relics, and Pilgrimage

The history of the veneration of saints in medieval Christianity frustrates any attempt at a brief and thorough analysis. Here we must satisfy ourselves with an account that evokes the nature of medieval sanctity, the motivations for the veneration of saints, and the functions saints satisfied in medieval Christianity. As we shall see, while medieval Christians did not invent the veneration of saints, it was utterly central to devotion in the Middle Ages. If evidence were needed for this assertion, the incalculable works of art, architecture, and sculpture dedicated to the saints—above all Mary—and the numerous prayers addressed to or invoking them attest quite conclusively.

The Saint and Ideals of Sanctity

In early Christianity, the word "saint" (Greek: *hagios;* Latin: *sanctus*) was given to any member of the church who had been baptized and died in the faith and was believed to be with God; this nomenclature was integrated into their piety in the modern age by some Protestant groups. Only later, in the age of persecution, did the name come to be set aside for a Christian who had died at the hands of the Romans: the martyr. Thus only a small fraction of those believed to be with God were venerated as saints. Incidentally, this argues very strongly against those who would say simply that the Christian cult of saints was somehow of pagan origin, that the saints were plainly successors to the gods and other heroes of Roman and Greek legend. For, as a noble and often courageous witness (for martyr means "witness"), martyrs were very early on remembered and venerated by Christians precisely because of their refusal to participate in pagan religion. This is not even to speak of Roman revulsion with the Christian veneration of the dead. In any event, martyrs were venerated at their tombs, some of which became elaborate shrines. These places Christians regarded as holy because of their association with the saint-martyr and because it was customarily believed that the saint dwelt, mysteriously, not only in the heavenly court but in his shrine as well. He or she was especially present, and powerful, on the day of his or her feast.

New ideals of sanctity emerged in late antiquity as monks replaced martyrs as the Christian heroes *par excellence*. Readers of the *Life* of St. Antony will perceive that as Antony multiplied his mortifications and as he lost bodily power, his supernatural, miraculous powers intensified. Conceptually, this transition simply sustained the ancient idea that the dead martyr, whose body was lifeless, radiated in death with supernatural power. In the third and fourth centuries, as Christianity gained toleration, the veneration of saints grew in geographical scope, visible acceptance (especially by the construction of large churches over saints' tombs), and the proliferation of those venerated. New categories of saints emerged: not just martyrs but also confessors, doctors, and bishops. Still, through the early Middle Ages, ascetics were preeminent; the dominance of ascetics is particularly marked in Hiberno-Saxon saints' lives. In the Merovingian period, as "social class" became a more important factor, most saints were drawn from the noble orders. It was best not to be from ignoble or unremarkable stock; the illustrious, the aristocratic, and the male were overrepresented in the canon of early-medieval saints. Also honored were those who spread the gospel among the unchristianized.

Much later, saints lives begin to be collected in single volumes for pious edification. Surely the most influential of these is the *Golden Legend* of Jacobus da Voragine (d. 1298). Thomas of Cantimpré (d. 1272), an Augustinian who became a Dominican, made gender a category central to the four lives *(vitae)* of holy women he composed in the thirteenth century. Until then, "female men of God," as women saints had been called, were relatively rarely memorialized in hagiography or lives, legends, and literature about the saints, though references to them are many. From the twelfth and thirteenth centuries, with the emergence of specifically female modes of piety (like the Beguinal movement, for example), this changes. Then we begin to see more lives and writings not only *about* but *by* women. Still, female saints were, statistically speaking, very likely to be virgins, even if, ironically, associated with fertility and importuned by women who were barren or childless.

In the later Middle Ages, saints tended to be members of religious orders. Indeed, religious orders were keen to celebrate their own saints and spent considerable time and treasure in having one of their own canonized by the pope. The key point is that saints both embody virtues that do not change with time *and* also reflect changing concepts of sanctity over the centuries. Similarly, the popularity of certain cults could fluctuate over time, or, as contemporaries might have seen it, the power of a saint could wax and wane as new holy competitors constantly entered the playing field and drew attention away from the tried-and-true performers. There is a curious geographical dimension also to the distribution of saints in western Christendom. Saints of Latin origin dominate, and among the Latins, Italians prevail. This is undoubtedly because of the closeness of Italian saints to the canonizing authority in Rome, especially as the papacy came to take control of the canonization process.

Specialization

Saints specialized, so much so that it has been argued, slightly implausibly, that the celestial specialization mirrored the development of economic specialization from the eleventh century on (implausibly, as saintly specialization began long before the economic). Not only did some cure infants, but some also cured particular infantile ailments. Some saints, like the Anglo-Saxon princess and abbess St. Frideswide (d. traditionally 735), whose cult was centered at Oxford, ministered, it seems, especially to women. Others patronized different occupations; still others, familial vocations, such as fatherhood. Almost every imaginable illness in the Middle Ages, almost every conceivable malady or adversity (storms, sudden death, snake bites, shipwrecks) had a saint to whom one could appeal if afflicted. At the beginning of life, in an age when infant mortality rates ran high, parents of infants could visit shrines where stillborn children could be temporarily "resuscitated" so that they could be baptized. The Benedictine shrine of St. Michael at Mont St. Michel, off the coast of Normandy, attracted many ill children, some of whom improbably and dauntlessly made the distant journey northward from southern France or even southeastern Germany. Many shrines specialized in one of the many ailments to which infants were prone. St. Hubert in the Ardennes (d. 727) was known to specialize in the cure of leprosy. Further on in the cycle of life, "marrying saints" could be visited by those seeking marriage; marriages were often arranged at the festivals of those saints. Others could help find articles that were lost or stolen. Many if not most archdioceses, guilds of workers, schools, clubs, universities, militias, monastic orders and particular monasteries, cities, countries, and regal dynasties had their patron saint.

Above all, saints were invoked and shrines visited for purposes of healing. Indeed, it has been suggested that the saint best be imagined as a physician. Some saints urged that the pilgrim visit a doctor; in practice, many supplicants had recourse to both medical and saintly cures. Some saints, like St. Lawrence (d. 258), cured the disease named after him. In some cases, a saint was believed to cause a disease so that he could cure it. In sum, over the course of the Middle Ages there evolved a division of labor, a highly developed celestial bureaucracy, that

27. The monastery of Mont St. Michel stands on a rocky island less than a mile from the Norman shore in France. Original foundation dates to 708; the later Romanesque construction was undertaken in the eleventh century by William de Volpiano. Photograph by the author.

ministered comprehensively to nearly every imaginable human illness, spiritual need, or association.

The Shrine and the Supernatural

The shrine could confer immense authority and prestige on a particular locus. Sts. Peter and Paul, both apostles and martyrs, endowed Rome with unparalleled sacred distinction, as St. Mark did with Alexandria and then Venice, St. James with Compostela in Spain, Becket with Canterbury, and Ste. Foy with Conques. The shrine usually contained either some or all of the saint's bones or a complete corpse or relics—namely, objects (such as pieces of clothing) linked with the saint. In this way, a practice centered initially on commemoration developed into a cult of veneration of saints who were believed to be capable of wielding supernatural power (effective especially at the shrine) and willing to perform miracles on behalf of those appealing for aid. The saint thus became a mediator between the transcendent, omnipotent God and the weak, vulnerable, and often suffering human.

The mighty acts performed by or through the saint overwhelmingly had to do with physical health; the well-being of fields and lands; the fertility of wives and animals; and the safety of villages and families. That is, there was an instrumental aspect to saint veneration (about which very few Christians felt any shame) in the Middle Ages. Some likely feared judgment and hoped to have a heavenly friend to help them make the perilous journey from earth to the heavenly court. Some early Christians attempted to be buried in close proximity to the shrines of the saints *(ad sanctos)* in the hope that at the last judgment, they would benefit from being close to a saint summoned by almighty power to eternal beatitude. Others passed a night at or in the shrine, a practice called "incubation" (which *does* have ancient precedent, as at the shrines of Aesculapius, the Greek god of healing), during which they often had a vision of the saint and experienced some sort of miracle.

Why was supernatural power focused at the site of bodily remains? Ancient Christians had a response to this question, one that applied especially to martyrs and then to monks. In their minds, there was an inverse relationship between the natural power of the body and the supernatural power of the saint. As noted above, as a martyr's or monk's natural powers dwindled and then disappeared, his or her supernatural powers mushroomed. A martyr, one second a mutilated corpse, was the next a wonder-working saint capable of expressing supernatural power. The severe asceticism of the ancient eastern monks, which made them seem corpse-like, similarly brought supernatural powers as their natural powers all but vanished.

According to a belief dating back to the first centuries of Christianity, the saints, in consideration of the merits they had acquired and the sufferings they had endured on earth, were believed to have been favored by God, as seen in the power, *virtus,* that continued to act after their death in the remains or an object that had been in contact with them. This grace was manifested by signs like a well-preserved body and, above all, the odor of sanctity, a smell radiating from the remains of the saints, or sometimes seepage of oil from the side of a tomb.

Saints manifested their power and proclaimed their saintly status through "miracles" experienced at their shrines. The majority of those who venerated saints or traveled to their shrines sought supernatural assistance. Miracles proved that God had favored a dead saint. Hagiographers and historians of sainthood stress that devotion to saints, and especially expectation of miracles (above all of healing), have to be understood on the model of a gift exchange, where the norms of reciprocity required some form of supernatural aid after acts of reverence, honor, and an appeal—especially when an appeal was, as was often the case, a *cri de coeur.* As Peter Brown has stressed, the receipt of supernatural benefits from a saint can also be understood on the late antique model of patronage. Saints of late antiquity were modeled on the Roman *patronus,* a patron who could advocate, plead, or intercede on behalf of a client. Later in ecclesiastical history, saints could be addressed using terms, like "lord," appropriate to secular or political deference. The language of heavenly courts was often used; medieval Christians undoubtedly conceptualized their relationships with saints in terms of petitions being given at celestial courts. Thus, in exchange for veneration, gifts, and alms, the saint was expected, like a great lord or patron, to produce the desired answer to a petition.

If he did not, he could be ritually humiliated. This is especially the case with saints with a reputation for delivering good weather in an agrarian culture; their images or statues might be dragged in the mud if the rain failed to fall or the sun to shine. This made a non-performing saint vulnerable to "market forces"; if he failed to deliver after an invocation, the disaffected petitioner could simply take his supernatural business elsewhere. On the other hand, some petitioners blamed themselves and their sinfulness for failed petitions.

Records of miracles *(miracula)* were usually kept at shrines by a custodian. The overwhelming number of these were healing wonders. Modern scholars have observed, not incorrectly, that many of these "wonders" are capable of natural explanations today. For example, we know today that headaches are self-limiting; medieval pilgrims did not and credited saints with miracles. Some cures were partial. Others were temporary. Yet all "counted" as supernatural incursions, *miracula;* all would have been celebrated, if the cure occurred at the shrine, on the spot. No pilgrim suddenly cured of a troublesome and refractory affliction was likely to seek a "natural" explanation of his cure when the cause of cure was all too clear: supernatural intervention by a gracious God or his servant-saint. Given how little even scientists and physicians know about the mechanisms involved in recovery from physical and mental illness, it would be hazardous for the historian to say, *tout court,* that nothing wondrous happened at medieval shrines.

Cures were achieved by pilgrims in a number of ways. Some pilgrims struggled to gain direct contact with the saint by touching the saint's clothes or traipsing over ground on which he was believed to have walked, the bed on which he had slept, the tomb in which he was buried, his relics, or even his image. A measure of the desperation of the very sickly can be caught in texts that tell us of a pilgrim consuming dust or chips he had scraped from the tomb. Wax or oil from the candles at shrines could be used to soothe an afflicted part of the body. Water used to wash the saint's corpse, relics, or tomb was also consumed in desperation. Builders of some shrines made access to relics easier by constructing holes that enabled pilgrims to see and even to touch the saintly remains.

Theological Issues and Problems of Authority

The question of whether the dead ascetic performed these miracles was sufficiently vexing as to have caused theologians to attempt some distinctions. For the theologian, the saint-as-mediator presented appeals to God on behalf of the supplicant. God would perform a miracle through the saint because of his *virtus*—a word that indicates both the holiness the saint exemplified in his life (virtue) and the power he had after it, for *virtus* is simply another Latin word for miracle. The early fathers and later Christian intellectuals, who, it must be emphasized, participated in the cult of the saints, were careful to insist that saints were conduits *through whom* God performed miracles. For this reason, they were to be venerated, not worshipped. True worship was due to God alone.

Almost needless to say, fine theological distinctions like these were not always appreciated, understood, or even disseminated to those who limped or crawled to shrines in desperation. Even lower clergy in the early Middle Ages and beyond were likely insensitive to them. The distinction between worship *(latreia)* and veneration *(dulia)* was worked out precisely in the East during the Iconoclastic controversy (ratified only at the Second Council of Nicaea in 767), and it underlines one of the major differences between eastern and western veneration of saints. In the Byzantine Empire, the veneration of icons, holy images of saints, was, on the whole, at least as important as the veneration of relics.

If theologians and bishops attempted to deliver authoritative verdicts on the issue of miraculous agency, they were also the ones who assumed the authority to decide who had satisfied the criteria for sanctity. The earliest martyrs were probably spontaneously venerated without the felt need of ecclesiastical approval; unprompted veneration was sufficient. Later liturgical celebration or veneration, however, required not only a community of saint-venerators, but increasingly bishops also came to control the list or canon of saints who could be worshipped in their dioceses. This recognition would be ritualized by the removal or "translation" of the saints' remains to a newer and usually far more elaborate burial site, one customarily built above ground. The clericalization of the saints' canon only intensified in the twelfth and thirteenth centuries, when the papacy seized authority to canonize and sanction cult. Then the criteria of heroic virtue in life and the accomplishment of supernatural acts, while either living or dead, became mandatory. Still, the reservation of such prerogatives to clergy hardly put a stop to the non-clerical celebration and recognition of saints.

Calendars and Feast Days

Feast days increased in number from the Carolingian period until the end of the Middle Ages. By the ninth century, nearly every church in the West celebrated the Feast of the Apostles and the Evangelists. Widespread also was the Feast of All Saints (November 1), St. John the Baptist (June 24), St. Lawrence (August 10), St. Michael (September 29), and St. Martin of Tours (November 11). Beginning in the eleventh century, the Feast of All Souls, invented by Abbot Odilo of

Cluny (d. 1049), was celebrated (November 2). The canonist Gratian specified in his book of canon law all the feasts that the faithful were obliged to celebrate. These remained more or less the same until Gregory IX in 1232 authorized a canon of saints and feasts nearly identical to Gratian's.

We grasp some sense of the scale of the celestial population when we perceive how the saints entered the liturgy and calendar of the church. This was one of the main ways that the church Christianized time. Actually, the link between saint and liturgy goes back to the second century. On the anniversary of a martyr's death (or "birth" into eternal life), Eucharist would be celebrated on his tomb. (This, incidentally, is the historical source of the practice of placing relics in altars.) In the high Middle Ages, the prayer consecrating the elements of the Eucharist came to include a section in which the saints were petitioned for aid; this took the literary form of a very lengthy litany of invocation. The church also developed liturgies for saints' feast days. These included readings from saints' *Lives* (or *legenda,* which means "ought to be read"). Homilies were given that focused on the saint's heroic virtue. The church also Christianized time by placing saints in its calendars. In early-medieval society, there were many such calendars. As they were exchanged, they eventually were merged into a general calendar and formalized in the West with the Roman Martyrology (1584). Every day of the year was linked with one or more saints so long as that day did not coincide with a feast linked with Christ or the Virgin Mary. These holy calendars merged with the social and economic calendars as feasts were set as days for payments, particular agricultural tasks, and other mundane responsibilities.

Children were of course named after apostles or martyrs in the early church. Canon law eventually required that children be christened with the name of a saint. This was a practice, however, that did not become widespread until the late Middle Ages. Children were often named after the saint on whose feast day they were born. That saint would then become his or her "patron." Some children were named after saints to whom parents had particular devotion. For example, if conception occurred after invoking a particular saint, the child conceived and then born would likely be named after the saint invoked.

Relics: Theft, Translation, Invention

The mention of bones requires us to appreciate that a suppliant at a shrine believed that he was venerating or praying in front of a saint who was very much alive in the divine court of heaven. In the case of a dead saint, sanctity was also concentrated in relics (*reliquiae*—things left behind)—that is, in bodily remains or objects associated with the saint and the place of burial. Relics included corpses or a piece of a saint's dead body or some article owned, handled, or used by the saint, such as his or her cowl or other piece of clothing. A new category of relics emerged when articles of fabric or sponges *(brandea)* were brought into contact with shrine relics. Relics were often preserved in splendid caskets placed in crypts or even beside the high altar. Some, like the statue of Ste. Foy, which still survives at Conques, were housed in a costly image of the saint. Reliquaries like these were among the finest art objects produced in the Middle Ages. One thinks of the reliquary for the Three Kings at Cologne or the arm-reliquary of Charlemagne at Aachen. Some of these were influenced, especially after the sack of Constantinople in the Fourth Crusade by western Crusaders, by reliquaries arriving from Byzantine churches. Relics were used in social and political transactions and when communities were endangered. Oaths were commonly sworn upon them. They were displayed in procession in times of epidemic, famine, and economic or social calamity.

Ancient and medieval Christians, not to mention modern ones in certain times and places, were very anxious to have contact with, or gain possession of, the corpses of reputed saints. Many Christians in the Middle Ages attempted to make a "pious theft"—*furta sacra*—of saints' remains, while other saints' bodies had to be guarded, lest they be stolen by or divvied up among the pious. The possession of relics of martyrs and saints by important cities was made possible by the transferral, discovery, or theft of sacred remains. For example, Constantinople, a new but important city, had no martyrs. Its saints, like Timothy, Andrew, and Luke, had to be imported. Technically (as noted above), this removal of a saint's body or remains is called "translation." It almost always involved removal to a more elaborate shrine. It was often initiated by the putative desire of the saint to be venerated elsewhere. Occasionally, a city without a saint, or one that wanted a higher-caste saint, "discovered" the tomb or remains of a saint who had not, until then, been known to have been buried there. This was the case with St. James at Santiago, whose shrine developed into one of the two most important pilgrimage destinations in the medieval West. Something similar occurred with the evangelist Matthew, whose body was fortuitously discovered in Salerno in 1080. Technically, this is known as "invention" (from the Latin word, *invenio*, "to find"), but the other meaning of invention—namely, "fabrication"—was certainly involved as well. Relics, like the saints with whom they were linked, could function to preserve health, to protect lands and treasure, and to prevent or punish crime. In this sense, the saint was not only the patron and protector of his church, but he was also a vigilant and often violent owner, ready to discipline, intimidate, and mutilate. Relics might be brought by a monastic community to a law court to help litigate for them. They were often brought into battle so as to mobilize the bellicose power of the saint; Emperor Henry IV did so regularly.

The prominence of relics swelled as canon law from the eighth century came to require that the altars of new churches be consecrated with them. The Crusades caused relics to be stolen, bought, and sold on a theretofore unknown scale. This was especially the case with the Fourth Crusade in 1204, when, with the devastation of Constantinople by western Crusaders, many eastern treasures made their way west. In 1248, King Louis IX finished the Sainte Chapelle (Holy Chapel), at once tiny and breathtaking, in Paris. It housed his own collection of relics associated with the Passion, including Christ's Crown of Thorns—this despite a Crown of Thorns lying in Paris just miles away at the Abbey of St. Denis. Fragments of the True Cross were later added. The chapel was also built in the form of a relic treasury, and its magnificent thirteenth-century stained glass is still visible for awed inspection by the modern tourist-pilgrim.

As the sermon became a normal part of the mass-going experience of the medieval urban parishioner, preachers used exemplary stories *(exempla)* accumulated (then collected and anthologized) from hagiographical literature. Another factor contributing to the proliferation of sanctuaries in the West after the year 1000 was the growing importance of pilgrimage in the religious life of the faithful.

Certainly there is evidence for Christian pilgrimage in the sources from late antiquity and the early Middle Ages, but these journeys, undertaken for devotional reasons, seem, after the eleventh century, to have changed in nature and even more in scale. In the Carolingian period, it was mainly great men (bishops, abbots, monks, lay luminaries) who went to Jerusalem, Rome, or Monte Cassino, accompanied by a small party of fellows, returning from their travels with precious objects. After the First Crusade pilgrimages became much more frequent and increasingly popular in social composition, even becoming meritorious acts strongly urged on the laity of both sexes, though not on monks. St. Bernard reminded the monastic order that the monastery was a true Jerusalem for those who had chosen a monastic life; it was pointless, even dangerous, for regular clergy to want to visit the Holy Land.

Pilgrimage

Almost all of the aspects of devotion to saints—miracles, cures, relics, shrine accounts—come together in the practice of pilgrimage. Pilgrimages can be considered in terms of graduated distances from the pilgrim's town to the shrine. Thus we can say that there were local, regional, and international pilgrimage shrines. As always, a pilgrimage could be undertaken to honor and venerate a saint. Yet at local shrines especially, many pilgrims hobbled, stumbled, lurched, or crawled to a saint's shrine in a quest, often anguished, for the alleviation of agony;

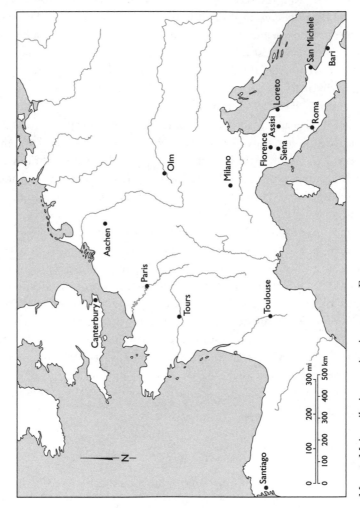

Map 6. Major pilgrimage sites in western Europe

others were carried in carts. Hagiographical literature suggests that such pilgrims could invoke a saint from a distance, yet it was believed that such invocations had less chance of a palliative outcome. The closer to the shrine a pilgrim could get, the better the chances for a cure. It was assumed by many medieval pilgrims that most saints had a certain radius of supernatural power; it weakened the further one traveled from center to periphery. Some saints were simply thought to be too far away to be effective.

Some pilgrims traveled not because they were ill or even because they wished to do so but to satisfy for a penance imposed by either ecclesiastical or secular authorities. For very serious sins, such as murder, bestiality, or sacrilege, pilgrimage to a distant, international shrine was prescribed as fitting penance. Those guilty of serious crimes could be identified: they were barefoot and fettered with chains. Murderers were required to attach their weapons to their fetters. The very worst crimes were occasionally punished with a sentence of perpetual pilgrimage. Many of these pilgrims simply wandered from shrine to shrine in the hope that a saint full of pity might miraculously break their chains, a sign that a murderer had been forgiven. Usually the chains were left at shrines in gratitude and as a sign of the power of the saint who had secured the forgiveness of God.

Penitential pilgrimages were of course not all compulsory. Many pilgrims, beginning in the tenth and eleventh centuries, undertook voluntary pilgrimages in the hopes that a saint at a shrine visited would intercede for them with God. Pilgrimage caused physical suffering, as much travel does, and the rigors of a long journey were imagined as an imitation of Christ; such rigors were thus thought to bring pilgrims closer to Christ and to have intrinsic religious value. Pilgrims to Jerusalem would interpret the intercessory act of a saint as a fresh beginning to be celebrated ritually by bathing in the Jordan. This was imagined as a second baptism, one that made the twenty-mile walk from Jerusalem to the Jordan well worthwhile. So many travelers to the Holy Land made the walk that one twelfth-century observer claimed to have counted no fewer than sixty thousand pilgrims on the banks of the Jordan. A similar ritual was practiced in a stream near Santiago de Compostela, one of the three great pilgrimage shrines in the Middle Ages.

Jerusalem

The earliest and most meritorious of pilgrimage destinations was of course Jerusalem. Pilgrims flocked to the Holy City in the fourth century after the construction of its most famous shrine, the Church of the Holy Sepulchre, the site of Jesus's crucifixion, burial, and resurrection. Many western Christians made the arduous trip to Jerusalem their last, on the belief that at the Last Judgment, it would be advantageous to be buried close to hundreds of martyrs and other saints. So many pilgrims flooded Jerusalem and environs that it was said, as early as the fifth century, that some two hundred monasteries or hostels were built to accommodate them. Again, Arab conquests put a temporary end to travel to Jerusalem, but revivals occurred under Charlemagne and especially in the eleventh century.

The increasing stress in the eleventh and twelfth centuries on the humanity of Christ made Jerusalem an even more popular destination for pious pilgrims. Now pilgrims traveled not just to famous shrines but also to all the places associated with Christ and the apostles, imbued with a newly intense aura of sanctity. It was as if the entire Holy Land was an extensive shrine and all of it a quarry for relic hunters. Pilgrims brought back bottles of water from the Jordan, dirt from Jerusalem, rocks from Mt. Sinai, and other kinds of relics. Such was the intensity of religious experience in the Holy Land that some were not capable of returning home to their normal lives and took up permanent residence. Similar psychological experiences, like the so-called "Jerusalem syndrome," affect pilgrims to the Near East today.

Rome

Rome was the most important pilgrimage destination in the West. The reason, of course, has to do with the city's status as capital of the ancient empire and the church's unparalleled collection of relics. The bodies of Sts. Peter and Paul were housed in basilicas dedicated to the founding saints of Rome's church. Their heads rested in the church of St. John Lateran. The remains of more than one hundred martyrs were housed in dozens of churches across the city. The remains had originally been placed in catacombs outside the city walls, but barbarian attacks encouraged Christians to bring them within the walls and to spread them across many churches. The veneration of relics and the canonical requirement that they be used in the altars of newly consecrated churches also led to the spread of the relics of illustrious saints.

Rome's preeminence was guaranteed by a number of accidental factors. First of all, the routes to Jerusalem were for several centuries cut off to potential pilgrims by Arab invasion and occupation. Second, Rome was much closer than Jerusalem for a western European traveler. Third, as we have seen, many Christians felt great affection for the Apostle Peter. That he possessed the keys to the kingdom of heaven only made a pilgrimage to his shrine more desirable. Needless to say, these religious motivations were enhanced by the classical aura, architecture, and art of ancient Rome. A guidebook entitled *The Wonders of the City of Rome*, a literary precursor to today's Blue Guide, catalogued and attempted to explain the marvelous remains of the city. That Rome was also the apostolic see increased pilgrim traffic, as liturgies were constantly being celebrated and relics were often displayed. Reliquaries were also carried in procession through the streets of the Eternal City on major Christian festival days.

Eventually, the papacy reserved to itself the forgiveness and absolution of very serious sin, like the murder of a cleric or the robbery of a church. Those who had committed such crimes were often required to go to Rome. Again, the papacy soon began bestowing indulgences for pilgrimages to certain churches, and the popes naturally selected many Roman shrines. Some pilgrims circulated to many of these churches to collect as many indulgences as possible. By the early fourteenth century, popes began granting indulgences for pilgrimages not just to churches but also to individual altars in the Basilica of St. Peter. This enabled a pilgrim, if in the city at the right time of year, to collect hundreds of years of indulgences. This process of inflation, which was driven by papal fiscalism, eventually caused strident criticism. Still, that did not stop the practice of granting a plenary indulgence—full remission of sin—to those who visited Roman basilicas in jubilee years, of which 1300 was one of the most famous.

Santiago de Compostela

Both Rome and Jerusalem attracted pilgrims in the ancient period of ecclesiastical history. Only in the ninth century did Santiago de Compostela become an international shrine. In 830, the discovery of the bones of St. James made the shrine immensely attractive. By the twelfth century, thousands of pilgrims, many of them French, were traveling to St. James by the five-pronged *camino de Santiago,* the most well-known and still used pilgrimage trail in the West.

The role of the invention of saints' bones in the instant and stunning popularity of Santiago was assisted by local bishops, who labored to publicize and promote the shrine by spreading the news of James's powerful ability to work miracles. Bishops worked with the kings of Navarre to ensure that the road to Santiago remained always passable and otherwise in good condition. Many churches, hospices, and monasteries housed or aided pilgrims, and all enjoyed material profits and prestige. Not only did the town of Santiago benefit economically, but also all small towns and even small shrines on the roads from France reaped the benefits of Santiago. Many of Cluny's houses lay on the roads from western France to Santiago. The monks of these houses likely wrote the *Book of Saint James,* a list of miracles that was spectacularly successful in promoting and publicizing the shrine. Without the monastic revival and the numerical growth of Cluny and its dependencies, it is unlikely that Santiago would have achieved such stunning success. Success led to more prestige. Santiago was in 1120 made a metropolitan see by the pope. Then, two years later, construction began on a glorious new cathedral. Soon kings would choose to be buried there, only enhancing its prestige.

28. Portico of glory, Santiago de Compostela, with a view of the central Romanesque nave and statuary. Compare with Gothic nave of Amiens (illustration 21). akg-images/ Jean Dieuzaide.

Conques: Ste. Foy

One of the most mysterious of all shrines in Christendom is that dedicated to Ste. Foy (Saint Faith) in Conques, France. The earliest reference to her is from Jerome, who makes a record of her martyrdom at Agen in Gaul. For a saint shrouded in legend, that she existed and was martyred are about the only two secure things we can say about her. Ducidus, the bishop of Agen, translated her relics to a basilica that he had constructed in honor of Ste. Foy and St. Caprasius. Many miracles were quickly believed to have occurred at Faith's shrine. She too specialized; she cured those with vision problems or blindness.

The monks at the nearby abbey of Conques were keen to acquire the relics of St. Vincent of Saragossa (d. 304) and then St. Vincent Pompejac in Agen, but they failed. At about the time St. James's relics were invented at Santiago, a monk was sent from the abbey of Conques to Agen. He is said to have remained at Agen for ten years, living in plain sight as a monk, until he had the opportunity to commit a "pious theft" and bring Ste. Foy's relics to Conques. Almost immediately, the pilgrim road through Agen to Santiago swung through Conques—precisely the outcome for which the monks filched the relics.

Conques was not only a stop on the road to St. James, but it also became a famous pilgrimage site in its own right. Indeed, Emperor Fredrick Barbarossa (r. 1155–1190) is only the most famous of the tens of thousands of pilgrims who made their way to venerate Ste. Foy. These pilgrims brought Conques the wealth they also wished for, and a large church began construction in the eleventh century and was finished in 1120. Many goldsmiths completed ornate reliquaries, and luminaries sent other golden treasures to the abbey.

Ironically, it is not at all clear that the main famous large reliquary at Conques contains any of the remains of Ste. Foy. Dating from around 900, the reliquary startles first by its dimensions, which are life-sized. Indeed, pilgrims to Conques will find themselves observed at eye level by Ste. Foy's famous blue eyes. Gold leaf and jewelry have been added to the reliquary over many centuries. Into a recess in the back of the figure, her relics were placed. Strangely, the head of the reliquary looks masculine. In the 1950s, it was determined that the head was in fact taken

29. Reliquary of Ste. Foy, ninth century, with Gothic additions. Treasury, Abbey Ste. Foy, Conques, France. Gilded silver, copper, enamel, rock crystal, precious stones, cameos, and wooden core. Many pilgrims would have seen this shrine en route to Santiago de Compostela. Photo credit: Erich Lessing/Art Resource, NY.

from a much older structure and may even—irony of ironies—represent the head of a Roman emperor.

The diffusion of Ste. Foy's cult throughout France and indeed all Europe, especially England, is quite remarkable. A shrine was set up to her by Benedictines near Norwich. Chapels were dedicated to her in Westminster Abbey and, later, St. Paul's Cathedral. Her cult survived the Middle Ages and even the French Revolution. The ancient "relics" still attract pilgrims, as Conques contains not only perhaps the most famous and mysterious reliquary in Christendom, but also a piece of the dragon-slaying saint, St. George.

Canterbury: Thomas

The importance of Canterbury Cathedral as a pilgrimage destination is entirely tied up with the murder of England's primate, or chief national bishop, Archbishop Thomas Becket (1118–1170). Before becoming the chancellor to King Henry II, Becket had spent most of his career as an official in the episcopal household of Archbishop Theobald (d. 1161). Henry made Thomas chancellor in 1155. Thomas was as talented a field general as he was a military commander, and he led campaigns in Anjou, Maine, and Toulouse. He served Henry as an itinerant justice, oversaw the activities and office of the exchequer, handled diplomatic contacts, and doled out patronage on behalf of the king. He was so intimate and trusted a friend of Henry that many have considered him the king's alter ego. For his fidelity, Henry named Thomas archbishop of Canterbury in 1162 (after, on consecutive June days of that year, he was ordained priest and consecrated bishop) on the assumption that he would remain Henry's trusted chancellor.

Once consecrated, however, Becket lived like, and may have become—for reasons not entirely clear—an entirely new man. Becket, to the king's immense surprise, resigned the secular role of chancellor. Almost immediately, the once worldly regal official became an ascetic. He prayed early in the morning, washed the feet of the poor, wore a hair shirt, scourged his body, studied scripture, prayed in private, and, even in the archbishop's household, ate a spartan diet. Whether he simply saw his new way of life as consistent with his new office, as his old way was with the chancellorship, or whether his soul had been transformed, we will never know. What is clear is that the resignation and the change that accompanied it augured trouble, which was not far off.

The issue that caused the two men to split was that of clergy who were guilty of secular crimes such as rape or murder. Ought they be tried in secular or ecclesiastical courts? At just that time, Henry was attempting to rationalize the English law and strengthen the court system. Henry claimed that clergy convicted and degraded from clerical status in clerical court should be punished by the state.

Thomas argued that degradation was a punishment that sufficed for a clergyman. Becket's position caused a division in the English episcopate. Opposition to him was led by Gilbert Foliot (d. 1187), bishop of London. Foliot's motives were not entirely pure, as he had wanted the primacy of England.

Henry insisted on the right of jurisdiction of royal courts to punish clerks degraded from clerical status. Becket reversed his position mysteriously several times. When the king refused a compromise, Becket fled in exile to France. From France, he appealed to Pope Alexander III for support. With Alexander's help, Becket was taken to the famous Cistercian abbey at Pontigny in Burgundy. There he remained for two years. Furious, Henry wrote to the general chapter of the Cistercians. He threatened to confiscate all the Cistercian lands in England if the order continued to give Thomas sanctuary. To the great relief of the abbots of the order, Becket volunteered to leave Pontigny. He moved to the Benedictine abbey of Sens.

In June 1170, Archbishop Roger of York (d. 1181), along with six of his episcopal colleagues, crowned the son of Henry II king. This was a deliberate usurpation of Thomas's primatial prerogative by a party of his episcopal opponents. Outraged and perhaps persuaded, then, that his dispute with the king could be resolved only by his own martyrdom, he returned to England. He excommunicated and suspended the bishops who had participated in the coronation. While in Normandy, the king, informed of the excommunications of the archbishops of York, London, and Salisbury, angrily queried why no one would rid him of "this foul priest." Taking a broad cue, four men did. With swords, the knights cut off the crown of Becket's head while he was saying mass at Canterbury Cathedral. One of them used his sword to spread the dying archbishop's brains across the floor of the cathedral, boasting that the traitor would not get up again.

The whole of Christendom was horrified as the story circulated throughout Europe. Henry suffered a personal interdict, and the archbishop of Sens imposed an interdict on Henry's continental holdings in France. Not wishing an interdict to be imposed on England and perhaps genuinely grieved, Henry reconciled himself to the church. As for the murder, he insisted that he did not send the knights to kill Thomas but conceded only that his angry words may have been misinterpreted. This was of course disingenuous. In any case, after Henry exempted clerics from secular courts and promised to go on Crusade to the Holy Land (a promise never kept), Becket had, if posthumously, won the feud that had separated two very stubborn and intemperate men.

Two years after Becket's death, Thomas was declared a saint and martyr on February 21, 1173. His feast is observed on December 29. In July 1174, Henry went to Canterbury as a penitent pilgrim. At the city gates, he removed his boots and made his way to Thomas's tomb barefoot. He then prostrated himself, admitted

30. Pewter pilgrimage badge depicting St. Thomas Becket's return to England from France *(regressio Sancti Thomae)* in December 1170, one month before his murder. The badge would have been purchased as a memento by a pilgrim who had visited his shrine. Badge dates from ca. 1350–1400. Photo credit: Museum of London / The Art Archive at Art Resource, NY.

his role (unwitting, he insisted) in the murder; he implored the monks of Canterbury to punish him. They did. Eighty monks each administered three strokes to the king's back. Henry remained at the tomb for the entire day and the following night. As with Emperor Henry IV at Canossa, it is difficult to say how genuine or calculated his penance was. Both men were humiliated, but both men were willing to suffer humiliation to preserve power.

Canterbury quickly became a shrine memorializing a priest-martyr who had challenged the power of the state over the church. For the next four hundred years, Thomas's shrine was the most important in England and among the three most visited in Europe. To be sure, this was a miracle-working shrine. Especially effective was Becket's martyr's blood. Pilgrims sought to obtain pieces of cloth soaked in his blood. Soon, monks at Canterbury Cathedral (cathedrals in England, by contrast to the continental model, were usually attached to a Benedictine monastery, not a house of canons) were selling glass bottles of Becket's blood. Becket, too, specialized. Pilgrims who managed to make contact with his blood were cured of blindness, epilepsy, and leprosy. Yet this was also an international pilgrimage destination. Many pilgrims, including an unusual number of continental and British prelates, abbots, and clerics, made the pilgrimage to Canterbury not for a miracle or cure but to honor the saint who had stood up to the king in order to preserve the liberty of the church.

Tours: Martin

Another immensely popular medieval saint was Martin of Tours, bishop of the city, monk, and missionary. Sometimes said to be the "Thirteenth Apostle" or "Apostle of Gaul," Martin established Tours as a major city in the religious geography of medieval Europe. He was the subject of an immensely influential biography by Sulpicius Severus (d. ca. 430), who knew Martin and composed perhaps the most famous incident in the history of hagiography. Approaching Amiens, Martin encountered a beggar, with whom he shared his cloak. This was a topos that was to be represented in much art and literature and was to influence the biographers of no less a saint than Francis of Assisi. During the Carolingian dynasty, by which time Martin had become the patron of Frankish kings, the most sacred relic of the palace, closely guarded by court clerics, was the cloak *(capa)* of St. Martin. (It was in fact at this time that clerics came to be known as *capellani,* or chaplains.) In his *vita,* Martin is represented as a sometimes violent destroyer of paganism, a missionary, a monk, a miracle worker, and a bishop. He thus exemplified almost all of the major saintly ideals in his person, and he was even willing to risk martyrdom in his missionary efforts among the pagans. On his feast day in November, he performed many miracles in Tours.

The shrine of St. Martin at Tours became an important sanctuary for pilgrims on their way to Santiago. Many churches in Europe were named after him, from St. Martin-in-the-Fields in Trafalgar Square to that in the Polish city of Poznań. These shrines and churches, as well as Tours itself, linked much of the religious geography of western Christendom. Another very popular French shrine was Vézelay, where the cult of Mary Magdalene was centered. In Italy, San Marco in Venice and St. Nicholas in Bari held pride of place behind Rome. Monte Cassino, the site of Benedict's monastery, was one of the most important medieval sanctuaries in Italy. In Germany, after the relics of the Three Kings in the Nativity story had been transferred by Frederick Barbarossa from Milan, Cologne Cathedral became an important pilgrimage destination. In this way, time was even more profoundly sacralized, and the very territory of Christendom was as well.

Women were particularly active in the late-medieval explosion of interest in traveling to the holy sites of Christendom. For example, St. Bridget of Sweden (d. 1373) traveled to Santiago and to Rome. She then visited most of the important shrines in Italy. Before she died, she traveled to the Holy Land. There she received visions, above all in Bethlehem. The English visionary and mystic Marjorie Kempe was also a tireless traveler to shrines. She seems to have visited every significant sanctuary in England before traveling to Rome and then to Santiago. Among the sanctuaries visited were those dedicated to the most widely venerated saint of the Middle Ages, Mary, the Mother of God.

"Virgin Most Powerful": The Special Place of Mary

It would be nearly impossible to exaggerate the place of Mary in the devotional imagination and acts of medieval Christians, the affection in which she was held, or the great deeds she inspired. In the industrial era, Henry Adams famously perceived of the profound adoration of Mary: "All the steam in the world could not, like the Virgin, build Chartres." Mary was commemorated, venerated, and beseeched not only throughout the ordinary year, but especially on her four feast days (the Purification, Annunciation, Assumption, and Nativity); in art, sculpture, and architecture; in written materials like legends and plays; in music and hymns; in sermons and homilies; in devotional and theological treatises; in prayers (especially the *Ave, Maria*) and special Marian devotions, like, in the later Middle Ages, the Rosary (a devotional practice generated by saying *Aves* scores of times on prayer beads while meditating on events from Mary's life); in supplications at countless wonder-working statues; and in the naming of many cathedrals and monasteries after her. The Cistercian Order dedicated every one of its hundreds of monasteries to her and named many for her.

Ironically, there was no international shrine dedicated to Mary in the Middle Ages that was the equal of Jerusalem, Rome, or Santiago. This is almost certainly because no single church could claim to house her remains. It was widely believed that Mary was assumed bodily into heaven. Thus, even while—and because—there was no body but only relics of her hair, vials of her milk, and pieces of her tunic, she was ubiquitously present. As such, she could be called on in times of distress from anywhere.

It has sometimes been argued that Mary functioned like a goddess in medieval Christianity. If so, it was as an extraordinarily compassionate and humane one, even as she was addressed with the honorific titles reserved for nobility: Our Lady, for example. The suffering Madonna was a kindred soul for the ordinary and the elite alike. She was a benevolent noblewoman who, when asked, would intercede with her more distant Divine Son. She was central not only to the religion of the people, but also to medieval devotion as such; her appeal cut through all social, religious, and economic strata; and shrines to the Virgin, and then, increasingly, artistic representations of Mary as Queen of Heaven, were found everywhere in medieval Europe.

No Marian feasts seem to have been celebrated widely in the West before the late seventh century. Around that time, certain commemorations seem to have become accepted at Rome: Mary's Purification (February), also celebrated as the Presentation of Christ and Temple; the Annunciation, celebrating the good news of Christ's birth by the angel Gabriel; the Assumption; and the Nativity of Mary (September). From Rome, these traditions spread, ultimately, to all areas of the West. In the late Middle Ages, other feasts were added. Certainly the most important and controversial of these was the feast of the Immaculate Conception. Based on the doctrine that Mary was conceived without original sin, its widespread observance by the fifteenth century can be explained in large part

31. Chartres Cathedral, lateral view from the south, as rebuilt after 1194. Notice the double flying buttresses as well as the conical south tower and highly articulated north tower. The crypt is said to hold the *sainte-chemise,* or holy tunic, of Mary. Hervé Champollion / akg-images.

by its promotion by the Franciscans. Some Dominicans opposed it; Albert the Great thought it "impious, heretical, and insane." Nonetheless, the feast day was established, even though the doctrine of the Immaculate Conception was not declared orthodox until 1854. Another important feast day established in the later Middle Ages was the Visitation of Mary to Elizabeth (July 2). In addition, many prayers, such as the *Salve, Regina,* came from this period. Many cathedrals were dedicated to Mary. Indeed, most of the French Gothic cathedrals we simply know as "Chartres" or "Amiens" are dedicated to Notre Dame, Our Lady. The great intellectuals of high-medieval scholasticism wrote prayers to Mary that achieved widespread use in the parishes, collegiate churches, monasteries, and cathedrals of medieval Europe.

That there was an explosion of Marian devotion in the final centuries of the Middle Ages is quite clear. The Mediterranean countries led in this respect. But, ultimately, Marian devotion spread to the entirety of western Christendom. It is interesting that the origins of many new Marian cults seem to have come from the laity. A simple believer might experience a revelation or apparition. Often the church approved the revelation or apparition as genuine, and a cult, with cultic buildings, was constructed; episcopal or clerical support usually followed.

Countless Marian sanctuaries were founded in this fashion, of which perhaps the most typical is that of Loreto in central Italy. A rural shrine to the Virgin was dedicated there in the twelfth century. By the fifteenth century, no less a personage than King Louis XI of France (r. 1461–1483) was a devotée. This example illustrates how the conceptual, two-tiered model of priestly religion and popular piety simply does not work. Marian devotion was embraced by all classes and by all strata in the church. It cut across the modern categories historians have sometimes tried to impose on medieval piety.

Critique

In the thirteenth century, shrines dedicated to the Virgin and to Christ proliferated. The great cathedral of Chartres, because it had (or so it claimed) the *sainte-chemise,* the tunic of Mary, became an early and perhaps the most important Marian shrine in France and among the most important in all of Christendom. Shrines dedicated to Christ usually centered, occasionally peculiarly, on pieces of his body, which of course was believed to have ascended to the heavens after his resurrection. Thus two abbeys at least claimed to have Christ's foreskin. One cloister was said to have his childhood teeth. Such claims sometimes led to critiques of relic veneration, of which *On Saints and Their Relics,* by the monk Guibert of Nogent, is the most well known. This text is often misunderstood as a proto-Enlightenment critique of superstition in religious practice. It is nothing of the sort. Though himself personally devoted to relics, Guibert deplored the practice of unsubstantiated sanctity. Neither opinion nor custom was sufficient for him. He depended on the "evidence of trustworthy writers" to guarantee the authenticity of a particular saint and called for greater clerical control over saints venerated without a shred of testimony to support their cult. Yet nothing Guibert said stemmed the swelling tide of devotion to all the saints, either in the Middle Ages or the Catholic Reformation.

A Lachrymose Age:
Christians and Jews, 1096–1492

As we argued in chapter 6, it would be quite wrong to conceptualize all of Jewish history or all Jewish-Christian interaction over the centuries as conflictual and "lachrymose." Even as, and very likely because, Europe became more unified religiously from the eleventh through the fifteenth centuries, relations with its Jewish communities generally deteriorated. Nonetheless, it would be wrong to imagine that Jews were continuously and ubiquitously persecuted. Still, in these centuries, Jews went from being a tolerated, if subservient minority, to an out-group that was increasingly marginalized, libeled, discriminated against, expelled, and massacred. One can only look back at the high and late Middle Ages, with respect to Jewish-Christian interaction, as a very sorrowful time indeed.

The Crusades

While it is true that ecclesiastically sponsored anti-Judaism predated the Crusades, it received new, hateful, and violent forms of expression in the First Crusade. In the German and Bohemian regions where Jewish communities were hardest hit by Crusaders, peaceful relations (despite occasional violence and repression) had by and large prevailed for centuries. This generally happy situation suffered reversal in the spring of 1096, as both Latin and Hebrew accounts testify, and many pogroms occurred. Jewish homes and cities were plundered, and fanatical Crusaders killed many Jews. The leaders of the main Crusader armies—high-ranking Frankish nobles mostly—arrived on the scene after the havoc had been wrought. Lower nobles, clerics, and many folk from the Rhineland cities had inflicted this damage, sometimes said to have occurred in the "pre-Crusades." The violence against Jewish communities was never sanctioned, and indeed was condemned, by Pope Urban II and several Rhineland bishops. However noble and even courageous their attempts to stem the violence and shelter the victims, they failed to stop an orgy of violence, desecration of holy places, destruction of homes, murder, mass suicide, and forced baptism. For this reason, some historians see the Crusades as a turning point in European history and have identified 1096 as the year when relations between Jews and Christians turned irreversibly hostile and often violent. Some historians, understandably but perhaps too simply, perceive in these episodes of mass violence the beginning of an interreligious hostility in Europe that was bound to result in the Holocaust under the Nazi regime in the twentieth century.

Why did an expedition undertaken against the Muslims of the Holy Land result in such desolation for European Jews? Some motivations, like greed and envy, were frankly secular. Yet one of the main reasons for the violence seems to have been that the Jew was so easily assimilated to the image of the enemy of God, the Muslim. Crusaders were also focused on the Church of the Holy Sepulchre and Jerusalem. There Christ had suffered, and there he had died. In the Middle Ages, Christians everywhere held Jews guilty for the death of the Son of God, the sin of deicide. Christians thought the Jews stubborn for not acknowledging the messiahship of Jesus. All of this took place in a religious environment of unholy enthusiasm, recent natural disaster, apocalyptic expectation (for both Jews and Christians), and anticipation that the Holy Land might be retaken, with full remission of sin (or, as some Crusaders undoubtedly understood the papal promise, the assurance of salvation). All of these factors only intensified the rhetoric and reality of religious persecution. In any case, the sources are unanimous on at least one sentiment: the Crusaders felt it senseless to undertake a long, dangerous journey to the Levant to fight a distant enemy while another, primordial religious enemy was left untouched at home in Europe.

At the time of the First Crusade, Jews in cities like Mainz and Worms formed perhaps one-sixth or one-seventh of the population. Many of the western Crusaders had never seen Jews before. Many themselves poor, they were probably taken aback to see many Jews living relatively prosperously. To anyone familiar with the Christian doctrine that Jews were to live in servitude, this was a cause of visible offense. Not only that; it was an offense to God, a violation of the divine will. Envy and greed indistinguishably merged with these religious motives, but the religious motivation alone could easily be invoked, implicitly or explicitly, for plunder. At Cologne in June 1096, the archbishop, Herman III (d. 1099), tried to protect the Jews of his diocese after their synagogue was destroyed and some died in the violence. Crusaders hunted them down nonetheless and plundered many Jewish homes. While many Christian chroniclers of these enormities refused to condemn anti-Jewish violence or plunder (some sympathized with it), one chronicler of the Crusades, Albert of Aachen (fl. twelfth century), stressed that greed was a major motivation for the Crusaders. The worst loss, though, was of life. At least 2,500 Jews died in German lands during the First Crusade.

The first communities assaulted by the Crusaders were in France, but it was in the Rhineland that Jewish communities suffered awful agony. It is no accident that these assaults occurred in the spring of Holy Week; they lasted until the end of June 1096. In the spring of 1096, the Crusade preacher Peter the Hermit (d. 1115) arrived in Trier with thousands of Crusaders. On May 3 (which fell on the Feast of the Finding of the Holy Cross) the Crusaders launched an assault on the city of Speyer during the Jewish Sabbath. Tragically, eleven Jews were killed. Yet the great majority of the city's Jewish population was protected by the sympathetic bishop of Speyer (who earlier had granted privileges and promised protection to the Jews). He even punished a number of the Crusaders. Roughly two and four weeks later the community at Worms was subject to two attacks. Here the bishop was absent and the slaughter horrible; some eight hundred Jews died. The infamous Rhenish count Emicho of Flonheim and his followers led these attacks. At Mainz, he annihilated a large portion of the Jewish community.

How did individuals and communities of Jews react to this threat to their and their children's survival? Many were faced with the prospect of baptism or death. A number of Jewish communities attempted to defend themselves. Some prelates, like Archbishop Egilbert (d. 1101) (who had preached against atrocity against the Jews) attempted to protect Jewish residents of his diocese by offering them shelter in his palace, which was fortified. Still, he urged them to consent to be baptized. Many consented to be. In other cases—as at Mainz, for example—Jews died at their own hands in an act of collective suicide or as a "sanctification of the Name of God" *(kiddush ha-Shem)*. More than one thousand died in this fashion.

In the Second Crusade (1147–1149), a Cistercian, Radulf, went to the Rhineland and preached virulently against the Jews, going so far as to call openly for killing them. Horrified, Bernard of Clairvaux, who had played a pivotal role in publicizing and preaching the Crusade, rushed to the Rhineland in an attempt to refute the preaching of his fellow white monk. It was during this Crusade that Jews were charged with killing a child whose remains had been found in the Main River. This was the first ritual murder ever alleged on the Continent; eight hundred years later, Nazi propagandists, in very different circumstances, would charge the Jews with the same crime. In 1146–1147, several cases of violence against Jews were reported from northern France, Germany, and England. One rabbi, attempting to return home from Cologne to England, was decapitated. In France, Crusaders killed the illustrious rabbi Rabbenu Tam (d. 1171) by inflicting five wounds in memory of the five wounds suffered by Christ "at the hands of the Jews." Only at the end of Holy Week 1147 did the Crusaders move on. It was during this Crusade that many Christians in fortified rural locations sheltered many Jews. One bishop, Siegfried von Truhendingen (d. 1150), washed, anointed, and buried in the grounds of his garden those Jews slain by the Crusaders who had tortured and killed in his diocese.

The fall of Jerusalem to Saladin in 1187 led to the call for a Third Crusade. In this case, while there were a few isolated incidents of violence in German lands, the emperors Frederick Barbarossa and his son effectively protected the vast majority of imperial Jewish subjects. Accordingly, the most horrific incidents occurred outside the empire, in England. After King Richard had left for the Levant in 1189, pogroms against Jews occurred in Lincoln, Lynn, Norwich, and Stanford. Perhaps the most memorable example of *kiddush ha-Shem* occurred in York in March 1190. There, in the city tower, the Jews gathered and committed mass suicide before an enraged mob could get to them.

In the case of the English pogroms, it seems as if many of those involved were indebted to Jews. This was an effect of the move into money lending by the Ashkenazic Jews of England, Germany, and northern France. That move was itself induced by the growing monopoly of trade by Christians and their guilds, a development that forced Jews into money lending and into the despicable role of creditors in the new money economy of western Europe. Not only was it an unpopular role, but it was also a dangerous one, and, as we see in the York incident, it made Jews vulnerable to mob or individual violence.

With the fall of Acre in 1291, the eight "numbered" crusades to the Holy Land came to an ignominious end. Yet crusades could be and were launched internally by so-called shepherds and others. Thus hundreds of Jews lost their lives in France, northern Spain, and the Netherlands in the thirteenth and early fourteenth centuries. Crusaders on their way to attack the Hussites of Bohemia (crusades against the Hussites are, while numerous, "unnumbered") again attacked communities of Rhineland Jews in 1421.

In the Crusades, then, a latent animosity toward a religious opponent and defenseless minority, long somewhat dormant, awakened with terrible ferocity. Economic motives (and envy) were mixed up with religious ones, especially as Jews assumed the role of creditors to Christians in the high Middle Ages. In many instances, bishops and secular authorities were able to protect Jews, but in their absence Jews were in great danger. These authorities not only protected Jews out of duty but also out of self-interest. They desired order and the economic services Jews could provide without church opposition (Italian and southern French bankers, as well as the Templars, also lent but did so in the face of ecclesiastical stricture). When faced with the choice of baptism or death, many Jews chose self-sacrifice so as not to surrender to the Gentile, to hurry the coming of the Messiah, to sanctify God's name, and to avoid apostasy. Whatever significance one imputes to the Crusades, it is clear that they can at least symbolize the beginning of a diminution of status of the Jews and their vulnerability to irrational violence and hatred in Christian Europe.

Anti-Semitic Myths

Blood Libel

In the wake of the crusades, as Ashkenazic Jews were forced to move into the business of money lending, a number of popular superstitious and legendary beliefs, some nourished by clergy and monks, began to appear and contributed not only to the medieval but also to the modern image of the Jew as an implacable enemy of Christians. Employed widely by the Nazis in the twentieth century (as noted) and still used against the Jewish community in the twenty-first, by far the most enduring and destructive of these is the so called "blood libel" or ritual murder charge.

Though Jewish law forbids the consumption of blood and despite the fact that no case of ritual murder or blood libel has ever been proven, the accusation that because of a felt obligation, Jews kidnapped, tortured, and ritually murdered Christian children (usually a young boy) originated in England in the case of William of Norwich (d. 1144) around the time of the First Crusade; it lasted until the early twentieth century and the Nazi period, where it was resurrected as a potent form of anti-Semitic propaganda. It has been suggested, quite controversially, that the blood libel originated in the wake of the First Crusade and acts of *kiddush ha-Shem*. If, the theory goes, Jews were capable of killing their own children, they surely could kill the children of Christians. Others have suggested, plausibly, that the image of a rabbi holding a knife near a child at the rite of circumcision, drawing blood, and then sucking on the wound gave rise to the libel in the Christian imagination. It is worth pondering that for all the many cases of ritual murder, we are entirely dependent on Christian sources, save for one exception.

Usually originating when a child was missing or died an accidental or inexplicable death, the ritual murder accusation, as distinguished from the blood libel, held that a young boy was abducted and killed as a reenactment and mockery of the crucifixion of Christ and as punishment for the claim in the Gospel of Matthew that Christ's blood be "upon us and our children" (Matthew 27:25). The closely related blood libel claim seems to have occurred first in Fulda, Germany, in 1235. Then the Jews of Fulda were charged with collecting blood and body parts for secret rituals, to make Passover matzah; some alleged the blood was used for medicinal or magical purposes. This was a very low, melancholy moment in the history of relations between Jews and Christians, especially as this libel would have a long, post-medieval afterlife.

Usually the children allegedly abducted became canonized and their tombs centers of cults. This was the case with William of Norwich, St. Hugh of Lincoln (d. 1255), and Simon of Trent (d. 1475), frequently represented in art in the Middle Ages and in propaganda in the Nazi period, as in a 1934 edition of Julius Streicher's *Der Stürmer,* a slanderous Nazi newspaper designed to encourage hatred of Jews (Streicher was convicted at Nuremberg for crimes against humanity and hanged in 1946). Their tombstones, and those of many other alleged victims, became objects of pilgrimage, and their relics were said to have performed miracles. Some pilgrims, such as those flocking to Norwich, where many artisans and townsfolk were indebted to Jewish moneylenders, may have come for perverse devotional reasons—namely, to sustain an anti-Semitic cult.

Almost always such allegations led to violence against the Jews and pleas on the part of popes, emperors, and kings to desist from such violence. The relationship among blood libel, ritual murder, and host desecration has been much debated. Obviously, they are related, but which one led to the other two is still unclear. Many scholars are convinced that all these libels originated from Christians struggling to comprehend the Eucharist, in which the actual physical body and blood of Christ were believed to be consumed after the consecration of the Eucharistic elements of bread and wine.

What were the motivations for these charges? Economic incitements loom large here. Some who made the accusation against a particular Jew coveted his property. Rulers who disbelieved the libel nonetheless invoked it in order to confiscate property, as well as to augment their prestige as protectors of Christians and a Christian commonwealth. Many wanted to establish shrines with wonder-working relics. This was, ironically, particularly the case when a body could not be found. Rumors of ritual murder and the establishment of a cult were in fact easier to establish if rumors alone could do the job.

Even after Jews were expelled from England and France, the narratives of ritual murder lived on in the imaginations of the folk and of literary geniuses. In "The Prioress's Tale," Geoffrey Chaucer depicts the reaction of Jews infuriated by a young Christian who sings a hymn while wandering through the Jewish quarter:

> From this time on the cursed Jews conspired
> This innocent boy out of the world to chase.
> A murderer for their purposes they hired
> Who in an alley had a secret place,

And as he went by at his childish pace,
The Jew seized on him, and held him fast, and slit
His neck, and threw his body in a pit.
Into a privy they threw the boy I say,
A place in which these Jews purged their entrails
O cursed people, unchanged since Herod's day,
What think you that your foul design avails?

It is of interest here that the fourteenth-century Chaucer repeats a myth that had a long pre-life and would have a catastrophic afterlife: the myth of the "eternal Jew," whose character could never change ("unchanged since Herod's day"), a trope that would be used to justify violence, and then much worse, against Jews. In Shakespeare, some claim to hear in Shylock's demand (in *The Merchant of Venice*) for a "pound of flesh" an allusion to Jewish blood thirst and blood vengeance. Ecclesiastics did what they could to support the charges enshrined in the classics of English literature. Franciscan and Dominican preachers spread the legend across Europe. The Premonstratensians, thick on the ground in Germany, composed a list of those supposedly ritually murdered by the Jews. One of the worst instances of devastation, the so-called "Prague Massacre," occurred on Easter Sunday 1389. A priest charged that the host had been desecrated and he pelted by rocks thrown by Jews. A prayer documenting these events has been left by the famous Prague rabbi and Kabbalist Avi Kara (d. 1439). Part of it reads as follows:

Towards the end of the holy Days
Of Passover blood stained our ways.
Without any reason they drew their knives.
And slaughtered our men, children and wives.
Our homes, our precious homes, they burnt.
Together with all our dear ones within
Helpless and shuddering we learned,
What it is to lose one's home and kin.
Woe to that day that made us to suffer
When wild grew the mob, the drunkard, the duffer
With axes and other weapons of dread
Our brothers' and sisters' blood was shed.

Several thousand Jews died in Prague on that day of resurrection. Some converted. Others took their lives. The synagogue was burned, and the books and scrolls within and gravestones were desecrated and destroyed. The secular authorities responsible for protecting them were so little interested in coming to the aid of the Jews that they helped themselves to their possessions. Charged with doing

32. Ritual murder of Simon of Trent. Detail image taken from Joannes Mathias, *Relatio de Simone Puero Tridentino* (Nuremberg: Frederick Creusner, ca. 1475), containing an account of the murder. © British Library Board/Robana/Art Resource, NY.

nothing to assist them, the Holy Roman emperor responded that they deserved their fate, for they had left their homes, when all knew it was forbidden to them to do so.

Certainly the most famous ritual murder accusation involved the infant boy Simon of Trent. The accusation began when the Franciscan preacher Bernardino da Feltre (d. 1494) arrived in the Tyrol and began preaching anti-Semitic sermons during Lent. He predicted something wicked was about to occur. Shortly, Simon, then aged two, disappeared on Maundy Thursday, which, in 1475, coincided with the Jewish celebration of Passover 5235. Andrew, the boy's father, immediately placed the blame on the Jews (one sign of how deeply the libel had penetrated the European Christian imagination).

After the boy's body washed up into the cellar of one of the leading Jews in Trent, seventeen Jews were tortured into a "confession." In this case, a prelate, Bishop Hinderbach (d. 1486), carried out the investigation and also served as the prosecution. Jewish protest of this arrangement brought a second trial but the same verdict. Jews protested again, bringing the case to Pope Sixtus IV (r. 1471–1484). A commission was appointed, but again the same verdict was reached. The result: the seventeen "guilty" Jews were burned at the stake. Simon was buried, and in normal medieval fashion, miracles were reported and attributed to the dead child. His cult was popular through northern Italy and Germany. Later Pope Gregory XIII (r. 1572–1585) recognized Bernardino as a prophet and canonized Simon as a martyr.

The ritual murder allegation involving Simon of Trent achieved such notoriety in large part because it occurred at the dawn of the printing age. As a consequence, many copies of the gruesome image, illustrated on a woodcut published in the *Nuremberg Chronicle* (1475), were published and circulated, and many mobs attacked innocent Jews. In the famous illustration, which was and is still often reproduced, nine Jews are depicted surrounding Simon. Holding him in the form of a crucifix on a table, they wound him in the side (where Christ was pierced by a lance) and collect his blood. They pierce his genitals, from which blood, also collected, flows copiously. This image and its many copies did immense work in spreading the story of Simon. Preachers spread the tale of Simon throughout Italy, and many Jews were attacked in the Veneto, Lombardy, and the Tyrol. Simon's fame only intensified with the visit of so many prelates, abbots, theologians, and clerics to the Council of Trent.

Thousands of Jews died in the Middle Ages after allegations of ritual murder, either following riots or judicial inquiries, which included the use of torture (under the agonies of which some Jews "confessed" to the crimes alleged). Though many cases were reported in Switzerland, Austria, and northern Italy, the allegations had a lengthy and destructive history in the lands of Germany. Such allegations occurred first near Berlin in 1243 and continued well into the nineteenth century. One of the most violent and destructive for German Jewry occurred after Easter 1298. Then twenty-one Franconian Jews in Röttingen were accused by a knight named Rindfleisch. Pogroms occurred then in nearly 150 communities throughout Germany. The toll was devastating. Some four to five thousand Jews lost their lives. The toll was particularly deadly to communities in the south. Seven hundred perished in Nuremberg and eight hundred in Würzburg. Included among the dead were some of the great intellectuals and rabbinic scholars of the era. Here the low and middle urban classes caused most of the mayhem, violence, and death. Yet secular rulers often quietly approved or even assisted. Some clergy attempted to stem the violence, with success only in Augsburg and Regensburg.

Rindfleish has been seen by some historians as marking an important turning point in the history of the persecution of the Jews. With him the allegations resulted in violence perpetrated not only in Röttingen or Franconia, but also jumped the borders of those locales and radiated outward to regions far removed from the center of the first allegations. Now Jews hundreds of miles from an allegation of ritual murder were in danger of violence that was as remote geographically from them as it was from their imaginations or intentions.

Host Desecration

The notion that Jews stole or purchased consecrated communion wafers, then stabbed, burned, or tortured the host and caused it to bleed was linked to the accusation of ritual murder and deicide. Depending on another anti-Semitic slur—namely, that Jews thirsted for blood (because anemic)—the emergence of the legend of Jewish host desecration coincided with the high-medieval debate on how, exactly, Christ was truly present in the sacramental host. The charge that the Jews caused the host to bleed served several functions in medieval Christendom. First, it allowed Christians to charge that Jews were reenacting the crucifixion. Second, it again demonstrated their status as witness people, illustrating a theological truth: Christ (as Jews knew) was truly and physically present in the consecrated host. Jews also witnessed to the divinity of Christ, a notion that they denied publicly but, as was obvious in desecrating a "live" host, they believed privately; this, incidentally, also made them duplicitous in character. Such a state of affairs assumed, preposterously, that Christian teaching was so evidently true that even Jews had to accept it. Third, it assured Christians who harbored doubts that Christ was indeed, through the miracle of transubstantiation, actually present in the Eucharistic elements, even though the "accidents" (taste, texture, color) of the elements had not changed. Fourth, it sanctioned crimes against Jews. Those who desecrated the host were the same deicide people who had killed the Son of God; one who punished a member of the deicide people became an instrument of justice in the hands of a just God.

Punish the Jews Christians did. Incidents of violence against Jews followed allegations of host desecration in Paris in 1290 and Bavaria in 1338. Of the latter episode, the chronicle of the Bavarian dukes for that year reports on the charge and its deadly consequences for Jews: "Jews cut up the Catholic host each in his synagogue and among other mockeries, pierced it with sharp thorns until it bled. As a result, around the feast of St. Michael in all the towns of Bavaria and Austria . . . they were miserably and cruelly killed by poor folk." Along with the charge of ritual murder, the charge of host desecration dramatically increased anti-Jewish sentiment in the thirteenth century and beyond. It helped cement the image of the Jew as the implacable enemy of the Christian and his religion and made him, thus, even more vulnerable to the sort of violence described by the Bavarian dukes.

Notable here is that the violence stemmed neither from official doctrine nor from ecclesiastical officials but from a local populace. Indeed, popes in the Middle Ages occasionally went to the trouble of officially denying the myths that led to anti-Jewish violence (though always emphasizing the disparity between Jewish prosperity and the Augustinian status of servitude they were supposed to maintain). Despite the efforts of popes, the blood ritual and host desecration charges would both contribute to the image of the Jews as an "other" so stubborn and evil that they were demonic or demonic in inspiration and thus a profound danger to Christian society.

Well Poisoners

It is widely known that Jews were charged with poisoning wells in the fourteenth century and causing, thus, the affliction of the Black Death. Yet the accusation antedated the plague by some three centuries. As early as the eleventh century, Jews were accused of well poisoning. When charged with ritual murder, they were accused also of having deposited the bodies of victims in wells. In the early fourteenth century, French Jews were accused of attempting murder on a widespread scale by poisoning wells. Along with lepers (with whom they were increasingly linked as outsiders in Christendom), they were accused of colluding so as to destroy Christian society. The charge led to and was repeated during the Shepherds' Crusade in 1320, when mobs of peasants attacked southern French Jews.

Over the decades, the stories took on details that were fantastic. One Jew confessed under torture that he had made poison from the remains of lizards, frogs, and the flesh and hearts of Christians. Some Christian chroniclers claimed that Jews brewed their poisons with ingredients that included the body parts of snakes, toads, and women. The charges became tinged politically when Jews were accused of conspiring with foreign powers, such as the monarchs of Tunis and Granada. In France, Jews were fined with the crime of insulting the monarch *(lèse-majesté)*. Many had their possessions confiscated or held for ransom. Impoverished Jews were simply expelled from the kingdom. These charges coincided with the need of the French for riches, at a time when the royal treasury had been depleted and with a seven-year famine (1315–1322). This is a textbook illustration of the ways that in conditions of adversity, widespread illness, panic, and governmental impoverishment, the myth of poisoning could emerge, reappear, and justify arrest, expulsion, and the confiscation of goods.

It was precisely in the context of deep and widespread terror in 1348, with the occurrence of the Black Death, that the well-poisoning charge returned—with a terrible vengeance. In this case, Jews were blamed (even though they were hardly spared by the disease that felled their Christian neighbors in such horrific proportions) and charged with causing the plague by well poisoning. In addition to the number of Jewish dead caused by the plague, thousands of Jews were killed by angry Christians. The entire town of Chinon in France was put to death in punishment. Terrified, now, of persecuting bands of angry Christians, some Jewish communities, like that at Vitry, committed mass suicide. Some 210 communities, small and large, were devastated by mob killings.

Again, the well-poisoning charge had a long life, and it exists today in anti-Semitic propaganda on the Internet. The Jewish protagonist of Christopher Marlowe's *The Jew of Malta* is depicted as taking active satisfaction in poisoning wells. Modern literature that portrays Jews as hazards to public health is very likely traceable to this medieval slur. But other slurs made the same point in caricature.

Caricature and Iconography

Many Jews were depicted in caricatures, perhaps none more disgusting than the Judensau, or Jew's pig. This customarily depicted Jews as offspring feeding from the teats of a sow, or pig, while other Jews are engaged in some form of labial or anal intercourse. Originating in thirteenth-century Germany, it was confined almost exclusively to German-speaking lands for the next six centuries. In its origins, it was intended as a Christian allegory representing supposed Jewish gluttony or carnality. The literary origins of this caricature are unknown, though John Chrysostom, in his infamous homilies, referred to Jews as gluttonous hogs. Over the course of the centuries, however, Judensau images intensified in their obscenity and anti-Semitic impact. Jews were sometimes depicted holding up the sow's tail while another Jew, occasionally identifiable as a rabbi, consumed its excrement. Often the Devil was represented, Semitic features emphasized, presiding over the proceedings with evident delight. Occasionally, this allegory was linked with ritual murder, with, for example, the body of Simon of Trent lying near the central action.

Such images were widely disseminated. The Judensau was represented not only on woodcuts, broadsheets, and playing cards, but also on the walls of several German cathedrals and churches, including one in Wittenberg. There Martin Luther

(d. 1546) dwelt bizarrely on the pig as the taproot of Jewish capacity and especially intelligence. On the Sachsenhauser Bridge in Frankfurt am Main, the Judensau was represented with the caption: "On Maundy Thursday in the year 1475, the little child Simon was murdered by the Jews." The widespread dissemination of an image that had hardened into a piece of anti-Semitic iconography reflected the worsening of the position of Jews in late-medieval Europe, above all in the lands of the German empire. One of the cruelest ironies of the images is that they depicted Jews feeding from and in some cases worshipping an animal that had always been for them an object of revulsion and religious prohibition.

Very frequently on medieval cathedrals the twinned pair of female statues of Ecclesia (church) and Synagoga (synagogue) was placed. Perhaps the most well known of these was placed on Strasbourg Cathedral in 1230. Such pairings occurred not just in sculpture but also in stained glass, friezes, and illuminated manuscripts. This iconographical image portrayed Ecclesia as vibrant and triumphant, usually a crowned woman holding a cross and chalice. Synagoga, dysphoric and defeated, is portrayed with a blindfold (signifying Jewish blindness to the reality of the Messiah). This portrayal perhaps depends on the words, universally thought to be Pauline in the Middle Ages, from 2 Cor. 3:13–16: "Not like Moses, who put a veil over his face to keep the people of Israel from gazing at the end of the glory that was being set aside. But their minds were hardened. Indeed, to this very day, when they hear the reading of the old covenant, that same veil is still there, since only in Christ is it set aside. Indeed, to this very day whenever Moses is read, a veil lies over their minds; but when one turns to the Lord, the veil is removed."

In addition to the sculpture at Strasbourg, an excellent example of statuary images of Ecclesia and Synagoga can be found on the exterior walls of the Cathedral of Bamberg. A wood carving in a choir bench at the Cathedral of Erfurt shows Ecclesia in pursuit of Synagoga, who is depicted riding on a Judensau. Here the image of the church triumphant and the dejected and blind synagogue merges with the trope of Jews consorting with swine. Almost all caricatures of the Jews in the modern ages used for purposes of defamation had their origins in the Middle Ages.

References to the Antichrist in the two New Testament Letters of John do not link him definitively with Jews. Nonetheless, early and medieval Christians did. In medieval thought about the end times, Jews would be the most loyal helpers of Antichrist, who would return shortly before the return of Christ to persecute the elect. Weaving together numerous scriptural passages, Christian interpreters argued that the Antichrist was to be a Jew of the tribe of Dan. He would be supported by the armies of Gog and Magog (Ezek. 38, 39; Apoc. 20). In the mid-tenth century, the Benedictine Adso of Montier-en-Der (d. 992) composed the definitive "biography" of Antichrist. This was the major source for religious and secular literature, sermons, theology, and visual representations of the Antichrist throughout the Middle Ages. One French play from the fourteenth century, entitled *The Day of Judgment,* suggested Antichrist had been conceived by a Babylonian Jewish prophet and the Devil. Medieval art reinforced this close connection between the Antichrist and Jews. Moralized Bibles in the thirteenth century depicted Jews as minions of Antichrist. Fifteenth-century German block books depicted his circumcision by a Jewish priest. He is pictured rebuilding the Temple in Jerusalem and, with his disciples, burning books of Christian theology. This piece of Christian lore and iconography also had a very long afterlife. In 1999, the evangelical pastor Jerry Falwell delivered a sermon that stated that the Antichrist, a Jewish male, was alive in Israel, a sign that the world was soon to end. Since the Antichrist was supposed to be Jewish, Jews, especially in art and iconography, came to be associated with the Devil, with horns, tails, and an odor all their own. Jews, in league with the Devil, now bore his characteristics or became blurred with the supernatural enemy in art and the imagination. If an enemy is diabolical, what reason would there be to tolerate him?

The Medieval Passion Play

Medieval passion plays occurred in large open spaces, with areas for performance and watching overlapping. This kind of staging was quite deliberate. It was intended to involve the spectators very intimately and emotionally in the drama of the crucifixion. In the plays that have survived, Jews are meant to embody the forces of Satan, as well as to illustrate their wanton tendencies to blindness and refusal to believe. In addition, they were portrayed as Christ killers and meant, thus, to bear all the guilt for the suffering and death of Jesus. They were murderers of God.

Directorial instructions for these plays have, in some cases, survived. They required the actors portraying Jews to pose awkwardly and menacingly, to gesture monstrously, to make fiendish noises, and to dance like animals to frightening music. During the scenes of crucifixion, they were asked to portray themselves as helpers of the Devil, delighting in torturing and executing Jesus. By the end of the fifteenth century, a stereotypical Jew had been established: he had unvarying physical attributes, acted and spoke with menace, and was in every way portrayed as vulgar, dangerous, and anti-Christian.

The character of Judas was almost always part of the *dramatis personae.* He was cunning, greedy, and a usurer. Occasionally, he was given the name of an actual Jewish moneylender from the region in which the play was staged. Needless to say, this highly provocative and negative view of the Jew often led to actual physical damage in many Jewish quarters. Some towns went so far as to post extra police to protect Jews from the fury of the mob. Other towns canceled performances, persuaded that a particular play's depiction of the Jew would result in too much destruction and death.

Of all the Passion Plays, the one staged annually in Oberammergau, a small town in the Bavarian Alps, has lasted the longest. At the dawn of the twentieth century, it drew some 175,000 spectators from Germany and all of Europe. In 1930, Hitler and Joseph Goebbels, propaganda minister in the Third Reich, attended the production. In 1934, a special tercentenary production was staged. Hitler again attended and was warmly welcomed at this Nazified version of the play. Even after the atrocities of World War II, Cardinal Michael Faulhaber in 1949 blessed the town and declared the play consistent with church doctrine. Though a new preface acknowledges the part past contributions had played in "preparing the soil" for the Holocaust, it was too late. The play did much to propagate a profoundly negative and popular image of the Jew. Because so many plays were staged annually, this was an image that could be, so to speak, consumed on a mass scale; it led to unimaginable consequences of which its originators could not have dreamt.

Innocent III and the Fourth Lateran Council

As mentioned above, Pope Innocent III announced the Fourth Lateran Council in 1213, and it convened in 1215. The seventy canons it issued have largely to do with reform and the recovery of the Holy Land. However, four canons (67–70) have to do with European Jews. Canon 67 regulated Jewish money lending, imposing severe restrictions on the rate of interest allowed; Canon 68 forbade Jews from appearing in public on certain holy days, criminalized Jewish expressions that satirized or otherwise derided Jesus and Christianity, and, most infamously, prescribed forms of Jewish dress; Canon 69 prohibited Jews from holding public office or exercising power over Christians; and Canon 70 forbade Jewish converts to Christianity from continuing to attend Jewish rites. These canons both reflected and contributed to the lowering of Jewish status in the high and late Middle Ages.

Certainly the decree on dress is the best known of the council's canons regarding Jewish life. It suggests that Jews and Christians could not be visually distinguished, so "it happens at times that through error Christians have relations with the women of the Jews." So that such "accursed intercourse" not recur, Innocent insisted that Jews "of both sexes in every province and at all times be marked off in the eyes of the public from other peoples through the character of their dress." He concluded by saying that this even had been "enjoined on them by Moses" (apparently a reference to Numbers 15:37–41). After the conclusion of the council,

Innocent wrote to the bishops of France. He demanded that so long as the code did not jeopardize the lives of Jews, the bishops enforce the canon requiring distinctive dress. It is clear, from the fact that the plea needed to be repeated by successive popes, that the decree on dress was neither observed instantly nor implemented ubiquitously. Where the decree was observed, there was a bewildering variety of styles (hats, patches) and colors. Still, the Jewish badge, which was the mark Jews were required to attach to their clothing when going out in public, for centuries distinguished and separated them from Christians. Needless to say, this decree, too, would have a terrible afterlife, especially in the twentieth century.

Money Lending and Usury

The growth of an urban mercantile class in high-medieval northern Europe had dreadful effects on Jews, both economically and culturally. As a consequence of being driven out of commercial trade, many Jews turned to money lending. Jews were not the only moneylenders in medieval society. Nor were they even the most important or influential ones. Groups of Christians in Italy and southern France, as well as the Templar order lent money as well, yet they did so at a time when the church was, officially, opposed to making profit off of loans, derided as "usury" or sometimes even "unreasonable usury" if fees were thought too steep. (Fees were condemned in three passages in the Pentateuch, and Jesus in Luke is depicted as saying, "Lend. Hope for nothing in return" [6:35]). Thus, sometimes Jewish merchants were, because of restrictions on guild membership and laws governing ownership of land, pushed into pawn broking and money lending. Although they were successful in this business, largely relying on capital they had accumulated as traders, it was culturally and sometimes physically disastrous, as it became, by the late Middle Ages, the primary occupation of Jews.

Money lending and usury came to be marks that signified and stigmatized the Jew. In an age of credit transaction, their services were desperately needed. For one thing, it strengthened the links between Jews and secular rulers, including powerful barons and kings (who took their share of the profits by routine taxes and "emergency" exactions). This association hardly made Jewish moneylenders more popular in the eyes of Christian creditors, who perceived that moneylenders were usually protected by secular authorities. Even some popes condoned Jewish money lending. Yet theirs was an occupation that was held in contempt, so much so that they could be expelled from secular realms once their financial services were no longer needed. Money lending was the Devil's work, and it made Jews, depicted heretofore as unbelievers and deicides, satanical in the eyes of Christians, demonically evil and treacherous. As early as the mid-twelfth century, Bernard of

Clairvaux used the Latin word for "to judaize" to mean—not to proselytize—
but to lend money at interest.

Scholarship in the past has suggested that it was money lending that led to the
rise of anti-Semitism in the high and late Middle Ages. Yet the picture is more
complicated than that. We know that some Christian borrowers and Jewish creditors had cordial relations over decades. More important, money lending came to
be linked up with the blood libel in ways that contributed to the satanic image
of the Jew. It can be no accident that the very first ritual murder accusation was
made by a knight who was heavily in debt to a Jewish creditor of Norwich; this
made William of Norwich's cult one particularly popular with artisans, workmen,
and small shopowners, who came to his shrine, in part, to sustain the image of
the Jew as ritual baby killer. Nor is it coincidental that the first expulsion from a
national kingdom occurred in France under Philip Augustus, when many French,
whose loans he annulled, were in debt to Jewish moneylenders; those in debt
charged the Jews with ritual murder, though it is not clear that the king believed
them, only that he profited by taking Jewish liquid and movable assets. Finally,
a pogrom launched against the Jews of York in 1190 was motivated by the desire
of local knights to burn lending records and to prevent foreclosures. Subsequent
riots were linked with ritual murder accusations and accompanied by the burning
of lending documents.

In the later Middle Ages, popular preachers linked Jews' supposed love for
money with other "Jewish" characteristics. Perhaps the most effective popular
preacher in this respect was the Franciscan Bernardino of Siena (d. 1444). Writing
at a time when commerce and the loans needed to make it work had been more
fully accepted by ecclesiastical authorities as necessary, this very popular preacher
nonetheless linked money lending, avarice, and blood lust; he thus viewed Jews as
an epidemic that threatened Christian society: "Money is the vital heat of a city.
The Jews are leeches who ask for nothing better than the opportunity to devour
an ailing member, whose blood they suck dry with insatiable ardor. When heat
and blood abandon the extremities of the body to flow back to the heart, it is a
sign that death is near. But the danger is even more imminent when the wealth of
a city is in the hands of the Jews. Then the heat no longer flows, as it does normally, toward the heart. As it does in a plague-ridden body, it moves toward the
ailing member of the body; for every Jew is a capital enemy of all Christians."

Money lending, finally, again violated the Augustinian witness doctrine, as
Jews were in a position of power, not servitude, in relation to Christians. The
Jews suffered for this, even though they had been pushed into the role. In iconography and literature, in sermons and theological tracts, Jews and money were
inevitably linked. As love of money was associated with worship of the Golden

Calf, Jews were charged with idolatry and sacrilege. A Jew holding a moneybag became an extremely common image in every medium of art. Usury was linked to avarice and thievery. The Jew as moneylender came to be assimilated to the image of all Jews and to Judas, the apostle who betrayed Jesus for love of money. Changing economic conditions in the age of emancipation proved how successful Jews would be in a wide spectrum of the occupational structure. Still, while later Jewish intellectuals complained, rightly, that if Jews could make a living in any other way than lending at interest they would, they were demonized as usurers, and *all* Jews were regarded as enemies of Christendom.

Talmud Disputations and Talmud Burnings

From the mid-thirteenth century to the end of the Middle Ages and beyond, the Talmud was at the center of many disputations, condemnations, acts, and burnings; the book was even put on trial at least once. The Talmud was known to Christians in the West before ca. 1240, and, in fact, two twelfth-century polemicists, Petrus Alfonsi (d. first half twelfth century), a convert from Judaism, and Peter the Venerable, abbot of Cluny, criticized Jews severely for not following biblical but rabbinic law. In a book entitled *Against the Inveterate Obstinacy of the Jews,* Peter argued that the Talmud was "a vast sea of impiety." Peter seems to have known only the legendary aspects of the volumes, not the extensive discussions of the Law. He branded the Talmud as blasphemous because, among other things, it depicted God in heaven studying it and pictured God as weeping daily. In addition, he charged, it was an obscene work because (he contends mistakenly) it contained the tale of Sirach's mother's impregnation. He also complained about a midrash in which Christians were punished in hell, a text that is, again, not contained in the Talmud. He concluded of the editors and writers of the "evil and filthy stories" of the Talmud that God would "justly condemn it and its authors to eternal fire." Peter's argument was, in effect, that Jews in his day need not be tolerated by the church for, as guided by the Talmud, which had been composed in the early centuries of the Common Era, contemporary Jews were different than those to whom the church had promised toleration. It was a dangerous attack, for it made the Talmud a weapon to be used in the hands of disputatious churchmen against "Talmudic Jews."

In May and June 1240, the Talmud itself became the subject of a trial at Vincennes. The "plaintiff" or accuser was Nicholas Donin of La Rochelle, a converted Jew, who had, in 1225, repudiated the Talmud. In 1238, Nicholas traveled to Rome. There he presented to Pope Gregory IX a list of charges against the Talmud. In response, the pope wrote many bishops and secular authorities. To his letter, he attached a list of some thirty-five offensive articles prepared by Nicholas and other apostates from Judaism. In June 1240, with Queen Mother Blanche of Castile (d. 1252) present and with several bishops as judges, the trial against the Talmud was conducted. It was the first trial of the Talmud for which any evidence exists.

Donin served as a sort of prosecuting attorney and Rabbi Yehiel ben Joseph of Paris (d. ca. 1265) as the defense. We do not have a deposition of the trial, but the outcome is clear. Some twenty cartloads of books, perhaps ten thousand volumes, were burned in Paris in 1242. Donin later composed a treatise of offensive and blasphemous extracts from the Talmud. Appalled, Jewish authorities in France appealed to Pope Innocent IV. In 1247, the pope asked Odo of Chateauroux (d. 1273) to form a commission of inquiry. He did. It included not only Nicholas Donin but also Albert the Great. Predictably, the committee report condemned the Talmud for containing offenses, errors, and blasphemies. To these conclusions, Innocent observed that in relation to normative biblical Judaism, the Talmud was heretical. In this burning of books, some have claimed to see the origins of western censorship.

Disputation at Barcelona

The mention of heresy and the involvement of Albert the Great require one to notice that Dominicans were heavily involved in bringing charges and participating in disputations between Jews and Christians in the thirteenth and fourteenth centuries. It was the Order of Preachers whose members set the stage for one of the most famous disputations of the high-medieval period. In this case, Pablo Christiani, again a converted Jew, was called upon to debate Moses ben Nahman (d. 1270), better known as Nahmanides. The issues to be resolved were whether the Messiah had come, whether he was divine or human, and whether the Jews or Christians possessed the true faith. Present at the debate was James I of Aragon (r. 1213–1276). Nahmanides cleverly exploited the king's presence in response to the second issue. He argued that the Messiah was less important to him than the king of Aragon. Why? Because it was a greater thing to obey the law of a Gentile king than the commands of a messiah. He also suggested influentially that the non-legal statements of the rabbinic writings were not binding. Indeed, one should imagine them as homilies to be reflected upon and even rejected.

Also present at the disputation was Raymond Martini (d. 1284). He too was a Dominican who had studied at an academy set up to study Hebrew, Arabic, and Aramaic by fellow Dominican Raymond of Penaforte, former minister general of the Order of Preachers who had also arranged the dispute with Nahmanides. In 1278, Martini would write a long book entitled *The Dagger of Faith*, written in Latin, Hebrew, and Aramaic. This book was unique for attempting to prove the truth of Christianity from Jewish sources. For this reason, it established a new paradigm, and many later-medieval polemics utilized this technique.

The aftermath was a travesty. At the conclusion of the dispute, King James declared that Nahmanides had won the debate. Outraged, the Dominicans, who had claimed victory, collected several excerpts from Nahmanides's now published version of the debate and sent them to Raymond of Penaforte. Nahmanides was brought before a specially called commission. There he confessed freely that he had indeed stated strong arguments against Christianity, yet he contended that he had recorded in a written document no statement not expressed at the dispute, where the king had granted him complete freedom of speech without fear of punishment. Again King James was persuaded by Nahmanides. This time, however, James felt compelled to quiet the angry Dominicans, and he exiled Nahmanides for two years and ordered that his written record of the dispute be burned. Under Dominican pressure, James was persuaded to convert this punishment into perpetual exile.

After Nahmanides left Aragon for Jerusalem (whence he never returned), King James appointed a committee of censors, which included a majority of Dominicans, to purge "offensive" texts from the Talmud. Many Dominican-authored texts, most of them composed by Jewish converts to Christianity, were composed. All used their intimate knowledge of Jewish texts against erstwhile co-religionists. Eventually, Dominicans would deliver sermons that Jews were forced to attend. Because such sermons, which had a conversionary purpose, never succeeded, the Dominicans became increasingly hostile toward and angry with the Jews and portrayed their Jewish auditors as irrationally stubborn. Some incited mobs to turn on their neighbors. The Dominican apocalyptic preacher St. Vincent Ferrer (d. 1413), preoccupied with the conversion of the Jews, brought with him hundreds of Christian flagellants. This time, out of frank fear, many Spanish Jews converted.

Dominicans were also involved in inquisitorial investigations of Jews that likely originated in fear that Christians would convert to Judaism. In 1267, Pope Clement IV (r. 1265–1268) issued a bull, *Turbato corde* (the title says it all: "With a Troubled Heart"). It required the mendicants to look into reports of Jewish attempts to proselytize Christians. Several popes repeated the order. Several members of the Inquisition actively intervened in Jewish attempts to influence former Jews who had converted to Christianity. Sexual relations between Jews and Christians now came to be considered a heresy; they were punishable by burning at the stake.

Expulsions and Massacre

In the period from 1096 to 1492, Jews were expelled from every major European country. By and large the agents of expulsions were regal or baronial, not ecclesiastical. Some nobles agitated for expulsion because they saw Jews as the king's loathed financial agents. Legally, it was the king's prerogative to expel. The church of course was not philosemitic, but in general the ancient doctrine that made a place for Jews, if the place was subservient, prevailed. The papacy, for example, never rejected the witness doctrine of Augustine. It called, as it always had, not for expulsion but for limitation. In addition, because Jews were regarded as servants or (as in England) even the "chattel" of the king, when kings had to prosecute wars or had other urgent financial needs, ridding a realm of the Jews was a simple way to fill the royal coffers.

Expulsion was thus often, if not always, motivated economically. In England, kings paid for fiscal deficits by repeatedly taxing Jews. Soon Italian firms began lending English kings money, making the situation of English Jews terribly parlous. Sure enough, in 1290, the king ordered all Jews to leave England. Their domiciles and capital went into the royal treasury, and most of the Jews moved to nearby France. As already noted, in 1182 King Philip Augustus expelled all Jews from the king's domains (which were small and concentrated around Paris). He confiscated Jewish property and canceled all debts owed to the Jews, except for a fraction of one-fifth, which was deposited in the royal treasury. In the thirteenth century, Jews were expelled again and again, only to be recalled. King Louis IX (later canonized) campaigned against usury and freed his subjects from debts to Jewish creditors. After several ritual murder and host desecration trials had been staged, popular hatred of the Jews was such that King Philip IV could issue an edict of expulsion (1306). Again, debts owed to the Jews went to the king. After several recalls, Jews were finally expelled from France in 1394. Again, Jews moved east, this time to Germany. There, because of a lack of central control, they were not expelled in the Middle Ages. However, they suffered agonizing massacres. One unprecedented massacre occurred in 1348–1349 (as mentioned, Jews were accused of well poisoning, leading to the Black Death), when many Jewish communities in Germany, Belgium, and Switzerland were slaughtered, sometimes by being burned to death. This precipitated yet a further move eastward, to Poland, where the future of the Ashkenazi lay. No expulsion, however, would equal in horror and scope that of the Spanish, where a massive and ancient community suffered grievously in the fourteenth and fifteenth centuries.

"Enough unto Our Sufferings": Spain

The Sephardic Jewry of the Iberian Peninsula was much larger than the Ashkenazic community of any one country. At least two hundred thousand Jews lived in the Christian kingdoms of Castile, Aragon, and Portugal. They occupied a much wider swath of the occupational structure than in the north: they were shopkeepers, artisans, physicians, and (relative to the north) there were a tiny number of moneylenders. Some small number of courtiers were royal councilors and financial experts, thought particularly trustworthy, as Jews could not aspire on their own to political office. In an era of widespread massacre in German lands, the kings of Castile and Aragon took effective action to prevent violence against Jews. As the Christian kings completed the Reconquista, they even gave large tracts of land to Jews to repopulate and develop.

The great reversal began in the fourteenth century. After concerns were expressed that converts to Christianity had apostatized, new rumors circulated: baptized Christians and born Jews retained unexpurgated copies of the Talmud. In 1391, riots spread throughout the Iberian Peninsula, especially in Castile and Aragon. Tens of thousands of Jews, fatefully, converted to Christianity to save themselves, along with their possessions. A public disputation held in the town of Tortosa in 1413–1414 resulted in another wave of conversions. Thus, within a quarter-century, there were many former Jews in Spain. They were called "New Christians" or Conversos. It has been estimated that they equaled in number those Jews who had refused to convert to Christianity. The presence of these two groups would shape the course of Spanish history into the early modern period.

As Conversos took jobs as tax collectors, popular hatred against them grew. Hostility to them was expressed in riots, first at Toledo and culminating in a terrible pogrom at Cordoba in 1473. To this popular hatred was added suspicion that the newly converted were continuing to practice Jewish ceremonies in secret. They began to be called Marranos, or swine, by their enemies. Within time this would cease to be a term of opprobrium from the point of view of the Jews and in fact became honorable among those faithful to Judaism.

After the marriage in 1469 of Isabella of Castile and Ferdinand II of Aragon resulted in a single Spanish kingdom, the rulers established the Spanish Inquisition to look into the charges of "Judaizing," especially blasphemy, among the New Christians. In 1482, seven inquisitors were appointed. These included the justly infamous Dominican Torquemada; he became the inquisitor general in Spain and wrote the first handbook of Spanish inquisitorial regulations. The following year, the new Spanish Inquisition was made a council of state, the Council of the Supreme (La Suprema) and General Inquisition.

In the first two decades of a history that would stretch for more than three centuries, the Inquisition claimed to have discovered several thousand secret Jews among the New Christians. Their property routinely confiscated, the Jews suffered various penances. Those refusing to repent were burned at the stake. In the late 1480s the use of torture resulted in confessions concerning a blood libel. Such confessions prepared the way for the expulsion of Jews from Spain. Once Ferdinand and Isabella subdued Granada in 1492, the last Muslim holdout on the Iberian Peninsula, they made Judaism illegal in Spain. Some Jews converted. But it has been estimated that 100,000–150,000 Jews departed from Spain in the summer of 1492. Many fled to North Africa, Italy, and Ottoman Turkey. An Italian Jew in 1495 completed his chronicle of the expulsions with this prayer: "He who said unto His world, Enough, may He also say Enough unto our sufferings." In four hundred years, the five greatest medieval European centers of Judaism—those in England, France, Spain, Portugal, and Germany—had been destroyed.

IV

Later-Medieval Christianity, ca. 1300–1500

Dark Ages? Popes and Councils,
ca. 1300–1450

By the turn of the fourteenth century, medieval society had begun to change in ways not always clear to contemporaries. By then, literacy had spread quite rapidly and had ceased to be a monopoly of Christian clerics. Now, many clerks used their skills on behalf of secular governments, whose claims they pressed with skill against those of Christendom. Many were trained in Roman law and knew Aristotle's thinking on politics, both of which viewed governments as autonomous units and in (what we would call) secular terms. In addition, changes in papal government and in papal monetary needs caused increasing resentment in Christendom. Expenses often outran revenues, and taxes were often raised to close the gap. Raises in taxes caused the papacy to lose not only political but also popular support. Much of the revenue was needed to protect regions of Italy and the off-shore islands to which both the papacy and secular powers felt they had legitimate claim. Thus, the papacy in the thirteenth century was in frequent conflict with the German empire over the Papal States, and it fought the French and Aragonese for control over southern Italy and Sicily.

Perhaps most significant, the idea of Christendom as a supranational entity toward which all Christians felt supreme loyalty and affection slowly collapsed. With the evolution of independent political and physical territories, soon to be called national monarchies or states, Christians began to choose between allegiance to state and devotion to church, and many chose the former. By the fifteenth century, the papacy ceased to function as a universal power and more and more like another regional Italian prince jealously guarding his fiefdom. While the

Hohenstaufen dynasty, against which the papacy had struggled mightily during the thirteenth century, slowly declined and the German empire broke up into smaller and smaller territories, France made itself felt as a new "national" power on the scene, to the detriment of the papacy's temporal claims to power and to the humiliation of a number of individual popes. Soon the historic dependency on the French evolved into crushing dominance by their king, and the papacy became the abject tool of French royal power. This transition would be dramatically symbolized by the removal of the papal curia from Rome to Avignon. While the abysmal quality of the French popes in Avignon has been often emphasized, recent scholarship has established that the traditional picture has been overdrawn and dependent on highly partial sources. Still, the removal from Rome of the pope and curia was a scandal to Christendom. All the more scandalous was the curia's return to Avignon, after having reestablished itself late in the fourteenth century in the Eternal City. Soon enough, two popes, each elected by the same College of Cardinals, and then each with its own bureaucracy and national supporters, caused a shocking and disastrous schism. A council called to heal the schism ended, tragicomically, by creating yet a third line of popes. Meanwhile, theorists of church power began to argue that ultimate power within the church lay not with the papal office but with councils. The movement they started, called "conciliarism," began powerfully, but popes soon began to reassert their own claims. Eventually, the popes would triumph in this conflict, but their victory was wholly pyrrhic. The papacy, having strayed so far from being reformed, lapsed into luxury and grandeur, seeming ever more like ancient emperors and ever less like shepherds of the church universal.

The Clash between Boniface VIII and Philip IV

The first severe friction between an emerging nation-state and the papacy was colored by a papal interregnum that preceded it, the desperation of cardinals who could not agree on a candidate, and finally the election of a man who, while surely holy, was perhaps among the most unsuitable men imaginable to be pope in the thirteenth century. From 1292 to 1294, the inability of the cardinals to come to an agreement led one exasperated prelate to utter aloud the name of Peter Murrone. Murrone was a holy man, a hermit—and completely innocent of administrative experience or aspiration. Nonetheless, once elected by the College of Cardinals, he took the name Celestine V (r. 1294). Under Celestine, the curia became utterly chaotic, so much so that the holy man quickly grasped how unsuitable he was for the office into which desperation and chance had thrust him. After several months, he abdicated, possibly with the encouragement of his successor, Boniface VIII (r. 1294–1303), whom the cardinals chose to succeed Peter. The odd circumstances of Boniface's election, as well as whispers that he had coaxed his predecessor to step down, would trail him throughout his pontificate.

Beyond the odd circumstances and whispers, Boniface found himself caught up in the struggle between the noble Gaetani family, of which he was a member, and the Colonna family, two of whom were cardinals. The Colonna were vexed that Boniface so openly practiced nepotism in the Papal States and loudly protested. They joined forces with the Spiritual Franciscans, who were crushed when Celestine V resigned. He had been a pope dedicated to their own religious ideals; some of their number even entered an academic debate about whether a pope could abdicate. When a dispute caused severe discord between the Gaetani and the Colonna, the latter withdrew to a family fortress in Longhezza. The Spirituals joined them there and then released a statement proclaiming that as Celestine had illicitly resigned, Boniface's election was ipso facto invalid. A general council ought to be invoked, they said, in order to consider the question of who was the rightful pope. Two more statements were released that contained charges that Boniface's secular enemies would soon use and expand upon: he was a heretic and a simoniac and he had hoodwinked Celestine into resigning, then had him murdered.

Boniface soon found himself deadlocked in a struggle of words, law, world-views, and, finally, minor force, with King Philip IV of France, with whom the Colonna joined hands. Philip was remorselessly ambitious, and he was surrounded by men at least as ruthless as he, especially William of Nogaret (d. 1313 or 1314). William might be imagined (for those who remember the Watergate trials) as a G. Gordon Liddyesque figure of pitiless dedication to the realization of the royal cause. Not unimportant, Nogaret and the other ministers who surrounded him were trained in Roman law. Among other things, this meant that they had studied a law that regarded the state in wholly secular terms. They were unimpressed with papal claims to sovereignty in the temporal realm and serenely unmoved by the excommunications and denunciations showered upon them by the pope. Boniface's temporal power had been severely diminished by the rise of national feeling, though he anachronistically acted as if he were lord of all the world.

The first conflict between king and pope originated as England and France were preparing to go to war with one another. Both the English and French kings taxed ecclesiastical property and wealth. As it happened, at the Fourth Lateran Council Innocent III had decreed that clergy were not to pay taxes to secular rulers without first securing the approval of the pope. So from Boniface's perspective, a point of canon law was at stake—even though, throughout the thirteenth century, kings had taxed clerical wealth without interference from the papacy. But for Boniface, who imagined himself as a mediator in such international disputes, such taxation was an intolerable encroachment on his prerogatives. Accordingly, he issued a bull, *Clericis Laicos* (1296). It forbade secular rulers from imposing and prelates from paying war taxes without his permission. He emphasized the duty of the clergy to disobey their kings if necessary and declared emphatically that lay rulers had no authority over ecclesiastical wealth or persons within their kingdom. This proclamation, of course, was a direct challenge to the king's view of national sovereignty.

Philip responded not with a royal rescript but with a practical response that had a triumphant effect. He simply issued a royal order that forbade the export to Rome from France of valuable metals and any negotiable currency. Since something on the order of one-fourth of annual papal revenues came from France, this order was a pragmatic blow with enormous negative impact. Boniface humiliatingly backpedaled, first declaring that *Clericis Laicos* had not been targeted at any particular king but was intended as a general statement applicable to all secular courts and powers. Indeed, he conceded, in an emergency in which there was no time to consult the pope, the king could tax the clergy. In a bull *Etsi de statu* (1297), Boniface completed his own humiliation by admitting that the king could himself declare when such a state of emergency prevailed in his kingdom without consulting the pope at all.

Even more awful mortification was to follow. The second skirmish between Philip and Boniface seems to have been deliberately provoked by the former to fabricate an occasion that would exhibit his unchallenged sovereignty over his kingdom. Thus, Philip ordered the bishop of Pamiers, Bernard de Saisset (d. 1314), whom the pope had recently sent to France as his ambassador, to be arrested. The trumped-up charges on which he was apprehended were that he was traitorous, heretical, and a blasphemer. Eventually, he was tried in the presence of the king. When found guilty, he was put into prison. This last action—incarceration—violated a principle of canon law—namely, that a bishop be tried only by the pope.

The king followed de Saisset's trial with a letter in which he laid out the supposed offenses of the bishop, embellished with charges that he had declared the Holy Father, Boniface, to be the Devil incarnate. Philip also demanded that Boniface assent to the action he had taken against de Saisset. To do so would, from the pope's point of view, concede entirely too much—namely, that in taking a bishop into custody, the king had absolute authority over the French episcopate. Accordingly, Boniface responded with a fusillade of letters in which he denounced the presumption of this royal action, demanded the release of de Saisset, and insisted that the entire French episcopate attend a council to be held in Rome to consider the state of Christianity in France. One of the letters began with the patronizing words, "Listen, my son" *(Ausculta, fili)* (1301). In it he warned Philip: "Let no one persuade you that you have no superior, or that you are not subject to the head of the ecclesiastical hierarchy. For it is [Boniface concluded] a fool who thinks so."

In the war of propaganda that ensued, Philip's agents would soon twist these words and use them against the pope. In a forgery purporting to be a letter from Boniface, the pope is pictured as thundering: "You are subject to us in spiritualities and temporalities." Another forgery, supposedly the king's response, includes the suggestion that "your great fatuity [that is, the pope] knows that, in temporalities, we are subject to no one." The pope was put on the defensive, all the more so when in 1302 Philip summoned the First Estates General, in which clergy, nobles, and commoners, all represented, would decide on the justice of Philip's antipapal policy. When it was assembled, the Estates General was informed falsely by one of the king's agents that the pope had asserted feudal lordship over the kingdom of France. France, he argued, held sovereignty from God alone. The assembly members then wrote a letter to the Roman cardinals, in which they stated their refusal to recognize Boniface as pope and demanded that the cardinals support them against the pope. In 1302, the council that Boniface had demanded was convened, yet fewer than half of the French bishops appeared. In the end, the council took no further steps against the kingdom of France.

In the wake of this failed council, Boniface, his notorious anger now out of control, issued perhaps the most famous bull of the entire Middle Ages, *Unam Sanctam* (1302). Gravely dissatisfied with the French episcopate and chagrined with the French royal power, the bull begins by reflecting upon the divinely ordained unity of the church and the Roman see as guardian of that unity. In recent days, when bishops had chosen allegiance to their king rather than the Vicar of Christ, the fabric of the church would tear along national lines and the church would cease to be an international body of Christians. In fact, that is precisely what had been happening over the past century; thus Boniface's bull can be interpreted as a loud jeremiad against the destruction of Christendom and its fragmentation into independent and hostile nation-states. Borrowing language from Thomas Aquinas, the bull famously declares, "It is altogether necessary to salvation for every human creature to be subject to the Roman Pontiff." Paradoxically, weapons of the spirit like this dogmatic definition and the excommunications with which popes would increasingly threaten their enemies were an indication of their dwindling real power in a world where few, even bishops, any longer credited the view that the power of their kings was delegated to them by the pope.

The bull marks a point of no return, diplomatically speaking, between pope and king. The king was not about to engage Boniface in a war of words over royal sovereignty. Instead, he employed the coarse tools of defamation, propaganda, and finally physical force. Before a second council, Nogaret presented Boniface to the French bishops as a usurper (here, the circumstances of Boniface's election came back to haunt him), a heretic, and a criminal. As Boniface left Rome for Anagni (his native city), a force of several hundred armed mercenaries led by Nogaret and a brother of Cardinal Peter (of the Colonna family) arrived in Anagni. A short skirmish ensued before Nogaret broke into the papal chambers. Boniface, draped in priestly robes and clutching a crucifix, stood defiantly in his room, at which point the French party insulted and perhaps struck him. Sciarra Colonna suggested that they kill him there. After a dispute among the leaders moved into its third day, the region retaliated against the French and routed them. Freed by his townsmen, Boniface returned to Rome, but, perhaps traumatized by the events that had transpired in Anagni, he died soon thereafter. With him, the temporal claims of the papacy would soon be buried, and the dreams of his predecessors for a universal polity of peace ordered by its supreme religious leader lay in ruins.

The Avignon Papacy, 1309–1378

Boniface's second successor, Clement V (r. 1305–1314), completed his predecessor's humiliation by reinterpreting *Unam Sanctam* in a sense opposite to that intended by Boniface, releasing Nogaret from the sentence of excommunication that had been imposed after the Anagni affair, and pusillanimously praising Philip for the fervor and piety with which he had confronted Boniface. These were just a few of the concessions the former archbishop of Bordeaux made to the French king. He also looked on as Philip, avid for the wealth of the Knights Templar, viciously suppressed the order (after the usual accusations and, more gravely, confessions pried from innocent knights by torture), then exonerated Philip for his appalling crimes. The papacy, already subject to the French king, was made its puppet when Clement francophonized the College of Cardinals and then, after four years of wandering around southern France, took up residence in Avignon, just across the Rhône River from French territory. It is true that Clement did not transfer the papal curia from Rome; nor did he imagine the move to Avignon as permanent. Still, it is customary to date the beginning of the Avignon papacy from that date and, following the lead of Petrarch (among others), to characterize the whole period of papal history from 1309 to 1378 as the "Babylonian Captivity"—a reference to the ancient period, almost identical in length, of Jewish exile. Petrarch was not the only one to perceive a scandal in the pope's removal to Avignon, inasmuch as the popes of this period were often humiliatingly subjected to the demands and needs of French royal power, and to see it as a dark tragedy, insofar as the papacy had been exiled from its historic home.

Yet the darkness of this period is the exact interpretation that historians have increasingly come to doubt and to complicate in the past century. The traditional view of the papacy, which might be called Petrarchan, was based almost entirely on the hostile views expressed in English, German, and Italian chronicles, as well as in the writings of St. Catherine of Siena and St. Bridget of Sweden (and, of course, Petrarch himself). As new materials in the archives of the Vatican were made available to historians some one hundred years ago, scholars have been forced to paint the lugubrious episode in hues of gray rather than in the traditional black.

One hastens to add that the curia and the College of Cardinals were decidedly French in composition. For example, some 134 cardinals were made by seven popes during the Avignon period. Of these, a staggering 112 were French. Of the curialists whose "national" identity can be ascertained, 50 percent were French. Still, even these apparently clear numbers need to be interpreted further. Almost all of the French cardinals and half of the curialists were from the Languedoc, a region culturally and linguistically distinct from the center of royal power in the north. One pope could not read letters composed in the language used at Paris without help. What is more clear is that nepotism was brought to a high art by the Avignonese popes, though perhaps less out of assumedly base motives than from a need to build a cardinalate and curia that would support them. Thus, popes appointed men from their own families or from regions in the south of which they themselves were native.

Some Avignonese popes were pilloried in their own day for unseemly sybaritic habits. Of these, one, Clement VI (r. 1342–1352), seems to have conceded as much, allegedly replying to his critics, "My predecessors did not know how to be popes." But it ought not to be assumed that the practice of nepotism inevitably implied luxury. Several of the seven popes in this period were notably simple and even spartan in their living styles. Three were reformers. Only Clement was an unapologetic *bon vivant*.

Even the removal to Avignon must be understood in context. In the centuries preceding the Avignon era, it was not uncommon for popes to reside in cities other than Rome. Several left Italy and spent time in France. Most of the popes at Avignon had not intended to make Avignon a permanent seat for the papacy. Only in the pontificate of Benedict XII (r. 1334–1342) did the papacy begin to reconcile itself to indefinite exile. Benedict was the pope under whom the fortress-like papal palace was constructed and under whose direction the papal archives, then deposited in Assisi, were transferred to Avignon.

Yet again, context matters. Conditions in Rome for some time were so anarchic as to render a return to the Eternal City unthinkable. Benedict's predecessor, John XXII (whom we have discussed in connection with the firestorm unleashed by the issue of Franciscan poverty), had attempted a military solution to bring order to the chaos then prevailing on the Italian peninsula. In so doing, he not only

33. The grand Palace of the Popes, Avignon. © Atlantide Phototravel/Corbis/Rights Managed (RM).

failed, but he also spent roughly two-thirds of the papal revenues. Thus Benedict XII's decision to remain in Avignon seems a defensible, if not an altogether sensible, response to the disastrous policy of his predecessor.

How, then, do we explain the loud criticism of the papacy during this period? Less and less, it seems, did it have to do with slavish subordination to the French royal power and more and more was it a response to actions and attitudes that even French contemporaries found intolerable. Chief among these was fiscal oppression and bureaucratic centralization. Because the papacy was involved in the pacification of the Papal States—sometimes, it seemed, unendingly—it had a fathomless need for revenue. It was the consequent "fiscalism," which involved hiring and sustaining mercenaries and amassing the huge apparatus of warfare, for which the Avignon popes were bitterly resented. This resentment was made even more acute by the common cultural assumption that rulers, sacred as well as secular, ought to live on customary rather than extraordinary or novel sources of revenue.

Yet it was on such extraordinary sources that the papacy increasingly and, in the eyes of contemporaries, appallingly relied. Especially offensive was the provision of benefices the papacy reserved for itself. With each appointment, some sort of financial benefit accrued to the papacy. Fees were set for every action it took, for every document issued, for every decision made. Most prelates during the Avignon period paid massive "benefice taxes." By the time the popes returned from

Avignon, these taxes counted for something on the order of one-half of all papal revenues. The material view of the benefice as a secular endowment and property and the corruption, pluralism (the holding of multiple benefices simultaneously), and absenteeism or nonresidence that followed—all harnessed to essentially political and military aims—were further reasons for which the papacy was so bitterly resented.

Eventually, and not surprisingly, there would be a negative response to all this. As indignation against papal fiscalism increased, so too did national feeling. As the papacy's need for money spiraled out of control, its reputation sank. As the papacy's style of living drifted further from the apostolic model (as then imagined), vociferous calls for total poverty increasingly began to be heard. Affection for the papacy dwindled rapidly and never more quickly than when excommunications were showered on the heads of those slow in paying taxes—or those who refused to pay them. The more ecclesiastical prerogatives and functions were centralized, the more local dignitaries nursed grievances against the central authority. The apostolic see of Peter had become an immense bureaucratic and fiscal machine. Once viewed as the leader of reform, the papacy came to be seen as the religious institution most in need of reform. Most thoughtful observers sincerely believed that reform could be accomplished only if the papacy returned to Rome.

Catherine of Siena

Born in 1347, Catherine was the twenty-fourth of twenty-five children of her bourgeois family. As we have already seen, she had a special relationship with the Dominican Raymond of Capua, who wrote her *Vita*. In 1365, surmounting the fierce objections of her family, she took a habit of pious women (often widows) and, for three years, took to her room. There she lived a life not unlike that of an anchoress or enclosed woman *(inclusa)*. During this time, she learned to read and prayed intensely. At about twenty-one, she had an experience of being wed to Christ, and she interpreted it as a call to serve the poor in Siena. Like many women in the high and late Middle Ages, she appealed to her direct experience of God to justify undertaking apostolic action.

Her fame and her scope of activity, both geographical and apostolic, grew rapidly. At the end of the Avignon papacy, Catherine urged Pope Gregory XI (r. 1370–1378) to return to Rome. She also urged him to lift an interdict on Florence. Conflict between the papacy and Florence was deep-seated, and in 1378 Catherine traveled to the Athens of the Middle Ages. Her aim was to reconcile the city with the papacy. Later, during the Great Schism, she wrote letters on behalf of the Roman claimant to the papal throne, even while deathly ill. At the age of thirty-three, she died (April 29, 1380).

The Great Schism, 1378–1417

In 1377, Gregory XI finally succeeded in returning the see of Peter to Rome. A number of French cardinals opposed the move, and some Roman nobles were so hostile that Gregory felt in danger for his life. He soon felt the return was a mistake, and he decided to return to Avignon. However, he died in March 1378 before he could depart for Rome. Fearing that the cardinals might try and remove the papacy from the Eternal City again, the Roman populace rioted outside the conclave of cardinals and shouted for a Roman pope to be elected. In this environment of external threat, as well as infighting among the cardinals, Bartolomeo Prignano, the archbishop of Bari, was elected. He took the name Urban VI (r. 1378–1389). It was the first time in over fifty years that a non-French pope had been elevated to the seat of Peter. He had served the Avignon curia faithfully, and the French cardinals hoped that he would be docile. In this hope they were to be gravely disappointed. Not only did he refuse to defer, but he also abused the cardinals verbally in ways that aggravated relations with them and even suggested madness.

In response, the cardinals present, with the exception of the Italians, left Rome for Anagni. In August 1378, the cardinals claimed that Urban's election had taken place in an atmosphere of intimidation (a claim that was probably sincere) and was thus invalid. Joined by three of the Italian cardinals a month later, they elected Cardinal Robert of Geneva as pope. He took the title Clement VII (antipope: 1378–1394). Clement tried to seize Rome but could not and, as a result, left Rome. He took up residence in Avignon. The so-called "Great Schism," which would last for forty years, had begun. This schism was "great" not only because of its length but also because of its character. There had been papal schisms before. What made this one unique was that the same College of Cardinals had properly elected two different popes. Now both popes proceeded to appoint rival colleges of cardinals and curiae. Churchmen and secular leaders pleaded with both to resign individually or at the same time, all to no avail. Meanwhile, rival nations lined up behind each of the two rival obediences. Most of Italy, Germany, Bohemia, Poland, Hungary, Scandinavia, and England championed the Roman line; the Avignon line was supported by France, Spain, Scotland, Naples, and Sicily. Yet all of Europe was scandalized. Existing resentment was deepened when taxes had to be increased to support two colleges of cardinals and two popes. Again, the damage to the papacy's popular reputation was considerable. The tragedy took on elements of farce when the Council of Pisa (1409), called to heal the schism, created yet a third line of popes.

The Emergence of the Conciliar Solution

When the Council of Pisa was called, the *via concilii* (conciliar solution) to the schism had already been formulated by distinguished theologians and canonists.

Since the twelfth century, canonists, relying heavily on the law of corporations, had contended that the actions of a corporate head or officers ought not to be allowed to damage the interests of the corporate body as a whole. (A large body of corporate law had grown up, as monasteries, hospitals, cathedral chapters, and other bodies were corporations that had officers, owned property, administered finances, and could be sued.) If an incompetent officer jeopardized the corporate good, the corporate body could protect its interests and existence, as a last resort, by deposing him. Minimally, but significantly, this implied that an officer held his authority by the will of the group. During the Great Schism, canonists and theologians argued between two entities that could be imagined as the corporate body of the Roman church empowered to take action. While some argued it was the College of Cardinals, the dominant view was that Christendom, the corporate body of Christians represented in a council, was that body so empowered. To be sure, the notion of representation was not the modern one that holds that each citizen had a right to vote. Rather, Christendom was represented according to "nations." This was to be a crucial feature of future councils, as it prevented any plurality from passing biased or unjust decrees.

Thus, the Council of Constance (1414–1418) was called not only to heal the schism, but also to deal with larger matters of reform, as well as to consider the problem of Bohemian heresy, especially as symbolized in the person of the leader of Czech reform, Jan Hus (d. 1415). All participants were organized first into four and finally into five nations: the Italian, German, French, English, and Spanish. It is very likely that Pope John XXIII (antipope: 1410–1415), who had been elected at the Council of Pisa, despite initial promises to resign, hoped to take action that would cause the Council of Constance to dissolve. This allegedly corrupt pope also hoped to secure the support of the many Italian cardinals present, along with a condemnation of his two rivals and support for his claim to the papal title. He hatched a plan that temporarily confused and stupefied the fathers at the council and very nearly succeeded in causing them to quit Constance. After promising to resign, John fled the council, along with a significant percentage of the curia. The council fathers, the majority of whom remained in Constance, were frankly confused about how to proceed in the absence of the pope who had brought the assembly together. At this point the decisive intervention of King Sigismund of Croatia and Hungary, later Holy Roman emperor (r. 1433–1437), was crucial. He prevented the fathers from becoming demoralized. Crucial, too, were the actions and words of Jean Gerson (d. 1429), the chancellor of the University of Paris. With his famous address, "Ambulate dum lucem habetis" (Walk while you still have the light; Jn. 12:35), he reinjected some modicum of self-confidence in the congregation. He also laid out the essential foundations of conciliar theory, which would be restated once the assembly began to act again with confidence: "The church, as the general council representing it, is a model or example so directed by the Holy

Spirit and influenced by Christ that *everyone of whatever rank, even the papal, is obliged to listen and obey it*" (emphasis added).

Emboldened by Gerson, and nearly giving up on Pope John's promise to resign, the fathers proceeded and began with a statement, *Haec Sancta*, in April 1415. It laid out their understanding of the authority of councils and the relationship of conciliar and papal power:

> In the name of the Holy and indivisible Trinity; of the Father, Son, and Holy Ghost. Amen. This holy synod of Constance, forming a general council for the extirpation of the present schism and the union and reformation, in head and members, of the Church of God, legitimately assembled in the Holy Ghost, to the praise of Omnipotent God, in order that it may the more easily, safely, effectively and freely bring about the union and reformation of the church of God, hereby determines, decrees, ordains and declares what follows: It first declares that this same council, legitimately assembled in the Holy Ghost, forming a general council and representing the Catholic Church militant, has its power immediately from Christ, and every one, whatever his state or position, even if it be the Papal dignity itself, is bound to obey it in all those things which pertain to the faith and the healing of the said schism, and to the general reformation of the Church of God, in head and members. It further declares that any one, whatever his condition, station or rank, even if it be the Papal, who shall contumaciously refuse to obey the mandates, decrees, ordinances or instructions which have been or shall be issued by this holy council, or by any other general council, legitimately summoned, which concern, or in any way relate to the above mentioned objects, shall, unless he repudiate his conduct, be subject to condign penance and be suitably punished, having recourse, if necessary, to the other resources of the law.

Just so there would be no doubt, the council fathers repeated that the papal dignity was subject to the representative authority of the council, and they also indicated that this would be the case not just for this individual council but all future councils. Accordingly, this document was the theoretical basis for the council that would soon be called at Basel as well.

Soon John was arrested and declared deposed—not on the grounds of the legitimacy of his election, but on scandalous misconduct, including simony and perjury. Several months later, Gregory XII (r. 1406–1415), the Roman pope already deposed at Pisa, resigned. In Avignon, Benedict XIII (antipope: 1394–1417) proved to be the most recalcitrant. He never gave up his claim to be the rightful pope, but he was deposed by Constance in July 1415. Finally, in November of that year, Odo Colonna was elected. He took the name of Martin V (r. 1417–1431). The schism, finally, had been healed.

34. Anathema on and deposition of Pope Benedict XIII at Council of Constance, 1415, a symbol of the triumph of council over pope. Illumination, second half of the fifteenth century. Illustration to *Chronicle of the Council of Constance,* by Ulrich of Richenthal. akg-images.

35. Capture of Jan Hus at Constance. From *Chronicle of the Council of Constance*, by Ulrich of Richenthal. Photo credit: Gianni Dagli Orti / The Art Archive at Art Resource, NY.

However, regarding the issue of heresy and the fate of Jan Hus, the council enjoyed much less success. Though given a safe conduct by Sigismund, Hus and his friend Jerome of Prague (d. 1416) were almost immediately executed, in large part to stop the spread of the ideas of John Wyclif. Their burnings caused a firestorm of resentment back in Bohemia and hardened Hus's enraged supporters in their commitment to indigenous reform in Bohemia. Hus had gone to the council hoping for vindication, but he was aware of the possibility of execution. The council could not distinguish his very nearly orthodox views and intent from the ideas of Wyclif; Hus paid the ultimate price for its inability to do so. Thus the conventional formula: Wyclif was the man for whose doctrine Hus went to the stake. Whatever the truth of that, it is clear that Constance's great victory in healing the schism was marred by burning a man to whom a safe conduct had been given and whose views were hardly distinguishable from its own.

Nor did the council enjoy success with the third of its aims: reform. Reformers at the council were anxious to limit fiscal and jurisdictional abuses by the papacy but were frustrated from doing so by the French and English nations, which, by this time, had concluded agreements with the papacy on the matter of taxation and preferment that they did not want to see reversed. The council did finally promulgate several reform decrees in October 1417, among which the decree *Frequens* was the most important. This decree required that future councils be assembled at regular intervals in the future. The requirement was intended to frustrate papal aspirations to ecclesiastical tyranny; for some time it succeeded. Had the decree actually governed ecclesiastical government in subsequent centuries, it would have profoundly reshaped the relationship of pope and council and would have caused theologians to reimagine the very definition of the church. At the end, then, Constance had restored ecclesiastical unity, but most of the work of reform would have to be accomplished by future councils if it was to happen at all. Before dissolving the council, Martin, according to the requirements of *Frequens,* called for a council to assemble in five years.

Later Councils

The new council that Martin had summoned was to meet in Pavia in 1423, but an outbreak of the plague caused the council to be transferred to Siena. Little of significance was accomplished there, and the pope brusquely disbanded the council. With negligible enthusiasm and under pressure from wars in Bohemia and the desperate need of the Byzantine Empire for western military help—not to mention the prospect of reunion with the Greek church—the fragile Martin summoned a council to meet in Basel in January 1431. He appointed Cardinal Giuliano Cesarini (d. 1444) his legate and gave him the power to preside over the council and, if he saw fit, to dissolve it. On this inspiring note, the pope launched a council he would never live to attend.

In two months, Martin was dead. He was succeeded by Eugenius IV (r. 1431–1447), who opened a council in Basel but held its purposes in suspicion. The assembled fathers suspected him, rightly, of profound ambivalence toward the conciliar cause; their ecclesiology disgusted him and he deplored their leaders. Just five months after he opened the council, he peremptorily adjourned it and ordered it to meet in 1433. This was a misstep. He had judged incorrectly the temper of the fathers and the conciliarists and especially that of the cardinals, most of whom sided with the council. For his part, Cardinal Cesarini also sided with the conciliarists. After an unsuccessful—indeed catastrophic—crusade against the Hussites, he hoped to conduct negotiations with the moderate Hussites, but Eugenius's attempt to dissolve the council would have rendered negotiations impossible. Cesarini, along with men the caliber of Nicholas of Cusa, again succeeded in rallying a council against a pope who was intent on causing the entire conciliar movement to fall apart.

Thus, in 1432 the council proceeded with its business, beginning by again promulgating the decree *Haec Sancta*. A successful agreement with the Hussites brought prestige to the council, as it brought great relief to central and eastern Europe and deprived the pope of his zeal for undermining the council. This time, the pope caved in. In December 1433, he issued the bull *Dudum sacrum,* in which he announced that his dissolution of the council had been illicit. In addition, he declared that the activity of the council had been, from its start, legitimate and binding. At this point, the future of conciliarism seemed secure, but this was to turn out to be illusory.

In retrospect, much of the council's energies seem to have been designed not to reform but to punish the papacy. In 1434, the council took a radical step in cutting off all papal revenue that came from outside the Papal States. It proceeded to organize committees that absorbed the functions of the pope, exercising such vital functions as appointments to benefices and dispensations. The recently established annates and other papal taxes, which had been paid begrudgingly, were abolished. This time, the conciliarists, who seemed to act more vindictively as time passed (perhaps expressing their long-suppressed and deep anger), took the crucial misstep. A number of the most distinguished council fathers had profound misgivings about the radicality of the conciliar actions in depriving the pope of his traditional administrative, financial, and executive powers. Eugenius IV protested but in vain. However, he would be saved by the pressure of world events.

As the Turks pressed their advantage in the East, the desperate emperor John VIII Palaiologos (r. 1425–1448), proposed, along with the patriarch of Constantinople, Joseph II (r. 1416–1439), negotiations for the reunion of the Greek and Latin churches. Eugenius enjoyed a stroke of luck when the emperor decided to treat with the pope rather than with the council fathers in Basel. In September 1437, Eugenius transferred the council to Ferrara, supposedly to be closer to the Greeks for the council of union. This time, many of the cardinals who had previously resisted Eugenius—including both Cesarini and Nicholas of Cusa (whom Eugenius called the "saner element")—obeyed the pope. In March 1438, they met with the eastern emperor and many important Greek ecclesiastics.

The forlorn fathers back in Basel stubbornly repeated their claim that the superiority of the council over the pope was an article of faith. They deposed Eugenius IV as a heretic. Then someone blundered. It was proposed that a new pope be elected, and soon the council elected the duke of Savoy, who took the name Felix V (antipope: 1439–1449). This was a fatal error. The council had caused a problem that conciliarism was conceived to solve and thus had brought severe discredit upon itself: it had triggered a new schism.

Basel lost even more influence when the council in Italy (transferred from Ferrara to Florence and lasting from 1438 to 1445) debated the theological and ecclesiological issues that had long divided the Greek and Roman churches. With concessions made on both sides, a decree of reunion, *Laetentur Coeli (Let the*

Heavens Rejoice), was announced in July 1439. The council then reached agreements with other eastern churches, but the reunions were not generally effective. Bitter memories of the Fourth Crusade in 1204 and the sacking of Constantinople caused the prized reunion with the Greek church to crumble almost right away. Still, from the point of view of the papacy, the council was a success. The pope's prestige was enhanced by the union, however ephemeral, and he seemed to have triumphed definitively over the conciliar theory. As the conciliarists deepened their radicalism, Felix V resigned, and in April 1449, the council dissolved itself. Meanwhile, the pope had negotiated a series of separate truces with the rulers of Europe, who had supported the conciliarists as a way to resist papal encroachment in their territories. In 1438, the pope concluded a concordat with the kingdom of France known as the "Pragmatic Sanction of Bourges." It restricted papal rights in France and gave legal sanction to what was, in effect, a fait accompli. Such agreements essentially authorized the status quo, in which national governments had a larger role in ecclesiastical appointments and a smaller papal tax burden. Similar agreements were concluded with other rulers in Europe. Once those rulers no longer needed the councils as a way to pressure the popes, the bottom fell out from the conciliar movement.

The Restoration Papacy

Historians usually view the denouement of Basel as symbolizing the collapse of the conciliar movement, even though conciliar theory certainly outlived the attempt to organize the church along constitutional lines. In 1460, Pope Pius II (r. 1458–1464) issued the bull *Execrabilis (Damnable,* 1460), which overturned the view of *Haec Sancta* and condemned the notion that councils were superior to the papacy. It also forbade appeals of papal decisions to a future council. Conciliarism had been defeated, and the papacy had triumphed. But almost no serious reform had been accomplished, and after the sound and fury of more than a century of schism and sparring between council and pope, Christendom was the entity that had lost most grievously.

Oddly enough, the unreformed papacy emerged from the struggle with the conciliarists with an elucidation of the nature of papal primacy. Imaginatively described by Hubert Jedin, the great historian of the councils, as "the *Magna Carta* of the papal restoration," it both communicated a lofty view of papal power within the universal church and offered a ludicrous, chimerical view of dominion in the temporal realm: "We define that the holy Apostolic See and the Roman Pontiff [so *Laetentur Coeli* asserts] hold the primacy over the whole world, that the Roman pontiff himself is the successor of Peter, prince of the Apostles, that he is true vicar of Christ, head of the whole Church, father and teacher of all

Christians; and [we define] that to him [in the person of] Peter was given by our Lord Jesus Christ the full power *[plenam potestatem]* of nourishing, ruling and governing the universal Church; as it is also contained in the acts of the ecumenical councils and in the holy canons."

Indeed, the expression of this highly theoretical view of Roman authority coincided with the loss of actual power in the provincial churches, as kings and secular lords asserted their jurisdiction within their realms and created national churches from the ruins of a Christendom that had crumbled. In this, they reversed trends initiated and supported by the papacy since the eleventh century, when the popes had struggled to free the local churches from secular control. The royal powers were helped enormously by the schism, which accelerated the process of the disintegration of Christendom into territorial and national churches. With these powerful and irreversible trends, the theoretical claims of *Laetentur Coeli* were in preposterous conflict. What seemed to matter to the popes was that claims be made as magnificent as possible, however impossible their chances of achieving actual expression.

As these grand claims were made, popes in the century between ca. 1430 and 1530 concentrated their efforts on protecting their Italian domain and in lavishly reconstructing the city of Rome. It is not for nothing that these pontiffs are often called "Renaissance popes." Posterity owes to them at least the glory of the Sistine Chapel and, more ambiguously, the construction of the new St. Peter's Basilica. But it seems these popes were constantly enmeshed in war; Italian politics; conflict with the city-states; trafficking in ecclesiastical offices; elevating their relatives (including their children, of whom one pope sired sixteen) to high office; and in the generation and accumulation of art and treasure. Almost nothing was accomplished by way of reform. The failure of reform and the eclipse of the universal claims of the papacy by the harsh realities of national feeling would last into the sixteenth century.

"Morning Stars" or Heretics?
Wyclif, Hus, and Followers

In the high Middle Ages, heresy had plagued the very heartland of Europe. In the later Middle Ages, it spread to the peripheries of Europe, to England, where Catharism could not get a toehold, and to Bohemia. In each country, the heresy was primarily associated with one man, John Wyclif in England and Jan Hus in Bohemia (though some of Wyclif's ideas were warmly received in Bohemia). Wyclif would eventually come to grief because of his views on Eucharistic presence, ecclesiastical dominion, the nature of the church, popular piety, and the authority of scripture. The indigenous movement of Czech ecclesiastical reform, of which Hus has become a symbol, while philosophically influenced by Wyclif, focused its efforts on clerical morality, access to the scriptures, and devotion to the Eucharist. As is obvious from even this brief introduction, the followers of Wyclif and Hus touched upon matters of theological and disciplinary importance—indeed of such significance that sixteenth-century reformers would reencounter and re-appropriate some of their late-medieval grievances and "heretical" ideas in an entirely new context and with significant influence.

John Wyclif: Life and Thought

John Wyclif (d. 1384) was born ca. 1330, likely in Yorkshire. Over the course of his early life, he was offered but (for reasons that remain mysterious) never received several promised canonries, rectories, and other ecclesiastical positions in various parts of England. Accordingly, Wyclif lived mostly in Oxford (1356–1381), and it is with Oxford that his name is indelibly associated. It is through his teaching and writing there that he exercised his extraordinary influence. Already in the 1360s, Wyclif had achieved considerable distinction as a lecturer and writer in philosophy, particularly logic and metaphysics. Early in the following decade, he set out to teach in theology; he incepted as a doctor in theology in 1372. Meanwhile, he was contemplating a prodigious *Summa* in theology.

Wyclif's years at Oxford, however, hardly make for a simple story of success, unconditional approval, and contentment. In 1365, Wyclif was elected warden of Canterbury College at Oxford. Fatefully, this election was dismissed by Pope Gregory XI, possibly for being somehow irregular. Around 1371 Wyclif became involved in the secular field of politics. Present at Parliament in that year, he witnessed two Augustinian friars debate the question of whether, in times of emergency, the state could legitimately seize the property of the church. Wyclif took a position there on dominion that would later cause him to be brought under ecclesiastical censure. In 1374, King Edward III (r. 1327–1377) granted him the parish of Lutterworth. He held the cure until his death in 1384, though he maintained his close ties with Oxford until 1381. His views on dominion were likely known by the crown when Wyclif received this appointment.

Wyclif developed his ideas on dominion in several works, including *De Dominio Divino (On Divine Lordship)* and *De Civili Dominio (On Civil Dominion)*. Wyclif took the view that as only God can vouchsafe property or power, he does so not by conferring permanent property. Rather, he does so in the form of temporary loans. It followed, for Wyclif, that these could be held only by men in a state of righteousness. The daring implication of this view was that authority over property was not intrinsic to any office. Thus no cleric, not even the pope, could claim dominion or sovereignty over lands or temporal powers simply because he held a position once occupied by the early apostles. Clerics and popes *could* exercise lordship but only *if* they were truly righteous; jurisdiction and clerical power were thus made conditional upon virtuous living. (With caution we can say this viewpoint is, and may have been recognized as, a form of neo-Donatism.) Any cleric living in a state of mortal sin would inescapably have forfeited his claims to ecclesiastical dominions or lands; these, Wyclif concluded, could then be taken, with justice, from the church by civil and secular rulers. This conclusion won Wyclif the appreciation of the nobility, of many ordinary critics of clerical wealth, and even of the mendicant orders, who of course wished, at least in theory, for those living the apostolic life to be poor.

Bishops and popes were considerably less exuberant. Indeed, in 1377, Wyclif was summoned to appear before an assembly of bishops in London. They wanted him to defend his views in person. In the event, he was protected by John of Gaunt (d. 1399), duke of Lancaster, and the proceedings never took place. The same year, Pope Gregory XI, perhaps encouraged by Benedictine antagonists of

Wyclif, published a list of eighteen errors in Wyclif's works. They also called for his examination and arrest. Again, Wyclif was protected by powerful figures.

Wyclif's denunciation of the monastic life can be found among his earliest writings; it consisted of several parts. First, Wyclif felt deeply that the monks of his day had departed reprehensibly from the ancient ascetical ideals their founders and rules had normatively expressed. Second, and not insignificantly, he insisted that those ideals were profoundly mismatched with the biblical patterns they claimed to embody. In his earliest writings on the regular life, the friars had, to some degree, eluded Wyclif's censure. Yet after 1380 they would become targets of Wyclif's comprehensive vilification of all forms of "private religion." For Wyclif, private religion suggested any form of religious life that segregated the individual from the communal life of the church. Other forms of contemporary piety Wyclif placed under reproach as well. These would ultimately include pilgrimages, indulgences and pardons, the worship of images, and—perhaps most serious to a church that felt implicated in and responsible for the eternal destiny of the deceased—prayers for the dead.

The popes were not wrong to be alarmed by Wyclif's ideas. Not only did they threaten papal temporal dominions and powers, but Wyclif would also ultimately question the divine institution of the papacy. With the occurrence in 1378 of the Great Schism, Wyclif's writings seem to have become more daring and radical, though again it is difficult to prove a simple cause-and-effect in this respect. Francis Oakley has convincingly observed that some of Wyclif's positions logically flowed from prior metaphysical and theological commitments.

Not in doubt, however, is that Wyclif's thought generally pursued a declensionist line—that is, Wyclif assumed a grievous decline in discipline, morals, and devotional and sacramental practice from the period of apostolic poverty and simplicity. As part of this view, his thoughts would develop in ways wholly inimical to the papacy; they would be subversive of some of the fundamental doctrines and practices of the late-medieval church. He would formulate views on the church, the authority of scripture, and Eucharistic presence that would all seem radical and even heretical to many who soon would judge them.

In short, for Wyclif, every practice not justified by scripture stood condemned by it. Ecclesiastical and clerical wealth—and especially a way of life divorced from not only ecclesiastical poverty but also the possession of all manner of secular jurisdiction—simply could not be justified by appeal to the gospels or the epistles. Wyclif made this point almost *en passant* in several of his biblical commentaries. In his book *De Veritate Sacrae Scripturae (On the Truth of the Sacred Scripture)* (1378), he systematically and forcefully argued that the unique, sole, and absolute source of Christian doctrine and practice was the Bible. Let us be clear. This was not a precocious form of the Reformation notion of "scripture alone" *(sola scriptura)*, according to which the scriptures functioned as the sole, unrivaled source of Christian doctrine and practice. (Incidentally, whether some reformers held this doctrine in this coarse form is itself more complicated than is often suggested.) Wyclif accepted that a complete view of the meaning of scripture may at times depend on the writings of the church fathers. He quoted Augustine voluminously to support his position. But he did regard the Bible as a certain kind of barometer or norm by which all papal claims could be measured, the authoritative point of reference by which claims made by the Roman church could be judged. This biblical norm, along with the ecclesiological thought of Augustine, deeply influenced his convictions on the church.

Crucial to Wyclif's views on the nature of the church, which he developed fully in 1378 in *De Ecclesia (On the Church)*, was Augustine's ancient, classic distinction between the heavenly and earthly cities. This distinction Wyclif pressed to extreme and tangible positions not clearly rooted in Augustine's own understanding. For Augustine, the damned and the saved were to remain indistinguishable, invisible, and nameless until the last judgment. Wyclif transformed this ahistorical distinction into something palpable and present. He was to insist that only the society of those predestined *(congregatio omnium predestinatorum)* were actually members of the church. This church had only one head, not the pope, but Christ alone. This was daring enough, but Wyclif went on to make explicit the implications of this idea. For Wyclif, the pope, the episcopate, and the priesthood held only an adventitious and provisional relationship to this true church. Indeed, for Wyclif the pope was, at best, the head only of the visible, Roman church, composed as it was of wheat and chaff. The elect were known to God alone, yet they could be identified (he held somewhat inconsistently), in part, by their fruits (as Matthew 7:16 suggests). As a mundane institution that was, more or less, coextensive with Christendom, the Roman church assuredly contained both the predestined and those ordained from all eternity to damnation. For this reason, it was not identical with the Body of Christ.

According to Wyclif, the Roman church ought not to hold jurisdictional or secular authority, much less civil dominion, which involved the holding of property and the management of revenues. These functions belonged properly to the secular authorities. They also prevented the clerical class from performing its authentic function, which was to follow Christ in poverty and suffering, as well as in preaching. It has been pointed out that Wyclif was among the first, thus, to propose a map of European territorial churches that would not only be protected and supported but also regulated by local lords and princes.

The following year, Wyclif would write a book entitled *De Potestate Papae (The Power of the Pope)*. Now he suggested that the visible church might well have a head or leader. Presumably he would be one of the elect. Yet *if* he were avaricious, craved power, or failed to follow Peter in apostolic simplicity and power, he, evidently, could not be one of the elect. Indeed he was surely an Antichrist. Needless to say, papal dicta need not be heeded in that case. A simple believer, Wyclif went on remorselessly, was nearer to God, by virtue of his membership in the true church, than a false pope. There was more. The papacy was not of divine institution but a human invention; it was founded not by Christ but the emperor Constantine. Though it now held temporal jurisdictions and lands, its proper purview was solely spiritual.

Again measuring current theological tradition against the dogma of the ancient church and the teaching of scripture, Wyclif boldly argued in *De Eucharistia (On the Eucharist)* against the now generally accepted view of sacramental presence in his day: transubstantiation. Transubstantiation, we recall, holds that in the consecration of the elements, the substance of the bread and wine is transformed miraculously into the flesh and blood of Christ; only the "accidents" (taste, color, texture, shape) of the Eucharistic elements remain. Wyclif would argue, and be condemned for contending, that the substance of the bread and wine remained after the consecration; this is a view technically known as "remanence." Wyclif went on to argue that no accident could truly exist apart from a real substance. It was not possible, in his view, for any real substance to be destroyed and miraculously transformed. How, then, was Christ present in the Eucharist? Wyclif argued that Christ was truly present but symbolically. He was not, and could not be, present in any fleshly or material sense. Later, he would be condemned for arguing that "Christ is not in the sacrament of the altar identically, truly and really, in his bodily person."

As daring as all of Wyclif's teaching had been, his views on the Eucharist were the ones that would eventually bring him misery in the form of an episcopal inquest. They also cost him the support of the friars, the court party, and his many sympathizers at the University of Oxford. Once he had lost the support of his defenders, who had shielded him on previous occasions from ecclesiastical probes, he was left naked to episcopal inquiry. Opposition to Wyclif strengthened in 1381 with a peasants' revolt, for which Wyclif's heresies were, somewhat bizarrely, blamed. However outlandish the connection, the revolt brought the secular and religious authorities into union against Wyclif. In 1382, William of Courtenay (d. 1396), the archbishop of Canterbury, convened a synod, and it resulted in the condemnation of twenty-four of Wyclif's propositions (as summarized, not always fairly, by the council of examiners). Courtenay was authorized to imprison anyone who defended theses that had been so condemned. Yet Wyclif was allowed to remain in his parish at Lutterworth, to which he had retired the previous year. While at Lutterworth, Wyclif wrote prolifically. He penned a number of polemical tracts on the ills plaguing the contemporary church and also wrote a great number of sermons. In addition, he authored the *Trialogus,* a brief but quite tendentious abbreviated version of his major ideas.

It is possible but remains unclear whether Wyclif also provided support and inspiration for the translation from Latin into English of the Vulgate Bible, which came to be known as the "Wycliffite Bible." He did not actually contribute directly to the work of translation, which was undertaken, after his death, by followers at Oxford and in his home parish. In November 1382, a stroke left him partially paralyzed; a second, suffered while hearing mass two years later, killed him. He was buried, for the moment, in the graveyard at Lutterworth church— that is, in consecrated grounds. In 1428, the bishop of Lincoln, obedient to an ordinance crafted at the Council of Constance in 1415, exhumed Wyclif's body, had it burned, and had the ashes deposited in the River Swift.

Criticism of Wyclif, which had begun early in his career, would intensify after his death. This cannot be surprising. Francis Oakley has briskly summarized the matter:

> We are left with . . . the radical nature of the conclusions he actually did draw. He periodically refused to accord efficacy to the ministrations of the sinful priest. More consistently he depreciated the function of the priesthood itself. He minimized the importance of the sacraments. He attacked the bases of the ecclesiastical hierarchy; he rejected the traditional claims of the papacy. He generally questioned, indeed, the mediatory function of the institutional church in the economy of salvation, and ascribed to the royal government a predominant role in the direction of that part of the visible church militant that he came to identify with the realm of England.

Still, despite the provocative and (in the eyes of many) heretical character of these propositions and the condemnation of his ideas by ecclesiastical judges, Wyclif retained support and certain interest in his work in England for decades to come. Both secular and ecclesiastical authorities felt it necessary to issue and reissue edicts against him, a certain sign that his works were still being read with appreciation or at least curiosity. The same conclusion is reinforced by a study in the history of books, which demonstrates that Wyclif's books continued to be acquired by individuals, libraries, and institutions, circulated and annotated by sympathetic readers as well as by the ill-disposed.

In 1401, an edict was passed by Parliament entitled *On the Burning of Heretics (De haeretico comburendo)* with the support of King Henry IV (r. 1399–1413). The edict was evidently aimed at Wyclif and his sympathizers. It was intended not only to threaten current followers but also to discourage potential sympathizers, as one of the concluding clauses makes quite clear. If a heretic refused to recant, then he

was to be brought "before the people in a high place to be burnt, that such punishment may strike fear into the minds of others." Six years later, an ecclesiastical judgment, the "Constitutions" of Archbishop Thomas Arundel (d. 1414) was
begun; they would take two years to complete. Their intent was, as we might say,
to chill speech on academic topics on which Wyclif had written so provocatively.
The Constitutions not only forbade Wyclif's books to be read, but they could not
even be owned. Discussion of controversial issues, like the mode of Eucharistic
presence, was discouraged. In particular, the philosophical and theological opinions of students at Oxford were to be examined regularly for correctness. Ownership of any translation of the Bible into English was made illegal. More denunciations followed in 1413, in the wake of a revolt by Sir John Oldcastle (d. 1417), an
enthusiast of Wycliffite opinion. The edicts against Wyclif's works were to have
their effect. By 1500 or so, it was difficult to find copies of Wyclif's writings in
England. The *Trialogus* would be printed in Switzerland in 1525. Yet no English
press would bring his works out before the Reformation.

The Lollards

In England, Wyclif's influence would be felt soon in the rise of the so-called
Lollard movement. From the first a term of opprobrium, the word was coined
in the late fourteenth century. Certainly Wyclif's followers were insulted by it.
They preferred to be called "true men." But opponents called them "Wycliffites"
(Wyclifistae) as well. Later both terms would be applied to the Bohemian reformer
Jan Hus and his followers. In any event, even during his lifetime, two of Wyclif's
close sympathizers were spreading his views outside the milieu of Oxford. That
they were doing so is clear, among other things, because an edict against them was
issued by the uncannily named Bishop Wykeham (d. 1404) in 1382. Copiers and
readers of the heresiarch's work were known to exist in Leicester by the same date.
A cascade of edicts was, in the end, to pour down upon these followers, beginning
in 1384, the year of Wyclif's death.

All of this evidence indicates that contrary to scholarly views expressed in the
1950s and 1960s, Wyclif's followers were organized, powerful, learned, and linked
by common appreciation of Wycliffite theological views and not, as had been
argued, by economic or social factors. Many students and enthusiasts were at
Oxford, where the aforementioned "Constitutions" of Arundel were exploited to
justify inquiry, every month, by wardens of the colleges regarding the theological opinions of undergraduates in their charge. Such actions suggest that in the
early fifteenth century, enthusiasm for Wyclif's writings was still high. Many texts
composed by Lollards, including biblical commentaries and *florilegia* (quotations
from the church fathers arranged by topic), were shaped decisively by Wycliffite

theological opinion, glossed gospels, and other sorts of works, all of which demonstrate an academic and learned background.

Given the length of time over which Lollardy persisted and the variety of texts it produced, it is not always easy to generalize about the relationship of Lollard ideas to Wyclif's. Nonetheless, there is no question but that they appropriated much of Wyclif's genuine thinking, though they developed some of it in ways probably not imagined by their originator. Surely the Lollards' characteristic denial of transubstantiation can be linked directly to Wyclif's own views. The worship of images Wyclif repudiated; the Lollards did as well. Support for the scriptures in the vernacular is again an idea held by the Lollards traceable to Wyclif. The Lollards took up but certainly embroidered upon Wyclif's ideas on "private religion," to all forms of which they were quite vigorously opposed. They also both drew and expanded upon his ideas on the papacy, ecclesiastical wealth and power, the efficacy of ecclesiastical absolution, and the use of excommunication. Some of their ideas on the priesthood they took far further than Wyclif. For example, they held that priests ought to devote themselves to preaching and to living so modestly that they would possess only what was needed to satisfy immediate needs. If food was needed, they should labor for it with their hands. Some denied the need for priestly baptism or any ecclesiastical involvement in marriage. Here, ironically, they had the long ancient and early-medieval tradition of the church on their side but not the support in Wyclif's writings for an idea that would, in the fifteenth century, have seemed clearly heretical. Some Lollards held clearly pacifist views, while others urged communal holding of property. Some of these views were not at all Wycliffite. Others were far-reaching extensions of Wycliffite ideas.

The Lollard contribution to the history of the book is significant, as Lollards produced the first finished and entirely vernacular translation of the Bible, which exists in an early and later version. Between two and three hundred of these manuscripts survive, a remarkable number given strenuous attempts by ecclesiastical authorities to suppress their dissemination. This is not even to count the usual losses to be expected over time. A large number of Lollard sermons survive, along with other tracts and texts. The so-called "Twelve Conclusions of the Lollards," a broadside on clerical disendowment, posted on the doors of Westminster Hall and St. Paul's Cathedral in 1395, received significant attention in the late fourteenth century.

Some of this attention came from the socially powerful, not the disenfranchised. It has recently been proven that some knights, who held power at the royal court, were favorably disposed to Lollard causes. These men helped underwrite the production and circulation of the many texts they composed. Episcopal registers suggest that many towns outside of Oxford, including London and some northern cities, harbored Lollard groups into the fifteenth century. As time passed, the social composition of these groups evolved. Initially, they infiltrated all classes, from laborers to gentry. By the 1420s, however, they were to be found almost exclusively in the lower classes. After the revolt of Oldcastle, many trials followed, and some Lollards were burned. Oldcastle himself evaded authorities for a long time, but he too was finally executed in 1417. The rebellion that he fomented was decisive for the fortunes of Lollardy. Lollards were henceforth regarded with immense suspicion and found themselves facing physical violence, as well as trials. Their fortunes were to change again, this time favorably, when, in the sixteenth century, reformers were able to drum up support for those views already associated with Lollardy. During the reign of Henry VIII (r. 1509–1547), Lollard texts were copied and printed, though again mainly on the Continent rather than in England.

Nonetheless, it would be on the other side of Europe, in Bohemia, that the term "Lollard" would be applied, again usually by the hostile, to the followers of Jan Hus. Thus, it would be on the opposite fringe of Europe that Wyclif's memory was most profoundly honored and his writings most carefully preserved and admired—and from which an indigenous reform movement would take new inspiration and supplement its store of philosophical and theological views.

Hus, Bohemia, and the Hussite Revolution

How was Wyclif's influence transmitted to distant Bohemia? One path was the establishment of a channel of literary and theological influence from Oxford to the University of Prague. In the wake of the Great Schism, as England fell under obedience to the Roman line of popes and France under those at Avignon, there was an exodus of Czech students, who quit the University of Paris for Oxford. There they would soon encounter the works of Wyclif and a significant body of fellow enthusiasts.

A second path has less to do with ecclesiastical politics than intellectual commitments, particularly the appreciation in Prague for Wyclif's philosophical views. A crucial factor here, one that would inform ecclesiastical and academic life in Prague in coming decades, was the desire of the Czech professors—or, as they were also called, "masters" *(magistri)*—to distinguish themselves, philosophically speaking, from their German counterparts. By roughly 1390, Czech students returning from Oxford had begun to acquaint their compatriots with Wyclif's epistemological views, which contrasted to the moderate nominalism embraced by most German masters. Well before Wyclif's theological works had begun to appear in Prague, his reputation as a bold and stimulating philosophical intellect was well established among the Czech masters.

Wyclif's theological works arrived in Prague early in the fifteenth century. When they did so, a robust indigenous movement of reform was already well under way. Wyclif's emphasis on a purified form of Christianity, one that patterned itself on the model of the age of the apostles, was certainly warmly received by leaders of the movement, including Hus, and those writings helped shaped the movement and inspire its ardent partisans. However, it must be stressed that the reform movement antedated the reception of Wyclif's writings and the leadership of Hus. The leading Czech reformers focused on issues touching on clerical morals, access to the scriptures (or as they might have put it, the "Law of God," especially as mediated and explicated in preaching), and devotion to the Eucharist. The reformers insisted that the lives of the clergy be improved morally. The principal obligations of the clergy were, or should have been, the study of the scripture and preaching. Second, the reformers wished to bring those scriptures to the faithful, not in the form of the Latin Vulgate but in the vernacular. Most strikingly, their movement was characterized by a profound devotion to the sacrament of the Eucharist. They underlined the importance of frequent reception of the sacrament, an idea that, embellished and amplified, would distinguish the Czech movement of reform for decades.

The launching of the reform suggested the role that political figures would play in the movement. Along with the archbishop of Prague, Emperor Charles IV brought to Prague the Austrian preacher Conrad of Waldhausen (d. 1369). Conrad helped set reform enthusiasms in motion by a campaign of popular sermons. The practice of delivering popular sermons would be continued by his successors, Milíč of Kroměříž (d. 1374) and Matthew of Janov (d. 1394). Matthew, a scholar of distinction, linked the burgeoning reform movement with key members of the faculty at the University of Prague.

As already suggested, another, politico-ethnic factor made this a reform that was animated by national sentiment and international tension: hostility between the indigenous Czechs and the immigrant Germans. Again, this hostility antedated Hus's arrival in Prague. It centered on university politics. The university was founded in the mid-fourteenth century by Charles IV, the Holy Roman emperor (1355–1378) and king of Bohemia (1346–1378). His objective in founding the university had been to strengthen his family's rule; Prague would be the capital of both the Holy Roman Empire and Bohemia. After the inundation of Bohemia with Germans, who received high positions not only in the university but also in the church and government, tensions generated by Charles's policy of Germanization erupted. After his death, his son, Wenceslas IV (r. 1378–1419), attempted to augment revenues and extend jurisdictions. His efforts were completely hamstrung by the Bohemian nobility's refusal to cooperate. Soon the Czech masters of the university organized to terminate the German monopoly on appointments. While not entirely unsuccessful, this initial effort left much of the university and Bohemian public life in Czech hands.

Still, the Czechs were motivated by determination to achieve political and social equality with the ruling Germans. In the late fourteenth century, meanwhile,
ties between Bohemia and England were strengthened when King Richard II
(r. 1377–1399) married the Bohemian princess Anne. This political union only
strengthened the influence of Wyclif at Prague. Among those it influenced was Jan
Hus, the man in whom the Czech reform movement would find its charismatic
leader, outstanding preacher, dedicated champion—and venerated martyr.

Born of a peasant family in the village of Husinec (from which his name of
course originates), Hus was destined early for a clerical career. After studying
Latin, he matriculated at the arts faculty of the University of Prague about 1390.
Three years later, he had earned his bachelor of arts; in 1396, the year in which he
took his master of arts, he began to teach in the arts faculty. Around 1400, he was
ordained a priest. He also began study in the faculty of theology. He proceeded
smoothly through the various stages to the doctorate and would undoubtedly
have earned his degree had not the more pressing agenda of reform reoriented his
energies toward purification of the church.

A teacher regarded by his pupils with great affection and a professor and man
trusted by his university colleagues, Hus served the arts faculty as dean for two
years (1401–1402). In 1402, his colleagues honored him by electing him preacher
of the Bethlehem Chapel; Hus replaced Stephen of Kolin, one of his professors,
who resigned so that Hus could take the position. For the next decade, Hus
taught, advised students, carried on with his activities, and preached to hundreds
of congregants (to many of whom he also served as spiritual director) who attended his popular sermons at the Bethlehem Chapel.

The chapel had been established in 1391, with the help of powerful members
of the king's court and the Prague bourgeoisie, as a center of preaching in the
Old Town of Prague. Hus's boundless energy, obvious earnestness, and attractive character won for him the respect and admiration of socially distinguished
citizens of Prague. These included the gentry and nobility, who sought out his
advice on a spectrum of issues, as well as members of the royal court. He also
won the admiration of the local ordinary, the archbishop of Prague, Zbyněk of
Hasemburg (d. 1411). The archbishop was impressed by his moral seriousness,
especially the gravity with which he demanded that diocesan clerics live a moral
life worthy of their high calling. On several occasions, the archbishop asked him
to preach before local synods. Hus accepted, and he did not hesitate from expressing his strong disapproval of the moral shortcomings of those he was addressing.
As Waldhausen had done before him, Hus criticized the local clergy not only for
religious mediocrity but also for specific sins, like the traditional medieval ones of
simony, concubinage, and a shockingly luxurious lifestyle. Fatefully, the prelates,
many canons of the Prague cathedral, retaliated by complaining to the papacy.

Hus's eloquence at the Bethlehem Chapel, the purity of his life, and his desire for reform and for Czech sovereignty in Bohemia all slowly worked together to crystallize his position as leader of a movement that was at once religious, national, political, and intellectual, as well as economic and social in character. In Hus's view, the Czechs should be considered first for offices in the Bohemian realm, just as the French were in France and the Germans in German lands. In Hus, the national program of sovereignty merged with the existing movement of religious reform and lay piety, of which Hus would presently become the international symbol.

Controversy has raged among scholars about the extent of Hus's dependence on Wyclif for his theological ideas and reform program. It is often said that Wyclif is the man for whom Hus went to the stake at Constance in 1415. It is true that Wyclif's epistemological "realism" was embraced by Hus, and this in contrast to the German preference for Ockhamist nominalism. So, too, was it taken up by the majority of Czech masters at the end of the fourteenth century (perhaps earlier). Still, Hus was more chary than many of his contemporaries about embracing some of Wyclif's condemned theological ideas. He never accepted the Eucharistic doctrine of remanence. Nor did he admit some of Wyclif's arguments regarding sinful clerics. Even if sinful, such a cleric held his office rightfully, if not worthily, and could hold and exercise its powers. On the other hand, Hus accepted Wyclif's repudiation of the divine institution of the Roman papacy and the Roman church. Eventually, Hus would have to respond to charges about his theological positions.

Meanwhile, there was still the work of the Czech reform movement to complete—and to transform. Now the Czech masters were determined to wrest control of the university finally from the German masters. They enjoyed the support of the Prague town government, which replaced the German minority with a Czech majority. More crucial still was the Kutna Hora Decree of January 18, 1409. This gave the Czech university "nation" three votes and the three German "nations" only one vote. This vote jiggering caused a mass exodus of the German professoriate and students. Roughly a thousand German masters and students left for existing German universities (some created the new one of Leipzig). Here the government intervened decisively, and in the view of Czech masters, appropriately. Czechs were then appointed by the government to all the places in the university. In his sermons, Hus made it clear that he and others had imagined this arrangement in terms of Wyclif's doctrine of the territorial church-state union under the secular prince. This won Hus even more support, and he was chosen as the university's new rector in 1409–1410.

This time support did not extend to the ecclesiastical realm. Alarmed at the extent of Hus's political Wycliffism, the archbishop of Prague, Zbyněk, complained to the Pisan pope, Alexander V. The archbishop insisted that ecclesiastical privileges were being transferred to civil authorities with Hus's approval; this claim was not untrue. In December 1409, the pope replied with a bull. It condemned Wyclif's forty-five articles and proscribed Hus's preaching in Bethlehem Chapel. The archbishop seized scores of copies of Wyclif's books and, in July 1410, burned them. For his part, Hus simply ignored the pope and archbishop and continued to preach. In 1410, he appealed to John XXII, the new pope. With the encouragement of Hus, Czechs from his congregation filled the streets. They militantly denounced the archbishop as a minion of Antichrist. This demonstration simply inflamed Rome, which summoned Hus to the papal court on charges of being a Wycliffite. Hus refused to go. In February 1411, he was excommunicated. Popular demonstrations recurred in Prague. Now the king compelled the archbishop to relent. He refused but was forced to flee Prague and died soon thereafter.

It seemed like an unequivocal victory for Hus and his movement. Yet by this point, his movement included men like Jerome of Prague, who would radicalize the movement and win many supporters. Still, Hus did not distance himself from him. Curiously, he refused even to disavow condemned Wycliffite doctrines that he had never held. In part because of this stance, he became the focus of the hostility and hatred of all those whom he had criticized, alienated, or sent away: the German masters, canons of the cathedral, and Czech anti-Wycliffites. All would speak against him at the papal court, and the German masters would testify vindictively against him at Constance.

Hus was unmoved and certainly not intimidated. In 1412, he made himself even more a *persona non grata* at Rome by criticizing the preaching of indulgences in Prague; the pope wished to use revenues from indulgences to underwrite his crusade against the king of Naples. Since the arrangement included the understanding that the revenues thus generated would be divided between pope and king, here the followers of Hus began to lose the support of Wenceslas IV. Again, demonstrations in the streets of Prague, which sometimes lapsed into violence, erupted. Placards depicting the pope as Antichrist were defiantly displayed. At this point, Hus may have begun to feel anxious about the intensity of the movement he had helped generate.

Finally, in September 1412, the definitive papal excommunication was pronounced against Hus in Prague. The pope put the city under interdict because Hus was there. Hus's response was to withdraw, and he spent most of the next two years in the castles of his noble supporters, first near Prague, then at Kozi Hradek in southern Bohemia, and finally at Krakovec in the west. It was in these years that he composed two of his most important works, one on the church, the other on simony. Inspired by Wyclif and written in the vernacular, *On Simony* vigorously assailed clerical corruption, the charging of fees for the administration of the sacraments, and and the receipt of revenues from church property. These, he concluded, could be taken away by the laity, especially noble patrons of the churches.

In 1414, as the Council of Constance got under way, Emperor Sigismund invited Hus to present his case before that council. He gave Hus a safe conduct composed of sympathetic Czech nobles. Hus accepted the invitation even before the safe conduct reached him. Several weeks after arriving in Constance, he was imprisoned. His adversaries, some of whom were sent money by the embittered Czech canons, persuaded the council leaders that Hus was a seditious Wycliffite. After months of interrogation and incarceration, he was finally given a sort of public hearing. Yet it was not a fair debate. Persuaded already that Hus was guilty of the charges on which he had been imprisoned, the Paris theologians Jean Gerson and Cardinal Pierre d'Ailly (d. 1420) demanded whether he could explain thirty articles taken from his works, all of which had a Wycliffite flavor, in an orthodox sense. Characteristically, Hus refused to abjure them, insisting that he could not disavow that which he had never held. That response sealed his fate. In July 1415, Hus was condemned as a heretic, stripped of his ecclesiastical vestments, and burned outside the city.

Radicalization in Prague

The decision at Constance radicalized the reform movement in Prague. A Wycliffite inspired by the ideas of Matthew of Janov, Jakoubek of Stříbro (d. 1429), a friend of Hus, took leadership of the movement. His ecclesiology, however, was more sectarian in nature than Hus's, and he viewed the true church as the congregation of holy men who had interiorized the norms and practices of Christianity as expressed in the gospel. In his view, the established Roman church had not, so all of its prelates and its pope were regarded as the corrupt and indeed evil instruments of Antichrist.

The sacramental hallmark of the radical movement was Utraquism, the giving of communion under both species *(sub utraque specie)*—that is, consecrated bread and wine. In fact, the chalice, which had during much of the Middle Ages been withheld from the laity, became the symbol of the movement. The practice of frequent communion, which, as we have seen, had deep roots in the reform movement, was encouraged. Utraquism, too, then, represented the rejection of late-medieval Roman practice—and not just Eucharistic practice but also the whole spectrum of non-evangelical devotional practices, the holding of property, and the exercise of jurisdictional power. Hus did support the Utraquists, if in lukewarm style, yet, again, he did not distance himself from them. Hus's letters from Constance do justify communion in both kinds. His concern (not unlike Luther's a century later) was that conservative practices not be overturned so rapidly as to antagonize traditionalists; rather, the practice should be introduced slowly and with feeling for conventional practice and its followers. Utraquism would be condemned by Constance with Hus, who favored it more strongly before his death. In any case, it was without doubt a popular religious practice among the laity of Prague and students at the university.

Sectarian emotions led the Hussites eventually to take their revenge against their martyred hero's death by taking over nearly all the churches in Prague. The radicalism of the movement led to a drastic pruning of the Roman mass. The new service replaced Latin with Czech. Many recitations were supplanted by hymns sung by the congregation, and communion, not surprisingly, was taken by the laity under both kinds at each service. Priests discarded their costly liturgical vestments with simplified clothing and their gold liturgical vessels with simple wooden or tin ones. The radicals rejected the veneration of the saints and a wave of iconoclasm destroyed many images. Many rejected the doctrine of purgatory. With that rejection went the support for masses for the souls of the dead and all liturgies designed to abbreviate the time of the beloved deceased in purgatory. All manner of blessings suddenly disappeared. Baptism now required unblessed water only; penance became a public rite, with no penitential prayers or works required.

Even more radical than the Utraquists were the Taborites, who took their name from Tabor, their fortress. Where the Utraquists would forbid only practices expressly prohibited by scriptures, the Taborites rejected all not explicitly commanded by the Law of God. The two sides quarreled but finally came together, adopting a religious program in common. Known as the "Four Articles of Prague," it demanded free preaching from the scriptures, the communion cup for the laity, the practice of gospel poverty, and rigorously ethical lay and clerical life. In common, too, they resisted several crusades designed to bring Bohemia under obedience to Rome. All of these resulted in bloody defeats for the Roman armies.

At the Council of Basel (1431–1449), the Hussites were granted use of the cup and some elements of the remaining four articles. Yet the Taborites refused to compromise, bringing them again into bellicose conflict with the more moderate Utraquists. Indeed, they were almost destroyed in 1434 at the battle of Lipany. At this point, in 1436, the Utraquists agreed to a "Compacta" with the Council of Basel and, under the terms of the compact, were brought again into communion with the Roman church.

Wyclif and Hus have often been styled "forerunners of the Reformation." Insofar as both promoted the Bible as the principal source of religious authority and expressed revulsion with ecclesiastical abuse, one can accept this categorization. Whether either should be styled a reformer or a heretic will likely depend on extra-historical considerations. There can be little doubt that each imagined himself as a reformer, primarily interested in restoring Christianity to the form it had taken in the centuries before medieval developments (to their minds) had perverted it. Certainly the union of imperial rule and ecclesiastical authority was, in their view, a monstrous development in the history of the church. The Bohemian revolution and especially the Taborite movement are sufficient evidence of this. The Bohemian church regarded the burning of Hus by a council as a form of violence that subverted the very authority of the reformers who had convoked it. To their mind, the Council of Basel went some way toward reestablishing that authority by ending the wars against the Bohemian church. Intriguingly, papal authority waned from 1417 to 1436, or even to 1462, when Pius II abrogated the Compacta, along with his decrees that appeals to councils were not licit. This decline of papal power is something of which Hus—not to mention Wyclif—could not have disapproved, and it might have seemed that the triumph of reform in Bohemia naturally paralleled the decline of papal authority throughout Europe in the early fifteenth century. In either event, each development should be studied in light of the other.

At the end of the day, nonetheless, neither Wyclif nor Hus was, strictly speaking, a "forerunner" or "morning star" of the Reformation. The theological doctrines of the magisterial reformers, above all justification, owed nothing to Wyclif, nor to Hus. Their teaching on grace was never imagined by either, and it was the inability to come to an agreement on this central issue that, in the first instance, caused the split between the Roman and reformed churches. Nor can it be said that Wyclif accepted the central doctrine of "scripture alone" as it was meant by the sixteenth-century reformers.

Late-Medieval Contours of
Reform, 1380–1500

Reform "in head and members" had, to the distress of many, failed. Not only had the conciliar theory for comprehensive reform suffered much damage in credibility, but even once staunch conciliarists had washed their hands of it. The papacy stood triumphant but manifestly unreformed. Even at the time of the Council of Basel, however, voices were heard that both expressed disappointment in general reform and hope in the possibility of *partial* reform. As Francis Oakley has observed, the Dominican Johannes Nider (d. 1438), for example, acknowledged that he had given up hope for "the general reform of the Church either at present or the near future." Yet he added: "On the other hand, a partial reform is possible in many countries and localities. We see it gaining ground day by day in monasteries and convents, though God knows amid what difficulties." Reform would also occur partially in a geographical sense: certain cities, notably Florence, would be reformed, if only ephemerally. Some reformers were sent around regions of Europe to oversee papally sponsored reforms. New religious groups and orders, notably the Sisters and Brothers of the Common Life were born and boomed. Most of the major religious orders attempted to recover the founding inspiration of their institutes and to observe it with new freshness and rigor, sometimes with the powerful aid of royalty. Without question, the later Middle Ages were centuries of ecclesiastical reform.

Partial Reform

Partial reform occurred in this era in a number of ways. Some few orders, like the Carthusian, underwent a significant expansion in the late Middle Ages—

indeed their largest ever in percentage terms. Yet they were quite exceptional. The most characteristic style of reform in the religious orders was not expansion in the number of postulants to new orders or in the creation of new ones. It lay rather in the infusion into existing, sometimes quite old, orders of what has come to be called the "Observant" or "Observantine" spirit. Nearly all the great orders of friars that originated in the Middle Ages—Dominican, Franciscan, Augustinian—made this an expression of the desire to recuperate what was widely felt to have been lost institutionally, morally, and in discipline over the prior decades. So, too, in the monastic orders, did the Benedictines and Cistercians. As the very word suggests, "Observantine" indicates a yearning to realize again the religious ideal that gave rise to a particular religious institute and to observe it, afresh, in its genuine and original form. Usually this effort entailed a renunciation of private possessions, rededication to the ideal of a genuinely communal life, and, at least among the Benedictines, commitment to the ancient ideal of strict inclaustration. Such changes sometimes occurred in the face of opposition, occasionally aggressive, from those not motivated by nor sympathetic with Observant passions.

As we have seen above, the question of the degree of Observance was a highly fraught one among the Franciscans, so much so that the order finally broke apart under the pressure of the questions involved in it in the thirteenth and fourteenth centuries. For that reason, the Observance was carefully and shrewdly moderated by its leaders, the illustrious preaching friars Bernardino of Siena and his friend John of Capistrano (d. 1456). Perhaps the outstanding preacher of the late Middle Ages, Bernardino, orphaned at age six, grew up with his maternal and paternal aunts, both quite pious. Their influence was strong. They may have sparked interest in Bernardino's religious calling; almost certainly they were the source of his interest, expressed often in his preaching, for the religious and moral lives of women. While living in Siena with his paternal aunt, Bernardino studied canon law for three years. After experimenting with several forms of the religious life and caring for the sick as a member of a noble flagellant community during a plague (an act of charity that almost caused his own death), he joined the Franciscans in 1402. Shortly thereafter, he joined the Observant branch of the order and moved into their friary south of Siena. Bernardino spent most of the rest of his life as a wandering preacher. It is interesting that it appears some of his sermons took the form of a running dialogue with his audience.

Though offered several bishoprics, including that of Siena, Bernardino declined them. Nonetheless, he held some significant positions within the order. As vicar general of the Italian Observance, he composed a new set of Constitutions in 1440. While hardly lax, the Constitutions gingerly attempted to avoid expressions that could be interpreted as critical of the Conventuals. Accordingly, the Constitutions accepted as normative papal decrees from the thirteenth century. At the same time, they attempted to restore the order's primitive commitment to the observance of poverty. For that reason, the Constitutions forbade the use of money and rejected all dispensations. The appeal of the Observant vision as expressed by Bernardino can be gauged in both the great expansion of the movement and its geographical reach. The Franciscan Observance was fantastically successful, reaching as far east as Poland and Hungary, west into Spain and Portugal, and north into England. It was especially strong in its traditional heartland of Italy, France, and Germany.

There were several historic nodes of regeneration among the Benedictine network of houses in the late Middle Ages. As was the case in other orders, observance implied an effort to require the brothers to honor the faithful and exact observance of a primitive *Rule*. Yet that is not all it meant. Two developments actually mark a move *away* from the strict observance of the Benedictine *Rule*. First, we observe the gradual erosion in the historic authority of the abbot in Observant Benedictine houses of the late Middle Ages. Second, the deep tradition of local independence gave way to new groupings of formerly autonomous houses; like more recently founded orders, they were now grouped into provinces. These were overseen by duly elected visitors in chapters that were now held every third year.

With the Benedictines and other Observant orders, certain outside authorities—including counts, secular lords, and some princes—made certain houses centers of renewal through exercise of their own will and power. The famous Benedictine house of Melk, to take one illustrious example, became a source of renewal for Benedictine houses in Austria, as well as Bavaria. This was largely because of pressure brought to bear by Albert V, duke of Austria (r. 1404–1439).

Some of the most impressive movements of reform in the high Middle Ages among the Dominicans took place among friars from the Roman province who were followers of Catherine of Siena. Raymond of Capua, Catherine's sometime confessor, played an important part in establishing the spirit of Observance in many leading houses in Germany, such as Colmar. Raymond's hope was that such a spirit would spread to other houses and provinces in the order. This was a hope that certainly found expression in Italy, where enthusiasm for and dedication to the preaching friars' early patterns and principles were established in many important houses. Again, a former disciple of Catherine, John Domenici (d. 1419), who would become vicar general of the Observants in Italy, led the way. Among the Dominican houses to have reformed according to the Observance was San Marco in Florence. Aside from providing a refuge for the great painter Fra Angelico (d. 1455), whose paintings in the cells, refectory, and walls of San Marco can still be admired, San Marco housed the apocalyptic reformer and incendiary preacher Savonarola. It was he who would lead yet another kind of reform—the local or provincial—characteristic of the late Middle Ages.

Local and Provincial Reform

In the wake of the Renaissance, many public preachers denounced the revival of classical or "pagan" literature and the production of literature that seemed too worldly. Similarly the production of art deemed lewd or prurient troubled many; they feared it would lead to impiety and godless license. Something like what we today call a culture war was being waged. Some Christians feared that enthusiasm for classical culture would simply overwhelm the normative authority of biblical culture; norms of thinking and acting would be molded by the irreligious and profane rather than by the sacred and ecclesiastical. Indeed, for some preachers, this threat was so real, so plausible, and indeed so imminent that they expected that the Antichrist was at hand. No such preacher received such contradictory treatment for his convictions, and few have so captivated historians, as Girolamo Savonarola (d. 1498). He was the penitential preacher most intent on creating a local culture based, negatively, on revulsion with the heathen culture of humanism, and, positively, on the revitalization of a Christian culture and a rigorous—today we might say "puritanical"—morality based on the language of the Bible and many of the components of traditional Christian asceticism.

Florentine Humanism and the Early Renaissance

The reaction of Savonarola is directly tied to the enthusiasm of the sovereign ruling classes of Florence, who were very passionate about the study of the classics. This enthusiasm is sometimes misunderstood. For the enthusiasts of Florentine humanism expected that the works of Cicero, Virgil, Livy, and others would lead one toward an active and good civic life and participation in reforming politics, as well as to writing and speaking eloquently. In other words, humanism in Florence grew as an educational program for citizenship in the city. The luminaries produced by Florence included Petrarch, Boccaccio, and Dante. But they also included artists and architects like Donatello and Brunelleschi. The latter's first building in "Renaissance" style was a hospital for foundlings, completed in 1424. Yet about the same time, he was working on the famous cupola of the Duomo, Santa Maria del Fiore, one of the great achievements of Renaissance architecture. Its campanile, or bell tower, would be built by Giotto, who had frescoed the interior of the Basilica San Francesco in Assisi. Artists the likes of Leonardo da Vinci and Michelangelo, who sculpted the famous David that came to symbolize Florence, flocked to the city. While the old view of Lorenzo de' Medici as lavish patron of the arts has been discredited, he knew many artists and patrons who wished to be brought to Florence by him. Lorenzo died before the fiery Dominican reformer Savonarola came to control the city in the late fifteenth century until, in 1512, the Medicis were restored.

36. Aerial view of the Cathedral of Santa Maria del Fiore, Giotto's Bell Tower, and the Baptistery of San Giovanni, Florence. Photo: Andrea Tradii, 2002. Alinari/Art Resource, NY.

Savonarola and Florence

The circumstances of Savonarola's attempt to establish in worldly Florence a "New Jerusalem" caused him to antagonize not only the ruling Medici family but also Pope Alexander VI (r. 1492–1503). His courage caused him to attract many supporters and enabled him to establish many elements of his reform vision. They in turn helped to persuade him of the central millennial role of the city of Florence. But the force and leverage of the papacy and of the most powerful family in Italy could be suspended only briefly. When these powers reasserted themselves, Savonarola would suffer cruelly and his movement of reform lose the traction it held, if only ephemerally, among the worldly Florentines.

Born in Ferrara, where he was also educated, Savonarola became a Dominican at Bologna in 1475. Early on, he showed signs of talent in preaching. Yet he was absorbed in positions both academic and administrative at Bologna and San Marco in Florence, of which he became prior in 1491. There he made San Marco a center for the study of the Bible. Each element of this briefly drawn background is critical for understanding his reform movement. As Francis Oakley has observed,

"The point of departure of Savonarola's reform was the Observantine movement of monastic reform that had earlier achieved considerable success in Italy and within his own order." A plague in 1448 had succeeded in reducing the numbers at San Marco and, then, the rigor of the Observance there. As prior, therefore, one of Savonarola's first aims was to restore the strictness of the Observance to his home convent. This he did successfully, and the numbers of postulants, many of them sons of prominent Florentine families, began again to grow. In addition, the spirit of Observance spread to other Dominican friaries in Italy (not to mention houses in Spain), including Fiesole, Pisa, Prato, and Sasso, all of which attached themselves to Savonarola's new congregation, of which Savonarola became the vicar general, having separated San Marco from the congregation of Lombardy in 1493.

Beginning some two years earlier, in 1491, Savonarola had begun to attract large crowds of Florentines to hear frighteningly vivid apocalyptic sermons, discourses indeed, as Savonarola tells us in his *Compendium of Revelations,* on the book of the Apocalypse. He first gave them at San Marco, and during Lent 1491 he came to give them at the city's Duomo. Thundering against corruption rampant in the church, he prophetically warned that the sword of the Lord was suspended, like Damocles's sword, above the earth. It would come quickly and bring terrible affliction, purifying the Italian church while worldwide tribulations marked the last days. Now, in this heated apocalyptic climate, it was quite evidently the time to repent, do penance, and purify one's life.

Savonarola's standing as a prophet only seemed strengthened and then guaranteed when, in 1494, Charles VIII of France (r. 1483–1498) descended the Alps and advanced on the city of Florence. Naturally, his arrival terrified the citizens of the city. Savonarola, persuaded that the king was God's divinely sent agent of reform, managed, in an approach to the king, to persuade him to spare Florence. To the Florentines, Savonarola had prophesied that a new conquering Cyrus would come down from the Alps, with an army none could hope to resist. Now, he linked Cyrus and Charles and the French army with the divine scourge about which he had already prophesied, a terror from which he would soon manage, through his formidable persuasive powers, to deliver them. To the Florentines who had heard him, these events could only seem like prophecy amazingly and precisely fulfilled, as they did to Savonarola himself. His faithful listeners, he boasted, knew how his scriptural interpretations read so faithfully the signs of the times.

With the fall of the Medici family, accomplished in part by popular revolt, the reforming Dominican's position as a visionary prophet grew immensely among the Florentines. His position as civic leader was cemented when he treated with Charles and secured the safety of Florence and freed the city, of which he was now recognized, almost messianically, as liberator and champion. Savonarola also suc-

37. Statue of Savonarola
preaching in fiery fashion
to the Florentines. akg-
images/Alfons Rath.

cessfully turned Florence into a penitential city. Many of its citizens chose a semi-
monastic life, and the carnival seasons of 1496 and 1497 famously saw the drama-
turgy of the "Bonfire of the Vanities," as Florentines deposited their playing cards,
dice, cosmetics, musical instruments, jewelry, wigs, books, and pictures—all occasions for sin in the eyes of Savonarola and his supporters—into the consuming
flames. Processions that were imagined as both penitential and celebratory were
led by young men in Florence.

Intriguingly, from this time forward, a new, far less pessimistic tone began to
be heard in Savonarola's sermons. Far from seeing Florence as a Sodom of sin, he
identified it as God's very own city, "one beloved of Christ," the "center and heart
of Italy." Indeed, Florence, now cleansed and renewed, was a New Jerusalem; it
would become "more glorious, richer, more powerful than ever before" (echoing
Is. 2:2). It was the heart of reform, from which religious and social regeneration
would flow out to the whole of Italy. Naturally, these panegyrics did nothing to
diminish Savonarola's popularity among the citizens of the city. Indeed, he created something like what we today would call a civic religion centered on the

greatness, election, and destiny of Florence. Perhaps not surprisingly, Savonarola began to imagine himself as a man sent by God, a seer appointed, like a modern-day John the Baptist, to exhort Florence to purity and to warn it of the tribulations to come. He imagined himself, as many presumed him now to be, the savior of Florence and the man who had delivered them from the frightening prospect of physical and spiritual annihilation.

Unfortunately for Savonarola, his very powerful and determined enemies had not forgotten him, nor had they ceded to him spiritual and secular control of Florence. These included the deposed Medici and, not least among his enemies, Pope Alexander VI, whose wickedness and supposed ineffectiveness as pontiff were favorite themes of the Dominican preacher. Worse, perhaps, in the eyes of the pope was that Savonarola had allied with the French king. Now, in 1495, the pope moved against his Dominican nemesis. He summoned Savonarola to Rome; Savonarola replied by indicating he was just then unable to leave Florence. In May 1497 papal agents excommunicated him, and the pope threatened to place Florence under interdict. Savonarola considered, but did not follow through on, an appeal to a council to the secular rulers of Europe. When a Franciscan preacher suggested that Savonarola's legitimacy as a prophet be tested by an ordeal by fire, the mercurial Florentine population turned against him. In May 1498 Savonarola was brought out to the Piazza della Signoria in Florence, where he, along with two other Dominicans, was condemned as a heretic and schismatic and then burned to death.

The Sisters and Brothers of the Common Life

The Sisters and Brothers of the Common Life were the institutional embodiment of a culture of conversion called by contemporaries themselves "the modern devotion" *(devotio moderna)*. This quite obviously signifies that the "devouts" (as American John Van Engen calls them in the most recent, and best, book on the movement) felt that *something* about them was novel. Historians, however, wrestling with that question, have felt hard pressed to say exactly what was new. Some have argued that the members of the Devotion and its founder, Geert Groote (d. 1384), were "forerunners" or "precursors" of the Reformation. Others have argued that it was essentially a backward-looking or at least certainly medieval and orthodox movement. Here we will follow Van Engen in avoiding that question and attempting to understand the Sisters and Brothers, who were after all the most innovative element of the Modern Devotion, in their high-medieval and almost exclusively urban and geographically focused context (for the Devouts were centered in the Low Countries).

The founder of the Sisters and Brothers, the Dutch reformer Geert Groote, studied arts and canon law in Paris. After returning to the Netherlands and accumulating prebends, Groote in 1374, in medieval fashion it should be observed, rather suddenly gave up his endowments. He then turned over his home to a group of women. They became the first Sisters of the Common Life. Because of this chronological priority and because female houses would always outnumber the male, it has become common, especially since Van Engen published his authoritative work, to refer to the Sisters first. In any case, Groote entered a Carthusian monastery. He there read the Flemish mystic Jan van Ruysbroec and translated one of his vernacular writings into Latin. Nonetheless, the great Flemish mystic's writings were to have little influence on the Devouts. Much more characteristic of their low-flying piety was *The Imitation of Christ*, written and its four parts gathered, almost certainly, by Thomas à Kempis (d. 1471). At the time, the proscription against the founding of religious orders was still in force, but sisterhoods and brotherhoods—which did not have to take vows—could be established. Accordingly, Groote established the Sisters and Brothers before dying of the plague at the age of forty-three.

As Van Engen observes, against the great panoply of high-medieval cultures of conversion and reform (Cistercians, Franciscans, and others), the Modern-Day Devout were neither lay nor fully clerical. They took no vows. Yet they lived lives that were quasi-monastic, pursuing chastity in communal households, rejecting the holding of private property, and producing textiles and books (part of the new urban entrepreneurial culture in which they were imbedded). They also ran schools for children of the rising bourgeois class but by and large did not aspire to university professorships. In this they certainly differed from the mendicant orders. They never aspired to higher learning and even had contempt for learning divorced from pious purposes. We might add that they also preferred a different style of devotion and piety than the monastic orders, whose hours they nonetheless observed. There is a meditative, simple, and direct quality to this sort of piety, as practically every line of *The Imitation of Christ* suggests. It would be true, also, to say that there was a mild obscurantism, as Thomas (here reminding us of Bernard of Clairvaux urging monks to flee the vain temptations of learning in Paris) enjoins his readers against "worldly" or "vain" learning—that is, learning not oriented toward the enrichment of the soul, or, as might be heard (sadly) on campuses today, "purely academic" learning. The Sisters and Brothers were urged to meditate upon scripture (yet it would be a stretch to say that this anticipated the world of the Reformation). Still, the greatest humanist of the age, Erasmus of Rotterdam, received some instruction from a Modern Devout, whom he nonetheless held in contempt and blamed for wasted years. Yet the mode of simple piety that Erasmus advocated was not unlike that of the Devouts, though the influence has not yet been proven. Erasmus did love learning, but he shared with the Devouts a frustration with the aridities and pettifoggery of late-medieval scholasticism.

Despite episcopal approval, the Devouts did kick up hostility from the mendicant orders (who were offended at the Devouts' rejection of begging). In response, some but not all of the Devouts took forms of life that increasingly resembled those of the historic monastic orders. Some placed themselves under the *Rule* of St. Augustine, which protected them from the charge of having formed a new religious order. In the end, though, we must understand the original impulse of the Devouts as one that attempted to live a simple, devout life *outside* the formal and legal structures of the traditional monastic order. That said, some Devouts, including Thomas, were in fact monks; he was committed to the ancient Benedictine ideal of stability. He wrote expressly for monks and aimed to excise anything from the monastic day that did not enrich monastic contemplation. The Devouts also reestablished labor, another Benedictine ideal. They aimed for virtue, not for flights of metaphysical speculation; catered to the literate bourgeois class, not to the nobility; settled in the city, not in remote rural areas; and taught in schools, not in universities.

The female Devouts took no vows and wore no habit. They worked for their bread and strove for a life of virtue and service to God with the support of other sisters. They read not scholastic authors but the scriptures above all and the classics of monastic spirituality, especially the works of John Cassian. Their reputation as leading humanists or Rhineland mystics has little foundation. Curiously, when attacked by such a personage as the Dominican Matthew Grabow, powerful allies Pierre d'Ailly and Jean Gerson protected them. In their piety they looked back to forms encouraged by the Cistercians and Franciscans. Still, the intensities of monastic life were not for them. As Francis Oakley has nicely put it, "For most of them their choice of life was . . . more moderate . . . more hesitant even. It was a choice that conveys a humble sense that the higher peaks of the spiritual life might well not be for them, that it was preferable to make the ascent step by cautious step and to take it day by routine day than to reach too high, as had so many religious before them, only to fall so very low." In the end, this was enough. Their culture of piety was a mode of reform that was local and popular in the Netherlands. They aimed neither to change the culture of Catholicism, nor to start an ecclesiastical revolution. It is quite clear that they satisfied their goals, as they contributed nothing of significance to the great sixteenth-century break in northern Europe.

Nicholas of Cusa's Papally Sponsored Reform

Born in the German town of Kues along the Moselle River, Nicholas of Cusa must be regarded as one of the most remarkable philosophers, theologians—and mathematicians—of the later Middle Ages. We know little of his early life, except that he was one of four children of a prominent shipper and his wife, John and Katharine Krebs. It used to be thought that he was trained by the Brothers of the Common Life in Deventer, but there is little to support that notion. We do know that he entered the University of Heidelberg in 1416; there he studied the liberal arts. Just one year later, he moved to the University of Padua, where he focused on canon law; he became a doctor of laws *(doctor decretorum)* in 1423. While in northern Italy, he learned much about mathematical and recent astronomical thinking. He also came under the influence of the Italian humanists and was impressed by their care for Greek eloquence.

Back in Germany in 1425, Nicholas enrolled at the University of Cologne. We assume that he delivered and attended lectures in canon law there. It was during his time in Cologne (about the length of which we are uncertain) that he began to live on ecclesiastical benefices given him by the archbishop of Trier. These were to bedevil his later reform efforts, not only because he was a pluralist, but also because he received these endowments before he was ordained a priest. Amazingly, he in 1428 discovered twelve lost comedies of Plautus (d. 184 BCE). Around the same time and again seven years later, he was offered a chair of canon law at the University of Louvain, and both times he turned the offer down.

Nicholas was to have a controversial history at the Council of Basel. While representing an associate's claim to the archbishopric of Trier at the council, he was drawn into the larger issues of ecclesiastical reform. He rose quickly to a position of leadership in the council. A prolific writer, he penned no fewer than five works on ecclesiastical unity, authority at the council, ecclesiology, and calendrical matters. These writings alone, which amount to a vigorous defense of the theory of conciliarism, along with his opposition to Pope Eugenius IV's efforts to dissolve the council, would have won him a permanent reputation as a staunch spokesman for the cause of conciliar superiority to the pope. Yet his sympathies suddenly changed when he voted in December 1436 to allow the pope to determine the site of the ecumenical council with the Greeks. In May 1437, the council formally split into two factions over the issue of site. Cusa now joined the papal party. On May 20, he embarked for Bologna. A little over a month later, the pope sent Cusa and two bishops as his official representatives to Constantinople. Their aim was to convince the patriarch to meet with the pope in the hope of bringing the divided halves of Christendom back into union. An agreement reached in July 1439 brought only a temporary reunion.

Why did Cusa, a conciliarist, choose to leave Basel? Apparently, he felt that the dissent expressed at Basel was threatening to dissolve the unity of the western church. That may well be, but many staunch conciliarists, who felt his betrayal keenly, identified Cusa as an opportunist who seized his chance to advance his ambitious personal agenda. Whatever the case may be, Pope Eugenius IV named

Nicholas cardinal in 1448 (sometime around 1426 he had been ordained a priest), a reward for his efforts at reunion. He was made cardinal after Eugenius's death by Pope Nicholas V (r. 1447–1455) and assigned the titular Roman church, San Pietro in Vincola (St. Peter in Chains).

It was under Nicholas V that Nicholas undertook a solo reform with papal authority, using the traditional vehicles of papal power: decrees, visitations, sermons, legislation, and, if need be, invocation of the whole spectrum of measures the secular power could bring to bear. Nicholas's undertaking had papal authority. The pope took the extraordinary step of making him *legatus a latere*—that is, a plenipotentiary legate appointed for a particular mission or assignment and not for indefinite residence abroad as the ambassador of the pope; in this sense, he was distinguished from a papal *nuncio*.

Nicholas's mission lasted roughly fifteen months; in that time he traveled nearly three thousand miles. He made his way through some of the largest dioceses in Germany and the Netherlands: Magdeburg, Mainz, Cologne, and many others. He held councils and synods, issued informal decrees, conducted scores of visitations, and preached something like fifty sermons. He attempted to arbitrate disputes and, when defied, threatened excommunication, interdict, or secular correction. He attempted to reform individual churches, both secular and regular. Traditional historiography has awarded him high marks for this reforming mission, because of both the epic aim and broad horizon of activity and his indefatigable energy in carrying out his assigned task.

Yet there is good reason that Nicholas achieved a good deal less than he, or his sponsor, had hoped. To be sure, there were some successes. First, Nicholas was particularly effective in the monastic realm, and he successfully supported reforms at some of the most important monasteries in his jurisdiction, including Melk. Yet with some monasteries he failed. With monks and clerics living with concubines, his successes were at best ephemeral; both regressed to form when Nicholas had departed. Second, his criticism of abuses in the benefice system cut no ice with those who understood that he himself was a shameless pluralist (he was drawing income from nearly twenty benefices at the time of his reform mission). Third, as his mission went on and he experienced hostility and defiance, he seems to have resorted more and more to the dark threats of intimidation, armed force, and excommunication. Beyond Nicholas's own failings, the very ecclesiastical context in which the cardinal undertook his mission made it almost impossible to fight for reform. In the wake of the dissolution of the Council of Basel, committed conciliarists, still convinced of the need for reform, thought the only instrument capable of it was a new council, and they were bitter at the failure of Basel and Nicholas's defection from it. Finally, some prince-bishops in Germany granted bishops and archbishops—those whom and whose dioceses Nicholas was striving to reform—exemption from the cardinal's reforming decrees. Their lack of cooperation doomed Nicholas's mission. Such reforms as endured in the provinces were often undertaken by prelates already conscientiously committed to the triumph of reform, however partial, in their own dioceses and locales, and these were usually accomplished without the aid, or interference, of the papal office and power.

Francisco Ximénez de Cisneros and the Reform of the Spanish Church

Just as Savonarola's reforms were entirely bound up with Florentine and papal politics, those of the Franciscan Francisco Ximénez de Cisneros (1436–1517) were deeply linked with the nationalizing process that occurred in Spain when, as is well known, two of the four most powerful kingdoms of the Iberian Peninsula were united by the marriage, in 1469, of Ferdinand, who would be king of Aragon, and Isabella, soon to be queen of Castile. These two monarchs (and their children) are well known for extending Spanish power into Italy, Austria, and the Netherlands and for supporting the voyage of Christopher Columbus to what soon came to be known as "the new world." But they were equally dedicated to mastery and reform of the church within their realm. Their framework of ecclesiastical jurisdiction and reform demanded the recruitment and ordination of clerics dedicated to the monarchy, distinguished for the fierceness of their discipline, and marked by a strain of profound piety. On all counts, Ximénez more than fit the bill.

Born to parents of the minor nobility, Ximénez studied theology and law at the University of Salamanca. In 1459 he began a period of service to the Roman curia. Six years later, he returned to Spain. After attracting the attention of several very important secular clerics there and holding a number of important positions in the secular hierarchy of the Spanish church, Ximénez in 1484 became a Franciscan friar of the Strict Observance. It was then that he took the name "Francisco" and for a while became a hermit. His reputation as a holy man, however, quickly spread, and it was not long before Queen Isabella appointed him her private confessor. She also made him archbishop of Toledo (1495), though he would continue to live a life of Franciscan simplicity and poverty as ordinary of that diocese.

At this point, Ximénez's life would take a momentous turn that resulted in his becoming the very exacting, militant, and occasionally intolerant overseer of the entire national church in the dawning age of Spanish ascendancy. Perceiving the need for an educated clergy, Ximénez established the University of Alcalá in 1508. This was to become a center of Christian humanism and a magnet for some of the greatest scholarly minds and products of this age in Spanish and European history. Among other things, the Polyglot Bible, to which Ximénez and his team of

Haec tibi pentadecas tetragonon respicit illud
Hospitium petri z pauli ter quinq3 dierum.
Namq3 instrumētum vetus hebdoas innuit: octo
Lex noua signatur. ter quinq3 receptat vtrunq3.

Vetus testamentū multiplici lingua nūc
primo impressum. Et imprimis
Pentateuchus Hebraico Gre-
co atq3 Chaldaico idioma-
te. Adiūcta vnicuiq3 sua
latina interpreta-
tione.

38. First page of Cardinal
Ximénez's Complutensian
Polyglot Bible. IAM/akg.

collaborators dedicated roughly fifteen years, was published at the university. This was the first complete edition of the Greek New Testament, and it was accompanied by versions of the Hebrew Bible in Hebrew, Latin, and Greek, along with the Aramaic Targum on the Pentateuch. The intellectual energies of Ximénez and the encouragement he gave to advanced study of theology also led to an important revival in the study of Thomas Aquinas at the University of Salamanca.

By 1494 Ximénez had become vicar general of the Observant Franciscans of Castile. The Dominicans had already been touched by the reform of Savonarola's congregation. Now Ximénez attempted to extend the Franciscan Observance with his characteristic energy, avidity, and—it must be said—tactics that were strong-armed and occasionally ruthless. He took friaries, not without resistance, from the Conventuals and simply put Observants in them. Because Queen Isabella supported him, he quelled the resisters, and by 1517 Conventual presence and influence in Spain had dwindled substantially.

Ximénez did not limit himself to reforming the regular clergy. Indeed, he demonstrated the same ferocious zeal in reforming the secular clergy. Though he failed to require the canons of the cathedral to live a communal life, he did manage, with the support of the Spanish monarchs, to appoint holy and worthy men to the episcopate. He convoked synods in 1497 and 1498. These not only addressed the usual abuses, like concubinous clerics, but they also attempted to impress upon the diocesan priesthood the nobility of their calling. As a result, decrees passed in these synods required priests to go to confession regularly themselves, to explain the gospel to parishioners on Sunday, and to ensure that children were being properly catechized. Ximénez himself produced a simple catechism to aid them with that last task. He also established a printing press that made possible the circulation of other kinds of pious and didactic literature. All of this activity reflected the assumption that members of the clergy had been insufficiently prepared to carry out their high calling and that they could be improved for pastoral care by education and reading.

In the long run, reform "in head and members" was to have little or no future in the Middle Ages. Yet we must recall that it was a pope who launched Nicholas of Cusa on his reforming mission. Other highly placed secular powers, like the Spanish monarchy, were crucial in consolidating reform in their own domains. Yet the picture, from this lofty altitude, is complex. One need only recall that the pope and the powerful Medici family conspired to bring Savonarola's reform to an abrupt and brutal end in Florence. In the end, it was men of individual genius, fervor, and conscience who were the primary movers of reform in the orders, in the cities and provinces, and in countries. In some cases, their reforms did not survive them; in others, they came to shape the destiny of national churches and even of the great Catholic reform of the sixteenth century.

Late-Medieval Piety and Its Problems

It has sometimes been suggested that the medieval church was treasured above all as an intercessor for the dead. If the suggestion is reductionist, there is none-theless something to it, and whatever insight it achieves pertains above all to the later Middle Ages. We see this notion of church-as-intercessor in the multiplica-tion and intensification of pious practices in the later Middle Ages, especially (and not surprisingly) after the scourge of the Black Death in 1348–1349. No act of devotion made this more visible than in the number of masses recited, requested, and paid for in the period ca. 1350–1500. Yet this is not the whole story. As Ber-nard McGinn and others have noted, there was a great "flowering" of mysticism in the fourteenth century, efforts to achieve unmediated experiences of the pres-ence of the divine. Intriguingly, women are among the most well remembered and important mystics of the era. In addition, books of hours were central to the piety of late-medieval Christians, especially to women. They provide us a glimpse into the domestic piety of the late Middle Ages. While some late-medieval Chris-tians found deep satisfaction in the pious practices, others felt oppressed by the medieval pastoral theology of the period. No volume of confessions, prayers, or practices could assure them of salvation. Thus, paradoxically, the decades of in-tense pious practice coincided with profound feelings and fears on the part of many. The pastoral theology of the period could comfort some; for others, it produced profound salvation anxiety. The stage was thus set for the splintering of Christendom.

The Flowering of Mysticism in the Later Middle Ages

In the fourteenth century, we witness a flowering of mysticism—the prepara-tion for, experience of, and reaction to the direct presence of God—especially in Germany and the Netherlands, but in England, Italy, and France as well. If mystics like Bernard of Clairvaux had spoken to an almost entirely monastic readership, those of the fourteenth century addressed themselves to a much wider audience. Many were women; not all were members of traditional monastic communities. Above all, many wrote in the vernacular rather than in Latin. This itself is strong evidence of hunger among the faithful for the very kind of writing, insight, and guidance in the mystical life that the mystic herself supplied in writing. Devout people had a hunger for the divine; that hunger was satisfied, in part, by the vernacular texts written by women mystics in the late Middle Ages. Guidance for the soul was provided not only by ordained priests and men, but it was also received from largely unlearned, un-Latinate women (though Hildegard of Bingen was neither). Their visions in turn often provided "texts" for reflection and exegesis.

Sybil of the Rhine: Hildegard of Bingen

The precursor of many significant German and Dutch women mystics of the thirteenth and fourteenth centuries, Hildegard of Bingen was perhaps the greatest woman of her age and one of the most accomplished and influential women in the history of Christianity. In October 2012, the Benedictine sister's genius and distinction were recognized when she was made a doctor of the church by Pope Benedict XVI. Born into a family of high nobility in the Rhineland, she was educated at the Benedictine cloister of Disibodenberg. So formidable was her character that she became prioress of her cloister in 1136. Soon she established a convent at Rupertsberg, near Bingen. In 1147, she and other nuns left for the newly founded cloister; Hildegard would stay there until her death.

The sheer range of Hildegard's capacities still beggars the imagination. Not only was she an abbess and a foundress of monasteries, but she was also a scientist, and during her lifetime she gained a reputation as a healer and physician. In the 1150s, she composed two books that supply the historian a clear picture of pathology, physiology, pharmaceutics, and therapeutics as practiced in Germany in Hildegard's time, particularly in convents. As late as the fifteenth century, the books were still in use among physicians. She was also a poetess, musician, and ecclesiastical activist. Some three hundred of her letters survive, many of them to secular and ecclesiastical worthies like Bernard of Clairvaux, Pope Eugenius III, and Frederick Barbarossa. Her visions and reputation for prophecy earned her the respectful sobriquet "Sybil of the Rhine." As we have seen, heretics were burned in Cologne in 1163. It is interesting that the burning of heretics was something to which she was deeply opposed on moral grounds, for, she argued, the heretic also was made in the image of God. She was also an active and original exponent of scripture and a preacher, an aspect of her genius often overlooked.

39. Miniature of Hildegard of Bingen dictating the contents of a vision to the monk Volmar (depicted in the corner of the frame) of God creating an angel to overcome the Devil. From eleventh- and twelfth-century Latin codex, *Visions of St. Hildegard of Bingen*. Gianni Dagli Orti/Art Resource, NY.

Hildegard's scriptural writings have been largely overlooked because of the interest in her prophetic, mystical, and visionary writings. From her early childhood, Hildegard experienced special gifts and visions, as well as auditions. These she kept from others, for she feared being considered freakish. Finally, at roughly the age of forty-three, she consulted her confessor, Godfrey; he in turn sought advice from the archbishop of Mainz. She then had a vision of God: "And it came to pass . . . when I was 42 years and 7 months old, that the heavens were opened and a blinding light of exceptional brilliance flowed through my entire brain. And so it kindled my whole heart and breast like a flame, not burning but warming . . . and suddenly I understood the meaning of expositions of the books."

After this vision and with the encouragement of the archbishop, Hildegard committed her visions to writing. This she did with the aid of a monk named Volmar. Volmar collaborated with the visionary Benedictine on her principal mystical and prophetic writing, *Nosce vias,* which is known better by the name *Scivias* or *Scito vias Domini (Know the Ways of the Lord)*. Written in Latin prose, the *Scivias* consists of twenty-six symbolic and allegorical visions (these were then translated artistically into thirty-five miniature illuminations under the direction of Hildegard), along with apocalyptic prophecies of corruption in the secular and religious realms. Many of her mystical visions center around the image of the Living Light of God, which appears to her in female form: "She is so bright and glorious that you cannot look at her face or her garments for the splendor with which she shines. For she is terrible with the terror of the avenging lightning, and gentle with the goodness of the bright sun; and both her terror and her gentleness are incomprehensible to humans. . . . But she is with everyone and in everyone, and so beautiful is her secret that no person can know the sweetness with which she sustains people, and spares them in inscrutable mercy" (*Scivias* 3.4.15).

Some historians of mysticism have observed that Hildegard's mystical writings are structured and written with such clarity and are so replete with original intellectual rumination that she must stand at the front of a German tradition of speculative mysticism that culminated in the writings of the great German mystic, the Dominican Meister Eckhart.

Eckhart was, without doubt, the most original and influential German mystic in the Middle Ages. Some of his most impressive and influential mystical writings were written not in Latin but Middle High German. Nonetheless, he was an accomplished scholastic and taught as a Dominican at the University of Paris in two periods in the early fourteenth century. The key mystical idea in Eckhart's writings is "the birth of God in the soul," and he develops a sophisticated anthropology to explain how this can occur. According to Eckhart, the soul is a spiritual organ capable of absorbing the divine light. In its very depths the soul has a locus where God and the human spirit touch. Eckhart also outlines how this process occurs. The human prepares for this experience of the divine by emptying himself of all desire. When the soul achieves a state of "nothingness," the spark of its soul "ignites." It is then that mystical union occurs. As he himself put it in one of his vernacular works: "When I preach, I usually speak of 'emptiness,' of the need for the human to rid him or herself of all things. I then speak of the possibility that one can be formed into entire goodness, a goodness that is God. And finally I say that one should reflect upon that great nobility with which God has endowed the soul. We are to use that quality as a miraculous link to God." The expression of this process in the vernacular, replete with creative metaphors, images, and paradoxes was wholly original; Eckhart created a vocabulary for subsequent mystics to use. They used the words and categories of this "God-intoxicated" mystic and absorbed his writings, anxious to share his experience of mystical union with the divine.

Hildegard's exceptional influence can be observed immediately in the writings of her contemporary, Elisabeth of Schönau. Born into a family of the minor nobility, she had relatives that included a bishop, abbots, priors, and other female nuns. Like Hildegard, Elisabeth was also a visionary, a forceful spokeswoman for ecclesial reform, and an opponent of capital punishment for heretics. Like Hildegard, she was an abbatial leader, and she served as the superior of nuns at the double monastery at Schönau, a cloister she had entered at the age of twelve in 1147. Between 1152 and 1160, she had mystical experiences, shortly after Hildegard published her *Scivias*. After an exchange of letters, Elisabeth visited Hildegard at Rupertsberg in 1156. Like Hildegard, she was ambivalent about her visions. In a letter to Hildegard, she reveals that an angel appeared to her and insisted that she reveal them and preach penance. One book, entitled *Visions,* includes reports of her visions and auditions of Christ, the Blessed Virgin, and saints. It is important that this book was recorded by her brother and secretary, Eckbert, who collected and likely edited her visions, as well as shaped her visions theologically. Another volume, the *Book on the Ways of God,* is very closely modeled on Hildegard's *Scivias*. Yet another book on her visions, *On the Resurrection of the Blessed Virgin Mary,* became attached to the book of visions; it concentrates on the theological idea of the Assumption of the Virgin. One of the best-known hagiographical works of the Middle Ages, it is about an ancient legend of Ursula and her band of virgin martyrs, along with Elisabeth's letters. Eckbert eventually added to this a description of his sister's death. These works were widely disseminated not only in Germany, but also in other parts of Europe, especially France and England, where they appeared within six years of Elisabeth's death. Although Elisabeth was never canonized, her name was entered into the Roman Martyrology in the sixteenth century, and when her works were published, the honorific "Saint" was placed before her name.

The convent of Helfta was an important intellectual, spiritual, and mystical center. It produced some of the great German mystics of the Middle Ages and is associated indelibly with the development of new forms of mysticism (sometimes simply called "German mysticism") and the development of vernacular mystical writings. Among the greatest female writers of vernacular mystical literature of this age is Mechtild of Magdeburg (ca. 1281/1301). Although Mechtild is sometimes referred to as the greatest German mystic of the Middle Ages, we know little about the facts of her life. Probably of noble lineage, she lived the life of a Beguine and a Dominican tertiary in Magdeburg before joining the Benedictine monastery of Helfta in southern Germany (1268). The date of her death is a mystery.

While a Dominican tertiary, Mechtild received spiritual guidance from Henry of Halle, a disciple of Albert the Great. She was almost certainly the first German to have composed her works, beginning in 1250, in the vernacular. The explanation for this is simple: she probably never mastered Latin. In any case, her visions and dialogues with God were collated and written down by Henry. They became famous throughout the Middle Ages under the title *The Flowing Light of Godhead*. It is this book that is sometimes said to have launched a new mystical tradition, "German mysticism," in the Middle Ages. It contains revelations about hell, purgatory, and paradise, not to mention judgments about contemporary political personalities and apocalyptic prophecies about judgment day. Through the text runs the crucial theme of "mystical union" *(unio mystica)*—namely, the possibility of intimate union with God while still in this world. The theme is expressed in notably literary language and in diction tied to the traditions of *minnesang,* German love poetry and songs, including chivalric categories that link the "bride," or the soul, with the "groom," Christ. It has been observed that Mechtild's experience, or rather depiction, of this union is highly affective and sensual. Some historians of mysticism argue that she is an affective mystic *par excellence (Gefühlsmystikerin)*. The master metaphor of her writings is *mâze,* a knowing and acting according to the conventions and norms of courtly society, transposed to a theological key.

Because of the ferocity of her vilifications of clerical and secular immorality, for which she was accused of heresy, Mechtild took refuge at Helfta around 1270. She soon lost her sight and dictated the conclusion of her book to the nuns. After her death, Henry produced a Latin translation of her book. Later Henry of Nördlingen (as we have seen, the spiritual adviser to Margaret Ebner) translated her book into High German. This translation circulated widely in southern Germany and Switzerland. There it became popular with the Friends of God (Gottesfreunde) movement. Led by important Dominicans, laypersons, nuns, and others, this movement, strengthened by the writings of Mechtild and others, emphasized the possibility of mystical union between God and humans, self-renunciation, and the essential equality of men and women. Like Hildegard, Mechtild combined in her writing striking and sometimes beautiful devotional and mystical writings with fierce denunciation of ecclesiastical and societal inequities. Although persecuted for this, she was also deeply admired, as is attested to by Dante, who immortalized her in *Purgatorio* 27:33 as "Matelda."

An important literary legacy of nuns from Germany are so-called *vitae sororum* (sister books), collections of spiritual and mystical biographies of sisters intended to provide edifying examples of the ascetical-mystical calling for nuns. Although such books have sometimes been derided for their simplicity, recent historians of mysticism have argued that to the contrary, they certainly made a contribution to the mystical language of the later Middle Ages by offering a comprehensive terminology of a less lyrical and less intense form of mysticism than that, say, of Mechtild. They exist in very large numbers in manuscript.

In the thirteenth and fourteenth centuries, many holy women in the Low Countries associated themselves with Cistercian or Dominican houses or the burgeoning Beguinal movement. Many women mystics of the Low Countries are known, with vocations as varied as laywomen, tertiaries, religious, anchoresses, and Beguines. All led lives of extreme asceticism, extraordinary virtue, and profound spirituality. Many were memorialized as holy women by male hagiographers of renown like Jacques de Vitry, Peter of Dacia, and Thomas of Cantimpré. Like their German sisters, they not only led lives of mysticism, but also campaigned against heresy, church negligence, and social immoralities. Many offered spiritual counseling or participated in social charity.

Perhaps the two greatest of these were the Cistercian nun Beatrice of Nazareth (ca. 1200–1268) and the Beguine Hadewijch of Antwerp (fl. 1250; d. ca. 1260). Both stood in the tradition of love mysticism, which drew upon concepts from Bernard of Clairvaux, as well as contemporary chivalric literature, in order to express the centrality of the love of Christ, the lover in the spiritual life. Author of a spiritual autobiography in the vernacular, Beatrice's book was later translated into Latin, as was an excerpt from it known as *The Seven Degrees of Love*. As the title suggests, this little tract silhouettes each of the states of a progressively more theopathic life. Slowly, the soul becomes more passive in the higher states of contemplation, annihilation, union, and finally a yearning for death, an end that alone would bring the soul into full union with God.

Not much is known of Hadewijch's life. Likely born into a noble family in or near Antwerp, she made her fame for her religious poetry and prose in the Old Flemish vernacular. For her part, Hadewijch left fourteen revelations, called the *Visions*, and more than thirty letters addressed to an anonymous young Beguine. She also wrote forty-five strophic poems, often thought to be her greatest work. In addition, she composed sixteen poems in sophisticated rhyming patterns. She knew and was influenced by many great male mystics, including Bernard and other Cistercians, as well as the Victorines, and she in turn may have influenced her fellow famous Dutch mystic Jan van Ruysbroec. She is one of the leading figures in the evolution of a woman's religious movement (Frauenbewegung) in the thirteenth century.

While the work of the soul is deification—namely, the striving for union with God—Hadewijch considered this very much an intellectual process, as well as an affective or emotional one. She sits astride a (somewhat artificial) boundary between emotional mysticism and speculative mysticism. Indeed, some have argued that she stands closer to the great speculative Dominican mystic Eckhart than any other contemporary, male or female. It is interesting that she imagines the soul not in the passive role of bride but very much in the active role of a fearless and determined knight traveling through a boundless wilderness, the domain of Love, until he eventually rides to the end of his journey and to his ultimate reward. Indeed, Hadewijch's poetry is suffused with the conventions of courtly love poetry: a lover suffers melancholy uncertainty, isolation, lack of companion-ship, and loneliness. His task is undertaken and continued alone; only his strong conviction and desire keep him from flagging. He hungers and thirsts. Hadewijch uses the concepts of jousting and dueling as master metaphors. These tropes were invented by the troubadours of Provence. It is in using their vehicle of secular love that Hadewijch develops her own highly elaborate and literary framework for the achievement of divine love.

Two women dominate later-medieval French mysticism. The first, Marguerite d'Oingt (d. 1310), was born into a noble Beaujolais family. She entered the Car-thusian house of Poleteins near Lyons, where she eventually became prioress, a position she held until her death. Among the most influential of her writings is her *Page of Meditations,* a collection in Latin on Christ's Passion, sin, hell, God's grace, and the Motherhood of Christ, a theme shared with other female mystics (like Julian of Norwich) but, as Caroline Bynum has shown us, many male mystics as well. Marguerite also left us a work called *The Mirror,* a collection of visions of Christ, heaven, and the Trinity, as well as a *Life of St. Beatrice of Ornacieux.*

Certainly the most famous—and ill-fated—French mystic of the later Middle Ages is Marguerite Porete (d. 1310). Almost certainly the author of a book entitled *The Mirror of Simple Souls,* she concentrates on the higher stages of contempla-tion, union, and mystical marriage. This book survives in its original Old French version, as well as in medieval Latin, Italian, and English translations. The book is replete with daring (some would say unorthodox) ideas bordering on the anti-nomian, the notion that the human could be deified in the present life and that the deification could be lasting as well as ephemeral. It also distinguishes between "Great Church" and "Little Church," the former of whose members are free to circumvent the sacramental media. Indeed, at one point in her book, Marguerite proclaims that the liberated soul "need not seek God by penance or by any sacra-ment of the Holy Church." It is doubly ironic then that both it and its author would be burned in 1310, while the book was preserved through the agency of the ultra-orthodox Carthusian order. Indeed, in 1927, an English version of the book was published and given the *nihil obstat* and the *imprimatur* (Catholic terms that established that the book was free of heterodoxy and therefore that nothing prevented its publication). Hardly any fact could demonstrate more clearly the conditional, fluid, and contextual definitions of orthodoxy and heresy.

Just as female mystics in Germany and Switzerland were often associated with Dominican or Franciscan orders, houses, or friars, so too were female mystics in Italy. In a spiritual autobiography, St. Angela da Foligno (1248–1309) represents her early life as a wife and mother in terms of a tepid Christianity. She was con-verted in 1285 to a more committed form by a dream of St. Francis, after which she confessed to her relative, Fra Arnaldo da Foligno, a Franciscan. Arnaldo then became her spiritual adviser, the transcriber of her revelations, and their Latin translator. After her dream and confession, Angela led a life of asceticism, penance, and contemplation, as well as of action; she worked at a leper hospital almost unceasingly. Following the death of her children, husband, and mother, she became a Franciscan tertiary. En route to Assisi, she received a revelation: she would become the instrument of God. At the insistence of her brother, she dictated the story of her spiritual journey from 1285 to 1296. This she organized into thirty steps of perfection, mirroring the hidden years of Jesus's life. After 1296, she devoted herself to circles of Christians in Italy, work that led her to the composition of pedagogical and catechetical materials, as well as to the composition of many letters. She is buried at the church of St. Francis in Foligno.

We have concentrated on Catherine of Siena as an activist, reformer, and leader in the cause to have the papacy return from Avignon to Rome. Yet she was a great mystic as well. At the age of twenty, she was "mystically married" to Christ, shortly after becoming a Dominican tertiary. Her works include nearly four hundred letters, many prayers, and a long dialogue between her soul and God entitled the *Book of Divine Providence*. Her mystical writings center on the salvific blood of Christ (a major theme, as Caroline Bynum has taught us, in the writings of mystics and in the piety of the later Middle Ages), the experience of union, and the translation of the love of God into service. Her writings and the *Vita* of Catherine, written by Raymond of Capua, circulated throughout continental Europe and England. In England, a Middle English translation was made. Catherine was canonized in 1461. Along with her patron, Francis of Assisi, she is a patroness of Italy, and she was proclaimed a doctor of the church in 1970.

Born into an aristocratic Genoese family, Catherine of Genoa (d. 1510) was pressured into a marriage at the age of sixteen. In 1473, she had a dramatic conversion to a life of asceticism, penance, and contemplation. Her husband agreed to a continent marriage, and Catherine and her husband dedicated themselves to nursing the indigent and ill, particularly victims of the plague. She also had mystical experiences. It is important to emphasize that these were associated with the Eucharistic Presence of Christ and are thus, in some sense, and in contrast to those of Marguerite Porete, very much tied to conventional institutional media for divine presence and grace. She soon attracted devoted disciples, one of whom, Ettore Vernazza, founded the Oratory of Divine Love, an institute dedicated to church reform and the care of the poor. Unlike virtually all of her fellow women mystics, Catherine had no spiritual director until roughly a decade before her death. She died surrounded by her circle of admirers and was canonized in 1733.

Married at fourteen, Bridget of Sweden traveled to Rome, after her husband's death and at the direction of God, in 1349. She intervened vigorously in secular and ecclesiastical, even papal, affairs. This earned her both hostility and the title "protectress of the Holy See." In Rome, she had several spiritual directors, one of whom edited her *Revelations* and led the cause of her canonization. Before her death in 1373, she made a trip to the Holy Land, the occasion of several visions of Christ and Mary. These and many other visions are recorded in her book of *700 Revelations,* widely circulated and especially popular in England. She died in Rome. The cause of her canonization was quite controversial. Even after her canonization in 1391, no less a figure than Jean Gerson opposed it. Yet her cause prevailed, and her canonization was reaffirmed.

Looking back on these remarkable women mystics, we can come to some generalizations. Many, as we have seen, were quite disinclined to record their mystical experiences. Many must have felt keenly their lack of education, their theological inadequacy, or fear of delusion or heresy. Most had to be encouraged by spiritual directors or a perceived divine mandate to dictate their accounts. As noted, many suffered with protracted and sometimes extreme illnesses. In modern interpretations, this has perhaps been overemphasized, as scholars have pointed to illness, reductionistically, as a cause of their visions and mystical experiences. Virtually all had spiritual guidance from learned directors, who, as Amy Hollywood has taught us, often assessed, and sometimes changed, the nature of the mystic's experience. Because most of these experiences were dictated in the vernacular, yet translated into Latin, historians have rightly raised the possibility that scribes could have emended the dictations or interpolated them. Yet these advisers were often able to turn the lack of schooling of many of these women to good effect, emphasizing that their experiences must be imputed to divine inspiration and infused knowledge. Despite the extraordinary nature of their experiences, their piety was highly Christocentric and, with few exceptions, these women mystics were orthodox in belief and in support of the institutional church. Julian of Norwich speaks for virtually all when she asserts that she would say nothing that holy church would not affirm. They, like most of their male counterparts, were essentially women of the church, despite their noninstitutional, individual, and direct encounters with God. Most, finally, linked their mystical experience with social obligation, and many condemned abuses and heresy and devoted themselves to corporal works of mercy. Indeed, their profound commitment to the indigent and the ill, perhaps more than any other characteristic, gives the lie to the old chestnut that mysticism necessarily implied separatism and withdrawal from the world. What these mystics and the consumption of their writing do imply is the widespread hunger for the divine in the Middle Ages, a hunger that could also be satisfied domestically or in church by reading books of hours. In the works of Caroline Bynum, we have learned that many women mystics and visionaries were encouraged to meditate on the "wonderful blood" dripping from the wounds of Christ and that some books of hours included illustrations of such distressing sanguinary quality as to

40. Late-medieval book of hours: Man of Sorrows. Crucified Christ is surrounded by twenty small compartments with instruments of passion. An example of late-medieval (ca. 1490) blood piety, there is evidence to suggest this book was owned by a woman. The indulgence, which promises roughly thirty-three thousand years of pardon, was defaced during the English Reformation. British Library, MS Egerton, 1821.

repulse the modern reader. Indeed, Bynum has proven that a "blood piety" prevailed in the later Middle Ages.

Books of Hours

One of the kinds of manuscript that has survived in very large numbers is the book of hours, so called because the book is organized around the eight "hours" or times of the liturgical day: matins, lauds, prime, terce, sext, none, vespers, and compline. These devotions are a major element in what historian Eamon Duffy has called "traditional religion" on the eve of the Reformation, and in a fine book on them, he views them as "windows" into the devotional intimacy of the literate pious in the later Middle Ages. Many of them are also spectacular works of art owned by the wealthy literate and the clergy, sumptuously illuminated, while others, owned by the literate bourgeois, had engravings. There is evidence to suggest that such private piety was associated particularly with women. If this is true, as it likely is, these books are indeed precious windows into what R. N. Swanson has nicely called "the creation of a domestic female spirituality" in the later Middle Ages.

These late-medieval texts originated in the Carolingian era with the compilation of the Office of the Virgin, probably by Benedict of Aniane. This office consisted of psalms, hymns, biblical texts, prayers, and antiphons. From the Continent, it moved to England. By the eleventh century, it was widely known and, in the next two centuries, used by canons in cathedrals across Christendom. Originally called the "Little Office of the Blessed Virgin Mary," it was indeed relatively small and grew over the centuries, first as a supplement to the canonical office and then as *the* preeminent prayer book of the laity. In any case, the Little Office formed the essential core of later devotional books.

Naturally what distinguishes the observance of the canonical hours is whether the book was used in public, as part of the natural (if compulsory) rhythm of the liturgical day in monasteries and regular communities, or privately by laypeople as a habit of domestic devotion. For the laity, this form of devotion achieved its greatest popularity in the fifteenth and sixteenth centuries. Many households owned just one book: the book of hours. Almost certainly, it is with this book that mothers taught their children to read. Many illustrators depicted the Virgin in the existing manuscripts reading the book of hours. It is not surprising that the book of hours has been called "the breviary of the laity." Yet the paradox here is that the pious laity, in reading a shorter breviary than the very complex and time-consuming clerical breviary, enacted their lay piety by attempting to imitate the lives of monks, clerics, and religious.

The structure and contents of the surviving books differ significantly. As mentioned, the Little Office of the Virgin is the central text. But many other prayers and services soon came to be considered indispensable. The inclusion of some texts depends very much on the saints, devotions, and prayers a particular owner wished to include. That said, a majority of the books of hours that exist contain a calendar of ecclesiastical feasts and saints days. Conventionally, a page was dedicated for each month. Artists indicated each month by a different color. Many of these books were copied and illuminated, then printed, in Paris. Also commonly included were a series of texts from the gospels. These were ones the laity knew well from hearing and memory, as well as from reading, each of them proclaiming one great Christian feast. Thus John 1:1–14 proclaimed the birth of Christ; Luke 1:26–38, the Annunciation of Gabriel to Mary; Matthew 2:1–12, the Epiphany; and Mark 16:14–20, the so-called "Dispersion of the Apostles." Very often a fifth text, John 18–19, was included, the story of the Passion. Two long prayers to the Virgin, one of which was often illustrated with the image of the owner kneeling before Mary, came right before the Little Office at the central part of the book.

Seven penitential psalms were sometimes added, along with the litanies of the saints and memorials addressed to particular saints for specific intercessions. These seem to reflect local conditions and vicissitudes. Many, for example, are prayers to saints asking for deliverance from the plague. In an attempt to place the reader in the milieu of Christ and his mother and to identify with the events of Christ's Passion, artists rendered biblical personae robed in contemporary clothing and posed in familiar local settings. This is a fine medieval example of art being harnessed to the service of devotion. Compendia of prayers and devotions, these books give us a view into possibly the most popular and beloved form of piety in the later Middle Ages. This is in part because they allowed for private or personal liturgy. While the books of hours could be and were used to augment devotion during the mass, it remains obvious that they offered a form of personal piety and a liturgy that was not inevitably tied to regular church services. An Office for the Dead could often be found, along with other prayers, some of which are in the vernacular and were written by patrons themselves. This brings us to the nexus of piety and purgatory in the later Middle Ages.

"Certain Mansions": Purgatory

It is impossible to avoid a discussion of purgatory in late-medieval piety. It touched upon most every aspect of the Christian's religious life, thought, and acts. More masses were almost certainly said to deliver souls temporarily marooned there than for all other purposes combined. Souls in purgatory were in the second stage of their journey to heaven. The first stage of that journey, life, was over. The final was heaven, and the fulcrum, so to speak, was death, which most medieval people dreaded, if the many, many books on the *ars moriendi* (art of dying) are any indication. Charity came to be expressed at death not through the giving of alms to the poor but through promises of intercessory prayer, above all masses, on the decedent's behalf.

Originating from the ancient Christian custom of praying for the dead (referred to as early as the second century), the church's doctrine of purgatory (there is an analogue in Islam) originally consisted of celebrating the Eucharist at a saint's tomb on the anniversary of his death. By the seventh century, the commemoration of the dead had become common at all weekday masses; by the fourteenth, at masses on Sundays and feast days. Prayers for the dead became increasingly prominent in the Carolingian period. Fraternities, as we have seen, were founded almost only to ensure that prayers for the dead would be recited for deceased members. At monasteries, many priests would pray for the dead all day long. It was at Cluny in the eleventh century that the custom of praying for All Souls on November 2 began. This practice would spread to all other monasteries.

Prayers for the dead merged with the notion that all sin was an offense to God for which some sort of satisfaction had to be "paid." Even as early as the Benedictine *Rule,* monks were urged to ponder past sins when saying Lenten penitential prayers. Still, it was recognized that few, even those whose sin had been utterly forgiven, would be able to pay the full debt incurred by sin to God. Thus the need for a post-mortem locus and time: purgatory. As the word implies, purgatory is a place of "cleansing," and II Maccabees 12:43–45 was used thus as slender scriptural evidence for a universal religious belief:

> He also took up a collection, man by man, to the amount of two thousand drachmas of silver, and sent it to Jerusalem to provide for a sin-offering. In doing this he acted very well and honorably, taking account of the resurrection. For if he were not expecting that those who had fallen would rise again, it would have been superfluous and foolish to pray for the dead. But if he was looking to the splendid reward that is laid up for those who fall asleep in godliness, it was a holy and pious thought. Therefore he made atonement for the dead, so that they might be delivered from their sin.

Late antique and early-medieval theologians struggled to understand whether purgatorial fires were real or not, how painful, and how related to venial and mortal sin. Pope Gregory the Great gave the doctrine authoritative outline by arguing that the imperfectly righteous remained for a time (in his aristocratic imagination) in "certain mansions." There they would be cleansed by purgatorial fire. As the centuries rolled on, little was added to the Gregorian vision. Always emphasis was laid on the efficacy of prayers and penances by members of the church in liberating the souls in torment from purgatory. To the traditional doctrine, Thomas Aquinas added only that venial sins were forgiven at death by an act of pure divine love. Debate among the scholastics on the duration and intensity of suffering was robust: did these depend on the number or gravity of sins? In his *Divine Comedy,* Dante of course drew liberally on the scholastic discussions. Only a few heretics, such as the Waldensians and Albigensians, denied the doctrine. It is generally agreed that the horrors of the Black Death in the fifteenth century focused the attention of survivors on the needs of the dead, especially the recently deceased. Accordingly, there is evidence for a great increase in the number of masses for the deceased.

The Mass and the Eucharist

A nickname for the central devotional act of the western churches—the term comes from the dismissal at the end of the liturgical service, *Ite, missa est* (translated, accurately if cryptically, as "Go, it is sent" or "It is the sending")—the

41. Eucharistic cup and paten given to and probably used by St. Francis and his followers. An important relic at the Basilica San Francesco, Assisi. akg-images/Gerhard Ruf.

mass is a re-creation of the Last Supper Jesus ate with his disciples. Yet it is also a memorial and, in the medieval western understanding, a reenactment of the sacrifice Christ offered for humanity. For this reason, it was understood as the most potent form of public liturgical prayer imaginable. It was therefore capable of being marshaled to help navigate the dead through the dangers of the afterlife to God's heavenly home. Even by the ninth century, western churches (by contrast with eastern) were being built so that large numbers of altars could be accommodated. This was so that priests could say as many masses as possible for the sake of benefactors deceased or about to die. The architectural infrastructure of the mass was further built up when institutions called "chantries" *(cantariae)* began to be built. These were places for singing the mass, some quite modest, others more elaborate, that an individual, family, or group would establish by paying a priest, or an entire staff of priests at deluxe chantries, a wage (an "obit").

Because of the supposed effectiveness of the mass, it was important to recite it often, actually as frequently as possible. Indeed, any one community such as the ones we have been describing—monastery, chantry, fraternity—can be imagined as a veritable factory of prayer, with priest-workers churning out salvific masses for those who provided the capital. This capital they transformed through prayer to efficacious supernatural intercession. Yet this economic language is not altogether appropriate for several reasons, one of which is that as solo performer, the priest's role was vital and emphasized his authority. No matter how wealthy or well born, those petitioning the priest depended on him. In any case, the powerful effect the mass was believed to have, and the conviction that it could help diminish purgatorial time, made it a central feature of the practice of late-medieval Christianity.

Yet the use of the mass in this way had some undesired and perhaps undesirable consequences. The mass came increasingly to be seen as an instrumental and functional rite. It lent a transactional view to the nature of the mass, by which God was bound to deliver the benefit for which the mass was recited. It generated an "arithmetical" view of piety, by which quantity trumped quality. King Henry VII (r. 1485–1509) made an endowment for ten thousand masses to be said for the repose of his soul. Colossal numbers of masses were said with embarrassing alacrity. The cash nexus that made the chantry industry flourish was also a source of potential criticism. Later-medieval theologians would argue that the mass-as-sacrifice derogated from the original sacrifice on Calvary and underlined the irrationality of offering Christ as a sacrifice to himself as Second Person of the Trinity. It all looked too much like commercial trade in the eyes of critics, with God as an equal partner in the transaction and bound by a covenant made by men. Intriguingly, this transactional view of the relation between human and divine tracks well with the emergence of something like (as its critics would have it) neo-Pelagian theology in the late Middle Ages.

The *Facere* Doctrine

In the fifteenth century, a number of theologians (philosophically often designated, though not entirely rightly, as "nominalists") developed a theory of salvation or justification that its critics hastened to label as "Pelagian" or "semi-Pelagian." The cornerstone of this doctrine was, again, a covenant between humanity and God, based, or influenced, it has been argued, on the contemporary development of economic theory based on covenants between two equal parties. Proponents of this covenant theory of justification, of course, argued that this covenant was imposed, not negotiated, by God. In their eyes, God could, should he wish to, save by any means that did not contradict his nature. According to the conditions of the covenant by which God had bound Himself (which theologians technically designated his "ordained" power), a human could be justified in the eyes of God so long as "he did whatever was within his power" (*facere quod in se est*) or did his very best to win the grace of God. By the terms of this covenant, God was obliged to accept the sinner's effort and to reward him with justifying grace, despite the recognition that those efforts were not, in terms of strict justice, sufficient to earn the sinner salvation. Indeed, "God would not deny grace to anyone who does what lies within his power": *facienti quod in se est Deus gratiam non denegat.* The late-medieval theologian Gabriel Biel (d. 1495) and other "neo-Pelagian" theologians like Duns Scotus and William Ockham specified that one attempting to do good and to resist evil action was doing his best and should try to do so: pray all you can, seek forgiveness in the confessional as often as possible, pile pious prayer upon pious practice, enjoin Mary and the saints to intercede constantly, and so forth. A believer would, with the help of God, in these acts acquire, if only ephemerally, an absolute love of God for God's sake alone. This in turn earned the sinner a "merit," which though strictly insufficient for salvation, God had bound himself to honor as a condition for being restored to a state of grace, following contrition in the sacrament of penance. In addition, the sinner then acquired a "habit" *(habitus)* of grace that allowed him or her, in accordance with the conditions that God had "ordained," to be accepted by God and justified. According to Biel, God had ordained a system to reward with grace those who had done their best and to reward those who persevered in grace and good works with the gift of eternal life. God had created a covenant, in his ordained power, by which ordinary good and moral acts could be accepted as worthy of an eternal reward.

Quite obviously, Biel was placing much of the onus for salvation on the shoulders of the individual sinner and implying that God was under an obligation to reward the sinner with justifying grace. In their critics' eyes, this notion sounded all too much like ancient Pelagianism, or semi-Pelagianism. Not surprisingly, critics raised vigorous objections to this view of salvation, for in their view, it failed to acknowledge how deeply humanity was damaged by the Fall, how ruinous to the soul Adam's sin was, and how little good humanity could actually do to achieve its own salvation.

Worst of all, it placed far too little emphasis on the free grace bestowed on the helpless sinner by a sovereign God. At no time, Biel's critics charged, could the sinner ever "merit" or deserve God's favor. The Augustinian Gregory of Rimini (d. 1358) was one who took a position involving these key elements. Biel and his critics responded to this charge, but they failed to persuade their most severe critics, especially those in the Augustinian order, including the observant German Augustinian, Martin Luther. From 1516, as is well known, Luther rejected this doctrine as in essence a Pelagian perversion of the gospel based on an unrealistic and unbiblical view of human capacity after the Fall and the absolute need of the human will of unmerited divine grace to achieve justification.

There is some reason to believe that northerners in Germany found this theology and the pastoral practice on which it was based, which urged the sinner to "do more," to be more unsatisfying than in the Latinate regions of Europe and in England. Be that as it may, it is clear that Luther spoke for many northerners in his anxiety at not knowing how many masses, how many confessions, how many prayers, novenas, pilgrimages, and pious actions were sufficient for salvation. How could one know? Many scholars have observed that in Germany in the long decades before the Reformation there was an intensification of pious practice. Some have called it among the most "churchly minded and devout periods of the Middle Ages."

The question is how to interpret these data. Medieval Christians and modern scholars have both interpreted them very differently. A medieval cleric might have seen this intensification of pious practices as an encouraging and cheering sign: the church's long effort to "Christianize" the populace was finally reaching fruition. Its attempts to internalize norms of conscience in the confessional stall were finally bearing fruit. Yet the experience of Luther and the many who responded to his protest suggests that the medieval church was making piety, for others, too burdensome psychologically. No matter how much one confessed, it was impossible to say if one was in a state of grace and justified in the eyes of God. Far from offering relief, the salvific instrumentalities of the late-medieval church could have encouraged hypersensitivity and doubt. In the end, what one group of Christians could feel as consolation, another could feel as anxiety-causing torment and, finally, un-Christian. When Christians split over this issue—on how they might be saved—when the same set of Christian practices and pastoral pieties could generate diametrically opposite emotional and religious responses; when one Christian, emerging from the confessional, could feel serene relief and another near-immediate doubt, the Christian Middle Ages can be said to have come to an end. It was profound disagreement over the issue of the media and mechanism of salvation, then, that did much to sunder the religious unity of the medieval Western church.

Chronology

107: Ignatius martyred in Rome

112: Christians tortured and persecuted by Pliny, governor of Bithynia-Pontus

144: Marcion excommunicated

155: Polycarp martyred in Smyrna

165: Justin martyred

177: Christians persecuted in Gaul; Montanus excommunicated

225: Death of Tertullian

254: Death of Origen

303: Great Persecution under Diocletian begins

313: Constantine issues the Edict of Milan, legalizing Christianity and ending the Great Persecution

ca. 324: Eusebius of Caesarea composes *Historia Ecclesiastica*

325: Council of Nicaea; Arianism declared heretical

ca. 341: Ulfilas converts to Arianism and launches preaching mission to Goths

356: Death of Antony

ca. 360: Athanasius composes *Life* of Antony

ca. 361: Martin of Tours establishes first monastery in Gaul

374: Ambrose becomes bishop of Milan

380: Edict of Thessalonica establishes Christianity as the official religion of the Roman Empire

382: Jerome composes Vulgate Bible

387: Augustine baptized by Ambrose

395: Augustine becomes bishop of Hippo

440–461: Reign of Pope Leo I

451: Council of Chalcedon

476: Romulus Augustulus, the last Roman emperor in the West, is deposed by Odoacer

496: Clovis and the Franks convert to Catholicism

ca. 524: Boethius publishes the *Consolation of Philosophy*

535–554: Gothic wars launched by Justinian to reclaim Italy from the Goths

ca. 550: Benedict composes his *Rule*

589: King Reccared I and the Visigoths convert to Christianity

590–604: Reign of Pope St. Gregory I the Great

597: Pope Gregory I sends Augustine to England to convert the Anglo-Saxons

601: King Ethelbert and the Anglo-Saxons convert to Christianity

632: Death of Muhammad

664: Synod of Whitby

711–716: Muslims conquer Visigothic Catholic kingdom of Spain

726–787: Iconoclastic controversy

731: Bede produces his *Ecclesiastical History*

732: Charles Martel defeats Muslim invaders at Tours

754: Pope Stephen travels to France to anoint Pepin king of the Franks

754: Boniface martyred at Frisia

782–796: Alcuin heads palace school at Aachen

800: Pope Leo III crowns Charlemagne emperor

909: Cluny monastery founded by William I, duke of Aquitaine

1012: Burchard of Worms compiles the *Decretum*

1012: Romuald of Ravenna founds the Camaldolese

1049–1054: Henry III appoints Leo IX pope. Leo invites prominent ecclesial reformers such as Humbert of Moyenmoutier, Hildebrand, and Peter Damian to join him as cardinals at Rome

1054: Great Schism occurs between Latin and Greek churches after Cardinal Humbert, the papal legate, and Michael Cerularius, the patriarch of Constantinople, excommunicate one another

1059: Synod of Rome under Nicholas II issues papal election decree

1075: Investiture controversy begins

1077: Henry IV flees to Countess Matilda's castle at Canossa, where he receives absolution from Gregory VII

ca. 1080: Hospital of Knights of St. John (Hospitallers) founded

1084: Bruno founds the Carthusian Order at La Grande Chartreuse

1085: Gregory VII dies in exile

1095: Urban II calls the First Crusade

1098: Abbot Robert of Molesme founds the Cistercian Order at Cîteaux

1099: Jerusalem falls to the Crusaders

1100: Abbey of Fontevrault founded by Robert of Abrissel

1108: William of Champeaux founds Abbey of St. Victor in Paris

1115: Bernard becomes abbot of Clairvaux

1120: Norbert of Xanten founds the Premonstratensian Order at Prémontré

1122: Concordat of Worms brings investiture controversy to a close

1128: Knights Templar approved at Council of Troyes

ca. 1130: Gilbert of Sempringham founds the Gilbertine Order

1142: Death of Peter Abelard

1145–1147: Bernard of Clairvaux preaches Second Crusade

1147: Hildegard establishes convent at Rupertsberg, near Bingen

1167: Cathar leader Nicetas preaches in Italy and southern France

1170: Thomas Becket martyred at Canterbury

1179: Alexander III convenes Third Lateran Council; forbids Waldes and his followers to preach without first obtaining episcopal approval

1179: Death of Hildegard of Bingen

1182 or 1183: Waldes excommunicated and expelled from Lyons after disobeying order not to preach there

1184: Lucius III issues *Ad Abolendam,* declaring the Cathars and Waldensians to be heretical

1187: Saladin recaptures Jerusalem from crusaders

1189–1192: Third Crusade

1198–1216: Reign of Pope Innocent III

1198: Innocent III determines that women are no longer to be admitted to the Premonstratensian Order

1204: Fourth Crusade; Crusaders sack Constantinople

1208: While attending mass at the church at the Portiuncula, Francis hears the gospel text of Matthew 10:7–14 and is inspired to adopt a life of apostolic poverty

1209: Innocent III launches the Albigensian Crusade against Cathar heretics and their protectors in southern France

1215: Innocent III presides over the Fourth Lateran Council

1215: Dominic launches anti-heretical preaching mission in Toulouse

1217: Honorius III approves the Order of Friars Preachers

1219–1221: Fifth Crusade

1219: Francis preaches at the court of the Ayyubid sultan al-Kamil in Egypt

ca. 1220: Cardinal Hugolino (later Pope Gregory IX) becomes protector of the Franciscan Order

1223: Francis composes the *Regula Bullata,* which is approved by Pope Honorius III

1227–1241: Reign of Pope Gregory IX

1230: Gregory IX issues *Quo Elongati,* which declares Francis's *Testimony* not binding on the Franciscan Order

1243: First ritual murder allegation in Germany leveled against Jews in Berlin

1245: Prebayon becomes first women's house to be admitted to the Carthusian Order

1247: Innocent IV declares the Talmud heretical

1250: Mechtild of Magdeburg begins to compose her works in the vernacular

1252: Innocent IV issues *Ad Extirpanda,* permitting inquisitors to use torture to extract confessions from heretics

1260: General chapter at Narbonne makes *usus pauper* normative for Franciscan Order

ca. 1265: Thomas Aquinas begins writing *Summa Theologiae*

1291: Crusader stronghold of Acre falls to Muslim forces

1302: *Unam Sanctam* issued by Boniface VIII

1303: Boniface VIII dies shortly after being arrested at Anagni by the forces of William of Nogaret

1307: Bernard Gui becomes inquisitor general in Toulouse

1309: Clement V moves the papacy from Rome to Avignon

1312: Clement V suppresses Knights Templar

1318: Four Spiritual Franciscans are burned at the stake

1323: Pope John XXII issues *Cum inter nonnullos,* which condemns as heretical the idea that Jesus and his apostles owned nothing and shared everything in common

1328: Death of Meister Eckhart

1348–1349: The Black Death

1349: Bridget of Sweden travels to Rome

1374: King Edward III grants Wyclif the parish of Lutterworth

1377: Gregory XI returns the papacy to Rome from Avignon

1378–1417: The Great Schism

1382: William of Courtenay, archbishop of Canterbury, condemns twenty-four of Wyclif's propositions

1414–1418: Council of Constance

1415: Jan Hus condemned as a heretic by the Council of Constance and burned at the stake

1439: *Laetentur Coeli* issued by Eugenius IV

1453: Fall of Constantinople to Ottoman Turks

1473: Catherine of Genoa converts to a life of asceticism, penance, and contemplation

1478: Queen Isabella and King Ferdinand launch the Spanish Inquisition

1492: End of the Reconquista; Ferdinand and Isabella expel all Jews from Spain

1498: Savonarola executed

1514–1517: Polyglot Bible published by Ximénez

Notes

This is a book for beginners. Therefore, I have kept references and suggestions for further reading to a minimum. I have referred only to secondary sources in English, with several exceptions. Where possible, I have indicated primary sources that can be accessed without cost and in English translation on Paul Halsall's Internet Medieval Sourcebook or other reliable online sources.

Throughout the notes, the abbreviation *PL* is used for *Patrologiae cursus completus, Series Latina*, Migne, 1844–64.

Preface

See R. W. Southern, *Western Society and the Church in the Middle Ages* (London: Penguin, 1970); Pelican History of the Church, vol. 2. On the identification of church and society, Southern remarks, "The identification of the church with the whole of organized society is the fundamental feature which distinguishes the Middle Ages from earlier and later periods of history" (*Western Society and the Church in the Middle Ages,* p. 16; see also pp. 17–18 and 20–21). See Robert Bartlett, *The Making of Europe: Conquest, Colonization and Cultural Change, 950–1350* (Princeton, NJ: Princeton University Press, 1993). See R. I. Moore, *The Formation of a Persecuting Society: Authority and Deviance in Western Europe, 950–1250,* 2nd ed. (Malden, MA: Blackwell, 2007). Caroline Bynum's contributions to the study of women in the Middle Ages are numerous. See her *Holy Feast and Holy Fast: The Religious Significance of Food to Medieval Women* (Berkeley: University of California Press, 1987). See Bernard McGinn's comprehensive history of mysticism, *The Presence of God: A History of Western Christian Mysticism* (New York: Crossroad, 1991–), of which five volumes of a projected seven-volume history are now published. McGinn's *Apocalyptic Spirituality* (New York: Paulist, 1979) is a good introduction with valuable translations of key texts. For a good example of how traditional documents can be used under the influence of the "cultural turn," see Miri Rubin, *Corpus Christi: The Eucharist in Late Medieval Culture* (Cambridge and New York: Cambridge University Press, 1991).

Chapter 1: Pivotal Moments in Early Christianity

For the Bauer thesis on orthodoxy and heresy, see Walter Bauer, *Orthodoxy and Heresy in Earliest Christianity* (Mifflintown, PA: Sigler Press, 1996); translated by a team from the Philadelphia Seminar on Christian Origins and edited by Robert A. Kraft and Gerhard Krodel. For a fine brief introduction to Gnosticism, see Christoph Markschies, *Gnosis: An Introduction* (London and New York: T and T Clark, 2003). Written sources from Gnostic teachers can be found in Bentley Layton, trans. and ed., *The Gnostic Scriptures* (Garden City, NY: Doubleday, 1987). This volume by Layton includes valuable annotations and introductions to difficult texts. Theodotus's remarks on the essence of Gnosticism are preserved only by Clement of Alexandria (ca. 150–215) in his *Excerpts from Theodotus,* found at http://www.gnosis.org/library/excr.htm. On Marcion, see Edwin Cyril Blackman, *Marcion and His Influence* (New York: AMS Press, 1978). On the Montanist movement, see Ronald E. Heine, *The Montanist Oracles and Testimonia* (Macon, GA: Mercer University Press, 1989), Patristic Monograph Series 14, which contains some interesting primary documents. On the development of the New Testament biblical canon, see Bruce M. Metzger, *The Canon of the New Testament: Its Origin, Development and Significance* (Oxford: Oxford University Press, 1987). The Roman creed is accessible at http://www.vatican.va/archive/ccc_css/archive/catechism/credo.htm. See an interesting juxtaposition of the Nicene Creed at this site. On the development of the early office of bishop, see W. Telfer, *The Office of a Bishop* (London: Darton, Longman and Todd, 1962); for interesting patristic reflections on the office, see Agnes Cunningham, *The Bishop in the Church: Patristic Texts on the Role of the Episkopos* (Wilmington: Glazier, 1985). An extensive treatment of Roman persecution of the Christians can be found in W. H. C. Frend, *Martyrdom and Persecution in the Early Church* (Garden City, NY: Doubleday, 1964). For Eusebius on Constantine, see Eusebius, *Ecclesiastical History* and *In Praise of Constantine,* both available in many fine editions. See also the study by T. D. Barnes, *Constantine and Eusebius* (Cambridge, MA: Harvard University Press, 1981). For an extensive treatment of the Arian controversy and Nicaea, as well as the long dispute over the Christian doctrine of God, see R. P. C. Hanson's magisterial study, *The Search for the Christian Doctrine of God: The Arian Controversy 318–381* (Edinburgh: T and T Clark, 1988). The best introduction in English to ancient Christian monasticism is D. J. Chitty, *The Desert a City: An Introduction to the Study of Egyptian and Palestinian Monasticism under the Christian Empire* (Oxford: Blackwell, 1966). For a superb study of the Christological controversy, see J. A. McGuckin, *Cyril of Alexandria: The Christological Controversy: Its History, Theology and Texts* (Leiden: Brill, 1994). Peter Brown, *Augustine of Hippo* (Berkeley: University of California Press, 2000), is a classic biography and study. Markus, *The End of Ancient Christianity,* was published by Cambridge University Press, 1990.

Chapter 2: Beginnings: The Conversion of the West and the Emergence of Celtic Christianity

For the quote from Gibbon on the barbarians, see Edward Gibbon, *The History of the Decline and Fall of the Roman Empire* (London: Strand, 1837), p. 612. For Pirenne's famous comments on the relationship between the rise of Islam and the Carolingian dynasty, see Henri Pirenne, *Medieval Cities* (Princeton, NJ: Princeton University Press, 1969), p. 27. The thesis is fully developed in Pirenne, *Mohammed and Charlemagne* (Totawa, NJ: Barnes and Noble Books, 1980). On Frankish Christianity, see J. M. Wallace-Hadrill, *The Frankish Church* (Oxford: Oxford University Press, 1983). On Clothilda's attempt to convert Clovis, see http://www.fordham.edu/halsall/source/gregory-clovisconv.asp#n30. For Clovis's conversion, see http://www.fordham.edu/halsall/source/gregory-clovisconv.asp#n31. The plea from the Irish to "come again and walk among us" can be found in *Confession* 23 at http://www.confessio.ie/etexts/confessio_english#01. Patrick's declaration that he had been "established as bishop" by God can be found in his *Letter to Coroticus* 1 at http://www.confessio.ie/etexts/epistola_english. For a brilliant introduction to early Irish society and the conversion of the Irish, see Kathleen Hughes, *The Church in Early Irish Society* (London: Methuen, 1966). For Celtic Christianity, see John T. McNeill, *The Celtic Churches: A History, A.D. 200 to 1200* (Chicago: University of Chicago Press, 1974). For a classic study of the Near Eastern "holy man," see Peter Brown, "The Rise and Function of the Holy Man in Late Antiquity," *Journal of Roman Studies* 61 (1971): 80–101. The penitential manual from which an excerpt is cited can be found in English translation at http://www.thehistoryblog.com/archives/4696.

Chapter 3: Foundations: Monasticism, the Papacy, and Mission

For a superb introduction to Benedict and to the practice of monasticism in Benedictine cloisters, see C. H. Lawrence, *Medieval Monasticism: Forms of Religious Life in Western Europe in the Middle Ages* (London and New York: Longman, 1984), ch. 2, and R. W. Southern, *Western Society and the Church in the Middle Ages* (London: Penguin, 1970), pp. 217–239. For a very fine edition of Benedict's *Rule*, see T. Fry, ed., *RB 1980: The Rule of St. Benedict in Latin and English* (Collegeville, MN: Liturgical Press, 1981). This edition is distinguished by the fullness and erudition of its voluminous notes. The same editor and publisher had come out with an English translation without notes. See T. Fry, ed., *RB 1980: The Rule of St. Benedict in English* (Collegeville, MN: Liturgical Press, 1982). This text, fundamental to an understanding of early-medieval Christianity, is available in Latin online in the Library of Latin Texts. For Gregory's reference to Benedict as "the finest teacher of the ascetical life" in his *Commentary on 1 Kings* 4.4, see J. Chamberlin, ed., *The Rule of St. Benedict* (Toronto: Pontifical Institute of Mediaeval Studies, 1982); Toronto Medieval Texts. The description of the monastery as a "school for the Lord's service" establishing "nothing harsh, nothing burdensome" can be found in Fry, *RB 1980: The Rule of St. Benedict in English,* p. 18. For Orderic, see *The Ecclesiastical History of Orderic Vitalis,* 6 vols., edited and translated with introduction and notes by Marjorie Chibnall (Oxford: Clarendon Press, 1969–1980), 1:xiv. On Gregory, see R. A. Markus, *Gregory the Great and His World* (Cambridge and New York: Cambridge University Press, 1997), and Jeffrey Richards, *Consul of God: The Life and Times of Gregory the Great* (London and Boston: Routledge and Kegan Paul, 1980). The quote from Pope Pelagius II is from a letter to his legate in Liguria. For Gregory's letter indicating he had heard of the earnest desire of the English to be converted, see P. H. Blair, *The World of Bede* (Cambridge: Cambridge University Press,

1990), p. 47. The "angels, not Angles" comment attributed to Gregory are words put in his mouth by Bede in *A History of the English Church and People* (Harmondsworth: Penguin, 1968), book 2, section 1. Bede's autobiographical remarks in the appendix to his *Ecclesiastical History* can be found at http://www.sacred-texts.com/chr/bede/hist141.htm.

Chapter 4: Holy Empire? Christianity, Charlemagne, and the Carolingians

Pepin III is not to be confused with Pepin I (d. 640), mayor of the palace, or his grandson, Pepin II of Herstal (655–714). For the major primary source on the Frankish-papal alliance, see http://www.fordham.edu/halsall/source/lorsch1.asp. See also Bernard Scholz, *Carolingian Chronicles* (Ann Arbor, MI: University of Michigan Press, 1970), in particular the *Royal Frankish Annals* for the year 749. The account given in these annals may not have been entirely reliable, but it soon grew into an authoritative account and was accepted as representing the origin of the Frankish-papal alliance. On Charlemagne's lives, see Einhard, *Life of Charlemagne* in Lewis Thorpe, ed., *Einhard and Notker the Stammerer: Two Lives of Charlemagne* (London: Penguin, 2008), ch. 26. On early-medieval civilization as "liturgical," see André Vauchez, *The Spirituality of the Medieval West: From the Eighth to the Twelfth Century* (Kalamazoo, MI: Cistercian Publications, 1993), pp. 15–19. On these incidents from Einhard, see Einhard, *Life of Charlemagne*, chs. 27–28. Charlemagne's views on the relationship of secular and sacred can be found in *Letters of Charles to Pope Leo*, in Monumenta Germaniae Historica, *Letter* 4 of *Epistolae Aevi Karolini*, vol. 2 (Berlin: Apvd Weidmannos, 1985), pp. 119–120. Alcuin's sympathetic remarks on the destruction of Lindisfarne are expressed in his *Letter* 24 in Stephen Allott, *Alcuin of York: His Life and Letters* (York: William Sessions, 1974), p. 31.

Chapter 5: Parochial Life and the Proprietary Church, ca. 700–1050

Much work done on the proprietary church has been in German. For a history of the proprietary church in English, see Susan Wood, *The Proprietary Church in the Medieval West* (Oxford and New York: Oxford University Press, 2006). For the priesthood in the Middle Ages, there is no work in English that approaches the invaluable and exhaustive *Le Pontifical romain au Moyen-Age*, by Michel Andrieu (Vatican City: Biblioteca Apostolica Vaticana, 1938–1941), 4 vols. For an excellent though naturally much shorter treatment in English, see Kenan B. Osborne, *Priesthood: A History of Ordained Ministry in the Roman Catholic Church* (New York: Paulist, 1988), chs. 6–7. Readers interested in Aelfric's sermons should consult Benjamin Thorpe, ed., *The Homilies of the Anglo-Saxon Church*, 2 vols. (London: Printed for the Ælfric Society, 1844–1846). For an early expression of medieval culture as "folkloric," see Jacques LeGoff, *Medieval Civilization, 400–1500* (Oxford: Blackwell, 1964). For the argument that Europe was not Christianized until the early modern era, see Jean Delumeau, *Catholicism between Luther and Voltaire: A New View of the Counter-Reformation* (London: Burns and Oates, 1977). The remark on the medieval church functioning as a reservoir of magical power can be found in Keith Thomas, *Religion and the Decline of Magic* (New York: Oxford

University Press, 1971), p. 45. For the odd cosmos of a sixteenth-century miller, see Carlo Ginzburg, *The Cheese and the Worms: The Cosmos of a Sixteenth-Century Miller* (Baltimore: Johns Hopkins University Press, 1992). The very oddity of this miller's cosmological views makes it a questionable work on which to base broader conclusions, however brilliantly the author evokes his subject's world. John Van Engen's article, a vigorous response to the French folklorists, is "The Christian Middle Ages as an Historiographical Problem," *American Historical Review* 91 (1986): 519–552. The Guinefort-as-Holy-Greyhound legend is analyzed in Jean-Claude Schmitt, *The Holy Greyhound: Guinefort, Healer of Children since the Thirteenth Century* (Cambridge: Cambridge University Press, 1983). It is Delumeau who argued that the veneration of Guinefort was a "species of paganism."

Chapter 6: Christians and Jews, ca. 400–1100

See the account in R. L. Wilken, *Christianity: The First Thousand Years* (New Haven and London: Yale University Press, 2012). For Jerome, See J. N. D. Kelly, *Jerome: His Life, Writings, and Controversies* (New York: Harper and Row, 1975). On Chrysostom and his anti-Judaizing sermons, see R. L. Wilken, *John Chrysostom and the Jews* (Berkeley: University of California Press, 1983), p. 159. This discussion of church councils is based on canons found in Harl Hefele, *A History of the Christian Councils from the Original Documents,* 5 vols. (Edinburgh: T and T Clark, 1871–1896). For secondary discussion, see Marcus Simon, *Verus Israel: A Study of the Relations between Christians and Jews in the Roman Empire, AD 135–425* (London: Littman, 1996). See Amnon Linder, *The Jews in Roman Imperial Legislation* (Detroit: Wayne State University Press, 1987). An indispensable study of Jewish policy in the Visigothic, Ostrogothic, and Frankish kingdoms, on which many of the following pages are largely based, is Bernard Bachrach, *Early Medieval Jewish Policy in Western Europe* (Minneapolis: University of Minnesota Press, 1977). These remarks from Bachrach can be found in *Early Medieval Jewish Policy,* pp. 5, 6, 36. On the possibility that anti-Judaism was racial, see Bat-Sheva Albert, "Christians and Jews," in *The Cambridge History of Christianity: Early Medieval Christianities c. 600 –c. 1100,* edited by Thomas F. X. Noble and Julia M. H. Smith (Cambridge: Cambridge University Press, 2008), p. 170. For Gregory and the Jews, see ch. 2 of Jeremy Cohen, *Living Letters of the Law: Ideas of the Jew in Medieval Christianity* (Berkeley: University of California Press, 1999); for Agobard, see ch. 4.

Chapter 7: Islam and Western Christianity, ca. 600–1450

A magisterial overview can be found in Sidney H. Griffith, *The Church in the Shadow of the Mosque* (Princeton, NJ: Princeton University Press, 2008). On the ideological origins of the crusade, see Carl Erdmann's classic study, *The Origin of the Idea of Crusade* (Princeton, NJ: Princeton University Press, 1977). For a shorter but very fine study, see Jonathan Riley Smith, *The Crusades: A Short History* (London: Athlone, 1987). Jonathan Riley Smith, *The First Crusade and the Idea of Crusading* (Philadelphia: University of Pennsylvania Press, 1977), is a study of the amazing obstacles and wonders encountered by the first crusaders. On Islam in European thought, see John V. Tolan, *Saracens: Islam in the Medieval European Imagination* (New York: Columbia University Press, 2002). For Francis's encounter with the sultan, see John V. Tolan, *St. Francis and the Sultan: The Curious History of a Christian-Muslim Encounter* (Oxford: Oxford University Press, 2009).

Chapter 8: *Libertas Ecclesiae*: The Age of Reform, ca. 1050–1125

The foundation charter for the house of Cluny can be found in Brian Tierney, *The Crisis of Church and State, 1050 to 1300* (Englewood Cliffs, NJ: Prentice-Hall, 1964), p. 28. The remark on the early-medieval period as being of "levitical" quality can be found in André Vauchez, *The Spirituality of the Medieval West: From the Eighth to the Twelfth Century* (Kalamazoo, MI: Cistercian Publications, 1993), p. 13. The remark on Leo IX's papacy can be found in Colin Morris, *The Papal Monarchy: The Western Church from 1050 to 1250* (Oxford: Oxford University Press, 1989), p. 87. The contemporary who dubbed Leo IX *papa mirabilis* was John of Fécamp, *Epistola ad S. Leonem 9*, in *PL* 143:797. The complaints about simony can be found in Humbert, *Adversus Simoniacos*, 2.36 and 3.7, and Peter Damian, *Vita Romualdi* 35 (*PL* 144:896). Damian's stigmatizing of clerical marriage as a heresy can be found at *De Celibatu Sacerdotum* 3 (*PL* 145:385). The contemporary who compared his denunciations to the roars of God was Udalric of Reims (*PL* 150:1547). The remark by Geoffrey Barraclough on the transformation of the reforming ethos as it reached the Mediterranean can be found in his book *The Medieval Papacy* (New York: Norton, 1968), p. 75. Burchard's *Decretum* has not been translated into English. But see Greta Austin, *Shaping Church Law around the Year 1000: The Decretum of Burchard of Worms* (Farnham, Surrey, and Burlington, VT: Ashgate, 2009). For the *Collection in 74 Titles*, see Kenneth Pennington's valuable translation at http://faculty.cua.edu/pennington/canon%20law/gregorianreform/74titles.htm. Quotes from Humbert's writings (which he takes to be authentic, obviously) occur in Tierney, *The Crisis of Church and State*, pp. 40–42. Humbert's complaints about the violation of the ancient canons can be found in *Adversus Simoniacos* 3.6. See also Tierney, *The Crisis of Church and State*, pp. 40–42. For the decree of 1059, see Tierney, *The Crisis of Church and State*, p. 42. The comment on Gregory VII's character can be found in Barraclough, *The Medieval Papacy*, p. 85. For the "Dictates of the Pope," see Tierney, *The Crisis of Church and State*, pp. 49–50. The remark that they were "emergency decrees" for the church in times of crisis can be found in Morris, *The Papal Monarchy*, p. 112. Gelasius's dualistic understanding of the powers can be found in Tierney, *The Crisis of Church and State*, p. 13. Henry's letter to the pope, calling Gregory a "false monk," can be found in Tierney, *The Crisis of Church and State*, pp. 58–59. Gregory's 1076 letter of deposition can be found in Tierney, *The Crisis of Church and State*, p. 61; Henry's riposte can be found on pp. 61–62. For Ivo of Chartres's view, see Tierney, *The Crisis of Church and State*, p. 82. Paschal's radical solution is expressed in Tierney, *The Crisis of Church and State*, p. 89. The Concordat of Worms is translated in Norton Downs, *Basic Documents in Medieval History* (Princeton, NJ: Van Nostrand, 1959), pp. 69–71.

Chapter 9: *Religiosi*: Monks and Nuns in the Monastic Centuries

For a stimulating study of five medieval anchoresses, see Anneke B. Mulder-Bakker, *Lives of the Anchoresses: The Rise of the Urban Recluse in Medieval Europe* (Philadelphia: University of Pennsylvania Press, 2005). For the anonymous rule, see Robert Hasenfratz, ed., *The Ancrene Wisse* (Kalamazoo, MI: Medieval Institute Publications, 2000). For a good selection of Peter Damian's writings, see Patricia McNulty, *St. Peter Damian: Selected Writings on the Spiritual Life* (New York: Harper and Brothers, 1959). For the quote from Guigo about the necessity of solitude, see *Guigonis I Consuetudines, PL* 153:703. Citation from Guigo found in C. H. Lawrence, *Medieval Monasticism: Forms of Religious Life in Western Europe in the Middle Ages* (London and New York: Longman, 1984), p. 135. Bruno's comment about the relative paucity of sons of contemplation can be found in *PL* 152:421. Guigo's comments about the fearful charms and deception of women can be found in *Consuetudines* 21.1. For Robert of Abrissel and his movement, see Jacqueline Smith, "Robert of Abrissel, Procurator Mulierum," in *Medieval Women*, edited by Derek Baker (Oxford: Blackwell, 1981), pp. 175–184; Studies in Church History, Subsidia 1. For the Gilbertines, see Brian Golding, *Gilbert of Sempringham and the Gilbertine Order, c. 1130–c. 1300* (Oxford: Clarendon Press; New York: Oxford University Press, 1995). For an analysis of the nun of Watton scandal, see Giles Constable, "Aelred of Rievaulx and the Nun of Watton: An Episode in the Early History of the Gilbertine Order," in *Medieval Women,* ed. Derek Baker. For the Martha-Mary remark, see R. W. Southern, *Western Society and the Church in the Middle Ages* (London: Penguin, 1970), p. 244. Southern's remark on the prolific observance of Augustine's *Rule* can be found on p. 249 of the same volume. His contrast between broad and severe schools of canonical life can be found on pp. 242–243. The comment on prevailing sentiment about unmarried women can be found in Lawrence, *Medieval Monasticism,* pp. 179–180. Early documents related to the founding of Cîteaux can be found in Louis J. Lekai, *The Cistercians: Ideals and Reality* (Kent, OH: Kent State University Press), pp. 11–32. Bernard's remark about the Cistercians as restorers of lost religion can be found in his *Letters, PL* 182:414.

Chapter 10: Heresy and Its Repression

The quote on the Gregorian movement being the source of heretical ideas comes from Colin Morris, *The Papal Monarchy: The Western Church from 1050 to 1250* (Oxford: Oxford University Press, 1989), p. 340. Two excellent sourcebooks with expert commentary for this material are R. I. Moore, *The Birth of Popular Heresy* (Toronto: University of Toronto Press in association with the Medieval Academy of America, 1995), and Edward Peters, *Heresy and Authority in Medieval Europe: Documents in Translation* (Philadelphia: University of Pennsylvania Press, 1980). Caesarius of Heisterbach's remark can be found at Caesarius of Heisterbach, *Dialogus miraculorum,* 2 vols., edited by J. Strange (Cologne: Heberle), 1, 5.21, 301–302. Material on Henry of Lausanne is based on documents found in Moore, *The Birth of Popular Heresy,* pp. 33–46; that on the Petrobrusians comes from pp. 61–62. The excerpt from the Assize of Clarendon can be found in G. B. Adams and H. M. Stephens, *Select Documents of English Constitutional History* (New York: Macmillan, 1920), p. 555. The ordinances were produced at the royal hunting lodge of Clarendon with many English lords present. The Assize was an attempt to improve criminal procedure, and one of its triumphs was the establishment of the jury system. My scattered remarks on the relationship of heresy and political authority are based on acceptance of the thesis of R. I. Moore, *The Origins of European Dissent*, 2nd ed. (Oxford: Blackwell, 1985; 1st ed., 1977). The book whose title suggests a historical continuity between the ancient Manichees and medieval Cathars was written by the great British historian Sir Steven Runciman, *The Medieval Manichee: A Study of the Christian Dualist Heresy* (Cambridge: Cambridge University Press, 1947). For a new, more reliable account, see Malcolm D. Lambert, *The Cathars* (Oxford and Malden, MA: Blackwell, 1998). Some of my analysis of Bogomil belief is based on "The Sermon of Cosmas the Priest against Bogomilism," in Peters, *Heresy and Authority*, p. 109. The three eleventh-century reports on western European groups that resembled Bogomil belief and practice come from Moore, *The Birth of Popular Heresy*, pp. 10–18. Eckbert's identification of heretics as "Cathars" and their burning in Cologne can be found on pp. 88–89 of this volume; the source for Niketas's debate on radical dualism can be found on p. 122. References to Cathar practice of the *consolamentum*, abstinence, and different "orders" are based on Moore, *The Birth of Popular Heresy*, pp. 133–134, 150, and 154. The sources for Waldes's life, late as they are—they were written, perhaps in 1218, decades after his conversion—are very likely a mix of pious fiction and fact, not easy to distinguish. For discussion of some of the problems with these sources, see Euan K. Cameron, *Waldenses: Rejections of Holy Church in Medieval Europe* (Oxford and Malden, MA: Blackwell, 2000), p. 336, and Malcolm D. Lambert, *Medieval Heresy: Popular Movements from the Gregorian Reform to the Reformation*, 2nd ed. (Cambridge, MA: B. Blackwell, 1992), p. 449. The latter volume is also an excellent survey of medieval heretical movements and figures from the eleventh to the sixteenth centuries. Étienne de Bourbon's report on the Waldensians and vernacular scripture, and that of the Passau Anonymous, can be found in Peters, *Heresy and Authority*, pp. 144, 151. For an account of the conversion of Waldes, see "The Conversion of Valdes and Its Consequences," in Moore, *The Birth of Popular Heresy*, p. 112. For Pope Lucius III's decretal *Ad Abolendam*, see Peters, *Heresy and Authority*, pp. 170–171. Some of my remarks on the Cathars depend on Raynier Sacconi's contemporary observations, found in Peters, *Heresy and Authority*, pp. 132–135. As Moore concludes in *The Origins of European Dissent*, 2nd ed., p. 282: "In seeking a correlation between the incidence of heresy and other phenomena one alone holds. It appeared sometimes among the poor, sometimes among the rich, sometimes in the backward regions if more often in the progressive, sometimes where the reform of the church was advanced and sometimes where it was retarded. It *always* flourished where political authority was diffused, and never where its concentration was greatest" (emphasis mine). The account of bishops being appointed to serve as inquisitors can be found in a canon from the Council of Toulouse (1229) in Peters, *Heresy and Authority*, p. 194. Some of my remarks on the formula for interrogation of heretics come from *A Manual for Inquisitors at Carcassonne* (1248–1249), found in Peters, *Heresy and Authority*, pp. 201–202. A superb short introduction is Bernard Hamilton, *The Medieval Inquisition* (London: E. Arnold, 1981).

Chapter 11: Dominicans and Their Sisters

A superb introduction to the origins and intellectual, religious, and cultural influence of the friars on western European society in the Middle Ages is C. H. Lawrence,

The Friars: The Impact of the Early Mendicant Movement on Western Society (New York: Longman's, 1994). A very fine introduction to the history of the Dominican Order is W. A. Hinnebusch, *The History of the Dominican Order*, 2 vols. (Staten Island, NY: Alba House, 1966). The early Dominican constitutions, including Dominic's distinct contributions, are discussed in vol. 1, pp. 44–47. A translation of the prologue to the original constitutions, in which the friars preachers dedicated themselves principally to being useful to the souls of neighbors, can be found at the excellent and reliable collection of Dominican documents at http://www.domcentral.org/trad/domdocs/0011.htm. Humbert's observations on the city's needs for the friars occurs in his book on the education of preachers, *Humberti de Romanis de Eruditione Praedicatorum II: Maxima Biblioteca Veterum Patrum,* edited by M. de la Bigne (Lyons, 1677), p. 491. The remark by Gerard of Fracheto concerning Jordan's tireless efforts to recruit students can be found in *Fratris Gerardi de Fracheto O.P. Vitae fratrum Ordinis Praedicatorum* (Louvain: E. Charpentier and J. Schoonjans, 1896), p. 529. Humbert's *Treatise on the Education of Preachers* can be found in English in *Early Dominicans: Selected Writings,* edited with an introduction by Simon Tugwell (New York: Paulist, 1982), section 3, pp. 179–370; Classics of Western Spirituality. This excellent volume of primary texts ably translated into English includes not only sermons and prayers by Dominic, but also texts on his life and canonization. It also has excellent translations of other thirteenth-century Dominican writings in addition to those of Humbert, including letters and other texts from Jordan of Saxony and a very valuable section on Dominican nuns, on which my account is partly based. Studies on the relationship of clerical men and saintly women, treated often in the past two decades, have never been so well examined as in John W. Coakley, *Women, Men, and Spiritual Power: Female Saints and Their Male Collaborators* (New York: Columbia University Press, 2006).

Chapter 12: *Fraticelli*: Franciscans and Their Sisters

The "Franciscan Question" began with the publication of Paul Sabatier, *Vie de s. François d'Assise,* édition définitive (Paris: Fischbacher, 1931). For an English translation, see *Life of St. Francis of Assisi* (London: Hodder and Stoughton, 1899). Interesting as it is, the thesis of this book ought not to be swallowed whole. For an authoritative analysis of the "synoptic problem," see W. R. Farmer, *The Synoptic Problem: A Critical Analysis* (Dillsboro, NC: Western North Carolina Press, 1976). For a fine, short, and authoritative view of the historical Jesus, see Dale C. Allison, *Jesus of Nazareth: Millenarian Prophet* (Minneapolis, MN: Fortress Press, 1998). For a collection of all thirteenth- and fourteenth-century lives, see Marion Alphonse Habig, *St. Francis of Assisi: Writings and Early Biographies: English Omnibus of the Sources for the Life of St. Francis,* 4th rev. ed. (Chicago: Franciscan Herald Press, 1983). For Thomas of Celano's two lives, see Thomas of Celano and Placid Hermann, *St. Francis of Assisi: First and Second Life of St. Francis, with Selections from Treatise on the Miracles of Blessed Francis* (Chicago: Franciscan Herald Press, 1963). For Bonaventure's life, see Bonaventure, *The Soul's Journey into God; the Tree of Life; the Life of St. Francis,* edited by Ewert H. Cousins (New York: Paulist, 1978); Classics of Western Spirituality. For the *Canticle,* see *Francis and Clare: The Complete Works,* translated by Regis J. Armstrong and Ignatius Brady (New York: Paulist, 1982), pp. 37–39; Classics of Western Spirituality. Francis's so-called *Testament* can be found in the same volume, pp. 153–159. The two existing *Rules* are translated, pp. 107–145. It is worth keeping in mind, especially when considering Francis, that medieval references to leprosy likely encompassed a wide spectrum of dermatological and other diseases. For an intricate, thorough analysis of changing views of poverty within the order and reaction extramurally to them, see Malcolm Lambert, *Franciscan Poverty: The Doctrine of Absolute Poverty of Christ and the Apostles in the Franciscan Order, 1210–1323*, rev. and expanded ed. (St. Bonaventure, NY: Franciscan Institute, St. Bonaventure University, 1998). Lawrence's comment on the "peculiarly Italian" and egalitarian nature of Franciscan fraternity can be found in C. H. Lawrence, *The Friars: The Impact of the Early Mendicant Movement on Western Society* (New York: Longman's, 1994), p. 35. The remark on the position of lepers in medieval society can be found in Robert Fossier, *The Axe and the Oath: Ordinary Life in the Middle Ages,* translated by Lydia G. Cochrane (Princeton, NJ: Princeton University Press, 2010), p. 6. Francis's question, "Who are these who snatched my Order and my Brethren out of my hands?" can be found in Thomas's *Second Life,* p. 188. For a fine study of the preaching of the Dominicans and Franciscans, see D. L. D'Avray, *The Preaching of the Friars: Sermons Diffused from Paris before 1300* (Oxford and New York: Clarendon Press, 1985). Francis's quote on being unlettered and in the service of all can be found in *Francis and Clare: The Complete Works,* p. 155. For the early development of the order and Elias, see Kajetan Esser, *Origins of the Franciscan Order* (Chicago: Franciscan Herald Press, 1970), and Rosalind B. Brooke, *Early Franciscan Government: Elias to Bonaventure* (Cambridge: Cambridge University Press, 1959); Cambridge Studies in Medieval Life and Thought, New Series 7. For Joachim's thought and influence, see Bernard McGinn, *The Calabrian Abbot: Joachim of Fiore in the History of Western Thought* (New York: Macmillan, 1985), and Marjorie Reeve, *Joachim of Fiore and the Prophetic Future: A Medieval Study in Historical Thinking,* new, rev. ed. (Stroud: Sutton Publishing, 1999). A magisterial account of the history of the Spirituals is David Burr, *The Spiritual Franciscans: From Protest to Persecution in the Century after Saint Francis* (University Park: Pennsylvania State University Press, 2001). For Guglielma and her followers, see Stephen Wessley, "The Thirteenth Century Guglielmites: Salvation through Women," *Studies in Church History,* Subsidia I, pp. 289–303, and Barbara Newman, *From Virile Woman to Womanchrist: Studies in Medieval Religion and Literature* (Philadelphia: University of Pennsylvania Press, 1995), pp. 213–214; Middle Ages Series; Malcolm D. Lambert, *Medieval Heresy: Popular Movements from the Gregorian Reform to the Reformation,* 2nd ed. (Cambridge, MA: B. Blackwell, 1992), pp. 200–202; and, most recently, Marina Bendetti, *Io non sono Dio: Guglielma di Milano e i Figli dello Spirito Santo* (Milan: Biblioteca Francescana, 1998). The best recent work on the secular-mendicant controversy has been written in French. For an adequate, if slightly outdated English account, see Decima L. Douie, *The Conflict between the Seculars and the Mendicants at the University of Paris in the Thirteenth Century: A Paper Read to the Aquinas Society of London on 22nd June, 1949,* vol. 23. (London: Blackfriars, 1954). Of the number of friars at the start of the *usus pauper* controversy, one-third of these were in Italy. This probably meant that one in every thousand Italians was a Franciscan in

1250. As David Burr has said of this development, "One out of every thousand people cannot be expected to emulate Saint Francis, even in Italy." See David Burr, *Olivi and Franciscan Poverty: The Origins of the Usus Pauper Controversy* (Philadelphia: University of Pennsylvania Press, 1989), p. 4; Middle Ages Series.

Chapter 13: The Philosopher, the Fathers, and the Faith: Scholasticism and the University

The classic study of monastic learning and teaching is Jean Leclercq, *The Love of Learning and the Desire for God: A Study of Monastic Culture,* translated by Catharine Misrahi, 3rd ed. (New York: Fordham University Press, 1982). For Anselm, see R. W. Southern, *Saint Anselm: Portrait in a Landscape* (Cambridge: Cambridge University Press, 1990). For a superb brief introduction to scholastic culture, including the cathedral school, see John W. Baldwin, *The Scholastic Culture of the Middle Ages, 1000–1300* (Prospect Heights, IL: Waveland, 1971). Abelard's *History of My Misfortunes* and the letters of Abelard and Eloise can be found in *The Letters of Abelard and Eloise,* translated and edited by Betty Radice; revised by M. T. Clanchy (London and New York: Penguin Classics, 1974). A brilliant biography is M. T. Clanchy, *Abelard: A Medieval Life* (Oxford: Blackwell, 1997). For the authenticity of Heloise's letters, see the work of C. J. Mews, who has also written a fine introduction: *Abelard and Heloise* (Oxford and New York: Oxford University Press, 2005). The letter of Bernard complaining about Abelard can be found in *Sancti Bernardi Opera,* 8 vols., edited by Jean Leclercq and Jean G. Hendrix (Rome: Editiones Cistercienses), 8:270–271. For histories of the medieval university, see Hastings Rashdall, F. M. Powicke, and A. B. Emden, *The Universities of Europe in the Middle Ages* (Oxford: Clarendon Press, 1987); Gordon Leff, *Paris and Oxford Universities in the Thirteenth and Fourteenth Centuries* (Huntington, NY: Krieger, 1968); and Alan Cobban, *The Medieval Universities: Their Development and Organization* (London and New York: Methuen, 1975). A fine collection of records having to do with medieval scholarly life can be found in Lynn Thorndike, *University Records and Life in the Middle Ages* (New York: Norton, 1975), Columbia Records of Civilization 38. For a study of the origins of scholasticism and its transmission from Mesopotamia to Europe, see George Makdisi, "Baghdad, Bologna and Scholasticism," in *Centers of Learning and Location in Pre-Modern Europe and the Near East,* edited by Jan W. Drijvers and Alasdair A. MacDonald (Leiden: Brill, 1995), pp. 141–157; Brill Studies in Intellectual History 61. An in-depth study of Peter Lombard has been made by Marcia Colish, *Peter Lombard,* 2 vols. (Leiden: Brill, 1994), Brill Studies in Intellectual History. See also Philipp Rosemann, *Peter Lombard* (Oxford: Oxford University Press, 2004). For the reception of Aristotle in the West, see Michael Haren, *Medieval Thought: The Western Intellectual Tradition from Antiquity to the Thirteenth Century,* 2nd ed. (London: Macmillan, 1992). For an earlier but still extremely useful view, see F. van Steenberghen, *The Philosophical Movement of the Thirteenth Century* (Edinburgh: Nelson, 1955), which usefully complicates the tripartite scheme of "Aristotelians," "Augustinians," and "radical Averroists." The definitive life and study of Thomas is now Jean-Pierre Torrell's *Thomas Aquinas,* 2 vols. (Washington, D.C.: Catholic University of America Press, 2003).

Chapter 14: The Bid for Papal Monarchy

The quotes from Innocent III on the extent of papal authority can be found in Brian Tierney, *The Crisis of Church and State, 1050 to 1300* (Englewood Cliffs, NJ: Prentice-Hall, 1964), pp. 131–132. For a fine introduction to canon law and its revival in the eleventh and twelfth centuries, see James Brundage, *Medieval Canon Law* (London and New York: Longman, 1995). Southern's remark on western inertia and papal impotence can be found in R. W. Southern, *Western Society and the Church in the Middle Ages* (London: Penguin, 1970), p. 107. For the rapidly accelerating volume in letters produced by the papal curia, see Southern, *Western Society and the Church in the Middle Ages,* pp. 108–109. For the process by which canonization became a papal prerogative, see Eric W. Kemp, *Canonization and Authority in the Western Church* (London: Oxford University Press, 1948). For Barraclough's remarks about the disparity of the atmosphere at the papal curia and what was imagined as the apostolic life, see *The Medieval Papacy* (New York: Norton, 1968), p. 128. The classic and still valuable study of provisions is Geoffrey Barraclough, *Papal Provisions* (Oxford: Oxford University Press, 1935).

Chapter 15: To "Deepen Understanding": Means of Christianization, 1050–1250

Mary Carruthers's remark on the memorial character of medieval culture can be found in *The Book of Memory: A Study of Memory in Medieval Culture* (Cambridge and New York: Cambridge University Press, 1990), p. 13. R. N. Swanson's remarks on "passive literacy" can be found in *Religion and Devotion in Europe, c. 1215–c. 1515* (Cambridge and New York: Cambridge University Press, 1995), pp. 79–80. For the comment on the hoped for blessings of the mass, see Odo of Cambrai, *Expositio in Canonem Missae* (*PL* 160:1058A). I found this quote in Colin Morris, *The Papal Monarchy: The Western Church from 1050 to 1250* (Oxford: Oxford University Press, 1989), p. 299. The argument that Romanesque sculpture communicated an anti-heretical message has been put forward by many medieval historians of Christianity and of art. However, this argument has been forcefully challenged by, among others, Walter Cahn in "Heresy and the Interpretation of Romanesque Art," in *Romanesque and Gothic,* edited by Neil Stratford (Woodbridge, Suffolk: Boydell and Brewer, 1987), pp. 27–33. Gregory the Great's famous remark can be found in his letters, Book 11, Letter 9. The letter is widely available. See http://www.newadvent.org/fathers/360211013.htm. Morris's remark on the people being witnesses of a ritual rather than holders of a faith can be found in *The Papal Monarchy,* p. 309. R. A. Markus's remark on Christian mediocrity can be found in his chapter on Augustine's "defense of Christian mediocrity" in *The End of Ancient Christianity* (Cambridge: Cambridge University Press, 1990), ch. 4. The Lateran IV decree on annual confession and communion can be found in Heinrich Denzinger, *Enchiridion symbolorum, definitionum et declarationum,* 34th ed. (Barcinone: Herder, 1967), p. 437. Lea's remark can be found in Henry Charles Lea, *A History of Auricular Confession* (London: Lea Brothers, 1896), p. 230. The remark on the "revolution" in pastoral care can be found in Leonard E. Boyle, "The Fourth Lateran Council and Manuals of Popular Theology," in *The Popular Literature of Medieval England,* edited by Thomas J. Heffernan (Knoxville: University of Tennessee Press, 1985), pp. 30–43;

Tennessee Studies in Literature 28. For a complete translation of the decrees of Lateran IV, see http://www.fordham.edu/halsall/basis/lateran4.asp. Peter Lombard's view on the cause of marriage can be found in *Sentences* 4.27.3. Peter Damian's remark on avarice can be found in his *Letter* 1.15 (*PL* 14:234B). For a somewhat controversial treatment of the relationship between the revolution in pastoral care and the new economy, see Lester K. Little, *Religious Poverty and the Profit Economy in Medieval Europe* (Ithaca, NY: Cornell University Press, 1983).

Chapter 16: Devotion: Saints, Relics, and Pilgrimage

For a superb text of sources for the topics treated in this chapter, see Thomas Head, *Medieval Hagiography: An Anthology* (London: Routledge, 2001). See Head's many interesting essays on sanctity at http://www.the-orb.net/encyclop/religion/hagiography/hagindex.html. See also John Shinners, ed., *Medieval Popular Religion, 1000–1500: A Reader* (Ontario: Broadview, 1997). On early Christian veneration of the saints, see Peter Brown, *The Cult of the Saints* (Chicago: University of Chicago Press, 1982). An indispensable introduction to hagiographical texts is Hippolyte Delehaye, *The Legends of the Saints* (Brussels, 1905); translated by V. M. Crawford; retranslated by Donald Attwater (New York: Fordham University Press, 1962); available online at http://www.fordham.edu/halsall/basis/delehaye-legends.asp. For an authoritative discussion of many aspects of sainthood from the twelfth century to the end of the Middle Ages, see André Vauchez, *Sainthood in the Later Middle Ages* (New York: Cambridge University Press, 1997). For how English saints like Frideswide "specialized" and came to have their distinctive "clientele," see Ronald Finucane, *Miracles and Pilgrims: Popular Beliefs in Medieval England* (Totowa, NJ: Rowman and Littlefield, 1977). For a fascinating treatment of "sacred theft," see Patrick Geary, *Furta Sacra: Thefts of Relics in the Central Middle Ages* (Princeton, NJ: Princeton University Press, 1978), particularly "Handlist of Relic Thefts (ca. 800–ca. 1100)," pp. 149–156. An excellent brief introduction to pilgrimage can be found in Diana Webb, *Medieval European Pilgrimage c. 700–1500* (New York: Palgrave MacMillan, 2002). Adams's remark on Mary and Chartres can be found in *The Education of Henry Adams: An Autobiography* (New York: Houghton Mifflin, 1918), p. 388.

Chapter 17: A Lachrymose Age: Christians and Jews, 1096–1492

On Jewish martyrs, see Robert Chazan, *God, Humanity and History: The Hebrew First Crusade Narratives* (Berkeley: University of California Press, 2000), and Jonathan Riley-Smith, "Christian Violence and the Crusades," in *Religious Violence between Christians and Jews: Medieval Roots, Modern Perspectives,* edited by Anna Sapir Abulafia (Basingstoke, UK: Palgrave, 2002), pp. 3–20; also, on *kiddush ha-Shem,* see Jeremy Cohen, *Sanctifying the Name of God: Jewish Martyrs and Jewish Memories of the First Crusade* (Philadelphia: University of Pennsylvania Press, 2000). See Alan Dundes, ed., *The Blood Libel Legend: A Casebook in Antisemitic Folklore* (Madison: University of Wisconsin Press, 1991), and R. Po-Chia Hsia, *The Myth of Ritual Murder* (New Haven: Yale University Press, 1989). Geoffrey Chaucer, "The Prioress's Tale," in Geoffrey Chaucer, *The Canterbury Tales,* edited by V. A. Kolve and Glending Olson, 2nd ed. (New York: Norton, 2005), p. 573. For the text of the Prague Massacre, see Abraham

David, *A Hebrew Chronicle from Prague, c. 1615* (Tuscaloosa and London: University of Alabama Press, 1993). On host desecration, see Robert Chazan, *Medieval Stereotypes and Modern Antisemitism* (Berkeley: University of California Press, 1997), pp. 71–72 passim. Citation from the Chronicle of the Bavarian Dukes can be found in Miri Rubin, *Gentile Tales: The Narrative Assault on Late Medieval Jews* (Philadelphia: University of Pennsylvania, 2004), p. 38. For the link between lepers and Jews, see R. I. Moore, *The Formation of a Persecuting Society: Authority and Deviance in Western Europe, 950–1250*, 2nd ed. (Malden, MA: Blackwell, 2007). See Isaiah Schachar, *The "Judensau": A Medieval Anti-Jewish Motif and Its History* (London: Warburg Institute, 1974). See Wolfgang S. Seiferth, *Synagogue and Church in the Middle Ages: Two Symbols of Art and Literature* (New York: Ungar, 1979); Ruth Mellinkoff, *Outcasts: Signs of Otherness in Northern European Art of the Late Middle Ages*, 2 vols. (Berkeley, Los Angeles, and London: University of California Press, 1994); Heinz Schreckenberg, *The Jews in Christian Art: An Illustrated History* (New York: Continuum, 1996); and Sara Lipton, *Images of Intolerance* (Berkeley: University of California Press, 1999). See Joshua Trachtenberg, *The Devil and the Jews* (New Haven: Yale University Press, 1943). This book was written in the shadow of the Holocaust and is an attempt by the author to find the roots for the Jew-hatred that had resulted in such calamity. See Sander L. Gilman, *The Jew's Body* (New York: Routledge, 1991). See James Shapiro, *Oberammergau: The Troubling Story of the World's Most Famous Passion Play* (New York: Vintage, 2000). See Norman Tanner, S.J., *Decrees of the Ecumenical Councils,* vol 1: *Nicaea to Lateran V* (Washington, D.C.: Georgetown University Press, 1990), pp. 227–272. See Guido Kisch, "The Yellow Badge in History," *Historia Judaica* 19 (1957): 89–146; cited in Dean Phillip Bell, *Jews in the Early Modern World* (Lanham, MD: Rowman and Littlefield, 2008), p. 216. See Joel E. Remaum, "The Talmud and the Popes: Reflections on the Talmud Trials of the 1240s," *Viator* 13 (1982): 203–223. See Haim Beinart, *The Expulsion of the Jews from Spain* (Oxford: Littman, 2002), and Kenneth R. Stow, *Alienated Minority* (Cambridge, MA: Harvard University Press, 1992). See "Jewish Conversion, the Spanish Pure Blood Laws and Reformation," in *Sixteenth Century Journal* 18 (1987): 3–29. The Spanish Chronicle of the Expulsions can be found at http://www.fordham.edu/halsall/jewish/1492-jews-spain1.asp.

Chapter 18: Dark Ages? Popes and Councils, ca. 1300–1450

My views in this chapter and indeed on the entire period ca. 1300–1500 are profoundly indebted to Francis Oakley's *The Western Church in the Later Middle Ages* (Ithaca, NY: Cornell University Press, 1979), perhaps the greatest work of synthesis in any language treating this period of history, to which Oakley himself has contributed innumerable stimulating and important studies. For an interesting biography, see T. S. R. Boase, *Boniface VIII* (London: Constable, 1933). For an authoritative, clear, and brief account of the struggle between Boniface VIII and Philip the Fair, see Brian Tierney, *The Crisis of Church and State, 1050 to 1300* (Englewood Cliffs, NJ: Prentice-Hall, 1964), pp. 172–179. In this volume, *Clericis Laicos* is translated on pp. 175–176; *Etsi de Statu* is translated on pp. 178–179; *Ausculta, Fili* is translated on pp. 185–187; the French forgeries against Boniface are translated on p. 187; *Unam Sanctam* is translated on pp. 188–189. *Unam Sanctam* takes from Thomas Aquinas, *Against the Errors of the Greeks* 2.38, which can be found at http://dhspriory.org/thomas/ContraErrGraecorum.htm#b38. The trumped-up charges against Boniface are translated in Tierney, *The Crisis of Church and State,* p. 190, and an eyewitness account of Boniface's humiliation at Anagni is translated on pp. 190–191. See Malcolm Barber, *The Trial of the Templars* (Cambridge: Cambridge University Press, 1978), for a horridly fascinating account. For an authoritative history of the Avignon period, see Guillaume Mollat, *The Popes at Avignon, 1305–1378,* translated by Janet Love (London: Nelson, 1963). See Walter Ullmann, *The Origins of the Great Schism: A Study in Fourteenth Century Ecclesiastical History* (London: Burns, Oates and Washbourne, 1948). For background on the conciliar movement and the ability of corporations to protect themselves from an incompetent executive, see Brian Tierney, *Foundations of Conciliar Theory* (Cambridge: Cambridge University Press, 1955), pp. 87–153. An English translation of *Haec Sancta* can be found at http://www.fordham.edu/halsall/source/constance1.asp. An English translation of *Frequens* can be found in C. M. D. Crowder, *Unity, Heresy and Reform: The Conciliar Response to the Great Schism* (London: Edward Arnold, 1977), pp. 128–129. The bull *Laetentur Coeli* can be found in Latin in Joseph Alberigo et al., *Conciliorum Oecumenicorum Decreta* (Basel and Rome: Herder, 1962), p. 504. Pius's bull *Execrabilis* is translated in Crowder, *Unity, Heresy and Reform,* pp. 179–181, a volume that is also a remarkable study of its topic. Another English translation of *Execrabilis* can be found at http://www.fordham.edu/halsall/source/p2-execrabilis.asp. I take my translation from Oakley, *The Western Church in the Later Middle Ages,* p. 71, n. 49.

Chapter 19: "Morning Stars" or Heretics? Wyclif, Hus, and Followers

For a brief but fine introduction, see Anthony Kenny, *Wyclif* (Oxford: Oxford University Press, 1985). A lengthy treatment can be found in Gordon Leff, *Heresy in the Later Middle Ages,* 2 vols. (Manchester and New York: Manchester University Press, 1967). See Francis Oakley, *The Western Church in the Later Middle Ages* (Ithaca, NY: Cornell University Press, 1979), pp. 192ff. See M. Hurley, "Scriptura sola: Wyclif and His Critics," *Traditio* 16 (1960): 275–352. See Wyclif's condemned assertions at http://www.fordham.edu/halsall/source/1382wycliffe.asp. For the bull, see http://www.ric.edu/faculty/rpotter/heretico.html. See Anne Hudson, *Lollards and Their Books* (London and Ronceverte, WV: Hambledon, 1985), and Margaret Aston, *Lollards and Reformers: Images and Literacy in Late Medieval Religion* (London: Hambledon, 1984). See Malcolm D. Lambert, *Medieval Heresy: Popular Movements from the Gregorian Reform to the Reformation,* 2nd ed. (Cambridge, MA: B. Blackwell, 1992), pp. 217–271, and Leff, *Heresy in the Later Middle Ages,* pp. 559–605. See Howard Kaminsky, *A History of the Hussite Revolution* (Berkeley: University of California Press, 1967). See William R. Cook, "John Wyclif and Hussite Theology 1415–1436," *Church History* 42 (1973): 335–349. David S. Schaff, trans., *De Ecclesia: The Church, by John Huss* (New York: Scribner, 1915; repr. Whitefish, MT: Kessinger, 2010). See Matthew Spinka, *John Hus' Concept of the Church* (Princeton: Princeton University Press, 1968). See Matthew

Spinka's fine if slightly biased and nationalistic records, *John Hus at the Council of Constance* (New York: Columbia University Press, 1968); Columbia University Records of Civilization 73.

Chapter 20: Late-Medieval Contours of Reform, 1380–1500

See Francis Oakley, *The Western Church in the Middle Ages* (Ithaca, NY: Cornell University Press, 1979), pp. 100–113 and ch. 5. Cited in Oakley, *The Western Church in the Middle Ages*, pp. 231 and 244. Text cited in Donald Weinstein, *Savonarola: The Rise and Fall of a Renaissance Prophet* (Princeton: Princeton University Press, 1970), p. 122; the language seems to be a play on Ps. 76:4. See John Van Engen, *Sisters and Brothers of the Common Life: The Devotio Moderna and the World of the Later Middle Ages* (Philadelphia: University of Pennsylvania Press, 2008). See Albert Hyma, *The Brethren of the Common Life* (Grand Rapids, MI: Eerdmans, 1950). See R. R. Post, *The Modern Devotion* (Leiden: Brill, 1968). See John Patrick Dolan, ed., *Unity and Reform: Selected Writings of Nicholas De Cusa* (Notre Dame, IN: University of Notre Dame Press, 1962). Oakley's observation on the humble and cautious spirituality of the Devouts can be found in *The Western Church in the Middle Ages*, p. 111.

Chapter 21: Late-Medieval Piety and Its Problems

See Francis Oakley, *The Western Church in the Later Middle Ages* (Ithaca, NY: Cornell University Press, 1979), pp. 100–113, for a stimulating discussion. See the classic article by Bernd Moeller, "Frömmigkeit in Deutschland um 1500," *Archiv für Reformationsgeschichte* 56 (1965): 3–31, p. 30. On the definition of mysticism and the history of mysticism in general, see the magisterial study by Bernard McGinn, *The Presence of God: A History of Western Christian Mysticism* (New York: Crossroad, 1991–). On Hildegard, see *Scivias*, translated by Columba Hart and Jane Bishop with an introduction by Barbara Newman and a preface by Caroline Walker Bynum (New York: Paulist, 1990), and Barbara Newman, *Sister of Wisdom: St. Hildegard's Theology of the Feminine* (Berkeley: University of California Press, 1987). On Elisabeth, see *Elisabeth of Schönau: The Complete Works,* translated by Anne L. Clark with a preface by Barbara Newman (New York: Paulist Press, 2000); Classics of Western Spirituality. For a study of Carthusian women and the experience of the divine, see Stephanie Paulsell, "*Scriptio Divina:* Writing and the Experience of God in the Works of Marguerite d'Oingt," PhD dissertation, University of Chicago, 1993. A good introduction to Eckhart is found in Bernard McGinn, *Meister Eckhart: The Man from Whom God Hid Nothing* (New York: Crossroad, 2001). See also *Meister Eckhart: The Essential Sermons, Commentaries, Treaties, and Defense,* translated and introduced by Edmund Colledge and Bernard McGinn (London: SPCK, 1981). On Mechtild, see *The Flowing Light of the Godhead,* translated and introduced by Frank Tobin (New York: Paulist, 1998). See *Hadewijch: The Complete Works,* translated and introduced by Mother Columba Hart (London: SPCK, 1981). For Marguerite, see *The Mirror of Simple Souls,* translated and introduced by Ellen L. Babinsky (New York: Paulist, 1993). See Paul Lachance, *The Mystical Journey of Angela of Foligno* (Toronto: Peregrina, 1990). For the ways in which hagiographers modified the lives and writings of the women about whom they wrote or whom they advised, see Amy M. Hollywood,

The Soul as Virgin Wife (Notre Dame, IN: University of Notre Dame Press, 2005). For the books of hours, see the lovely volume by Eamon Duffy, *Marking the Hours: English People and Their Prayers* (New Haven and London: Yale University Press, 2006). For the *facere* doctrine, see Heiko Oberman, *Forerunners of the Reformation,* translated by Paul L. Nyhus (Philadelphia: Fortress, 1981).

Glossary

Abbot/Abbess: The highest ranking monk or nun in a monastic community or order.

Absolution: The remission of sin.

Albigensians/Cathars: A heretical group popular in southern France and Italy during the twelfth and thirteenth centuries. Albigensians maintained a highly organized ecclesial structure, subscribed to a dualist theology, and were committed to rigorous asceticism.

Anchoress: A female anchorite. During the Middle Ages, they were known for enclosing themselves in a single room and dedicating their lives to contemplation and prayer.

Anchorite: One who voluntarily withdraws from society with the goal of achieving salvation through the disciplines of prayer, asceticism, and mortification.

Apostasy: The deliberate renunciation of the faith.

Arianism: An ancient heresy that held that Christ was not by nature divine but rather an exalted creation of God the Father. The view was championed by Arius, a priest from Alexandria, and was condemned at the Council of Nicaea in 325.

Autohagiography: An autobiographical account of a saint's life.

Avignon papacy: The period from 1309 to 1377 when seven consecutive popes reigned in Avignon (technically then within the boundaries of the German Empire) rather than in Rome.

Baptismal church: A church founded by a bishop, endowed with a baptismal font, and legally empowered to collect tithes and fees from parishioners.

Beguines: A community of laywomen who were voluntarily committed to piety and chastity but did not take formal vows or join a religious order. Consequently, they were free to engage in commerce, to possess private property, and even to marry. They were condemned in 1311–1312 at the Council of Vienne.

Benefice: A benefit due to the holder of an ecclesial office.

Bishop: The highest ecclesiastical authority in a diocese.

Blood libel: The myth that Jews secretly kidnapped and murdered children for ritualistic purposes. The blood libel myth was widely held by Christians in medieval Europe and led to the persecution and murder of many Jews.

Bogomils: A dualist sect originating in Bulgaria in the tenth century. Like the ancient Manichaeans before them, Bogomils denounced the material world and practiced rigorous asceticism. The sect spread throughout Asia Minor, the Balkans, and finally to Europe, where it influenced the Cathars of France and Italy.

Canon law: A collection of laws that govern ecclesial life, organization, and practice.

Canons regular: A body of secular clerics who live in community and follow the *Rule* of St. Augustine. They are also known as Augustinian canons.

Carthusian: A monastic order founded at the Grande Chartreuse in 1084 by Bruno of Cologne. Carthusian monks take a vow of silence; live alone in simple, one-room houses on the grounds of the monastery; and dedicate their lives to prayer and contemplation; they are, however, permitted to gather with fellow monks to recite the daily office, attend mass, share meals, and even socialize on liturgical feast days.

Cenobite: A monk who follows a *Rule* and lives in community with other monks.

Cistercian: A monastic order founded at Cîteaux in 1098 by Robert of Molesme. Cistercians are characterized by their strict adherence to the *Rule* of St. Benedict and, in contrast with the Cluniac order, their preference for simplicity and austerity in liturgy and architecture.

Cluny: Burgundian monastic house founded in 909 by Duke William of Aquitaine. Its freedom from lay control and interference allowed it to develop into a vital and independent center for monastic and ecclesiastical reform during the tenth and eleventh centuries. Cluny established the first monastic order, was famous for its highly elaborate liturgical practices, and was the head of hundreds of daughter houses throughout western Europe.

Conciliarism: The belief that church councils, rather than the pope, should exercise supreme authority in matters relating to ecclesial doctrine and practice. Conciliarism was especially popular during the period of the Great Schism (1378–1417), when as many as three men, each with his own curia, simultaneously claimed to be pope.

Confessor: A Christian who has been persecuted and tortured for his faith but not killed.

Confirmation: A sacrament administered by a local bishop by which an already baptized Christian receives the grace of the Holy Spirit.

Confraternity: An organized association of lay Christians who gathered for prayer, fellowship, and the performance of charitable deeds.

Conventuals: The branch of the Franciscan Order that permitted friars to use (but not own) private property and favored a flexible interpretation of the *Rule* of St. Francis.

Conversi: Lay brothers who work as manual laborers at monastic houses in order to allow choir monks the freedom to dedicate themselves fully to prayer and other liturgical duties.

Conversos: Muslims and Jews of Spain who converted, often through coercion, to Christianity during the fourteenth and fifteenth centuries. Conversos were frequently persecuted by secular and ecclesial authorities who doubted the sincerity of their conversion.

Convivencia: Period during the Middle Ages when the Muslims, Jews, and Christians of Iberia lived together under Muslim rule.

Council/Synod: An official meeting of bishops and other church authorities who gather for the purposes of ruling on matters of faith, practice, and canon law.

Creed: A concise statement of belief—for example, the Apostles' Creed.

Deacon: An ordained minister who ranks below an ordained priest. While deacons are permitted to read the gospels and distribute the Eucharist during the mass, they are not permitted to consecrate the Eucharist or to grant absolution.

Docetism: A heresy that holds that Christ did not exist as a human person but was rather a divine spirit who only appeared to be human.

Donation of Constantine: A medieval forgery that alleged that Constantine had voluntarily transferred temporal authority of the western empire to the papacy. During the Middle Ages, the Donation of Constantine was frequently cited to support the claim that the papacy should hold temporal authority over secular rulers.

Donation of Pepin: The donation of land made to the papacy by Pepin the Short, king of the Franks in 756. The territory, located in central Italy, was known as the Papal States.

Donatism: A heretical sect that flourished in Africa during the fourth and fifth centuries after the Great Persecution under Diocletian. Donatists considered any sacrament performed by a priest or bishop who later apostatized from the faith, even under threat of persecution, torture, or death, to be invalid. The Donatists were opposed by Augustine, who argued that sacraments received their validity through the grace and power of God and not the moral condition of the minister performing the sacrament.

Dualism: The belief that the cosmos is divided into two equally powerful, constantly dueling, forces of good and evil.

East-West Schism: Formal split, often said to date from 1054, between the western Catholic and eastern Orthodox churches.

Eremitic: A form of monasticism in which a monk renounces the world and seeks to live alone in the wilderness as a hermit.

Friars: Name for members of the mendicant orders, especially the Franciscans and Dominicans, who renounce ownership of private property and rely solely on charity for their basic needs.

Gilbertines: An order of women religious and canons regular founded in 1131 by Gilbert, a parish priest from Sempringham, England, in response to the desire of several women under his spiritual care to enter cloistered life. After 1147, men were permitted to join the order to provide for the spiritual and sacramental needs of the women. The order grew rapidly and was very popular in England.

Gnosticism: A diverse group of heretical sects that were united by their rejection of the material world and their belief in the necessity of attaining secret knowledge *(gnosis)* to achieve salvation.

Gregorian reform movement: A movement named for Pope Gregory VII, the most influential and prominent papal reformer of the eleventh century. The term applies to a diverse spectrum of ecclesiastical reform currents that appeared during the tenth and eleventh centuries.

Hagiography: A written account of a saint's life. Hagiographies typically followed a standard formula and were written not for biographical purposes, but for the spiritual edification of the reader.

Iconoclasm: The act of destroying icons and the condemnation and suppression of the practice of venerating them.

Icons: A venerated image of Christ, the Blessed Virgin Mary, or a saint.

Indulgence: A dispensation from the punishment due for sin in exchange for the performance of specific acts of penance, including pilgrimage or monetary donation.

Joachites: Spiritual Franciscans who follow the eschatological teaching of the apocalyptic biblical exegete and visionary Joachim of Fiore.

Lay investiture: Act whereby lay rulers appoint clergy to their ecclesial positions and invest them with the symbols of their office.

Leprosaries: Colonies of lepers.

Lollards: Followers of the teachings of John Wyclif.

Marcionism: An early Christian movement named for the second-century heretic Marcion, who subscribed to a dualist theology whereby he accepted the God of the New Testament and rejected the God of the Old Testament as an inferior, malevolent being. Marcion was one of the first to compile a canon of New Testament books.

Martyr: A person who is killed for refusing to renounce his faith.

Mendicant: A member of one of the "begging" orders, such as the Franciscans or Dominicans, who eschews the ownership of property and possessions and relies on charitable giving for his basic needs; also known as friars.

Metropolitan: A bishop who oversees a group of dioceses.

Military orders: Martial monastic orders, such as the Knights of St. John and the Knights Templar, that were founded during the Crusades to protect and defend Crusader territory in the Holy Land.

Montanism: An early Christian movement named after the second-century heretic Montanus. Montanus and his companions Priscilla and Maximilla believed themselves to be the direct recipients of divine, ecstatic, prophetic revelations from the Holy Spirit. Also known as Phrygians.

Nag Hammadi: A collection of Gnostic texts composed sometime in the second century and discovered in 1945 in Nag Hammadi, Egypt.

Nominalism: The idea that universal concepts and categories do not exist in reality and that all things are reducible to their individual particulars; contrasted with Realism.

Oblate: A child who is donated by his parents to a monastery.

Observantine: A reform movement in the Franciscan Order that insisted upon a literal observance of the *Rule* of St. Francis.

Orthodoxy: Correct belief in matters of faith and practice.

Pallium: A woolen liturgical vestment given to a bishop by a pope as a symbol of his authority.

Papal legate: An ambassador sent to represent papal interests outside of Rome.

Papal States: The states in the Italian peninsula that were ruled by the pope.

Patriarchate: One of the five ancient episcopal sees located in Alexandria, Antioch, Constantinople, Jerusalem, and Rome. Due to their historical connection to the early church and, in the cases of Rome and Constantinople, their connection to centers of power and influence, patriarchs were the most respected and highest-ranking bishops in the ancient world. The patriarchates of Alexandria, Antioch, and Jerusalem were eliminated during the Islamic conquests of the seventh century.

Pelagianism: A fourth-century heresy promulgated by Pelagius, who taught that Christians were capable of attaining holiness through the exercise of their own free will. This view was opposed by Augustine, who taught that Christians were entirely dependent upon the grace of God for both the desire and ability to attain holiness.

Pilgrimage: A journey taken to a shrine or holy place for the purpose of supplication or penance.

Pluralism: The practice of holding multiple ecclesiastical offices or benefices at once.

Pogrom: A pre-planned, organized massacre of Jews.

Premonstratensian: An order of canons regular founded in 1120 by Norbert of Xanten; also known as the Norbertines.

Prior/Prioress: One who occupies the rank below an abbot or abbess in a monastic house or order.

Proprietary church: A church built, endowed, and maintained by a secular lay lord, although formally under the supervision of the local bishop. Often, proprietary churches would come into legal conflict with baptismal churches over the right to collect tithes and fees from parishioners.

Purgatory: The idea that those who have died in a state of sin may undergo purgative cleansing before being admitted to heaven. Later understood to be a place where the soul was purified from all sin before being granted admittance into heaven.

Realism: The idea that universal categories and concepts exist in reality despite the presence of individual particulars; the opposite of Nominalism.

Reconquista: The period from ca. 722 to 1492, when Christian monarchs in Iberia undertook a sustained military campaign to conquer territory under Islamic rule.

Relic: A part of a deceased saint's body or an item that was owned or used by the saint that is considered holy and is preserved for the purpose of veneration.

Remanence: The idea that the *substance* of the Eucharistic bread and wine does not transform into the real body and blood of Christ at the mass. The idea was promulgated by John Wyclif and was declared heretical in 1382.

***Rule* of St. Augustine:** *Rule* adopted by the canons regular.

Sacrament: There are seven sacraments: baptism, Eucharist, penance, confirmation, holy orders, anointing of the sick, and matrimony; they are said to give sanctifying grace to those who receive them.

Schism: A split within the church due to differences over matters of faith or practice.

Simony: The act of purchasing an ecclesiastical office, based on the New Testament story of Simon the Magician (Acts of the Apostles 8:18–24), who attempted to purchase spiritual powers from St. Peter the Apostle.

Soteriology: In theology, the study of salvation.

Spirituals: The branch of the Franciscan Order that championed poverty, eschewed ownership of property, and insisted on a literal interpretation of the *Rule* and *Testament* of St. Francis. Spirituals were often suppressed by the institutional church.

Talmud: A collection of Jewish rabbinic commentary; it is considered a sacred text in Judaism.

Tertiary (third order): A lay organization associated with a monastic order, particularly one of the Mendicant orders.

Translation: Refers to the movement of a saint's relics from one location to another.

Transubstantiation: The doctrine that the *substance* of the Eucharistic bread and wine transforms into the body and blood of Christ during the mass while their *appearance* remains the same.

Trivium: The subjects of grammar, rhetoric, and logic.

Quadrivium: The subjects of geometry, arithmetic, astronomy, and music.

Usury: The practice of charging interest on a loan.

Victorines: Canons regular of the former Abbey of St. Victor in Paris. The abbey was founded in 1113 by William of Champeaux and renowned for producing some of the greatest scholars of the Middle Ages.

Vita apostolica: A revival movement that occurred during the eleventh through thirteenth centuries as certain books of the New Testament, particularly the gospels and the Acts of the Apostles, assumed a place of primacy in ecclesiastical life and imagination. The life and deeds of Christ and the apostles recorded in these texts, particularly those dealing with renunciation of property and wealth, preaching, suffering, and chastity, were emulated by many Christians.

Waldensians/poor of Lyons: Followers of Peter Waldes who were committed to poverty and preaching. They were condemned in 1184 for preaching without first obtaining local episcopal approval.

Index

Maps and illustrations are indicated by italic page numbers.

Aachen Cathedral (Palatine Chapel), *76*, *76*–77, 328
Abbasid Caliph, 101
Abbots' role, 52, 123
Abelard. *See* Peter Abelard
Abstinence, 88. *See also* Fasting
Acre, 114, 346
Acts of the Apostles, 124
Ad Abolendam (Lucius III), 193, 202
Adam, 8, 25, 176, 249
Adams, Henry, 340
Ad Conditorem Canonum (John XXII), 256
Adeodatus, 23
Ad Extirpanda (Innocent IV), 205, 224
Adrianople, battle of (378), 34, 37
Adso of Montier-en-Der, 355
Aelfric, 87
Aesculapius (Greek god of healing), 324
Against the Inveterate Obstinacy of the Jews (Peter the Venerable), 360
Against the Petrobrusians (Peter the Venerable), 176
Age of Faith, 93
Age of Reform, 119–147; canon law developments, 131–132; Cluny and papal reform, 123–124; conflict of papacy and empire (1075–1100), 139–143; consequences of reform, 145–147; Gregory VII and, 134–139; investiture, 132–134; moderate papal reform, 126–130; monastic reform, 120–122; New Testament's role, 124–126; Norman alliance, 134; pamphlet war and compromise, 143–145
Agobard, archbishop of Lyons, 101–102
Aidan, Saint, 43, 48
Ailred of Rievaulx, 150
Alaric I (king of the Visigoths), 26, 37
Alberic, 166
Albert V (duke of Austria), 405
Albert of Aachen, 345
Albert the Great (Albertus Magnus), 94, 219, 277, 279, 283, 341, 361, 422
Albigensians. *See* Cathars
Alcuin of York, 73, 77, 78
Alexander II (pope), 128, 134, 315, 317
Alexander III (pope), 159, 191, 261–262, 294, 337
Alexander IV (pope), 206, 253
Alexander V (pope), 399
Alexander VI (pope), 407, 410

Alexander of Hales, 252, 253, 280
Alexandria, 6, 21, 103, 104, 323
Alexius, Saint, 188
Alexius I (emperor), 203
Alexius Angelus IV, 115
Alfonso VIII (king of Castile), 171, *172*
al-Kamil, 116
Ambrose, 23, 39, 56, 65
Amiens Cathedral (France), *284*, 341
Amulets, 88
Anchorites, 149–150
Ancient Christianity, 3–30; Augustine
    of Hippo, 22–28; Constantine, 20–22,
    72, 196, 391; creeds and rules of faith,
    11–13; end of, 29–30; gnosticism, 4–7;
    Marcionism, 7–9, 13, 114; Montanism,
    9–11, 17; normative Christianity, 11–15;
    Roman persecution of Christians, 15–20
Ancona, 152
Ancrene Wisse (*Ancrene Riwle*), 150
Andrew, Saint, 112
Angela da Foligno, Saint, 425–426
Angels, 90
Angles, 34, 62
Anglo-Saxons, 46, 50, 61, 62–64, 66, 67,
    79, 120
Anselm of Bec, 260, 262
Anselm of Laon, 262, 264, 276
Antichrist, 135, 136, 224, 250, 255, 256,
    355–356, 391, 400, 406
Antioch, 21, 103, 104, 111, 112, 113, 114
Anti-Semitism, 95, 99, 170, 209, 347–356.
    See also Jews and Judaism
Antitheses (Marcion), 8
Antony, Saint, 22, 321
Apocalypse, 13, 196
Apocalypse of Pseudo-Methodius of
    Patara, 105
Aquinas. *See* Thomas Aquinas
Aquitaine, 97, 120–121
Arab empire, 34, 103–104. *See also* Mus-
    lims and Islam
Arabic language, 34, 50, 104, 105, 106
Aragon, 203, 209

Architecture, 54, *55*, *82*, 82–83, *167*, 306,
    323, *334*
Arians/Arianism, 21, 25–26, 34, *36*,
    36–40, 50, 97–98, 183
Aristotle, 39, 218, 272, 274–276, 279–282,
    317–318, 369
Arius, 21
Arnald Amaury (abbot of Cîteaux), 200,
    214
Art. *See* Icons, images, and pictorials
Arundel, Thomas, 393
Asceticism: canons and, 162; Gaul, male
    and female ascetics in, 42–44; of
    Gregory I, 57; in Ireland, 47, 49; Pela-
    gius and, 25; practices of, 10, 22; *Rule*
    and, 52; supernatural powers of ancient
    eastern monks, 324; in Western culture,
    29–30. *See also* Hermit lifestyle
Ashkenazic Jewry, 100–101, 346, 347, 363
Asia Minor, 9–12, 111, 112
Assisi, 231–232, 246, 248
Assize of Clarendon (1166), 178
Assumption of the Virgin, 340, 422
Astrology, 89
Athanasius, 14, 22
Atheism charge against early
    Christians, 16
Attila the Hun, 37
Augsburg council (1077), 140
Augustine of Canterbury, 50, 63
Augustine of Hippo (saint), 18, 22–28,
    37, 39, 44, 56, 98, 161, 261, 281, 390. See
    also *Rule* of St. Augustine
Augustinian canons, 161, *161*
Avarice as sin, 318
Ave Maria, 313, 340
Averroës and Averroists, 275, 279, 282, 283
Avicenna, 275, 279
Avignon, 70, 200, 370, *376*
Avignon papacy (1309–1378), 374–378;
    Council of Constance (1414–1418) and,
    379–383; Council of Pisa (1409) and,
    378–379
Ayyubid sultan al-Kamil, 238

"Babylonian Captivity," 374
Bachrach, Bernard, 98
Baldwin of Boulogne, 111
Balthild, 42, 43
Baptism, 92, 176, 182, 401
Baptismal churches, 81
Baron, Salo, 95
Barraclough, Geoffrey, 130, 295
Basil (patriarch), 53
Basilides, 18
Bavarians, 68, 73, 101, 352
Beatrice of Nazareth, 424
Becket, Thomas, 323, 336–338, *338*
Bede, the Venerable, 46, 50, 54, 63,
    64–65, 78
Beguines, 209, 220–223, 321, 424
Belisarios, 39
Benedict XII (pope), 375–376
Benedict XIII (pope), 380, *381*
Benedict XVI (pope), 419
Benedict Biscop, 65
Benedictines and Benedictine monas-
    teries, 122, *122*, 152, 156, 160, 164, 166,
    169, 336, 404, 405. *See also* Monks and
    monasticism
Benedict of Aniane, 75–76
Benedict of Nursia (saint), 42, 50,
    51–53, 54, 258. See also *Rule* of
    St. Benedict (RB)
Benefice, 84
Bernardino of Siena, 404
Bernard of Chartres, 174
Bernard of Clairvaux: on Abelard, 265;
    on Anselm, 262; Carthusians and, 153,
    155; Cistercians and, 166–167, 169–171;
    on monastic life, 329; monastic schools
    and, 259–260; on money lending,
    358–359; mysticism and, 419, 424; on
    papal power, 297; Peter Lombard and,
    273; on Petrobrusians, 176; preaching
    tours of, 308; Second Crusade and, 345;
    Templars' *Rule* prepared by, 114
Bernard of Quintavalle, 235
Béziers, 183, 188, 200

Bible. *See* Hebrew Bible; New Testament;
    Old Testament; Scripture
Biel, Gabriel, 434
Biller, Peter, 184, 190
Bishops: complaints at Council of Lyons
    (1245), 298; control of list of saints, 326;
    election and consecration of, 133, 144;
    in Ireland, 46; lay appointment of, 79;
    map of Europe with major bishoprics
    (ca. 1250), *296*; municipal authority
    assumed by, 29; role of, 61, 294; in
    Roman cities, 21; synodical legislation
    and, 311
Black Death, 28, 271, 353–354, 418, 431
"Blood libel," 347–352, *350*
Bobbio monastery, 46
Boccaccio, 406
Boethius, 38–39
Bogomils, 181–183, 203
Bohemia, 107, 193, 343, 382, 395, 402
Bohemond of Sicily, 111
Bologna, 216, 217, 219, 224, 239, 266,
    268–270, 276
Bonaventure, 229, 246, 253–254, 280–281
Boniface (Winfrith), 68
Boniface VIII (pope), 370–374
Book of Divine Providence (Catherine of
    Siena), 426
Book of Kells, 65
Book of the City of Ladies (Christine de
    Pizan), 318
Book on the Ways of God (St. Elisabeth),
    422
Books of hours, 428–430
Boyle, Leonard, 310
Bridget of Sweden, Saint, 339, 375,
    426–427
Britain. *See* England
Brittany, 46
Brown, Peter, 324
Brunelleschi, 406
Bruno, Saint (Bruno of Cologne), 153,
    153, 156
Bruno of Toul. *See* Leo IX (pope)

Bubonic plague, 58
Bulgars, 180
Burchard of Worms, 88, 99, 131
Burgundy, 42, 130, 166, 171
Burr, David, 254
Bynum, Caroline, 151, 425, 426, 427–428
Byzantine church, 86, 109
Byzantine Empire: Charlemagne and, 74–75; ecumenical councils of, 21, 292; Islam and, 103; Lombards and, 58, 70–71, 72, 99; Normans and, 130; Orthodox Christianity in, 50; Roman emperors presiding over, 34; Theodoric's relations with, 38; veneration of icons in, 326
Byzantium, 20, 105. *See also* Constantinople

Caecilian of Carthage, 23–24
Caesarea, 103, 113
Caesarius of Heisterbach, 174, 177
Cain and Abel, 27
Calendar, 326–327
Calixtus II (pope), 102, 292
Calpurnius, 44
Camaldolese order, 152, 167
Canon law, 21, 69, 75, 79, 87, 99, 130, 131–132, 144, 190, 206, 292; *The Body of Canon Law* (*Corpus Iuris Canonici*), 292; *Collection in 74 Titles*, 131; feast days, 327; Jews and, 357–358; *Omnis utriusque sexus* (Canon 21), 310; relics used to consecrate churches, 329
Canonries, 160–162
Canossa meeting of Henry IV and Gregory VII (1077), 140–141
Canterbury Cathedral, 307, 323, 336–338
Canticle of Brother Sun (Francis), 229
Carcassonne, *200*, 203
Cardinals, 126
Carloman, 73
Carolingian dynasty, 39, 69–80, 86, 100–102, 258, 329, 339, 429, 430
Carolingian miniscule, 78

Carolingian Renaissance, 77
Carruthers, Mary, 300
Carthage, 17, 23, 25, 103
Carthusians, 152–157, 177, 403
Cassiodorus, 38, 39
Cathars, 178–188, 190, 192, 199–200, *200*, 203, 205, 207–209, 211–213, 431
Catherine of Genoa, 426
Catherine of Siena, 222, 375, 377, 405, 426
Catholic Christianity: Boethius and, 38; Clovis and, 40–41; conversion of Reccared I to, 98; Franks and, 71–73; Gallo-Roman culture and, 34, 37; Magyars converting to, 79; Protestant intolerance of, 201; after Roman Empire, 50
Celestine (pope), 45, 370–371
Celibacy, 83, 125, 128, 131, 145, 186
Celtic Christianity: Abelard and, 265; Easter controversy and, 43–44; emergence of, 46–49; Gertrude and, 43; Roman missionaries and, 66–67; use of term "Celtic," 46
Cerdo, 8
Cesarini, Giuliano (cardinal), 383
Chalcedon, 21
Chaplains, 339
Charities, 314–315
Charlemagne, 73–76, *76*, 101, 242, 328
Charles IV (Holy Roman emperor), 396
Charles VIII (king of France), 408
Charles Martel, 69–71
Charles the Great. *See* Charlemagne
Chartres, 261, *285*, 286, 341, *341*, 342
Chaucer, 245, 348–349
Children: book of hours used to instruct in reading, 429; charges of ritual murder against Jews, 345, 347–352; child oblation, 258, 316; monasteries as safe havens for, 54; named after saints, 327
Christendom (Christianitas), 145–146, 291, 369, 373, 379, 386
Christianized culture, 91–94
"Christian mediocrity," 309
Christine de Pizan, 275, 317–318

Christine of Stommeln, 221

Christology: Cathar, 184; Docetic, 7, 8; synoptic gospels and, 227

Christopher, Saint, 90, 306–307

Church decoration, *306*

Church of the Holy Savior (Spoleto), *63*

Church of the Holy Sepulchre (Jerusalem), *108*, 109, 113, 332, 344

Cicero, 23, 77, 406

Circumcellions, 24

Cistercians, 164–173, *167*, *172*; anti-schools stance of, 259; Carthusians and, 152; *conversi* and, 216; devotion to Virgin Mary, 340; Devouts and, 412; Dominican universities and, 215; in England, 337; female mystics and, 423; Gilbert and, 159; heresy, role in suppression of, 177–178, 198, 202, 211, 212–214; as itinerant preachers, 215; poverty and, 233; on purgatory, 309; rejecting child oblation, 316; Templars' *Rule* and, 114; Thomas's *Lives* and, 229

Cîteaux, 152, 166, 169, 171

Cities: structure and ecclesiastical organization, 20–21; urban schools, 260–262

The City of God (Augustine), 26–27

Civitate, battle of (1053), 131

Clairvaux monastery, 166–167

Clare of Assisi, 236–238, *237*

Classicism, revival in early Renaissance, 406–410

Clement (Willibrord), 67–68

Clement III (pope), 142

Clement IV (pope), 362

Clement V (pope), 374

Clement VI (Avignon pope), 375

Clement VII (antipope), 378

Clergy: Cathars, 187; celibacy of, 83–84, 125, 128, 131, 145; Charlemagne and, 74; education of, 83–85; hierarchical line under pope's direction, 144; instruction through worship, 300–301; in Ireland, 46; lay appointment of, 79, 119, 132, 144–146; marriage of, 83–84, 119, 128, 152, 175; misconduct of, 79, 311, 336–337; model for, 14–15; papal reform of, 126–130; pastoral care (1200–1250), 309–312; purchase of offices by parish clergy, 119–120, 125, 127, 131, 175; role of, 83–84, 86. *See also* Bishops

Clericis Laicos (Boniface VIII), 371–372

Clermont, 109, 110

Clothilda, 40–41, 42

Clovis I (Merovingian king), 40–42

Clovis II (Merovingian king), 42

Cluniac order, 111, 123, 130, 333

Cluny (Benedictine abbey), *122*, 122–124, 167–168, 170, 259, 266, 430

Code of Canon Law, 274

Codex Argenteus, *36*

Codex Theodosianus (Theodosian Code), 96, 99–100

Cohen, Jeremy, 28

Cohen, Mark, 105

Collection in 74 Titles (canon law), 131

Colman, Bishop, 67

Cologne, 183, 219, 220, 328, 339, 344

Colonges convent, 173

Colonna family, 371

Columba, Saint, 48

Columbanus, 42, 43, 48

Columbus, Christopher, 415

Commentary on the Sentences (Thomas Aquinas), 277, 278

Communal lifestyle, 22

Compendium of Revelations (Savonarola), 408

Conciliarists after Great Schism, 385–386, 414

Concordat of London (1107), 144

Concordat of Worms (1122), 144

Concord of Discordant Canons (*Decretum*, Gratian), 274, 276, 292

Conduct of Inquiry Concerning Heretical Depravity (Gui), 224

Confession (St. Patrick), 44

Confession and confessors, 244–245, 310–312, 417

Confessions (Augustine), 23, 25

Confirmation, sacrament of, 83

Conques (France), 323, 328, 334–336, *335*

Conrad of Marburg, 209

Conrad of Waldhausen, 396, 397

Consolamentum (laying on of hands), 184, 185

Consolation of Philosophy (Boethius), 38–39

Constantine (emperor), 20–22, 72, 196, 391

Constantinople: Aristotle's works in translation and, 274; Crusades and, III, 115; Islamic armies attacking, 103; Niketas and, 185; papal reform and, 130; patriarchate of, 21, 104; Roman rule over, 34; sack of, in Fourth Crusade, 328, 329, 385; seeking aid from Clermont, 110

Constitutions (Bernanardino), 404–405

Constitutions of Arundel, 393

Consuetudines (*Customs*, Guigo I), 154–156

Convents. *See* Monasteries; Monks and monasticism; Women and nuns

Conventuals, 252, 255–256, 416

Conversi. See Lay brethren

Conversion of the West, 33–49; conversion of the Arians, 36–40; conversion of the Franks, 40–42; emergence of Celtic Christianity, 46–49; Gaul, male and female ascetics in, 42–44; Ireland and St. Patrick, 44–46

Conversos (Spanish and Portuguese converts to Catholicism), 313–314, 364

Coptic documents, 4

Coroticus, 44, 45–46

Corpus Iuris Civilis. See Justinian Code

Council of Agde (506), 97

Council of Basel (1431–1449), 383–384, 401–402, 403, 413, 414

Council of Constance (1414–1418), 379–383, *381–382*, 392, 400

Council of Ferrara (1437), 384

Council of Florence (1438–1445), 384

Council of Lyons (1245), 297

Council of Pisa (1409), 378–379

Council of Soissons (1121), 264

Council of Trent (1545–1563), 84, 91, 245, 351

Council of Troyes (1128), 114

Council of Verona (1184), 235

Covenant of 'Umar, 104

Creationist, 26

The Creed, 92, 307, 309

Creeds and rules of faith, 11–13

Crescentius of Iesu, 228, 249, 252

Criminals as pilgrims, 331

Crosses, *304–305*, 305–306

Crusades, 107–115; Augustinian doctrine and, 28; Bernard and, 170; against Cathars, 199–200, *200*; Crusaders' Chapel of the Virgin Mary (Church of the Holy Sepulchre), *108*, 109; Fifth Crusade, 238; First Crusade, 109–111, 343, 345, 347; Fourth Crusade, 114–115, 328, 329, 385; incentives for Crusaders, 107–113, 115, 344; Jews and, 170, 343–347; negative conclusion of, 115, 146; papal powers and, 104, 136, 146; relics and, 112–113, 115, 328, 329; Second Crusade, 345; taxes to pay for, 295; Third Crusade, 114, 346; vow of Crusaders, 108–109

Cult of Mary, 94–95, 171

Cult of the dead, 88

Cum inter nonnullos (John XXII), 256

Cusa. *See* Nicholas of Cusa

Customs (Guigo I), 154–156

Cyprian of Carthage, 18

Dacia, 36

The Dagger of Faith (Martini), 361–362

Dalmatian Coast, 38

Dante, 226, 249, 274, 282, 406, 423, 431

Dark Ages, 369–386

Decius, 18

De Civili Dominio (*On Civil Dominion*, Wyclif), 388

Decree of 1059, 134

Decretum (Burchard of Worms), 131

Decretum (Gratian), 274, 276, 292

De Dominio Divino (*On Divine Lordship*, Wyclif), 388

De Ecclesia (*On the Church*, Wyclif), 390

De Eucharistia (*On the Eucharist*, Wyclif), 391

de Mille, Cecil B., 15

Denis the Carthusian, 155

De Potestate Papae (*The Power of the Pope*, Wyclif), 390

de Saisset, Bernard, 372

Desecularization, 29

Desert life, 22, 151–152. *See also* Hermit lifestyle

De Veritate Sacrae Scripturae (*On the Truth of the Sacred Scripture*, Wyclif), 389

Devil. *See* Satan

Devouts, 410–412

Dhimmitude, 106

Dialogues (Gregory I), 51

Diana d'Andalo, 221

The Dictates of the Pope (*Dictatus Papae*), 137–139

Diego d'Azevedo, 212–214

Diocese, 21, 144

Diocletian, 19–20

Dionysio-Hadriana (canon law), 75

Divine Comedy (Dante), 431

Divorce, ban on, 316

Docetic Christology, 7, 8

Doctrine of apostolic succession, 14

Dome of the Rock (Jerusalem), 104

Dominicans, 211–225; Aristotelian thinking and, 281–282; Catherine of Siena and, 405; in competition with Friars Minor, 247; confession and confessors, 244–245; elimination of social distinctions among, 216; female mystics and, 423; founding and growth of, 211–218; heresy, role in suppression of, 198–199, 202, 208, 211, 212; on immaculate conception, 341; in Inquisition, 223–225;

Jews and, 361; as learned order, 218–219; Manichees and, 180; Muslim conversion and, 116; nuns, 219–223; Observance and, 404–405, 408; preaching by, 242–243; as spiritual men, 250

Dominic of Caleruega, 212–214, *213*

Donatello, 406

"Donation of Constantine," 72–73, 131

"Donation of Pepin," 72

Donatism, 24–25, 28, 175, 182, 185, 195. *See also* neo-Donatism

Donatus, 24

Dorlaeum, 111

Drama, 301–302, 307–308

Dualism of good and evil, 23, 184, 185, 187

Duns Scotus, 434

Dunstan, Saint, 120

Early-medieval Christianity (ca. 600–1050), 31–116; Benedict, Abbot of Monte Cassino, 50–56; conversion of the West, 33–49; Gregory I (pope), 55–62; Islam's relationship with Christianity, 103–116; Jews' relationship with Christianity, 95–102

Easter, celebration of, 300, 310

Easter controversy, 43–44, 66–67

Ebner, Margaret, 221–222, 423

Ecclesiastical History (Eusebius), 10

Ecclesiastical History of the English People (Bede), 64

Ecclesiastical organization. *See* Clergy

Eckbert of Schönau, 179–180, 183

Eco, Umberto, 201

Ecumenical councils, 21

Edessa, 111, 114, 170, 188

Edict on the Jews (Theodoric), 99

Education, 257–286; Aristotelian thought and, 274–276, 279–282; of clergy, 83–85; mendicant orders and, 276–277; monastic schools, 258–260; teaching and learning, 271–274; university, 266–271; urban schools, 260–262

Edward III (king of England), 388

Egilbert (archbishop), 345

Egypt, 22, 103, 111, 148, 238

Einhard, 74–76, 77

Eleanor (duchess of Aquitaine), 158

Eleutherus, 14

Elias, 239, 246, 248

Elisabeth of Schönau (St. Elisabeth), 179–180, 421–422

Elizabethan England, 201

Emmaus, 113

The End of Ancient Christianity (Markus), 29

Endura (fasting to death), 186

England: ascetics in, 42; Celtic missionaries to, 48; Charlemagne and, 73; church construction in, 83; Cluny's influence on cloisters in, 122; conversion of Northmen in, 79; Dominicans in, 215, 217; double monasteries in, 43; Franciscans in, 405; Gregory the Great and, 61; heresy in, 178; Jews in, 346, 363; lay churches in, 81; monasteries and nunneries in, 164; monastic reform in, 120; Roman missionaries to, 50, 62–64; St. Patrick and, 44; Viking incursions in, 79

Erasmus of Rotterdam, 411

Ethelbert, King, 64

Etsi animarum (Innocent IV), 253

Etsi de statu (Boniface VIII), 372

Eucharist, 85–88, 176, 327, 348, 391, 426, 430, 432

Eugenius III (pope), 419

Eugenius IV (pope), 383, 384, 413

Eusebius of Caesarea, 20

Eusebius of Nicomedia, 36

Eve, 5, 6. *See also* Adam

Eve of Wilton, 150

Excommunication: of Cathars, 183; of Cerularius, 130; of Elias, 248; of Henry IV and clergy by expelled Gregory VII, *141*, 143; of Montanists, 10; of Otto, 289; of Raymond VI (Count of Toulouse), 199; of Savonarola, 410; of Waldensians, 193

Execrabilis (Pius II), 385

Exiit qui seminat (John XXII), 255–256

Fabian, 18

Facere doctrine, 433–435

Falwell, Jerry, 356

Fasting, 47, 49, 88, 186

Feast days, 326–327, 340

Feast of the Dispersion of the Apostles, 112

Felicitas, 17

Felix III (pope), 56

Felix V (antipope), 384

Felix of Apthungi, 23–24

Ferdinand and Isabella, 203, 209, 364, 415

Ferdinand of Castile, 107

First Life (*Vita Prima*, Thomas of Celano), 228

Fleury abbey, 42

Florence, 377, 403, 405, 406–410

The Flowing Light of Godhead (Mechtild of Magdeburg), 423

Folkloristic culture, 91–94

Fonte Avellana, 152

Fontenay Abbey (France), *167*

Fontevrault monastery, 157–158, 159

Forty Gospel Homilies (Gregory the Great), 242

Fossier, Robert, 234–235

"Four Articles of Prague," 401

Four Books of Sentences (Bernard of Clairvaux), 273, 274

Fourth Council of Toledo (633), 98

Fourth Lateran Council (1215), 54, 214, 236, 238, 249, 310, 315, 357–358

Foy, Sainte, 323, 328, 334–335, *335*

Fra Angelico, 405

France: Avignon papacy and, 378–385; Beguines in, 220; Bernard and, 170; Cathars in, 185–187, 199; Cluny's influence on cloisters in, 122; conversion of Northmen in, 79; Crusade in, 107, 345; Dominicans in, 215; Franciscans in, 238, 405; heresy in, 178, 180, 185,

186, 193; Inquisition in, 203, 223; Jewry in, 100–101, 209, 345, 353, 358, 363; La Grande Chartreuse (France), 153, *153*, 155; Leo IX's travel in, 129; monastic reform in, 115, 120; power at end of Middle Ages, 370; Romanesque architecture of Abbaye aux Hommes (Caen), *55*; Romuald's monasteries in, 152; Visigoths in, 70

Franciscans, 226–256; Aristotelian thinking and, 281; conflict and controversy (1226–1274), 245–249; "Donation of Constantine" and, 73; elimination of social distinctions among, 216; growth of order, 203, 246, 254; heresy, role in suppression of, 208, 211; on immaculate conception, 341; Inquisition and, 223–224; Joachites and, 249–250, 255; Muslim conversion and, 116; Observance and, 404–405; pastoral mission to the cities, 241–245; poverty and, 217, 233, 255–256; secular-mendicant controversy, 251–253; Spirituals vs. Conventuals, 209, 252, 255–256, 371, 404, 416; use of goods (*usus pauper*), 253–255

Francis of Assisi, 116, 188–189, 226–233, *240*

Franks: Carolingians and, 69; conversion of, 40–42, 68; Crusades and, 111; defeat of Huns, 37; defeat of Lombards, 40; defense of Rome, 107; dominance of, 34; First Crusade and, 109, 343; Jews and, 100–101; lay churches and, 81; Muslims fighting, 103; relationship with Catholic Church, 71–73; relationship with Rome, 41. *See also* Charlemagne

Fraternities, 312–315, 430

Frederick II (excommunicated emperor), 248, 289

Fredrick Barbarossa (emperor), 335, 339, 346, 419

French language, 41

Frequens decree (1417), 383

Friars Minor, 233–234, 235, 238, 247

Frideswide, Saint, 322

Friends of God (Gottesfreunde) movement, 423

Frisia, 67–68

Fulbert, 263

Fulk (bishop of Toulouse), 214, 215

Gaetani family, 371

Gallienus, 19

Gallo-Roman culture, 37, 41

Gaul, 40–44; Celtic missionaries in, 48; first monastery in, 22; Franks in, 40; male and female ascetics in, 42–44; mob violence in, 17; monasteries in, 42–44, 46; Papal States in, 59; prosecution in, 17; repudiation of Augustinian views, 26; simony in, 127; Visigoths in, 97

Gelasius I (pope), 139

General Admonition (Charlemagne), 75

George, Saint, 112, 336

Gerard of Borgo San Donnino, 250, 252, 253

Germanic peoples, 33–36, *35*, 50, 61, 67, 81

German language, 50, 98

Germany: Beguines in, 220; Cluniac empire and, 122, 123; crowning of emperors in, 132; Crusades and, 170; *The Dictates of the Pope* (*Dictatus Papae*) and, 138–139; Dominicans in, 217; Franciscans in, 238; Franks in, 40, 73; Frisians in, 67; Henry VI and, 288; Henry VII and, 141–142; Inquisition in, 203, 209; Italy in competition for papacy with, 79; Jewry in, 100–101, 343, 348, 351, 354–355, 363; Leo IX's travel in, 129; monasteries in, 46; monastic reform in, 120; nunneries in, 172; pious intensification prior to Reformation, 435; schism in relations with, 146; simony in, 127

Gerson, Jean, 379–380, 400, 412

Gertrude, 43

Gibbon, Edward, 33

Gilbertines, 158–160, 171

Gilbert of Sempringham, 158–160

Giles of Assisi, 235

Giotto, 406

Gloria Patri, 86

Gnosticism, 4–7, 9, 10, 12, 184

God: Cathar dogma and, 184; of the Hebrew Bible, 8, 11; Muslim vs. Christian God, 115; of the New Testament, 8

Golden Legend (Jacobus da Voragine), 321

Good Friday, celebration of, 300

Gospel of Philip, 4

Gospel of Thomas, 4

Gospels, 6, *36. See also* New Testament; Scripture

Gothic architecture, 283–284, *284–285*

Gothic Architecture and Scholasticism (Panofsky), 283–286

Gothic language, 36

Goths, 36. *See also* Ostrogoths; Visigoths

Grabow, Matthew, 412

Grace, 25–26

Graetz, Henrich, 95

La Grande Chartreuse (France), 153, *153*, 155

Grand Inquisitor for Lombardy, 181

Gratian, 99, 274, 315, 317, 327

Great Persecution under Diocletian, 19, 23

Great Schism (1328–1415), 378, 389

Greek churches, 130, 385

Greek language, 34, 50, 77, 105, 106

Gregorianism, 143, 175–178

Gregorian Reform, 123–124, 175. *See also* Age of Reform

Gregory I, Pope (Gregory the Great), 50, 55–62, 65, 99–100, 242, 306, 431

Gregory II (pope), 68

Gregory VI (pope), 134

Gregory VII (pope), 107–108, 123, 126, 128, 130, 133, 134–143, *141*, 175, 290

Gregory IX (pope): Beguines and, 220; Benedictine *Rule* and, 236; canonization authority reserved to pope, 294; Elias and, 248; Franciscans and, 239, 246, 247; Inquisition and, 178, 203, 223;

saints and feasts, list set by, 327; Talmud and, 360–361; Thomas's *Life* and, 228; university governance and, 269, 279

Gregory XI (pope), 377, 378, 388

Gregory XII (pope), 380

Gregory of Rimini, 434

Gregory of Tours, 41

Groote, Geert, 410–411

Guglielma of Milan, 250–251

Gui, Bernard, 201, 224

Guibert (antipope), *141*

Guibert of Nogent, 150, 342

Guigo I, 153–155

Guigo II, 155

Guilds, 267–268, 312–315

Guinefort, Saint, 93

Hadewijch of Antwerp, 424–425

Haec Sancta (Council of Constance), 383–384, 385

Hairshirts, 154

The Hammer of Witches (*Malleus Maleficarum*), 209

Hausheiliger (house saint), 43

Hebrew Bible, 23, 124–125, 176, 184

Heloise and Abelard, 262–266

Henry II (king of England), 158, 178, 336–338

Henry III (emperor), 126, 131

Henry IV (emperor), 130, 131, 139–143, *141*, 328

Henry IV (king of England), 392

Henry VI (emperor), 288

Henry VII (king of England), 433

Henry VIII (king of England), 395

Henry of Halle, 422

Henry of Lausanne, 176, 192

Henry of Nördlingen, 221, 423

Henry of Suso, 222

Heresy, 174–210; of Abelard, 264; of Augustine's opponents, 23; burning as punishment for, 182, 193, 200, 202, 208, 209, 255; Cathars and, 178–188, 190, 192, 199–200, *200*, 203, 205, 207–209; confiscation of property for, 198–199,

207; Crusade against Cathars, 199–200, *200*; Guglielma of Milan's followers, 251; historians' view of, 3, 94; Hussites, 346, 382, *382*, 387, 393, 395–400; icons and religious images as, 71; Islam and, 104, 105, 116; Lollards, 393–395; nuns and, 164; radical Gregorians and, 175–178; repression of, 198–210; Savonarola, 410; sexual relations between Jews and Christians as, 362; simony as, 127; sinful priests and, 147; use of term, 197–198; Waldensians and, 73, 187, 188–198, 199, 209; Wyclif, John, 382, 387–393, 395

Herman III (archbishop of Cologne), 344

Hermit lifestyle, 22, 48, 148, 152–153, *153*, 157–158

High-medieval Christianity (ca. 1050–1300), 117–365; Age of Reform, 119–147; Dominicans, 211–225; Franciscans, 226–256; heresy, repression of, 174–210; Jews' relationship with Christianity, 343–365; means of Christianization, 299–319; monks and nuns in monastic centuries, 148–173; papal monarchy, 287–298; saints, relics, and pilgrimage, 320–342; scholasticism, 257–286

Hilda, 43–44

Hildebrand, 126, 129, 131, 132, 134–139. *See also* Gregory VII (pope)

Hildegard of Bingen, 180, 234, 242, 419–422, *420*

Hippo, 23, 37

Historia Scholastica (*Scholastic History* of Peter Comestor), 218

A History of My Calamities (Peter Abelard), 262

Hohenstaufen dynasty, 297, 370

Hollywood, Amy, 427

Holocaust, 95, 344, 357

Holy City of Zion. *See* Jerusalem

Holy Land, Crusades in, 104, 108, 109, 112–114. *See also* Crusades

Holy Sepulchre. *See* Church of the Holy Sepulchre (Jerusalem)

Holy Spirit, 250–252

Honorius III (pope), 214, 229, 239

Hortensius (Cicero), 23

Hospitallers (Knights of St. John), 114

Hubert, Saint, 322

Hugh (Augustinian canon), 161, *161*

Hugh of Cluny, Abbot, 141

Hugh of Grenoble, 153

Hugh of St. Cher, 223, 276

Hugo, Victor, 209

Hugolino, Cardinal, 236, 238–240, 246. *See also* Gregory IX (pope)

Huguccio, 288

Humanism, 406–410

Humbert of Romans, 217, 223, 242

Humbert of Silva Candida, 126, 130, 132–133, 175

Hungary, 79, 193, 217, 238, 405

Huns, 33, 36, 37

Hus (Jan) and Hussite Revolution, 346, 382, *382*, 387, 393, 395–400

Iberian Peninsula, 37, 70, 73, 97, 98, 103, 106, 261. *See also* Spain

Icons, images, and pictorials, 302–303, *303*; Cathars and Bogomils rejecting veneration of, 181; didactic purpose of, 306; iconoclastic controversy, 71

Ignatius of Antioch, 11–12, 14

The Imitation of Christ (Thomas à Kempis), 411

Immaculate Conception of Mary, 94, 340–341

Incubation, 324

Indulgences, 313, 333, 399

Infallibility of pope, 256

Ingeborg of Denmark, 290

Innocent II (pope), 154, 170, 266

Innocent III (pope), 287–290, *289*; Albigensian Crusade and, 198–199; cathedral schools and, 262; on consent to marriage, 316; Fourth Lateran Council and, 357–358; Francis of Assisi and, 235; heretics, suppression of, 178, 191, 192, 197, 213–214, 310; on moneylenders and

Innocent III (pope)(*continued*)
merchants, 311; Norbertines and, 164;
Rule of St. Francis and, 239
Innocent IV (pope), 205, 224, 237,
247–248, 253, 295, 297, 361
Inquisition, 178, 187, 197, 201–210,
223–225, 363–365
Institutions (Cassiodorus), 39
Introduction to the Eternal Gospel (Gerard
of Borgo San Donnino), 252
Investiture, 132–134, 145
Iona, 48, 78
Ireland, 44–47, 47. *See also* Celtic
Christianity
Irenaeus, 4, 7, 14
Irene, Empress, 74–75
"Ishmaelites," 105
Isidore, archbishop of Seville, 98–99
Islam. *See* Muslims and Islam
Istanbul. *See* Constantinople
Italy: appointments by imperial authority
in, 126; Camaldolese order in, 152; Caro-
lingians in, 69; Cathars in, 183, 186–188;
Cluny's influence on cloisters in, 122;
defeat of Lombards by Pepin in, 72–73;
Dominicans in, 215, 405; First Crusade
and, 109; Franciscans in, 238, 405; Ger-
many in competition for papacy with,
79; heresy in, 180–181, 193; hermetical
life, revival of, 151; Inquisition in, 203,
224; Jews in, 99, 101, 351; Justinian's
campaign in, 39–40, 58; Kingdom of
Italy, establishment of, 38, 79; Latin use
in Greek churches in, 130; lay churches
in, 81; Lombards in, 55–56, 58, 70, 97;
monasteries in, 46; Normans in, 134;
Ostrogoths in, 58, 99; simony in, 127;
Visigoths in, 37
Itta, 43
Ivo of Chartres, 99, 143

Jacques de Vitry, 171
Jakoubek of Stříbro, 400
James, Saint, 107, 323, 328, 333

James I of Aragon, 361–362
Jan van Ruysbroec, 411, 424
Jedin, Hubert, 385
Jerome, 39, 44, 56, 65, 98
Jerusalem: bishop in, 21; Crusaders'
Chapel of the Virgin Mary (Church of
the Holy Sepulchre), *108*; destruction of
Temple, 27, 98; Dome of the Rock in,
104; fall to Muslim rule (1187), 103, 346;
Fifth Crusade and, 238; First Crusade
and, 109–113, 344; Jews and, 27; kingdom of, 114; patriarch in, 104; pilgrimages to, 329, 331–332; processions in,
303–304; St. John the Baptist hospital,
114; Saladin and, 114
Jesus Christ: Bernard on, 171; at Cana, 317;
divinity of, 184; Francis's reenactment
of birth scene of, 240; Gnostic view of,
11; Jews' responsibility for death of, 28;
Muslim view of, 104; Nicene creed and,
21; relics of, 77, 329; suffering on cross,
305–306; virgin birth of, 182
The Jew of Malta (Marlowe), 354
Jews and Judaism: Ashkenazi, 100–101,
346, 347, 363; Augustine's view of,
27–28; "blood libel," 347–352, *350*;
caricature and iconography of, 354–356;
Christian theology of, 23; Crusades' effect on, 170, 343–347; in early Frankish
and Carolingian era, 100–102; expulsion of, 362–363, 364–365; Gnostics
compared to, 5; in Gothic kingdoms,
96; historical view of, 95–96; host desecration, 352–353; Joachim prediction of
conversion of, 251; Marcion's rejection of apostles as Judaizers, 9; money
lending and, 346, 347, 357, 358–360;
in Ostrogothic kingdoms, 99–100;
passion plays and, 356–357; relationship with Christianity (ca. 300–1100),
95–102; relationship with Christianity
(1096–1492), 343–365; under Roman
rule, 27–28; sectarian influence, 4;
Spanish Inquisition and, 209; in Visig-

othic kingdoms, 97–99; well poisoning, 353–354. *See also* Talmud

Jihad, 107

Joachim of Fiore and Joachites, 249–251, 252, 253

Joan of Arc, 209, 318

John (king of England), 290

John, gospel of, 227

John VIII (pope), 107

John XII (pope), 79

John XXII (pope), 255, 293, 375, 399

John XXIII (antipope), 379

John VIII Palaiologos (Byzantine emperor), 384

John Cassian, 53, 412

John Chrysostom, 354

John Domenici, 405

John Kamateros, 291

John Lateran, Saint, 235

John of Capistrano, 404

John of Damascus, 105, 116

John of Gaunt, 388

John of Parma, 250, 253

John of St. Giles, 252

John of Salisbury, 171, 262

John Paul II (pope), 129

John Tauler, 222

Jordan of Saxony, 215, 217, 218, 221, 222

Joseph II (Constantinople patriarch), 384

Judaism. *See* Jews and Judaism

Judas, 356

Judgment day, 11

Julian of Eclanum, 26

Julian of Norwich, 150–151, 427

Julian the Apostate (emperor), 40

Justinian I, 37–38, 39–40, 58, 304

Justinian Code, 96–97, 100, 276

Justin Martyr, 8

Jutes, 34, 62

Kara, Avi, 349

Kempe, Margery, 150

Kings considering themselves as quasi-clerical sacred officeholders, 120

Knights of St. John (Hospitallers), 114

Knights Templar, 114, 170, 346, 358, 374

Kutna Hora Decree (1409), 398

Kyrie, 86

The Ladder of Monks (Guigo II), 155

La Ferté monastery, 166

Lambert, Malcolm, 189

Languedoc, 180, 187, 190, 191, 199, 200, 203, 375

Laon, 163, 261, 262, 264, 276

Last rites, 92

Last Supper, 432

Lateran II (1139), 128

Lateran III (1179), 191–193, 318

Lateran IV (1215), 214, 236, 238, 249, 310, 315, 357–358

Lateran Palace, 72, 142

Later-medieval Christianity (ca. 1300–1500), 367–435; Avignon papacy (1309–1378), 374–377; Boniface VIII vs. Philip IV of France, 370–374; Catherine of Siena, 377; Dark Ages, 369–386; Florentine humanism, 406–407; Great Schism (1328–1415), 378; Hus and Hussites, 346, 382, *382*, 387, 393, 395–400; local and provincial reform, 406; Lollards, 393–395; Nicholas of Cusa, 73, 383, 384, 412–415; piety, 418–435; Prague, radicalization in, 400–402; reform (1380–1500), 403–405; Savonarola, 407–410; Sisters and Brothers of the Common Life, 410–412; Wyclif, 387–393; Ximénez de Cisneros, Francisco, 415–417

Latin language, 41, 50, 77, 84, 86, 87, 106, 127, 130, 258–259, 261, 268, 274–275, 300, 310

Lawrence, C. H., 234

Lawrence, Saint, 322

Lay brethren, 169, 216

Lay churches and lay control, 81, 119, 132, 144–146

Lea, Henry Charles, 310

Leo I (pope), 61, 129, 318
Leo III (emperor), 71
Leo III (pope), 74–75, 76
Leo IV (pope), 107
Leo IX (pope), 124, 126, 129–131, 134, 135, 136, 145
Leo XIII (pope), 283
Leonardo da Vinci, 406
Leonidas, 18
Leprosy, 314, 316, 322, 338
Letter 40 (Gregory I), 61
Letter to Coroticus (St. Patrick), 45–46
Levant, 107, 110, 111, 114, 238
Levitical period, 125
Liège, 171, 182
Life (Athanasius), 22
Life of St. Antony, 321
Life of St. Benedict (Gregory I), 51, 52
Life of St. Francis (Bonaventure), 229, 253
Life of St. Hugh of Grenoble (Guigo I), 155
Lindisfarne, looting by Vikings, 78
Lindisfarne Gospels, 65–66, *66*
Little Flowers, 228
"Little Office of the Blessed Virgin Mary," 429
Liturgical drama, 301–302
Liturgy and sacraments, 85–87
Lives (read on saints' days), 327
Lives (St. Patrick), 45
Livy, 406
Loans, interest on, 318–319, 358–360
Lollards, 393–395
Lombards, 34, 40, 55, 58–59, 70–73, 97, 99
Lombardy: Guglielma of Milan's followers in, 251; Inquisition in, 203, 205, 224; Jews in, 351
Lord's Prayer, 92, 309
Lorenzo de' Medici, 406
Lorenzo Valla, 73
Lorraine, 124, 126, 127, 130
Lothario da Segni. *See* Innocent III (pope)

Louis VII (king of France), 170
Louis VIII (king of France), 201
Louis IX (king of France), 269, 297, 329, 363
Louis XI (king of France), 342
Louis the Bavarian (emperor), 256
Louis the Pious, 75, 78, 101
Low Countries, 163, 172–173, 220
Lucius III (pope), 193, 202
Luther, Martin, 354–355, 434
Luxeuil monastery, 42, 43, 46
Lyons, 17, 93

Magic, 88–91
Magyars, 79
Maifreda da Pirovano, 251
Mainz, 68, 101, 129, 344, 345
Manichaeans, 23, 26, 135, 180, 181, 183
Maps: Europe at time of Gregory the Great (ca. 600), *60*; Europe with major bishoprics (ca. 1250), *296*; Germanic pattern of settlement, *35*; monasteries of medieval Europe, *165*; pilgrimage sites in western Europe, *330*
Marches of Ancona, 249, 251
Marcionism, 7–9, 13, 114
Marcion of Pontus, 7–9, 14
Margaret (queen of France), 173
Margaret of Scotland, Queen, 67
Marguerite d'Oingt, 425
Marguerite Porete, 425, 426
Marian apparitions and Crusaders, 112
Marjorie Kempe, 339
Mark (Cathar bishop), 185
Mark, Saint, 323
Markus, Robert, 29, 309
Marlowe, Christopher, 354
Marranos, 364
Marriage: Cathars on, 186; ceremonies, 317; of clergy, 83–84, 119, 128, 131, 175; divorce, ban on, 316; Henry of Lausanne on, 176; indissolubility of, 131, 316–317; meaning of, 315–318
Martha, 160, 162

Martialis, 18

Martin V (pope), 380, 383

Martin of Tours, 22, 338–339

Martyrs: anniversary of death, celebration of, 327; Crusaders and, 112; feast days of, 29; pilgrimage sites to tombs of, 18; remains among churches of Rome, 332; as saints, 17; veneration of, 320–321, 326

Mary, Blessed Virgin: Assumption of, 340, 422; Bernard on, 171; cult of, 94–95, 341; devotion to, 339–342; "Little Office of the Blessed Virgin Mary," 429; monks and, 160; relics of, 77, 340. *See also* Immaculate Conception of Mary

Mary Magdalene, cult of, 339

Masses, 53–54, 86–87, 431–433; Lord's Prayer and the Creed as part of, 92; monastery funding tied to, 164; prayers for the dead, 430; votive masses, 90. *See also* Prayers

Matilda of Canossa, 137, 140–141

Matthew of Janov, 396, 400

Maurice (emperor), 61

Maxentius, 20

Maximilla, 10

McGinn, Bernard, 418

Mechtild of Magdeburg, 422–423

Medici family, 406–407, 408, 417

The Medieval Manichee (Runciman), 180

Meister Eckhart, 222, 421, 424

Merovingians, 40, 42, 43, 70, 321

Metaphysics (Aristotle), 275

Metropolitans, 21

Michael, Saint, 322

Michael Cerularius (patriarch of Constantinople), 130

Michael of Cesena, 255, 256

Michelangelo, 406

Millers, 91–92

Miracles, 324–326, 333

The Mirror of Simple Souls (Marguerite Porete), 425

Misericordia Maggiore, 315

Missionaries: British missionaries on the Continent, 67–68; Celtic missionaries, 66; Franks and, 41; in Ireland, 48; Roman missionaries, 50, 66

Modern Devotion, 410–412

Modes of instruction, 299–319; images and pictorials, 302–303, *303*; learning through texts, 300; liturgical drama, 301–302; religious drama, 307–308; stained glass, 306; worship as, 300–301. *See also* Preaching

Monasteries: abbot's role, 52; daily tasks in, 52–53; double monasteries, 42–44, 163; Gregory's founding of, 57; in high-medieval Christianity (ca. 1050–1300), 148–173; iconoclastic controversy and expropriation of lands, 71; in Ireland, 46; map of medieval Europe's monasteries, *165*; prayers and masses in, 53–54, 55; role of, 53–55; Romanesque architecture, 54, *55*, *82*; as safe havens for children, 54; Viking attacks on, 78. *See also* Monks and monasticism; *specific names and locations of monasteries*

Money lending, 346, 347, 357, 358–360

Monica, 23

Monks and monasticism, 52–53, 54, 123; anchoritic life, 149–150; apostles, monks considered to be, 125, 160; Benedictinization of, 75; black monks (Benedictines), 166; Carthusian order, 152–157; Cistercian order, 164–171; Cluniac monks, 123–124; desert tradition and, 22, 30, 151–152; Franks and, 41; in Ireland, 47; in monastic centuries (ca. 1050–1300), 148–173; monastic schools, 258–260; Observant or Observantine, 404; prayers and, 52–55; white monks (Cistercians), 166, 168, 214. *See also* Hermit lifestyle; Monasteries; *specific monks, orders, etc.*

Montanism, 9–11, 17

Montanus, 9–10

Monte Cassino monastery (Italy), 43, 51, 55, 329, 339

Montpellier, 203, 219, 261, 266

Mont St. Michel (France), 322, *323*

Moralia in Job (Gregory I), 57

Morality plays, 307–308

Morris, Colin, 126, 174, 306, 309

Moses ben Maimon (Maimonides), 275

The Mother of Sciences (*Parens Scientiarum*) (Gregory IX), 269

Muhammad (prophet), 34, 116

Muratorian Fragment, 13

Musical plays, 301–302

Muslims and Islam: attacks on Europe, 25, 70, 78, 79, 103–104; conversion to Christianity, 116, 251; distorted Christian views of, 115–116; Francis of Assisi and, 238; intellectual exchange with, 275; Reconquest, 106–107, 108, 212, 364; relationship with Christianity, 34, 50, 104–116, 146; Saladin and, 114; in Spain, 98; Spanish Inquisition and, 209. *See also* Crusades

Mysticism, 418–419; female mystics, 419–428

Mythology of Gnostics, 5–6

Nag Hammadi library, 4

Nahmanides, 361–362

The Name of the Rose (Eco), 201

Narbonne, 70, 215, 253, 255

Nec insolitum (Alexander IV), 253

neo-Arianism, 21

neo-Donatism, 128, 133, 146–147, 175, 177, 183, 186–187, 192, 195, 388

neo-Gnostic, 182

Newman, John Henry, 51

New Rome, 21. *See also* Constantinople

New Testament: Cathars and, 184; development of, 13–14; John, gospel of, 9, *66*; John, letters of, 13, 355; Jude, letter of, 13; Luke, gospel of, 9; papal reform and, 124–125; Paul, letters of, 6, 9, 13; Revelation, book of, 9–10; synoptic

gospels of, 227; translation into Gothic, 36

Nicaea, 21, 111, 112, 326

Nicene Creed, 21, 24, 25

Nicholas II (pope), 132–134, 135

Nicholas V (pope), 256, 414

Nicholas Donin of La Rochelle, 360–361

Nicholas of Cusa, 73, 383, 384, 412–415, 417

Nider, Johannes, 403

Niketas, 185

Nirenberg, David, 105

Norbertines, 163–164

Norbert of Xanten, 162–164

Normans, 54, 130, 131, 134, 142

Normative Christianity, 11–15

Northmen (Vikings), 78–79

Northumbria, 43, 66–67, 78

Norway, 79

Nuns. *See* Monasteries; Monks and monasticism; Women and nuns

Oakley, Francis, 389, 392, 403, 407–408, 412

Oberammergau, 357

Observant or Observantine, 404–405, 408

Occitania, 178, 180, 185, 187, 188, 198

Ockham, William, 434

Odoacer (Germanic king), 38

Odo of Chateauroux, 361

Office of the Virgin, 429

Oldcastle, John, 393, 395

Old Roman Creed, 12–13

Old Testament: Daniel, book of, 105; Job, book of, 57, 112; kingship models in, 125. *See also* Hebrew Bible

Omnis utriusque sexus (canon decree of Innocent III), 310

On Christian Teaching (Augustine), 261

On Contemplation (Denis the Carthusian), 155

On Saints and Their Relics (Guibert of Nogent), 342

On the Burning of Heretics (edict 1401), 392

On the Cathars and the Poor of Lyons (Raynier Sacconi), 181

On the Catholic Faith against the Jews (Isidore), 98

On the Education of Clerics (Ailred of Rievaulx), 150

On the Heresies (John of Damascus), 105

On the Instruction of Preachers (Humbert of Romans), 242

"On the Jews" (Justinian), 97

On the Mysteries of the Mass (Innocent III), 288

On the Resurrection of the Blessed Virgin Mary (St. Elisabeth), 422

On the Unity of the Intellect against the Averroists (Thomas Aquinas), 283

Opera Omnia (*Collected Works*, Thomas Aquinas), 278

Orange, 26

Orderic Vitalis, 54

Ordinem Vestrum (Innocent IV), 247

Organon (Aristotle), 274

Origen, 18

Orléans, 182, 261

Orthodox Christianity, 50

Orthodoxy: Gnostic views of, 10; historians' view of, 3; Inquisition and, 210

Orthodoxy and Heresy in Earliest Christianity (Bauer), 3

Osma Cathedral, 212, 214

Ostrogoths, 33, 34, 40, 58, 99

Oswiu, King, 43

Otto I (German king), 79, 126

Otto IV of Brunswick, 289

Ottomans, 106, 115, 365

Ovid, 259

Oxford, 266, 268, 269, 322; Dominicans in, 216, 219

Pachomius, 42

Paganism: of ancient Roman literature, 77–78; classics of pagan antiquity, study of, 259; Constantine and, 20; folkloristic remnants in Middle Ages, 93–95; Franks and, 42; revival of classical (pagan) literature, 406; rituals held over from, 88

Page of Meditations (Marguerite d'Oingt), 425

Palestine, 19, 27, 103; loss to Muslims (1291), 115

Palladius of Auxerre, 45

Palm Sunday, 304, 305

Panofsky, Erwin, 283–286

Pantheon, 15

Papacy: absolution of serious sin and, 333; Avignon papacy (1309–1378), 374–377; centralization of "church" in, 294, 297; conflict of papacy and empire (1075–1100), 139–143; functioning like a regional fiefdom, 369; heresies and, 175; instruments of papal power, 292–295; legates, appointment of, 293; moderate papal reform, 126–130; papal curia, 257, 287, 291, 292–293, 370, 374–375; papal monarchy and supremacy, 287–298; papal resentment, 295–298, 376–377; prestige and status of, 145–146; universities and, 269; vested ownership of all properties and goods in, 247, 256

Papal Inquisition, 202

Papal States, 59, 73, 288–291, 369, 371, 376

Parable of the Prodigal Son, 188

Paradiso (Dante), 226, 249, 274

Paris, 128, 215, 219, 266, 268, 269; Sainte Chapelle, 329

Parish churches, 81, 145

Parishes, 82–83

Parochial life, 80

Paschal II (pope), 143–144, 158

Passion plays, 356–357

Pastoral Care (Gregory I), 59, 61

Patarines, 178, 180

Paternoster, 155, 182, 183, 185, 307, 313

Patriarchates, 21

"Patrician of the Romans," 72

Patrick (saint), 44–46

"Patrimony of St. Peter," 59

Paul (Saul) of Tarsus, 9, 14, 323

Paulicians, 203

Paul the Deacon, 77

Pavia, 129

Pelagianism, 25, 433–434

Pelagius, 25–26

Pelagius II (pope), 57

Penance, 48–49, 53, 55, 86, 206–207, 245, 311, 331

"People of the Book," 104, 105

Pepin III, 70, 71–73

Péronne monastery, 46

Perpetua, 17

Persecution of Christians, 15–20

Persia, 103

Peter, the Apostle: Celtic Christianity and, 67; Charlemagne and, 74; Crusaders and, 112; Gregory IX and, 136; Irenaeus on, 14; Leo believing Peter speaking though him, 129; New Testament and, 125; pilgrimage to shrine of, 332; Rome and, 323; Waldes and, 196

Peter Abelard, 170, 262–266, 272–273, 276

Peter Comestor ("Peter the Eater"), 218

Peter Damian, 126, 128, 131, 132, 135, 152, 318

Peter Lombard, 155, 273, 282–283, 316, 317

Peter of Bruys, 176, 192

Peter of Castelnau, 199

Peter of Cattani, 235, 239

Peter of Dacia, 221

Peter of Pisa, 77

Peter of Verona, 224

Peter Olivi, 254–255

Peter the Chancellor, 287–288

Peter the Hermit, 345

Peter the Venerable, 116, 155, 176, 266, 360

Petrarch, 374–375, 406

Petronille de Chemillé, 158

Petrus Alfonsi, 360

Philip II (king of France), 199, 290

Philip IV (king of France), 114, 363, 371

Philip VI (king of France), 370–374

Philip Augustus (king of France), 363

Philip of Swabia, 289

Phrygia, 9–10

"Phrygian heresy," 9

Piacenza council (1095), 110

Picts, 48

Pierre d'Ailly, 400, 412

Piety, 258–259, 303–307, *304*, 418–435; blood piety, 428, *428*; books of hours, 428–430; female mystics and, 419–428; purgatory and, 430–431. *See also* Eucharist; Masses; Prayers

Pilgrimages, 305, 325, 328, 329–342; to Canterbury Cathedral, 336–338; to Chartres, 341, *341*, 342; to Jerusalem, 329, 331–332; map of sites in western Europe, *330*; to Monte Cassino monastery, 339; to Rome, 329, 332–333; to Tours shrine of St. Martin, 338–339; by women, 339

Pippin the Elder, 43

Pirenne, Henri, 34

Pirenne thesis, 34

Pistis-Sophia (Coptic document), 4

Pius II (pope), 152, 385, 402

Plato, 275

Plautus, 413

"Plentitude of power," 291

Pliny, 16, 17

Pogroms, 343, 351, 363, 364

Poland, 79, 193, 217, 363, 405

Poll-tax required for People of the Book, 106

Polycarp, Bishop, 14

Polyglot Bible, 415, *416*

Pontigny monastery (Burgundy), 166, 337

Posterior Analytics (Aristotle), 39

Po Valley, 40

Poverty, 190, 207; Dominicans and, 214, 217; Franciscans and, 233; society for "Catholic poor," 199

"Pragmatic Sanction of Bourges," 385

Prague, radicalization, 395, 400–402

"Prague Massacre," 349

"Prayer of Charlemagne," 90

Prayers: Christian, 53–54, 55, 80, 85–87, 90; for the dead, 430–431; Henry of Lausanne on prayers for the dead, 176; Islam, 105; Peter of Bruys on prayers for the dead, 176; Virgin Mary and, 341

Preaching, 87–91, 128, 215, 242–243, 308–309

Prebayon, France, 156

Predestination, 26

Premonstratensians, 162–164, 171, 172, 349

Priests. *See* Clergy

Prior Analytics (Aristotle), 39

Priscilla, 10

Processions, 303–307, *304*, 333

Profession of Faith, 192–193

Proprietary church, 80–82

Proselytizing: by Jews, 27, 362; for Muslim conversion to Christianity, 116; in second century, 16. *See also* Missionaries

Protestants and suppression of heresy, 201

Proto-orthodox Christianity, 3

Prouille, 214, 215, 223

Pseudo-Pauline letters, 13

Purgatory, 94, 195, 309, 311, 401, 430–431

Quasi lignum vitae (Alexander IV), 253

Quo Elongati (Gregory IX), 247, 256

Qur'an, 104, 105, 106, 115, 116

Rashi, 101

Ravenna, 29, *36*, 38, 40, 57, 58

Raymond VI (count of Toulouse), 199

Raymond Martini, 361–362

Raymond of Capua, 222, 377, 405, 426

Raymond of Penaforte, 218, 219, 244–245, 361–362

Raynier Sacconi, 180–181, 188, 204, 223–224

Reccared I (king of the Visigoths), 37, 98

Reformation, 23, 160, 193, 210, 389, 393, 401

Reims, 129, 153, 261

Relics, 29, 327–329; of Benedict, 42; Charlemagne's collection of, 77; critique of, 342; Crusaders taking, 112–113, 115, 328, 329; of Martin of Tours, 339; in Rome, 332; sacramental use of, 88; shrines and, 323; theft of, 42, 328

Remigius (bishop of Reims), 41, 129

Renaissance, early, 406–410

"Renaissance popes," 386

Revelations (Margaret Ebner), 221–222

The Revelations of Divine Love (Julian of Norwich), 150

Richard I the Lionhearted, 114, 346

Richard II (king of England), 397

Richard of Capua, 134

Rich Young Man story, 188–189

Rievaulx monastery (Yorkshire), 170

Rindfleisch, 351–352

RM. See *Rule of the Master*

Robert Grosseteste, 220, 248

Robert Guiscard, 134

Robert le Bougre, 223

Robert of Abrissel, 157, 162

Robert of Molesme, 166

Roderick (Visigothic king of Spain), 98

Roman Empire, 14, 15–20, 33, 37, 50, 56, 96–97, 303–304, 324

Romanesque churches and art, 306, *323*, *334*

Roman temples converted into Christian churches, *63*

Rome: Benedict in, 51; bishops of, 21, 29, 59, 70, 127; Celts' relationship with, 46; Charlemagne and, 74; Franks' relationship with, 40, 43, 107; Gregory I's role in, 56–59; Henry III and, 126; Henry IV expelling Gregory VII from, *141*, 142; Justinian conquering, 39–40; Lombards' defeat of Ostrogoths for, 57–59; Muslim raids in, 104; Normans taking back from Henry IV, 142; papal reform and, 130; Papal States claimed by, 59, 72; Pelagius in, 25; pilgrimages to, 329,

Rome (*continued*)
332–333; sack of (410), 26, 37; synod in
  (1059), 128, 129, 133
Romuald of Ravenna, Saint, 152
Romulus Augustulus (emperor), 34, 38
Rosary, 340
Royal theocracy, 119–120
Rubrics, 302
Rudolf of Swabia, 141, 142
Rule of a Father for Virgins (Walbert of
  Luxeuil), 43
Rule of Bernard of Clairvaux, 114
Rule of St. Augustine, 149, 161–162, 212,
  214, 412
Rule of St. Benedict (RB), 42, 43, 51–53,
  56, 69, 149, 152, 154, 158, 162, 167–169,
  170, 216, 236, 258, 405, 431
Rule of St. Francis, 239, 241, 247, 250, 253
Rule of the Master (RM), 52

Sabellianism, 264
Sacralization of secular office, 72
Sacramentals, 89–91
Sacraments, 85–87, 92, 247
St. Agnes convent (Bologna), 221
St. Andrew's monastery (Rome), 57
St. Denis abbey (Paris), 72, 285, 329
St. Gildas monastery (Britanny), 265
St. James of Compostela cathedral, 107
St. John Lateran church (Rome), 332
St. Martin of Tours monastery, 42
St. Paul's Cathedral (London), 336, 394
St. Peter's (Rome), 78, 333, 386
St. Ruf Abbey (Avignon), 162
St. Victor Abbey (Paris), 160–161, *161*
Saints, 320–322; female house saints, 43;
  Hussites' view of, 401; invocation of,
  89–90; martyrs as, 17; meaning of term
  "saint," 320; patron saints, 322, 327;
  recognition of, 294, 327; saints' days in
  church calendar, 326–327; specialization
  of, 322–323; supernatural powers and
  miracles, 324–326, 331. *See also names of
  specific saints;* Pilgrimages

Saladin, 114, 346
Sanctus, 86
San Marco (Florence), 405, 408
Santa Maria del Fiore (Florence), 406
Santa María la Real de Las Huelgas Abbey
  (Burgos), *172*
Santiago de Compostela, 333, *334*
Saracens, 107
Satan, 53, 89, 184, 185
Savonarola, Girolamo, 405, 406, 407–
  410, *409*, 417
Saxons, 34, 42, 62, 73, 101, 140
Schmitt, J.-C., 93
Scholasticism, 257–286. *See also* Education
Scivias (Hildegard of Bingen), 420, 422
Scripture: Genesis, 5–6, 181, 184;
  Numbers 15:37–41, 357; II Maccabees
  12:43–45, 431; Psalm 15:5, 318; Psalm 59,
  28; Psalm 59:12, 27; Psalm 118, 52; Eze-
  kiel 38–39, 355; Matthew 2:1–12, 429;
  Matthew 7:16, 390; Matthew 10:7–14,
  235; Matthew 13:24–30, 24; Matthew
  16, 61; Matthew 16:14, 235; Matthew
  19:21, 189, 235; Matthew 27:25, 347;
  Mark 6:6–13, 125; Mark 16:14–20, 429;
  Luke 1:26–38, 429; Luke 6:35, 358; Luke
  9:3, 235; Luke 14:23, 24; Luke 15:11–32,
  188; Acts 2:45, 175; Acts 4:32–5, 125; Acts
  8, 120; John 1:1–14, 429; John 18–19,
  429; 1 Cor. 3:11–15, 309; 2 Cor. 3:13–16,
  355; Galatians 1:8–9, 9; Ephesians 3, 316;
  Philippians 2:21, 135; 1 Tim. 6:10, 318;
  Philemon 1:6, 299; Apocalypse 9:13–15,
  226; Apocalypse 12, 10; Apocalypse
  20, 355
Second Council of Nicaea (767), 326
Second Lateran Council (1139), 128
Second Life (*Vita Secunda*, Thomas of
  Celano), 228–229, 239
Second Vatican Council (1962), 130
Secret Book of John, 4
Self-flagellation, 47–48
Sentences (Peter Lombard), 155, 267, 277,
  278–279

Septuagint, 13, 97

Sermo Generalis, 206

Sermons. *See* Preaching

"Servant of the servants of God," 57

The Seven Degrees of Love (Beatrice of Nazareth), 424

Shakespeare, William, 349

Shepherds' Crusade (1320), 353

Showings (Julian of Norwich), 150

Shrines, 323–324

Sic et Non (Peter Abelard), 264, 272, 276

Sicily, 57, 103, 109, 203, 274, 288–290, 297

Sickness, cure at shrines, 323–324

Sicut Iudaeis (Calixtus II), 102

Sicut Iudaeis (Gregory I), 100

Siegfried von Truhendingen, 346

Siger de Brabant, 281–283

Sigismund (Holy Roman emperor), 379, 382, 400

Silence, 53, 154, 163

"Silver Bible" (Arian), 36

Simon de Montfort, 200

Simon Magus, 120

Simon of Trent, 350, 350–351, 354, 355

Simony, 119–120, 127, 131, 145, 152, 175, 399

Sin: absolution for, 311, 333; Augustine's view of, 25–26; avarice as, 318; commercial activity and, 318–319; crucifixion as atonement for, 10; crusaders receiving remission of, 107, 111, 112; Islamic conquest as punishment for, 105, 115; martyrs and, 17; monks' prayers as satisfying, 53; Pelagius's view of, 25; penance for, 48; pilgrimage as penance for, 331; renunciation of Christianity and, 19; William I founding monastery to atone for, 120–121

Sisters and Brothers of the Common Life, 410–412

Sixtus IV (pope), 351

Smyrna, 14; Ignatius's letter to, 12

Solignac, charter of, 42

Solomon ben Isaac of Troyes (Rashi), 101

Sophia (Wisdom), 5–6

Southern, R. W., 162, 292, 293

Spain: Camaldolese monasteries in, 152; Charlemagne's conquest of, 73; Cluny's influence on cloisters in, 122; Crusades to free, 110–111; Dominicans in, 215, 219; Franciscans in, 238, 405; heretics in, 202; Inquisition in, 203, 363–365; intellectual exchange in, 274; Jews in, 98; lay churches in, 81; Muslims in, 34, 104, 105; Reconquista, 107, 108, 212, 364; reform of Spanish church, 415–417; Visigoths in, 37

Squillace, 39

Stained glass, 306

The Standard Gloss (*Glossa Ordinaria*), 276

Stephen II (pope), 72

Stephen IV (pope), 75

Stephen Harding, 166

Stephen Langton, 287, 290

Stephen of Bourbon, 93

Stephen Tempier, 282, 283

Sulpicius Severus, 339

Summa contra Gentiles (Thomas Aquinas), 278

Summa Theologiae (*Handbook of Theology*, Thomas Aquinas), 274, 278–279, 285

Summers, Janet, 171

Supernatural, 89–91, 112

Supernatural powers of saints, 324–325, 331

Superpositio (fasting), 47

Superstitions, 88–91

Sutri, bishop of, 129

Swanson, R. N., 300, 429

Switzerland, 82, 193, 351

Sylvester (pope), 72

Synod of ___. See *specific name of synod*

Syria, 11, 22, 103, 105, 112, 148, 274

Syriac language, 105, 106

Taborites, 401

Tacitus, 40

Talmud, 97, 209, 360–362, 364

Tam, Rabbenu, 345–346
Taxation, 287, 295, 369, 376–377
Templar Knights. *See* Knights Templar
Tertullian, 10, 16–17
The Testament of St. Francis, 229, 231, 232, 240, 241, 247, 250
Theodora (empress), 203
Theodore of Canterbury, 48–49
Theodoric (Ostrogothic king), *36*, 38, 99
Theodosian Code (*Codex Theodosianus*), 96, 99–100
Theodosius I (emperor), 20, 37
Theodosius II (emperor), 96
Theodulph, 77
Theologia (Peter Abelard), 264
Third Council of Toledo (589), 37
Third Lateran Council (1179), 191–193, 318
Third orders, 244
Thomas à Kempis, 411–412
Thomas Aquinas, 215, 225, 233, *243*, 274, 275, 277–281, 373, 416, 431
Thomas of Cantimpré, 321
Thomas of Celano, 228–229, 235, 239, 246
Three Books against the Simoniacs (Humbert), 132
Toledo, 261, 275, 313, 364
Torquemada, 209, 364
Toulouse, 37, 176, 183, 185, 187, 200, 201, 203, 205, 214–216, *243*, 269
Tours, battle of (732), 70, 103
Tours shrine of St. Martin, 338–339
Transubstantiation, 352, 391, 394
Trialogus (Wyclif), 392, 393
Trinity, doctrine of, 104, 182–183, 185, 249–250, 433
"Twelve Conclusions of the Lollards," 394

Ulfilas and conversion of Arian kingdoms, *36, 36*
Unam Sanctam (Boniface VIII), 373
Universities, 266–271
University of Paris, 252, 270

Urban II (pope), 109–111, 113, 123–124, 136, 143, 153, 344
Urban VI (pope), 378
Use of goods (*usus pauper*), 253–255
Usury, 318, 358–360
Utraquism, 400–401

Valens (emperor), 34
Valentinus, 6
Valerian, 19
Vandals, 25, 34, 37–38
Van Engen, John, 92–93, 410, 411
Vatican Library, 13
Vauchez, André, 74, 85
Venice, 40, 115, 339
Vernacular, 86, 87, 92, 105, 189, 190, 242
Vernazza, Ettore, 426
Victorines, 160, 424
Vienne, 17
Vikings, 78–79
Vincent Ferrer, Saint, 362
Virgil, 406
Virgin and Child images, 302–303, *303*
Virgin Mary. *See* Mary, Blessed Virgin
Visigoths, 33–34, 36–37, 40, 42, 70, 97–98, 103, 107
Visions (Hadewijch of Antwerp), 424
Visions (St. Elisabeth), 422
Vita of Catherine of Siena, 377, 426
Vivarium, 39
Volmar (monk), 420
Vulgate Bible, 44, 65, 392

Walafrid Strabo, 276
Walbert of Luxeuil, 43
Waldensians, 73, 187, 188–198, 199, 209, 215, 431
Waldes, 188, 235, 318
Waldhausen. *See* Conrad of Waldhausen
Walter Map, 191–192
Wearmouth, 65, 78
Weber, Max, 227
Wenceslas IV (Holy Roman emperor), 396, 399

Westminster Abbey (London), 336, 394
Whitby: abbey, 43–44; Synod of (664), 43, 66–67
White monks. *See* Cistercians
Whom Do You Seek? (*Quem quaeritis?*), 302
Wibert of Ravenna (later Pope Clement III), 142
William I, duke of Aquitaine, 120–121
William of Champeaux, 160
William of Courtenay, 391
William of Nogaret, 371, 373–374
William of St. Amour, 252
Willibrord (Clement), 67–68, 69
Winfrith (Boniface), 68
Wisdom (Sophia), 5–6
Witches, 209
Women and nuns: as abbesses, 43; as anchorites, 149–150; aristocratic women in nunneries, 54, 173; as Carthusians, 156–157; as Cathars, 186; charities founded by women, 315; as Cistercians, 171–173, *172*; in desert monastic establishments, 22; as Devouts, 412; as Dominicans, 214, 219–223; in Fontevrault monastery, 158; in Gaul, 42; as Gilbertines, 158–160, 171; heresy and, 164; inferiority of women and exclusion from universities, 275; marriage rights of, 317–318; in monastic centuries (ca. 1050–1300), 148–173; as mystics, 419–428; pilgrimages by, 339; Premonstratensian, 163–164, 171, 172; as prophetic leaders, 10; as saints, 321; as Waldensians, 191
The Wonders of the City of Rome (guidebook), 332
Worms: Jewish population of, 344, 345; Synod of (1076), 140
Wyclif, John, 382, 387–393, 395
Wycliffite Bible, 392

Ximénez de Cisneros, Francisco, 415–417, *416*

Yehiel ben Joseph of Paris, 361

Zachary (pope), 71–72
Zanchi, Jerome, 210